SMETANA

Bedřich Smetana, 1860

BRIAN LARGE

SMETANA

PRAEGER PUBLISHERS

New York · Washington

BOOKS THAT MATTER

Published in the United States of America in 1970
by Praeger Publishers, Inc., 111 Fourth Avenue,
New York, N.Y. 10003

Library of Congress Catalog Card Number: 78-100938

Printed in Great Britain

TO MY PARENTS

WITH GRATITUDE AND AFFECTION

CONTENTS

LIST OF PLATES

PREFACE

A FEW DAYS after Smetana's body had been laid to rest in the Vyšehrad Cemetery, Prague, Franz Liszt sent word to Karel Navrátil: 'In haste I write to tell you that the death of Smetana has deeply affected me. He was indeed a genius!' Ironically, with his death Smetana was proclaimed the founder of modern Czech music, but only a few years before he had been spurned, labelled 'Wagnerian' and accused of impeding the way of musical progress. Like Verdi, Smetana was a confirmed patriot. Dramatic music was his platform and his greatest ambition was to see the Prague National Theatre become the permanent home of Czech opera. This he witnessed, but not without making countless enemies and spending years of bitterness in arduous struggle. Smetana's life was one long struggle and sadly he never lived to reap the rewards of his efforts. He developed late. Like Schumann, his early works were almost exclusively for the piano: like Dostoevsky, his first important essay appeared only in middle life. His output was relatively small. Few of his scores found their way into print and, apart from *The Bartered Bride* and *The Kiss*, little of his music was performed with any regularity during his life. After ten busy years, during which he wrote five operas and worked as Musical Director of the Prague Provisional Theatre, he was halted by deafness. There followed a further ten years in which illness and mental disorder made composition increasingly difficult. Yet despite this he produced three more operas, two string quartets and the symphonic cycle *Má Vlast*; but of the six poems only *Vltava* and *From Bohemia's Woods and Fields* are well known in this country. While Zdeněk Nejedlý and Vladimír Helfert have carried out a considerable amount of Smetana research and published their findings in Czechoslovakia, comparatively little has appeared elsewhere and, surprisingly, England has produced no full study of the composer or his music. In writing this book I have attempted to give an insight into the composer's life and work with the help of letters, diaries and other documents preserved in the Bedřich Smetana Museum in Prague. Smetana was always a diligent writer and his letters show him consistently noting personal details in addition to daily events which throw as much light on the social scene of nineteenth-century Bohemia as on himself. No single volume can emphasize more than a few facets of a composer's work, and when the life was as full as that of Smetana it is impossible to produce an exhaustive study. Instead, I have endeavoured to discuss the music in some depth and place the compositions against the background and times in which they were written.

Anyone who attempts to write a book on this scale must inevitably incur a considerable number of debts. I am no exception and am particularly grateful to Dr. Miloslav Malý, Director of the Smetana Museum, Prague, for providing excellent working facilities with access to scores and other documents, and for advice in the preparation of this book. I must acknowledge my gratitude to Smetana's grandson, Mr. Erik Graf, who kindly placed at my disposal a wealth of family letters and manuscripts not previously known to Smetana scholars. I am indebted to my friends in the Czechoslovak Embassy, to Dr. Josef Urban of the Prague National Theatre; to Dr. Václav Holzknecht of the Rudolfinum, Prague; to the Librarians of the Music Section of the National Museum, Prague; to Dr. Strnad, Dr. Dam, Dr. Smola, Mr. Rothbauer and Mr. Vinařický of Supraphon for their interest and cooperation, and to Mr. Josef Bernáth for exceptional kindness; and to the Supraphon Music Publishing House, Prague, for permission to reprint in this work extracts from Smetana's compositions. Many others have contributed to this book but mention must be made of Miss Zdenka Podhajská for her painstaking research and invaluable help in documentation; and to Professor and Mrs. Karel Svolinský, Mr. Jaroslav Vogel and Miss Geraldine Thomsen I owe an especial word of thanks for providing hospitality and much-needed help during my visits to Prague. Dr. Gerald Abraham has made a number of important documents available to me and offered friendly suggestions throughout; and Mr. Cupak and Dr. Zouhar of Radio Brno have supplied various recordings unobtainable in the West. Mr. Vic Dowdall has kindly helped with the music examples; Miss Katharine Wilkinson has prepared the manuscript and in addition to her time-consuming task as typist has added much useful comment for which I am grateful. Apart from initiating this book Mr. John Warrack has read the typescript and generously offered scholarly advice and penetrating criticism. His interest and encouragement have certainly enriched it.

London BRIAN LARGE
January 1970

INTRODUCTION

BEDŘICH SMETANA has rightly been called the founder of Czech music. However, the dawn of a new period began not with his birth in 1824 but thirty-eight years before. 1786 marks the spiritual awakening of music in the Bohemian lands: the year Prague was conquered by *Le Nozze di Figaro*, the year in which the city became 'Mozart's Prague', where, according to the delighted composer, 'nothing was played, sung or whistled except *Figaro*.' Twelve months later the Stavovské Divadlo saw the birth of *Don Giovanni*, and Mozart's presence in the city was 'like a ray of sunshine falling on an old grey ruin'. But Prague was in fact far from being a clutter of grey ruins. It was, and is, one of the most beautiful capitals in Europe, and through the achievements of such architects as Marini, Kilian Dienzenhofer, Hildebrandt and Fischer von Erlach, it had flowered into a superb architectural show-piece sheltering the Belvedere, the Powder Towers, the Kinsky and Nostitz Palaces, the Bertramka, the Church of St. Nicholas and a host of smaller Baroque buildings. Beneath the Charles Bridge flowed the Vltava, majestically dividing the city, and high above towered the impressive outline of Hradčany and the as yet unfinished Cathedral of St. Vitus.

This was Mozart's Prague. It was also the Prague of Josef II and the period of enlightened despotism. Reform was in the air. Prague witnessed the abolition of serfdom, the decree of religious toleration, the publication of a Czech newspaper, the foundation of the Bohemian Society of Sciences, and later the establishing of a chair of Bohemian language at the Charles University. To Josef II can be attributed the birth of Czech Nationalism, to him also the revival of interest in the literature and history of Bohemia. Though Burney had declared the Bohemians to be among the most musical people in Europe, composition was almost an imported art and the leading force who had endowed a new musical impetus in Prague was not the Emperor, but Mozart. The Mozart cult was no fleeting whim. It flourished well into the nineteenth century when the gospel was preached and propagated by devotees like Tomášek, Vitašek and Dionys (Divis) Weber.

His memory was revered and his music kept alive despite new tendencies which were beginning to stir in other capitals; and it is not surprising that Prague remained the 'spiritual hospital of Mozart' (C. M. Weber), for with no Bohemian composer to break the shackles of classicism imposed by Tomášek, an Absolutist rule was maintained.

Just as restricting was Italian opera, which played with alarming regularity and indifferent standard until 1807. In 1808, however, a German House opened and the first steps were taken to inaugurate the Prague Conservatoire. There was hope. Under Černohorský's direction the Prague Organ School had struck out on a more progressive course before being closed in the latter part of the eighteenth century. It was believed that the Conservatoire would continue the work of Černohorský, but with Divis Weber's appointment as Principal in 1811 hope faded. He slumbered peacefully without making any startling pronouncements apart from one to the effect that Beethoven's Third Symphony was an utter abortion. Though fine instrumentalists graduated from the classes of Pixis and Mildner with formidable techniques and enviable reputations—among them Paganini's rival Josef Slavík, Kalivoda and Laub—no composer emerged since composition was not part of the curriculum. Though composers of the preceding generation, including Stamic, Mysliveček, Benda, Tůma and Zelenka, had written a wealth of scores, their destiny was to flourish on foreign soils with little of their music being known in Prague. Bohemian by birth, but émigrés by choice, in Paris, Milan, Vienna and Mannheim, they forfeited their birthright, renounced their native expression and were swallowed up in the flood-tide of classicism.

Beethoven's emancipation of art, spreading through Vienna, was greeted in Prague with suspicion, even distrust. To Tomášek all progressive ideas were anathema. The lack of musical thought and activity which descended over the capital in the early years of the century was due essentially to his conservatism. Tomášek had set himself up as the high priest of classicism, impeding progress, refusing to move from his entrenchments; and though he had admired Beethoven as a performer, had known Weber personally and witnessed the birth of the Romantic era, he remained obstinately loyal to the eighteenth century.

Gradually, with the disintegration of feudal order, the rise of industrialization, and a desire among the middle classes to equal the wealthy and culturally more mature German burghers, the need for a distinctly national school of music was recognized. Musicians were faced with new problems. Patrons receded as executants sought new spheres of expression and outlets for their work. Societa, the first musicians' benevolent organization, was set up in 1803 and under its auspices concerts and recitals were given as well as performances of oratorios and choral works, though these were arranged biennially at this time. In 1808 an association for the improvement of musical arts in Bohemia was established and this, together with the growing national awareness which was beginning to manifest itself in Bohemia as it was in Russia and Poland, led to a demand for songs and choruses for male voices. Czech songs on patriotic, social and comic themes were composed by Pavel Křížkovský, who not only imitated folk idiom but incorporated it into his music. Others followed his example. Short symphonies, serenades and overtures poured from the pens of Václav Veit (a dilettante, and judge by profession), and Leopold Měchura (an amateur musician and lawyer by vocation); Josef Labický and František Hilmar provided music for dances at the Czech Society Balls which were growing in popularity. But despite this activity, opera in Prague as played at the Stavovské Theatre was a disappointment. There was no parallel to the work of Křížkovský, and the level of performance under Václav (Wenzel) Müller had degenerated to abysmal depths. However, with the new guiding hand of Karl Liebich (Director from 1808 to 1816), and under Carl Maria von Weber's baton (1813–1816), the standard was raised to an impressive degree. Weber rescued opera in Prague by improving and broadening the repertoire and removing the sense of apathy that had befallen the operatic life of the city. In 1816 his place was taken by Triebensee who, as Kapellmeister, extended the operatic horizon with the introduction of works by Auber, Rossini, Cherubini, Hérold and Boïeldieu; and under František Holbein, Weber's *Der Freischütz* and *Euryanthe* were added to the repertoire. Despite this, Czech opera remained unrepresented simply because no Czech operas existed to challenge the works of Bellini and Meyerbeer which were currently fashionable.

Following the appointment of Johann Stöger, times were to change. František Škroup, a lawyer with an interest in operatic singing, began to foster Czech Singspiele of his own composition. Modelled on Viennese examples, the Singspiel was imported into Bohemia around 1810, when J. N. Štěpánek mounted simple folk plays at amateur theatres called 'bouda' (literally 'booth' or 'trestle stage') in an attempt to awaken interest in Czech art and language. The number of Singspiele was few and in order to strengthen the repertoire foreign works were adapted in Czech versions and popular additions included Brož's *Persefone* (1820), Hanka's *Božena* (1821), and Weigl's *Die Schweizerfamilie*. Though the last-named was the work of a foreigner, it soon established itself in the vernacular as a 'Czech opera', and in 1824 Cherubini's *Les deux journées* (translated into Czech by K. S. Macháček) was accepted as thoroughly 'Czech'. In 1824 Štěpánek introduced 'Czech' performances of *Der Freischütz* and Méhul's *Joseph* (translated by Štépánek and Chmelenský) on Sundays and feast days, but such performances were mounted only in the afternoons. In the evenings opera reverted to German, even if the same works were repeated. Opera in Prague was like a mirror presenting a reflection of its own image but split in two languages: Czech for the Bohemians and German for the burghers.

After a while the public began to tire of mere translation and to thirst for genuine Czech stage works. Škroup, in collaboration with the librettist Chmelenský, produced the first native opera in Bohemia entitled *Drátenik* (*The Tinker*) on February 2, 1826, when its reception surpassed all the enthusiasm its authors could have hoped for. A second venture, *Oldřich and Božena* (December, 1828) fared less well and of *Libuše's Wedding* (1832) only Act III reached the stage in 1835, the remaining acts being given fifteen years later. *Fidlovačka* (1834) endeared itself with the song 'Kde domov můj?' ('Where is my home?'), which was adopted as the national anthem; but this apart, the generally weak nature of the libretto and uneven quality of the folk music contributed little to Czech theatre and came nowhere towards establishing a Czech operatic tradition. *Žižka's Oak* by Klicpera with music by Jiří Macourek (1847) was likewise a failure and, disillusioned, Škroup virtually retired from composition and devoted his talent to conducting; but instead of favouring the scores of other Czech composers, such as they were, he reverted to German opera, to Duke Eugen of Württemberg's *Geisterbraut* and to his own *Die Meergeuse*. Under Škroup Czech opera all but disappeared. Clearly he had neither the creative capacity nor the individuality to become the leader of a national school of music, and none of his contemporaries could offer a more hopeful solution. For Führer, Horák, Kolešovský, Mašek and Krejčí were church musicians and completely outside the national revivalist movement. Apart from Tomášek, who lived to 1850, but whose narrow-mindedness prevented his making the break from tradition, only one man could have led a campaign for Bohemian opera, and that was Bedřich Kittl (1809–1868). Kittl managed to grasp and understand what Czech music should be about; but he was an eclectic, too much involved in academic circles and Mendelssohnian Romanticism to create a new school. Unfortunately neither Kníže, Veit, Jelen, Vorel nor Martinovský had sufficient talent or imagination to take up the torch. Music in Bohemia was still-born. Before any real native voice could emerge, Prague was invaded by a number of visiting artists, notably Berlioz, who came at the request of Kittl and Ambros, leaders of a dissatisfied clique forced to look abroad for relief and inspiration. Though bitterly opposed by a conservative element led by Veit (he parodied the *Symphonie Fantastique* under the title *Episode in the Life of a Tailor*), the public responded warmly to Berlioz. Clearly Berlioz's visit had opened up new vistas for other artists who had something fresh to offer 'Tomášek's Prague'. The city became more progressive. After Berlioz came Liszt, then Wagner. Music was reborn but not by Bohemians—by French, German, and Hungarian visitors whose influence began to stifle everything Czech. Prague may have worshipped Mozart, acclaimed Berlioz, toasted Liszt and applauded Wagner, but it thirsted for music of its own. People began to look to the folk-song for salvation, but it was no guarantee of establishing a distinct national school of composition. It served as a punitive weapon against foreign influence; but no great art grew from its seeds. Only one man was able to cut a path out of the wilderness and transform Czech music into the vehicle of cultural and national ideas. This was Bedřich Smetana.

SMETANA

ONE

CHILDHOOD

1824–1843

SOME EIGHTY-FIVE miles south-east of Prague at the foot of the Czecho-Moravian highlands lies the small border town of Litomyšl. Today it remains much as it did at the beginning of the last century—pleasantly walled, with Austrian-style houses, cobbled streets and a fine Renaissance castle, the seat of the Wallenstein family. As well as supporting the castle and the rich social life which nobility brought to the community, Litomyšl was the centre of a thriving woollen and jute industry. It boasted a theatre, an imposing square, a large park, rich surrounding farmland and, on the gently rolling hills overlooking the town, the renowned Piarist School. Directly opposite the castle stood the local brewery, to which, in the autumn of 1823, Count Wallenstein appointed a new manager, František Smetana,[1] son of Václav Smetana (1730–1779), a cooper and barrel binder from Sádová near Králové Dvůr, and Ludmila (1734–1806), daughter of the miller Václav Konárovský. Born on October 26, 1777, and brought up in a poor environment, František had been apprenticed as a gamekeeper's assistant on an estate in the upper Elbe. At the age of thirteen, however, he left in search of adventure, making his way through Lower Austria to Vienna and back to Bohemia where he took up brewing in 1780. He settled for a while at Česká Skalice. Here he met and married his first wife, Anna Bartoníčková, but their years together were neither long nor happy. In 1805 she died in childbirth and shortly afterwards Smetana moved to Neise in Silesian Prussia where, during the Napoleonic wars, he abandoned his profession in order to supply the French Army with provisions and clothing. As a keen and ambitious business man he made the most of the political turn of events. He acquired a certain wealth which later enabled him to return to Bohemia and brewing, no longer as apprentice, however, but as leaseholder. In 1809 he

[1] The Smetana family tree will be found in Appendix A.

remarried, choosing as his wife the daughter of the Burgomaster of Jaroměř, Ludmila Exnerová (1779–1820) who over the next few years bore him no less than eight girls. On July 7, 1811, Smetana received the title Master Brewer from the Guild in Chvalkovice, which had become the family home the year before. Here they lived until 1820 when František's second wife died. Later he rented a brewery in Nové Město nad Metují and it was from this small town that he took his third wife, Barbora Lynková (1792–1864), a handsome woman fourteen years his junior and the daughter of a coachman in the employ of nobility in Hořice. The couple were married on November 21, 1820, and set up house in Nové Město.

Barbora Smetana was a good wife and kind mother to František's already large family. Of his children, five daughters by his second wife were then alive, the two children of his first marriage having died in infancy. To these were added two more girls, Albertína and Františka, born in 1821 and 1823 respectively. Life in Nové Město was pleasant; but it was in Litomyšl, which became the Smetanas' new home in 1823, that the family was really to flourish. As Master Brewer, Smetana was now raised to a social level which gave him an entry to noble society such as he had never known before; and he joined in this new life with the greatest enthusiasm. He was a genial, energetic man who knew how to enjoy himself. His favourite pastime was hunting, and the thick forests and beautiful countryside surrounding Litomyšl gave him every opportunity to indulge it. Although he had never had the chance of studying seriously (he learned to read and write only in later life), he was very fond of music and had taught himself to play the violin. In the evenings, by way of recreation, the family would either make music or entertain their friends with good food and lively conversation. Barbora Smetana and her husband were particularly keen dancers, and soon after their arrival, they established themselves as colourful figures at all the social events in Litomyšl. It is even said that at the Shrove-tide Ball on March 1st, 1824, Smetana's wife danced well into the early hours of the morning. There would appear to be nothing extraordinary about this had she not at ten on the morning of Shrove Tuesday (March 2nd) given birth to a boy. František Smetana's happiness knew no bounds: at last he had a son. Although his wife was to bear him seven more children over the next nine years (bringing the total to eighteen), none ever won the same affection in his father's eyes as did the first boy. He was christened Bedřich.

In the Litomyšl Register of Births the child's name is recorded in the German form 'Fridrich' [*sic*]. At this period it was customary for

Bohemians to adopt Germanic forms of spelling. In a country which had known the oppressions and restrictions of the Hapsburgs for nearly three hundred years, it is not surprising that German should have become the accepted language. As early as 1780 Czech had been abolished in Grammar Schools, and four years later German was decreed the official tongue. University lectures were no longer delivered in Latin. Though Czech was spoken by peasants and artisans, elsewhere there was a feeling that it could never survive, and significantly there was no major dictionary of the Czech language until Josef Jungmann's[2] appeared in the second quarter of the nineteenth century. František Smetana certainly knew Czech, but his position and connexions demanded that he did not use it. The business of the brewery was conducted in German, and even in the Smetana household the children remained ignorant of Czech for many years.

Bedřich, the eldest son, was a frail child whose favoured position in the family remained unshaken even though Barbora Smetana was to give birth to three more boys.[3] The home in which he grew up was unusually agreeable, and though his parents were not rich they enjoyed a comfortable position, as can be judged from their fine clothes shown in the portraits painted by Antonín Machek. Of other composers, possibly only Mozart can have known such a contented youth; but there was one important difference. On displaying signs of musical talent, Mozart found his artistic life fostered and shaped by his father. František Smetana, no professional musician like Leopold Mozart, recognized Bedřich's gifts, but regarded music as something that would give the boy pleasure in later life—nothing more. He firmly believed that to know how to play for the dance was a social asset, an attribute that would eventually ease his son's entry into noble circles, but that to know more was undesirable.

In his first years Bedřich probably heard a great deal of music. Apart from the popular songs of the young brewers there was always the sound of his father's violin. He enjoyed playing duets by Pleyel

[2] Josef Jungmann (1773–1847), scholar and writer, was responsible for bringing new vigour and flexibility to the literary Czech language. He produced a great five-volume Czech-German Dictionary (1835–1839) partly based on an earlier compilation by Dobrovský and a Polish Dictionary of Linde. Jungmann did not hesitate to borrow Polish and Russian words, adapting them to the Czech phonetic system. He was also active as a translator and was responsible for Czech versions of Milton's *Paradise Lost*, Goldsmith's *Traveller*, Gray's *Elegy*, Chateaubriand's *Atala* and Goethe's *Hermann und Dorothea*. Later he translated poems by Schiller, Klopstock and Herder and directed the school in the centre of Prague to which Smetana was later admitted.

[3] Antonín (1825–1881); František (1826–1827); Karel (1830–1907).

and the music of Jírovec, but above all he admired Haydn's Quartets. He and his family performed them so regularly that they must have formed an important part of Bedřich's listening. Small wonder that in such an environment the boy, who inherited his father's intense feeling for music, rapidly acquired a keen ear.

In his first Diary (written in German and dated May 1, 1840) Bedřich records that he was three when his father taught him to 'keep time to music'. His father also showed him how to handle a violin and read notation, and his progress was such that by the time he was four he had mastered the fundamentals of playing and could take the leader's place in a Haydn Quartet to celebrate his father's fifty-first birthday. At the age of five he became a pupil at the local Piarist School, where he continued to study the violin, and at his father's suggestion began to learn the piano from Jan Chmelík (1777–1849), a well-schooled musician but one who was little above the average level of town cantors. Bedřich's progress, however, was prodigious, and on October 14, 1830, he made his first public appearance. At a concert given to celebrate the name day of the Emperor, and held in the local school hall, Bedřich played a piano arrangement of the striking overture to Auber's *La Muette de Portici*—just two years after the Paris première. So warm was the reception which Litomyšl gave the six-year-old boy that Count Wallenstein's secretary had to lift him into the air to allow the crowd to see him more easily. Bedřich was hailed as a child prodigy and many of the local inhabitants believed that he should give himself entirely to music. His father was less certain. Bedřich's talents had appeared spontaneously at a relatively early age, but not unnaturally František had misgivings. In the 1830's the life of a professional musician was precarious: to František it seemed safer to have his son acquire a good basic education rather than attend a music school. And so it was that Bedřich devoted as much time to general studies as he did to music.

In 1831 František Smetana was offered an appointment as brewer on Count Czernin's estate at Jindřichův Hradec. Since the conditions were more attractive than those in Litomyšl, he accepted the post and with his family moved south into a region which had once been the seat of the famous Rožmberk family. Its connexions with nobility apart, the town had been in coaching days one of the halting places between Vienna and Prague, and was delightfully situated, with fine old houses surrounded by downs and thick woodlands. In Jindřichův Hradec, Bedřich attended first the elementary school, then the gymnasium. He continued his musical studies with the local organist, František Ikavec (1800–1860), a sound musician and the first to insist on the boy's following a systematic course of study. It was Ikavec who introduced him to the music of Mozart, Beethoven and Hummel, and Ikavec who laid the foundations of his vocal technique.

Little is known of how Bedřich spent his leisure hours in Jindřichův Hradec but it is certain he joined the local church choir, where he sang regularly as a treble, and sometimes as soloist. It is likely that his first compositions date from this period. The earliest extant work is a simple piano piece called *Kvapíček* (*Little Galop*) written in 1832, but this is only a copy of dance music and in no way suggests an outstanding talent. Although he probably composed other miniatures of a similar nature, nothing has been preserved and the next compositions appear from the year 1839.

In Jindřichův Hradec, František Smetana's keen business sense enabled him to accumulate a considerable fortune; in 1835 he fulfilled one of his most cherished ambitions and bought a farm at Růžková Lhotice, near Čechtice, in a region dominated by the legendary Blaník Mountain. Here the Hussite army was supposed to have concealed itself in order to emerge in the country's darkest days of suffering and defeat the enemy. In such surroundings,[4] rich in historical events, Bedřich found much that fascinated him, much that furnished him with ideas for later compositions. He was attracted by stories of the past as he was by natural phenomena. The Hussite Wars, the figure of Žižka, the Táborites and great castles like Wallenstein's in Litomyšl within whose shadow he had been raised, were impressions he drew on many years later in *Blaník*, *Tábor* and *Wallenstein's Camp*. Similarly the huge wall of rock, stretching across the Vltava at Vyši Brod, which local tradition says was thrown down by the Devil in prehistoric times, the swiftly flowing Vltava itself, and the beautiful Bohemian landscape with its deep forests and rolling hills were part of a picture which was stored up and reproduced in the opera *The Devil's Wall*, and the tone poems *Vltava* and *From Bohemia's Woods and Fields*.

With this move to Růžková Lhotice, the Smetanas' life assumed a character far more fitting for nobility than farmers; and they lived accordingly. Bedřich was very happy on the farm, spending much of his time getting to know the life and work of the peasants and local people. He became aware of their customs, their songs and something of their language; he grew friendly with the itinerant bands of musicians who passed Lhotice on their way to Jihlava, for the farmhouse

[4] Some thirty years later the same geographical region helped to colour the sensibility of another Bohemian composer—Gustav Mahler.

was large and František Smetana loved to play host to these strolling troupes. In return for a night's lodging they would perform sketches, sing folk songs or make music for dancing. These gay scenes undoubtedly coloured the imagination of the eleven-year-old boy, who possibly recalled them when characterizing the strolling comedians in the third act of *The Bartered Bride* and Skřivánek, the ballad singer in *The Secret*. Apart from these wandering groups of entertainers, other travellers passed near Růžková Lhotice especially at Easter when pilgrims made their way through the neighbouring countryside to the shrine at Loreta near Vlašim. Bedřich certainly witnessed their processions and may well have drawn upon his memories of them for scenes in *Dalibor*, *Libuše* and *The Secret*.

As there was no school in the area, Bedřich was obliged to leave the farm and travel to Jihlava to continue his education. Accompanied by Antonín, his brother, he attended a German school with the sole purpose of acquiring a fluent knowledge of that language. Although he was entrusted to Viktorín Mat'ocha (1801–1862) for his musical studies, he made little progress, and being away from home for the first time became unhappy and depressed. In the second term his father removed him from Jihlava and enrolled him as a pupil at the gymnasium in Německý Brod (now Havlíčkův Brod), where he was placed in the first form. Here the boy settled down well, and his three years at the school were to be among the most formative of his entire childhood. Outside his normal studies, he became intimately acquainted with the popular Bohemian plays of the folk puppet master Matěj Kopecký (1762–1846), whose simple tales made such an impression on him that he came to know them by heart and re-enacted them for his friends. In later years they led him to write two small orchestral works based on Kopecký's versions of *Dr. Faust* and *Oldřich and Božena*. Two enlightened teachers, Václav Divok and Karel Šindelář, did much to encourage Bedřich at this time. Father Karel, Professor of Grammar and Classics, was no professional musician but he greatly enjoyed music, particularly that of Weber (whose name was still very much alive in Bohemia ever since his years as Director of the Prague Opera from 1813 to 1816). Unfortunately Bedřich received no musical instruction at Německý Brod, but Father Karel did introduce him to Weber's *Der Freischütz*, which made a profound impression on him. During his holidays he spent countless hours coming to understand the music as best he could. At school he struck up a friendship with a fellow pupil, Karel Havlíček[5]

[5] Karel Havlíček Borovský (1821–1856). The first great Czech journalist and leader of public opinion. He was trained as a philosopher at the Charles Uni-

Borovský, his senior by three years and even at this time an uncompromising political publicist. Later, Havlíček was to become one of the leaders championing the cause of Czech Nationalism and to play an important part in the uprising of 1848. The two boys became good friends, and when in 1839 Havlíček left Německý Brod for Prague, he sent Bedřich glowing reports of the city which at that time was not only one of the largest in Central Europe but the economic and cultural hub of Bohemia. By now Bedřich had begun to realize how restricted and narrow his life had been. Prague, as seen through the letters of Havlíček, seemed to draw him irresistibly. Finally in the autumn of 1839, besieged by his son's persistent entreaties to be allowed to join Havlíček, František Smetana gave way.

Hitherto the boy had known many small Bohemian towns, but nothing of the size and grandeur of Prague. With a population exceeding three hundred thousand, spacious streets, new buildings, an opera house (basically German but with a large repertoire), a lively social life enhanced by concerts given by outstanding virtuosi, it is no wonder Smetana was exhilarated by his new surroundings. Prague was one of the most beautiful cities in Europe, ancient and majestic, with the great Vltava flowing through its centre, a skyline broken by spires and towers, and a monumental panorama dominated by Hradčany. Smetana was probably much too absorbed with this inspiring atmosphere to become aware of the restrictions and persecutions which Metternich's rule of Absolutism brought to the city. Indeed, he found it very difficult to give himself to his academic studies. On the recommendation of his Plzeň cousin, Dr. Josef Smetana,[6] he was admitted to the Prague Classical Grammar School in the Old Town—directed by the celebrated Josef Jungmann and for entry to which competition was naturally great. The majority of the pupils stemmed from prosperous German burgher classes and had been brought up in sophisticated homes. Smetana, a shy, frail

versity and became a priest. Later he taught in Russia but turned to journalism in 1845, becoming Editor of *Pražské Noviny* and *Česká Včela*. In 1848 he took an active interest in politics and founded the newspapers *Národní Noviny* and *Slovan* in which he became well known for his satirical and witty epigrams abusing Austria's reactionary clerical régime, the Church and Czech society of the day. In 1851 he fell foul of the police and was deported to the Tyrol where he produced his most sarcastic and humorous literary works. Notable among his output are *Tyrol Elegies*, *King Lávra* and *The Conversion of St. Vladimír*.

[6] Dr. František Josef Smetana (1801–1861) was the son of Bedřich's uncle, Josef. He later became a teacher in Plzeň specializing in philosophy, theology, history and astrology.

country boy, the son of a brewer, did not fit in. Jungmann's school was founded on a rigid German educational system, and though Smetana had known that language since birth he had never mastered it grammatically. Lessons became a burden. He could not express himself clearly, he was humiliated by his teacher, Professor Chýle, and mocked by the class for his country manners. Sensitive at all times, he decided to tolerate this no more and without permission absented himself.

Although he had occasional piano lessons from Jan Batka (1795–1874), Smetana spent most of his time in the company of František Butula (1820–1885), whom he had known in Německý Brod and who had left the school there to seek his fortune in Prague. Butula was a philosophy student who later became a teacher in Chotěboř, and in his spare time he formed a String Quartet[7] (it met every evening) of which Smetana was the leader, František Kostka and Antonín Vlček the other members. Havlíček attended as the respectful listener. Life was certainly happier away from Jungmann's school, but it was also harder. He found it difficult to make ends meet, and as he had little money for food and clothing, could ill afford to purchase new music. A certain amount of improvisation was therefore necessary and from a Diary entry we can get some idea of his ingenuity:

> . . . from our joint funds the Quartet would give me the price of a ticket for the Žofín Hall or a concert at a beer-house where new music was being played. As I was gifted with a good memory I noted the pieces down after only one hearing. Later Butula arranged them for the Quartet to play.

On the Žofín Island[8] Smetana became acquainted with the popular

[7] At this time quartet playing was so popular that at least ten groups are known to have existed in Prague alone.

[8] Smetana was unable to hear any of the Žofín Philharmonic concerts at this time since they were essentially for a society audience who could afford tickets far beyond his pocket. The Philharmonic concerts were arranged by the brothers Scraub; the younger directed a ninety-strong choir, while the older conducted an orchestra drawn from the Opera. According to Berlioz, who attended several of these concerts in 1846, they were great occasions:

> . . . prepared with exemplary care a long time in advance, they always attract a large élite audience for whom music is neither recreation nor a tiresome duty, but a serious passion demanding and receiving all one's powers of intelligence, concentration, ardour and sensibility. . . . I had never heard and have not heard since such pungent vocal writing performed with such dash, precision, accuracy of intonation, command of vivid contrasts and splendidly sonorous tone. . .

(*Memoirs:* Sixth Letter from Prague to Humbert Ferrand.
In the translation by David Cairns.)

tunes of the day as well as the marches which formed the core of most programmes given there by the Band of the Prague House Regiment conducted by Emil Titl. As these pieces were generally of little musical value, and consequently of less interest to the Quartet, Smetana could not resist composing for his own group.

Unfortunately only the sketch of the first violin part of a set of Waltzes has come down to us. We know from his first catalogue (dated April 3, 1841) that in the five months between October 1839 and Easter 1840 he wrote at least six works for the group, but from the remarks recorded there it seems unlikely they were on a very ambitious scale:

1 Polka for Quartet.
2 Two Polkas for Quartet—I call the second one Osmanen (Turkish).
3 String Quartet in D flat minor [*sic*]. (This Quartet is my first: the workmanship is poor, there is not much harmony in it nor much pleasure to be gained from it.)
4 Waltzes for Quartet. (An introduction with five waltzes—and not very good!)
5 Overture for Quartet. (In the style of Mozart: everyone at the time though it to be good.)
6 Fantasy for Quartet. (Based on a motive from the second act of Bellini's opera *Il Pirata*.)[9]

Apart from these early attempts at composition,[1] Smetana devoted himself to piano playing. Up to now his development had tended to move erratically, and being without supervision for long periods he had learnt as much from listening to performers as he had from his mediocre teachers. Avidly he devoured all that he could lay his hands on—Mozart, Beethoven, Hummel, Schubert, even the *Études* of Bertini. On Sundays, the great theatre-going day of the week, he went to the Opera or to concerts—that is, when he could afford to—in the hope of coming to know the best that musical life in Prague could offer. Fate was certainly on his side. Early in 1840 Franz Liszt visited the city and gave five recitals which captivated Smetana, and convinced him that only in music could he find satisfaction. His Diary records that these concerts were the most beautiful days ever spent in Prague. It is hard to estimate the profound effect Liszt's playing had on him; for he was not only the great magician of the

[9] Only the first violin part was noted down, but from this is established the basic key of D minor which swings in the second part into D major.

[1] Six duets for two violins under the name 'Smetana' are not genuine.

keyboard, but a composer of the Romantic school and a hero to be emulated. Smetana can have had no idea that the virtuoso whom he revered so greatly was to become his adviser, friend and confidant. At this time he had only one aim: to become as prodigious a technician as Liszt, and the *Études* of Chopin became the object of his untiring practice.

In February, 1840, Smetana planned two piano compositions on a grand scale, the first to be written since the *Little Galop* of 1832 and modelled on Liszt's bravura style. At each concert Liszt had performed his dazzling arrangement of airs from Bellini's opera *I Puritani*. Profoundly impressed, Smetana now began to sketch two sets of variations which also took their themes from a Bellini opera —in this case, *I Capuletti ed i Montecchi*. Neither is complete, but sufficient is preserved to show the Lisztian influence—brilliant cadenza-like passages, rolling arpeggio accompaniments, glittering filigree embellishments, all in the style of the best paraphrases. Vacuous they may be, but one fact emerges: to perform them as he certainly did, Smetana, at sixteen, must have possessed a formidable technique.

In the following month Smetana's father paid an unexpected visit to Prague and was horrified to learn from Josef Jungmann that his son had absented himself from the school several weeks before. Instead of a conscientious student, František Smetana found a wild rebel, and immediately a rift developed between father and son. Having no means of supporting himself, Bedřich was obliged to leave Prague and journey south to Nové Město where his uncle Václav was the local brewer. After the excitement of city life, he was able to relax in the pleasant countryside and here it was that he became involved in his first romance. Smetana was not a handsome youth. Short of stature, slim, with brown hair, a prominent nose and large forehead, he did not make a very impressive figure. (There may well be some truth in Balzac's theory that the great men of history have generally been small: 'the head has to be near the heart if the two powers that govern the human organization are to function well'). His bluish-green eyes were invariably hidden by the thick-lensed spectacles he used to aid his short sight; and in later years he grew a small beard and wore a top hat with a narrow crown, which lent him a somewhat eccentric appearance. Yet there was something about him which women found attractive, perhaps it was his gaiety and *joie-de-vivre*. Whatever it was, his cousin Louisa, his senior by one year, was the first to fall for him. Smetana wrote and dedicated two pieces to her. The first, now lost, was a set of eleven short movements

PLATE I

František
Smetana

Barbora
Lynková
(Smetana's
mother)

PLATE II

Two views of the Smetana brewery at Litomyšl

for piano, four hands, called *Vzpomínka na Nové Město* (*Memories of Nové Město*). The second, which has been preserved, is *Louisa's Polka*. Modest in aim and achievement, it is nevertheless a delightful drawing-room dance in ternary form that has the air of an improvization about it. Although he was a considerable pianist, he knew little if anything of the technical side of composition, and most of the juvenilia are fashioned on the music he must have heard around him. Smetana himself thought highly of this piece, and a year later wrote:

> Without flattery to myself I can say that this Polka has hardly any equal. Each bar is charming and lovely and all those in Plzeň who know it cannot praise it enough. I can't play any of my pieces without tiring of them; but this one I can play repeatedly.[2]

Louisa's Polka became so popular that it was later orchestrated by Pavel Svoboda and played at a ball in Plzeň in the autumn of 1840. This was the first occasion on which Smetana heard one of his own compositions in orchestral form, and the Diary reveals his displeasure:

> At the Philosophers' Ball my *Louisa's Polka* was played, but it did not sound well, as the conductor—from Baron Fleischer's Infantry Regiment—had not arranged it satisfactorily.

After his stay in Nové Město Smetana returned to Růžková Lhotice, where his parents were toying with the idea of binding him to farming. Their deliberations were interrupted by Josef Smetana—a professor at the Premonstratensian Grammar School in Plzeň—who offered to place the youth under his care and supervise his studies. In Plzeň Smetana enrolled at the gymnasium, joining the fourth form where he was one of the oldest pupils.[3] That he began to take his studies more seriously we know from the Diary:

> During June and July life was very easy-going—I didn't do a thing. In October, November and December, however, I did penance and changed sloth to diligence and in that way gave myself great pleasure.[4]

Smetana's teachers, drawn from the Tepl Monastery in Western Bohemia, were initially successful in capturing the boy's attention:

[2] Diary: August, 1840.

[3] In his first year he lodged with one of his teachers, Father Jan Sýkora, but in 1841 he moved to the house of the widow Mrs. Wildmannová, who offered accommodation in return for piano lessons for her son.

[4] Diary: December, 1840.

> At the examination in Latin and history they were satisfied with my progress. Please God may I always be able to write this in my Diary.[5]

But his willingness to study diligently was not to be maintained:

> I am persecuted by misfortune in my studies. When I am asked a question I never know the answer, even when I've prepared my work. I think my marks will be less than excellent this term . . . If only I were not so overtaxed I could compose more often and with greater attention to detail, but Professor Graumann gives us so many exercises that I can spare only a few moments for playing my pieces and even less for hunting which has become my favourite pastime.[6]

Indeed, his marks were less than excellent but the fault was not entirely his own. His musical talents had been discovered soon after arriving in Plzeň, and one of his teachers, Father Gustav Beer, a man of huge physique, began to introduce him to society. Smetana showed such a command of the keyboard and played the music of Chopin and Liszt with such mastery that he swiftly came to be regarded as a distinct social asset in the town. Though Father Beer was responsible for suggesting the composition of *Píseň o Sv. Janu Nepomukém* (*Song to the Memory of Jan of Nepomuk*),[7] he continued to exploit the boy in this way, but mostly so as to further his own connexions and at the expense of his charge's academic studies.

In Plzeň, the contemporary bourgeois circles were neither particularly distinguished nor highly original in devising forms of entertainment. Life was gentle and unhurried and much time was devoted to music. There was the Opera, but in Bohemia, as in Italy, the *prima donna* reigned supreme. In so-called 'academies', recitals were given by visiting celebrities and alleged virtuosi who would astound their audiences with daring pyrotechnics and feats of bombast. Symphonies and long orchestral works were rarely performed and the planning of Plzeň's musical evenings was generally

[5] Diary: *op. cit.*

[6] Diary: April 3, 1841.

[7] Unfortunately the *Song to the Memory of Jan of Nepomuk* has not been preserved, but from the Diary, where its composition is noted as being completed within two hours, it seems unlikely it was very substantial. The legend of Jan of Nepomuk, as recorded by the chronicler Hajek of Libocan (1383) describes him as a Jesuit priest who, for refusing to disclose the secret confessions of the Queen, was chained and thrown into the Vltava by Wenceslas IV. As the Bohemian Saint of bridges, his martyrdom is commemorated by a statue on the Charles Bridge in Prague.

PLATE III

Daguerreotype of Smetana in 1843, aged 19

First known manuscript—Galop in D major

Tyn Church and Old Town Square

Vltava River and Charles Bridge

PLATE IV. Views of Old Prague

in the hands of local dilettanti whose taste and musical knowledge were more often not so much suspect as simply negligible. Short overtures, fantasias, sets of variations, transcriptions, characteristic salon pieces and, above all, dances formed the popular programme items. The cultivation of music in the home was something which stemmed originally from the drawing-rooms of the aristocracy, where dancing was regarded as the principal pleasure. During the 1830's the first Czech Society Balls had won enormous success, the favourite items being those of native origin such as the třasák, rejdovák, skočná and sousedská. Imported dances like the waltz were performed but the step which became something of an epidemic was the polka (of Polish origin). This was made popular by František Hilmar (1803–1881), a music teacher from Kopidlny whose *Prague*, *Libuše*, *Přemysl*, *Amazon*, *Esmeralda* and *Silvester* Polkas were in vogue and formed the basic repertoire of Josef Labický's touring Carlsbad Spa Orchestra. These Polkas were certainly known in Plzeň and were important in serving to introduce young people to each other. Any young man who could sweep his partner off the floor and then sit at the keyboard to make music for dancing was in great demand. Smetana had just these gifts, and it is not surprising that he became a welcome guest in the majority of homes. His life developed into a round of pleasure. Soon he became acquainted with every type of musical entertainment, and being himself a keen dancer he wrote a number of pieces especially for dancing. Most of these were composed for the piano and are important not so much for the value of the music as for the emergence of certain musical features which in later years became marks of his style.

The *Galop di Bravoura* and *Jiřinková* (*Dahlia*) *Polka* were written soon after Smetana's arrival in Plzeň in 1840 and intended for domestic consumption there. The *Galop*, as its title suggests, is a brilliant piece with strong overtones of Liszt's *Grande Valse di Bravura*, written four years earlier. It is of virtuoso character, calling for good octave work throughout and a single extract (Example 1) will show how much the piece was designed for showing off a superlative technique.

The Polka entitled *Dahlia* is quite different from the one Smetana wrote for his cousin Louisa some months before. This is a remembrance of an event—a flower exhibition and the dance festivities following it in Česká Skalice in 1839. The piece has two trios, the second of which is interesting for the appearance of the augmented sixth chord—a harmonic feature that characterizes the scores of the final years. The Polka is a gay, busy piece written in the style of

Example 1

Liszt, and for all its immaturity has something of the awkward charm of adolescence. Following this, Smetana produced his *Grande Polka* in B flat which is also known as *Polčinka*. Written for Lida Bradáčová, 'one of the finest pianists in Plzeň, next to me', only a sketch exists, but from this we can see it was to be not a single polka but a chain of five with introduction and coda. The sketch, which dates from February 3, 1841, is described in the Diary as being 'too difficult for dancing' and is worked out on an ambitious, almost heroic scale with bravura keyboard writing and daring key schemes which anticipate Smetana's later adventurous modulations. There followed two Waltzes, two Galops, and a Polka and Nocturne,[8] but unfortunately none of these has been preserved. In the autumn of the same year, however, there appeared *Three Impromptus* which are intact and which Smetana regarded in a different light:

> These are the first of my pieces to be written in a decent way: that is not in a dance style. Only gnomes and ghosts could possibly dance to them. I hope to see them in print and at the same time to begin real composition.[9]

As a set the *Impromptus* are not particularly striking, but they are of interest for the various features of his style which are beginning to

[8] Diary: February–June, 1841. [9] Diary: February–June, 1841.

emerge, if only in embryo. The first, in E flat minor, a Romance marked Andante, is the most original composition that he had so far produced. The initial melodic material is in the style of the Russian folk song known in English as 'Black Eyes' while the part writing suggests Field or Mendelssohn. Yet beneath the surface there is an underlying personality which is essentially Smetana's own—the subtle use of shifting harmonies over sustained pedal notes, the fondness for swinging between dominant seventh and tonic chords, and the modulation method of sliding up or down a semitone. The second *Impromptu*, Allegro Moderato in B flat minor, acts as a foil to the first, and again the idiom is entirely personal. In the outer parts he pays respect to Beethoven, in the chromatic middle section to the virtuoso display of Liszt. Here, for the first time, the composer discovers the power of dramatic contrast and exuberantly calls for sudden dynamic graduations ranging from *ppp* to *fff*. Also remarkable is the first appearance of one of Smetana's characteristic markings, 'praecipite e con tutta forza'. The last *Impromptu*, in A flat, dates from January, 1842, and is in the style of a lullaby, recalling one of Mendelssohn's *Lieder ohne Wörte* with a sense of flow that is never forced. Technically it is far less demanding than either of the preceding pieces and here Smetana possibly made concessions to the amateur pianists of Plzeň who may have found the earlier *Impromptu* taxing. The use of dynamic markings and irregular phrase lengths shows how his style was forming; and the return of sustained pedal harmonies in the coda was to become a distinct musical fingerprint.

In the spring of 1842 Smetana turned to writing dance forms again. The Diary for March mentions the composition of a *Quadrille* and a *Bravoura Waltz* in C sharp minor. Neither is extant. He followed these with a brilliant Polka which has been preserved and reflects the gaiety and exuberance of his days in Plzeň. *Ze studentského zivota* (*From a Student's Life*)[1] is a lively piece which has all the wit of a Mendelssohn *Scherzo* and the élan of a Liszt *Étude* (see Example 2 overleaf).

After completing this Polka, Smetana turned his hand to orchestration, choosing his own *Minuet* in B flat and *Galop Bajader*. Here for the first time we see him groping to solve the problems of instrumentation. Apart from the string writing, which is accomplished (the violins being occasionally in double and triple stopping), Smetana's most obvious weakness is in the handling of the woodwind. Of this it seems he had little working knowledge; in the *Minuet* he called for two oboes

[1] Some sixteen years later Smetana revised this work, giving it a 'vivo' marking which not only alters the nature of the Polka but makes it difficult to dance.

Example 2

in E flat,[2] but writes the score in the first section as if for oboes in F. On the original manuscript of the *Galop*, he indicates that clarinets 'a 2' are to be used, but from time to time we find four-part writing. Similarly in the *Galop*, the bassoons are pitched outside their range (especially in the tutti passages) and the notation is in the treble clef as if for violins. In spite of thick scoring and congested textures which occasionally obscure the melodic lines, both compositions are eminently danceable.[3] The *Minuet* shows an influence of Boccherini more than Mozart or Haydn, while the *Galop*, by far the most successful, displays a lively temperament, anticipating the spirited and boisterous character of the mature works.

Smetana composed with great facility during his Plzeň years, but the inspiration behind much of his music was not exclusively the dance. When he wrote *Louisa's Polka* it was something other than his cousin's musical talent which interested him. He was no stranger to feminine company: he had been brought up in a family of girls and in the Plzeň society his acquaintances had generally been female. Smetana was excitable, impulsive, irascible; he read all the contemporary literature, full of passion and intrigue; he was an ardent romantic; a follower of Hector Berlioz, whose temperament and eroticism were close to his own; he was able to love intensely, but his

[2] Though oboes in E flat were used in continental military bands (see Forsyth: *Orchestration*, p. 229) their appearance is very rare and one wonders if Smetana really intended to use them here. Writing for them in F is more likely to have been an error of transposition than a lack of woodwind knowledge. The clarinet and bassoon mistakes, however, are certainly the result of ignorance.

[3] The Diary for June 8, 1843, records that Smetana danced these 'fashionable' pieces himself.

feelings, though genuine, were of a short-term character. At this time the names of many young ladies appear in the Diary and from some of the accompanying entries it seems he changed his sweethearts more frequently than he did his shirts. After Louisa, and Lida Bradáčová he became infatuated with Elizabeth Gollerová, a young beauty for whom he composed *The Elizabeth Waltz*; but Elizabeth proved to be nothing more than a fleeting whim, and her place was taken first by Marie, sister of the Plzeň Smetana, to whom he dedicated *The Marina Polka*, then by Kateřina Corvinová for whom he wrote *The Kateřina Polka*. She, too, failed to hold his attention, and a successor was found in Clara (her surname is not known)—a sixteen-year-old pupil at the Plzeň Art School. To her he dedicated a *Quadrille* (now lost) and sang her praises in his Diary. But as was usual with him, his feelings were short-lived and when after a few months he sought to terminate their romance, Clara objected. She clung to him, pleaded with him, refused to leave him—but to no avail:

> My heart, so deeply troubled, is quiet at last. It has born so many sorrows; but now I am vindicated. Hot and destructive was the fire but all is extinguished and there is nothing left it can destroy. Clara conquered me but now I am released. I shall celebrate my victory in freeing myself from her destructive clutches which would otherwise have held me prisoner and tortured me. We have separated. Adieu, Clara![4]

The reason for his break with Clara was Kateřina Kolářová (1827–1859), daughter of Karel Kolář (1800–1853), a food-tax commissioner, and Anna Mixová (1804–1880), whom Smetana had known in his childhood days at Jindřichův Hradec. At that period Kateřina had been something of a tomboy and her exuberance had led to her becoming known everywhere as 'wild Kate'. In Plzeň Smetana found no harum-scarum girl but a young lady with a beautiful slim figure, a lovely face and deep, expressive eyes. She was three years his junior and the only pianist whom he regarded as his equal: 'Today I was playing with Kate some four-handed pieces—she plays well and is best of all the ladies here'.[5] Soon after their meeting he arranged to take up lodgings in the Kolář's household, where, before long, he became captivated by Kateřina's charms. 'When I am not with her I am sitting on hot coals and have no peace'.[6] That he looked upon her as different from his previous friends we know from another entry:

[4] Diary: April, 1842. [5] Diary: May 31, 1842.
[6] Diary: June 29, 1842.

> Slowly that strange feeling has blossomed into love. May it flower for ever! You are curious, dear little book, to know who it is that lives in my heart. Let me tell you . . . it is Kate, yes Kateřina—a virtuoso who with her heart has captured my affections![7]

Not unnaturally he began to write music with Kateřina especially in mind, and in the autumn produced his *Overtures*, designed in a four-handed version so that he could become more closely acquainted with Miss Kolářová. It is evident from the inscription which was added to the manuscript six years later that Smetana did not then value these pieces highly:

> Composed in Plzeň in the darkness of the most complete ignorance of all musical science and saved from destruction by fire only thanks to the intercession of the owner who was anxious to keep this effusion as a curiosity of its kind.

The *Overtures* are neither distinguished nor memorable, the arrangement being sometimes thick and ineffective. In both pieces the form is the same: a slow introduction followed by a number of faster episodes which are musically uneven.

The next creations for Kateřina, *Two Quadrilles*, are on a much higher level. The quadrille (a form of square dance) had become popular at the court of Napoleon I and then in France generally; imported into Bohemia in the 1820's, it soon became fashionable and possibly Smetana had danced it in Plzeň himself. The original quadrille or contredanse was a five-section piece, but Smetana extended his to include a sixth. The *Quadrille* in F has each movement titled in French. The underlying musical influence is undoubtedly Robert Schumann, and Smetana must certainly have had the Opus 9 *Carnaval* pieces at the back of his mind when composing it: the trick of doubling the right hand melody in octaves comes directly from Schumann's 'Valse Noble' or 'Estrella'; and the darting left hand accompaniments possibly find their origins in 'Reconnaissance'. Schumann's influence apart, there is much here that is typical of Smetana himself: the movement of the melody in parallel sixths in 'Pantalon'; the stream of running thirds in 'L'Été'; the sustained pedal harmonies of 'Poule'; the polka-like character of 'Pastourelle'; the appearance in 'Trenis' of a theme which looks forward to the great Polka in the opera *The Two Widows*. The *Quadrille* in B flat is musically less rich than the first; but this, too, seems to have been written under the influence of Schumann, and contains marks of the composer's maturing style

[7] Diary: June, 1842.

similar to those found in the F major work including one not noted before—the abrupt changes of mode from major to minor, a feature returning in the works of the last years which may well have developed unconsciously from his knowledge of Schubert's piano music.

Apart from a delightful miniature for piano called *Duo beze slov* (*Song Without Words*), an incomplete *Étude* for the left hand and a *Romance*, all for Kateřina, Smetana wrote nothing more during his school days. In June, 1843, the Kolář family moved from Plzeň to the small town of Mladá Boleslav twenty-five miles north of Prague, and in July he spent a happy holiday with them during which his feelings for Kateřina became certain:

> When I look at Kate my heart begins to beat, but there's nothing of Clara's blazing flame—just a sea of heavenly warmth. I have reached a peak from which no mortal power can throw me down. Slowly, very slowly I am kindled by a pure and blissful love that will warm me for ever . . . She has become something unearthly for me and if I had a picture of her I would kneel before it for hours and hours.[8]

At the end of the summer term he left the Premonstratensian Grammar School without any noticeable distinction and was faced with the problem of finding some means of livelihood. He could expect little financial assistance from his parents, who during his Plzeň days had fallen upon hard times and been obliged to sell the farm at Růžková Lhotice to pay off debts caused by crop failure. František Smetana had been forced to lease a small brewery at Obříství on the slopes of the Mělník vineyards where, as manager, he eked out an existence which barely kept the wolf from the door. He had hoped that Bedřich might enter the Civil Service or become a brewer, as had Antonín the younger son; but the Plzeň Smetana, Bedřich's cousin, was convinced that he was fit only to become a musician. František, while loath to see his son struggle in what he considered to be a precarious profession, refused to stand in the boy's way and was obliged to give his consent for Bedřich to follow a musical career. So it was that Smetana left for Prague. Hopeful of renewing his friendship with Kateřina (who had enrolled at a music institute there), confident that the city would recognize his gifts and certain that he would fulfil his ambition he wrote:

> By the grace of God and with His help I shall one day be a Liszt in technique, a Mozart in composition.[9]

[8] Diary: September, 1843. [9] Diary: January 23, 1843.

TWO

YEARS OF APPRENTICESHIP
1843–1846

THE STERN POLICE absolutism, which had been established throughout the Hapsburg Monarchy after the French Revolution and maintained and administered by Metternich, pressed heavily on Bohemia. In Prague the general oppression was most acute: the Czech language was excluded from public affairs and education and Austrian domination of the Czech masses continued everywhere. Not even the institutions of art and learning were really of Czech character: the Royal Bohemian Society of Sciences, though founded in 1774, was only chartered in 1790; and the Stavovské Divadlo (also known as the Stände, Nostitz and Tyl Theatre) had been created to house Italian opera in 1783. Gradually, however, the longing for political liberty and freedom of expression led to a revival of national consciousness among a handful of patriots. As the Austrian police were endowed with the power of expulsion, there were constant persecutions; but a few young men braved the authorities and managed to obtain the support of the more enlightened members of Bohemian nobility who attempted to revive enthusiasm for the Czech language. It was largely through the support of such people that new scholarly institutions were established. In 1793 a chair of Czech Language and Literature was established at the Charles University in Prague and in 1818 the Museum of the Kingdom of Bohemia (later the National Museum) was founded with a rich library. From 1827 to 1832 the Museum published two journals, one in German, the other in Czech, but after 1832 only the Czech version was continued under the title *Časopis českého musea*. The first Czech newspaper had appeared in 1786 (from 1824 known as *Pražske Noviny*) and a number of others were brought out in the 1820's: important being *Krok*, *Čechoslav* and *Česká Včela*. In 1831 the Česká Matica Society was established with the sole purpose of supporting the publication of books devoted to Bohemia's past, and the movement for a National Revival (Národní Obrození). A spirit of enlightenment spreading from France and Germany began to awaken Bohemian men of letters who, with tremendous energy, unearthed and studied the medieval literature of the Czechs; and the language was thus revived by people who most naturally spoke German even among themselves. Czech and the study of national history were fostered by the aristocracy, the Thun, Wallenstein, Sternberg, Černin and Kinsky families, who were as much interested in tracing their lineages as they were in encouraging pioneers such as Dobrovský,[1] Jungmann the indefatigable translator and scholar, Palacký,[2] Puchmajer,[3] and later Karel Havlíček. Along with the rehabilitation of Czech literature and history came the discovery of many ancient documents dealing with the history of Bohemia. In 1817 a manuscript was brought to light at Králové Dvůr (Königshof), and a year later another was found at Zelená Hora (Grunberg). These famous collections of medieval epic and lyric poems, though recently thought to be the work of the forgers Václav Hanka and Josef Linda, did as much to make the people aware of their past as the *Kalevala* did for the Finns or *The Epic of the Army of Igor* for the Russians. With these and other manuscripts like the *Kiev Letters* (900), the *Legend of St. Wenceslas* (940) and the Glagolitic *Prague Fragments* came the rediscovery of folk songs[4] and the chorales of Hus.[5]

[1] Josef Dobrovský (1753–1829) was the first man to begin a scientific study of Czech language and literature and the founder of Slavonic philology (including old Slavonic). A historian and writer whose influence on Czech literature was immense, he attempted to codify the Czech language in a number of grammars and prepared a Czech-German Dictionary (1802–1821) which became the basis of Jungmann's five-volume Dictionary of 1835–1839.

[2] František Palacký (1798–1876) was the greatest of all Czech historians and author of a vast Czech History.

[3] Antonín Puchmajer (1769–1820), priest, patriot and follower of Dobrovský, was a writer who assisted Dobrovský in his dictionary work and prepared on his own a Czech-Russian Speller, a Russian Grammar (in German), and a Grammar of Gipsy language and of criminal jargon. These were followed by a rhyming dictionary and a volume of sermons and religious odes that are deistic in spirit. Puchmajer also produced a collection of Fables and a number of patriotic idylls.

[4] The first volume of Bohemian folk songs had been made in 1825 by Johann Ritter von Rittersburg but the most important is that by Karel Erben (*Folk Songs of Bohemia*, 1842) which contains more than two thousand, two hundred songs and variants. Erben (1811–1870), philosopher, poet and official archivist of the City of Prague, was one of the most important workers in the field of folk lore. Apart from collating folk melody, he gathered folk tales and ballads of the Slavonic peoples which became the definitive collection in Bohemia.

[5] Jan Hus born 1369 (1376?) at Husinec in Southern Bohemia, priest and revivalist who codified the written Czech language in treatises, sermons and letters and established a new orthography. Rector of Prague University and confessor to Queen Sofia, he was burnt at the stake in Constance (1415) for alleged heretical views.

Generally there was a musical reawakening. On April 9, 1825, Mozart's *Don Giovanni*, the première of which had been staged in Prague some thirty-eight years earlier, received its first performance in the Czech tongue, and in 1826 the earliest opera by a Bohemian composer was written and given in Czech—Škroup's *Drátenik* (*The Tinker*). Music and books began to be printed more freely and between 1836 and 1841 there appeared Volumes 1 and 2 of Palacký's epoch-making *Geschichte von Boehmen* (*History of Bohemia*). Even though this was brought out in a sternly censored German edition, it was eagerly studied by a public which had grown accustomed to reading between the lines. Czech scholarship was developing and the study of Czech literary history was begun by the writers Václav Bolemír Nebeský (1818–1882) and Karel Sabina (1813–1877), both of whom insisted on a knowledge of European literary history. Jungmann's Dictionary was followed by further developments of language. The terminology of law, government and school was created, revised and standardized; and orthography was given its present-day form. Clubs and associations, like the Concordia, were established where intellectuals such as Jan Kollár,[6] Pavel Šafařik,[7] František Čelakovský,[8] Karel Mácha[9] and other leading spirits in the National Revival movement could meet.

The Prague which Smetana found on his arrival in August, 1843, was certainly not the moribund capital it had been decades before. He had come at a time when new hope and life were spreading through the old city. With only twenty gulden to his name, he shared a small room with two lawyers in the home of his cousin, Pepi. His life, he tells us, was simple, even hard:

[6] Jan Kollár (1793–1852), clergyman, patriot, philosopher, antiquarian, collector of folk songs and the leader of a Pan-Slav movement, was one of the greatest of Czech pre-Romantic poets. His *Daughter of Sláva* (1824) contains fifty sonnets which are among the finest poems ever written in Czech.

[7] Pavel Šafařík (1795–1861) was second only to Dobrovský as a student of comparative Slavonic studies. His *Slavonic Antiquity* (1837) laid the foundations of Slav archaeology and explained the Slavonic share in and contribution to the civilization of Europe.

[8] František Čelakovský (1799–1852), a collector of folk verse and a Pan-Slavicist, published a three-volume anthology of *Slavonic Folk Songs* which was the first work to be compiled with Czech translations. He also produced a collection of proverbs called *Folk Wisdom of Slavonic Peoples*. Later he wrote a number of sophisticated pastiches and imitations of folk songs called *Echoes of Czech and Russian Songs*.

[9] Karel Mácha (1810–1836) was a poet who worked under Jungmann's influence. His most significant works, *Maý*, *Krokonoše Pilgrimage* and *The Gipsies* are remarkable for their surrealistic imagery and romantic passion. He also wrote a number of lyrical tales and a historical novel on the Hussite period.

> I took my meals at an inn at twenty-one kreutzers a day for as long as the money lasted. Often I went to bed hungry and on one occasion had only a mug of coffee with a roll for breakfast and nothing else for three days. I was very badly off in every respect and spent nine weeks without being able to get hold of a piano. I could neither buy nor borrow one and it was only at the beginning of December that I managed to get one from a dealer at six gulden a month and on a six-monthly contract. At last I started practising and did nothing but play all day long, for I wanted to become a real virtuoso and not a mere pianist![1]

Although nineteen years old and by all acounts an outstanding performer, Smetana was completely ignorant of musical theory. He was more or less self-taught as a composer and later confessed that at the age of seventeen he had been unable to distinguish the difference between one note and another.[2] His dance music for the Plzeň bourgeoisie had taxed him considerably; but somehow he had mastered a style of writing which allowed him to capture the zest and gaiety of the Galop and Polka, the dances he knew well. In Prague, he realized that without systematic and thorough tuition he could never achieve the goal he had set himself. He was without connexions; he was too old to be accepted at the Conservatoire, too poor to study privately. What is more, he was desperately unhappy. One of the reasons for his coming to Prague was to be near Kateřina (who was a pupil at the Music Institute owned by Josef Proksch and situated in the Old Town Square). Their relationship had suffered considerably since the Plzeň days, and Kateřina, perhaps embarrassed by Smetana's curious appearance and passionate and excitable outbursts, appeared to have cooled in her feelings towards him:

> Kateřina lived with the Prokschs but for me she was further away than if she had been in America! At that time I never went to see Proksch because we did not know each other and even had I gone there Kateřina would have remained invisible since she was anything but well disposed towards me. If I chanced to see her in the street she never condescended to speak but would hurry by . . . she hardly seemed to notice me![3]

By December he was in a state of utter depression, but happily Anna Kolářová, Kateřina's mother, arrived in Prague and immediately set

[1] Diary: August 16, 1843. [2] Letter to Franz Liszt: March 3, 1848.
[3] Diary: August 16, 1843.

about finding a solution to his deplorable state of affairs. She quickly arranged for Bedřich to meet Kateřina's teacher:

> I went with her to see Proksch, played him a few *Études* and waited for the verdict. He praised my touch, but no more. After having enquired into my earlier studies in music and on learning that I was self-taught he smiled at me despairingly. . . . Finally Kateřina's mother asked Proksch to take me as a pupil for theory only, which, after much pleading he consented to do, solely in consideration of my talent. The fee was fixed at one gulden a lesson. Although I knew very well that I could not pay him this sum I accepted and placed myself entirely in heaven's hands.[4]

Josef Proksch was by general consent one of the finest musicians in Prague. Born in Liberec of a German family in 1794, he had been blind since his thirteenth year. Despite this he had become an outstanding pianist, a fine clarinettist, a celebrated theorist and respected teacher. In his early days in Vienna he had known the poet Zacharias Werner who had not only introduced him to the world of the Romantics but to Weber, of whom he became a close friend. In Berlin he had studied with the pianist Johann Logier and on returning to Prague in the 1830's had opened a school based on Logier's methods, which he extended and perfected. Proksch was a man of experience and wide knowledge and his Institute, which was thought to be more progressive than the Prague Conservatoire under the former Directorship of Divis Weber, enjoyed great renown, not least for its musical evenings where pupils played programmes of modern music. He admired the works of Bach and Mozart, and saw Beethoven as the climax of past and present and the pointer to the future. For Kalkbrenner, Thalberg, Herz and Czerny he had little time. He found their music shallow and the composers themselves ripe only for pension. In Italian opera he could see no future. He dismissed Bellini's scores as music of fashion, preferring instead the world of Auber, Halévy and Cherubini. He was a champion of Chopin, Schumann, Berlioz and Liszt: furthermore, he knew his four contemporaries personally, and on their trips to Prague Liszt and Berlioz generally found time to visit the blind musician and hear concerts given by his students.[5]

[4] Diary: August 16, 1843.

[5] In August, 1846, Berlioz visited Proksch's Institute and was moved to express his sentiments in the visitors' book:

> I can only compliment Mr. Proksch on the talent of his pupils. He has not only made them good pianists but excellent musicians who feel as well as understand their art. They will make the best contribution to the science of music by emulating their Master.

From some programmes preserved in the Smetana Museum in Prague we know that Bedřich played at several of Proksch's musical soirées; but he was not a regular performer, appearing only as accompanist or partner to Kateřina in four-handed duets.[6] After all, he had come for theoretical instruction, not to perfect his keyboard technique, and from the very beginning he set about his exercises with an enthusiasm and diligence which was quite remarkable. The matter which caused him most anxiety was the payment for his lessons. Proksch, however, was a kindly man who well understood his pupil's difficult financial position, and at the Concordia Club he touched on the subject to the Director of the Prague Conservatoire, Bedřich Kittl,[7] who consequently recommended Smetana for the position of music teacher to the family of Count Leopold Thun and Hohenstein:

> One day when neither Nesvadba[8] nor myself had a kreutzer between us and our luncheon tickets were used up and we could no longer have credit, the servant of the Director of the Conservatoire came to me and asked if I would care to take up the post of music teacher at the home of Count Thun. . . . No-one could have been more surprised and without a moment's thought I jumped at the offer.[9]

[6] On March 9, 1845, he partnered Kateřina in a performance of the Rondo from Herz's Fourth Concerto and two weeks earlier (February 23) had accompanied a Professor Vogel in a recital of Handel arias.

[7] Bedřich Kittl (1809–1868), teacher and scholar, had been a pupil of Tomášek, a follower of the new Romantic School, and was a friend of Liszt and Berlioz. He composed a *Hunting Symphony* and the opera *Bianca und Giuseppe* (subtitled *The French before Nice*) to a libretto by Wagner; but he preferred to devote himself to academic study, becoming Director of the Prague Conservatoire in 1843. Of him Berlioz wrote:

> The Prague Conservatoire, to boot, is directed by a talented composer, a man with a passion for his art, energetic, enthusiastic, untiring, capable of being severe on occasion but lavish with his praise when praise is due—and young. Such a man is Kittl. They could so easily have found some plodding mediocrity hallowed by time . . . and appointed him to do what he could to paralyse the progress of music in Prague. Instead they chose Kittl, who is thirty-five, and music in Prague is flourishing.
>
> (*Memoirs:* Fifth Letter from Prague to Humbert Ferrand. In the translation by David Cairns.)

[8] Arnošt Nesvadba was a violinist and fellow student who supported Smetana financially during his early days in Prague. Earlier the two had given a recital in Rokycany (July 5, 1843). On coming to Prague, it was Nesvadba who recommended Smetana for membership to the Concordia Club.

[9] Diary: January, 1844.

On January 18, 1844, Smetana duly presented himself at the Thun's beautiful palace in the Malá Strana. At first the young musician's wild appearance raised doubts in the Count's mind as to his suitability for the post, as Countess Elizabeth Thun was later to recall:

> When he came to introduce himself my father was somewhat distrustful of him. His very youthful appearance gave my father no great confidence in his knowledge and he placed before him a very difficult composition by Pius Richter[1] who had been our previous teacher. This Smetana played brilliantly at sight. His whole manner was so simple and modest that my parents decided to engage him as our teacher. We had arrived at scales and exercises, and every day he had to give the five children a lesson lasting one hour each. In addition, four of us were not at all musical![2]

Smetana was appointed to the Thun household with board and lodging and a salary of three hundred gulden a year. In the winter he lived with the family in Prague, but when the city became too hot they all moved to a summer residence on Ronšperk, in the Šumava Mountains or to the Thuns' country seat, Bon Repos, on the Jizera River some thirty-two miles north-east of Prague between Nové Benátky and Lysá near Mladá Boleslav, the home of Kateřina's parents.

With these lengthy summer sojourns at Bon Repos Smetana came to love a part of Bohemia previously little known to him. His childhood, spent in the south around Litomyšl and Německý Brod or in the rural district of Jihlava and Blaník Mountain, had introduced him to two typical landscapes. In Plzeň he had explored a third: the western expanses of deep forests. Now, in the romantic north-eastern region, he came to know another, Bezděz Mountain, an area which became so much part of him that when he was engaged on his opera *The Secret* he looked no further for his setting.

At Bon Repos Smetana was happy. He was companion as well as tutor and probably enjoyed playing games and going for walks with the children far more than giving lessons. He made no secret of the fact that he was obliged to teach music for financial and not vocational reasons. He was not a pedant, but a cheerful young man who with passionate absorption acquainted his pupils with the classics as well as contemporary music:[3]

[1] Pius Richter was a pupil of Proksch who later became court organist in Vienna.

[2] Countess Elizabeth Thun: *Memoirs.*

[3] The contemporary music which he invariably used for teaching consisted of Henselt's characteristic pieces *Eroica*, *Witch's Dance*, *Ave Maria*, *Lost Father-*

> Although Smetana revered Liszt deeply, for him Beethoven stood out far above everybody else. He taught me to appreciate and understand the spirit of Beethoven's music through his wonderfully lucid explanations, as he did the music of Bach and Scarlatti which he discussed thoroughly. He made me learn a great deal of Chopin, but when he performed Meyerbeer's *Robert le Diable* and *Les Huguenots* he thrilled me as no-one before had done . . . When he played scales and arpeggios it was as if a little mouse was running over the keyboard.[4]

Having found security with the Thun family, Smetana was able to devote himself wholeheartedly to theory and composition. Even during the long periods when he was away from Prague he continued his studies, working countless exercises which were bundled up and sent by post to Proksch for correction.

Proksch based Smetana's course of instruction on the best and most extensive text book of the day, Dr. A. B. Marx' *Theory of Musical Composition* (Volume 1) which he adapted and extended to his pupil's needs; but it is likely he also had recourse to a systematic study of harmony and composition by the important Bohemian theorist Antonín Rejcha,[5] whose writings served as textbooks for Conservatoires throughout Europe. First Smetana came to grips with the fundamentals of harmony, and though he did not find this particularly stimulating he worked diligently so as to progress to the study of counterpoint in species, canon and fugue. Václav Zelený[6] confirms that the young composer committed himself tirelessly to working the dullest and most difficult exercises so as to achieve complete contrapuntual mastery[7] and many of these have been preserved in the Smetana Museum in Prague. They include various harmonic motives, the text of Marx's chapter dealing with the completion of a movement, a series of themes with variations, attempts to master triple

land and *Play of the Dwarfs*. He found the programmatic nature of these miniatures particularly successful with young pupils and may well have chosen to model his own cycle *Bagatelles and Impromptus* on similar lines.

[4] Countess Elizabeth Thun: *op. cit.*

[5] Antonín Rejcha (1770–1836) was a composer, theorist and professor at the Paris Conservatoire, where Berlioz, Liszt, Gounod and César Franck were among his pupils. His *Traité de Mélodie* (1814), *Cours de Composition Musicale* (1818) and *Traité de Haute Composition Musicale* (1824–1826) laid down the basic rules of harmony, counterpoint and instrumentation.

[6] Václav Zelený (1858–1892) was one of the writers and journalists who worked hardest for the recognition of Smetana's work.

[7] Zelený: *On Bedřich Smetana* (1894).

invertible counterpoint, augmentation and diminution. Most of the exercises[8] are in two or four-part settings for piano or vocal quartet, and the only time any instrumentation is specified is in the accompaniment of two Offertories. As for exercises in which the young musician worked out the possibilities of orchestral instruments, all that has come down to us is a table of transpositions for valve horns, a fragment of a piece for woodwind instruments with double reed mouthpieces, a chorale for two clarinets and bassoons, and sixty-three bars of a fanfare-like movement for four horns. Following these are Smetana's only known attempts at orchestrating the works of other composers: Škroup's *God We Praise Thee* and Mozart's *Fantasia* in C minor (K. 475). Škroup's piece is simply set for strings, chamber organ, trumpet and drums. The Mozart, on the other hand, is far more ambitious, and though only the initial ten bars have been preserved in full score (double woodwind, two horns, two trumpets, three trombones, timpani and strings) they are imaginatively arranged. An interesting point about this fragment is the position on the page of the timpani part: not in its usual place, below the brass, but on the stave immediately above the flutes (in later compositions Smetana made a *volte face* and generally indicated the percussion lines on the bottom stave normally reserved for the double basses). That Smetana was wholly dependent on the classical composers for his models of orchestration we know, for he copied out in full score certain passages, some long, some short, in an endeavour to come to grips with different styles, groupings, effects and tone-colours. In his copying he was very selective, and fourteen extracts have been kept in the Smetana Museum Archives. From Beethoven, whom we know he revered above all other composers, he selected:

Symphony No. 2.................First movement, bars 1–9
Symphony No. 9................First movement, bars 1–27
Leonore Overture No. 1..........Bars 1–16 and 57–64

From the works of Weber he chose the first twelve bars of the *Jubel-Ouvertüre*, and from the Overture to *Der Freischütz* bars 1–17 and 73–85. Three sections attracted his attention in Mendelssohn's *Die schöne Melusine* Overture, bars 1–11, 49–57 and 68–71; and from the same composer's *Meeresstille und glückliche Fahrt* bars 1–17, 49–63 and 279–92. The only composition reproduced in its entirety was Leopolda de Meyer's *March Marocain*, not for the quality of the music, let it be said, but for the superb orchestral treatment by Berlioz.

[8] The most interesting of these exercises is based on a study theme of Rejcha. It is in four parts and bears the date 'Prague 1845'.

Interesting as these fragments are, we can discover far more about Smetana's growth in composition from the various choral exercises written between 1845 and 1846. These are mainly worked to Latin or German words and are a mixture of studies in liturgical musical forms. Among motets, psalms and offertories, we can see that Smetana was taking as his models the scores of Palestrina, Lassus, Bach and Handel in an attempt to gain a reliable vocal and choral technique. On January 6, 1845, he began simple harmonizations of chorales in the style of Bach and soon moved on to more adventurous settings. Six months later he turned to a series of choral figurations on protestant chorales in which the part writing is freer, the harmony bolder. Two chorales in the form of arias followed in August: 'Jesu my strength' and 'My hope stands firm' both elaborate a *cantus firmus* and display a certain advance in the handling of vocal lines.

The next intensive period of study seems to have been the spring of 1846, when he was again in Ronšperk with the Thun family. Here he worked a number of exercises, including a motet 'Jesu meine Freude' and an impressive fugue 'Ich hoffe auf den Herrn' ('I hope in the Lord'). Another fugue, this time with introduction and called 'Lobet den Herrn' ('Praise ye the Lord'), shows his growing technical assurance. The introduction is homophonic, and the fugue displays a fine understanding of polyphonic textures not found in the previous exercises. The climax is a broad 'Hallelujah' which returns to the choral style of the opening. The high level set by this piece is not maintained and a 'Sanctus' for double chorus is little more than a contrapuntal exercise in the handling of antiphonal choral effects. The coda, contrived over sustained pedals, is particularly weak. Two undated Offertories, however, show a much firmer grasp. The model for the form and instrumentation in both 'Scapulis suis obumbrabit' and 'Meditabitur in mandatis tuis' is clearly Handel, the former acknowledging the influence with a rigid dotted quaver-semiquaver rhythm that seems to have come from 'Surely He hath borne our griefs' from *Messiah*. In the second piece Smetana introduces a figured bass and writes melodic lines close to Handel's 'If God be for us, who can be against us?'; but these similarities fail to hide the augmented seconds and unprepared consecutive dominant sevenths which appear from time to time in the part writing. Nevertheless, these Offertories demonstrate that had Smetana continued in this field he could well have become an accomplished composer of church music.

Four songs[9] written as exercises on German texts between April

[9] Smetana's first attempt at song writing, *Poutník* (*The Wanderer*), dates from 1840 when he tried his hand at a setting of Schiller's *Der Pilgrim*.

and December, 1846, show a fully-fledged understanding of the genre. The manuscript of *Der Liebsten Augen* (*My Sweetheart's Eyes*), to a poem by B. Breiger, is simply marked 'Gesang composition.' *Lebewohl*, a through-composed song based on Wilhelm Melhop's *The Farewell*, is notable for a scheme of modulation swinging between E minor and E major, that anticipates the string Quartet *From my Life* where the same device returns. *Schmerz der Trennung* (*Sadness of a Deserted One*), to words by Christoph Wieland, owes a debt to Schumann: the song is haunting, with a sense of atmosphere, a severity of detachment and a beauty of line which mark it out from the others. *Einladung* is a personal arrangement of Johann Jacobi's *Invitation*. In matters of inflexion, the marriage of vocal line to piano accompaniment, the richness of allusion and greater tonal enterprise, this song, standing on its own merits, can no longer be regarded as an exercise. Clearly, had Smetana's writing progressed on this level he might possibly have developed into a significant composer of *Lieder*.[1]

Instead he returned wholeheartedly to writing for the piano—not that he had ever really given up composing for the instrument, for there exists a whole collection of sketches dating from his first lessons with Proksch which testify that most problems of form and content were studied first on the keyboard. These are far too numerous to describe in any detail, but among the many marches, sets of variations, canons, fugues and attempted sonata movements, are a number of works which warrant closer examination. A group of *Five Marches* (1845) is remarkable for the way the young composer transforms a basic ternary structure into a number of well contrasted pieces of real musical value. Particularly interesting is the *March* in C minor which foreshadows by seventeen years the motive of Tausendmark in the opera *The Brandenburgers in Bohemia*.

The set of *Five Waltzes*, written at the beginning of 1844, is modelled on Chopin's famous collection, but in his pieces Smetana introduces a basic thematic element which returns from time to time, binding the movements together and looking forward to his working with monothematic ideas.[2] The final piece is especially interesting for the appearance of a lilting phrase in sixths which was to develop twenty years later into the motive of 'faithful love' between Jeník and Mařenka in the first act of *The Bartered Bride*. The popularity

[1] Smetana only returned to song writing nine years later when he chose to set Rückert's *Liebesfrühling* (*Spring of Love*) and dedicated it to the tenor František Stégr-Stažiček before his departure to the Vienna Hofoper.

[2] Notably in the symphonic poem *Richard III*.

of the fifth *Waltz* was such that it was performed in February, 1844, in an orchestral version (now lost) at the Artists' Ball in Prague, and here it reaped great success—a fact which had considerable influence on Kateřina and probably resulted in their relationship regaining its former warmth.

In 1843 Smetana wrote the Polka *Memories of Plzeň*, probably for Kateřina's birthday. In the clarity of piano writing, this piece shows Smetana's determination to emulate the style of Chopin. It is no boisterous, heavy dance, but a light, airy scherzo. Here we see for the first time that Smetana was beginning to transform the polka from the one he had known in Plzeň to something quite different—a scherzo-polka which was to be a vehicle for virtuoso display and not for dancing. While this Polka looks forward to one of Smetana's works of mature style, the *Bagatelles and Impromptus* look back to an older technique: a scheme of working through the major and minor keys. Bach and Chopin had fully exploited the possibilities of this device, but where they both systematically progressed through all keys Smetana chose only eight. The pieces are conceived as an entire cycle and not isolated items as his previous compositions had been. What is more important, however, is that a new, individual form of expression here emerges to bind these miniatures in a unity of style. The pieces are named and the musical content of each corresponds most aptly to the title. The *Bagately a Impromptus* (*Bagatelles and Impromptus*) are of an intimate nature, reflecting the state of relations between Smetana and Kateřina Kolářova. As such, the cycle is almost certainly programmatic in its expression, though no definite programme is known to exist. The numbers, naïvely labelled 'Innocence', 'Dejection', 'Idyll', 'Desire', 'Joy', 'Fairy Tale', 'Love', and 'Discord', evoke the image of the beloved, the charm of the girl herself, the exuberance and impatience of the youth—but they do more. Each piece complements the succeeding one and acts as a foil to it. Smetana almost certainly modelled this cycle on the characteristic compositions of Henselt[3] or Schumann; but where Schumann's are dream-like, more chimerical, Smetana's are less fanciful, and more definite. At the age of twenty he created a piano work of which there was hardly any equal in Bohemia at the time of its composition.

[3] It is interesting that many of Henselt's marks of style are to be found in Smetana's cycle: the melody in the inner voice supported by chords in syncopation, the placing of the climax on the subdominant, the use of scales for the basic melodic formation all point to the fact that Smetana may well have had Henselt's miniatures in mind. The influence becomes more certain when we remember that Smetana frequently used Henselt's pieces as teaching material for the Countess Elizabeth Thun.

But the value of the cycle in the study of Smetana's catalogue lies in its demonstration of his particular cast of thought and emotion. The work shows for the first time the germ of his entire art—his ability to compose his most significant pieces when the impulse was one of musical portraiture, autobiography or an expression of literary ideas. Herein lies the substance of the mature Smetana, the programme composer, the disciple of Liszt and Berlioz.

Apart from the great promise which this cycle of simple love poems displays, it shows other marks of Smetana's style emerging for the first time, not least the extraordinarily rich harmonies. The dissonance in the very first bars of 'Innocence' with an exposed interval of a seventh (C to B) and the subsequently shifting harmonies, moving in the bass in fourths, does much to destroy the tonality of C major before it is even established. This was a technique little known to Smetana's Bohemian predecessors and its recurrence in the later piano works (notably the Opus 2 *Preludes* and the 'small' *Étude* in C) makes it a distinct musical fingerprint. Smetana's fondness for pedals can be traced in the fifth piece, built entirely on three sustained notes; the characteristic melodic movement in thirds and sixths returns in the sixth piece, 'Fairy Tale', as does the composer's tendancy to write melodies on scales. But above all it is the daring clashes of sevenths and seconds in the tempestuous final 'Discord' that shows the originality of the cycle and points to the advanced harmonic thought.

The trend of these pieces was continued in a group of miniatures for piano called *Lístky do památníku* (*Album Leaves*). Though Smetana wrote nearly forty pieces bearing this title, these are spread, sporadically, over a period of forty years. The first compositions form an independent group somewhat apart from the further line of development and arose either in response to a direct request, or as a tribute to friends or nearer acquaintances. As a relaxation from academic exercise they provided the opportunity for freer flights of imagination and independent expression. Again the influence is Schumann; again the impulse Kateřina (in the first piece at least). Within twenty-six bars Smetana succeeds in creating a delicately etched impression of the girl he so much admired (*Leaf* in B, July 22, 1844). The remaining *Leaves* are no less personal. They date from April and June, 1845, and were intended for persons whom Smetana knew at Proksch's Institute or in the family of Count Thun. The E major *Leaf*, composed for a fellow pupil, Josefina Finkeová, is in the style of a drawing-room ballade; the *Leaf* in C minor inscribed to Jean Kunz, who had come from Russia to study with Proksch, is basically a study in two-part invertible counterpoint; the E flat minor *Leaf*, written for Václav

Ulwer, a teacher at Proksch's Institute who died in the cholera epidemic of 1850, is an exercise in variation. One of the most charming *Leaves*, however, is that inscribed to Smetana's pupil Countess Elizabeth Thun. Together with the *Leaf* in C, dedicated to Marie, Proksch's daughter, and wittily built on four notes, the first, eighth, sixth and second degrees of the scale and representing the year of its composition (1862), these pieces show the wide range of moods Smetana was able to capture in the space of a few bars.

Example 3

Of his other works dating from his apprenticeship with Proksch, mention must be made of three movements written during August-September, 1845 especially for the Countess Elizabeth Thun. The *Vivace*, *Andante* and *March* are all in F major and linked by a common theme, a descending three-note germ which is transformed to take on a different character in each piece. These show Smetana's growing pleasure in monothematic composition and anticipate a feature of his mature working method. Another feature which points forward to the later composer is the melodic turn of phrase at bars 21–4 of the *Andante*, directly anticipating Jeník's aria 'Utis se dívko' ('Calm down and trust me') in the third act of *The Bartered Bride*. In October, 1845, Smetana produced a delightful miniature called *Pensée Fugitive*, again for the Countess. This follows the pattern set by the *Bagatelles and Impromptus* and is essentially lyrical, with a melody which the composer regarded with fond affection: it reappears in the incomplete piano fantasy *Cid and Ximene*, written in Sweden some fourteen years later. Another *morceau charactéristique* which furnished him with material for the same work is the third of *Four Rondos* dating from February, 1846. The habit of borrowing a phrase from one work and using it in another is one in which Smetana frequently indulged: from the *Characteristic Variations on a Czech Folk Song* he earmarked the fugato figure which was put to good use in the finale of the G minor Piano Sonata (written the same year) and incorporated in the last movement of the G minor Piano Trio some ten years later. The importance of these variations, however, lies not so much in the thematic similarities but in the folk song itself. *S'il jsem proso na souvrati* (*I was sowing millet*) is the song Smetana deliberately chose as his theme.[4] Four years previously he had incorporated the same melody into the *Fantasia* for Violin and Piano. During the 1840's the song played an important role in the rebirth of the nation on account of the comment which the text made on the social life of the day. The underlying subject of thought of Polak's poem can be judged from the first line: 'I tried to love and sow, but I neither loved nor sowed!'—a symbolic expression of the failure of the peasants to achieve success in the cause for which they were fighting. In choosing this particular folk song Smetana was openly declaring his sympathies with the young Czech radicals and their campaign for the end of Absolutism, the restoration of the Czech tongue and freedom of expression.

This particular set of variations was not the first composition to reflect his feelings towards movements of political unrest. As early as

[4] At Německý Brod *I was sowing millet* had become accepted as the unofficial school song and was popularized by Karel Havlíček.

October, 1845, he had created the *March of the Warrior*, which, apart from a fanfare figure that returns in the first act of the opera *Dalibor*, is full of a heroic conflict quite new to Smetana's vocabulary. Even in the *Étude* in A minor (January, 1846), basically an exercise for the wrist in presto staccato chords and closely modelled on Liszt's *Étude Gnomenreigen*, there is a daring, fighting quality and one commentator, Mirko Očadlík, has even gone so far as to interpret the quiet cadence which ends the study as an expression of the composer's sympathies towards the abortive insurrection in Galicia of 1846.[5] Whether this be so or not, it is certain that he was acutely aware of the tense political situation which had led to serious rioting and that he belonged to the Prague Repeal, a radical association organized by a number of young Czech artists. It was probably in this company of fellow patriots that he first became aware of the importance of Berlioz's music. For Smetana and his colleagues, Berlioz was the supreme symbol of the Romantic revival, an iconoclast who was breaking conventional forms and forging new ones. Painters, poets, politicians—everyone was excited by him, sensing that his art came directly from the depths of a revolutionary spirit. Smetana saw in Berlioz a revelation, an apostle of the new, a leader of those who cultivated an art which was the expression of an awakened life in Europe. On March 31, 1846, Berlioz visited Prague to conduct performances of his own *Symphonie Fantastique* and *Carnaval Romain* overture in the Stavovské Theatre. The success of the concert was enormous and represented a break in the otherwise conservative musical life of Prague (where admiration for Mozart was stifling the growth of new music). The reception of Berlioz's concert was symptomatic of the growing strength of the younger generation of Czechs, and on Smetana the effect was total and complete. Flexing his creative muscles, he set to work on a Sonata which is nothing less than a tribute to the French master.

The basis of the Sonata's first movement is the *idée fixe*. It should not be assumed that Smetana came to appreciate this technique of composition only following Berlioz's concerts in Prague: on the contrary, the cycle of *Waltzes*, and the *Vivace*, *Andante* and *March* all show a leaning towards monothematicism. In the *Triumphal March* in A (December, 1845) he had begun to experiment with the *idée fixe* as the core of his composition. The Sonata, however, provided him with the opportunity of putting this working method into practice on a grand four-movement scale and also of incorporating much that he had learnt over the previous three years with Proksch.

[5] Mirko Očadlík: *Klavírní dílo Bedřicha Smetany* (*Smetana's Piano Works*) (1961).

The first movement begins with a four-bar motive which undergoes metamorphoses:

Example 4

Smetana later worked the *idée fixe* into the sketch of the first act of *Dalibor*, where it appeared in precisely the same key and notation as in the Sonata. In the final version of the opera, however, he modified it and though the harmony, tonality and mood remain the same, the initial melody notes have been transformed (the theme appears in the second scene of Act I immediately following King Vladislav's denunciation of Dalibor and before the arrival of Milada). The second movement is a set of variations. The influence is Schubertian, the mood nocturnal. The piece is built into a grandiose, almost monumental climax which finds its resolution only in the following scherzo. Originally at this point Smetana had written a Polka in E flat, but Proksch, doubting its suitability within the sonata framework, suggested a formal scherzo and trio. Smetana duly complied, but the result is musically less inspired than his first thoughts. The Polka was not designed as dance music but as a scherzo-polka with interesting cross-rhythms that suggest a furiant. The final movement of the Sonata is a rondo and a *tour de force* for the pianist. It takes as its principal theme an idea which reappeared in the G minor Piano Trio, and may even have been inspired by the 'Cimbalom' motive in the finale of Schubert's E flat Trio (Opus 100). There are two episodes, one fugal and angular, the other lyrical and based on the *idée fixe*, but now in augmentation. Throughout, Smetana's marks of style, pedals, melodic movement in thirds and sixths, wild, tempestuous keyboard writing, daring harmonic clashes, are omnipresent; and it seems that here he throws off his student fetters and comes of age. As a whole, the Sonata is clearly defined, thoroughly pianistic and never less than workmanlike. It was the last piece to be produced under the guidance of Proksch, and with it Smetana completed his apprenticeship and emerged technically proficient in his trade.

In the many works which he wrote during his three years' study we see a great deal which represents little more than the student's indefatigable endeavour to master a craft. In other cases his growing musical personality sometimes raises an exercise to the level of a composition, as is certainly the case in the *Bagatelles and Impromptus.* Smetana was very self-critical, and did not regard these exercises as representative of his real creative ability. Although pleased to turn to several of them for certain ideas in later life, he never regarded any of his study-tasks as worthy of publication, nor even of bearing any opus number (the *Six Characteristic Pieces*, Opus 1, was written two years later).

When examining Smetana's course with Proksch, it can be seen that it did not include only the mere copying of various techniques but an intensive analysis of works by Bach, Mozart and Beethoven. It led also to the appearance and development of a number of musical characteristics, peculiarities almost, which were to become established points of his mature style. At this stage five distinct features are apparent: his leaning towards monothematicism, and the acceptance of the *idée fixe*; his skill in polyphony and daring harmonic progressions; his highly personal form of piano writing which is technically so demanding as occasionally to restrict the use of conventional ornamentation; a proclivity towards the epic and heroic; the ability to create music inspired by portraiture, autobiography or literary ideas.

During this time with Proksch, Smetana's interests had undergone a complete *volte face*: his attention had switched from performer to composer. By 1846 he felt fully prepared to stand on his own feet as an artist, but realized that as a composer he would experience enormous difficulties in making a livelihood. Since 1844 he had known the security of Count Thun's household; but now he felt the need for greater freedom in order to develop artistically and embark on his own creative path. He resolved to establish himself as a concert pianist and on June 1, 1847, resigned from the service of Count Thun.[6] With Kateřina, whom he hoped to marry, recommended as his successor, he set out on his first concert tour of Western Bohemia eager to make a name for himself, positive he would find the success his talents deserved.

[6] As a tribute to his employer Smetana dedicated a set of *Six Preludes for Organ* (written towards the end of 1846) to Count Thun. This was the only occasion on which Smetana composed for the instrument.

THREE

YEARS OF STRUGGLE 1846–1856

THE NEW PERIOD of Smetana's life did not begin with the success he had expected. An impressive tour, planned to take in Eger (now Cheb), Plzeň, Mariánské Lázně, Františkovy Lázně and Karlovy Vary absorbed him completely, and he flung himself into practising for the event with enormous enthusiasm. Though he had played in Litomyšl at the age of six, appeared as soloist in Hořálek's Piano Concerto in Cectice at fifteen, and performed Henselt's *Fantasia on Slovak Themes* in Plzeň at nineteen, he had never before tackled anything on the scale of a recital. In July, 1846, he informed his cousin of his intention to visit Plzeň and asked him to rally support in bourgeois musical circles. Josef Smetana agreed and added:

> There's another wish I would like to offer for myself and for our homeland: [in Czech] that you travel as a Czech artist! [in German] If you understand and feel these words then my wish is fulfilled . . . You, a Slav by birth and nationality, will, if you travel as a German virtuoso, forfeit all rights to national recognition—of far greater value than money, even though honours be showered upon you. . . . In Plzeň you can expect little appreciation from the people—this you already know—but your concert will not pass without arousing vivid interest.[1]

Unfortunately Smetana never encountered the Plzeň reception, for his first concert on August 7th was such a financial disaster that he was obliged to cancel his other appearances. In Eger he had reserved the Bohemian Crown Hall where he presented a programme of contemporary music:[2] the first movement of Beethoven's A flat

[1] Letter to Smetana: July 10, 1846.

[2] Possibly the people of Eger failed to support Smetana's concert not because he was unknown but since his programme was too modern.

Sonata (Opus 26); two of Mendelssohn's *Lieder ohne Wörte* and his *Presto* in F sharp minor; two Chopin *Études*, Liszt's transcription of Schubert's *Serenade*, and a *Fantasia on Bohemian Melodies* 'by the Concert Giver and Piano Virtuoso'. For this he took four folk songs, *Chytili jsme lososa* (*We caught a salmon*), *Kde pak jsi, má milá?* (*Where are you my sweetheart?*), *Chovejte mne, má matičko* (*Rock me mother dear*), *Kdybys byl Honzíčku?* (*Where would you be, John?*), which he elaborately treated in the style of a quodlibet. Apart from the paraphrases of Liszt, Smetana possibly had in mind the fantasy Škroup had arranged from incidental music to the play *Fidlovačka* (*The Fiddler*) which included the song *Kde domov můj?* (*Where is my home?*), later to become the National Anthem of Czechoslovakia. Although the admission prices had been only twenty and thirty kreutzer, Smetana made a considerable loss, and was forced to abandon his project and return to Prague. He eked out a living as best he could. Secretly he had hoped to lay the foundations of an independent existence; and from the proceeds of his concerts had planned to set up home with Kateřina, whose financial position as a teacher was far superior to his own. He was doomed to disappointment. He could find a post neither as conductor nor organist and only after several months did he attract attention as an accompanist and pianist in chamber music circles. Through these appearances he secured some pupils and a monthly pittance of twelve gulden. But this was barely enough to keep him alive, let alone fulfil his ambition: to open a music school. With no capital and few connexions the prospect was dark. Nevertheless, on January 28, 1848, he filed an application to establish a private institute in Prague.

The year 1848 brought Smetana no new hopes for improving his miserable lot. He continued to teach, to play and compose, and between January and March produced a set of *Šest charakteristických skladeb* (*Six Characteristic Pieces*) for piano, the first to bear an opus number (Opus 1). It was this collection he sent in desperation to Liszt with an urgent plea for help:

> Up till now no one has done anything for me . . . my parents have sunk so low as to become almost beggars. I cannot get my compositions printed because I need to put up money for them. Unfortunately I am unable to save anything and don't know when I shall be able to repay my debts. I am a creative artist and a pianist yet I possess no instrument. A friend allows me to practise in his room. Truly my fate is unenviable![3]

[3] Letter to Liszt: March 23, 1848.

Königl. Stadt Eger.

Friedrich Smetana

Piano - Virtuose

wird

Samstag den 7. August 1847 um 8 Uhr Abends

im Saale zur böhmischen Krone

ein

CONCERT

zu geben die Ehre haben

PROGRAMM:

N. 1. As dur Sonate (1 Satz) von L. van Beethoven.

N. 2. Lieder ohne Worte (E dur, C dur) von F. Mendelssohn-Bartholdy.

N. 3. Etüden, 1 und 2 von Fried. Chopin.

N. 4. Presto, Fis moll von F. Mendelssohn - Bartholdy.

N. 5. Das Ständchen von F. Liszt.

N. 6. Böhmische Melodieen von dem Concertgeber.

Sämmtliche Piecen werden vom Concertgeber vorgetragen.

Preise der Plätze.

Cercle 30 kr. Erster Platz 20 kr. C. M.

Programme of Smetana's first professional concert appearance in Eger (August 7, 1847)

Smetana continues by confiding his plans of making a livelihood from an Institute on the lines of Proksch's. In addition he asked Liszt to accept the dedication of his Opus 1, find a publisher for it, and requested a loan of four hundred gulden which he pledged to repay:

> I have no guarantee, only my word which to me is sacred and therefore possibly better surety than a hundred guarantors. I have confided my distress and wretchedness to no other living soul except yourself. In whom should an artist confide if not in another? In the greatest perturbation of spirit I ask you not to delay your answer but deliver me from doubt, for in a few weeks Smetana may no longer be![4]

This pathetic plea reached Liszt in Krzyzanowice just before his departure for Vienna. His reaction to it and to the twenty-four-year-old unknown writer is remarkable. On March 30 he acknowledged Smetana's dedication, suggested a change in the title of the first piece, and promised to recommend the work for publication. At the same time he expressed the hope of meeting him on his next visit to Prague. Liszt was as good as his word. Several months later he made the acquaintance of the young composer and arranged for the Leipzig publisher, Franz Kistner, to bring out the pieces in two parts. Though Smetana received neither fee for the *Six Characteristic Pieces* nor loan from Liszt, he was more than rewarded by recognition; for Liszt described Smetana's Opus 1 as 'the most outstanding, finely felt and finely finished pieces that recently have come to my note'.[5] Such was praise indeed, and an examination of the set shows that this judgement was not without foundation.

The *Six Characteristic Pieces* begin where the *Bagatelles and Impromptus* and Sonata in G minor leave off. The set is based on a sequence of keys arranged in a cycle of fifths in which major and minor modes alternate (that is C major-minor, G major-minor, D major-minor). He also introduces a monothematic compositional method looking back to the *idée fixe* scheme of the Piano Sonata. The *idée fixe* was originally to be announced in a sixty-seven-bar Prelude in C sharp but Smetana abandoned this as the key did not fit his harmonic plan. The motive, a descending scale, appears in all six pieces sometimes as melody, sometimes as episode or counter-subject, but never in the same form. The opening piece, 'In the Forest', shows Smetana treating the motive canonically. Originally his title had included the name Gretel, but after perusing the score Liszt explained

[4] Letter to Liszt: March 23, 1848. [5] Letter from Liszt: March 30, 1848.

that canon seemed 'too scientific a form to portray a girl like Gretel'.[6] Obediently Smetana withdrew the name, but remained uneasy about it. Possibly he saw the composition as a musical evocation of a young person wandering through woods and not merely as a picture of wooded landscape.

Throughout the set Smetana's typical fingerprints are in evidence and in 'Shepherdess', the third piece, there is even a suggestion of a polka. While the underlying influence is nearer Schumann than Chopin, the harmony is very much Smetana's own with a greater emphasis on dissonance than had appeared in anything before. Apart from the sequence of major-minor keys, the most remarkable feature is the wide range of moods which he is able to convey. The set opens full of optimism, but in the second piece 'Rising Passion', an aggressive note is sounded which grows in the fourth ('Desire') and penultimate composition ('Soldier'), to dramatic, almost heroic proportions. 'Despair', the final piece, completes the gamut of moods, being predominantly tragic and pessimistic. In this cycle Smetana, consciously or otherwise, seems to be commenting on the growing tension and political unrest which was spreading throughout Europe and making itself manifest in Bohemia in numerous incidents.

At the time he was composing his Opus 1 clouds were gathering over the continent to break into the spring storm of revolution. The news of the February insurrection in France soon spread to Austria, where as early as March Metternich was defeated and the Emperor Ferdinand forced to abdicate. The time seemed ripe for political emancipation and in Prague it was hoped to set up a Federal Austria that would give autonomy to the Bohemian people. By April the young Czech radicals were using the turn of events to make petitions and gain concessions for political and religious liberty. They looked forward to the end of Absolutism, the abolition of serfdom and freedom of expression. The most ardent and enlightened leaders of the movement, Palacký and Havlíček, urged a more democratic understanding between Vienna and Prague, and during May articles especially written by Havlíček with the purpose of inciting the people appeared in the Press. The situation became tense, and when on June 11, Prince Windischgrätz, Commander of the Prague Garrison, ordered a military revue as a show of strength, panic seized the populace, who saw his action as a move to re-establish Absolutism by force. Demonstrations followed. Barricades were hastily erected by students and enthusiastic patriots. Though no revolt as such had been planned, Windischgrätz began a general bombardment during

[6] Letter from Liszt: March 30, 1848.

which Prague was fired. On the morning of June 16, the city capitulated unconditionally. Once again it was under Absolutist rule. Persecutions and reprisals followed and Metternich's place was taken by a new Minister, Alexander Bach. In Prague the atmosphere became more stifling than before as the foremost leaders of the uprising were either exiled or flung into prison. For the time being the movement for a free Bohemia was at an end. The harsh Austrian reaction which followed the unsuccessful revolution dealt a blow to national development and especially to the process of bringing Czech national culture up to date in the international European scene. Bohemia now became isolated for more than a decade from non-Austrian Europe as censorship was tightened and restrictions placed on travel.

Not much is known of Smetana's participation in the revolution. Certainly he sympathized with the writings of the priest and revivalist Jan Jindřich Marek, whose verses under the name of Jan of Hvězdy, were recited at patriotic meetings during this time.[7] It is likely he took an active part in manning the barricade on the Charles Bridge and, being a member of the armed Citizen Corps called Svornost,[8] probably carried powder to the forces on the old Chain Bridge as well. Svornost means 'united', and it was while in this society that he became acquainted with one of the leading representatives of the Czech radical movement, Karel Sabina, later to be the librettist of his first two operas.[9] Following the Whitsun uprising Smetana fled to his parents' home in Obříství where he stayed for several weeks, even though he had received official permission to establish his Institute in Prague as early as May 18 and needed to remain in the city to make preliminary arrangements for its opening.

By the beginning of 1848 Smetana had written some forty works, mainly for piano and intended for the drawing-rooms of the aristocracy. Now, following the spring insurrection, he found inspiration in the revolutionary spirit that was shaking the feudal rule of the Hapsburgs. He responded with *Two Marches* for piano which were brought out immediately by the Prague music publisher J. Hoffmann; but as their character and purpose urgently called for a more effective treatment than Smetana had envisaged, the bandmaster, Jan Pavlis, made an arrangement for military band. The first, *Pochod národní gardy* (dedicated to the Czech National Guard which had been

[7] Marek's papers had appeared in print as early as March 26, 1840, when the magazine *Květy* included a selection of his verses edited by Josef Tyl.

[8] The Svornost Corps was created on March 18, 1848, and founder members included Tyl, Havlíček, Kollár and Sabina.

[9] *The Brandenburgers in Bohemia* and *The Bartered Bride*.

formed in Prague as it had in other European cities at the beginning of the year), is a stirring piece in which Smetana not only demonstrates his loyalty by quoting as a theme for the middle section of his trio the last phrase of Haydn's tune adopted for the Imperial Anthem: 'Eternally with Hapsburgs' crown the fate of Austria is united', but anticipates by five years his own *Triumphal Symphony* where the same melody appears in three of the four movements.

The second *March*, *Pochod pražské studenské legie* (dedicated to the Legion of Students[1] in the University of Prague), makes use of the celebrated tune *Gaudeamus Igitur* (a) as well as the German students' song (b) *Was kommt dort von der Hoh?* (*What's coming there from above?*). This has something in common with another students' song *Das Frischlied* (*The Freshman's Song*), which together with the *Gaudeamus* was incorporated into the *Academic Festival Overture* some thirty-two years later. The following shows how far Smetana anticipated Brahms:

Example 5

(*a*)

(*b*)

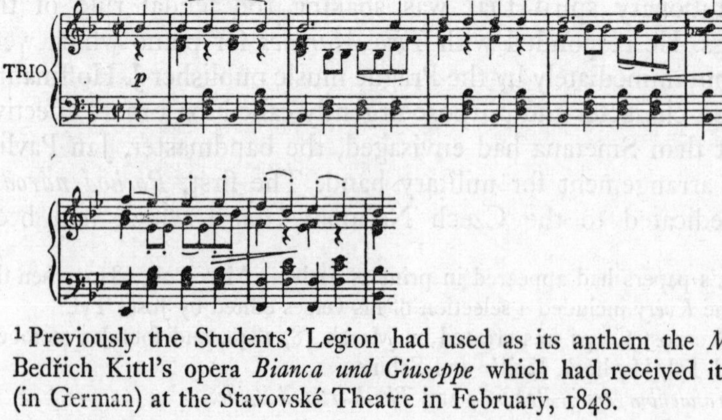

[1] Previously the Students' Legion had used as its anthem the *March* from Bedřich Kittl's opera *Bianca und Giuseppe* which had received its première (in German) at the Stavovské Theatre in February, 1848.

Kateřina Kolařová, 1858 (Smetana's first wife)

PLATE V

Smetana in 1866

PLATE VI

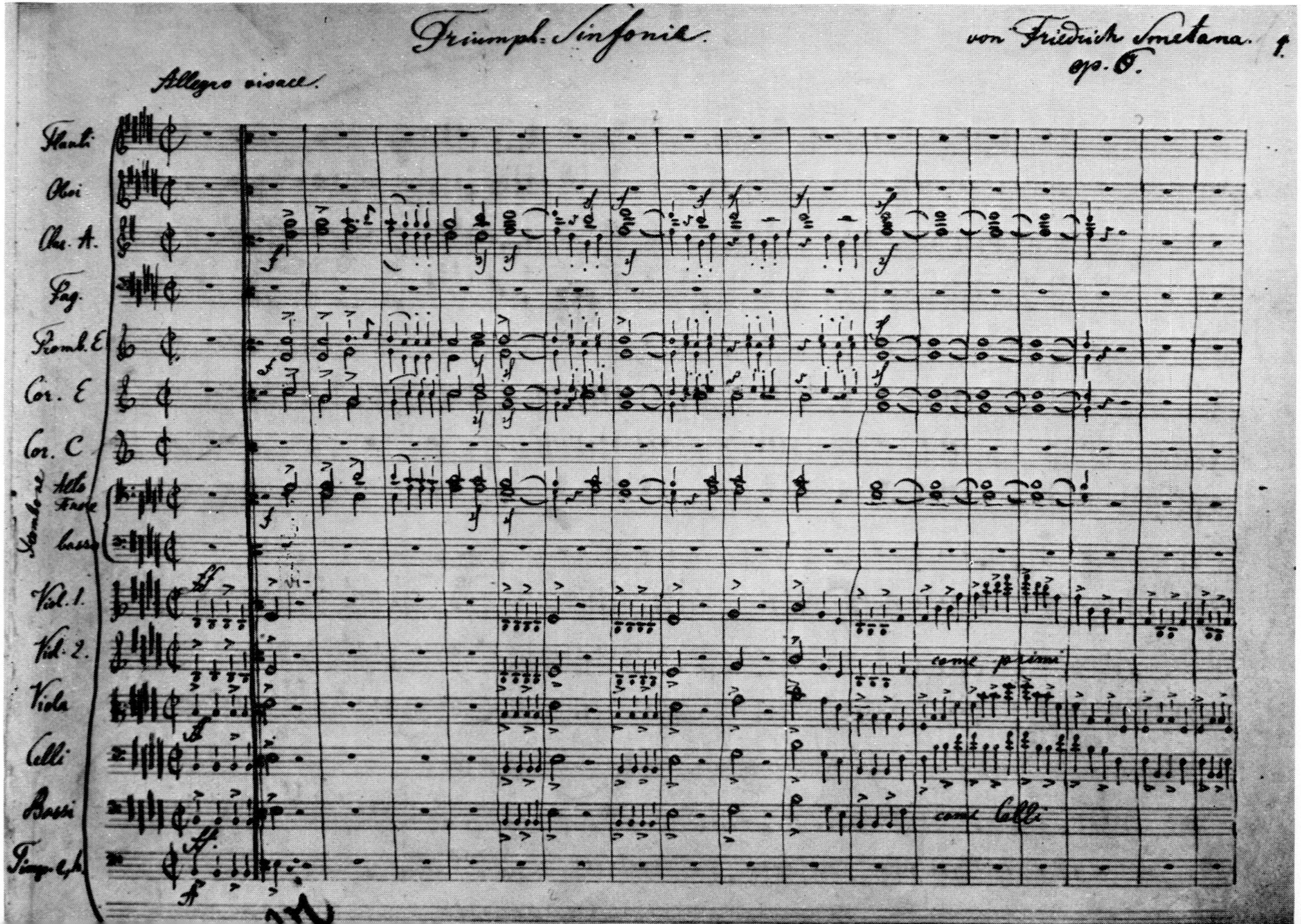

Smetana's autograph of the Triumphal Symphony

Apart from the striking similarity between the two compositions one may question why Smetana was moved to include a German song in Czech revolutionary music. Possibly he was commenting on the young Emperor's promise of a constitutional régime; for although Smetana, like most young Czechs, had grievances with the government of the day, he nevertheless hoped for a just settlement with Austria and welcomed the new eighteen-year-old monarch Franz Josef. The people of Prague saw in him a guarantee of a reorganization of the State which would allow for the free development of Czechs within the framework of Austrian policy. The quotation of the Austrian National Anthem in Smetana's *Triumphal Symphony*, and the composition of a *Hymn in honour of the Bohemian King*[2] to words of Václav Pok-Poděbradský, leave us in no doubt as to his sympathies at the time of the accession. Faith in the person of the monarch was enormous and held good for several decades in the minds of the Czechs. For them Franz Josef was not only Emperor of Austria but the future King of Bohemia.

About this time Smetana arranged two revolutionary songs, *The Death of Jan of Husinec* (Jan Hus) and *Patriotic Chorus* to words of Siegfried Kaffer. Neither has been preserved. A third piece which also reflects the events of revolution and has come down to us is *Píseň svobody* (*The Song of Freedom*), perhaps the most interesting of all the works Smetana wrote in the Spring of 1848. For the first time he set a Czech text written by Jan Kollár, and the direct references to Svornost suggest the poem was intended to be the hymn of the organization. The theme was simple: to arouse the Czechs and evoke in them feelings of national pride and freedom.

War! War! does the flag fly?
Rise up ye Czechs, for God is with us!
Stand firmly for your rights.
Guard your country and the glory of the Czechs!
The clamour that fills the air is
The sound of Žižka and of Tábor!

Whosoever is Czech must wield a sword!
Let there be blood and slaughter.
Let there be anger and terror.
Let there be cruel Hussite deeds!
Awake, take up your weapons you Czech lions!
God commands you to the Holy War!

[2] The opening lines of the text, 'Hail Josef, King of the Czechs, glorified by the faith of your people', point the reference.

With stirring lines and references to Jan Hus, Žižka,[3] the Hussite leader, Tábor,[4] the symbol of freedom, the Czech lion, the emblem of supremacy in Slavonic heraldry, and elsewhere to Svornost, it is little wonder that people were incited to rebellion. Smetana was obviously excited by the poem and responded with a simple but impressive setting for massed voices. The harmony may be diatonic, but the fanfare-like phrases, triadic melodies, and occasional clashing seconds of the accompaniment make it particularly effective and suitable for outdoor performance. From this time the march seemed to take on a new significance for Smetana; it was no longer the characteristic salon piece it had been but became linked with impressions of heroism and splendid processions as well as those of popular riots and gathering revolutionary forces.

The events of the Whitsun uprising are again reflected in Smetana's first large-scale orchestral work, the *Velka předehra* (*Grand Overture*). He had begun to sketch this during the summer of 1848 while staying with his parents in Obříství and although it was not completed until the following March, when it was performed by Škroup, it is important since it arose as a direct result of revolutionary events.

> The *Overture* was written at a time when rebellion was in the minds of the people—the revolt of 1848 which I witnessed and lived through. The form of the piece is old and so is the instrumentation, but its agreeable, gay, happy character remains . . . That at the time I did not care for it was only my negligence and carelessness. Besides giving daily piano lessons I did duty as conductor, and as I wanted to capture in my work an orchestral style which at that time was new I realized I would have to attain a higher standard of composition . . . It was my first orchestral work of a symphonic nature[5] and because of this I don't want it to rot in a corner. Let it live![6]

[3] Jan Žižka was born in 1378 in southern Bohemia. After losing one eye fighting for King Wenceslas against Bohemian nobles he was appointed Chamberlain and courtier to Queen Sophia (1412). Later he became leader of a party directed by priests which continued the principles set out by Hus during the Hussite Wars.

[4] Tábor was the town that became the centre of the more advanced Hussites, including Žižka. Later Žižka's warriors were known as Táborites and as a result of their religious campaigns Tábor became the symbol of freedom and the Táborites the bringers of liberty.

[5] Apart from this admission the manuscript score, preserved in the Smetana Museum in Prague, reveals signs of the composer's immaturity and lack of experience. Over the trombone parts he writes: 'If the players are uncertain of the intonation it is better not to play the notes at all.' Elsewhere he devised easier alternatives.

[6] Letter to Josef Srb-Debrnov: April, 1883.

The old form and instrumentation which Smetana mentions refer to a sonata movement and classical scoring, while the new orchestral style was possibly that of Berlioz. We have already noted the enormous impact that the French composer's visit had on Smetana in 1846: two years afterwards the same spirit, élan and youthful zest is to be found in the D major *Overture* where they seem to recall *Le Corsair* or *Carnaval Romain*; but the vitality and optimism with which the score is imbued is pure Smetana. Throughout, the typical features of his style are in evidence, including one which appears for the first time: it is an echo effect, built on a three-note pattern repeated at a different interval and in a new scoring, which gradually achieves prominence in later works.

At the end of July Smetana returned to Prague to make arrangements for the opening of his Institute. Having found accommodation in an apartment in the Old Town Square, on August 8 he inserted the following notice in the city's newspapers, in both Czech and German:

Nowě zřizený

ústaw

k wyučowání

na Piano-Forte.

Bedřich Smetana, zabýwajíc se po mnoha leta wýhradně wy-
ním w elementární i wyšší hudbě s nejlepším prospěchem, jsa i ze mnoha
wyzýwán, by z ohledu swého nawodu prospěšně se oswědčiwšího okres
ti swé ku podporowání zájemnosti hudebních užitečněji porozšířil, domníwá
ato žadostem wyhowěti zřízením nowé školy k wyučowání na Forte-Piané,
mladež oběho pohlawí w teto hře dokonale a dle nejlepšího náwodu wy-
na bude.

Wyučowaní nebude obmezeno toliko na počáteční předměty hudby, budeť
owat i theorii we wšech jejích oddílech, učení o skladbě, o souzwuku,
punktu, učení o formách, hudební krasowědu a t. d. wyšší hru na kla-
ojímání hudebních kusů, a uměleckého jich přednosu.

čební tento ustaw dělí se tedy we dwě třídy, w kteréžto prwní učití
le počatkům hudby theoreticky a prakticky, w druhé pak nawod k wyšší
a klawír a wyšší theorie hudby přednasetí se bude.

Chowanci tohoto ustawu budau třikrat w temdni po dwau hodinach wy-
ni, tak že zákyně počateční třídy wždy w pondělí, we středu a w patek
do 12 hodin, z wyšší třídy ale w ty samé dny odpoledne od 2 do 4
wyučowany budau. W tom samém pořadku budau žací w ostatních dnech
ně cwičeni, by se literními wyučowaní zawada nečinila.

Plat za jednoho žáka je měsíčně 4 zl. stříbra, jenž wždy napřed odwádí.

stаw tento nachází se na staroměstskem naměstí číslo domu 548, w tak
ném Nro. 1 w druhém poschodí pres dwůr, kdez se ohlasiti neciwě žadá
k wyučowaní w tento ustawu jest na 8. Srpna t. r. ustanowen

Bedřich Smetana.

Neu errichtetes

Lehr-Institut

im

Pianoforte-Spiele.

Friedrich Smetana, durch eine Reihe von Jahren sich ausschliesslich mit dem Elementar- und höheren Musik-Unterrichte mit dem besten Erfolge befassend und von vielen Seiten aufgefordert, in Betracht seiner sich so vortheilhaft bewährten Unterrichtsmethode seinen Wirkungskreis zur Förderung der Musikinteressen gemeinnütziger zu erweitern, glaubt diesem für ihn so schmeichelhaften Wunsche durch die Errichtung einer **Pianoforte-Schule** entgegen zu kommen, in welcher von ihm die Jugend beiderlei Geschlechts im Pianoforte-Spiel gründlich und nach bester Methode unterrichtet wird.

Der Unterricht beschränkt sich nicht nur auf die musikalischen Elementar-Gegenstände, er umfasst die Theorie in allen ihren Abtheilungen, Compositionslehre, Harmonie, Contrapunkt, Formlehre, musikalische Aesthetik u. s. w., das höhere Clavier-Spiel, Auffassung der Musikstücke und ihren kunstgemässen Vortrag.

Die Lehranstalt zerfällt also in 2 Klassen, in deren erster der Elementar-Unterricht theoretisch und praktisch vorgenommen wird, und in deren zweiter das höhere Clavierspiel und die höhere musikalische Theorie gelehrt wird.

Die Zöglinge erhalten dreimal der Woche, immer zu 2 Stunden Unterricht, so dass die weiblichen Zöglinge der Elementarklasse ihren Unterricht Montag, Mittwoch, Freitag früh von 10 bis 12 Uhr, jene der höheren Klasse hingegen an denselben Tagen Nachmittags von 2—4 Uhr erhalten. Ebenso die männlichen Zöglinge an den übrigen Tagen der Woche, um mit dem literarischen Unterricht nicht in Collision zu gerathen.

Das in Vorhinein zu berichtigende Honorar beträgt monatlich für einen Zögling 4 fl. C. Mze.

Das Instituts-Lokale befindet sich am altstädter Ring Nro. 548, im sogenannten Nro. 1 im 2. Stock rückwärts, wo man gefälligst die Anmeldungen zu machen hat. Der Zeitpunkt der Eröffnung dieser Musikschule ist am 8. August d. J.

Friedrich Smetana.

Press Notice announcing Smetana's intention to establish a Piano Institute in Prague (1848)

A NEW INSTITUTE FOR PIANOFORTE PLAYING

> Friedrich [*sic*] Smetana who over the last few years has been occupied in teaching music has, as a result of his excellently proven method, been asked to widen his circle of activity and help interest young people in music. He believes he can establish a school where young people of both sexes will be taught according to the best pianoforte method of the day. The Institute will not confine its teaching to the elementary but will include advanced tuition as well. The curriculum embraces theory, composition, harmony, counterpoint, form, musical aesthetics, the higher degrees of piano playing, musical appreciation and an artistic standard of performance. The Institute will have two classes: one for beginners, the other for experienced players. Junior pupils are invited to attend three times a week on Mondays, Wednesdays and Fridays for three hours each day, and senior pupils for two hours on each of these days. Payment is requested in advance at the fee of four gulden a month.

By the end of the month Smetana had recruited a dozen pupils but during the early stages he faced many obstacles. He was financially ill-equipped to set up a school on the scale he wanted and was able to provide neither heating nor sufficient pianos for practice. By Christmas more than half his clientele had left. In 1849, he managed to organize himself more successfully and found rooms with Kateřina's parents who had come to live in Prague. During his second season he attracted a number of young pupils from the nobility including Auguste, daughter of the playwright Kollár, Marie, daughter of the politician František Palacký, Ferdinand, son of the *prima donna* Kateřina Podhorská, and Marie, daughter of the painter Hellich. Later, he cultivated the interest and support of the aristocracy and was favoured by his former patron Count Thun as well as the Nostitz, Spork and Bellegarde families. Generally the Institute won a fashionable reputation not only as a house of learning but as a forum for new ideas where Czech nationalism was freely expounded:

> It is interesting that my former private pupil, Smetana has opened an Institute which he will direct on the basis of my system. With his presence being increasingly felt and his support for the cause of his people, he could well become the transformer of my ideas in the Czech language.[7]

The majority of pupils were young ladies, for at this time the piano

[7] Letter from Josef Proksch to his brother: August 5, 1848.

was taught not at the Conservatoire but at the Prague Organ School which was open only to men. Consequently instruction in a keyboard instrument was organized privately and 'piano' establishments[8] were often of a doubtful musical standing. Smetana's was certainly above the average level and though Proksch, with whom the young composer remained on the friendliest of terms, regarded it as one of the more radical institutions it nevertheless did much to further Czech music.

During 1849 Smetana's affairs improved and on August 27 he married Kateřina Kolářová at the church of St. Stephen, Prague. She was twenty-two and at the height of her beauty. He could not have wished for a more understanding partner. The couple lived with her parents, and according to Smetana's sister-in-law, Anna Ponc, they were very contented:

> Financially Smetana was at that time fairly well off and when Bedřiška, Gabriela and Žofie were born[9] his happiness was complete. . . . With the exception of music he lived only for his wife and children, he was gay and loved to join in the children's games wholeheartedly. . . . As time went by he welcomed distinguished guests to his home. Liszt liked to be one of his intimate circle and would often play cards with the family, and even the Emperor Ferdinand himself attended matinées at the Smetanas' home.[1]

The Emperor, who had abdicated during the 1848 uprising, now lived in retirement in Prague, and in the summer of 1850 Proksch recommended Smetana for the post of Court Pianist to the former King; consequently two or three times a week he played for the Emperor's amusement, partnering him in four-handed duets. As Ferdinand had only recently begun to take an interest in music his standard was low and the repertoire rarely went beyond Diabelli exercises. Smetana usually emerged bored and weary from these experiences, tolerating them only for the fee, and though he received four ducats every visit, he begrudged the hours involved in this royal chore. More stimulating, however, was his work for the magazine *Cecilia* with which he was associated from its inception. He worked closely with the Editor, Josef Krejčí, whose aim was to make more widely known the church compositions of Horák, Mašek and Kolešovský. Occasionally

[8] Apart from Smetana's, there were at least ten music institutes in Prague of which those run by Proksch, Chládek, Hodic and Horák were the most reputed.

[9] Bedřiška was born on January 1, 1851, Gabriela on February 26, 1852, and Žofie on May 24, 1853.

[1] Bartoš: *Letters and Reminiscences* (1955).

the magazine included music of a non-liturgical nature, and in the supplement for December, 1849, Smetana's own *Polka* in D appeared. But this was an exception. Krejčí, a traditionalist and Director of the Prague Organ School, found the enthusiastic young man too progressive for his liking and before long their association was brought to an abrupt end.

Smetana now concentrated on composing and arranging music for his Institute, which was beginning to enjoy a certain artistic and social success. Within a few months the students' concerts had won remarkable attention, and were considered to be outstanding as much for their unconventional character as for their musical standard. Into each concert he now introduced movements of piano quartets[2] by Beethoven, Mendelssohn and Schumann performed by Němec (violin), Král (viola) and Träg (cello), with Smetana himself at the keyboard.[3] Alongside these works his pupils played solo items, but as the number of students increased Smetana was obliged to make arrangements of well known orchestral scores for two or four pianos, so as to involve as many players as possible. He began with eight-handed versions of famous overtures, *Fidelio*, *Coriolan* and *Fingal's Cave*, and followed these with Webster's *Jubel-Ouvertüre* and Schumann's *Canonic Studies*; but as his forces grew he turned to sixteen-handed arrangements including one of Wagner's *Tannhäuser* Prelude which won enormous popularity. As much as he enjoyed making these versions he could not resist composing three original pieces[4] himself; and between November, 1849, and April, 1850, he produced a *Rondo* for two pianos, eight-hands, subtitled *Mládí* (*Youth*), written in the style of Mozart and sometimes called the *Mozart Rondo*; a one-movement Sonata[5] in E minor for the same combination; and a three-movement *Well of Melody*[6] for two pianos, eight hands, 'designed to encourage and refresh pupils'. Though intended for home and school consumption these are raised to a level of distinction by the freshness of melodic ideas and ingenious distribution of texture.

Apart from the chamber music items, the highlight of all the students' concerts was undoubtedly Smetana's own solo contribution.

[2] Smetana's chamber music evenings were described in the magazine *Cecilia* as an essential part of Prague's musical life.

[3] After 1849 the Quartet members changed, Němec's place being taken by Königslöw, that of Král by Goltermann. Träg, the cellist, stayed on.

[4] Earlier in 1846 Smetana had tried his hand at his first *Rondo*, for one piano, four hands, but this proceeded no further than a rough sketch.

[5] In 1851 he began to sketch a second Sonata for two pianos, eight hands, but unfortunately this did not materialize.

[6] The three movements are marked *Prelude*, *Capriccio* and *Finale*.

Up to this time he had made no professional public appearance in the city and consequently he used these soirées as a vehicle for displaying his own talents, imprinting himself on the mind of musical Prague as a pianist of immense technical ability. Smetana once confessed to his pupil Leopold Hruš that he had gained far more from listening to Liszt play for half an hour than from any other teacher. Curiously, contemporary accounts suggest that his own style of playing was far nearer that of Chopin than Liszt. While he had a remarkable command of the keyboard, his manner was elegant and possibly more refined than Liszt's grandiose and extravagant style. Smetana did not have a heavy hand, but a delicate, crystalline touch wedded to the bravura of Thalberg and the gentle poetry of Clara Schumann. As a technician he was one of the foremost of his day and the composer Josef Rozkošný (1833–1913) confirms that even towards the end of his life, and when deaf, Smetana was able to play the left hand part of Chopin's *Revolutionary Study* as Liszt had when in Prague in 1840—not as the composer had written it, but in octaves. Yet despite his formidable technique Smetana was not ideally fitted for the life of a concert pianist. He was small and weak and tired easily in performance. The critic Emanuel Chvála believed that his physical build was a serious disadvantage to him and for this reason Smetana may well have thought himself more suited to teaching than performing.

As a teacher, he was highly regarded by his pupils. He was a kindly man who achieved more by occasional irony than stern discipline. He laid great stress on theoretical instruction and adhered closely to the Marx method from which he had learned so much. He gave most of the instruction himself, but beginners were placed with a graduate from the Conservatoire or with Kateřina who deputized for her husband when the number of pupils grew unmanageable. Smetana always kept a study-cum-workroom apart from the school, and it reflected his musical tastes. On the walls hung pictures of Liszt, Berlioz, Schumann and his wife, whom Smetana had met during his last month in the employ of Count Thun, and Wagner, whose *Tannhäuser* had made an impression on him at its Prague première in November, 1854. Surrounded by these musical giants, Smetana would practice or compose.

Since his marriage he had concentrated on writing piano music, the first cycle to appear being *Svatební scény* (*Wedding Scenes*), a gift for a former pupil, Marie Thun. The three pieces are conceived in a relatively simple and direct style, and when he wrote them he possibly had in mind a series of rustic wedding festivities such as he may have witnessed during his childhood in Růžková Lhotice. The cycle is important since it is the first of Smetana's 'Czech' compositions to depict popular scenes from peasant life. It owes much to Schumann. The first movement, 'Wedding March', is remarkable for its use of pedals. Here the composer imitates the *dudy*—a bagpipe played by folk-musicians from Strakonice in Southern Bohemia. The *dudy* emits a drone on the interval of a fifth and it is this primitive sounding bass which forms the foundation of Smetana's 'March'. The next piece, 'Bride and Groom', is rich in modulation and close to a polka. The characteristic melody, formed on a descending scale, is delightfully treated in dialogue between soprano and tenor lines, portraying the newly wedded couple. The finale, 'Wedding Merry-making', is a chain of dances which suggests all the gaiety of the marriage celebrations. After a wild stamping dance the music gives way to a more relaxed waltz-like section, called sousedská. A polka follows, and over long, sustained harmonies Smetana introduces a theme later reworked in *The Bartered Bride* (it reappears in the introduction of the opening chorus to Act I). The polka from the second episode, 'Bride and Groom', is repeated, as is the sousedská, and 'Wedding Merry-making' ends as it began, with the stamping dance. Apart from the polka which returned in *The Bartered Bride*, the most interesting feature of the cycle is the appearance of the sousedská. Like the skočná, it is a folk dance rarely used by Smetana and, the operas apart, the only other piano set to include it is the *Czech Dances* written some thirty years later.

Smetana followed *Wedding Scenes* with a number of smaller pieces grouped under the collective title *Lístky do památníku* (*Album Leaves*), a description he had used for an earlier collection written in 1844–1845. Work on this first set had been, to a certain extent, influenced by the climate of Smetana's studies with Proksch, but they had not greatly affected the main line of his artistic development. The opposite is true of the large group of piano pieces written between 1848 and 1850 which also bear the name *Album Leaves* but otherwise have little in common with the usual run of works in this genre.

The primary impulse behind these pieces was probably one of experimentation, and the small scale forms enabled Smetana to test the appropriateness and effectiveness of various thoughts, moods, and musical impressions. Where the earlier *Album Leaves* were set out with some form of designation, here Smetana had no such scheme in mind: on the contrary, the cycle was to be based on the use of all twenty-four major and minor keys in a rotation dictated by the cycle of fifths, and Bach's *Das wohltemperierte Klavier* was clearly to be the model. This was not, however, the first time Smetana had chosen such a procedure: the *Bagatelles and Impromptus* (1844) and *Six Characteristic Pieces* (1848) show his leaning towards this device (though in both sets the key scheme while maintaining the cycle of fifths is arranged in a series of alternating major and minor modes).

The *Album Leaves* came to mind in quick succession during the autumn of 1848 and spring of 1849, following the revolutionary period when Smetana had had little time for concentrated work. Few of the *Leaves* are dated, but one in B flat is headed 'May, 1849'. It is also marked as 'Number 22' which suggests that the composer had not been idle during the winter months. Most of the *Leaves* exist in two versions: the original in which he noted down his thoughts in their first spontaneity and freshness, and a second in which he revised and recast the balance, harmony and figuration until they assumed their definitive form, ready for publication. But the plan to work in all twenty-four major and minor modes was not realized, and a number of pieces exist in which the key is duplicated. Instead of twenty-four *Leaves* there are thirty-two. That the original intention was unfinished was probably due to the uncertain prospect for publishing the collection as a whole. Smetana lost interest in them and devoted himself to other works.

Not that he had omitted to bring the *Album Leaves* to the attention of various publishers. He had. And in order to make them more attractive, he selected and freely arranged a number of pieces in the following forms, thus obscuring the original key scheme: a collection of six *Leaves* which he called Opus 2; a set of three, Opus 3, to which he added subtitles: 'Robertu Schumannovi' ('To Robert Schumann'), 'Píseň pocestného' ('Song of the Wayfarer'), 'Je slyšet tu hukot a sykot a svist' ('A roaring, hissing whirling can be heard') after Schiller's poem *The Diver*; and two groups each of four pieces called *Črty* (*Sketches*) Opus 4 and Opus 5 which also received characteristic titles.

Through these efforts he succeeded in interesting the publisher Franz Kistner, who brought out the Opus 2 pieces as a selection labelled Volume 1 (July, 1851); but although these were favourably reviewed by the music critic František Ulm,[7] Kistner made no move to print the rest and Volume 2 never appeared. Hopeful that Clara

[7] *Bohemia*: December 11, 1851 (No. 194/195). After analysing the pieces Ulm found the *Leaves* 'most accessible'. Numbers 2, 4 and 5 he considered to be 'full of unusual poetry, short but expressive, with unexpected harmonies and modulations which are unforced and spontaneous'. He concluded by expressing the view that further success awaited Smetana in the not too distant future.

Schumann might find a publisher for him, Smetana dedicated and sent the Opus 5 pieces to her; but though she replied with a certain interest there was no recommendation:

> If I may be so free I would say the *Album Leaves* described as 'romantic' are those that please me least, and I believe it would be better not to have them printed as they are too bizarre, so that neither listener nor pianist can derive peaceful enjoyment from them. It does not seem right to seek the romantic in the bizarre. In other pieces, too, I could wish to find a bar here or there more harmonically pleasing.[8]

At their first meeting in 1847 Clara Schumann had found it difficult to warm to Smetana's idiom; above all she had never become reconciled to the influence of Berlioz in his music, and the *idée fixe* which was discernible in many of his pieces. Undaunted, Smetana tried Liszt. Though complimentary he, too, was unable to suggest a publishing house, but offered to meet the young composer for a 'working consultation' in Weimar where they could put right those pieces which were found to be less distinguished than others.[9] Smetana declined Liszt's invitation. Instead, he stayed in Prague where he hoped to interest another publisher, Marco Berra. But Berra also rejected the *Album Leaves*, preferring to present to the public the *Salon* and *Poetic Polkas* (1855). In 1856, however, Smetana managed to have one *Leaf*, the *Andante* in E flat, included in the *Festive Music Album* published in honour of the silver wedding of Emperor Ferdinand and Maria Anna; and the following year two more *Leaves* were placed in Hallberger's collection, *Das Pianoforte* [*sic*], edited by Liszt. But in order to have these accepted Smetana was obliged to split the Opus 3 group, omitting 'A roaring, hissing whirling can be heard' which only received the distinction of print posthumously. Though another publisher, Viet, accepted the Opus 4 and Opus 5 *Sketches* (in a revised form) in 1858, the other *Leaves* remained unpublished during Smetana's lifetime except for the *Andante* in F minor which appeared as a contribution to a *Memorial Folio* published in aid of the National Theatre Building Fund, and the *Romance* in G minor included in a *Festive Album* prepared to commemorate the Jubilee Wedding of Crown Prince Rudolf in 1881.

Despite their chequered history,[1] the *Album Leaves* are delightful

[8] Letter from Clara Schumann: May 18, 1852.

[9] Letter from Liszt: April 12, 1854.

[1] A table showing the various arrangements of the *Album Leaves* and their keys will be found in Appendix B.

miniatures, and charming poetic tone pictures which follow closely the tradition of Schumann's characteristic piano works. They are rich harmonically, abound in exquisite detail, and cover a wide range of moods. Most important, they show Smetana gaining practice in writing pieces on single thematic ideas. The *Leaves* are often concise, almost terse, and their economy of thought and monothematic technique, on a reduced scale, must be singled out as a developing mark of style that looks forward to the symphonic poems, notably *Richard III* where the composer exploits this as a personal working method. Noteworthy, too, are the musical seeds that were to flower in many of Smetana's later works; for by examining these pieces we can see how his melodic thought developed and crystallized from one work to the next. Consider bars 30–35 of the *Leaf* in G major which were later reworked to provide material for the Dance of the Reapers in Act II of *Libuše* (full score p. 362); and from another *Leaf*, 'The Wanderer's Song', Smetana extracted a fanfare (a) which appeared in (b) the F sharp major Polka of 1852 (*Salon Polka* No. 1), in (c) 'Thoughts for a Symphony' (1852–3) and the sketch of the symphonic poem, *The Vikings' Voyage* (d):

Example 6

(a) Allegro moderato

(b)

(c)

(d)

The *Leaf* 'To Robert Schumann' also furnished Smetana with another motive for *Libuše*: the opening bars were transformed and lengthened to form Přemysl's love theme:

Example 7

After sketching *Album Leaves*, Smetana turned his attention to the polka. Over the years he had gradually changed its character from the fashionable dance of the bourgeois drawing-rooms to a scherzo—a vehicle for virtuoso display in the music-rooms of his Institute. Between 1849 and 1854, however, he was concerned with another idea: to raise the polka from the level of a showpiece to a musical tone poem. His model was certainly Chopin, whose Mazurkas and Polonaises had transformed prosaic dances into personal and sophisticated art forms in which he could express everything that was most directly linked in his mind with his native Poland. Smetana aspired to do the same and saw the polka as a suitable outlet for voicing his growing enthusiasm for everything Czech—the people, the countryside, the way of life. Czech optimism was a characteristic ideally suited to the bright and joyful dance element of the polka; but gradually Smetana began to extend the range of moods so that it became a highly stylized and subjective genre reflecting his most ardent nationalistic thoughts. During these years he produced two cycles of Polkas, apart from a number of individual pieces which bear that name. In *Tři polky salónní* (*Three Salon Polkas*) (Opus 7) and *Tři polky poetické* (*Three Poetic Polkas*) (Opus 8), he succeeded in giving the form a special meaning, displaying on the one hand the zest and jubilant vitality of the society in whose midst he had grown up, and on the other, a depth of feeling which goes so far as to include sorrow and wistful loneliness. Two examples from the Opus 8 pieces will show the wide area that these pieces cover. In the G minor *Polka* a sad melancholic mood permeates the music, while in the one in A flat Smetana is at his happiest and most lyrical with a theme which has enormous élan even though it depends on an endlessly rising scale for its impetus:

Example 8

(*a*)

(*b*)

Between 1849 and 1854 he began to cast his net further afield, turning from compositions for piano to orchestral works on similar lines as the D major *Overture*. Three unconnected fragments have survived; but apart from knowing that they were intended for use in a *Prelude* in D minor for large orchestra it is difficult to guess to what impulse they owe their origin. Thematically they correspond to neither sketch preserved in the Prague Museum, nor are there any written references to it in the Diary or letters. It seems likely, however, that they were drafted before the *Slavnostní symfonie* (*Triumphal Symphony*) (1853); for on one of the manuscript pages are pencil sketches for material that was later worked into the first movement. The idea of writing a symphony had occupied Smetana some time before 1853 and while composing the *Album Leaves* and *Poetic Polkas* he had set down a few 'Thoughts for a Symphony' (Gedanken zu einer Sinfonie) possibly on a Shakespearean theme (one of the 'thoughts' was to be worked into the *Album Leaf* called 'The Wayfarer's Song'). It is hard to know when Smetana began his *Triumphal Symphony* or, indeed, what prompted him to write it. He later confessed that the impetus for the work had stemmed from the announcement that the Emperor Franz Josef was to marry Princess Elizabeth of Bavaria. The engagement was announced on August 1, 1853; but according to Smetana's catalogue of compositions, drawn up in 1858, the *Triumphal Symphony* was completed in February 1853. Almost certainly his catalogue can only have indicated that the sketch was finished; for in Kateřina's Diary there exists an entry from the 'beginning of the year 1854' which tells us:

> Bedřich was occupied all day with lessons, and after dinner worked diligently on the Symphony written to commemorate the wedding of Franz.

Possibly he had decided to write a symphonic work before August 1, and the announcement of the engagement prompted him to use the event as a peg upon which to hang his new composition. Thus he not only dedicated the work to the Emperor and his bride, but confirmed his allegiance to the Monarchy by incorporating in the score direct references to the Austrian Anthem.

The Czechs placed enormous faith in the person of Franz Josef and despite the darkest oppression of Bach's police régime they set great store by the Emperor's engagement and subsequent marriage, looking forward to his initiating a series of radical social reforms, and effecting a political settlement. Most of all, they hoped for the time when the coronation of Franz Josef as King of Bohemia would confirm the rights of the Czech Crown. But by quoting part of the Austrian Imperial Hymn in the *Triumphal Symphony* Smetana did not automatically place the seal of success on the work. On the contrary, the use of the Anthem was fatal. He had hoped that the piece would be performed on the occasion of the solemn wedding which was to take place on April 24, 1854, and hopefully sent the work to Vienna with a request that he be allowed to dedicate it to the royal couple; yet even this manifestation of Czech loyalty failed to arouse any response. Kateřina believed that the equerry to the Imperial Court, a Count Lanskoronsky, was responsible for ignoring the score:

> In spite of what he has been promised by all the important men, my good husband has had no success with the *Symphony*. Two years have passed and Bedřich still has no answer.[2]

He never did receive an answer from the Imperial Court, and it is interesting to speculate on what grounds the work was set aside. It is difficult to imagine the composition was rejected on an assessment of its artistic values, for it undoubtedly bears witness to Smetana's talent and his skill in handling symphonic form and textures. It is more likely that the work was considered unsuitable because the Anthem had not been given the outstanding place that was expected; for although the melody appears briefly in three of the four movements it is not used as organic thematic material. In the first, the opening four bars of Haydn's tune appear only once, and then very discreetly, before the recapitulation. In the original sketch, however, Smetana had been even more circumspect in outlining the theme thus:

Example 9

In the second movement, a majestic Largo, the Imperial Hymn recurs more forcibly: Example 10 (p. 61). In the Scherzo, however, it does not appear at all, and only once in the Finale where it is solemnly given out in the closing bars in truncated form.

Since the Imperial Court had ignored the *Triumphal Symphony* Smetana had little hope of hearing his new work unless he mounted a performance himself. This he now attempted to organize in his Institute where he set up a music society which was open to amateur

[2] Kateřina's Diary: August, 1856.

PROGRAMM

zu dem

CONCERT von FRIEDRICH SMETANA

den 26. Februar Nachmittags 5 Uhr

im

CONVICT-SAALE.

Erste Abtheilung.

Triumph-Sinfonie mit Benützung der österreich. Volkshymne für das grosse Orchester bei Gelegenheit der feierlichen Vermählung I. I. M. des Kaisers **Franz Joseph** und der Kaiserin **Elisabeth** eigens componirt vom Concertgeber.

Zweite Abtheilung.

1. a) **Fuge**, Fis-moll, von Seb. Bach.
   b) **Variationen**, E-dur, von Fr. Händel, vorgetragen vom Concertgeber.
2. **Lied** von Schubert, vorgetragen von Herrn Lukeš.
3. **Trio** von Beethoven, G-dur op. 1. für Piano, Violine und Violoncello, vorgetragen von der 11jährigen Auguste Kolar, Schülerin des Concertgebers, Herrn Bennewitz, und Herrn Prof. Goltermann.
4. a) **Canon**, H-moll von Rob. Schumann.
   b) **Polonaise**, Cis-moll von Fr. Chopin.
   c) **Lied ohne Worte**, Nr. 6. V. Heft, von F. Mendelssohn.
5. a) **Lied** von Löwe, b) **Lied** von Veit, } vorgetragen von Frau Botschon-Soukup.
6. a) **Trois Polka de Salon**, op. 7. Nr. 1.
   b) **Trois Polka poëtiques**, op. 8. Nr. 3. componirt und vorgetragen vom Concertgeber.

Frau Botschon-Soukup, Herr Lukeš, Herr Orchester-director Prof. Mildner, Herr Prof. Goltermann und Herr Bennewitz haben bereitwilligst ihre Mitwirkung zugesagt.

Eintrittskarten in den Cercle zu 2 fl., in den Saal zu 1 fl., auf die Gallerie zu 40 kr. sind in der Kunst- und Musikalienhandlung von **Marco Berra**, Egydi-Gasse Nr. 453—I, so wie im Musik-Institute des Fr. Smetana, Zeltnergasse Nr. 596, 2. Stock rückwärts und Abends an der Cassa zu haben.

Druck von C. W. Medau in Prag 1855.

Programme for the concert in which Smetana's *Triumphal Symphony* was played for the first time in Prague (February 26, 1855)

Example 10

instrumentalists as well as advanced pupils. Though he experienced difficulty in recruiting players prepared to give up their leisure time purely for the enjoyment of music, he devised a scheme whereby friends and musical acquaintances would join with the Theatre Orchestra to perform his Symphony. In spite of enormous expense the Konvikt Hall was booked for February 26, at 5.00 p.m. Smetana was to conduct his *Triumphal Symphony* in the first half of the programme and perform numerous solos in the second. This was to be his first concert appearance in Prague, and a subscribers' list was circulated among the aristocracy with considerable response. Smetana had selected the date most carefully so as not to clash with the opera performance, but an unfortunate change of programme at the Stavovské Theatre resulted in *Tannhäuser*, then at the height of its fame, being given the same evening. This not only harmed Smetana's concert, but thoroughly disorganized it. He was unable to prepare the *Triumphal Symphony* with the Theatre Orchestra until the *Tannhäuser* rehearsals were finished; moreover the programme had to be changed so that the tenor, Jan Lukes, who was to appear in the concert, could appear as Walther von der Vogelweide in *Tannhäuser*. Kateřina later recalled:

> The concert had one fault: it was too long.[3] This apart the success was considerable. The *Symphony* was well received,

[3] Smetana also played Bach's Fugue in F sharp minor, Handel's Variations in E, Schumann's Canon in B minor, Chopin's C sharp minor Polonaise, Mendelssohn's *Spring Song*, and his own *Salon Polka* in F sharp minor and *Poetic Polka* in A flat.

> particularly the Scherzo. Bedřich's playing was generally applauded and though he performed well, he tired towards the end since he had conducted the *Symphony* twice in one day. . . . The oil in the lamps which lit the hall gave out at the same time as his strength, and an unpleasant smell took some of the joy out of the concert. Alas the financial success was not particularly brilliant: Bedřich handed me as my share, twenty-five gulden.[4]

Apart from the Scherzo, the other movements of the *Triumphal Symphony* failed to make much impression on either audience or critics, and Smetana's disappointment at the work's reception developed into antipathy. The *Triumphal Symphony* was not to be heard in Prague for twenty-seven years, and it was only when the composer examined the score in 1881 (renaming it *Festive Symphony*) that he recognized the qualities of the music:

> The *Symphony* is something I can be proud of even though it is on a vast scale and worked out in classical form; it has power and something good to say in content, style and originality. Let the entire *Symphony* be performed with the full anthem and let it be victorious![5]

The *Triumphal Symphony* was his first serious attempt to write a work in this genre, and its very origins seem to be a paradox. Rosa Newmarch dismisses it as 'an epithalamium for a Hapsburg Prince, written by a Czech musician on an Austrian national hymn composed by a Croatian'.[6] But the *Triumphal Symphony* is far more than this. It is a fully accomplished piece which shows no lack of conviction in grappling with symphonic form. Clearly his model was the large scale symphonies of Schubert and Mendelssohn but the character is typically Smetana's. This delightful theme, from the first movement development, shows a melodic competence quite new in his expression:

Example 11

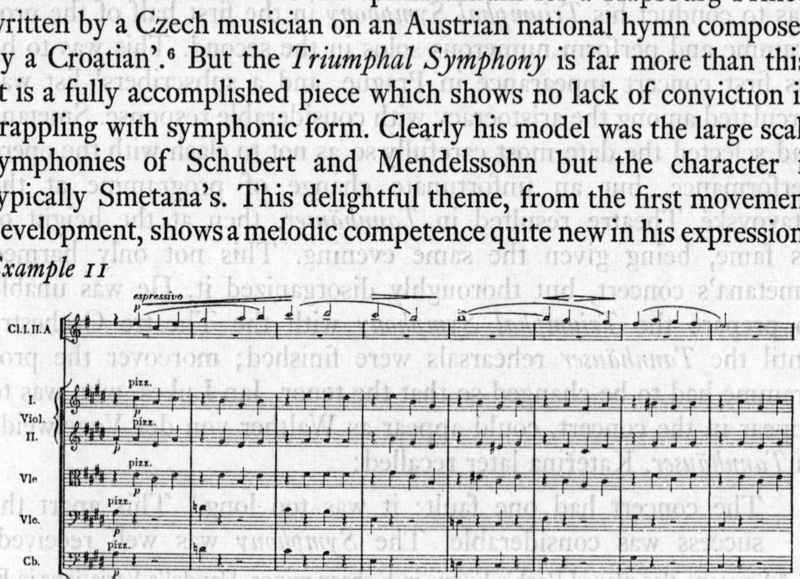

[4] Kateřina's Diary: February, 1855.
[5] Letter to Srb-Debrnov: November, 1881.
[6] Newmarch: *The Music of Czechoslovakia* (1942).

Throughout there are aspects of the working-out, the manipulation of material, that predict much which becomes characteristic of the composer in later years: the busy instrumental parts, the bouncing rhythms, the movement in thirds and sixths, the inclusion of the marking 'con tutta la forza', before the triumphant statement of the Imperial Hymn in the Finale, all point to the composer's increasing maturity. The instrumentation (with echoes of Mendelssohn and Gade) is particularly successful, and nowhere more so than in the Scherzo, which is remarkable for its clarity and well-graded climax. The principal theme of this movement, an alternating four-note pattern, is especially interesting in that its basic shape anticipates the phrase with which Dvořák chose to begin his *Requiem* some thirty-five years later. Although Smetana indicates a trio section in this movement this is given a marked individuality by being in $\frac{2}{4}$ and in the style of a polka. If the *Triumphal Symphony* has a fault it is its length. Smetana realized this, for when re-examining the piece in the winter of 1881 he marked a number of optional cuts in the outer movements which do much to strengthen the work as a whole.

Shortly after completing the *Triumphal Symphony*, Smetana's happiness was completely shattered. On June 9, 1854, his second daughter, Gabriela, died. His grief was enormous, but nothing compared to the profound personal suffering which followed the loss of his eldest daughter, Bedřiška, who died from scarlet fever on September 6, 1855. Smetana had nicknamed her Fritzi, and of all his children she, a talented girl who could speak German at the age of two, sing with good intonation at three, and play simple pieces on the piano at four, was his favourite. Although on October 25, 1855, his wife had given birth to another girl, whom they named Kateřina, she too died within eight months. 'Nothing can replace Fritzi, the angel whom death has stolen from us' is the pathetic entry in Smetana's Diary at this time. His tragic loss threw him into the depths of despair, and only in composition could he find consolation. He worked feverishly, and within two months produced a work which was to be his first mature artistic achievement, the Piano Trio in G minor.

It is an ironic fact that in the most tragic events of his life Smetana was to find inspiration for some of his most important compositions. The Piano Trio is but the first of a line of works which arose out of suffering. There is no doubt that his daughter's death, his later financial hardships, his deafness and personal unhappiness dragged from him the real stuff of composition. And there is no mistaking the force behind the Piano Trio:

PROGRAMM

zur

4ten SOIRÉE

für Kammermusik,

Montag den 3. December 1855 präcise 4½ Uhr

im

CONVICT - SAALE.

Unter Mitwirkung der Herren Director **Smetana** und **Wiedemann.**

1. **Trio** für Pianoforte, Violin und Violoncell von *Fr. Smetana.* (G-moll. Manuscript).
   - *a.* Allegro moderato ed energico.
   - *b.* Non troppo agitato, Andante, Maestoso.
   - *c.* Finale, Presto.
2. **Quintett** für 2 Violinen, Viola und 2 Celli von *Fr. Schubert,* (C-moll Op. 163).
   - *a.* Allegro ma non troppo.
   - *b.* Adagio.
   - *c.* Scherzo, Presto, Trio, Andante sostenuto.
   - *d.* Allegretto.
3. **Quintett** für Pianoforte, 2 Violinen, Viola und Violoncell von *R. Schumann,* (Es-dur, Op. 44).
   - *a.* Allegro brillante.
   - *b.* In modo d'una Marcia.
   - *c.* Scherzo, Molto vivace.
   - *d.* Allegro ma non troppo.

O. von Königslöw. A. Bennewitz.
A. Paulus. J. Goltermann.

Programme for one of Smetana's Chamber-Music Evenings at which the Piano Trio in G minor was given for the first time (December 3, 1855)

> The loss of my eldest daughter, an extraordinarily gifted child, inspired me to compose my chamber work in 1855. In the winter of the same year the Trio was performed publicly in Prague with poor success.[7] The critics condemned it harshly, but a year later we performed it in our home for Liszt, who embraced me and expressed his congratulations to my wife.[8]

Smetana's grief for his daughter colours most of the score and is epitomized in the chromatic descent of a fifth which is to be found extensively in the first two movements, and less predominantly in the Finale, where it is somewhat disguised. The first movement, in sonata form, begins with a solo violin plaint suggesting the composer's mental struggle, his grief and remorse. The opening is characterized by a pentatonic-type melody, a prophetic touch that looks forward to the initial bars of *The Bartered Bride* overture, the principal theme of *Vyšehrad* and to Martinka's aria in Act I of *The Kiss*. The mood is one of intense gloom, and the music proceeds with a feeling of resigned melancholy. The harmony is searchingly chromatic, the textures richly contrapuntal (the development provides examples of both canonic imitation and augmentation). A calmer atmosphere is found, however, in a theme that suggests the remembrance of Smetana's daughter herself; but this is only an interlude. There is no respite and the aggressive and powerful opening material returns in a compelling argument.

The second movement also depicts the composer's recollections of Bedřiška's childish playfulness. It is episodic with the principal theme, a scherzo-like Polka, interrupted by two serious trios called, in the old style, *alternativo*. So as to bring unity to the Trio Smetana derives the principal theme itself from the 'plaint' motive of the previous movement (Example 12). But this technique is not extended to either *alternativo*, the first pastoral and reflective, the second mournful and characterized by a heroic march rhythm that seems to summon death.

The Finale, on the other hand, is full of restless energy and defiance. The rondo theme is taken from the Sonata in G minor written

[7] The Piano Trio was first given on December 3, 1855, in the Konvikt Hall, when Smetana was joined by Antonín Bennewitz (viloin) and Julius Goltermann (cello).

[8] Letter to Procházka: September 26, 1877. Ludevít Procházka (1837–1884) was one of Smetana's most faithful friends. He studied the piano with him at the age of seventeen, but their relationship began only in 1860. Between 1866–1883 he was his confidant and advisor. As a journalist he contributed articles on Smetana's work in *Dalibor* and *Hudební Listy*. He was also responsible for introducing Smetana's opera *The Two Widows* to Hamburg.

Example 12

(*a*)

(*b*)

under Proksch's guidance in 1846, and here Smetana not only quotes the idea itself but the first hundred and eighteen bars in which persistent ostinatos and turbulent cross rhythms (couplets against triplets) anticipate the fantastic Bezděz Mountain scene in his opera *The Secret*. Here, however, the abrupt rhythmic patterns possibly suggest the irregular heart beats of the dying child. In contrast, the episodes are warmly lyrical and full of sad memories such as this phrase in which we sense his own voice has begun to emerge, asserting itself as a force to be reckoned with:

Example 13

Despite the underlying sorrow which embraces this music the basic minor tonality is somehow defeated in the final bars, and the whole work ends triumphantly in the major, as if the composer had finally found reconcilation with fate. This change of mode from minor to major, accompanied by a feeling of optimism in the final bars, is a characteristic feature of Smetana's style which can be found time and again in many of the later works, particularly the operas.[9]

But the show of optimism with which the Piano Trio ends was only on the surface. Smetana found life difficult during 1855 and 1856. Although his Institute flourished and the number of private pupils from aristocratic circles increased, he remained depressed, unhappy, disillusioned. Around him the revolutionary spirit, burning so brightly in 1848, had dimmed. The Emperor Franz Josef had failed to fulfil any of Smetana's hopes for social reform and had broken all

[9] Despite the diverse nature of his operatic plots, which cover the whole gamut of moods from comedy to tragedy, seven of the eight end in a similar celebratory way. *Dalibor* is the exception.

promises to reorganize the state. In 1856 Josef Tyl,[1] one of the most enlightened writers of the day, died; in the same year Karel Havlíček, Smetana's lifelong friend, also died after being imprisoned for four years by Bach's police régime at Brixen in the Tyrol. Moreover, Smetana had failed to make the impact on Prague he had hoped for. Although he had won a sizeable reputation as a pianist, he had captured neither the people nor the city. Apart from isolated recitals, he had given only one concert in Prague, and thereafter had found it difficult to make headway against the tides of oppression and prejudice. What is more he had serious competition in the person of Alexander Dreyschock,[2] a pianist of national renown.

Smetana had met Dreyschock at the Concordia Club in 1848 and had gone out of his way to cultivate his support for his Institute. Later he had written a brilliant *Allegro Capriccioso* especially for him, but the motive behind the piece remains obscure. The obvious explanation is that it was intended as a tribute to Dreyschock, but the prodigious virtuosity, the extreme technical demands, and the marathon-like nature of the piece (three hundred and thirty-three bars—the longest piano work that Smetana had produced to date) seem to suggest it was designed more as a challenge than an acknowledgement. There is no evidence that Dreyschock ever performed it; but the wild character of the music hints that relations between the two pianists may have been tense and that Smetana regarded Dreyschock as a rival to his advancement.

In January, 1856, however, Smetana at last found an opportunity to display his talents. For the hundredth anniversary concert celebrating Mozart's birth, he was chosen to be soloist in the D minor

[1] Tyl (1808–1856) was an actor, novelist and playwright whose plays voiced the contemporary democratic ideals of the rebirth of the nation.

[2] Alexander Dreyschock (1818–1869) had been a pupil of Tomášek and friend of Spohr and was later Professor at the Conservatoire in St. Petersburg. He composed one hundred and twenty piano works as well as chamber music and an opera. He was one of the best piano technicians of his generation and almost rivalled Liszt. He became famous for his rendering of Chopin's *Revolutionary Study* in which he played the left hand part entirely in octaves. Of him Berlioz writes:

> I would single out Dreyschock . . . it seems that he was badly handled by his compatriots on his first appearance there [in Prague] and vowed never again to expose his talents to the disparagement of a Bohemian audience. . . . However the Praguers are taking note of the admiring reports coming in from all points of the compass that Dreyschock is an admirable pianist. . . .
>
> (*Memoirs:* Sixth Letter to Humbert Ferrand. In the translation by David Cairns).

Piano Concerto (K. 466), and to mark the occasion wrote his own elaborate cadenzas. His success was considerable. At last he enjoyed public recognition and his achievement was regarded by many to have equalled, if not surpassed, that of Dreyschock. Gratifying as this was to Smetana, it was too much for his jaundiced rival, who had recently returned from a concert tour of Scandinavia. Dreyschock set about goading Smetana with accounts of his reception and success; he urged him to leave Prague and to take up residence in Göteborg, where he promised to recommend him to a teaching post.[3] Smetana hesitated. In September Liszt visited Prague to conduct performances of some of his works, and though he stayed just over a week he managed to see Smetana every day. Smetana had always cherished an unlimited respect for the Hungarian composer, and had become one of his most ardent followers. Now the two artists spent countless hours together discussing the neo-Romantic school[4] and the writings of Wagner, whose *Lohengrin* and *Der fliegende Holländer* had been staged for the first time in Bohemia earlier in the year. These conversations may well have aroused in Smetana a desire to test his creative abilities elsewhere. Whether the impulse came from Dreyschock, from Liszt or from the idea of escaping from his home where the sad and lonely atmosphere following the deaths of his three daughters was made worse by the inability of his ailing wife to fill his life with the happiness of former years, we do not know. All that is certain is that on October 11, 1856, Smetana left for Sweden, alone.

[3] In the Göteborg *Morgonposten* of November 20, 1897, Smetana's friend and compatriot Josef Czapek recalls that Dreyschock was invited by Mrs. Dickson to find some able piano teacher to come to Sweden and make his home in Göteborg.

[4] The neo-Romantic or new-German school of composers centred around Weimar and had Liszt and Wagner at its head. The term was coined to distinguish the work of these composers from others who, to some extent, drew their inspiration from classical models—namely Schumann, Mendelssohn and Brahms.

FOUR

YEARS ABROAD
1856–1859

ALTHOUGH SMETANA had travelled widely in his own country he had seldom ventured outside it. He knew little of Europe, and his journey in the autumn of 1856 introduced him to many new sights. He had never before seen Dresden, Leipzig or Hamburg, and his arrival in Kiel on October 13 made a deep impression on him:

> Nobody can possibly imagine how the sea and large ocean-going vessels surprise one for the first time. The steamers which used to leave from Obříství here seem like the little toy pleasure boats on our Bohemian fish ponds.[1]

He stayed in the port only a few hours before embarking for Copenhagen and Göteborg which he reached on October 17.

The old town of Göteborg (literally Gothic Castle) had been founded by Gustav Adolf as the first fort against the Danes after the Thirty Years' War, and as a result of its geographical position had grown into a busy commercial centre, being one of the richest ports in Sweden. With a population of over forty thousand it was the largest town after Stockholm; but in 1856 it was mainly the home of seamen and merchants who depended on the harbour for their livelihood. Few of them, however, were Swedes. Only the Lindström and Reuström families were of Swedish origin; for the rest, the leading figures were either Dutch immigrants, like the Wijks who had been responsible for rebuilding the harbour after the Napoleonic invasion, English, like the Dicksons (a reminder that the town had been the chief British depot in Northern Europe after 1806), or of German extraction like the Koch, Röhss and Kraft families. The most important community, however, was the Jewish one, and as a result of their skill in trading

[1] Letter to his parents: December 23, 1856. This is the first known example of Smetana adopting the Czech language, and throughout the style is often stiff and ungrammatical.

Göteborg had grown prosperous. The Magnus, Fürstenberg, Pinaes, Valentin and Gumpert families had all flourished and accumulated a certain wealth. These people had not only formed the tone of society but had been instrumental in setting up the first synagogue (1855) which quickly became the most important building in the town. As a result of their keen business sense they had learnt to live well, but they existed for their livelihood and little else.

In Göteborg Smetana enjoyed a freer life than he had known in reactionary Prague; but everything was so governed by the power of money and property that he found the cost of living much higher than before:

> Life is expensive, living quarters particularly so, but the food and beer are good. Mostly English porter and ale are drunk. To all appearances my standing here is better than in Prague.[2]

The social life of the local bourgeoisie was similar to that which Smetana had known in Plzeň—whist, dancing, and the consumption of wine seem to have been the main pastimes. Home music-making was cultivated among the female members of rich families, but only to ward off boredom while their menfolk were occupied with business affairs. Music was regarded as an accompaniment to a reception or an At Home, as a social grace rather than an artistic activity. Musically, in fact, Göteborg was far more backward than Prague: there was no properly established opera house (only the local theatre where the standard was very low), little concert life and no regular orchestra. Göteborg depended on the occasional appearances of visiting artists and mediocre touring companies for its music, and it is not surprising that in this culture-starved society Smetana made an immediate impact. His first recital, on October 23 at the Blom Assembly Room,[3] just six days after his arrival, led to his being recognized as a virtuoso. His programme comprised two of Mendelssohn's *Lieder ohne Wörte*, Handel's E major Variations, Schubert's *Serenade* (arranged by Liszt) and his own F sharp minor *Salon Polka*. The audience was enthusiastic; and even the local music critic praised his polished technique and method of interpretation.[4] He followed this with other recitals on November 6 (the anniversary of Gustav Adolf), 12 and 17, and was so warmly received that he considered making his home in

[2] Letter to his parents: December 23, 1856.

[3] The Assembly Room was the accepted place of Göteborg's entertainment of all kinds including music, and was part of Blom's Hotel. According to the Göteborg music critic it was dirty and uncomfortable, with a poor piano and rickety music stool.

[4] *Commercial and Navigational Newssheet*: October 24, 1856.

1. Soiree

Sonntag den 6ten April 1856

Nachmit. um 4 Uhr

Programm.

1. Jubel-Ouverture von C. M. v. Weber aufgeführt von 8 weiblichen Zöglingen der Harmonie-Schule.
2. Capriccio von Fr. Smetana, vorgetragen von Franz Brava.
3. Impromptu von H. Litolff, vorgetrag[en] von Fräulein Louise Sieger
4. Rondino von Diabelli für 2 Claviere, gespielt von Sophie und Nikolaia Gillich, Marie Hellich und Marie Weihrauch
5. Les adieux, Fantasie von C. M. v. Weber, vorgetragen von Fräulein Anna Mai.
6. Finale aus Beethovens Dmoll-Sonate, vorgetragen von Auguste Kolar.
7. Ballade von Fr. Chopin, Op. 23, vorgetragen von Herrn Ludwig Prochaska.
8. Fingalshöhle, Ouverture von Mendelssohn aufgeführt von 8 weiblichen Zöglingen der Harmonie-Schule.

Programme of one of Smetana's Prague 'Pupils Evenings' (April 6, 1856)

Göteborg. On arrival he had taken quayside lodgings at the Hotel Garni, Skeppsbron, and it was from here he hoped to establish a Music School:

SCHOOL OF MUSIC

> Provided that pupils apply in sufficient numbers I, the undersigned, who have been Director of a School of Music in Prague, intend to found a similar School in Göteborg at which instruction will be given in piano playing and the theory of music, beginning with basic rudiments and proceeding to the study of harmony and composition. Lessons will be given in groups of six or eight pupils. Halfway through each course the pupils' parents and guardians will be invited to observe their progress for themselves, and at the end of the term a full examination will be held, both in the theory of music and practical exercises. The fee, payable in advance, will be eight *Rdr Bco* for each pupil per month to include one hour's daily instruction. Application forms are obtainable at Gumpert's bookshop and those who wish to attend the proposed School are requested to send their names before the 15th of the month.
>
> Göteborg, November, 1856
> Freidr. [*sic*] Smetana,
> Director.[5]

Within three weeks he had received so many applications that his future seemed assured:

> A School of Music will be opened by the undersigned on December 1, 1856. Detailed arrangements may be made at my apartment between the hours of 5.00 and 6.00 (p.m.)
>
> Freidr. [*sic*] Smetana,
> Director.[6]

By Christmas the School had come to be regarded as the most exclusive in Göteborg. It was also the most expensive. But though Smetana earned a considerable sum each month he was unable to save much,[7] being obliged to provide not only for himself and his

[5] *Commercial and Navigational Newssheet*: November 4, 1856.
[6] *Commercial and Navigational Newssheet*: November 21, 1856.
[7] Between January and March, 1857, Smetana kept a careful record of his monthly expenditure which affords a glimpse of his daily life:
40 Swedish dollars for two rooms at the Hotel Garni.
25 Swedish dollars for dinners at the Exchange Restaurant.
20 Swedish dollars to a lady assistant teacher at the school.
15 Swedish dollars for a blackboard.

wife in Prague, but to repay a loan of four hundred gulden which his parents had advanced towards his travelling expenses. However, an opportunity to supplement his income came with an invitation to become conductor of the Göteborg Society for Practising Classical Choral Music (*Måndagssångövningssällskapet*). The group, which was amateur, had been founded in January 1855, from the remains of the old Mozart Association, and held its rehearsals on Monday evenings in the Exchange Hall. At this time it was customary for social activities to play as important a part as the musical proceedings themselves, and all concerts and practices were followed by refreshments in the Exchange Restaurant. The Director and leading force behind the Society was Mrs. Jeanna Åckerman (1790–1859), a Stockholm music teacher and Editor of *Ny Tidning för Musik*, who on discovering Smetana's rare musical gifts was moved to hand the baton to an artist for whom she felt an intense admiration. It was probably this offer which persuaded Smetana to stay in Göteborg for one year, and when, in 1857, the Choral Society joined with another amateur association, the Harmonic Society (*Harmoniska sällskapets sångavdelning*) which was short of members, Smetana saw great possibilities for gaining wider experience. The Harmonic Society was, at this time, in two sections, one choral, the other instrumental, the latter being under the conductorship of Josef Czapek (1825–1915), a fellow Czech who had studied with Pixis in Prague as violinist, organist, conductor and bandsman before settling in Göteborg some nine years earlier. The two compatriots immediately became close friends, agreeing to divide the Harmonic Society between them: Czapek remained conductor of the instrumental section; Smetana assumed the directorship of the choral section.

At the modest fee of twenty-five Swedish thalers a week (the account book of the *Måndagssångövningssällskapet* refers to 'a cash payment to Fr. Smetana for December/January of 200 *Rdr Bco*') the post offered enormous scope and infinitely greater opportunity than anything he had known in Prague. To conduct a group of inexperienced amateurs such as belonged to the Harmonic Society called for a deal of hard work and placed an enormous strain on Smetana from the start; but he was able to adapt himself to his new conditions and the atmosphere at rehearsals was said to be relaxed and stimulating. He was free to choose his own programmes and could mould public taste as he thought fit. His first concert was on March 16 in the Exchange Hall when two hundred and seven relatives and friends heard a performance of *Elijah* (Part 1). Numerous rehearsals preceded the event and despite last-minute cuts[8] the concert was a success. Afterwards, Smetana noted that he had felt ill from all the exertion and nervous tension;[9] and that this first venture had caused him certain setbacks we know from a letter to Liszt:

> The people have become tightly wedged in an antediluvian conception of art. Mozart is their idol, but not yet understood; Beethoven is feared, Mendelssohn declared indigestible and newer composers are unknown! I even had to introduce Schumann's music here. . . . The choral work we studied first of all was *Elijah*. . . . It was performed publicly but you can have only the haziest notion of what it means to prepare a score with singers who are untrained or amateur, with runaway soloists, an orchestra consisting partly of unpractised dilletanti, partly of the military. . . . Apart from this I have rehearsed Gade's *The Fairy King's Daughter* which was much liked. In smaller circles I have played a great deal of Wagner and your own compositions, and I have found what I have been looking for—a receptive public. The people here have been left so much to themselves that they have no idea what is happening in music. . . . I hope for better and wider results next season.[1]

Despite his enthusiasm, the musical standards of the society remained low and results were often more approximate than precise. As well as chorus master and conductor, Smetana was teacher and educator; but his task was often made difficult by his inability to express himself in Swedish. Even with a keen ear such as his he could never master the language and had to make himself understood in German. This led to his being considered somewhat eccentric, a view supported by his loud voice, long dark hair, and fiery temper; yet his wide musical knowledge and uncompromising artistic standards soon impressed the town.

When he was not rehearsing, his social engagements occupied most of his time, and according to Eduard Magnus[2] he was from the first regarded as a member of every Göteborg household. His Diaries are full of the functions he attended: a banquet with the

[8] The contralto soloist Hilda Lamm wrote to her husband directly before the performance: 'Smetana was here in the afternoon and went through with me all that I have to sing. Now still more is to be omitted, so what I have to perform will not take longer than five minutes.'

[9] Diary: March 17, 1857.

[1] Letter to Liszt: April 10, 1857.

[2] Eduard Magnus (1800–1879) was an industrialist and merchant who played an important part in the commercial and municipal life of Göteborg.

Russian Consul, a gentleman's dinner party at Oscar Dickson's,[3] various *kalas* (parties), dinners, soirées and balls at Prytz's,[4] James Dickson's, F. A. Dahlgren's,[5] Heymen's and other families. He often went to S. Hedlund's[6] or R. Koch's[7] home to play cards and never refused an invitation to make music. To Smetana it was of great importance to be asked to play and his temperament demanded that he be involved in society. Some fifteen years before he had exclaimed:

> A society where there's dancing and there's music, but where there is no Smetana, is no society of any importance! I must be everywhere![8]

And in Göteborg he lived up to his boast. Smetana made friends with everyone but he kept a special place for the Jews, not only because they spoke German and were among the most culturally advanced in the town, but because they were in a position to favour him with loans and to finance the more ambitious of his musical projects. Among his closest friends were A. M. Nissen, a singing teacher and choir trainer at the local synagogue; Valentin, a merchant who contributed funds towards his trips to Prague; and two painters, Geskel Saloman (1821–1902), who later became Professor at the Stockholm Academy and whose portrait of the composer was copied and widely circulated throughout the region; and J. P. Södermark (1822–1889), whose portraits of Smetana and his first wife are preserved in the Smetana Museum in Prague. This small circle would often dine together, go for walks along the seashore or make excursions to the Trollhätta Falls. On Easter Sunday they went to watch bonfires flaming on the hill above the town and even travelled by train to the nearby town of Jonsered, well known for its friendly inn and local beer. It was probably in their company that Smetana conceived the idea of arranging chamber music evenings with Czapek and the local cellist, August Meissner[9] (1833–1903), who was of German origin. Their

[3] Oscar Dickson (1823–1897) was an industrialist and benefactor well known for his support of the voyage of the 'Vega' (1878–1880) which led to the discovery of the North-east Passage.

[4] Adolf Prytz (1813–1870) was a tobacco factory owner whose favourite pastime was to invite the Harmonic Society to his home to make music.

[5] F. A. Dahlgren, author and playwright.

[6] S. A. Hedlund (1821–1900) was a renowned publicist and politician, and Editor of the Göteborg *Commercial and Navigational Newssheet.*

[7] R. Koch (1802–1876) was a wine merchant who later became librarian to the Harmonic Society.

[8] Diary: April, 1842.

[9] Meissner left Göteborg in 1860 for Helsingfors and Stockholm, where he formed an orchestra which won considerable success at Bern's Restaurant. He was made a member of the Swedish Academy of Music in the 1890's.

PLATE VII

The Prague Barricade in 1848

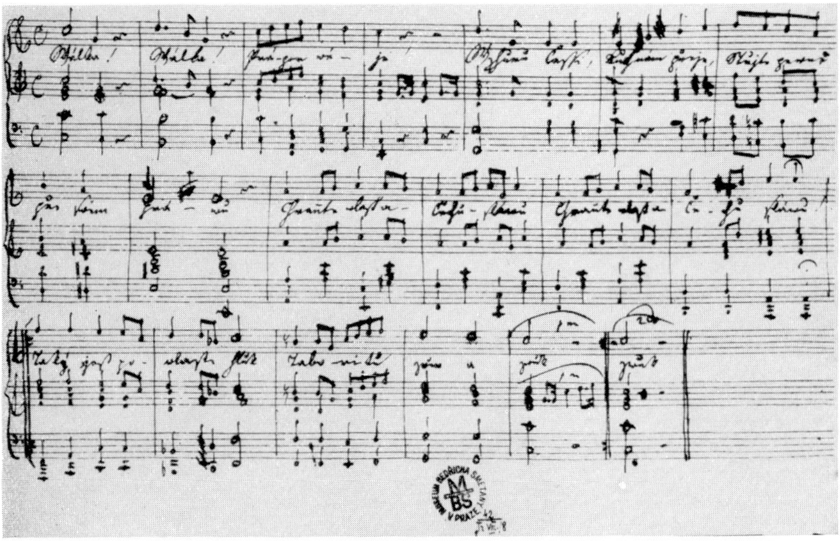

Smetana's manuscript of *The Song of Freedom* inspired by the 1848 uprising

PLATE VIII

Lithograph of Göteborg, *c.* 1854

first soirée took place on January 31 in the Freemasons' House and included Beethoven's C minor Trio (Opus 1, No. 3) and Mendelssohn's D major Sonata for violin and piano (Opus 58). A week later the trio presented a second programme comprising Beethoven's D major Trio (Opus 70, No. 1) and Mendelssohn's Third Piano Quartet (Opus 3). Both recitals were warmly received and as well attended as space would allow.[1] A third soirée was arranged for February 28 when the programme included Beethoven's B flat major Trio (Opus 97) and Mendelssohn's C minor Trio (Opus 66). On the following day Smetana recorded that the concert had been so well supported that people were obliged to stand.[2] Generally the success of these musical evenings was such that a new series had to be arranged, this time on a subscription basis. Extra players were recruited and the repertoire enlarged to nearly forty works including some by Anton Rubinstein, Hummel and George Onslow. Smetana was greatly encouraged by the way the people of Göteborg had responded to his efforts and increasingly he showed himself willing to be associated with any serious musical event, whether to perform himself or co-operate with artists either living in or passing through the town. During the early months of 1857 there was hardly a concert in which Smetana did not participate. On February 12 he played the last movement of Beethoven's D minor Sonata (Opus 31, No. 2) and conducted the Harmonic Society in excerpts from *Die Zauberflöte*; on March 12 he accompanied Czapek's recital at the Blom Assembly Room; on April 14 performed Beethoven's C minor Concerto and Liszt's Second *Hungarian Rhapsody*, and after the interval conducted Gade's cantata *The Fairy King's Daughter* to raise funds for the destitute of Lapland; finally on April 27 he arranged another chamber music evening in which Beethoven's B flat major Trio (Opus 11) was the main work. With so much musical activity it is little wonder that people believed 'Göteborg to be keeping up with the musical life of Stockholm'.[3] Indeed it was. But it allowed Smetana little opportunity for real creative work. In his Diary, however, there is an entry which suggests he was looking for a subject for composition, and was willing to be influenced by his new surroundings:

> Today I discovered Teigner's wonderful poem—*The Saga of Frithjof* in Berger's German translation. I hope to set it to music for chorus, soloist and orchestra.[4]

[1] *Commercial and Navigational Newssheet*: February 9, 1857.
[2] Diary: March, 1857.
[3] *Ny Tidning för Musik*: No. 123, 1857.
[4] Diary: January 3, 1857.

Despite his initial enthusiasm he was still searching for something which had connexions with his northern working milieu three weeks later:

> Mrs. Dahlgren[5] brought me several Nordic poems, but I did not like them except for Nicander's *Runes*.[6]

After a while he returned to his first choice and worked a hundred and seventy-four-bar orchestral fragment in full score, the first page of which bears the faintly pencilled title, *Frithjof*. It is impossible to date this accurately, but it can only have been made in Göteborg since the principal melodic material, a seven-bar passacaglia theme (the earliest example to occur in his works), reappears in another incomplete sketch, dating from April, 1857, called *Plavbě vikingů* (*The Viking's Voyage*). Possibly Smetana changed his mind about the form *Frithjof* should take, as the existing manuscript accounts in no way for the chorus and soloist referred to in the Diary—unless, of course, the fragment was intended only as an introduction. *The Viking's Voyage*, on the other hand, was to be conceived programmatically as an overture or fantasy but the orchestral parts are indicated in less detail than in *Frithjof*. Apart from the reappearance of the passacaglia theme in bar 120, the most notable feature is the reworking of a motive which Smetana had marked down in 1852–1853 among his 'Thoughts for a Symphony' and had put to good use in the F sharp major *Salon Polka* of 1854.

Unfortunately he completed neither *Frithjof* nor *The Viking's Voyage* and may well have abandoned work on them to return to Bohemia in 1857. After stopping in Copenhagen to meet Gade, Smetana arrived in Prague on May 24, but his home-coming was not a happy one. His wife, who had never regained her health following the loss of her three daughters, was ill with consumption. The infection, which had first shown itself after her wedding, was by this time in an advanced condition, and she barely had enough strength to tend Žofie who was recovering from an acute attack of scarlet fever. This sad atmosphere was made more acute on June 20 by the news that Smetana's father had died, at the age of eighty.[7] His personal situation was

[5] Bina Dahlgren (1831–1921) was a teacher of water colour painting at the Art School of the Göteborg Museum. She was a good pianist and one of Smetana's better pupils. She had a lively interest in *belles-lettres* and often recited Swedish poems to him in order to find one suitable for musical setting.

[6] Diary: *op. cit.*

[7] Following the death of František Smetana his widow, Barbora, went to live with her son Karel, a game-keeper in Loučený. She died in Mladá Boleslav in November, 1864.

depressing and he could find no hope in the state of music around him. Little, if anything had changed in Prague during his absence. Life was still gloomy and every attempt to establish a more liberal attitude was nipped in the bud. Göteborg may not have given him the outlet his art thirsted for, but it did offer him more opportunity to make music, and he resolved to return there before the winter. Having closed the school which Kateřina had supervised single-handed he set out for Sweden at the beginning of September, this time accompanied by his family. Though his wife was ill and feared the damp northern climate would accelerate her complaint, she agreed to travel with her husband.

Their route took them first through Dresden then to Weimar, where at the invitation of Liszt they broke their journey to attend the Karl August Goethe-Schiller Jubilee celebrations which were held between September 3 and 7. After the provincialism of Göteborg and the restrictions of Prague, Smetana discovered an atmosphere which almost turned his head. Everything he had ever dreamed of seemed to have found its realization here. The musical life was at its most flourishing, and Liszt, who was at its centre, had made the city the heart of the neo-Romantic movement. Everyone appeared to make the pilgrimage to Weimar as the Rome of music, and during his visit Smetana met many of Liszt's pupils and followers—Peter Cornelius, Feodor Milde (Wagner's first Telramund), his wife Rosa (the first Elsa), Edmund Singer, leader of the Weimar Orchestra, Bernhard Cossman, the cellist, Hoffmann von Fallersleben, the poet, Carl Tausig and Hans von Bülow. Devoted to Liszt's ideals, they had come to Weimar to champion his crusade for neo-Romanticism which was spreading throughout Europe. The climax of the proceedings was the first performance of the *Faust Symphony* and the symphonic poem *Die Ideale*, and in these works Smetana found an answer to many of the questions which for some time had concerned him. Through literary influences and the stimuli of works of art, Liszt's tone poems seemed to suggest a solution to the problems of outer structure and inner musical texture. Even in his approach to life Liszt offered a new way of combining a triple existence as pianist, teacher and composer. Invigorated and inspired by new artistic ideas, Smetana left Weimar determined to emulate his friend and mentor.

He arrived in Sweden on September 17 and set up house in Storanygatan, but despite a friendly reception and the excitement of a new environment Kateřina did not settle well in her new surroundings. The climate was rougher and more extreme than that of Bohemia; it was bitterly cold and the snows lasted from November until the end of May. She was ailing and her health rarely allowed her to venture out of doors. She made few friends, could not communicate easily with those who visited her and grew sad with nostalgia. The rich local food sickened her and the dull forms of entertainment depressed her. She spent many hours in her own company, cheerless and unhappy. The only thing in her life was Žofie to whom she clung desperately. Smetana was rarely at home. He was either teaching, rehearsing the Choral Society in Mozart's *Requiem*, the main work of the season,[8] or organizing a ladies' school of singing where lessons were to be given three times a week on Tuesdays, Thursdays and Saturdays between 4.30 and 6.30 p.m.[9]

On his return from Prague his pupils had increased considerably: for the year 1858–1859 his register contained twenty-six names, ten in the junior class, sixteen in the advanced. Though the level of attainment was not high, the variety of teaching was enormous and generally the students held their teacher in great esteem.[1] Despite a casual approach and the fact that he often kept pupils waiting,[2] he never spared his own efforts in playing to them. As had been the case at home, his students were mostly young ladies, and one in particular found her teacher more attractive than the subject he taught. She was Fröjda Benecke,[3] twenty-one and married. From the start Smetana was attracted to her. Piano lessons soon gave way to a round of social engagements and in turn to an intimate friendship with a strong emotional background. A deep understanding grew between them and Smetana came to regard her as something special. She became a medium through which the artist and thinker in him could pour out the fullness of his soul. She was not the generator of lightning but the conductor of it. To Smetana there was nothing unusual in being able to exist mentally in two dimensions at once. Kateřina was his wife and affectionate domestic partner, but Fröjda was his muse and mistress.

Their relationship soon became evident in Smetana's compositions, and the first piece to reveal his sentiments for her was a transcription of Schubert's 'Der Neugierige' ('Curious One'), the sixth song from

[8] Rehearsals began on October 19 and Smetana also prepared choruses from *Fidelio* and *Lohengrin*.

[9] The Ladies' School of Singing was eventually opened on December 1 at Mr. Blomberg's house in Stora Torget.

[1] According to Georg Brandes (1842–1927), copies of Smetana's portrait were to be found in all his pupils' homes.

[2] Letter written by Hilda Magnus: December 14, 1856.

[3] Fröjda Benecke (1836–1923), *née* Gumpert, a niece of Nissen. She later married a Jew called Rubenson.

Die schöne Müllerin cycle. It was not by chance that Smetana hit upon this piece and he probably chose it more for the words than for Schubert's melody. The latter part of the text in particular seems to mirror his own thought:

Brook of my love,
how silent you are today!
I only ask one thing,
a single word one way or the other.
One word is 'yes',
the other, 'no';
These two words include
the whole world for me.[4]

This could well be interpreted as a direct comment on the love he felt for Fröjda, a love which in the winter of 1857 was assumed rather than declared. Smetana followed this transcription with another, also taken from the same Schubert cycle. Unfortunately his arrangement of 'Thränenregen' ('Teardrops') has not been preserved, but a cursory glance at the opening lines of Müller's poem is sufficient to show how aptly it epitomized his feelings:

Cosily we sat together
under the cool roof of the alders,
and gazed together,
into the rippling stream.
The moon had come out too,
followed by the stars—
they looked down together
into the silvery mirroring water.[5]

A third piece, also inspired by Fröjda, that has come down to us is the polka-rhapsody *Vidění na plese* (*Ball Vision*). While outwardly painting a musical picture of a ball and the excitement of the onlookers as a lovely girl joins the dance, the piece is really an affirmation of love. Smetana more or less indicated this by signing his name on the manuscript in the personal form, 'Bedřich' instead of 'Friedrich', the practice he generally adopted for other compositions at this period—furthermore, he incorporated into the score a cryptogram on the letters F E D A, built around Fröjda's name. His model was almost certainly Berlioz's *Symphonie Fantastique* in which the second movement 'At the Ball' contains references to Harriet Smithson in

[4] Translated by S. S. Prawer: *The Penguin Book of Lieder* (1964).
[5] S. S. Prawer: *op. cit.*

the use of the *idée fixe*; but there are other precedents, for instance in the works based on the B A C H theme (Beethoven's String Quartet, Opus 59, and Liszt's organ *Fantasia and Fugue*). The most likely model, however, was Schumann's *Carnaval* where the tenth piece, 'Lettres Dansantes', is based on the cipher A S C H – S C H A. In Smetana's polka the F E D A motive appears five times: first in the introduction in octaves, then in arpeggios and augmented, later in the opening bars of the polka proper where it is chromatically altered, and at bars 58–9 and 117–18 where it is incorporated into the texture in its original form. The extracts on the next page (Example 14(a) and (b)) show the composer's simple but telling use of the musical monogram as well as his adventurous harmonic thought.

Not everything that Smetana wrote at this time was the direct result of his affair with Mrs. Benecke. In the winter of 1857 he discovered a collection of Herder's poems which made a profound effect upon him. Although these had found their way to Göteborg in a translation by the Crown Prince of Sweden, Smetana had become acquainted with them in the original German and one poem in particular absorbed him so much that he decided to set it to music—the legend of Cid Campeador and Ximene. Herder's epic *Der Cid* tells how the popular Spanish hero, while fighting to free his country from the yoke of the oppressors, kills his future father-in-law in a duel fought to avenge the family name. Ximene, the Cid's betrothed, though faithful to her lover, is overcome with misgivings and sees her husband to be only as her father's murderer. The climax of the poem occurs at the wedding ceremony where the Cid, racked by qualms of conscience, confesses his guilt and binds himself to Ximene with the words: 'All that you have lost will I be to you—both father and friend, relative and servant, your husband and consort.' Despite an obvious similarity to Da Ponte's *Don Giovanni*, Smetana saw *Cid and Ximene* as a dramatic fantasia for the piano. Coming direct from Weimar he no doubt had in mind Liszt's huge programmatic work *Mazeppa*, now expanded from its piano version, and possibly *Prometheus* which also owed its origins to Herder. From the outset Smetana engages our attention with piano writing that is majestic and grand. Hitherto, his instrumental pieces had been of a charming, intimate nature; but here he steers clear of the drawing-room polka style and for the first time commands a new and impassioned means of expression worked on a vast canvas. *Cid and Ximene* is really an experimental work, but it shows few signs that Smetana was grappling with new principles of composition. There is no move to illustrate the detailed description of the poem, merely an attempt to establish

Example 14

(*a*)

(*b*)

the general mood of the underlying dramatic action. Smetana moulds his fantasy in two movements, one depicting the Cid, the other Ximene, and at no point is the musical form conditioned by the literary programme. Here we can recognize immediately that the overriding influence was the *Faust Symphony*, which Smetana had heard barely three months before, and in which each section is devoted to a portrait of one of the principal characters of the drama. Unfortunately Smetana never completed this composition: a hundred and seventy-six bars of the first part are intact, but only ninety-two of the second. These fragments, however, are not without interest. Fröjda may have inspired the impassioned nature of the writing, but it is unlikely she was the force behind Smetana's dramatic musical structures, monumental climaxes and powerful melodies. These are all quite new in his language, and so is the broad C major theme for the Cid which seventeen years later flowered into the motive symbolizing Vyšehrad in the first part of the cycle *Má Vlast*. The mood of the Ximene fragment is warmly lyrical and serenely calm, and here Smetana adapts material previously put to good use in the *Pensée Fugitive*. It is to be regretted that so little of this movement is extant; for the subject of Ximene, the girl who loves her father's murderer, in some ways anticipates by a decade the character of Milada in the opera *Dalibor*, though there the situation is different. Excited by the enormous scope opened up in this piece, Smetana decided to try his hand at an orchestral composition based on other literary ideas. Apart from a bundle of pages containing *Frithjof* and *The Viking's Voyage*, sketched the year before, he had produced nothing for orchestra since the ill-fated *Triumphal Symphony*. Now he had been recognized in Göteborg and enjoyed a position better than anything he had known in Prague. He had at his disposal a band of players, admittedly of poor standard, who nevertheless offered him a chance to perform Mozart's *Requiem*, Mendelssohn's *St. Paul* and Wagner's *Tannhäuser* and *Lohengrin*, extracts of which he conducted during the 1857–1858 season.

Busy as he was preparing these, he found time to search for a suitable subject for composition, and eventually his choice fell on Shakespeare's *Richard III*. At first sight it seems curious that a Bohemian, resident in Sweden, should have selected the work of an English dramatist; but we must not overlook the great popularity which Shakespeare's plays enjoyed in Europe during the first half of the last century. One has only to consider *Hamlet*, *King Lear*, *Romeo and Juliet*, *The Tempest*, *A Midsummer Night's Dream* and *Macbeth* to realize the impact these had on Berlioz, Liszt, Mendelssohn and Verdi. The texts of Shakespeare's plays had been translated into French, Italian and German, in which language they had become known in Bohemia. In 1851, the publishing house Česká Matice began to bring out a complete Czech edition of all the dramas and the first volume to appear was *Richard III*. This had been staged in Prague with considerable success by a company directed by Jan Kollár. He had been partly responsible for making the translation and it was mainly due to his efforts that the play achieved an immediate success. For the Czechs Shakespeare became a symbol of great art overnight; and people eagerly flocked to rediscover his works, not only for the intrinsic value which they recognized at once, but as a stand against the lions of German literature whose anniversaries were made so much of by the German bourgeoisie in Prague and whose plays were forced upon them. Naturally Smetana had attended the first Czech performance of *Richard III* in Prague before leaving for Sweden, and had enthusiastically followed everything that Berlioz had written on Shakespearean themes. He certainly knew *Lélio*, the overture *King Lear* and *Roméo et Juliette*, extracts of which he later performed in 1864; but these scores, influential though they were, did not provide the model on which to work. He looked instead to Liszt's tone poems, to *Tasso*, *Prometheus*, *Les Préludes*, *Orpheus*, *Mazeppa* and *Festklänge*, all of which had appeared in print in early 1856. In 1857 *Hungaria*, *Héroïde Funèbre* and *Ce qu'on entend sur la montagne* were published, and Smetana had examined these works with the composer in Weimar, before bringing a number of the scores with him to Sweden.[6] Subsequent study had convinced him of the possibility of expressing literary subjects in music; and in 1858 he confessed as much to Liszt:

> Just a year has passed since I spent those unforgettable days with you in Weimar which had such a deep and beneficient effect on me. . . . I cannot describe the soul-stirring impression your music has made on me. . . . Art as taught by you has become my credo. Please regard me as one of the most zealous disciples of your artistic school of thought, who will champion its sacred truth in word and deed.[7]

Smetana began *Richard III* towards the end of 1857 and took as the basis of his work two ideas sketched in Prague several years before the *Triumphal Symphony*. He spent six months shaping the score, and finished it on July 17 at Särö, the Spa to which he had taken his wife for convalescence. Marked as Opus 11, there is no mention on the title page of *Richard III* being a symphonic poem; and eight weeks later he was still at a loss to know what to call it:

> It's something after the fashion of a musical illustration but is neither overture nor symphony and in fact needs only one name. . . .[8]

[6] Smetana performed *Tasso* in a two-piano version at his Institute on April 30, 1858, and *Les Préludes*, similarly arranged, on March 17, 1859.
[7] Letter to Liszt: October 24, 1858.
[8] Letter to Proksch: September 9, 1858.

In his letter to Liszt he refers to it simply as 'music for Shakespeare's Richard III'; but in the Diary for 1858 it is entered as 'Symphony'. At the first performance in Göteborg on April 24, 1860, *Richard III* was given in an arrangement for four pianos and described as a 'Symphonic Work'; yet at the orchestral première in Prague on January 5, 1862, he labelled it 'Fantasia for full orchestra'. Despite these uncertainties the work is a precise attempt to suggest in musical terms Shakespeare's tragic figure and is not a psychological study, as is Liszt's *Hamlet*:

> It consists of a single movement and the mood more or less follows the action of the play—the attainment of a goal after all obstacles have been surmounted—the triumph and final downfall of the hero. This theme in the bass

Example 15

> represents the main character, and the second motive

Example 16

> his adversaries. The work is finished but not doomed like my *Symphony* . . . to while away its existence in my cupboard, to serve as a resting place for dust and an asylum for moths. A great deal of courage and self-denial is needed to write for moths![9]

Towards the end of his life Smetana again attempted to explain the intention behind his work:

> I can say that the personality of Richard III begins in the very first bar and that his theme predominates in various forms throughout. The middle section depicts Richard victoriously crowned King. Towards the end, I have tried to picture the terrible dream he has in his tent before the battle when his victims appear as ghosts to foretell his doom.[1]

The division of the work into three sections might lead us to expect a fully worked out sonata movement, and the motives representing

[9] Letter to Liszt: October 24, 1858. [1] Letter to Srb-Debrnov: 1881.

Richard and his adversaries could well have served as first and second subjects (the key schemes, tonic and dominant of A minor, even support this argument). But this is not the case. Smetana had no intention of employing a classical form, especially one he had found so unsuccessful in the *Triumphal Symphony*. Instead, he adopts an episodic technique which repeats the 'Richard' motive in a number of variants and different orchestral guises, and thus reverts to a working method used by Liszt. Although Smetana had learnt a great deal from Liszt, he was not always discriminating in what he imitated; and in *Richard III* we see him emulating one of his mentor's more serious weaknesses: repetition. Liszt once declared it to be 'a mistake to regard repetition as poverty',[2] and in his own compositions he occasionally carried the device so far as to produce entire movements from a handful of phrases repeated mechanically in different keys and scoring. Smetana never goes this far, but he does have a tendency to write musical paragraphs which are either repeated, elaborated, juxtaposed, or merely joined by sustained timpani rolls or trumpet fanfares. In *Richard III* the links are often noticeable and the formal outline is so confused that it is best shown by the caption: Introduction A B A C D E C B F B Coda. In spite of its episodic structure *Richard III* is important; for it is the first significant orchestral work in Smetana's catalogue that can be regarded as monothematic. Clearly Richard and his adversaries are inter-related thematically and developed in relation to each other. But though this makes for greater musical unity, Smetana had not yet learnt to use the idea as a means of formal integration. In handling the orchestra he was not a Berlioz, but time and again he shows how well he had mastered his craft with clear, bright and highly effective colouring. Occasionally his scoring resembles that of Liszt in its general pianistic origins, but the textures are never thick and usually include imaginative touches.

With *Richard III* Smetana declared himself to be a disciple of Liszt;[3] but while recognizing the source of his inspiration he did not automatically see himself continuing on the same lines. In *A Hundred Years of Music* Gerald Abraham has pointed out how Liszt was able to translate into musical terms any idea that fired his imagination, whether from literature, sculpture or painting, and that under the banner of programme music, Liszt wrote only two genuinely programmatic tone poems, *Mazeppa* and *Hunnenschlacht*. In these it

[2] Liszt: Essay on Schumann's Piano Works. (*Gesammelee Schriften* Vol. II.)

[3] The score was composed not for Göteborg but with Weimar in mind and Smetana hoped the first performance would be given there under Liszt's direction. (Letter to Liszt: October 24, 1858.)

can be argued that the musical form was conditioned by the programme, but elsewhere, in *Die Ideale*, *Les Préludes*, *Hungaria*, *Festklänge* and *Ce qu'on entend sur la montagne*, he was transcribing generalized ideas into sound; for in spite of their titles these pieces are without real programmes. Smetana realized the danger of this superficial characterization and, typical of the future opera composer, found himself intuitively drawn towards the stage rather than to paintings and poetry. Like Liszt, his creative imagination had been stimulated by extra-musical forces, as shown by piano pieces written for his cousin Louisa, for Fröjda, for his wife and the Students' Legion in the 1848 uprising. At this period, however, he was captivated by the plays of Schiller.

The incentive came from an invitation to write incidental music for a production of Schiller's *Wallenstein* trilogy. Smetana spent the summer of 1858 collecting ideas, and later expressed his intention to set '*Wallenstein's Camp* as a first part and *The Death of Wallenstein* as a second'.[4] Unfortunately the schemes did not materialize as a whole and instead he planned an overture. As with *Richard III* Smetana did not call his piece a symphonic poem, but saw it as a fantasy on Schiller's tragedy. His enthusiasm for this project, and complete involvement in it, stemmed from the fact that the play was set on native soil, around Plzeň where he attended the gymnasium, and Eger where he had given his first recital. Furthermore he had been raised in the shadow of the Wallenstein family seat in Litomyšl. All this and the Slavonic elements of the plot stirred him considerably, though not sufficiently to allow him to introduce indigenous folk melody anywhere in the score. But, inexplicably, there is a generalized feeling of something Czech, an element quite absent in *Richard III*. There, Smetana was concerned mainly with the figure of the King, whom he made much more of a hero (as it then seemed to the Czechs) than the villainous and gloomy figure of Shakespeare's tragedy. In *Valdštýnův tabor* (*Wallenstein's Camp*) he was more interested in capturing the atmosphere of Czech life, of people gathering, soldiers dancing, listening to a sermon, the battalion moving off. The splendour of fluttering flags, the trumpet fanfares, the triumphant processions, the massed forces, were part of a scene which appealed to Smetana all his life. The harsh realities of the revolution in Prague had led him to produce marches and war songs and in the bustle of *Wallenstein's Camp* we can see the emergence of a typical Smetana picture that looks forward to the spectacular pageantry of the operas *The Brandenburgers in Bohemia*, *Dalibor* and *Libuše*.

[4] Letter to Liszt: October 24, 1858.

In this score Smetana was anxious to suggest the various incidents described in Schiller's play and consequently he designed a sequence of musical pictures built on a carefully conceived framework which looks back to Liszt's B minor Sonata and the tone poem *Die Ideale*, both of which were originally designed in several short movements before being compressed into one. In *Wallenstein's Camp* there are four clearly defined sections and each in its own way corresponds to the movements of a miniature symphony. The first episode (bars 1–185) introduces the boisterous, unbridled manner of army life in Wallenstein's Camp; the second (bars 186–434) has the function of a scherzo and trio and represents the soldiers' merrymaking, the friar's sermon against the godless amusement of soldiery and a reprise of their dance; the third part (bars 435–474), a nocturnal intermezzo as the sentry mounts guard, corresponds to a slow movement, while the final section (bars 475–638) suggests reveille, dawn and the regimental march.[5]

Although *Wallenstein's Camp* is a well designed structure it must not be assumed that Smetana was accepting conventional form. He was not. The only part of the score to have any thematic unity is the second, where the soldiers' dance and friar's recitative are built on identical material, a working out similar to the one Liszt used in the *Faust Symphony*:

Example 17

(*a*)

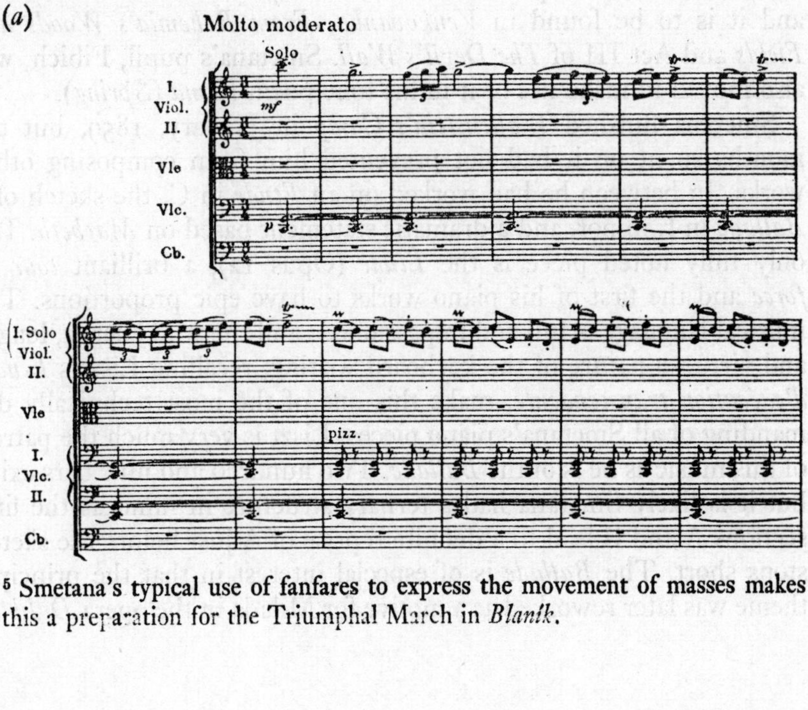

[5] Smetana's typical use of fanfares to express the movement of masses makes this a preparation for the Triumphal March in *Blaník*.

(*b*)

In Example 17 (a) the pedal bass plays as important a part in the overall effect as the violin theme, and it is likely that Smetana was deliberately imitating the *dudy* in an attempt to give his score a flavour of folk music. He admirably captures a folk idiom in the soldiers' dance which returns as the friar is dismissed. Here Smetana may have had in mind an obkročák (a type of folk-polka); for he writes a phrase which bears a certain rhythmic similarity to the folk song 'Our tom cat has broken his leg':

Example 18

The song has a rhythmic pattern of which Smetana was especially fond: he later incorporated it into his opera *The Bartered Bride* and it is to be found in *Venkovanka*, *From Bohemia's Woods and Fields* and Act III of *The Devil's Wall*. Smetana's pupil, Fibich, was also moved to make use of it in his tone poem *Vesna* (*Spring*).

Smetana finished *Wallenstein's Camp* in January, 1859, but the months spent on it had not prevented him from composing other works. In between he had worked on an *Étude* in C, the sketch of a *Ballade* in E minor, and a dramatic statement based on *Macbeth*. The only fully noted piece is the *Étude* (Opus 12), a brilliant *tour de force* and the first of his piano works to have epic proportions. The musical language is full and impassioned; and the wild energy, length and virtuoso nature of the keyboard writing, recalling Liszt's *Études d'exécution transcendente*, make this one of the most technically demanding of all Smetana's piano pieces. Liszt is very much the patron of this music as he is of the *Ballade*. Two hundred and nine bars exist, but it is likely Smetana had a ternary structure in mind as the first sections A and B lead to a definite reprise of A just before the sketch stops short. The *Ballade* is of especial interest in that the principal theme was later reworked as a motive for Milada in the opera *Dalibor*:

Example 19

(*a*)

(*b*)

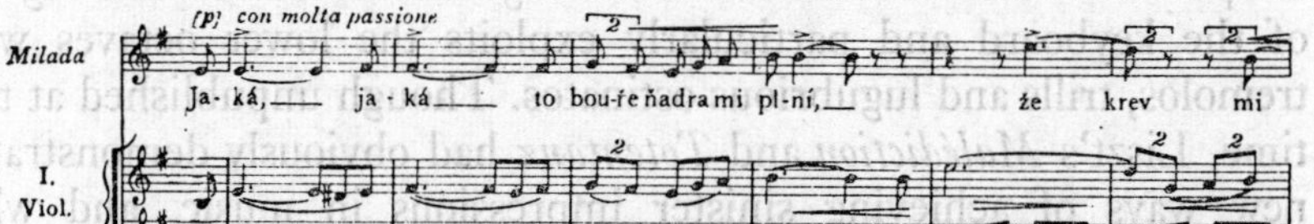

Though only a few months separate the *Ballade* from *Macbeth*, the opening bars alone emphasize the immense distance Smetana had travelled in self-discovery. *Macbeth* is inspired by Shakespeare's play, which had been revived in Prague on February 8, 1852. Though Smetana's pencil sketch is complete, no fair copy was ever made. The manuscript, marked with a blue cross dating from his last years, also bears the words 'will be accepted', presumably an indication that the work was fit for publication; but it appeared in print only posthumously. Towards the end of his life Smetana revised the piece and altered the title to *Macbeth a čarodějnice* (*Macbeth and the Witches*), which offers a clue to what he was trying to express. Though continuous it can be divided into two parts, the first dealing with Macbeth's confrontation with the witches, the second with the fulfilment of their prophecies.

In the opening bars he introduces the three hag-like creatures in a series of dramatic cadenzas which sweep up the keyboard like forked lightning; Macbeth is announced by fanfares leading to a heroic march; the witches' cadenzas return as they make their prophecies and dance before him; he urges them to foretell the future; they agree and the music builds to a climax depicting Macbeth triumphant. At no point does Smetana's composition imply that this is only an illusion. Instead he concentrates on producing effects which suggest evil and the powers of darkness. He makes a savage assault on the outer regions of the keyboard and particularly exploits the lower octaves with tremolos, trills and lugubrious ostinatos. Though unpublished at this time, Liszt's *Malédiction* and *Totentanz* had obviously demonstrated new ways of achieving sinister impressions in music, and what Smetana writes here is derived from those scores (it is unlikely that Liszt's first *Mephisto Waltz*, written during 1859, had reached Sweden before Smetana completed *Macbeth*). Apart from the complexity of the writing, *Macbeth* is important for showing the advanced nature of the composer's harmonic thought. Despite a key signature of two flats the first part appears to be keyless. He uses the diminished triad—the stock in trade of all romantic horrors—as a harmonic commonplace and treats it with such freedom that it can no longer be regarded as a discord to be prepared or resolved. His basic vocabulary is built on chromatic passing notes, suspensions, clashing sevenths, ninths and thirteenths, false relations and the simultaneous use of appogiaturas and their resolutions. These passages are typical of his writing and indicate his progressive style:

In the latter half of the piece Smetana swings into the key of C sharp

Example 20

(*a*)

(b)

minor and works more rigidly within it, though there is a great deal of sliding chromaticism and an appearance of the whole-tone scale which tends to weaken the tonal system (see Example 21).

Effective here though the whole-tone scale undoubtedly is, its use is not as original as might at first seem. One has only to compare Example 21 with Liszt's *Grand Galop Chromatique* written some twenty years

Example 21

before, to see the patronage. It is not only in the harmony that Smetana's expression is more daring but in the rhythmic patterns as well. Particularly remarkable is his use of irregular septuplet groups of semiquavers; this was to become a fingerprint that reappears in *Prague Carnival* of 1883–1884, written at a time when the composer was suffering considerable nervous tension and experiencing signs of mental collapse. Since *Macbeth* was also sketched in a period of great emotional strain, during the illness of his first wife, could not similar neurotic conditions have led him to create similar rhythmic patterns in two essentially dissimilar works—works that are among the most advanced compositions in his entire catalogue? How far the ideas of discord and of rhythmic irregularity were connected with his nervous disorder it is impossible to say. By no means diabolic throughout, *Macbeth* shows Smetana to be a master of dramatic expression. Essentially it is a tone poem, the descendant of *Richard III*, and as such deserves orchestral treatment.[6] Unfortunately Smetana never achieved this, possibly through shortage of time: his teaching and work at the Harmonic Society were occupying him fully, and his relationship with Mrs. Benecke absorbed not a little of his leisure.

Towards the end of 1858 he began to realize how seriously ill his wife was. She had spent the summer making excursions to Partille, where the Langes,[7] had a summer house, or to Liseberg where the three Nonnen sisters[8] lived. Occasionally she had travelled on the new railway as far as Jonsered and in July she had spent several weeks at the Spa at Särö; but her cure had been ineffective and the tuber-

[6] An orchestral realization of *Macbeth* has been made by O. Jeremiáš.

[7] The Langes were an important merchant family in Göteborg.

[8] The Nonnen sisters were pupils at Smetana's School.

cular complaint was now in an acute stage. Being weak, she could neither leave the house nor be left. She was often delirious and lived only for one thing—to return to Bohemia. In January, 1859, Smetana, having broken off his association with Fröjda, wrote to his mother-in-law in Prague informing her of Kateřina's frail condition:

> She is not only no better, she is worse. . . . The greatest blame attaches to me in that I came to live here. It was to be expected that the climate, strange customs and people would make the loss of all that was familiar hard to bear. She longs to return home and her dissatisfaction with present conditions has aggravated her illness. I came to improve my own condition and have everything to deplore. It is my unalterable wish to leave Göteborg for ever and return to Prague in the hope that it will have a beneficent influence on Kateřina's health. . . . There will be time enough for me to think about my future when we arrive, but on no condition shall I again start a school. Perhaps I shall go on a concert tour next winter.[9]

Anna Kolářová promptly made the journey to Sweden to be with her daughter while Smetana made preparations to leave Göteborg; yet curiously these difficult family problems seem to have had no adverse effect on either his disposition or his work. He arranged a series of six subscription chamber concerts at one of which he had to play to a sparsely-filled house—an unfamiliar experience;[1] continued rehearsals for the Harmonic Society concert[2] at the Exchange Hall on February 11; performed Hummel's Septet at the Assembly Room on February 15; conducted excerpts from *Elijah* and *Tannhäuser* at the Assembly Room with the Harmonic Society on February 22; and took part in a concert[3] arranged by the Band of the Göta Artillery Regiment on March 4, to raise funds for the Band's pension fund. Shortly after, Smetana terminated his music lessons and prepared to return to Bohemia; but before he could leave he had to fulfil his outstanding engagements—three farewell concerts.

[9] Letter to Anna Kolářová: January, 1859.

[1] Smetana dwells on this incident in his Diary and comments that subscribers were either prevented from attending since two *kalas* (parties) were arranged on the same evening, or stopped by 'the clerk of the weather who sent the January gales, suddenly driving the water up the canals so that it was impossible to walk in the streets.'

[2] The concert included choruses from Mendelssohn's *Ruy Blas*.

[3] Smetana's contribution was a performance of Weber's *Aufforderung zum Tanz* and the Schubert-Liszt *Serenade*.

ADVANCE NOTICE

> Tomorrow evening Mr. Smetana will give a full concert which at the same time will take the form of a farewell from the people of Göteborg, in whom his excellence as composer, performer and teacher has caused a musical awakening, although for it to develop into a real musical education they would still need the Master's help. Surely it will be the wish of every music lover at the concert to be allowed to show Mr. Smetana the approval and gratitude which he so richly deserves from us.[4]

The concert, which took place in the Blom Assembly Room, was largely in the nature of a demonstration of Smetana's achievements as teacher and conductor. The Choral Section of the Harmonic Society sang Beethoven's *Choral Fantasia* (with Smetana playing the piano and Czapek conducting) and excerpts from *Messiah*; the Ladies' Singing School performed a chorus from *Ruy Blas* and three members, Hilda Lamm, Amalia Lindgren and Adelaide Leuhusen, sang the Trio from Rossini's *Guillaume Tell*; four pupils from the Music School played Beethoven's *Coriolan*, arranged for two pianos by Smetana; this was followed by Liszt's *Les Préludes* in a two-piano version; and to conclude Smetana performed two fantasies—one by Mozart (in C minor, K. 475), the other by Liszt (on the Sextet from Donizetti's *Lucia di Lammermoor*.)

Afterwards Smetana wrote that the Assembly Room had been filled to capacity, that he had been recalled six times, and played two encores in response to the applause which was loud and prolonged.[5] A similar ovation greeted his second farewell concert, a soirée by the Harmonic Society whose programme included choruses from *Elijah*, the Trio from *Guillaume Tell*, the Furies' Chorus from *Orfeo* and the finales to Act II of *Tannhäuser* and Act I of *Fidelio*.

On March 29 the Music School bade farewell to its Director, and on this occasion the musical items consisted of eight- and sixteen-handed piano versions of famous overtures—Beethoven's *Egmont* and *Coriolan*, Mendelssohn's *Hebrides* and Spontini's *Ferdinand Cortez*. Smetana recorded in his Diary that Saloman had delivered an address on behalf of his pupils, who in appreciation and affection presented him with a silver baton. He adds:

> I was so deeply moved that I could only express my thanks in a few words.[6]

By April 8 the weather had improved. On the evening of the 9th

[4] *Commercial and Navigational Newssheet*: March 16, 1859.
[5] Diary: March 18, 1859.
[6] Diary: April, 1859.

Kateřina was brought in Mrs. Dickson's carriage to the boat; and on the following day she was in Copenhagen. The journey was difficult and trying. It was bitterly cold, and Kateřina fainted repeatedly. After four days they arrived in Dresden, where they were forced to halt. Next to Prague it was the city she loved most, but she was too ill even to know she was there. Her condition rapidly deteriorated. She grew weaker. On April 19, Smetana sorrowfully entered in his Diary:

> It is consummated! Kateřina, my darling, dearly beloved wife died early this morning at five o'clock, gently, without our knowing anything until the quiet drew my attention to her. Farewell my Angel!

FIVE

YEARS OF TRAVEL
1859–1862

At thirty-five Smetana returned to Prague a widower. After arranging for Kateřina's body to be transported to the Olšany Cemetery where it was buried on April 22 alongside the grave of his daughter Bedřiška, he placed Žofie in his mother-in-law's care and wandered from place to place in the depths of despair. His sorrow was profound. He reproached himself for having taken his wife to Sweden, for having deserted her in the final months. His grieving was in vain. There were many tragic features in Kateřina's life, but none more so than her end. At the time when Smetana was developing as an artist, his faithful companion, the inspiration behind so many of his youthful works, was fading away, a shadow of the girl whom he had so passionately adored at the beginning of his artistic career. Mournful and aimless, he went first to Mladá Boleslav, then to Česká Lípa, to Liberec, to Prague, to Valtusy and to Nové Město nad Metují. He could rest nowhere.

Towards the end of May he received an invitation to attend a meeting of young musicians arranged by Liszt to celebrate the twenty-fifth anniversary of the Leipzig newspaper *Neue Zeitschrift für Musik*. Smetana, who had been unable to muster any interest in music, accepted, and on the 29th journeyed to Leipzig where he joined Hans von Bülow, Alexander Serov (the Russian composer and critic nicknamed 'The Tartar') and Johann von Herbeck, the Viennese conductor, in vigorous discussions on the future of the neo-Romantic movement. In between he attended concerts, at one of which the Prelude to Wagner's *Tristan und Isolde* was performed. Later, in St. Thomas's Church, he heard Bach's B minor Mass and Liszt's *Gran* Mass, and on June 4 Schumann's opera *Genoveva* in the Gewandhaus. To complete the celebrations, Liszt invited Smetana and a group of friends to his home in Weimar, where they stayed for ten days. In this inspiring atmosphere Smetana heard a performance of his own Piano Trio, played Liszt his latest piano works, and put before him his most recent scores, *Richard III* and *Wallenstein's Camp*. Previously he had hoped that Liszt would conduct these symphonic poems, but no performance had been forthcoming.[1] In fact, Liszt had been unconvinced by them as they then stood and recommended a number of cuts, particularly in *Wallenstein's Camp*, which Smetana agreed to make the following autumn. Among the personalities he met at this time were the historian K. F. Weitzmann, the choir trainer Hans Bronsart, the pianist Karl Tausig. He played cards with Carl Pohl and Louis Köhler, and chess with von Bülow; and with Liszt's nineteen-year-old pupil, Ingeborgh Stark,[2] he struck up a special friendship. He also became acquainted with the music of Peter Cornelius, whose *Der Barbier von Bagdad* had had its première the year before. The work was badly received by the Weimar audience. It had had no further hearing and a war raged over its merits. Like Berlioz's *Benvenuto Cellini*, it was an early attempt by a member of the neo-Romantic group to write opera in a new style. Liszt, for all the qualities he recognized in Nicolai's *Lustige Weiber von Windsor* and Lortzing's *Czaar und Zimmermann*, considered both works as belonging to an older school. On seeing how superbly Wagner had solved the problems of music drama, he had urged his pupils to exploit the sphere of music comedy, but on Wagnerian principles. Despite the paltry success of his own operatic venture, he encouraged Cornelius, the brightest of his followers, to create a comic work for the stage. *Der Barbier von Bagdad* is a score of considerable achievement: it is witty and shows a fine grasp of neo-Romantic harmony and orchestration married to a Rossinian lightness and gaiety; yet the demonstration following the first night caused the true value of the piece to be underrated for many years. Smetana found himself in sympathy not only with Cornelius' music but with the whole idea of modern comic opera founded on a warm and optimistic attitude to life. Though he did not immediately try to put this theory into practice, it took root and years later inspired parts of *The Bartered Bride* and *The Kiss*.[3]

On June 12 Smetana held a reception for Liszt and his friends which did much to help future relationships, and two days later,

[1] Letter to Liszt: October, 1858.

[2] Ingeborgh Stark was the composer of a Sonata and a series of Fugues and Toccatas. Smetana became so attracted by her beauty that he dedicated his *Concert Study* in C to her.

[3] Cornelius later attempted to learn Czech so as to appreciate more fully Smetana's *The Bartered Bride*.

after lunching with Liszt (during which he was presented with a copy of the *Dante Symphony*) he set out for Bohemia. His weeks spent in the company of artists with similar opinions enabled him to find his way back to life more rapidly than expected, and in Prague he began practising for a recital hastily arranged in Boemisch Alcha for the 29th. Though the programme was easy on the ear—Chopin's *Berceuse*, two of Mendelssohn's *Lieder ohne Wörte*, Schumann's *Nachtstücke* and Liszt's transcription of the Sextet from *Lucia di Lammermoor*—the financial and artistic results were not outstanding; and somewhat crestfallen he travelled south to stay with his brother, Karel, a forester in Chlomek. In these friendly surroundings Albertína, his sister-in-law, introduced him to her father, František Ferdinandi, Director of the Mělník Estate, and owner of a small holding at Lamberk, near Obříství. This region was one in which Smetana always felt at ease; his parents had lived in the neighbourhood for many years, and he now spent the summer in the peaceful countryside, wandering through woods and shooting partridge. Jan Rys,[4] a fifteen-year-old servant whom Smetana befriended and later took to Göteborg as general factotum, recalls that he was not only a bad shot but 'uncommonly queer' to look at.[5] He dressed in a mohair jacket, cut like a shirt with wide sleeves. He was thin, wore gold-rimmed spectacles, had grown a moustache and goatee beard and invariably sported a blue Swedish cap to prevent his long, oily hair blowing about. Eccentric he certainly appeared, but he still made a considerable impression on the opposite sex and it is not surprising that he felt particularly at home in the company of Ferdinandi's daughters.

It was at this time that Smetana became aware of Barbora, nicknamed Betty. She was nineteen, the youngest of seven girls, and very beautiful. Although Kateřina had died only three months before he now fell passionately in love. He found Betty refined, cultured, intelligent. She had the manner and instincts of a lady and seemed born to live in society; she was a skilled painter,[6] well-read and spoke several languages; but though she had a pretty voice she was not particularly fond of music. At first she regarded Smetana more as a mature relative than an admirer and was unable to return his affections. When in August he proposed marriage, she made no secret that her feelings were of friendship and respect rather than love. The

[4] Jan Rys (1843–1914) was a servant in the family of Smetana's brother, Karel, who lived in Chlomek.

[5] Memoirs of J. Rys: *Hudební Revue* (No. 5—1912).

[6] Betty Ferdinandi had been a pupil of the artist Antonín Waldhauser.

Ferdinandis, however, with half-a-dozen daughters still unmarried, were so favourably impressed by Betty's eligible suitor that they fostered the relationship and gave their consent to the engagement. Betty, out of deference to her parents, agreed to the union and Smetana convinced himself that he could win her heart one way or another.

Shortly after, he left for Göteborg, where on September 30, the following notice appeared in the *Commercial and Navigational Newssheet*:

> Teaching at the Music Institute will be resumed on October 1st.
> Friedrich Smetana,
> who will be in residence at Mr. Jährig's house,
> Holländaregatan, 2nd floor.

On reopening the Institute he engaged a young Swedish teacher to help with the twenty or more pupils who attended lessons two or three times a week. He now increased his fee to two thalers for an hour's individual tuition, and five thalers for weekly class instruction, and by the end of the year his receipts totalled nearly twelve thousand thalers, not counting sums he received from the Choral and Harmonic Societies. There, for the main works of the season, he selected Schumann's *Paradise und Peri* and choruses from *Messiah*, and within a few days had arranged a full series of concerts. On October 5 he performed Schumann's Piano Concerto at the Blom Assembly Room; on November 12 he commenced his chamber music evenings with the first of three recitals[7] devoted to Trios and Quartets[8] by Beethoven, Mendelssohn, Schubert, Schumann and Onslow; on December 10 he organized a complete performance of Mozart's *Requiem* to commemorate the death of the late conductor of the Harmonic Society, Mrs. Åkerman. As a result of this performance the singing members increased[9] considerably and Smetana was encouraged to prepare Mendelssohn's *Elijah*, the second part of which was given with orchestra on January 23. There were also a number of informal musical evenings over the New Year which Smetana spent at the

[7] The second chamber concert was given on December 15; the third on February 8.

[8] On February 8 Smetana entered in his Diary that the concert had been noteworthy since Czapek had, for the first time, included a Quartet (without piano) in the programme. In a letter to Fröjda Benecke (February 10) Smetana wrote about this 'novelty' in Göteborg's life. All three soirées differed from those of previous years in that the middle item was a pure string quartet.

[9] In January, 1860, the Society numbered fifty-nine members: twenty sopranos, nineteen altos, twenty basses. There seem to have been no tenors in Smetana's choir at this time unless the male section also included the tenors.

Magnus' home. Throughout January and February he attended banquets and balls at the Langes',[1] the Robinsons' and Fürstenbergs'. Respite from work continued with a birthday celebration at the Levissons', a drawing-room charade at the Dicksons', a dinner party at Mrs. Gumpert's and a 'most enjoyable evening at Mrs. Benecke's'.[2] Later, Smetana threw a supper for the élite of the town at the 'Prins Karl', Göteborg's most fashionable restaurant. But despite the wealth of social entertainment, the numerous musical activities and his impending marriage to Betty Ferdinandi, Göteborg seemed to open afresh the wounds which Kateřina's death had inflicted a year before. Jan Rys, who now kept house for Smetana, testified how depressed he used to be, especially when alone. Within seconds his mood would change from good humour to melancholy as his thoughts alternated between his former wife and his bride-to-be. Possibly he had misgivings about his forthcoming marriage, for he had known Betty but a few months and knew little of her character. All he realized was that she was different.

Indeed, the women in his life could not have been more dissimilar in personality or ways, and the only attribute they had in common was beauty. Kateřina was simple and good-natured, ordinary yet devoted. Fröjda excited him: she was strange and remote like a being from another world; but Betty, for all her finesse and social brilliance was thoughtless, cold and hard—a fact born out by her tactless refusal to accept the *Bettina Polka* Smetana had written especially for her soon after arriving in Sweden:

> I cannot tell you how sorry I am that my Polka failed to make you happy. Not that I regret the piece . . . just strike out your name from the title, I would not want it to appear on something you do not like. Perhaps you will dance the piece when I play it for you. . . . It only annoys me in so far as I have served you ill.[3]

It is hard to know what Berry objected to, for the Polka which bears her name is a delightful miniature in the most lyrical vein. Smetana had designed it not only as an affirmation of love, but as a musical portrait of his future wife, and in some respects it is almost onomatopoeic in function with descending triplet figures that admirably convey her girlish laughter. That he was hurt by her rejection we know, for the next two compositions were dedicated to Fröjda. Smetana had written nothing in dance form for some time and we can imagine with what pleasure he worked on two Polkas, *Vzpomínky na Čechy*

[1] Lange was the Göteborg Customs Surveyor. [2] Diary: January, 1860.
[3] Letter to Betty Ferdinandi: January 30, 1860.

(*Memories of Bohemia*). These are rich in Czech spirit and were prompted in part by his voluntary exile, in part by his pupil, Mrs. Benecke, whose cypher F E D A is incorporated into the texture of the A minor Polka (left hand—bars 1–2) as it is in the earlier *Ball Vision*. Smetana swallowed his pride and followed these pieces with a further two, this time dedicated to Betty. Though the four Polkas are unrelated thematically they are bound by a confident, optimistic temper and this characteristic syncopation,  — sometimes in the accompaniment, sometimes in the melody. Throughout, Smetana's musical fingerprints are very much in evidence—the warm lyricism, abrupt changes from major to minor mode, echo effects, pedals, movement in parallel thirds and sixths, modulation by sliding up or down a semitone and melodies formed on scales.

After this excursion into piano music Smetana turned once more to orchestral works. In his motive book, given to him by Kateřina on the occasion of his thirty-fourth birthday, there is an entry dated January 6, 1860, which shows a seven-bar theme intended for use in a fantasy based on Schiller's *Maria Stuart*:

Example 22

The idea was abandoned almost immediately; for on the opposite page, also dating from January 6, is a sixty-four-bar piano sketch above which are the words 'Hakon Jarl'. The first mention of this composition is in a letter to Ludevít Procházka (March 11, 1860), but the inspiration, a play by Oehlenschläger,[4] dates from 1859 when it was performed at the Göteborg Theatre on December 9 in a translation by Smetana's friend, Hedlund:[5]

> I can assure you the impression it made on me was so powerful that I wished to present at least the plot of the tragedy in

[4] Oehlenschläger's play was in fact based on an Icelandic Saga recorded by the medieval historian, Snorre.

[5] Hedlund had translated the play for its first performance at the Stockholm Theatre in 1848.

symphonic form . . . it was the impressive figure of this epic hero that moved me to make a musical interpretation.[6]

Smetana designed *Hakon Jarl*, his first completed composition based on mythology, on similar lines to those of *Richard III* and *Wallenstein's Camp*, but it shows a considerable advance in technique, content and planning, which is far more comprehensive. Work on the composition caused trouble and it was not finished until March 24, 1861, when he hoped to dedicate it to the King of Sweden. On visiting Stockholm he saw for himself how inadequate the orchestra was and the lack of interest shown by the Royal Court. He therefore changed his mind, offering it instead to the people of Göteborg as a token of gratitude for their hospitality and for giving him the chance to employ his musical gifts there. Smetana had long wanted to write music on a Scandinavian theme. Happily this project proceeded further than either *Frijthof* or *The Viking's Voyage*, and he may well have been drawn to Oehlenschläger's tragedy for the affinity it has with the Norse myth that inspired Wagner's *Der fliegende Holländer*. It should not be thought, however, that Oehlenschläger's play is Wagnerian; and neither is Smetana's approach to it. It concerns the victorious struggle of Christianity over Paganism. Towards the end of his life the composer outlined his idea of the work to Adolf Čech, who was preparing the score for performance in Prague:

> Jarl, a Norwegian usurper, can no longer endure the weak rule of Olaf, the rightful heir to the throne. Consequently he drives him out and has himself crowned King. Olaf flees to seek support among neighbouring princes. Jarl, victorious in battle, immediately wins the people's support and leads them to worship heathen idols, but later he rouses their anger by introducing and enforcing severe measures. Olaf, meanwhile, gains the help of Christian princes abroad and makes a surprise attack, offering the Norwegian people concessions. Jarl is betrayed by his own subjects and Olaf is declared King. In the course of the battle, Jarl takes refuge in a cave high in the mountains where he believes himself to be invulnerable to attack. But he is murdered by members of his own band.[7]

Though Smetana was raised in the Roman Catholic faith, he rarely went to church. He believed in fate, and in life after death, but little else; and it is not surprising that in this score he stressed the attitude of Jarl and the pagan people, rather than Olaf and his allies. Instead

[6] Letter to Adolf Čech: May 7, 1883.

[7] Letter to Čech: *op. cit.*

of an apotheosis of Christianity he writes an extended elegy on the destruction of the pagan hero, interpreting the plot as a tragic struggle in which Jarl represents a national element, Olaf an intruding Christian one. Consequently, Jarl is depicted with powerful, heroic music, Olaf somewhat indifferently. Nothing could point the contrast more than the strong healthy lyricism of (a) Jarl's motive (used to identify rather than symbolize) and the victorious chorale-like march of Olaf and his supporters (b), built on a repeated chord pattern which is almost a complete negation of melody:

Example 23

(*a*)

(*b*)

In the peaceful coda, Smetana's sympathies are clearly with the usurper, and in *Hakon Jarl* we see the creation of a prototype of his later national heroes which anticipates Dalibor in particular. After the experience gained in the earlier symphonic poems he was well equipped to start on this work. From the outset there is a growth in confidence and expression and throughout one senses a marked rhetorical emphasis. The score divides into four episodes of which the first introduces the protagonist, the others describe the battle, Olaf's triumph and Jarl's assassination. Nowhere is there a feeling that here one section ends, there another begins. The workmanship never obtrudes and the music grows in a continuous and expanding flow of ideas from the dark opening, full of foreboding, to the poignant lament accompanying Jarl's death. Smetana makes no attempt to give his score local colour. He avoids Norwegian folk melody and spurns a traditional chorale for one of his own invention. He favours modal harmonies to suggest former times (he was later to use the same device in *Vyšehrad*, *Tábor* and *Blaník*) and binds his various lines with a symphonic thinking that looks forward to the other movements of *Má Vlast*. From the point of view of orchestration *Hakon Jarl* shows a development beyond his previous works. The forces are larger than before and the bass clarinet, which makes its first appearance in this score, is put to telling effect in the early pages. (Possibly Liszt's use of this instrument in the *Dante Symphony* coloured Smetana's imagination at this point.) For the chorale Smetana achieves a remarkable organ-like sonority in which woodwinds and horns are supported by muted strings. But it is noticeably in the violin writing that his command is surer, more mature. Divided and unison parts make for enormous variety in the colouring, while the harp, with extended solo recitatives (foreshadowing *Vyšehrad* and the harp of Lumír) adds to the richness of the textures, evokes pictures of the Slavonic bards (whose symbol it was) and expresses the mythological character of the past. In *Hakon Jarl* Smetana produced a work worthy of the title 'Symphonic Poem'. The broad lines, powerful lyricism and majestic sweep are the musical analogue of a great fresco of Michelangelo. But because of its originality, the work was misunderstood. Those who examined the score merely labelled it 'music of the future'. Similar views had been expressed about *Wallenstein's Camp*, and following an attack in the Czech magazine *Lumír* (Autumn, 1859), the score had been dropped from the projected stage performance of Schiller's play in Prague.

While Bohemia continued to ignore Smetana's works, Göteborg, at least, showed some appreciation of his talent. On March 31, the ill-

PROGRAM

till

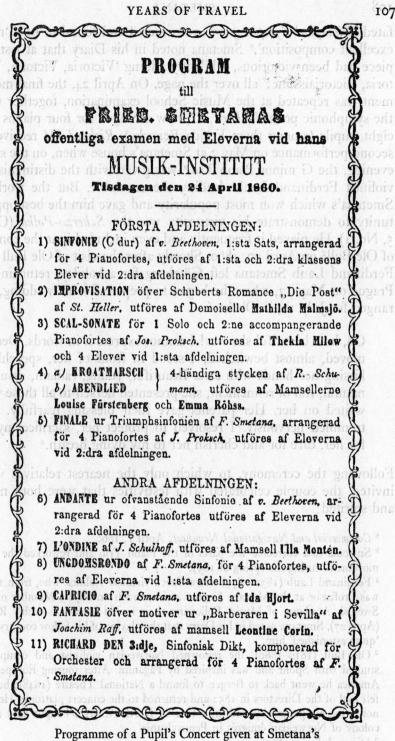

FRIED. SMETANAS

offentliga examen med Eleverna vid hans

MUSIK-INSTITUT

Tisdagen den 24 April 1860.

FÖRSTA AFDELNINGEN:

1) **SINFONIE** (C dur) af *v. Beethoven.* 1:sta Sats, arrangerad för 4 Pianofortes, utföres af 1:sta och 2:dra klassens Elever vid 2:dra afdelningen.

2) **IMPROVISATION** öfver Schuberts Romance „Die Post" af *St. Heller,* utföres af Demoiselle **Mathilda Malmsjö.**

3) **SCAL-SONATE** för 1 Solo och 2:ne accompangerande Pianofortes af *Jos. Proksch.* utföres af **Thekla Milow** och 4 Elever vid 1:sta afdelningen.

4) *a)* **KROATMARSCH** } 4-händiga stycken af *R. Schumann.* utföres af Mamsellerne
b) **ABENDLIED** }
Louise Fürstenberg och **Emma Röhss.**

5) **FINALE** ur Triumphsinfonien af *F. Smetana,* arrangerad för 4 Pianofortes af *J. Proksch,* utföres af Eleverna vid 2:dra afdelningen.

ANDRA AFDELNINGEN:

6) **ANDANTE** ur ofvanstående Sinfonie af *v. Beethoven,* arrangerad för 4 Pianofortes utföres af Eleverna vid 2:dra afdelningen.

7) **L'ONDINE** af *J. Schulhoff,* utföres af Mamsell **Ulla Montén.**

8) **UNGDOMSRONDO** af *F. Smetana,* för 4 Pianofortes, utföres af Eleverna vid 1:sta afdelningen.

9) **CAPRICIO** af *F. Smetana,* utföres af **Ida Hjort.**

10) **FANTASIE** öfver motiver ur „Barberaren i Sevilla" af *Joachim Raff,* utföres af mamsell **Leontine Corin.**

11) **RICHARD DEN 3:dje,** Sinfonisk Dikt, komponerad för Orchester och arrangerad för 4 Pianofortes af *F. Smetana.*

Programme of a Pupil's Concert given at Smetana's Institute in Göteborg (April 24, 1860)

fated *Triumphal Symphony* was resurrected and found to be a 'most excellent composition'.[8] Smetana noted in his Diary that at last the piece had been victorious, jubilantly adding 'Victoria, Victoria, Victoria, Victoriaissime!' all over the page. On April 24, the final movement was repeated at the Music School examination, together with the symphonic poem *Richard III*, now arranged for four pianos and eight pupils (among them Fröjda Benecke). *Richard III* received a second performance on May 2 at Smetana's house when, on the same evening, the G minor Piano Trio[9] was given with the distinguished violinist Ferdinand Laub[1] leading the ensemble. But the work of Smetana's which won most popularity and gave him the best opportunity to demonstrate his virtuosity was the *Scherzo-Polka* (Opus 5, No. 1). He played it frequently and even included it at the concert of Ole Bull[2] on April 20, 1860. Shortly after the visit of Ole Bull and Ferdinand Laub Smetana left Göteborg for a holiday, returning to Prague on May 13, where he began to prepare for his wedding, arranged for July 10, in Obříství:

> Oh, how beautiful she was! I cannot express it in words. Deeply moved, almost bewitched, I stood in front of her, speechless, kissing her hands with awe. Beautiful, young, radiant, assured, natural, full of refinement, she presented herself to all those who waited on her. Her parents gave their blessing tearfully. She trembled nervously. I resolved to protect her, sacrifice myself for her, care for and cherish her to my dying breath.[3]

Following the ceremony, to which only the nearest relatives were invited, the couple celebrated with festivities that were both noisy and spirited:

[8] *Commercial and Navigational Newsheet*: April 1, 1860.

[9] Smetana had corrected the parts of the Piano Trio and reworked the first movement during the spring of 1857.

[1] Ferdinand Laub (1832–1875) was a Czech virtuoso violinist who, from 1866, was Professor at the Moscow Conservatoire, and from 1870 a Member of the Swedish Academy of Music. Following their recital in the Assembly Room (April 27), Smetana noted in his Diary that the playing of his fellow countryman 'quite astonished' him.

[2] Ole Bull (1810–1880), the renowned Norwegian violinist and composer, studied with Spohr and was inspired by Paganini. After touring Europe and America he went back to Bergen to found a National Theatre (1848); but he fell foul of the Directors in 1852 and returned to the concert platform. He was noted for his generosity and on a tour of North America bought land for a colony of Norwegian émigrés in Pennsylvania.

[3] Diary: July 11, 1861.

PLATE IX

Smetana in 1880

Betty Ferdinandi
(Smetana's second wife)

Fröjda Benecke

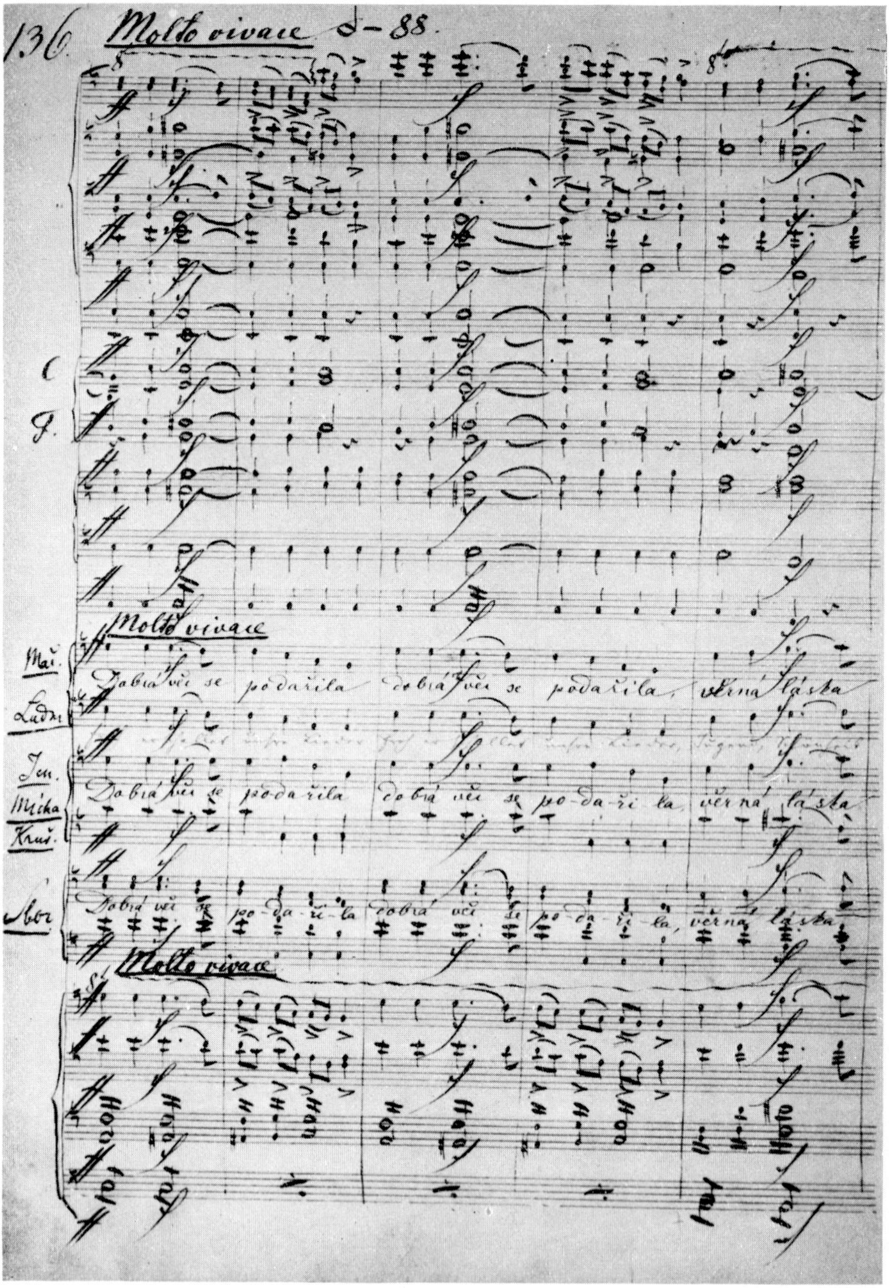

PLATE X. Manuscript of *The Bartered Bride*, Act III

Smetana radiated happiness and humour everywhere. While the bride's sisters took turns at the piano, the groom danced; but his dancing was characterized not so much by grace as by the rapidity of his movements. He danced passionately, continuously, and with such abundance of temperament that there was hardly room for anybody else in the hall. The guests contented themselves by watching the newly-wedded couple perform solo after solo. Rarely had Smetana been so gay.[4]

After the wedding, the Smetanas stayed but a few weeks in Bohemia before setting out for Sweden at the beginning of September:

It is sad that I am forced to seek my living in foreign lands, far from my home which I love so dearly and where I would so gladly live. But perhaps it will not be for long.[5]

Here, for the first time, we sense his dissatisfaction at leaving his homeland. Before he had never voiced doubts about Göteborg and it is possible that for these Betty was partly responsible. She was anxious to remain in the country of her birth and had misgivings about the voyage, as he recorded in his Diary. Other entries underline his sadness and point to his growing feeling of national pride:

Shall I—and when?—see those dear mountains again? My heart is heavy as I take leave of those places. Be happy, my homeland, which I love above all, my beautiful, my great, my only homeland. I would gladly rest in your lap—your soil is sacred to me.[6]

After a stormy crossing from Copenhagen, Smetana and his wife arrived in Göteborg on September 5. From the start Betty was ill at ease. Though she adapted herself well to local surroundings and was an asset to her husband at the various social gatherings they attended, she made it abundantly clear that her presence was as a visitor and not as a resident. She was young, immature and jealous. She resented Fröjda Benecke and the other attractive women who followed her husband admiringly at parties, and accused him of encouraging them. A number of domestic scenes followed. At work Smetana looked forward to another successful season, but he was faced with several setbacks. On October 1 the Music School reopened but with fewer pupils than he had expected; on October 4 the cellist Meissner gave a farewell concert before moving to Helsingfors to better his position; on October 13 a meeting arranged by the Directors of the New Theatre

[4] Bartoš: *Letters and Reminiscences* (1955).
[5] Diary: September 3, 1860. [6] Diary: September 4, 1860.

and the Harmonic Society failed to make any progress in setting up a full-time permanent orchestra. Further, Grosse, Meissner's successor in the Trio, was found to be disappointing. He belonged to the 'old school, had little technique, was musically uneducated and could hardly come up to Göteborg's expectations'.[7] More serious was Czapek's lack of interest in participating in soirées and the fact that his energy in helping to procure new music had diminished. Despite this, Smetana arranged five chamber concerts, but the programmes were mostly repetitions from previous years, and consequently less well attended. Less well attended, too, were the Harmonic Society's rehearsals for Haydn's *Die Schöpfung* (*The Creation*) which began on October 29. Smetana was growing restive; he had noted in his Diary that 'it is now no longer worthwhile living my life in Göteborg'.[8] He began to feel he could achieve a more satisfying existence elsewhere and following the New Year banquets, balls, *kalas* and sleigh-rides, he tendered his resignation to the Choral and Harmonic Societies to take effect from April 3.

A farewell concert, arranged in the New Theatre on March 19 included Beethoven's C minor Piano Concerto (with Smetana's own cadenzas), a Chopin Mazurka and Liszt's paraphrase of *God Save the King*. In addition Smetana conducted Schumann's *Zigeunerleben* and the 'Solemn March' from Beethoven's *Die Ruinen von Athen*. Each item won an ovation, and in his Diary he recorded that the audience had showered upon him so many flowers and bouquets that he did not have vases enough to put them in, and that the pupils, young and old, shed tears when they said goodbye. On April 3 at the time of his resignation he received a testimonial (in French) from James Dickson, on behalf of the Music Committee, and the following day set out on a concert tour to Stockholm and the neighbouring district:

> It is a great loss to Göteborg that he is leaving, for it will never have another teacher with such musical ability and enthusiasm; and cannot expect it, since it would be a pity if any gifted young artist were to remain in a place where there are few prospects and where no development is possible . . . so it was easy to guess that sooner or later he would leave Göteborg; however, he had nothing to complain about for few have been fêted there as much as he has, nobody has earned as much money as he by his sort of work, and wealth and appreciation are not easily found in other places. I told him what was in store for him the first day he came here, and our hopes have been realized beyond all expectations.

[7] Diary: January, 1861. [8] Diary: October, 1860.

> Perhaps Göteborg will in future provide greater and more varied opportunities for a musician, but that may still be a long way off, and cannot be achieved without several years of educating pupils. . . . It will be interesting to hear about Smetana's success in Stockholm, about which there can be no doubts.[9]

Despite Saloman's optimism Smetana did not find the success that had been forecast. After nearly five years' residence in Sweden he was known hardly at all outside Göteborg. He had explored little of the surrounding country and had appeared nowhere else either as soloist or conductor. On April 10, however, he made his début at the Stockholm Court Theatre; but the circumstances were different from those to which he had grown accustomed, or expected. At the Court Theatre music served one specific purpose—it made the intervals less tedious and drowned backstage noise during the scene changes:

> The King and his family were present at the Theatre, but the Intendant objected to my playing with the orchestra on the grounds that there was insufficient time for rehearsal. Instead I had to perform a group of solo pieces between the first and second acts. I played the *Berceuse* of Chopin, Handel's E major Variations, and the *Serenade* and *God Save the King* in Liszt's arrangements. To begin with there was little response but the applause grew piece by piece and at the end I was called back. According to my agreement I received no fee, but contented myself with the artistic success. However, the Intendant has suggested I should play again—next Sunday, the 13th—this time with orchestra and fee![1]

Grateful as Smetana was for the opportunity of playing before Royalty, he was incensed that people should think him 'a pupil of Dreyschock, but recently graduated from the Conservatoire in Prague, and other nonsense'.[2] He particularly disliked the idea of performing between acts as he felt the audience had come to see a drama and not him; he also objected to the convention whereby the public was obliged to hear music they did not expect. In Stockholm this was the fashion and even movements from Beethoven Symphonies were given as entr'actes. On the 13th Smetana returned to the same theatre to play Beethoven's C minor Piano Concerto between the first two acts, and his own F sharp minor Polka and the transcription of Schubert's

[9] Letter from Geskel Saloman to Evelina Abramson, the sister of Fröjda Benecke: April 30, 1861.

[1] Diary: April 11, 1861.

[2] Diary: April 12, 1861.

'Der Neugierige', as well as Liszt's second *Hungarian Rhapsody* in the next interval. He described his reception as:

> Brilliant! This evening the Beethoven Concerto, with my long cadenza, had the biggest success. At the end of the opening movement I had to bow many times because the public continued to applaud wildly.[3]

For this appearance Smetana received only a third of the fee he had expected but stayed in Stockholm to give another concert, at the Salle de Bourse, ten days later.[4] On this occasion he was joined by members of his Trio from Göteborg and a singer named Walan. Their programme comprised Rubinstein's Trio, Beethoven's 'Kreutzer' Sonata and a group of songs. Apart from the accompaniments, Smetana's contribution was Chopin's Tarantella, two of Mendelssohn's *Lieder ohne Wörte* and the Gigue from the F minor Suite by Handel. Again the success was considerable; but so was the deficit, and Smetana's position was made sound only by Miss Walan's refusal to accept her fee. Undaunted, he made his way to Norrköping where on May 3 he had arranged another concert. The journey from Stockholm was not an easy one; he disliked travelling in cold weather and was forced to wait at Norsholm from ten in the morning until four in the afternoon. From falling snow and wild winds he sheltered in a hut where he lamented his miserable condition:

> Cold, alone, hungry, thirsty, bored to death, since 10.00 a.m.—it is now 2 o'clock—I wait and the boat still does not come—I die![5]

In Norrköping, a town of two thousand inhabitants, he presented a recital which included Beethoven's Sonata, Opus 10, Chopin's *Berceuse*, Mendelssohn's *Spinnerlied*, Handel's E major Variations, Liszt's Second *Hungarian Rhapsody* and his own F sharp minor Polka. He played to an audience of a hundred and fifty and, for the first time in his life, made a profit:

> I have managed to give my name wider publicity and some little extra weight—by accomplishing this I have gone some way towards making a good beginning for the coming autumn. Now I am hurrying home to my angel and then with her to Bohemia.[6]

[3] Diary: April 14, 1861.

[4] The only event which refreshed Smetana from the tedium of ten days spent in the capital was a performance of Gade's *Spring Message* conducted by Ludvig Norman (1831–1885), whom he had met in Göteborg in 1860.

[5] Diary: May 1, 1861.

[6] Letter to Betty Smetana: May 1861.

On the afternoon of May 11, Smetana and his family left their apartment for the last time:[7]

> The boat sailed at night and the period of my life in Göteborg from October, 1856, to April, 1861, is closed. It belongs to the past, and a new life is beginning. But for me the remembrance of many beautiful things from the old life will remain alive.[8]

Smetana's period of creative activity in Sweden ended with *Hakon Jarl*. His time spent in this northern backwater had made an extraordinary impact on him and it was during this period that he made the transition from a composer of charming piano pieces in the Chopin-Schumann school, to a true disciple of the neo-Romantic music as exemplified by Liszt. In these years his means of expression had broadened, becoming more mature; and those features which have been noted as occurring in early works now became crystallized and confirmed as distinct personal marks of style, characteristic of the composer and the seal of his individuality. Before Göteborg, Smetana was regarded almost exclusively as a writer of piano music; in 1861 he was returning to Prague richer for his experiences abroad and the author of several large-scale orchestral scores which exploit the latest forms and musical concepts. He had arrived at a stage when the suggestion of folk idiom, the march and the polka elements as demonstrated in the three tone poems, and in *Macbeth*, *Cid* and the *Ballade*, were anticipating *The Brandenburgers in Bohemia*, *Dalibor* and *Libuše*; but before these works could be written it was necessary for him to breathe the air of Bohemia again. Could he, one wonders, have produced such scores and developed into the father-figure of Czech music had he stayed in Göteborg? It seems unlikely. At thirty-seven, he was a fine pianist, a respected conductor, a successful teacher and a composer with a number of unpublished works to his credit; but he was neither known nor recognized outside Göteborg. His years there had brought him into contact only with pupils and amateurs, and the level of attainment, for all his efforts, had remained provincial. Göteborg could never have become the Weimar of the north, and it is almost certain that, had he stayed, his situation would have changed hardly at all. Both his wives realized this: but Kateřina was too ill to do anything about it, and Betty was too ambitious for her husband to let him try. Although she did not love him, her respect and loyalty

[7] His post in Göteborg was eventually filled by another Czech musician, V. Hřímalý, who stayed from 1869 to 1873 when he returned to Prague to lead the orchestra at the Provisional Theatre, under Smetana's baton.

[8] Diary: May 12, 1861.

to him knew no bounds. She was determined he should not become another Czapek and was anxious to see his talents acknowledged. It was Betty who suggested the concerts in Stockholm and Norrköping, and it was Betty who urged his return to Prague:

> Recently I have a different goal before my eyes. Whether luck will favour me I know not, but I cannot remain buried in Göteborg. I must try to see that my compositions are published, and that I am given an opportunity for new activities and more far-reaching work with my pen. I must go out into the wide world and as soon as possible. Betty is looking forward to living at home again and so am I.[9]

In fairness to Betty we have to admit that her urgings did not fall on unsympathetic ears. Smetana had never lost touch with his homeland. He had returned regularly every summer and had even come to grips with the Czech language (his Diary and letters of this period cease to be written in German). He kept abreast of events at home through the newspaper *Bohemia*, which was regularly sent to him, thereby maintaining a lively interest in political matters and the course of the Austro-Italian War. The military defeat inflicted on Austria by Italy in 1859 had weakened the Hapsburg Empire considerably. Thereafter the Central Government in Vienna was forced to take a more liberal attitude towards the political aspirations of the non-Germanic peoples, and, consequently, Bach's rule of absolute power was weakened. On October 20, 1860, the Emperor issued a decree announcing the end of Absolutism and the setting up of a constitutional monarchy. This opened the way for a new stage in the National Revival Movement in Bohemia. Imprisoned leaders of the 1848 uprising were released and a period of feverish patriotic activity began first and most vigorously in the field of culture. As there was no Czech institution to deal with concert life in Prague, new musical organizations were formed and over two hundred small choral societies sprang up including a larger Czech union of singers called Hlahol ('Sound'). Smetana followed these proceedings with great interest, as he did the activities of two main political groups—the Old Czechs (Staročeši), a party led by František Rieger[1] who approved the constitutional régime of the Austrian Government and

[9] Diary: March 31, 1861.

[1] František Rieger (1818–1903) was Palacký's son-in-law and a man of letters who published, between 1860 and 1874, an eleven-volume encyclopaedia called *Slovník Naučny*, in which he made a summary of world knowledge available to the Czechs. He was also an influential politician and, later, Intendant of the Prague Provincial Theatre.

whose policy was the unification and Germanization of the entire Empire; and a more radically minded body, the Young Czechs (Mladočeši), guided by a number of brilliant political journalists with Jan Neruda[2] and Karel Sladkovský[3] at their head. The relaxation of political Absolutism manifested itself in the granting of freedom of association and the Press, and three new Czech newspapers had been brought out, *Čas* (*Time*), *Hlas* (*Voice*) and *Národní Listy* (*National Newssheet*) which won enormous popularity not least for their topicality and sarcastic, hard-hitting comment. In Göteborg Smetana, who subscribed to *Národní Listy*, read in the issue of February 20, 1861, details of a competition organized by Count Jan Harrach[4] for the two best operas composed on national Czech themes. A prize of six hundred gulden was offered to the winners. This announcement coincided with another stating that a Provisional Czech Theatre was to be constructed which would not be reserved exclusively for drama, but would be the home of opera until a permanent National Theatre could be erected. At this time nearly all the institutions of art in Prague, including the old theatres, were in the hands of the Austrians. There was no state support and the Czechs were forced to raise funds for their own theatre by public subscription. A site for the Provisional Theatre had been found adjoining the remains of the old Salt House on the banks of the Vltava, overlooking Hradčany, the seat of the Czech kings. Plans were drawn up by Hynek Ullman, who estimated that a sum of a hundred thousand gulden[5] would be needed to construct a temporary building, suitable for plays and opera. This wealth of activity, together with the improvements in political and social measures, coupled with Betty's persistent entreaties to leave Göteborg, finally provided the incentive for his departure. He left on May 19, arriving in Prague on the 27th. He was surprised to find the atmosphere in the old city much as it had been before. Furthermore, there was a certain degree of disloyalty and intrigue among a number of chauvinistic patriots

[2] Jan Neruda (1834–1891) was an outstanding Czech poet and publicist who was one of Smetana's most sincere friends. He often took up his pen in *Národní Listy* in defence of Smetana and was active in popularizing his music.

[3] Karel Sladkovský (1823–1880) was outstanding as a politician, journalist and orator, and became one of Smetana's most faithful followers.

[4] Count Harrach (1828–1899) was a Czech patriot who, after an army training, became a diplomat active in national enlightenment. He was Chairman of the Building Committee for the National Theatre and founder of a patriotic group called Česká Matice.

[5] In the event, the Provisional Theatre took six months to build and the cost was 106,626 gulden, 82 kreutzer.

who saw the country's good only from the narrowest cultural point of view.

Smetana began to draw together the threads of a new life but was disturbed that the newspaper *Dalibor*, referring to his return, should describe him only as a 'piano virtuoso' and not as a composer. However, there was much to occupy his mind. He renewed contacts and resumed piano lessons; but since these did not provide for him a secure artistic existence, he planned a concert tour of Germany. At this time he particularly needed money, for on September 25 his wife had given birth to a daughter, whom they named Zdenka. In October he set out for Leipzig, hopeful of establishing himself as a virtuoso, confident that the people whom he had met two years before would rally to his side. He was numbed by disappointment. Despite a certain friendliness, neither Brendel nor Bronsart (who had since married Ingeborgh Stark) could offer any help. No opening could be found for Smetana and the impresario Carl Reinecke was unable to promise anything, not even for a soloist whose repertoire included twenty-four pieces of Liszt (Rhapsodies, Studies and Transcriptions), thirty-one compositions of Chopin (eight Mazurkas, seven Nocturnes, five Waltzes, three Polonaises, four Études, one Ballade, one Impromptu, the *Berceuse* and the E minor Piano Concerto), and twenty works of Schumann. Clara Schumann herself was engaged to play in November, and at the Euterpe Music Society Ingeborgh Stark, protected jointly by Bronsart and Reinecke, reigned supreme. Smetana stayed in Leipzig ten days, during which the only music he heard was a performance of Chopin's First Piano Concerto, with Ingeborgh as soloist, and the sound of his own practising at Blüthner's workshop. Smetana grew impatient. He hated waiting on people for introductions and recommendations, and became nostalgic for his home:

> If only I could remain in Bohemia! These foreign countries are odious to me . . . after all home *is* home, and if I had a fitting position in Prague I would stay there.[6]

By November 3 he could tolerate Leipzig no longer. He moved to Cologne where he stayed with O. Köningslöw (leader of his Prague String Quartet in 1849) who introduced him to the composer Waldemar Bargiel, and August Kömpel, a violinist from the Hanover Opera Orchestra (he later performed Smetana's First String Quartet for Liszt in Weimar), and to the pianist Ferdinand Hiller. Smetana and Hiller immediately struck up a friendship which developed even though Hiller, a conservative musician by all accounts, did not adhere

[6] Letter to Betty Smetana: October 31, 1861.

to the neo-Romantic School of thought. In Cologne Hiller was the centre of all musical activity, and soon after Smetana's arrival he invited his new Czech friend to play to an all-male musical society on November 9:

> . . . four hundred members were present and after Beethoven's C minor Concerto I received a wonderful ovation which became fantastic for my three solos.[7]

Ludwig Bischoff, the leading critic, favourably reviewed Smetana's recital, singling out his performance of the A minor Polka, the *Étude, Na beřhu mořskem* (*On the Sea Shore*) and Liszt's *Rigoletto Fantasy*. Warmed by this reception, Smetana travelled to Rotterdam where he hoped Škroup, the conductor, and Hřímalý, leader of the theatre orchestra, would offer him work. In Rotterdam, however, the majority of concerts were arranged by the impresario Jean Verhulst, nicknamed *den groote* ('the big one') who, unfortunately, had no time for the Czech pianist. After an unsuccessful meeting Smetana christened him *der grobe* ('the rude one') and stayed on only to audition for Tours, Manager of the Eruditio Music Society. Here, too, he failed to make any impression:

> What would Nissen say if he could see me so unhappy? Surely he'd scold me. 'And you left Göteborg where you were so much appreciated and held in such high esteem! It serves you right.'[8]

Crestfallen, he decided to try his luck in The Hague, but to his dismay, all music was again controlled by Verhulst, and after only a few hours, Smetana journeyed to Amsterdam where the impresario Land had promised him a recital on December 13, and suggested that he should play for a student organization called Sempre Crescendo, in Leiden. Smetana willingly agreed, and on November 26, presented a programme similar to the one he had given in Cologne, but this time including Liszt's six *Hungarian Rhapsodies*:

> When I came onto the platform there was such applause, even before I played, that it seemed as if it would never stop. Perhaps the Committee Members (present at rehearsal) told the others how well I played. Afterwards the President came on to the platform to give me a diploma, making me an Honorary Member of their Society, and a fee of sixty gulden.[9]

[7] Diary: November 10, 1861.
[8] Letter to Betty Smetana: November 21, 1861.
[9] Diary: November 28, 1861.

With fourteen days before his next engagement he was at a loss to know how to pass the time. That he was unhappy in Holland we know from another Diary entry:

> Let me quickly leave this country! I had hoped the state of music here would have been favourable, but I am much disappointed. Apart from a few subscription concerts, the Dutch have nothing. There is not the slightest suggestion of native opera and only German and French works are played. The Swedes are more musical, more poetic than are the Dutch, and they certainly have more feeling and heart! No! I would not stay here![1]

Bored by his surroundings, Smetana decided to visit Bonn where he felt certain his wife's relatives would arrange a concert for him; but here, too, he failed to make any headway and was forced to return to Cologne. Once again Hiller came to his rescue but the only engagement that could be found at such short notice was at the Hotel Disch where, on December 10, Smetana was obliged to join the resident 'palm court' instrumentalists for a performance of Beethoven's Piano Trio (Opus 97). Later the same evening he played solos by Mendelssohn, Chopin and Schumann, but was happy with neither his reception nor the Erard piano, whose mechanism he found too noisy and too tiring. He was even less happy the following morning when he received a letter from Land cancelling his Amsterdam recital. Deeply offended, Smetana packed his belongings and returned home, where he had to admit his tour had been a financial failure and a complete débacle. He had set out with no real plan and had achieved no great artistic success; he lacked all business sense and had barely covered his expenses. Yet within days of his arrival he was arranging to storm the Prague musical circles with an ambitious concert which was to include the first performance of *Richard III* and *Wallenstein's Camp* as well as Beethoven's C minor Piano Concerto, Schumann's *Frauenliebe und Leben* (sung by Miss Mick), and a group of solos including his recently-composed *Étude*, *On the Sea Shore*. Long though his programme was, Smetana felt sure of success. He had last appeared in Prague as a conductor seven years before, and his playing had not been heard there for more than six. He was convinced that the musical world would flock to hear him, but his optimism was not to be fulfilled. His name was either forgotten or unknown. At the morning rehearsal members of the orchestra are said to have enquired who Smetana was, and questioned his ability to conduct. The actual concert was far from the triumph he had hoped for:

[1] Diary: November 30, 1861.

> It was Sunday the 5th on which my concert was launched in the large precincts of the Žofín Hall. Outside, snow was falling fast and it soon covered up the tracks of the few people who came because they had been given free tickets; shortly after the concert had begun nobody could have traced their footprints in the snow. Yes, indeed, a prophet is without honour in his own country. I had hoped, if only out of curiosity, that people would have wanted to hear a compatriot who, after years abroad, was visiting his home town once more. Not at all! The programme consisted of big pieces, yet the hall was nearly empty. I had to pay a deficit of two hundred and eighty gulden myself. Prague does nothing to help her artists![2]

In spite of unfavourable reviews Smetana negotiated for another concert twelve days later, this time a solo recital in the Konvikt Hall. The Konvikt was the smaller of Prague's two halls and accommodated two hundred people, a hundred less than the Žofín. On this occasion a large public turned out to hear him play Beethoven's Sonata (Opus 26), a Bach Gavotte and Gigue (unspecified), the *Nachtstücke* of Schumann, a Chopin Étude and his own *Memories of Bohemia*; but his profit was only twenty-four gulden. Depressed by the lack of attention which Prague showed him it is little wonder he jumped at an offer to return to Göteborg for eight weeks with all expenses paid by Nissen. He left on March 8:

> I was never so sad or depressed. Yes, I wept on leaving Prague as I never did before! If only the financial situation were not so gloomy then no one in the world would force me to make this journey.[3]

In Berlin he heard Spontini's opera *Ferdinand Cortez*, and in Copenhagen met Gade; but he derived little pleasure from either event. He arrived in Göteborg on March 17 and set about teaching and giving recitals in the Blom Assembly Room as on previous visits. Life in the old port was much as it had always been and Smetana's programmes included many of his favourite party pieces. There was, however, a novelty: Mendelssohn's G minor Concerto given with Czapek at a second piano on March 26. But to the people of Göteborg it mattered little what Smetana played: they were simply grateful for his return and warmly showed their appreciation with an overwhelming number of bouquets. Göteborg fêted him. All the fashionable families invited him to be their guest. Rudolf Koch celebrated his visit with a champagne supper at the Exchange Restaurant and Governor Fåhraeus arranged a lavish reception in his honour.

[2] Diary: January, 1862.
[3] Diary: March, 1862.

But in spite of the round of social engagements and colourful *kalas*, Smetana found Göteborg much less to his taste than formerly. He now saw it for what it was—a provincial backwater. He longed to return to Prague:

> If only I could be sent home by telegraph! My home has rooted itself into my heart so much that only there do I find real contentment. It is this to which I will sacrifice myself.[4]

His last appearance[5] in Göteborg was on May 2, and soon after, he made his farewells to the town that he had known for nearly six years. He was never to return and never to perform outside his own country again. His years of wandering were at an end.

[4] Diary: April, 1863.

[5] At his matinée in the Freemasons' Hall Smetana performed Beethoven's Piano Trio (Opus 9, No. 1) and a solo by Handel, Chopin's Mazurka in C sharp minor, Schumann's *Nachtstücke* (Opus 23) and his own *Memories of Bohemia*.

SIX

HOME FOR GOOD
1862–1866

'THE BRANDENBURGERS IN BOHEMIA'

SMETANA RETURNED to Prague at the beginning of June and immediately became involved in as many musical activities as he could, both amateur and professional. His efforts were unceasing. He seemed to be obsessed with a mission to establish a musical life that was Czech in language and spirit. But as his reputation as a composer was insufficient to ensure the realization of this idea, his only option was to found a Music Institute from which he could organize the various streams of Prague's musical life. The Directorship of the Provisional Opera offered the widest scope; but for Smetana this was little more than a wild ambition. He was unknown, unrecognized, and in the eyes of the musical bourgeoisie, unimportant. No one seemed to take him seriously, not even his friends, who regarded his ideas as fantasies. Although there was no Czech Opera (the Provisional Theatre was still incomplete), he devoted himself to the service of any serious music society that was struggling for survival, and within a month had arranged a number of recitals to swell the funds for the building of the Provisional Theatre. The first, at Mladá Boleslav on July 6, raised a hundred and twenty gulden, and the result of his next appearance, at Nymburk on August 21, was even more encouraging. Worthwhile as these recitals were, Smetana felt able to contribute more in other fields and the opening to attract him was by way of the Hlahol Choral Society to which he had been appointed Chorus Master soon after his return from Göteborg. His first appearance was on July 13 when, following the musical proceedings, the Society flag (specially designed and painted by the Czech artist Josef Mánes) was presented in solemn procession to Rudolf Thun-Taxis, Mayor of Prague, to the accompaniment of the chorale *Kdož jste Boží bojovníci* (*Ye who are God's Warriors*), a significant revolutionary hymn of the time of Jan Hus, which Smetana was to incorporate into *Libuše* and *Má Vlast*. Apart from experience in choir-training, the Hlahol offered him an opportunity of promoting his own composition; but except for the *Song of Freedom* (1848) he had written only one choral work, *Česka píseň* (*Czech Song*) (the result of an invitation from Ludevít Procházka, who in 1860 had requested a four-part male chorus for a collection being prepared under the title *Záboj*). Smetana had selected a text by Jan Jindřich Marek, but his inexperience in setting Czech words led to an awkwardness of style. The tenor line was written an octave too high and the bass parts outside the voices range. The work was not published.

During 1860 and 1862 Smetana gained greater fluency in the Czech language and also discovered the works of Karel Křížkovský, many of which he performed at the Hlahol concerts. Křížkovský (1820–1885) was one of the first musicians to appreciate the Moravian folk idiom. He entered the Augustinian Community of St. Thomas in Brno, where he later directed the choir (his pupils included Vojaček and Janáček), but his importance was as a collector and arranger of folk songs. He was one of the earliest composers whose understanding of music and profound insight into the spirit and traditions of folk idiom enabled him to reconcile the two. In a way, he was the precursor of Smetana, who confessed that only through Křížkovský's scores had he grasped the true significance of folk melody. Where other composers were emulating folk song in simple and sometimes naïve treatments, Smetana approached his work for the Hlahol in a different way. His basis was the text, which he treated, as Janáček was to do, by transforming the intonation and rhythmic stress of the language into melody. He described this method of working years later to Josef Srb-Debrnov:[1]

> I read the poem many times then I declaim it—simply pacing to and fro in my room until the words change into rhythm and melody.[2]

The first chorus Smetana wrote for the Hlahol was *Tři jezdci* (*The Three Riders*), a dramatic setting of Jiljí Jahn's ballad (based on Lenau). The piece, which was printed at Smetana's expense, is a tribute to the memory of Jan Hus, and concerns three Czech nobles who bring to their homeland the tragic news of the burning at the stake of their hero. Smetana paints a vivid picture of the envoys

[1] Srb-Debrnov (1836–1904) was a Czech writer and organizer who became Smetana's closest friend and adviser during the last years of his life.

[2] Letter to Srb-Debrnov: October 16, 1880.

journeying from Constance to Prague, and dramatizes their conversations in three solos, before ending with a powerful coda glorifying Hus. Unaccompanied, and for male voices only, *The Three Riders* is remarkable for the composer's handling of words. Only two years before Smetana had written to Procházka:

> I would ask you to excuse my mistakes both in spelling and grammar, of which you will certainly see plenty, for up to the present I have not had the good fortune to perfect myself in our mother tongue. Educated from my youth in German, both at school and in society, I took no care . . . and to my shame I must confess I cannot express myself adequately or write correctly in Czech. . . . But I am Czech, body and soul, and I am not ashamed to assure you, albeit imperfectly in my native tongue, for I am proud to show that my homeland means more to me than anything else.[3]

Now the choral writing in the work, though basically homophonic, is technically far more demanding than anything of Smetana's that had appeared before from the point of view of rhythm and melodic interval. Although it was designed for amateurs (there were no professional choirs in Bohemia in the 1860's), he made few concessions:

> I never take into consideration the standard of the small-town chorus because when I compose I never make the piece deliberately simple. It is based on true expression as I feel it without bearing in mind who will perform it.[4]

One of the most striking features of the score occurs during the solo narrations where the music is supported by a hummed accompaniment, and suggests that the composer may well have had an 'orchestral' colouring in mind:

Example 24

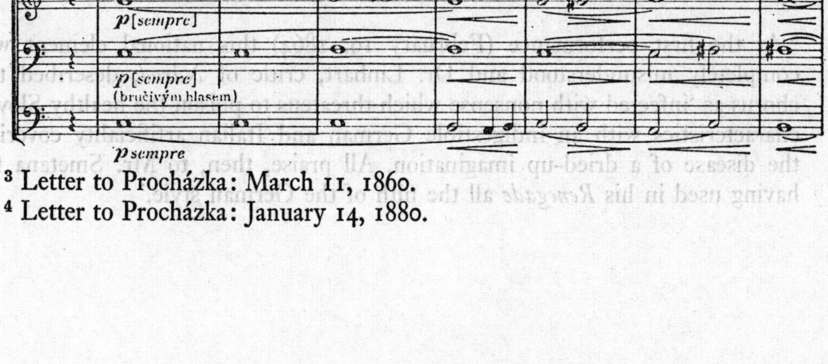

[3] Letter to Procházka: March 11, 1860.
[4] Letter to Procházka: January 14, 1880.

The Three Riders received its first performance under Ferdinand Heller at a Hlahol concert on February 27, 1863, and within weeks of the première Smetana had completed a second chorus, this time to a text by the Ukrainian poet Ambrož Metliński, translated into Czech by Čelakovský. In *Odrodilec* (*The Renegade*) Smetana was more ambitious and called for an eight-part unaccompanied male chorus. The poem condemns all those who deny their nation and describes the people's joy on learning that the traitor in their midst has been punished. Smetana's is a powerful, compelling setting in ternary form exploiting all the possibilities of a double chorus: stirring unison passages alternate with broad harmonized phrases, cross-rhythms, antiphonal effects, pedals and dramatic dynamics are all elaborately juxtaposed. There is even a strong national[5] feeling in this music with a vigorous polka-like finale reflecting the people's joy at the renegade's capture (see Example 25 on next page).

If this chorus has a weakness it is in the word setting, where the rhythmic stress is sometimes incorrect. Smetana was often troubled in this way, even in *The Bartered Bride*. Occasionally he falsely accented inner syllables, instead of the first as is customary in Czech. A year after its completion Smetana simplified *The Renegade*, re-arranging it for mixed voices and a quartet of soloists to make it suitable for massed performance. At the same time he added an optional brass accompaniment, an idea that may well have suggested itself following his study of Křížkovsky's cantata, *Cyril and Methodius*, where the same combination is employed. (*The Renegade* was given

[5] At the first performance (February 19, 1864) this national element was completely misunderstood and Dr. Linhart, critic of *Národ*, described the chorus as 'infected with nonsense which threatens to poison the healthy Slovak characteristics with an indigestible German and Italian artificiality covering the disease of a dried-up imagination. All praise, then, to Mr. Smetana for having used in his *Renegade* all the filth of the German style.'

Example 25

in its new version in May, 1864, when fifteen hundred singers participated.)

Through his work with the Hlahol, Smetana made many new contacts. The President, Dr. Thun-Taxis, invited committee members to dine at his home every Tuesday, and here Palacký the historian, Erben the poet, Rieger the politician and Intendant-elect of the Provisional Theatre, Sklenář,[6] Wocel[7] and Tonner[8] were regular visitors. In spite of opportunities to cultivate influential members of society, Smetana could not better his position; he seemed unable to turn social events to his own advantage and tactful petitions for the post of Conductor at the Provisional Theatre fell on deaf ears. Prague was Rieger's stronghold and an assault on it was a hazardous one; for he had not only the Theatre, but the bulk of the Press in his pocket.

[6] Josef Sklenář (1838–1890) was Secretary of the Provisional Theatre and husband of the celebrated Czech actress Otilie Sklenář-Malá.

[7] Jan Wocel (1802–1871) was a poet and writer who held an archaeological post in the University of Prague.

[8] Emanuel Tonner (1829–1890) was an educationalist and writer.

Certainly Smetana's reputation went against him. He was known to be a follower of Liszt and Wagner and was considered too progressive. More damaging was his support for the Young Czech Party and it was this which aggravated Rieger, leader of the Old Czechs and spokesman for the bourgeoisie. The two men were bitterly opposed and openly clashed not only on politics but on musical points as well. Matters were brought to a head during the summer, when work on the Provisional Theatre was completed and an official opening announced for the autumn. Smetana hoped his name would be selected for Conductor, but as a result of various intrigues Rieger offered the post to Jan Nepomuk Maýr.

Born in Mělník in 1818, Maýr had begun his studies as a boy chorister in the U Křizovníků Church in Prague. Later he became organist there, but being able to earn more with his pleasing tenor voice he toured Budapest and what is now Yugoslavia with an Italian opera company. He made his first appearance in Prague as Nemorino in *L'Elisir d'Amore* in 1842 and later joined the company at the Stavovské Theatre. In 1849 he attempted to widen his activities by conducting concerts on the Žofín Island, but as these were not a great success he returned to the Church, becoming Choirmaster of Panny Maria Sněžné (the Church of Our Lady Mary of the Snow) in 1853. The following year he was appointed Master of the Choristers at St. Thomas's Prague, remaining there until Rieger called him to the Provisional Theatre. Despite his wide practical experience, from the artistic point of view Maýr was barely of average standard.

And so it was that the Prague Provisional Theatre—a stopgap house on the banks of the Vltava, holding eight hundred people with standing room for an additional three hundred—opened its doors on November 18, 1862, with the tragedy *Král Vukašin* and two days later with the inaugural opera, Cherubini's *Les Deux Journées*, accompanied by an orchestra formed from Karel Komzák's dance band.[9] For the people this was an auspicious occasion: at last Czech art could flourish independently of German direction. For Smetana, however, the event brought bitter disappointment. Most of all he regretted that the theatre on which he had set his heart should have begun to function on the basis of mediocrity and convention.[1]

[9] Komzák's band, of which Dvořák was a member, provided music in Prague's larger inns and restaurants. When the Provisional Theatre opened the band became the nucleus of the pit orchestra and since opera was presented only three or four times each week, players were able to continue with their former engagements during the daytime.

[1] Initially opera was presented every other day but from the beginning of 1864 performances were given daily. The Theatre existed for twenty-one years

For the time being life was uneventful. He resumed his duties as Court Pianist to the former Emperor, Ferdinand V (who had grown more senile and less musical over the years), and continued to receive pupils privately, teaching with neither enthusiasm nor interest. In December, however, his spirits rose at the suggestion of establishing a Society for Czech artists, later known as the Umělecká Beseda (Society of Arts) which, it was hoped, would bring together writers, painters, doctors, men of letters, musicians and lay readers of the nation:

> Before our draft statutes were approved by the Government we would gather at the Jerusalem Inn, where we hired a separate room and spent happy hours . . . We celebrated the New Year together and also arranged collections for the new National Theatre, passing round the plate among ourselves. Sometimes we would go to a club in Příkopy where we, the younger ones, had our table and were gay . . . we often played billiards for funds for the National Theatre![2]

Early in 1863 the Umělecká Beseda was officially set up and on March 13 Smetana was elected President of the Music Section with Procházka, Pivoda,[3] Zvonař[4] and Kolešovský[5] as committee members. Before this, however, the Society had celebrated Silvester, the New Year festivities, in typical fashion, and for the occasion Smetana wrote the first of two short overtures intended to be of a 'lighter tone'. The inspiration behind *Doktor Faust* was the puppet play of Matěj Kopecký which had impressed him in his youth. In the early 1860's Kopecký's plays had returned to vogue and were being issued in Czech newspapers and magazines in instalments. By far the most popular was *Faust*, and in December, 1862, Smetana set to work on a version which the Society presented on New Year's Eve. *Faust*

during which five thousand, one hundred and thirty-five performances were staged including the premières of four of Smetana's operas. Prices of admission ranged from eight gulden for a lower box to thirty kreutzers for a standing place in the third balcony. Standing places in the stalls were fixed at one gulden and a seat in the gallery was marked at sixty kreutzers.

[2] Diary: January, 1863.

[3] František Pivoda (1824–1898) was a composer and teacher of singing. He later founded the Prague Singing School and was partially intrumental in seeing Smetana appointed chief Conductor at the Provisional Theatre in 1866. He later turned against Smetana and became an implacable opponent of his work.

[4] Josef Zvonař (1824–1865) was a Czech composer and musicologist.

[5] Zikmund Kolešovský (1817–1868) was a minor Czech composer and musical scholar.

could not have been a more popular choice. Earlier in the year Gounod's opera had played to packed houses at the Stavovské Divadlo. In 1861 the Czech Dramatic Theatre had mounted Goethe's tragedy with enormous success, and the St. Cecilia Music Society had performed Schumann's *Scenes from Faust* as recently as December 6, 1862. Moreover, they had held their rehearsals in the Jerusalem Inn, the very place Smetana selected for his own performance. But whereas these previous ventures had been mounted as serious entertainment, Smetana's intention was burlesque. *Faust* was to be presented with neither players nor puppets, but Beseda members imitating the stiff movements of Kopecký's marionettes. For Smetana, however, the work had a serious side and offered him a chance of returning to his childhood memories as well as re-examining Gounod's opera, a score he particularly admired.[6]

As a preliminary, he noted in his motive book thirty-seven bars taken from the introduction of Gounod's score, and though this is not quoted note for note, one section of his parody seems to have been worked out with Gounod's model in mind (bars 25–67). Throughout there is a light-hearted quality and natural wit which shows as much in the melodic ideas as in the scoring (two horns, trombone, triangle, bass drum, strings and piano). The special effects, between bars 107 and 110, where the strings are required to play *col legno* and strike the bow on the music desk, were possibly intended to accompany some theatrical business.

The success of *Doktor Faust* led to the entertainment being repeated the following year (December, 1863) but with a new Kopecký play, *Oldřich and Božena*. Again Smetana entered into the spirit of the piece, this time the comedy being at the expense of the itinerant bands of musicians whom he possibly heard in his childhood at Růžková Lhotice. In this overture he gently mocks amateur and less practised players by writing music which is deliberately hesitant, jerky and ragged, especially between bars 57 and 61 and in bar 98 (where the clarinet is instructed to anticipate the ensemble). There is nothing malicious in this score: the effects are kindly meant and may well have been modelled on Mozart's *Ein musikalischer Spass* (K. 522), which distorts popular music in an artistic way and even parodies the clumsiness of village instrumentalists.

Though the Hlahol and Umělecká Beseda provided Smetana with a chance to get to know people and be known, neither gave him the

[6] After a performance of *Faust* which Smetana attended with Heller he is reported to have said: 'Wonderful! I have only one wish: to write something similar one day.' (Aleš Heller: *Memoirs of Ferdinand Heller*.)

opportunity of making public his views on the state of Prague's musical life. He now looked for a platform from which he could communicate with the public, and found an outlet for his high-voltage dynamism, allied to an illimitable and unshakeable belief in himself, in the Press.[7] His contributions to various magazines nearly all deal with the same topic: the low standard of city music-making and the need to fight for the recognition of Czech music. An extract from one of his articles will give an idea of the forcefulness behind his argument:

> If I have set myself the task of bringing concert life here, which as regards programmes and execution is to proclaim a striving after the preservation of the sacred rights of art, yet I am far from attempting to set myself up as a reformer. . . . I am simply making a beginning. . . . The programmes I suggest are to include masterpieces by heroes of every nation, but particular attention will be given to the works of Slavonic composers. And rightly so. Have works by Russian, Polish or Southern Slav composers ever been heard in Prague? I hardly think so. Indeed, it is a rarity to meet one of our own people's names in our programmes. . . . As a Czech I arrange Czech concerts. Surely we Czechs are allowed to have our own concerts. Or is the Czech public not fit for this? I think our reputation as a musical nation is sufficiently old and well known to justify this. As for me, I am merely making a beginning![8]

Smetana's aim was to attack as sharply as he could the deficiencies of music around him. We must not forget that in Prague there was as yet no full-time symphony orchestra and consequently no regular concerts. Smetana was fighting for both. His experience in Sweden had shown him the benefits to be gained from musical evenings arranged on a subscription basis, and he now endeavoured to introduce concerts sponsored by the Umělecká Beseda.[9] Though he found

[7] Through his friendship with František Liegert, Director at the Provisional Theatre, Smetana was recommended to become Music Critic for *Národní Listy*. Liegert had an agreement with the paper whereby a certain amount of space was guaranteed for the coverage of musical and theatrical events. Smetana became a regular contributor from 1864 and worked alongside other journalists such as Julius Gregr, Vítězslav Hálek and Ervín Špindler.

[8] *Slavoj*: October 1, 1862.

[9] Smetana also attempted to organize, through the Umělecká Beseda, a school of theatrical and dramatic art. Although a Committee was established including Smetana, Pivoda and Zvonař, the project failed to materialize because of lack of finance.

little support, he refused to be defeated and continued campaigning in *Národní Listy*; here he won a great following as well as making a large number of enemies who resented the drive with which, by seemingly radical measures, the young Czech was trying to change the face of the city.

Apart from the publicity his writings brought, Smetana was grateful for the remuneration. He was still poor, and with the arrival on February 19, 1863, of another daughter, who was named Božena, he was obliged to reopen his Institute. During the summer he found accommodation in Lažanský House where he received his first pupils on September 1. On this occasion Smetana, whose business sense was not particularly keen, had formed a partnership with Ferdinand Heller, the violinist and first Conductor of the Hlahol. But unfortunately Heller was even less astute than his colleague and before long it became clear that the Institute was not a paying concern. Smetana could hardly have expected otherwise. Apart from the two partners, three other teachers, Marie Roubal, Jindřich Pech[1] and Karel Bendl[2] had to be paid before accounting for the rent and repayment of a loan for the purchase of three grand pianos. That the Institute failed to make money was not due to any dearth of pupils. On the contrary, the results as demonstrated at pupils' concerts won many new recruits. The fact remained that fees were too low. For eight collective lessons Smetana asked only three gulden, while individual tuition was fixed at the rate of one gulden an hour. At first Smetana seemed to enjoy teaching, particularly if he liked the pupil or if he or she were talented; but later, in periods of increased activity and composition, he lost interest, becoming absent-minded and oblivious to much of what was going on around him.

On October 23 Smetana succeeded Heller as Director of the Hlahol, and in the following months arranged his first public event at the Umělecká Beseda. From the start members had pressed for this venture to be on a scale and of a kind befitting the importance and cultural aims of the recently formed Society, and Smetana was charged with the task of finding a suitable theme which would involve as many artists and musicians as possible. One of the determining factors was the desire of the Czechs to surpass the Schiller celebrations held by the Prague Germans a few years before; and by turning to the

[1] Jindrich Pech (1837–1905) was a singing teacher and brother of Eliška Krásnohorská-Pech, who wrote librettos for three of Smetana's operas.

[2] Karel Bendl (1838–1897) was a composer, choirmaster and conductor who taught the piano at Smetana's school and was a warm supporter of his work. He later composed the Romantic opera *Lejla* (1868).

three hundredth anniversary of Shakespeare's birth Smetana was certain of support. His admiration for the plays of Shakespeare[3] has already been mentioned and the scores of *Richard III* and *Macbeth* show his willingness to be influenced by them. He now threw himself into devising a festive programme to mark the occasion. Karel Purkyne was to be responsible for scenic presentation, Smetana for the music. The Novoměstské Divadlo[4] (New Town Theatre) was reserved for April 23 as was the Provisional Theatre Orchestra; but as this totalled no more than twenty-nine[5] players Smetana was obliged to enlist the services of thirty-one instrumentalists from the Conservatoire to swell the numbers. In the first part of the programme he planned to conduct extracts from Berlioz's *Roméo et Juliette* (heard previously in Prague when the composer conducted it in 1846) and incidental music especially written by Vilém Blodek[6] for a series of *tableaux vivants* based on scenes from *The Merchant of Venice*, *Richard III*, *Coriolanus*, *Cymbeline* and *A Winter's Tale*. The culmination of the proceedings was to be Mendelssohn's music for *A Midsummer Night's Dream*.

The celebration called for enormous organization on Smetana's part and made great demands on his time. For Berlioz's work (which

[3] The year also saw the millennium celebrations of the arrival of the two Slavonic missionary saints, Cyril and Methodius, on the soil of Moravia. It is curious that this event should have taken second place to the Shakespeare celebrations and that it did not draw from Smetana a huge musical celebration on a national theme.

[4] The Novoměstské Divadlo, also known as the Zabranské Divadlo (Suburban Theatre), opened in 1858 as an overflow house to the Stavovské Divadlo. It seated three thousand people and was used for circuses, ballets, balls and bazaars. Opera was played there on Thursday and Sunday afternoons, but after 1862 Tuesday performances were also arranged. The Theatre had a sliding roof and notices were displayed advising the public that opera would be given only at the New Town Theatre in fine weather, and at the Provisional Theatre when it was inclement. Another system was later devised whereby flags, if flown before 2.00 p.m., denoted a performance in the New Town Theatre. If no flag appeared until after 2.00 p.m. the performance was understood to be in the Provisional Theatre. Up to 1876 only six hundred and forty-five opera performances were presented at the New Town Theatre which continued to operate until 1885. Thereafter the site was used to accommodate the present Smetana Theatre.

[5] The orchestra at the Provisional Theatre consisted of double woodwind, two each of horns, trumpets and trombones; timpani, harp and strings (four first violins, four second violins, two violas, two cellos and one double bass).

[6] Vilém Blodek (1834–1874) was a flautist and a professor at the Prague Conservatoire, a contemporary of Bendl and Fibich and the composer of a one-act rustic opera *In the Well* (1867).

was to be staged) he required a chorus, and while the Hlahol provided the nucleus of his singers, these were only men. Prague possessed no established female chorus, and consequently he was forced to recruit voices from churches, the Sokol[7] and St. Cecilia Societies and the friends of music, all of whom he rehearsed privately at his Institute. Finally he gathered eighty women and a hundred and fifty men, to which Purkyne added fifty others for the *tableaux*. Encouraged by these arrangements, Smetana felt disappointed not to be contributing music to the proceedings himself. So obsessed did he become with composing something for the occasion that eventually he was unable to resist setting to work, and barely seven days before the Festival produced his *Pochod k slavnosti Shakespearové* (*Shakespearean March*) which he substituted in place of the Mendelssohn:

> Great celebration[8] of Shakespeare's three hundredth birthday. Music, *tableaux* and the strains of a march created by me to accompany a magnificent procession of the most outstanding characters in Shakespeare's play.[9]

Despite its intentions, Smetana's *March* does not rise to the level of his *Richard III*. This could hardly be expected, for it was designed as a *pièce d'occasion*[1] and as such sacrifices originality for effect. The most interesting feature of the score is the manner in which the composer captures the qualities of a formal festive occasion with solemn fanfares, powerful drum-rolls and portentous climaxes. Yet beneath the square rhythms and persistent perfect cadences there is a fleeting hint of the broad lyricism that was to flower in the pageant scenes of *Dalibor* and *Libuše* (Example 26).

The *Shakespearean March*, the last piece to bear an opus number (20), was favourably reviewed by *Slavoj* (May, 1864) but did not make Smetana a celebrity overnight. In the Press he continued to act for Czech art by citing his work in connexion with the Shakespeare Festival, but to no avail. At the Umělecká Beseda he became acquainted with representatives of Czech literary life. He cultivated

[7] The Sokol, founded in 1862, was a society which combined physical training with the theory of mental discipline and had a popular, democratic, as well as nationalistic, basis of membership.

[8] In Berlioz' *Roméo et Juliette*, Smetana began the third part, *Scene d'Amour* before the chorus were fully on stage and was forced to stop and start the piece again. This unfortunate incident was later used by Smetana's adversaries to illustrate his shortcomings as a conductor.

[9] Diary: April, 1863.

[1] In the original manuscript score, Smetana added a remark whereby several bars in the coda can be repeated to allow the procession to assemble on stage.

Example 26

leading figures like Sladkovský, Tonner, Kučera, Sabina, Wenzig and Neruda, and he invited them regularly to his flat on Sunday afternoons in an attempt to establish himself as one of their circle and gain their support in his fight to remove from his nation the reproach that it could produce only executant musicians.

In May he renewed his attacks on the standard of music in Prague, his criticisms ranging from the low level of singing to the fact that posters advertising events at the Provisional Theatre were printed in German as well as Czech. Gradually, however, he was winning attention and was able to organize a trial programme of three subscription concerts which were sponsored by the Umělecká Beseda. Though these represented a breakthrough in the customs of Czech musical life and did much to establish a standard for the future they ended in financial disaster and failed to make Smetana the household name he had hoped.[2] On the contrary, his articles earned him a good deal of hostility, a litany of complaints and a host of enemies. He seemed no nearer to achieving his goal than he had been on his return from Sweden three years before:

[2] Subscription concerts given by the Umělecká Beseda were held on December 28, 1864, and March 4 and May 16, 1865, and ended with a deficit of 622 gulden.

> Attacked by many, misjudged by others, whether purposely or otherwise is of no importance, I see all my endeavours in the field of art postponed to some distant and indefinite date when the present deplorable conditions give way to new and better ones. Perhaps this will soon happen. But until today my motto has been: 'Patience always'. From the national point of view the post of Conductor at the Czech Theatre is no doubt most important. From here one really has a direct influence on the public in the broadest sense and would be able to influence to the greatest possible extent the refinement of artistic taste as well as the trend of art. . . . This post would certainly suit me. But as long as Dr. Rieger is the Intendant it is useless even to think of it, as the present Conductor [Mayŕ] appears to him to be a model for all Conductors in spite of his oft-proved uselessness. A more promising hope now appears. . . . It is the post of Director of the Conservatoire which has been left vacant by the resignation of Kittl. My friends are trying to persuade me that this post might have been specially created for me, since it is not only really the first post in rank, but the most brilliant as regards endowment . . . I'm doing everything my friends advise me. Pivoda makes propaganda for me, since the position depends on the favour of the aristocracy from whom I have recently become somewhat estranged. Now it is a question of donning a tail-coat again, paying visits, catching up with composition and a thousand and one other unpleasant things.[3]

Despite his efforts to win favour with the aristocracy, his application was rejected. Though Pivoda had loudly sung his praises, this was insufficient to erase the doubtful reputation he had already earned; and from the testimonial, delivered in support of Smetana's application by Dr. August Ambros,[4] he was clearly regarded with undisguised coolness:

> I know all that is good about Smetana as pianist, conductor and composer, but he wants to proceed with the composition of symphonic poems in the same direction as Liszt. This is basically suspect and can only provoke more enemies.

[3] Letter to Valentin: April 20, 1865.

[4] August Ambros (1816–1876) was a historian and music critic who later taught in the University of Vienna. Though he opposed Smetana in favour of Krejčí in the competition for the Directorship of the Prague Conservatoire his attitude changed to a friendlier one, and in Harrach's opera competition he was a member of the jury who awarded Smetana first prize.

It is little wonder that the post was offered to Dr. Josef Krejčí, a traditionalist from the Prague Organ School who was so soaked in conservatism that he regarded the work of Liszt as 'Turkish music' and urged his pupils to avoid Wagner at all costs. He remained in charge of the Conservatoire until 1881 and during this time warmed neither to Smetana nor his music.

Stung by a rejection which he interpreted as a personal slight, Smetana resumed his column in *Národní Listy*, attacking the Provisional Theatre and the bad conditions which prevailed there:

> . . . Enthusiasts exclaim 'Thank God we have a Provisional Theatre!' But let us pray to God to deliver us from it soon! . . . How can we possibly play opera in a house as small as ours? In *Les Huguenots* the armies barely number eight on each side . . . and thus provoke laughter. The singers are pressed so closely together in the foreground that everyone must be careful not to hurt his neighbour when he turns. As for the chorus—they stand either in a straight line at the footlights or in a semicircle at the back packed tightly against each other, singing their parts without movement of leg or arm for fear of injuring the adjoining person. . . . The narrowness of the stage is to blame, and behind it is even worse, for singers have no room to prepare an entrance. The acoustics are very different from those of our larger houses and when an artist has grown accustomed to a small stage area it takes many tiring hours and many errors before they become used to a larger one. Another evil is the orchestral pit—a space which barely deserves that name! Whoever hears the strings when their numbers are barely suitable for the production of chamber, let alone garden, music! There are four first violins, four seconds, two violas, two cellos and one double bass only! We can never hear the musicians play as a body or in their correct proportions. The brass and wind smother the strings completely. In such conditions it is hard to speak of higher artistic standards. The most important ingredient of the opera house, the pit, they forgot when building the theatre. Perhaps they never considered opera at all. I'm reminded of that town hall in — where the building was erected without doors or windows. It was a great success! If we are to build a Czech Opera we must build a theatre which is suitable for opera and the sooner the better.[5]

Apart from the stage and orchestra pit, which Smetana condemned,

[5] *Národní Listy*: July 22, 1864.

he more than once criticized the appalling heat which was generated during the course of the evening:

> Who makes the greater sacrifice: singers or public? If they decide to endure almost three hours of Turkish Bath with a temperature of 25 or 30 Rëaumur[6] in our narrow theatre, then it must be the public. And it must be recognized that in spite of this tropical heat the public gathered to hear *Die Zauberflöte* and even stayed to the last notes.[7]

But the aspect of the Provisional Theatre which aggravated him most was its neglect of Czech opera; for as Maýr had grown hoary with routine and mentally flaccid with the years the repertoire had become more conservative and financially dependent on the gratification of mob taste:

> . . . To foster a dramatic art is the most important task of our Opera . . . and when the Directors have mounted two native works in a year they feel they have done enough. . . The public always thirsts for something new and will support two or three performances and thus pay all expenses. The Directors must not forget that they have a duty to educate the public and that our public is always ready to sacrifice itself especially if it is for a good cause.
>
> The second task is not to neglect the older native composers. All foreign works need to be translated into Czech so why do they not do the same for our own composers who wrote operas on a German text, like Škroup's *Colombus* which would be something of a novelty. Why do they ignore Kittl's *Bianca und Giuseppe*, a work that is so much better than many others they stubbornly produce now? And is it not also time to make the public aware of the scores of our brothers—Glinka, Moniusko and Rubinstein, whose *Die Kinder der Heide* (*Children of the Heath*) has been given in Vienna with outstanding success? As for the classical and romantic composers, where are they? Where is *Figaro*, so long available in a Czech version and unperformed here for years? Where are *Don Giovanni* and *Fidelio*? If we can perform Gounod's *Faust* why should we fear other large-scale dramatic works? Could we not even perform Wagner? But in our Theatre, no! There is a rich quarry of opera and all the Directors have to do is mine it. . . . The final thing we ask

[6] 25 or 30 Réaumur=about 34° centigrade.

[7] *Národní Listy*: August 3, 1865.

is that the performances of conscientious, truthful, genuine and pure works are given by artistic minds. Not only external duty is sufficient. What is needed is inspired action. Operas are not only musical productions where singers sing for singing's sake, where music continues bar by bar, where the main thing is the baton. Opera must be raised to the level of drama, so let us forget external mechanical guidance (baton, bars, corporal's sticks and everything) and go ahead to win honour for the Czechs.[8]

With 'baton' and 'corporal's stick' Smetana was referring to Maýr, whom he considered to be his 'personal and unreconciled enemy'.[9] In his reviews he often drew attention to Maýr's stick technique or lack of it, to his 'unnecessary and pretentious display which suggests more a corporal's stick than a baton':

Maýr in his excitement, knocked the desk and hit the score, in an effort to attract attention to himself and to the difficulties of being a conductor . . . even in the simple passages he created an enormous amount of superfluous arm movement. Why does the Kapellmeister shift his baton so much? Does he want to draw more attention to himself than to the stage so that one can see how much perspiration it costs and what effort is needed to conduct a simple chorus?[1]

Such critiques were hardly likely to establish good relations between the two men and not unnaturally Maýr retaliated with a campaign designed to obstruct Smetana's progress as a composer at the Provisional Theatre. Nettled, he reciprocated with a series of punitive counter-attacks that found their target not in Maýr's musicianship but in his frequent lapses of good taste:

To Mozart's masterpiece was added an appendix: the last scene of Vaccai's *Giulietta e Romeo*.[2] And Kapellmeister Maýr says it was by 'popular request'. We have no words to express this breach of taste. No, not even the time-worn phrase 'by request' can condone this erroneous choice. After *Don Giovanni* nothing can follow![3]

But this was not Maýr's worst offence. At the Provisional Theatre it was customary for the management to provide some form of

[8] *Národní Listy*: July 15, 1864.
[9] Letter to Benecke: October 12, 1863.
[1] *Il Trovatore—Národní Listy*: May 2, 1864.
[2] The final scene of Vaccai's opera was often substituted for the finale of Bellini's *I Capuletti ed i Montecchi*.
[3] *Národní Listy*: July 15, 1864.

entr'acte so that patrons did not find the intervals too wearisome. At the Court Theatre in Stockholm Smetana had once been called upon to provide the entertainment himself. In Sweden he had detested the convention: in Prague he abhorred it.[4] The public, on the other hand not only appreciated it but expected it and flocked to see the supporting attraction as much as the advertised opera. It was quite usual for variety acts to be sandwiched between serious musical items, and thus we find programmes in which, for example, Ferdinand Laub shared his violin recital with a one-act farce *Žensky plác* (*Weeping Women*) described as 'the most frivolous comedy on the stage'.[5] On another occasion Mlle. Milaszewsky, a Polish music-hall artist, provided bawdy songs between acts of Bellini's *Norma*. Worse, Maýr actually allowed two American acrobats (Mr. Walkes and Mr. Newman) from the Cirque Napoléon in Paris to present a high-wire act called *Life in Dreams*. At a height of sixty *stop*[6] one of the artists walked from the gallery of the Novoměstské Theatre across the auditorium and onto the stage—all this between the acts of Halévy's *La Juive*.[7]

Much as Smetana condemned this, he reserved his saddest comments for a spectacular one-legged dancer Julian Donato, whom Maýr invited to enliven Rossini's *Otello*:

> Should Mr. Donato embellish the opera or should the opera win a large audience for the dancer? . . . Why are we so enthusiastic about Art? Are we idealists or dreamers? Why don't we sing Osannas to Maýr and the directors of our Opera? . . . Mr. Donato has become the nightly attraction. Why else would one third of the audience leave after the third act interval? He won enthusiasm as much for his presentation as for his virtuosity and execution. Wreaths and flowers and unending cheers were his reward. . . . For *Otello* it would do no harm if the singers would learn to look at each other when one has to tell the other something instead of staring at the public who are quite innocent of their disputes![8]

Donato provided one of the most popular acts at the Provisional Theatre. He had lost his right leg fighting at the King's School of

[4] Despite his caustic attacks Smetana was unable to ensure that entr'acte music would cease and the practice continued at the Prague Provisional and National Theatres until the end of the century.

[5] *Národní Listy*: January 15, 1865.

[6] *Stop*—an old linear measure of approximately one foot.

[7] *Národní Listy*: October 17, 1864.

[8] *Národní Listy*: August 14, 1864.

Toreadors in Madrid; and following this had turned to entertainment, visiting Budapest, Germany and England, where he appeared at a Covent Garden pantomime on Boxing Day, 1864. He was one of the highest paid artists in Europe: at Krolls Theatre, Berlin, he received six hundred gulden a night and in Prague took fifty per cent of the box office takings (approximately eleven hundred gulden each evening). His success was so certain that Maýr and his colleagues quickly re-engaged him, this time for a season. Smetana despaired:

> . . . we have previously spoken about Mr. Donato's agility. On one leg he can not only perform the possible but the impossible! But we cannot help feeling sorry that art gains nothing from his act. One may admire his neck-breaking evolutions but one cannot avoid a certain monotony. It is as if someone was playing the piano with only the left hand. There, as here, it is only agility; for when the curiosity of the spectator is appeased, nothing remains. Now Mr. Donato dances nightly. If this must be so then we pity him because the same dance is not suited to works of tragic content and anyone with the slightest aesthetic education will agree. . . . What would they say if he danced between the acts of *King Lear* or *Hamlet*? Surely they would protest! And so do we! If Maýr and the Directors are bound to allow Mr. Donato to appear every evening, then the management should perform lighter operas, like *Alessandro Stradella*, *Martha* and *Il Barbiere di Siviglia*! We must not let our Art be trampled on—not even with one foot! For Halévy's *La Juive* all is as bad as before. Clarinets play for cor anglais and so on! Why? But then in our Theatre one gets used to anything.[9]

In most of these reviews we can sense Smetana's intense animosity to Maýr and his policy at the Theatre. Though he was right to draw attention to the depressing state of music in Prague, it is questionable whether he should have struck out on a personal level or used the columns of *Národní Listy* to petition for his own appointment to the staff of the Provisional Theatre. Yet at the time when he was expressing these views he was not entirely without means of supporting them. Few acknowledged his talents, but he was, nevertheless, a competent conductor and a proven choir trainer: he possessed indefatigable energy and wide experience in the planning and organization of concerts. What is more, he had completed his first opera, *Braniboři v Čechách* (*The Brandenburgers in Bohemia*), the year before.

The announcement of Count Jan Harrach's Opera Competition,

[9] *Národní Listy*: August 21, 1864.

together with the decision to present music as well as drama at the Provisional Theatre, had filled Smetana with the desire to write a large dramatic work for the stage. So intent was he on winning the prize that he had pulled up his Swedish roots and returned to Prague where, on the day following his arrival (May 28, 1861), he had discussed with a friend the possibility of collaborating on a historical opera. Six months elapsed and still Smetana was without a text. Impatient as always, he looked everywhere for a libretto. His concern was natural, for the Competition closing date was September 30, 1862, barely eight working-months away. Towards the end of December Procházka recommended Smetana for membership to the Prague Měšt'anská Beseda (Citizens' Society) and it was here he made the acquaintance of Karel Sabina (1813–1877), a journalist, poet and supporter of the Young Czechs. The two men struck up an immediate friendship and Sabina agreed to provide the required text. He was as good as his word:

> Today I received the opera in two acts from Sabina. The plot is taken from the time when Bohemia was invaded by Otto of Brandenburg, following the death of Přemsyl Otakar II.[1]

The problems facing Smetana were enormous. In 1862 there was no model for Czech opera to which he could turn, and though he knew the conventional repertoire this did not offer a solution. It was not simply that Czech opera was unperformed, but rather that no Czech opera existed. Smetana certainly knew Škroup's *The Tinker* and *The Fiddler*, but these were so slight that they could hardly be considered prototypes. No Czech had really explored the field, and one could hardly have expected otherwise in a country where political and social matters were so unsettled. Prague was unprepared for the cultivation of a home-grown product and it is not entirely Maýr's fault that during his four years as Conductor at the Provisional Theatre, only two Czech operas were staged there: Skuherský's[2] *Vladimír—Chosen by God* (September 27, 1863) and Šebor's *The Templars in Moravia* (October 19, 1865) also to a text by Sabina. On the other hand, he hardly went out of his way to foster the work of Czech composers and it was his flagrant refusal to acknowledge local talent which enraged Smetana. At first he hesitated, not knowing in which direction to

[1] Diary: February, 1862.

[2] F. Z. Skuherský (1830–1892) was Director of the Prague Organ School from 1864 and one of the most progressive teachers of his day. He was an ardent follower of the works of Wagner, the author of two books on composition and later Janáček's tutor.

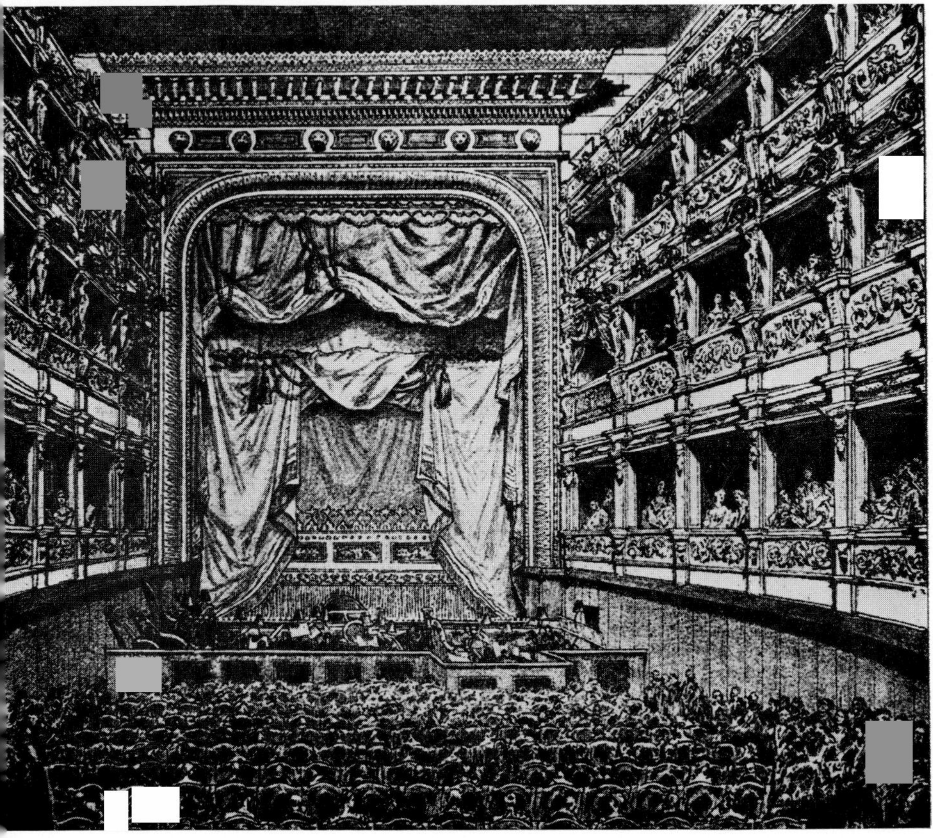

PLATE XI. Prague Provisional Theatre

PLATE XII

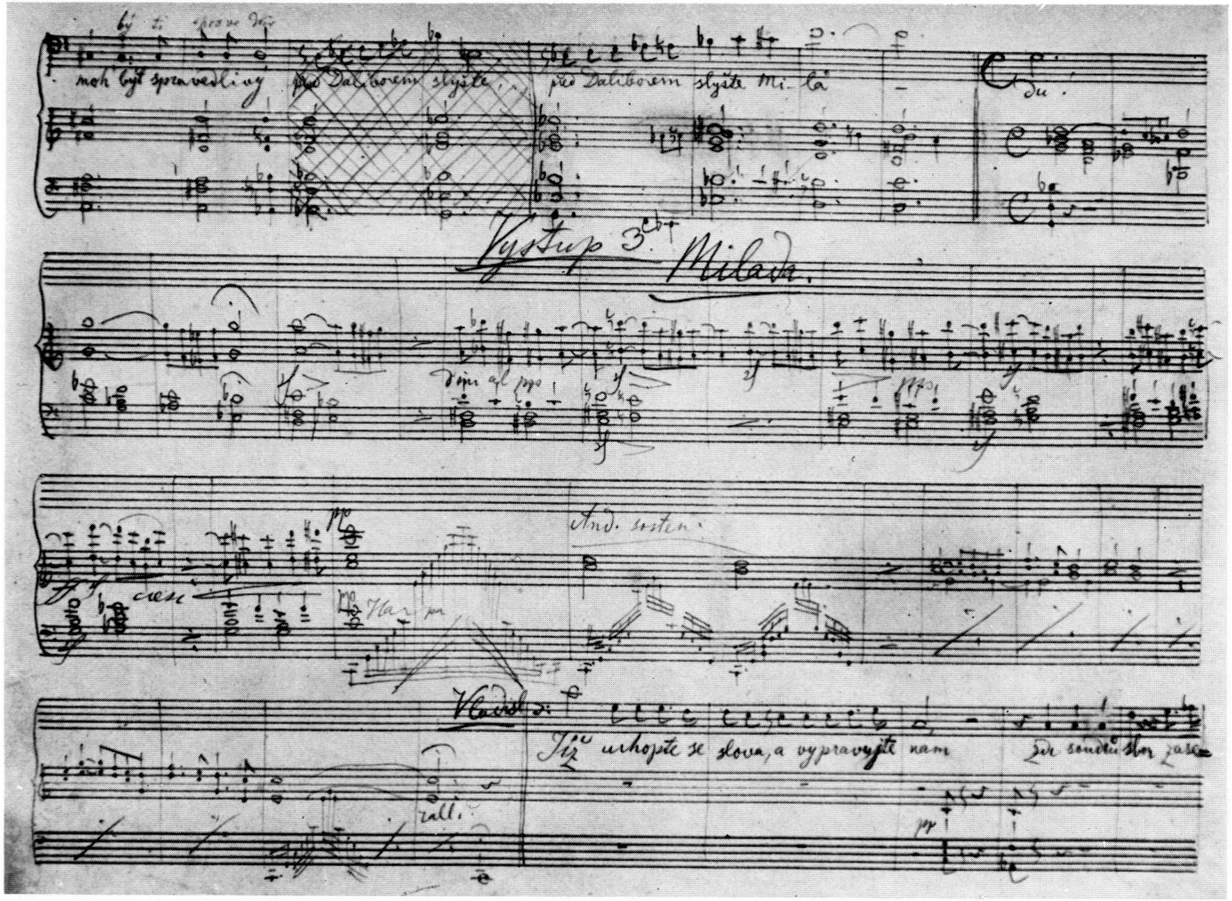

Dalibor
Act I. Scene 3

turn. Should he follow convention or strike out on new ground? His decision to forge ahead, irrespective of operatic forms around him, was made more difficult by the conditions of Count Harrach's competition which, though set out with the intention of providing a guide to the Czech opera of the future, for Smetana became something of a barrier:

OPERA COMPETITION

There is no nation who loves song and music in greater measure and at the same time could prove themselves with a treasure of genuine songs and delightful melodies than the Slav in general, and the Czech in particular.

. . . I want to encourage the composition of Czech National Opera, and therefore announce two prizes, each of six hundred gulden, for the two best two-act scores, and two prizes, each of two hundred gulden, for the best Czech texts to these. The first of these operas is to be based on the history of the Czech people; the second should be of gay content and taken from the national life of the people in Bohemia, Moravia or Silesia.

The composers are free to choose their texts and their librettists so that each can work out, in collaboration with his own poet, his own treatment. It is not necessary to remind the entrants that the selected plot must be simple but sufficiently dramatic, at the same time rich in lyric and pathetic moments so that there can be an adequate basis for song and music. The characters should be lightly drawn and well contrasted; the verses must be fluent and singable; rhythm and form moulded to the mood and situation; the diction should be poetic, natural, easy and correct and the whole content imaginative, emotional and above all musical.

Concerning music and song, I stipulate that the opera shall be based on a diligent study of the national songs of the Czech and Slovak peoples. The music must have a real national identity. The chorus in gay operas should not cause boredom among the audience, but rather a vivid reflection of national songs which stimulate a lively interest. In gay operas national dances may also be introduced to advantage. To what extent historical operas employ old chorales as themes for the chorus is left to the discretion of the composer according to his chosen plot.

A basic condition is that the composer should by birth belong to the lands of the Czech Crown. The composition, text and music should be delivered at the latest on September 30, 1862, to my address in Prague. On the first page should appear a motto which at the same time should be written on the envelope of a letter in which is sealed the name of the poet and the composer, his position and address. Manuscripts and compositions not awarded a prize will be returned by means of this motto. The jury that will make the decision for the successful composition and the best text will be called together officially and announced at a later date. The poet whose text will be recognized by the jury to be the best will receive a premium even if the musical setting is not awarded a prize, and he will be free to do as he wishes with his text. The prize-winning opera shall remain the exclusive property of the composer with one condition that the first performance shall be given in a Prague theatre. And so I invite my dear compatriots, wherever they may be, to participate enthusiastically in this Czech enterprise—to produce a real national work that will glorify the Czechs!

JAN HRABE HARRACH

February 10, 1861.

Though well intentioned, Count Harrach's articles of faith contained nothing new, and were designed on lines which had conditioned Italian opera for years. Had they been followed to the letter, it is likely that they would have produced little more than a Czech version of standard operatic form. The actual quotation of folk song and dance may lend local colour to a dramatic work, and at times be a desirable ingredient, but in itself it is insufficient to establish a national school of opera. Smetana, realizing the inherent weakness of Count Harrach's scheme, argued that a pseudo-Scottish décor, a Highland dance and a few kilts and sporrans did not *ipso facto* make *Lucia di Lammermoor* a national Scottish opera nor Donizetti, for that matter, a typical Scottish composer. Anxious as he was to develop a school of Czech opera, Smetana could not subscribe to the note-for-note quotation of folk melody. This was no sudden decision on his part. In *Wallenstein's Camp* and *Hakon Jarl* he had deliberately avoided the use of indigenous folk elements, and he now sought to solve his operatic problems in a way that contradicted Harrach's conditions.

From the start Smetana was aware that he had to work in his own style and follow his own course:

If the new German School is proclaiming progress then I am their disciple—but otherwise I belong only to myself. I try to write only as I feel in myself.[3]

[3] Diary: January 6, 1862.

He began the piano sketch[4] of *The Brandenburgers in Bohemia* in February, 1862, incorporating into the score three ideas noted in his motive book in November, 1860. A letter to Fröjda Benecke (dated February 25) contains a progress report: by the first days of March he had arrived at the Act I finale which he played to Procházka 'who liked it'. Despite a trip to Sweden between March and May, which interrupted his thought-process, he managed to complete 'half the opera' by June 16 (so he wrote to Valentin in Göteborg), and by January 1863, Act I was ready. The instrumentation of Act II was completed on February 16 and the finishing touches to Act III were made on April 23, 1863, when he submitted the score to the organizers, with 'Music—the language of feeling, words—the language of ideas' inscribed on the title page.

The Competition was due to close at the end of September, 1862, but as no entry had been received, it was decided to extend the time by a further twelve months. The jury, announced in December, 1863, included Kittl, Principal of the Conservatoire, Krejčí, Director of the Organ School, and Ambros, the critic and historian. Though Smetana was the first to submit a score, his was not the only entry. Two others were received: Adolf Pozděny's *The Treasure* and Jan Maýr's *Horymir's Jump*; but neither was publicized as much as *The Brandenburgers in Bohemia*. Both *Slavoj* and *Lumír* gave considerable attention to Smetana's first opera and in the newspaper *Dalibor* it was announced that Liegert[5] intended to open his season with it. Unfortunately Liegert's scheme failed as the only score was with the jury, still deliberating the result. During the summer, however, Smetana succeeded in making a copy and Liegert once again renewed his efforts to mount the production. This time Maýr was the stumbling block. He refused to find anything of value in the score and to the charge that he was obstructing the way to the works of native composers he

[4] Sixty-two pages of piano sketches for *The Brandenburgers* have been preserved in the Smetana Museum in Prague. Of all his operas this is the most fully worked. As he became more experienced the sketches tended to become shorter: *The Bartered Bride* is contained on thirty pages, *Dalibor* on eighteen, *Libuše* on thirty-two, *The Two Widows* on four, *The Kiss* on thirteen, *The Secret* on eleven. For *The Devil's Wall*, with which he experienced considerable difficulties, there are, however, thirty-one sheets but most of these are crossed through and full of alterations. With the exception of *The Secret* and *The Devil's Wall* each sketch stops short well before the definite end. It seems as if Smetana may well have grown impatient to start composition proper.

[5] František Liegert (1803–1881) was German by birth. A draper by profession, he had little theatrical experience but a keen business sense. He was appointed Director of the Provisional Theatre in 1863 and was responsible for changing its name to Král Zemské Česke Divadlo (The King's Czech Country Theatre).

hastily responded with a performance of *Eva Hlínová, Daughter of the Prague Shield-Bearer*, an opera in five acts by the forgotten composer Dörstling.

In December, Smetana presented extracts from *The Brandenburgers* in concert version. The reviews were favourable and Liegert, who had enormous faith in Smetana, announced his intention to present *The Brandenburgers* on St. Wenceslas' Day (September 28, 1865) followed by new productions of Mozart's *Figaro* and Nicolai's *Lustigen Weiber von Windsor*. Maýr objected, and protected by Rieger, refused to conduct Smetana's work. Matters were brought to a head when Liegert, supported by Thomé,[6] overruled Maýr and insisted that the opera be mounted. Having placed himself in the invidious position of refusing to acknowledge *The Brandenburgers* Maýr could hardly retract. The only person capable of directing the work was the composer himself, who jumped at the opportunity. The problems facing him were considerable and his letters and Diary for 1866 give some idea of what he had to face:

> . . . . they arranged that I should produce my own opera, that is to say I should see to both piano and orchestral rehearsals because, as Thomé explained: 'Maýr will have nothing to do with it'. He told me the conditions under which the opera should be put on: the first three performances to go to the Directors, the fourth to me, and after the fifth, if it runs that long, I am to have ten-per-cent of the gross takings.[7] I accepted full of joy because my opera, after lying around for three years was to be staged at last. I chose Miss von Ehrenberg[8] as principal soprano as she held sway over Maýr at this time and therefore over the entire company. Although the role was not meant for her, I hoped . . . she might help my work onto its feet . . . but during the first piano rehearsal she sang through the part, threw down the score disdainfully and exclaimed derisively: 'And you expect me to sing that? Why, there's not a single *coloratura* passage in it and I'm engaged exclusively for *coloratura*!' She stormed out and when Thomé heard about this he advized me to give the part to Miss Ferenczy. This I did and it was a good thing for me.

[6] František Thomé (1807–1882) had been Manager and Director of the Stavovské Theatre but was forced to relinquish this post because of financial ruin. He was appointed Second Director of the Provincial Theatre, remaining there until 1866.

[7] In the event Smetana received between fifty and sixty gulden for each performance.

[8] Eleonora Gayer von Ehrenberg (1832–1912).

The first performance was on January 5, 1866, and I conducted for the first time at the Theatre. The house was packed and the applause exceptional.[9]

... the opera was liked and was excellent. I was called on stage nine times. I conducted myself, but the work was tiring to prepare, especially with the singers. I had to hammer the parts into their heads note by note. There were rehearsals with the soloists and chorus for six days from 10.00 a.m. to 4.00 p.m. and I returned home each evening quite exhausted. . . . Even though I did not expect it the house was sold out and critics, both Czech and German, are full of praise.[1]

The success of *The Brandenburgers* was real and immediate. Eleven performances were given in the first two months and Thomé also kept his word about royalties and allowed Smetana a Benefit at the third performance as well as the fourth.[2] *The Brandenburgers in Bohemia* not only surpassed everything that had been previously created in the field of Czech opera, but confounded a number of Smetana's adversaries. Critics and public were stirred by the popular choruses, the patriotic nature of the plot, the vitality of the music:

We now know Mr. Smetana to be a man of great gifts. He alone has the vocation to make the name of Czech music glorious. The public received his opera with enthusiasm and the work should indicate to the Directors the way in which national opera must proceed.[3]

Generally, it was felt that Smetana had won a great victory for Czech music but there were some who failed to acknowledge his triumph. Rieger objected to an *avant garde* style smacking of Wagner and avoiding Bohemian folk melody; Mayr found the idiom too advanced, the harmony too dissonant, the plot too complex; and Count Harrach's jury, who had delayed their decision, detected weaknesses in the vocal writing and counterpoint. More serious, they considered the subject insufficiently national. Czech or not, they could hardly deny that *The Brandenburgers* was a box-office success at the Provisional Theatre and that its composition marked the inauguration of a new epoch in Prague's music. Reluctantly, the judges agreed to award the first prize to Smetana, and on March 27 he received a letter from Count Harrach:

[9] Diary: January, 1866. [1] Letter to Benecke: January, 1866.
[2] The fifth performance was a Benefit for the baritone Josef Lev, the seventh for the tenor Polák; the remaining performances were for subscribers.
[3] *Národní Listy*: January 16, 1866.

> Your score has complied with the rules of the competition and the judges have been unanimous in their decision to award you the Prize of six hundred gulden. My heartiest congratulations!

But the judges did not award a prize for the best operatic text, and Sabina's libretto failed to gain even honourable mention. Instead, a consolation of one hundred gulden was given to František Šir whose *Drahomír*[4] was considered to be the most distinguished poem of those submitted.

Weber once told Schubert that he thought first operas and puppies should be drowned; and as his own earliest attempt has disappeared, he presumably acted on this advice. Smetana's first opera has fortunately been preserved and is the work of no puppy composer. Though he was coming to the form for the first time, he was already very experienced and *The Brandenburgers in Bohemia* continues a style previously exploited in the three Swedish tone poems. It is a score that was born of a revolutionary spirit of its time, and in it Smetana and Sabina were united in their intentions.

The opera is set in the thirteenth century during a difficult period of Czech history. After the death of the Bohemian King, Přemysl Ottokar II (1278), the widowed Queen, Kunhuta, invoked the aid of Otto V, Margrave of Brandenburg, to halt the advances of her husband's murderer, Rudolf of Hapsburg. The Brandenburgers, behaving as if they were in enemy territory, plundered the land and murdered the Bohemians. Their leader, Otto, not only quarrelled with Queen Kunhuta, but held her and her seven-year-old son and heir to the Crown captive in the fortified Bezděz Castle outside Prague. A Hapsburg-Brandenburg agreement gave Otto mandatory power over Bohemia for five years, during which time the Brandenburgers massacred and caused widespread misery that was aggravated by famine. Moreover, the Brandenburgers favoured German citizens resident in Prague at the expense of the defenceless Bohemian population, and thus deepened the existing antagonism between the two nations. Though based on these historical events, Sabina's plot is imaginary. At a time of ardent nationalism and of a new-culture movement, the recollection of the Brandenburger reign of terror and of its downfall was both topical and a symbol of national awakening. Although Tyl had drawn on the same historical background in one of his dramatic works,[5] both Sabina and Smetana saw the subject as a

[4] *Drahomír* was later reworked by Böhm and set to music by Karl Šebor.

[5] In 1834 Tyl had attempted to use this historical situation for his play *Zapuzení Braniborů* (*The Driving out of the Brandenburgers*). Though it was never finished, Sabina may well have been impressed by the way Tyl based the action on the

vehicle for new comment on the political and social problems of the nineteenth century contemporary scene, at a time when all Bohemians were striving to break from the Hapsburgs and establish as independent national identity. The theme of Smetana's first opera therefore reflects these struggles and aspirations, and indicates that only the Bohemians themselves were capable of saving the country.

Apart from Tyl's play, which Sabina probably knew, another contributing source may well have been the rhymed *Chronicle of Dalimil*[6] (c. 1316), the work of an anonymous poet but attributed in the early nineteenth century to either the monk Dalimil or a Bohemian noble belonging to the northern districts.[7] The book describes the close of King Ottokar II's reign (1253–1278) and voices the patriotic, anti-German feelings of Bohemian noblemen who resented the arrogance of German burgers in Bohemia, and, concerned with the independence and future of the Czech people, attempted to oust them from their lands. While Dalimil probably provided substantial material for Sabina's setting, his treatment of the plot is not always historically correct and one of his most serious mistakes was to make Volfram Olbramavič leader of the Czech bourgeoisie when, in fact, the Olbramavič family was historically of German origin. Although the libretto is undistinguished as literature, it does provide a number of interesting

treatment of masses rather than individuals and incorporated a similar element into his libretto.

[6] Dalimil's *Chronicle* is one of the most important works in Bohemian literature and one of the earliest works written in the Bohemian language. In spite of wholesale destruction of Bohemian writings in the fourteenth and fifteenth centuries, nine manuscript copies have been preserved. The *Chronicle*, which is plentifully supplied with dates, was probably begun in 1308 and finished in 1315; of the events after 1280 the author writes as an eye witness. The first part of the book records the deluge and founding of Bohemia, and relates the semi-mythical tales outlined by Cosmas two centuries before which Hajek was to repeat two centuries later. The book closes with the reign of Henry of Carinthia (1310).

[7] Dalimil, who always writes as the champion of the Bohemian aristocracy, expresses contemporary feeling in his report of the Bohemian Prince Ulrich's indifference thus:

> Rather would I entrust myself to a Bohemian peasant girl than I should take a German queen for my wife. Every heart clings to its own nation; therefore would a German woman less favour my language. A German woman will have German servants. German will she teach my children. Then there will be division and thereby certain ruin to the State.

Elsewhere Dalimil records Rudolf of Hapsburg's hatred of the Bohemians:

> When I return from the wars I will inflict much evil on the Bohemians. I will stain the Petrin [place of execution] with their blood so that no Bohemian will any longer be seen on the Bridge of Prague.

thumb-nail sketches upon which Smetana was able to build. Certainly the first act is swift-moving in action and full of promise, but thereafter real development and detailed characterization are rarely to be found. Volfram and Oldřich merely set and settle the plot; Děčana and Vlčenka spend most of their time being abducted; the old man, a relic from earlier days of Romantic opera, is a type of patriarch whose static qualities are nearer the world of oratorio than opera; and Junoš, for all his comings and goings, is a lay figure—a tenor lover, and a cardboard one at that. The Brandenburgers fare little better. Both Tausendmark and Varneman are singularly unvillainous, evoking more pity than fear.[8] But there are two characters who stand out from the rest—Jíra and Liduše. Jíra is the hero of the opera, a serf and man of the people whose large heart responds to Liduše's plea for help against Tausendmark. Sabina makes him a social revolutionary who proclaims his own opinion on the equality of men and claims justice for the humble and despised. He is the representative of the populace, their mouthpiece and the defender of Volfram's daughters. Most of the dramatic action revolves around him, and it is when he is active that the music assumes a particular significance.

Liduše is also a positive character. She is fearless, brave, outspoken. She abhores Tausendmark for what he is—a liar, a cheat and a coward. She dominates the scene because her lover Junoš is weak and in this there is a parallel between *The Brandenburgers in Bohemia* and *Der fliegende Holländer*, where a similar mixture of the conventional and original is to be found (Daland is a lay figure and Erik a weak tenor lover, while Senta is a completely rounded character). But if Sabina's plot resembles any other, it is Pushkin's *Boris Godunov* rather than Wagner's work. The two poets were concerned with similar situations: both evolve their plots around a prince in his minority and a ruthless guardian; Otto's Brandenburg hordes pillaging Bohemia are analogous to the Poles striving to overcome Western Russia, and in both operas the real protagonist is the people rising in protest against oppressors.

But Smetana was less fortunate in having Sabina as his collaborator than was Mussorgsky who had Pushkin as his model; further, he was posed a problem which both Glinka and Dargomijsky had to some extent solved—namely, the question of declamation. Smetana came to understand the Czech language late in life, and this did not make

[8] Their scene together at the beginning of Act III is the only exception: possibly Smetana and Sabina had Beethoven's *Fidelio* in mind; for Pizarro and Rocco seem to have been the models for Tausendmark and Varneman, who are, however more menacing.

his task of bringing musical declamation into closer relationship with speech any easier. The most serious problem at this time concerned Czech prosody, which was in a much less settled condition than it was in Russia. No fixed rules of pronunciation existed. Carelessness and an inconsistent approach to accent and stress resulted in considerable variation, because the Bohemian philologist Dobrovský had devised a system of word emphasis which Jungmann, author of the first Czech dictionary, contradicted. Smetana, at first by intuition and later by trial and error, was obliged to evolve his own technique of musical declamation. In *The Brandenburgers* we see this in embryo. He is coming to grips with it for the first time and gaining experience as he writes (in some cases the pencil sketches, which are worked in considerable detail, differ from the definitive manuscript and it seems likely that he may have realized that his first thoughts were in many ways impracticable). But this was not the only problem he was forced to solve. For Smetana, the most serious question was the form his score should take. As a follower of Wagner, he saw his reforms as the salvation of opera and subscribed to the belief that stage works should be built on a dramatic framework rather than in a series of lyric numbers; but if he sympathized with Wagner on the questions of method and approach, his ideals concerning dramatic material were completely different. Where Wagner was drawn to myth, Smetana opted for dramatic realism. His choice of subjects and characters is taken from history and everyday life, and thus comes closer to the form of opera favoured by Weber, whose *Euryanthe*, with its technique of through composition, certainly influenced Smetana in *The Brandenburgers*. Though the two scores differ widely in manner, they have much in common, not least their musical continuity. Arias, duets, trios, ensembles and choruses all lead into one another in a continuous flow; spoken dialogue is superseded by integrated accompanied recitative, dramatically conceived and swift in action; both composers adopt a system of *Leitmotiv* to represent characters, but these identify rather than symbolize. In his handling of motives Smetana was at this stage less practised than Weber. Apart from an initial clumsiness he seems unaware of the possibilities of underlining fragments of the plot or characters by thematic transformation. It is not that his ideas are unsuitable for variation: on the contrary, many of them are particularly well drawn and those representing Tausendmark (a) (the villain who, as his name tells us, would sell his reputation for a thousand marks), Varneman (b), the strutting Captain, and (c) the Brandenburgers themselves are especially memorable:

In the first few pages Smetana introduces a number of striking ideas

Example 27 (*a*)

(*b*)

(*c*)

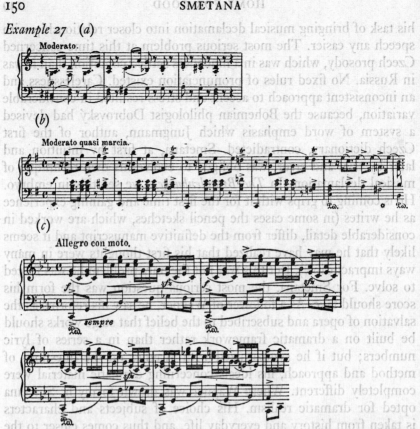

which depict the Bohemians (bars 45–52, strings and woodwind), the young heir to the throne (bars 90–95, clarinets) and Prague, the glory of the Czechs (bars 115–121), horns and strings; but these do not return with any consistency nor are they present in the finale when the Bohemians triumph over their invaders. Nor is there any reason why the two villains (Tausendmark and Varneman) should each have definitive motives when Liduše and Jíra have not. Instead Liduše is characterized by warm and lyrical lines: with one exception her music revolves around major keys (A flat and A in Act I; E flat, F and G in Act II; and B flat, F and C in Act III) and this makes for a marked contrast with Tausendmark, whose music is invariably minor in mode. Tonality apart, Smetana reserves some of his most poignant moments for Liduše herself: these bars from her Act I aria (a) and the trio in Act II, Scene 6 (b), are typical of her music (see Example 28 on next page).

Though *The Brandenburgers* is a rich quarry for lyricism, it is in the handling of the dramatic situation and the creating of atmosphere that Smetana strikes an original vein. Within the space of thirty bars the

Example 28 (*a*)

(*b*)

Prelude to Act I succeeds in conveying the uneasy current which existed in Prague under the Brandenburgers: immediately we sense the dark foreboding, the restless despair and terror of the oppressed people. Similarly, at the beginning of Act II, he captures the sorrow and misery which the peasants feel on being uprooted from their homes in a simple chorale-like melody. But it is not only in the orchestra that Smetana is able to paint evocative scenes. The chorus writing shows him to be a master of effect, and nowhere more so than in Act III (Scene 6) where the people describe the stillness of the night. Though *The Brandenburgers* was written at a time when no large choirs existed, Smetana here incorporated an *a capella* style more suited to the local choral society than the opera house, and in so doing produced one of the most hauntingly beautiful sections in the score:

Example 29

For Smetana the question of making his opera sufficiently 'national' was a burning one, especially as he had no intention of incorporating actual folk melodies[9] into the piece. His ideas of nationalism had been modified by Liszt's and furthermore he believed that national character in music could only be shown in the thought and substance of the composition and was not something to be achieved by the reproduction or superimposition of local colour as an ethnographical

[9] 'Copying of the melodic contour and rhythm of our folk songs does not create in itself a national style—at best a weak imitation with no dramatic truth.' (Letter to Procházka: 1862)

curiosity. Though he included a folk-scene in *The Brandenburgers* which foreshadows the one Mussorgsky used in *Boris Godunov*, he shunned traditional dances and thus left the naïve ideal of Škroup far behind. Instead he created naturalistic lines based on folk idiom which suggest folk origin without actually drawing on folk melody. In the mob scene in Prague Square (Act I, Scene 7) Smetana takes a basic polka rhythm but transforms it into a scherzo so that it assumes the vitality and energy of a skočná (a folk polka), depicting the triumph of the underprivileged as they raid the food supplies of the rich. This scene is among the most original in the score, not least for the way in which it anticipates the dance sequences in *The Bartered Bride*:

Example 30

Elsewhere Smetana evinces a sense of nationalism but nowhere more vividly than in the choruses. From the outset he had aimed to make an opera of and for the people, and for the first time in Czech music the people emerge as the protagonist with a genuine dramatic function. Here they became the revolutionary rabble, fighting for freedom with full-throated vigour, forceful rhythms and passionate melodies:

Example 31

The characteristic which gives this music its national flavour is the rapid quaver movement in thirds and sixths, and it is this above all which Smetana uses to depict all things Czech. The Act II love duet between Liduše and Junoš (Scene 7) shows an extension of this. As the couple express their feelings and look forward to the time when the storms and stresses of invasion will leave their country free, the sliding thirds and sixths pattern emerges as a distinct mark of style (the love duet is headed 'Molto vivace' and thus breaks Czech convention by expressing sentiments of emotion in an energetic vein) (see Example 32 on next page).

Another feature which contributes a personal flavour to this duet is the long pedal point. The significance of this device in Smetana's style has already been suggested: in *The Brandenburgers* it begins to

Example 32

assert itself more forcibly and hardly an aria passes without its appearance. In Act II, Scene 6, Smetana carries the technique to new limits by building the whole of Děčana's aria, some one hundred and thirty bars, on five sustained notes. Despite the healthy lyricism which distinguishes the music, Smetana saw *The Brandenburgers* as a dramatic opera, and the dramatic sections of the score are not only the immediate and most memorable but the most skilfully contrived and vigorous in action. For the historical court scenes he doubtlessly drew on his experience gained in the employ of Ferdinand V; but when he came to depict ordinary people—characters like

Liduše and Tausendmark when they were not involved in great crowd scenes but expressing simple sentiments in simple situations —he was faced with another problem. This was outside Smetana's experience, and consequently he looked to Italian composers for a solution. Varneman's Act II aria (*a*) has a Rossinian lightness quite out of character for a villain about to dispose of Volfram's three daughters, while the sisters' lament (*b*) (Act I, Scene 10) has a strong suggestion of Verdi:

Example 33 (*a*)

(*b*)

In Tausendmark's Act III aria we find another echo of Verdi in the way the broad vocal line is doubled first by solo cello then by violins.

Example 34

This passage demonstrates the demanding bass-baritone tessitura which Smetana writes. Perhaps a more practised hand would have pitched the aria lower or arranged the melodic line differently. This was a problem Smetana ran into time and again and only learnt to solve by trial and error. But for all its uneven qualities, *The Brandenburgers* is a remarkable opera. For a composer who was coming to the stage for the first time, Act I sets an unusually high standard. Act II drags somewhat and Act II descends to the conventional; but nevertheless the work remains highly effective in the theatre. Though Smetana was to outgrow his teething troubles and become more assured, *The Brandenburgers in Bohemia* is important in establishing a number of principles which return in the succeeding works. While he explored a different type of opera in *The Bartered Bride* (comic), *Dalibor* (tragic), *Libuše* (epic-patriotic), *The Two Widows* (drawing-room comedy-cum-Bohemian Singspiel), *The Kiss* (folk), *The Secret* (romantic) and *The Devil's Wall* (heroic-fantastic), each is based on history or everyday life (the exception is *Dalibor*, which is founded to some extent on mythology). Each opera expresses a similar motive of good triumphing over evil and ends joyfully or optimistically (again, the exception is *Dalibor*). This convention was one Smetana certainly inherited from *Don Giovanni* and *Der Freischütz*, where both plots are contrived to facilitate a happy close. Of the women it is invariably the soprano who leads the action and is more firmly drawn: Liduše (*The Brandenburgers*), Milada (*Dalibor*), Libuše (*Libuše*), Vendulka (*The Kiss*), and Hedvika (*The Devil's Wall*) all belong to a type and follow a pattern. Of the men it is the baritones who emerge more distinctly. Tausendmark apart, King Vladislav (*Dalibor*), Přemysl (*Libuše*), Kalina (*The Secret*), and Vok (*The Devil's Wall*) all belong in a tradition of virtuous baritone-do-gooders: they are all of noble birth (in Přemysl's case he is elevated to a noble station) and are invested with honourable qualities. Similarly, half Smetana's plots revolve around trial or judgement scenes.[1] In *The Brandenburgers* Jíra is brought to book before Volfram; in *Dalibor* it is the hero who is tried by Vladislav; in *Libuše* the brothers Chrudoš and Sťáhlav are brought to judgement for quarrelling over their father's estate; and in *The Two Widows* there is a mock trial when Podhajský is interrogated by Karoline imitating a judge.

Musically each opera continues to identify and develop the *dramatis personae* on the *leitmotiv* system, but unlike Wagner, where the heart of the music-drama is the orchestra, in Smetana's scores it lies with the chorus. His climaxes invariably depend more on rhythm than melody, while in the coda sections he explores the possibilities of new modulations and different scoring. Generally his orchestral palette is bright and effective but never as exciting or as overwhelming as Wagner's, nor as subtle and opulent as Dvořák's. Smetana could hardly expect such sophistication: he had at his disposal a force of barely thirty players and the limitations of pit and stage at the Provisional Theatre no doubt account for the occasional small-scale conservatism of the scoring. Even so, certain features stand out as distinct marks of his instrumental style: the use of bowed tremolo to swell sonority and add background to recitatives; the solo clarinet to suggest things Czech; the horn to evoke nature; the cymbal and bass drum to represent mob activity.

[1] In later years Smetana became conscious of this recurring feature and instructed Eliška Krásnohorská to avoid all court-room incidents in her librettos. So conscientious was she that in the case of *Vlasta* (1871) she felt it her duty to warn him that the text included his pet aversion. His reply sums up his feelings on the subject:

> I really don't know how to make judgement scenes in music any more, neither do I wish to. (Letter to Krásnohorská: January 19, 1871)

The spontaneous success which greeted *The Brandenburgers* at the beginning of 1866 did not last long. Though it was Smetana's greatest triumph to date, the patriotic zeal, youthful energy and daring originality of the score did not carry all the Prague public away. There were many who found the music heavy, Germanic in style, insufficiently nationalistic; yet it received thirteen performances up to May, 1866 (an astonishing number for a new work) before making way for another score.[2] If *The Brandenburgers* dropped from the repertoire, the fault was to some extent Smetana's own. Two months earlier he had completed *The Bartered Bride* which, after its première on May 30, eventually led to his being regarded as the founder of Czech opera. From this time he saw it as his life's task to produce the series of dramatic works which became his legacy to the nation.

[2] *The Brandenburgers in Bohemia* received twenty-six performances in Smetana's lifetime. After the first season it was played three times in 1867, three times in 1869, once in 1870, twice in 1877 and in 1880, four times.

SEVEN

'THE BARTERED BRIDE'

1866–1867

> *The Bartered Bride* is only a toy and composing it was merely child's play! I wrote it not out of ambition but simply tossed it off after *The Brandenburgers* to spite those who accused me of being Wagnerian and incapable of doing anything in a lighter vein. At the time of writing *The Bartered Bride* it was my opinion that not even Offenbach could compete with it!

SO SMETANA described his second opera on the occasion of its hundredth performance on May 5, 1882. We must allow for a little exaggeration here. The score was not written solely to placate critics who had condemned his first opera, for in one form or another *The Bartered Bride* had existed long before *The Brandenburgers of Bohemia* was staged, and some years before Smetana was publicly labelled Wagnerian.[1] In fact *The Bartered Bride* was kindled from a spark which was first struck on one of his visits to Weimar where he had become acquainted with the music of Peter Cornelius. In *Der Barbier von Bagdad* Cornelius had created something of a comic pendant to Wagner's music dramas; and impressed by this, Smetana was moved to work in the genre himself, but with less sophistication and with a more down-to-earth, even racy plot. But *Der Barbier von Bagdad* was not the only contributing factor behind *The Bartered Bride*. During his stay in Weimar in 1857 Smetana had been offended by Herbeck, the Viennese conductor, who tactlessly remarked that the Czechs, generally fine instrumentalists though they were, seemed incapable of composing scores of their own. Piqued, Smetana vowed to dedicate himself to the creation of national music.[2] Though several years had passed since Weimar, he never

[1] The campaign to tag Smetana 'Wagnerian' only began after the first night of *Dalibor* in 1867.

[2] Václav Novotný: *Memoirs and Reminiscences*.

lost sight of this promise and ten weeks after submitting *The Brandenburgers in Bohemia* to Count Harrach's Competition he noted:

> In Obříství, today I received from Sabina the text of the comic opera which so far has no name.[3]

We know little of how Sabina came to write his text, but it seems unlikely Smetana gave him any detailed instructions. When the libretto was handed to him it was but a short sketch, in German and in one act. Ferdinand Heller confirms that Sabina was paid no more than ten gulden for his plot and that Smetana began work on it almost immediately.[4] After an initial period, however, further progress became impossible: the action was too scanty, the characters too faintly sketched. Sabina was asked to rework the text, filling in detail and adding new verses for arias and choruses; but several months elapsed before Smetana saw the new two-act version. When it was returned to him it came piecemeal and in a number of differing hands; and it may well be that Sabina dictated the additions himself, for one page seems to have been written in a script resembling Betty's. Elsewhere Smetana added several verses himself and though a Czech translation was appended, notes describing the action and setting remained in German (Smetana's Czech was far from fluent at this time and a German text was a necessary guideline to all he wrote).

While Sabina was remodelling his libretto Smetana had not been idle, and during the autumn he had set to work on an overture. His usual practice was to leave this until last, but on this occasion he completely changed his course of action. In December, 1863, *Slavoj* reported:

> A comic overture by Bedřich Smetana was played on the piano to mark the thirtieth anniversary of the actor Jan Kaser at the Umělecká Beseda on November 18.

This was probably the overture to *The Bartered Bride* and though Gerald Abraham has pointed out that the performance could well have referred to the puppet play *Doktor Faust* it seems unlikely;[5] for the only overture to exist in a piano arrangement is *The Bartered Bride*, made by the composer in 1863.

There is no mention of Smetana's progress on the score until August 20, 1864, when the magazine *Národ* (No. 209) announced

[3] Smetana's Diary for July 5, 1862, records that he himself chose the title *Prodaná nevěsta* (literally *Sold Bride*) as 'the poet did not know what to call it'.
[4] Aleš Heller: *Memoirs of Ferdinand Heller*.
[5] Abraham: 'The Genesis of The Bartered Bride' in *Music and Letters* (1947); reprinted in *Slavonic and Romantic Music* (1968).

Nové české divadlo.

Dnes v neděli dne 7. května 1882.

Mimo předplacení.

Na všeobecnou žádosť

sté opakováni opery

Prodaná NEVĚSTA.

Komická zpěvohra ve třech jednáních. Slova od K. S.

Hudbu složil Bedřich Smetana. Nové ve scénu uvedl regisseur p. Hynek.

Krušina, sedlák	p. Stropnický.	Kecal, dohazovač	p. Hynek.
Ludmila, jeho manželka	pí. Fibichová.	Komediant, principal,	p. Mošna.
Mařenka, jejich dcera	sl. Sittova.	Esmeralda, jeho dcera	pí. Maislerová.
Micha, statkář	p. Koubek.	Indián, komediant druhý	p. Zápotocký.
Háta, jeho manželka	sl. z Ehrenbergů.	První } selský kluk	m. Špaček.
Vašek, jejich syn	p Krössing.	Druhý } selský kluk	m. Ryél.
Jeník, selský hoch	p. Vávra.		

Selská chasa, komedianti, kluci. Děj v čas pouti.

TANCE: V 1. jednáni „Polku tanči sl. ze Schöpfů, Zieglerova a sbor baletni. V 2. jednání „Furiant" tanči slečny Kepplerova, Zieglerova a sbor baletni. V 3. jednání „Produkce kejklířů" provedou sl. Kepplerova, Zieglerova, ze Schöpfů a sbor baletní.

Tance uspořádal baletní mistr pan Reisinger.

Pan Kolár ochuravěl, pan Čech jest churav.

Začátek v 7 h. **Konec o půl 10. h.**

Zítra v pondělí dne 8. května 1882. **153 hra v předplacení.**

Třetí pohostinská hra pana Navrátila

člena carské opery v Oděse

a

pohostinské vystoupení pana A. ZÍTKA.

Trobadour.

Knihtiskárna „Politiky" v Praze. — Nákladem vlastním.

Poster announcing the 100th performance of *The Bartered Bride* in the New Czech Theatre, Prague (May 7, 1882)

that his comic opera in two acts was complete; but there is some confusion here, because another four months were to pass before he could actually note:

> I have been working on my opera, to a text by Sabina, in two acts. I have tried to give it a popular character because the plot in which the bridegroom sells his bride is taken from village life and demands a national treatment.[6]

The *Národ* article almost certainly refers to the rough sketches which, we know Smetana brought daily to play to his friend Heller.[7] The existence of a carefully preserved manuscript piano version of *The Bartered Bride* substantiates this and suggests that it may have been composed at the keyboard. Both Heller and Smetana's housekeeper, Johanka Vaněček, confirm that this was his usual working-method, though Srb-Debrnov asserts:

> Smetana never used the piano for composition; only when the piece was finished did he sit down at the keyboard and play it. If he had to set something to music he would walk up and down . . . before beginning to write. Most of *The Bartered Bride* originated on the bank of the Vltava where the Master strolled every day towards evening. After reading Sabina's text the tunes would come into his head . . . and on arriving at his flat he would sit at the table and draft what he had thought out.[8]

We know that between 1874 and 1884 Smetana had no need to compose at the piano, for the last three operas and *Má Vlast* were written at a time when he was completely deaf. Yet the evidence of Smetana's nephew, Alexandre Kniesl, contradicts Srb's statement completely:

> He would call me, a six-year-old boy sitting on a chair, to listen. 'Do you like that?' my uncle would ask. . . . Naturally at six I had no critical judgement, but it was music and I would say 'Yes'. Yet without realizing it I was witnessing my uncle compose. On the desk lay manuscript paper, partly written on, and I saw how he would write notes in pencil with the right hand while playing with the left what he had jotted down. . . . As a child I did not pay much attention to this but I later learned from my cousin, Zdenka Smetana, that these sketches were the humble beginnings of *The Bartered Bride*.[9]

[6] Diary: December, 1864. [7] Heller: *op. cit.*
[8] Srb-Debrnov: *A Friend of Smetana tells his Story* (1945).
[9] Letter of Alexandre Kniesl: January 1, 1941.

Whatever the method, Smetana worked quickly: the pencil sketch was completed in October 1865, when it was laid on one side 'to make way for *Dalibor*'.[1] There is no other reference to *The Bartered Bride* until February, 1866, when, following the success of *The Brandenburgers in Bohemia*, Thomé, Director at the Provisional Theatre proposed mounting Smetana's new opera, and negotiated an agreement with the composer:

> I propose *The Bartered Bride* be given to me for the period that I am Director of this Theatre in Prague. I shall provide both orchestral and vocal material which shall remain my property. In return for these rights, I shall give you for the first ten performances, a fee of thirty gulden each night. The eleventh performance is to be your Benefit and you are to have one half of the gross receipts. For each of the subsequent ten performances you will receive fifteen gulden and for each of the following ten performances the fee is to be ten gulden. It is a condition of contract that you prepare and conduct the opera yourself and your advice in all matters will be valuable. Apart from performances in Prague and in Czech, I have no rights and these remain entirely yours.[2]

Encouraged by the reception which the current performances of *The Brandenburgers in Bohemia* were receiving, Smetana was prompted to demand a more realistic fee and on February 20, Thomé drew up a new contract agreeing to pay fifty gulden a night for each of the first six performances and twenty-five for the remainder. Contented, Smetana threw himself into scoring the work, which he completed on March 16. Rehearsals began at the end of April and the première was announced for May 30.

After *The Brandenburgers*, Smetana had little difficulty in recruiting the services of Eleonora Gayer von Ehrenberg to prepare the part of Mařenka and, tactfully, he invited three other principals who had sung in his first opera[3] to join the cast. But this in itself was no guarantee of success. Assuming that *The Bartered Bride* would at least equal, if not surpass *The Brandenburgers* in general acclaim and attendance, Smetana had pressed Thomé to increase his royalty from fifty gulden to a hundred for each of the first six performances. But neither composer nor Director was able to forecast public response and in the event

[1] Letter to Benecke: October 12, 1865.
[2] Contract between Thomé and Smetana: February 19, 1866.
[3] Jindřich Polák, sang Jeník, František Hynek took the part of Kecal and Josef Paleček the role of Krušina.

both men were disappointed. The Prague audience not only failed to respond to the new work, but, coming as they did from society or middle-class circles, found the plot too naïve, even too rustic. *The Bartered Bride* was, after all, one of the earliest Czech operas to be set in a village milieu where the *dramatis personae* were ordinary folk and not the conventional aristocratic characters whom the public were used to seeing on the stage. Possibly the good humoured plot in which true love overcomes all obstacles failed to win their favour, simply because it was unfamiliar and outside their experience. Whatever the reason, few bothered to attend the first night and from those who did the reception was barely luke-warm. Though not at the première himself, Srb-Debrnov questioned members of the audience as they left the theatre: 'A few praised it but most shook their heads.' he recorded;[4] and Josef Krejčí, a member of the jury in Count Harrach's Competition who knew Smetana's style well, curtly dismissed it:

> That's not a comic opera—it's a failure and will never hold its own. The opening chorus[5] is good but for the rest—I did not like it![6]

The Bartered Bride was misunderstood. Subsequent performances failed to convert the public:

> Great heat and an empty house, but recalled after each act. . . . Poor Thomé has been forced to pay me two hundred gulden out of his own pocket and receipts have failed to cover the costs. He has since asked me to terminate my contract for all further performances. . . . As he has been so considerate to me over *The Brandenburgers* I must be considerate to him. I shall do as he asks.[7]

While the first night of *The Bartered Bride* was something of a fiasco the fault was not entirely Smetana's own. By an unforunate coincidence the première had clashed with an official holiday which, by custom, was reserved for society and club outings. Furthermore, May 30 was one of the hottest days of the year: most people had made excursions into the country and the few that remained in the city refused to perspire in a hot and stuffy theatre. More serious was the political situation. Relations between Austria and Prussia had always

[4] Srb-Debrnov: *op. cit.*

[5] In his Diary Smetana noted that the opening chorus had been encored; but though he was called on stage three times after each act this was the only item to make an immediate impression.

[6] Bartoš: *Letters and Reminiscences* (1955).

[7] Diary: June, 1866.

been strained and in recent months passions had been rising. There was a deal of unrest and many feared the outbreak of war, which if it materialized, would inevitably affect Bohemia. In this tense and uneasy atmosphere *The Bartered Bride*, with its feeling of relaxed comedy, hardly stood a chance; and seventeen days after the first performance the Provisional Theatre closed its doors.

On June 16 war was declared. The campaign was short—a mere seven weeks—but bitter. The Prussians, directed by Bismarck and led by Count von Moltke, invaded Bohemia and on July 3 overwhelmingly defeated the Austrian armies at Sádová, near Hradec Králové, some sixty miles east of Prague. Austria had finally lost her hegemony in the German states to Prussia. The subsequent setting up of a dual Austro-Hungarian monarchy linking the two countries had little effect on Bohemia, which merely retained the political concessions gained in 1860. Though the Czechs had grievances with the Austrian Government, they had learnt to accept their conditions, but for the Prussians there was nothing but deep hatred. They were regarded as a greater enemy than the Hapsburgs and were traditionally loathed as the destroyers of the Slavs and the perpetrators of the rape of Silesia. It was against them that Smetana had launched his attack in *The Brandenburgers in Bohemia*; and now, fearing persecution and reprisals as the Prussians invaded Prague, he decided to leave the city. Marie Roubal, a teacher at his Institute, suggested he took refuge at her father's brewery at Nová Hut' near Beroun; and from Josef Jiránek, Smetana's eleven-year-old pupil, we learn something of the haste with which he evacuated:

> He was afraid that when the Prussians came to know he was the author of *The Brandenburgers in Bohemia* they would shoot him. Failing this he was convinced he would be placed in a labour camp, pulling down the ramparts, digging or carrying away bricks with his bare hands. With the greatest speed, therefore, all essential items including feather beds were packed into cases, and the day after the report of the battle we went to Smíchov Station. The crowds were indescribable. Everyone was moving and it was impossible to pass for cases, crates and packages . . . finally we managed to get on a train and only the cook Baruška [Pospíšil] remained in the Prague flat. When the Prussian officers were billeted there she was able to save damage and looting only by pretending the apartment was owned by some German professor or other.[8]

[8] Josef Jiránek: *Vzpomínky a Korespondence* (*Memoirs and Letters*) (1957).

Smetana stayed at Nová Hut' until the end of July when he moved to Obříství. On returning to Prague five weeks later he was surprised to find the city had changed in its attitude to the arts and to music in particular. Following the war, the numerous bodies who had previously administered the Prague theatres individually reorganized themselves on a group basis where policy was set out and governed by a co-operative movement known as Družstvo. Through friends on the Theatre Committee Smetana's name was proposed as a replacement for Maýr, and his nomination was backed by Liegert, Thomé and Skrejšovský. An election was held on September 15, and after almost five years of petitioning, Smetana attained his goal:

> It has happened! I am conductor! Skrejšovský has taken over the theatre as Director and the Committee has chosen me. It matters little that these gentlemen offer me a salary of twelve hundred gulden a year and one Benefit—altogether fourteen hundred gulden. They make excuses on the grounds that they can give me no more. . . . Later, as soon as it is at all possible, they say they will see what they can do to make it more. . . . Well we shall see. For the moment I have to be content. My duties have already begun. . . . I am engaging singers and we shall start work when we have a company.[9]

For Smetana, 1866 was one of the happiest years he was ever to know. He took up his duties on September 27 but at that time had no premonition of the hardship, conflict and misery his new position would bring. He regarded the theatre as the centre of Czech musical life and flung himself enthusiastically into rehearsing a basic repertoire. On September 28, he made his début as chief Conductor with a new production of Weber's *Der Freischütz*. Mozart's *Die Zauberflöte* followed on October 3, and Halévy's *La Juive* on October 10. Bellini's *Lucrezia Borgia* was added to the repertoire on the 14th, Rudolf Kreutzer's *Das Nachtlager von Granada* on the 21st, and on the 27th *The Bartered Bride* returned to the stage. Ten days later he directed *Il Trovatore* and on November 7 Auber's *La Muette de Portici*. Between performances he was preparing for *Guillaume Tell* (December 14) and a revival of Glinka's *A Life for the Tsar* (January 4, 1867).

Despite the care which Smetana lavished on *The Bartered Bride*, the work remained a disappointment and he now decided to reshape it in an attempt to remove certain uneven qualities in both acts. The score as it then stood differed considerably from the one we know today, and a great deal of repolishing was required before it appeared, four years

[9] Letter to Betty Smetana: September 15, 1866.

later, in its definitive form. As the work proceeded from one stage to another it inevitably became more involved in the working out and a table showing its five versions will be found in Appendix C.

In its earliest state *The Bartered Bride* was nearer operetta than comic opera. The piece was divided into two acts, and with the overture comprised twenty musical items linked by spoken dialogue. There was only one set, a village green. The original version received two performances, but for the third, which was to be given before the Emperor Franz Josef, Smetana made further alterations. Apart from reducing some of the prose between numbers the main difference concerned the couplet near the beginning of Act II. At the première, five months before, Jan Neruda had expressed doubts about the value of this duet,[1] and now, fearing its inclusion might offend the majesty of the Emperor, Smetana decided to omit it completely. Since there was no time to write an alternative he substituted the ballet music from *The Brandenburgers in Bohemia* (Act I, Scene 5), adding the descriptive title 'Gipsy Dance' at the top of the score (as the couplet had been written in C major, the ballet music in A minor, the relative minor key, probably fitted without too offensive a bump). Enterprising as Smetana's scheme was, his efforts were in vain: the Emperor, though present for part of the performance, left before the end of Act I. It was felt that the inclusion of the ballet in the second act strengthened the piece as a whole and all subsequent performances up to January 29, 1869, were given in this form, but with the couplet restored. Though the opera was played thirteen times, neither ballet nor couplet brought box office success to *The Bartered Bride*.

The next development dates from February, 1869, when Smetana had the text translated into French so that it could, as he wrote to Valentin on February 13, 'go out into the world and gain recognition beyond our frontiers and perhaps earn some money for me too'. On August 14 he dispatched the score to the Paris Opera following a recommendation by the Intendant of Prague, Dr. Rieger:

> Dr. Rieger assures me you gentlemen will be favourably disposed to protect my work and I send to your esteemed address my *Bartered Bride* and submit to accept your conditions. That is to say:
>
> (a) To divide the royalty between the Theatre and myself for a period of one year for Paris and the French provincial towns.
>
> (b) To divide the profits from sales of my score and piano reduction which you shall publish with French, German and Czech texts.

[1] See pp. 183–84 and 409–13.

To which Paris theatre this Czech Bride shall be engaged for the sophisticated and fashionable French audiences I leave entirely to your judgement.
Bedřich Smetana, Chief Conductor, Czech Theatre, Prague.

What the management of the Paris Opera thought of *The Bartered Bride* we do not know. It seems unlikely that they were impressed, for no attempt to mount the work was ever made in Smetana's lifetime. Meanwhile, Prague had received his third opera, *Dalibor*, with a blaze of enthusiasm, and though public opinion rapidly changed after the first performance Smetana decided to re-examine its unfortunate predecessor. During the autumn he reworked the score (for the third time) dividing the first act into two. Part I now ended after the Mařenka-Vašek Duet; he specified a change of scene (the Inn) for Part II, adding an exultant beer chorus by way of introduction. Thereafter Part II adhered exactly to the remaining items of the former first act finale. For Act II (which is again set on the village green) Smetana composed an original Polka to replace the 'Gipsy Music' previously borrowed from *The Brandenburgers* and this he inserted before Vašek's aria. He restored the couplet and extended Mařenka's aria 'O jaký žal' ('Oh what grief') with another section, 'Ten lásky sen' ('Dream of love'). Smetana conducted four performances of this version between January and May, 1869, but he continued to have misgivings about the score. The couplet still seemed to be a weak spot, and after the performance on Februrary 7, 1869, he removed the controversial duet for all time. Yet for Smetana the score remained flawed. The arrival of new scenery for Act I seemed to point the general weakness all the more, and for another production planned for the Novoměstské Theatre on June 1 he resolved to recast the work in three acts. In the fourth version Acts I and II correspond to the first act of Version No. 3, with the exception of a newly composed furiant which was placed next to the Polka from the previous second act to form a resounding if long, drawn out finale. Having repositioned the Polka, Smetana allowed the curtain to go up on Act III with Vašek's solo, but extended the scene with a march for the entry of the Comedians. He replaced the ill-fated couplet with a Skočná which today is known as the 'Dance of the Comedians' and thereafter Act III followed the usual pattern.

This fourth version[2] was presented nine times at the Novoměstské

[2] The fourth version was also played in Plzeň by a touring company directed by Švanda and conducted by Mořic Anger. Though the work had been well received the standard of performance had not been outstanding and Smetana noted as much in his Diary on November 9, 1869.

Theatre between June, 1869, and August, 1870, and it is unlikely Smetana would have revised the score again had he not received an invitation from Eduard Nápravník, Conductor at the Maryinsky Theatre in St. Petersburg, to send *The Bartered Bride* to Russia for consideration. Smetana complied, but Nápravník was unconvinced:

> As you know the public here does not like Russian opera with spoken dialogue and I'm sure there would be great difficulty in presenting your *Bartered Bride* in this form. It would first be necessary for you to replace the prose with newly composed recitatives and send them on later.[3]

Smetana did not respond immediately to Nápravník's request; for on May 11 he received a second letter from Russia, this time written by the bass, Josef Paleček:

> Please send as soon as possible the score and piano reduction of *The Bartered Bride* to the Director of the Maryinsky Theatre.... For the recitatives, I hardly dare advise you, but I speak for us all when I say it would be to our advantage if they were not of a *secco* variety but, in some places, especially for Kecal, of an accompanied type, like those for Falstaff in Nicolai's *Lustigen Weiber von Windsor*. At the same time I beg you not to make them too short in duration. I would remind you that it is the custom here for the opera to last more than three hours. Failing this the management will consider *The Bartered Bride* a 'small' work and will place another opera alongside it in the same evening, thus causing the percentage to be drastically reduced.

The promise of one production abroad was hardly likely to make Smetana take up his pen on a score which had already caused him enormous pains. Surely there was another reason. When reviewing the first performance of the opera, the Prague critic Otakar Hostinský had suggested that *The Bartered Bride* would be enormously enhanced if the spoken dialogue were to be replaced by musical recitative.[4] Whether the incentive came from Hostinský, from Nápravník or from Smetana himself is doubtful. All that is certain is that in July he began work on the score for the fifth time. He started by writing the additions in a three stave piano arrangement which, when orchestrated, was inserted into his own full score at a cost of thirty-seven gulden.[5] The Czech text was translated into Russian in August

[3] Letter from Nápravník to Smetana: April 21, 1870.

[4] *Dalibor*: June 10, 1869.

[5] In the manuscript full score the Czech version of the recitatives are written in black ink, while below a German translation is added in red.

and a duplicate score made in September; but before sending it to St. Petersburg he decided to test its practicability and on September 25 conducted a performance in the Provincial Theatre, not only with sung recitatives but with the Furiant repositioned as the second number of Act II. In its fifth version *The Bartered Bride* began to attract larger audiences. The public responded to the gay and colourful score and Sabina boasted that he would have provided a more accomplished libretto had he known what Smetana was finally to make of his feeble text.

While Prague was warming to *The Bartered Bride*, St. Petersburg was less appreciative. The opera was given there on January 11, 1871, but its reception was far from favourable. Though Smetana had received a congratulatory telegram[6] after the first night, this was little more than courtesy, for general opinion in Russia was negative. Professor A. S. Fanitsin writing in the St. Petersburg *Muzikalny Sezon* described the work as

> ... approaching the genre of Offenbach with whom Mr. Smetana could not otherwise be compared in piquancy or originality of motives.

Smetana was deeply hurt by this remark, as he was by others reprinted in *Hudební Listy*. At heart he held Balakirev, the Russian composer, responsible for inciting feeling against *The Bartered Bride*. Relations between the two composers had not been good and now they were barely on nodding terms. Balakirev had never forgiven Smetana for his alleged attempts to sabotage the Prague performances of Glinka's *A Life for the Tsar* and *Ruslan and Ludmila* in January and February, 1867. His animosity towards the Czech composer is well known,[7] and Balakirev could easily have been instrumental in inciting feeling in his turn. It is unlikely, however, that he allowed his personal enmity to influence his musical judgement or that he shared the views of Hostinský who described the Russian performance as 'banal, common and ordinary', declaring it to be no better than the work of a gifted fourteen-year-old boy.[8] History has proved *The Bartered Bride* to be far more than this, and while the plot revolves on an almost Gilbertian legal twist, the characters are

[6] This telegram arrived on the morning of January 12 signed by Paleček: Splendid success of *The Bartered Bride*. Overture and every number applauded. Polka repeated. Nobility present: heir-apparent Konstantin, Grand Duke Vladimir, Nikolay, Grand Duchess. Highest prize. Packed to overflowing. Benefits, wreaths. Repeat Friday. Glory yours!

[7] See Chapter 9, pp. 209–10. [8] *Hudební Listy*: February 15, 1871.

real and their predicaments serious. *The Bartered Bride* is not *opera buffa* but *opera semi-seria*, a pastoral *Figaro* rather than a boisterous *Barbiere*.

The Bartered Bride has such impetus and spontaneity that it is hard to believe it was not created in one period and without interruption. Despite its chequered origins, some of the thematic material dates from the time when Smetana was completing *The Brandenburgers in Bohemia*. As early as October, 1862, he noted in his motive book the bars which were to become the basis of the opening chorus. Now there would appear to be nothing unusual about this, except that in the margin are written the words 'chorus to comedy' which suggests he had a comic work in mind long before Sabina's text existed. Two other ideas jotted in the motive book also furnished useful material for the score: an eight-bar rocking phrase dated May 13, 1863, was eventually placed in the first act Mařenka-Jeník duet; and a nineteen-bar fragment in A major dated September, 1864, was incorporated into the third act duet for Esmeralda and the principal comedian. But Smetana also drew on earlier ideas. From the piano suite *Wedding Scenes*, written in 1849, he extracted the polka melody in the third movement ('Wedding Festivity') and inserted it note-for-note into the opening chorus between bars 10–75 and 443–460. Here it is used rather like the waltz in Weber's *Der Freischütz*—as an invitation to dance. The same chorus also betrays another influence: the beseda. The beseda,[9] a ball-room dance similar to the lancer, won enormous popularity at the Prague Národní Beseda on January 16, 1864, when Heller and Smetana with their wives had attended the first public performance. According to Heller, Smetana was so enthusiastic about the new dance that he conscientiously attempted to incorporate it into his new opera.[1]

As had been the case in *The Brandenburgers*, Smetana builds *The Bartered Bride* on a number of simple but characteristic motives of which only three are heard in the overture. This can be explained because it was written some months before the bulk of the score and at a time when Smetana had formulated few definite ideas for the principal characters. The themes which appear there are associated with Kecal, his contract and Jeník (see Example 35 on next page). For the rest, Smetana is content to let the piece set the scene. It bubbles over with good humour and exuberant vitality and in its

[9] Beseda means party or club house, and the dance, which was designed by Karel Link with music by Heller, took its name from the social gathering where it was performed.

[1] Aleš Heller: *Memoirs of Ferdinand Heller*.

Josef Wenzig

Eliška Krásnohorská

Karel Sabina

PLATE XIII. Smetana's librettists

The Bartered Bride, 1882

The Kiss, 1876

PLATE XIV. Early stage sets

Example 35 (*a*)

Vivacissimo

(*b*)

(*c*)

brilliant, inexhaustible energy is not far removed from the overtures to Mozart's *Figaro* and *Die Zauberflöte*.[2] It is the musical analogue of what Smetana's contemporary, Josef Mánes, was depicting in his colourful paintings based on rustic life and what Božena Němcová[3]

[2] It is particularly in the rapid violin movement, with its light contrapuntal lines and canonic imitations, that *The Bartered Bride* overture resembles those of Mozart.

[3] Božena Němcová (1820–1862) was one of the most important writers of the Romantic revival. In her poems and novels she described the folk rites and customs observed on her travels throughout Bohemia and Slovakia. Most of her folk tales are set against a background of village life and tradition and are almost ethnographic sketches or direct recordings of folk narratives. Her most important work is *Babička* (1855), subtitled *Pictures of Country Life*, which became the prototype of a long series of village novels in Czech literature.

was describing in her folk novels. Each in his own way was contributing to national art.

Apart from the ideas announced in the overture there are three other motives which have specific connexions: the first represents faithful love, and the second and third depict Mařenka herself:

Example 36 (*a*)

(*b*)

(*c*)

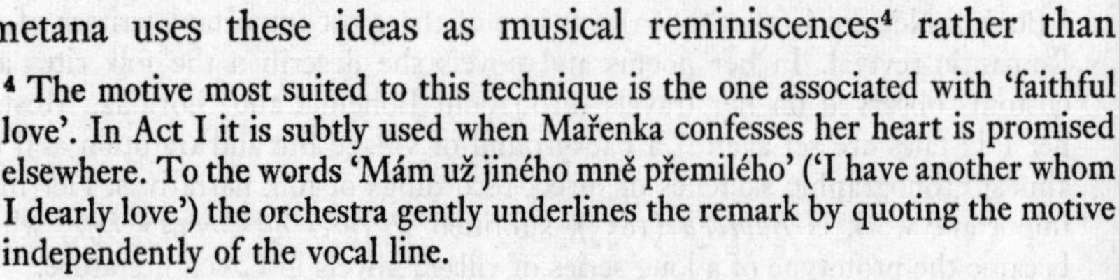

Smetana uses these ideas as musical reminiscences[4] rather than

[4] The motive most suited to this technique is the one associated with 'faithful love'. In Act I it is subtly used when Mařenka confesses her heart is promised elsewhere. To the words 'Mám už jiného mně přemilého' ('I have another whom I dearly love') the orchestra gently underlines the remark by quoting the motive independently of the vocal line.

fully worked out symbolic *Leitmotive* and in so doing remains closer to the French school of opera than to Wagner's. One could hardly expect weighty and dignified thematic transformations in a work that in its first draft purported to be little more than an operetta. Although some of the music has a Rossinian patter, there is little in the way of characterization. Mícha, Háta and Krušina remain conventional operatic parents, appearing only in pairs or ensembles and rarely coming to life on their own account. Ludmila is the exception. Smetana endows her with distinct marks which cast her as a particular type: the easy-going mother, concerned for her daughter's happiness, she directly anticipates another figure, Martinka in the opera *The Kiss*, and the melodic lines with which he invests both characters are very similar.

The troupe of travelling players, though they make an amusing diversion in the third act, remain little more than penny-plain figures and neither the principal comedian nor Esmeralda break through their theatrical masks. From the first sketches of the score (preserved in the Smetana Museum in Prague) it seems likely that both characters were conceived as non-singing roles: the second act begins with Vašek's lament and leads directly to the ensemble 'Aj, Jakže jakže!' ('He does not want her!') without music for either of the players. From the same sketch we can see it is the person of Kecal who dominates the opera and of all the characters he is the most colourfully realized. In the first draft he remained unnamed and is referred to simply as Dohazovač (Broker), sometimes abbreviated to 'Doh'. This jabbering braggart (could the Baron in Cimarosa's *Matrimonio Segreto* have been Smetana's model?) is typified in continuous quaver movement often on consecutive degrees of the scale or on notes of the triad. Significantly, he never sings the bustling motive that is associated with him or his marriage contract. Instead, at his first entrance he is given a series of octave leaps and elsewhere a number of busy rhythmic units that move sideways by semi-tones. Smetana depicts his pig-headed insistence by a four-fold repeated sequence which becomes one of his most prominent musical characteristics (see Example 37 overleaf).

Kecal's rapid patter songs are invariably in a major key and even at the point of his discomforture in Act III his music remains firmly anchored around F major. But it is in the flexible recitatives of the fifth version that he is seen as a loquacious bumbler. For the most part the quaver movement persists, but in the finale of Act II the lines take on a pompous nature as quavers are replaced by minims; and in Act III (Scene 4) at a reference to the marriage contract his

Example 37

music takes up a motive from *Das Rheingold* used by Wagner to symbolize the contract of the Giants:

Example 38

Smetana

Wagner

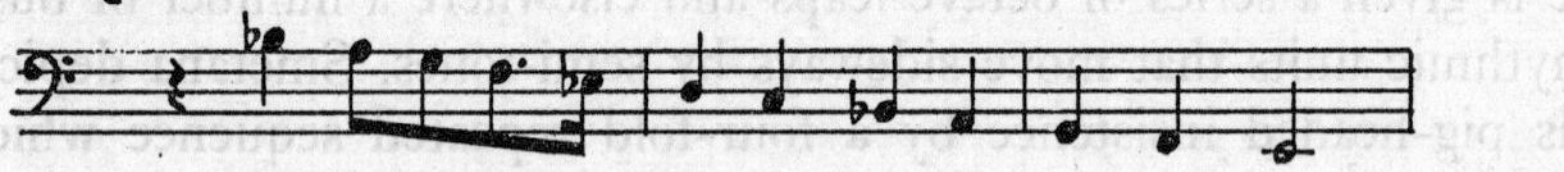

After Kecal it is Jeník and Mařenka who are the most memorably depicted. As hero and heroine they have well defined personalities, drawn on Mozartian lines, combining both humour and seriousness. Mařenka could almost pass for Smetana's country cousin: their natures sometimes spirited, sometimes stubborn, are very close. Mařenka's temperament is shown in the delightful vocal flourishes, the *coloratura* runs and sustained high notes with which Smetana endows her part. She loves life, has common sense and remains thoroughly credible throughout. Her music is associated with B flat, the key of her first aria, and the motive of 'faithful love'; and her lyrical melodies, accompanied by a flowing movement in thirds and sixths, tend to hover around the first degrees of the scale:

Example 39

Occasionally her song-like lines have a distinct folk flavour (the irregular three-bar phrase lengths of her first aria are especially typical) and though she never sings an actual folk melody, as does the heroine in *The Kiss*,[5] she is the figure upon whom, some nine years later, Smetana was to model Vendulka.

Similarly, Jeník is the prototype of Lukáš, his counterpart in *The Kiss*. Both men have the same ambition, to win their sweetheart one way or another. Jeník is a good-hearted fellow whose phrases reflect his confident, forthright and vigorous character. His enterprising nature is matched by music of great inventiveness and his presence is felt by a simple harmonic progression, the so-called 'horn passage' the interval of a sixth, followed by a fifth and then by a third. This is heard beneath his first utterance and returns sufficiently often to be regarded as a subsidiary motive. His music favours G minor (the relative minor of Mařenka's B flat), but when he outwits Kecal, Smetana swings into the major (G and C) to point the moment of triumph.

His step-brother Vašek is more than a humorous foil and is depicted simultaneously as a comic and pathetic character. This dual personality allows Smetana to create a double musical image in which

[1] See Chapter 12, pp. 313–14.

Vašek becomes the object of ridicule and the subject of pity. Again there is no characteristic motive, and again the composer depends on a simple key change to describe the two sides of the coin—major for humour, minor for sorrow; yet though the idea is well-worn there is a light and assured touch which ideally epitomizes the gauche, tongue-tied bridegroom-to-be who has never been into a tavern in his life because his mother's apron strings have never before stretched that far:

Example 40

Vašek's impediment provides ample opportunity for definite musical description; and though Smetana may not have been the first to use a stammer[6] in music, he is successful in providing effective stuttering phrases which never wear thin. Consequently, the inarticulate Vašek is given lines which are sometimes more rhythmic than lyrical and in his Act II duet with Mařenka it is the orchestra that provides the flowing melody, not the singers. Instead he is given a number of irregular staccato patterns anchored on a monotone that erratically flower into a melismatic phrase. Like Kecal's part, this is written in notes of predominantly short value, favouring semi-quaver units. Similarly there are cadential repetitions which probably stem from a knowledge of folk idiom. That Vašek's stuttering music caused Smetana considerable thought we know from an examination of the

[6] Could the musical stammer which Mozart gives Don Curzio in *Figaro* have been Smetana's model for Vašek?

original draft. Certainly the end result was only arrived at after a deal of trial and error. The pencil sketch of his first aria illustrates how different it was in its first form:

Example 41

This opening phrase was abandoned after ten bars or so but elsewhere the sketches, which sometimes look like written improvisations, show interesting variations. The sextet in Act III (was the sextet in *Don Giovanni* the model for this?) began life as an ensemble for 'Mícha, Háta, Vaš, Kruš and Doh' (the direction written in the margin in Smetana's hand). (See Example 42 (a), (b).)

Example 42 (*a*)

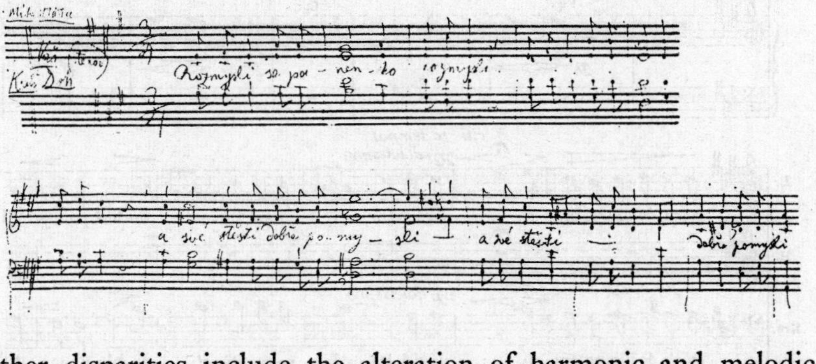

Other disparities include the alteration of harmonic and melodic detail but, generally, Smetana tried to keep his rhythmic patterns constant. In Act III (Scene 9) where the chorus of villagers sing the words 'Jak jsi se, Mařenko, rozmyslila mluv' ('Mařenka have you made up your mind, speak'), he originally produced a simple, direct setting but later revisions and a change of key resulted in the transformations shown in Example 43, pp. 181–8.

Example 42 (b)

Lento, ma non troppo ♩= 63
LUDMILA
pp dolce
ben cantando
Rozmysli si, Ma-
HÁTA
KRUŠINA
pp dolce
Rozmysli si, Ma-
KECAL
pp dolce
Rozmysli si, Ma-
Lento, ma non troppo ♩= 63
p
L.
řen - ko, rozmysli, rozmysli si, Ma - řen - ko, rozmysli, na své
H.
pp
Rozmysli_ si! rozmysli_ si,
Kru.
řen - ko, rozmysli, rozmysli si, Ma - řen - ko, rozmysli, na své
K.
řen - ko, rozmysli, rozmysli si, Ma - řen - ko, rozmysli, na své
Fag.
p
Cor.
p
sf
rit.
[a tempo]
pp dolcissimo
L.
štěstí do - bře po - my - sli,_ na své ště - stí, na své ště - stí_ do - bře po - my - sli!
H.
Kru.
pp dolcissimo
štěstí do - bře po - my - sli, na své ště - stí, na své ště - stí do - bře po - my - sli!
Mí.
rit.
pp dolcissimo
K.
štěstí do - bře po - my - sli, na své ště - stí, na své ště - stí do - bře po - my - sli!
[a tempo]
rit.
pp dolcissimo

Example 43

(*a*)

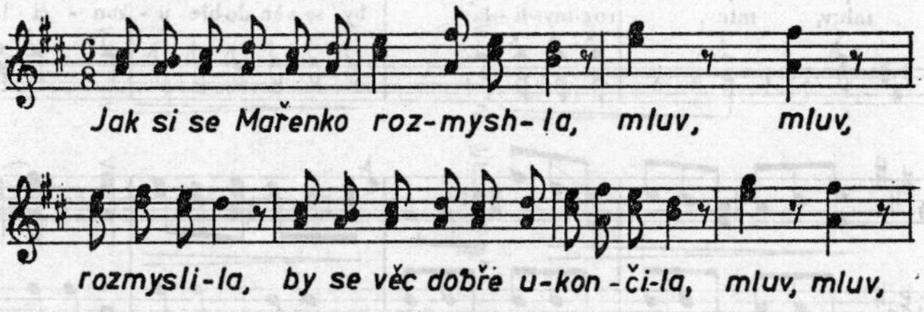
Jak si se Mařenko roz-mysh-la, mluv, mluv,
rozmysli-la, by se věc dobře u-kon-či-la, mluv, mluv,

(*b*)

(*c*)

Allegro vivo
SBOR
S.
A.
Jak jsi se,Ma-řen-ko, roz-mys-li - la? Mluv! mluv! roz-mys-li - la,
T.
B.

Example 44

(a)

(b)

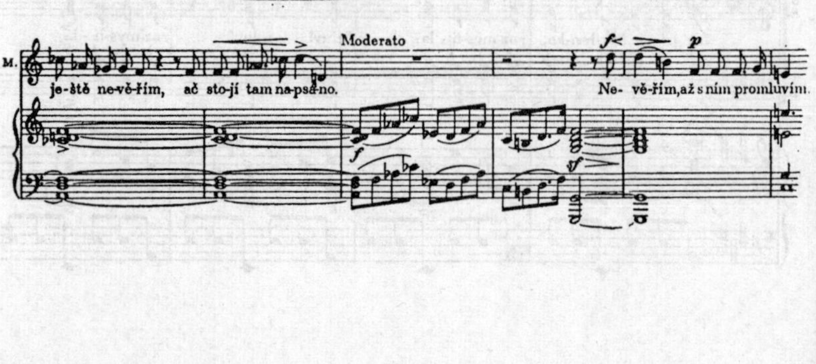

Other numbers were similarly affected. Mařenka's Act I aria 'Kyd bych se cos takového' ('If I should ever learn something like that about you'), without introduction in the first draft, was later altered and her 'O jaký žal' ('Oh, what grief'), the first phrase of which initially encompassed a diminished fifth, was later expanded to cover a tenth to make the part more easily singable. (See Example 44 on previous page.)

Most of the alterations are relatively small, second thoughts perhaps to improve melody or harmony; but the sketch does reveal an instance where the composer changed his entire conception. In the Mařenka-Jeník duet 'Jako matka požehnáním' '(While a mother's love means blessing') only the text and key remain common to first draft and final version:

Example 45

(*a*)

Despite various revisions in the arias, the choruses and ensembles remained virtually untouched, and it is in these sections rather than in the solos that Smetana's growth as an operatic composer can best be measured. Where the choruses in *The Brandenburgers* were often independent numbers placed on to a musical canvas, in *The Bartered Bride* they are far more integrated. There is a sense of progression, a continuity of ideas, a flow of dramatic action accompanied by a musical impetus which finds its resolution in the finales to each act. Here Smetana comes close to the finales of Mozart's *Figaro*, and though the two works are separated by eighty years it is upon Mozart's masterpiece that *The Bartered Bride* is modelled.

Apart from the numerous pieces of dance music which are obviously missing from the first version of the sketch, the most serious omission is the couplet for Esmeralda and the principal comedian which was originally placed at the start of Act II. Recently the manuscript of the orchestral score of this couplet has come to light among the composer's papers in Prague, and it is reproduced in Appendix D. This discovery allows us to assess the value of the duet which caused so much uncertainty in Smetana's mind and a deal of controversy at its first performance. Though on a low literary level, it is hard to understand how the text could have caused so much offence.

Verse I — One chap acts like a hypocrite and rolling his eyes up and down,
Tries to hoodwink the crowd!
Another chap looks as if he's got thousands in his pockets.
Though he's got horses and servants at home he's got mostly debts all around!

Chorus — Thus everywhere behind a masque another face is hidden
Thus everywhere before the world it's only a comedy that is given!

Verse II — Though many sit at home caressing their wives all day,
others on the streets start chasing the chicks away.
Look, over there's a blockhead rubbing himself with polish,
and over there's another who thinks that pince-nez's a sign of culture!

Chorus — Thus everywhere behind a masque another face is hidden
Thus everywhere before the world it's only a comedy that is given!

(*b*)

The couplet runs to fifty bars, and being in C major we can appreciate how the A minor ballet music from *The Brandenburgers* fitted on to it. Unfortunately the piece is neither as accomplished nor as attractive as the duet which now stands in its place, but it is nevertheless interesting, not least for the five-bar phrase structure which introduces each verse. Melodically it is playful and makes an excellent companion-piece to Esmeralda's 'Milostné zviřátko' ('We shall make a pretty little bear of you'). The delightful imitation between the parts is typical of the composer and might have been written under the sign of Offenbach. There is no suggestion of folk idiom anywhere in the piece and the only trace of folk element in the opera, apart from a *dudy*-like drone in the opening chorus and an occasional pentatonic flavouring in the melody, is to be found in the Polka, Furiant and Skočná. Of these only the Furiant is based on a traditional folk melody, 'Sedlák, sedlák, ještě jednou,'[8] though it is unlikely that the folk of Smetana's day had ever heard it harmonized quite as chromatically as this:

Example 46

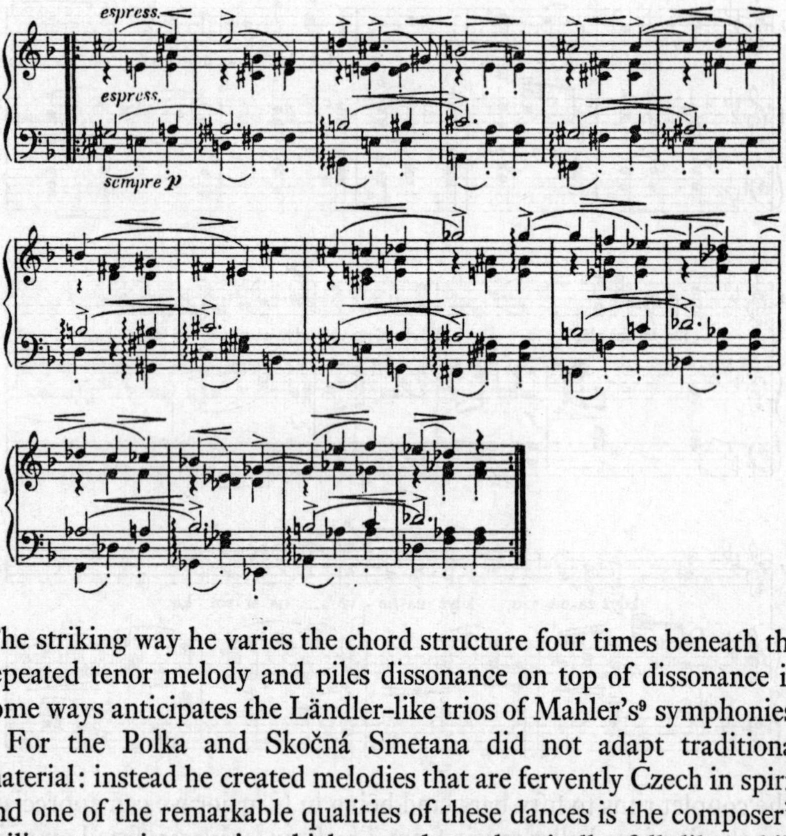

The striking way he varies the chord structure four times beneath the repeated tenor melody and piles dissonance on top of dissonance in some ways anticipates the Ländler-like trios of Mahler's[9] symphonies.

For the Polka and Skočná Smetana did not adapt traditional material: instead he created melodies that are fervently Czech in spirit and one of the remarkable qualities of these dances is the composer's ability to write music which sounds authentically folk-like while springing from his own pen. Though he had written numerous Polkas before, they all fell into one of two types—the social ball-room dance

[8] Erben: *Nápěvy prostonárodních písní Českých* (1862).

[9] Mahler, who was Bohemian by birth (1860), had a deep admiration for Smetana's work. He introduced *Dalibor* to the repertoire of the Vienna Opera shortly after his appointment as Director there. He knew and loved *Má Vlast*, and *Tábor* and *Blaník* may well have inspired parts of the Sixth Symphony.

or the characteristic piano composition reflecting some personal whim or suhjective idea. In *The Bartered Bride* Smetana writes a piece that belongs to neither of the above groups. The Polka in Act I becomes a whirling village dance for mass merrymaking by country-folk, a transformation of the folk dances he may have witnessed as a boy in Růžková Lhotice. It was certainly in this district that he became acquainted with groups of itinerant musicians whom he portrays in the Skočná ('The Dance of the Comedians'). From the same region he drank deep of the rustic streams of a language that was the very essence of the Bohemian ethos; and in this lies his greatest strength. Few people, however, realized that Smetana was speaking to them about their own countryside, and his first audiences failed to appreciate the obvious features of the landscape. Despite its uncertain start, *The Bartered Bride* has become Smetana's most successful work. He conducted it forty-nine times himself and lived to see the hundred and seventeenth performance in Prague; but paradoxically it was its very popularity which proved to be Smetana's downfall. Within a few years it had overshadowed his other operas and so charmed the public that they failed to respond to the later scores which he himself felt to be among the most significant contributions to Czech music. Such a work was *Dalibor*, the composition of which overlapped that of *The Bartered Bride*.

EIGHT

'DALIBOR'
1867–1868

SMETANA BEGAN THE sketches for *Dalibor* on April 15, 1865, while scoring *The Bartered Bride* and waiting for an opportunity to mount *The Brandenburgers in Bohemia*. At a time when he had little hope of seeing these operas staged it is remarkable that he should have been preparing a third, belonging to neither the historic nor comic types in which the previous works are cast. This outburst of creative activity cannot easily be explained. For Smetana it was part of an inevitable process in his musical development: he seems to have been driven by some inner force to produce work after work no matter what became of them. *Dalibor* is important not because it is his first tragic opera but because its dramatic expression shows a marked advance on the earlier scores before he had had the opportunity of putting to the test, through actual stage presentation, the effectiveness of his dramatic ideas.

The opera is based on an event linked with one of the towers of Prague Castle called Daliborka and the legend,[1] which was well known in Smetana's day, became the basis of a freely arranged libretto by the poet and writer Josef Wenzig (1807–1876). A German by birth, Wenzig was Director and founder of one of the first technical schools in Prague. He was a teacher of history but became more widely known as an advocate of equality of Czech and German languages, being one of the foremost figures in the nineteenth-century Czech renaissance movement. As President of the Umělecká Beseda he had made Smetana's acquaintance in 1863 and had invited him to read his treatment of *Dalibor* some time towards the end of 1864. How quickly the opera grew is not known (the diaries are less informative on this work than they are about *The Bartered Bride*); for of the pencil sketches, only the first act and the beginning of the second have been pre-

[1] The composer F. B. Knott (1808–1884) had set the subject as an opera in 1846 and some six years earlier George Sand had based her novel *Consuelo* on the same legend, though the hero is interned not in a tower but a subterranean cave.

served. The pages contain no dates, and the only indication we have of Smetana's rate of progress is to be found in his correspondence:

> I am working at the opera, *Dalibor*. The text is really excellent and one for which a composer can be grateful. The poet is Wenzig—Councillor to the Ministry of Education.[2]

By October 12 he was able to report the completion of the Act I sketch in a letter to Fröjda Benecke; and by the following April, so he told her, he was well advanced in drafting the second. Little else is known about the composition apart from the dates on which he finished the scoring of the individual acts—I: September 15, 1866; II: October 24, 1867; III: December 29, 1867.

Ervín Špindler[3] had been invited to make a Czech version of the text (as with all his poems, Wenzig wrote it in German) but the original remained Smetana's guideline as it had in *The Bartered Bride*. In this case, however, he placed more dependence on it, scribbling occasional German phrases under the vocal line, but in a different coloured ink. It may well be that he was counting on the opera being produced abroad, and he suggested as much in the letter to Valentin referred to above; yet this must have been a distant hope when neither of his previous operas had been staged, even in Prague. Inexplicably, the German text, which was never wholly continuous, breaks off two-thirds of the way through Act I[4] and thereafter only Czech is used, even for the stage directions. At first Smetana had reservations about the poem, but having identified himself with its powerful and tragic possibilities he threw himself into composition with enormous energy. On completing the score, he looked for a chance to mount *Dalibor* and the occasion of the laying of the foundation stone of the National Theatre, on May 16, 1868, offered a most appropriate opportunity. As he wrote to Valentin on February 13, he planned to present the work as a 'gala with the best cast available'. He was to rehearse and conduct himself, and Josef Kolář was to produce.

During the four years in which the Provisional Theatre had operated, many shortcomings on the stage and in the pit had become apparent; and the Czechs had always dreamt of the day when the wooden building on the site of the old Salt House would be replaced by a permanent one more suited to be the home of Czech music and

[2] Letter to J. P. Valentin: April 20, 1865.

[3] Špindler (1843–1918) was a politician and writer who also provided the Czech version of Smetana's fourth opera *Libuše*. His translation of Wenzig's text was made and delivered in instalments.

[4] In Dalibor's solo (bar 608 of the final version).

Poster announcing the première of *Dalibor* in the New Town Theatre, Prague (May 16, 1868)

drama. The collecting of funds had never ceased. Smetana had organized numerous concerts himself to raise sufficient money to buy land for the new building. A willing architect had been found in the person of Karel Liebscher, who during 1867 had prepared proposals for a magnificent modern theatre on the banks of the Vltava, adjacent to the Provisional Theatre.[5] Liebscher's plan was to erect the new Theatre backing directly onto the existing house so that both buildings could be joined and utilized. Early in 1868 the ground was pegged out.

As the arrangements went ahead for the ceremony of laying the foundation stone, Smetana became deeply excited and his creative faculties were stimulated accordingly. For all Czechs May 16 promised to be a memorable day; for Smetana, however, it was not just another solemn formality but a significant event, unique in the history of the nation. Naturally he was stirred by the implications, and responded characteristically by writing a relatively short, but extraordinarily expressive piece to mark the occasion.

[5] Originally the Theatre Committee attempted to acquire the land on which the Slavia Café stands today.

The *Slavnostní předehra* (*Festive Overture in C*), completed six days before its performance, is distinguished by a grandeur and power seldom felt in Smetana's previous works. The grave yet calm opening builds through stirring string sequences and blazing trumpet fanfares to a triumphant C major climax with massive pillars of sound that thrust their way through the orchestra like the very supports of the National Theatre itself. Here Smetana anticipates the monumentality of *Libuše* and creates a musical landmark to commemorate a moment of history. For the Czechs the foundation stone of the new Theatre was more than a marker: it was the root of the spiritual and cultural independence of the nation and the official ceremony found them united as a vast movement for the revival of music and literature.

The proceedings on the morning of May 16 began with a procession in which a thousand people drawn from guilds, societies, choral and student unions, marched to the accompaniment of bands towards the site of the new theatre. Here more than sixty thousand guests from the Slav countries were gathered to witness the ceremony. Among the foremost men who approached the foundation stone was Smetana, the representative of his country's music. As he performed the symbolic act of driving the stone into the earth with ceremonial trowel and mallet he delivered the slogan: 'In music is the life of the Czechs'. The festive morning mood in which the people of Prague manifested their spiritual awareness of nationhood was carried over into the evening performance at the vast Novoměstské Theatre where the *Festive Overture* was heard for the first time. Next was performed an allegory called *Libušin soud* (*Libuše's Judgement*), devised from the medieval manuscript of Zelená Hora, the climax of which was a dramatic apotheosis and a vision of the future National Theatre. Finally there followed the première of Smetana's new opera *Dalibor*.

On May 17, the *Festive Overture* was repeated in the same theatre but this time by Karel Bendl, who directed a mixed programme presented by the massed Prague choral societies, including the first performance of Smetana's new male-voice chorus *Rolnická* (*The Peasant*). To words of Václav Trnobranský he composed a panegyric to the Czech farmer and the countryside that was his home, and though he was probably unaware of it, he was expressing sentiments similar to those which Vivaldi had celebrated in *The Seasons*. The text, which is notable for its descriptive qualities, had a special significance at this time when rural areas were being liberated from the feudal law and serfdom that had suppressed the people for centuries. *The Peasant*, which is programmatically conceived as a musical evocation of the Czech patriot faithful to his country, falls into four main sections, each corresponding to a season of the year. There is also a coda which incorporates material from the previous parts. The first describes ploughing in springtime; the second, an impressive scherzo, depicts the reaper harvesting his crop; part three paints a colourful picture of threshers at work; while in the final section Smetana underlines the farmer's loyalty to his country, even in the hardships of a cruel winter. Technically, the music is on a high level and the contrasting season and moods are skilfully suggested by subtle variations of basic tonalities (A major for spring; D major for summer; G major for autumn and A major for winter). *The Peasant* develops the rich, lyrical choruses in *The Brandenburgers* and *The Bartered Bride*, and is imaginatively worked out with delightful pictorial touches. Indeed, the writing in Part III is virtually onomatopoeic in the sharp rhythmic ostinatos that admirably convey the sound of flails:

Example 47

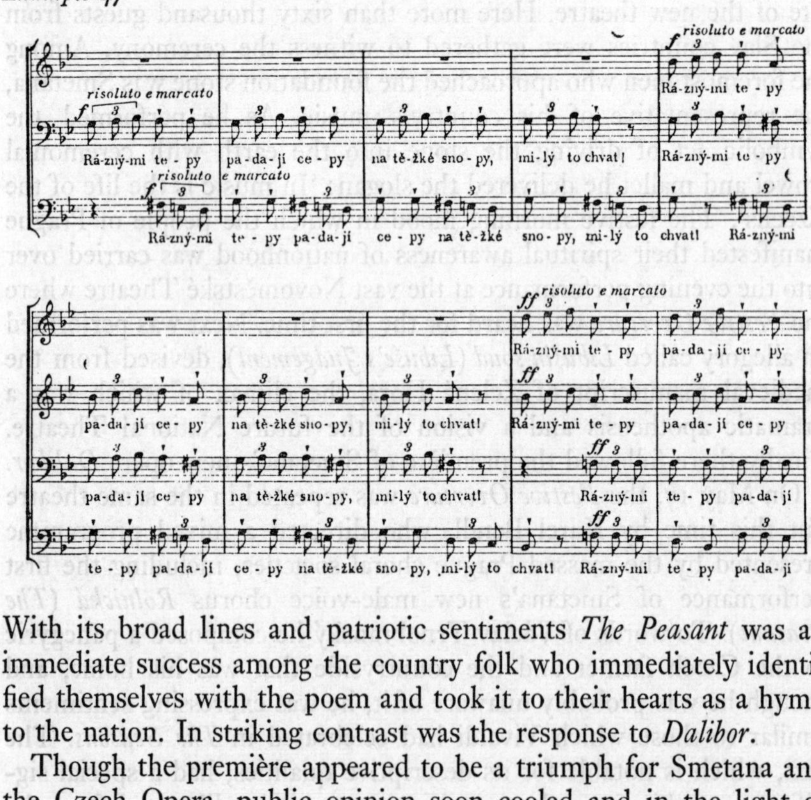

With its broad lines and patriotic sentiments *The Peasant* was an immediate success among the country folk who immediately identified themselves with the poem and took it to their hearts as a hymn to the nation. In striking contrast was the response to *Dalibor*.

Though the première appeared to be a triumph for Smetana and the Czech Opera, public opinion soon cooled and in the light of subsequent performances he realized that the score was not the success it had appeared to be. Doubts, encouraged by a hostile press, grew into vicious attacks. Against a strong political background

Smetana was accused, tried and found guilty of Wagnerian associations, and the fact that *Dalibor* is taken from legend, albeit Czech, was enough to condemn him for contaminating national art with Germanic novelties. These reproaches[6] were not so much caused by a lack of understanding of Smetana's music as by a spiteful retaliation campaign on the part of Mayŕ, Rieger and Pivoda. Affairs were aggravated by Smetana's supporters whose defence of their champion overemphasized his progressiveness. They were biased in their valuation of Wagnerism as the only possible basis of modern opera. In fact Smetana's relationship with Wagner was never as close as it was with Liszt. The two composers had not even met:

> I am now rather sorry I am not in closer contact with Wagner. But knowing the stories about his overbearing and rude behaviour towards the musical world with the exception of Liszt, I did not care to become acquainted with him, indeed I avoided it on every occasion for I am also sensitive and cannot stand rudeness. Thus I have never met Wagner personally. I do know his wife, however, but am sure she is too proud to put in a word for such an unimportant artist as I doubtless am in her eyes.[7]

Despite this Smetana had an enormous respect for Wagner as a musician and had become acquainted with his works at the earliest opportunity.[8] In 1857 he had conducted excerpts from *Tannhäuser* and *Lohengrin* in Göteborg; and in 1859 he had heard the first performance of the Prelude to *Tristan und Isolde* in Weimar. Although he never conducted any of the music dramas himself, he was certainly aware of Wagner's activities and followed his work with considerable interest and understanding. In 1870 he travelled to Munich to attend performances of *Das Rheingold* and *Die Walküre* in the company of Liszt; in 1871 he returned to Munich to hear *Tristan*, and later the same year went to the German Theatre in Prague in order to hear *Die Meistersinger*.

Sympathies apart, the two men could not have been more diametrically opposed and the only feature which they had in common was the use of the *Leitmotiv*. Even here, however, the idea of representing a character or object by a musical theme was known long before

[6] See also Chapter 10, page 233.

[7] Letter to Bendl: July 24, 1875.

[8] *Tannhäuser*, the first Wagner opera to be given in Prague at the Stavovské Divadlo on November 25, 1854, was followed by *Lohengrin* (February 23, 1856) and *Der fliegende Holländer* (September 7, 1856). In each case Škroup was the conductor.

Wagner. The technique of musical reminiscence had been practised in the French and Italian schools for many years and had been incorporated into the orchestral works of Berlioz and Liszt with considerable success. Wagner had adopted the principle as a basis of his music dramas, and though Smetana was not consciously creating music dramas *per se* he did employ a system of motive working, similar to Wagner's, which in *Dalibor* dominates the score far more than anything in *The Brandenburgers* or *The Bartered Bride*. In Smetana's operas the motive is never used as subtly nor with such sophistication as in Wagner's. Neither does it assume a symbolic significance because Smetana regards it purely as a means of identification and little else. In *Dalibor*, however, he introduces a technique of thematic transformation which makes the score apparently the most Wagnerian in his output; so much so that critics argued it had become a 'monothematic' opera since the bulk of the musical texture can be seen to be drawn from one basic motive. It was this aspect of the score which Smetana's adversaries seized as ammunition for their attack and which led them to castigate the opera as turbulent, boisterous, passionate and insufficiently Czech. Instead of echoes of folk song they heard only strains of Wagner and their negative and condemnatory tone soon made its influence felt on the public. A second hearing on May 29, 1868 was poorly attended: three repeat performances in October fared no better, and even the presence of the Emperor on June 28, 1869,[9] failed to make the opera a triumph. In July, 1869, *Dalibor* disappeared from the repertoire and was not revived again until Smetana chose it for his Benefit[1] on December 2, 1870. For this occasion he revised certain sections of the score, making substantial cuts in Act II and reworking the close of Act III. But he was no more successful in placating hostile criticism than before. The opera failed to make any notable impression and was withdrawn after the sixth performance. The composer was never again to hear his score.

Clearly *Dalibor* was a disaster, and for Smetana this was the bitterest blow of his artistic career. He firmly believed in the work and was convinced that the criticisms were groundless. Though general opinion contradicted him he clung to this belief, revising[2] the score again

[9] On this occasion only the first act of *Dalibor* was presented, the remainder of the evening being devoted to Act II of Šebor's *Drahomír* and Act II of Bendl's *Lejla*.

[1] According to the terms of his contract, Smetana was allowed the proceeds of one benefit night in addition to his yearly salary.

[2] The 1875 revisions are of a minor nature and mostly concern points of declamation.

in 1878. As an act of charity *Dalibor* was mounted in the New Czech Theatre by Adolf Čech in October, 1879, when Smetana noted in his Diary that he was called on to the platform nine times. Despite this, the opera was indifferently received. The reviews were barely lukewarm and the box office takings hardly covered expenses. Those members of the audience who attended did so as a tribute to a composer who could now no longer hear and whose health was failing fast. This third production survived for only two performances and was never revived in Smetana's lifetime. During a period of sixteen years *Dalibor* was staged only fifteen times—a depressingly low figure compared to *The Bartered Bride*, which was performed a hundred and seventeen times up to 1883. Bitterly disappointed, he resigned himself to the opera's failure; yet he maintained that the time for *Dalibor's* recognition would come. Ironically he never lived to see it. In December, 1886, just two-and-a-half years after his death, *Dalibor* was revived and warmly received. Next to *The Bartered Bride* it became one of his most frequently performed works. It went from success to success until its triumph at the International Theatre Exhibition in Vienna in 1892 paved its way to foreign stages.

The legend on which the opera is founded concerns the rebellious knight, Dalibor, imprisoned in the Daliborka Tower near Hradčany, by Vladislav of Jagellon in 1498 for leading an uprising for the recognition of peasant brewing rights. During captivity, Dalibor learnt to play the violin so beautifully that people came from all over the city to hear him. Though tortured on the 'skřípec'[3] and later executed for his part in inciting serfs to rebel against their tyrannical masters, Dalibor became a symbol of just revolt against royal power.

In Wenzig's freely adapted version only the basic outline is preserved, the plot being motivated in another way. Dalibor is involved in disputes with the Council of Litoměřice and their ally, the Burgrave of Ploškovice. When, however, the Burgrave's soldiers attack Dalibor's household they take by force his friend and companion, Zdeněk,[4] a violinist whom they put to an ignominious death. Dalibor becomes an avenger plundering the castle of Ploškovice and killing the Burgrave himself. His spiteful action is seized upon by Milada, the Burgrave's sister, who denounces him to the King. Dalibor is imprisoned and put on trial before the Royal Court of Judges.

[3] 'Skřípec' means 'rack' and is derived from the old Czech 'skřípky'—literally 'scraping'. The torture instrument was sometimes called the 'violin that stretched' because the word was also used to denote a form of stringed instrument similar to the violin.

[4] In the original draft Dalibor's companion was called Jarek, not Zdeněk.

No doubt the plot of Wagner's *Lohengrin* (the helpless Elsa seeking a king's justice for the death of her brother) which to some extent anticipates *Dalibor* (Milada begging Vladislav to punish the knight for the murder of her brother) strengthened the attacks of Smetana's enemies. It is curious that his critics, so blinded by prejudice and the conviction that he was imitating Wagner, failed to realize that the most influential source behind *Dalibor* was Beethoven's *Fidelio*.[5] When Wenzig wrote *Dalibor* it is almost certain he had *Fidelio*, or a similar pain-and-torment story of a type popular after the French Revolution in mind.[6] Possibly Smetana helped to shape some of the dramatic points himself, for there is a marked affinity between the characters of Milada and Beethoven's Leonore, while the disguise, the deception of the gaoler Beneš on the one hand, Rocco on the other, and the prison scene all resemble each other too closely to be explained on grounds of coincidence alone. Unfortunately Wenzig, an amateur librettist with an inexperienced eye, was unable to detect the flaws and similarities in this work which were partly concealed by some good points: thus the greatest weakness, Dalibor's ability to learn to play the violin like a virtuoso within the space of one long day, stands uncorrected. However, the Beethoven influence remains, not only in plot but in working method as well. In *Dalibor* Smetana was predominantly concerned with achieving maximum inner unity by the greatest possible concentration of musical expression: consequently the appearance and reappearance of a motive and its transformations characterizing individuals and situations helps to preserve continuity and makes for a symphonic texture that becomes almost Beethovenian—especially in the way the musical fabric seems to grow from one single root, announced in bar 16:

Example 48

The simplicity of the theme, with its scalic construction is typical of

[5] *Fidelio*, the first German opera to be translated into Czech, had been introduced by Weber during his term of office in Prague.

[6] It is quite possible that Weber's *Euryanthe* provided Wenzig with the knightly, chivalrous background of his plot, and Smetana with a model of through-composed opera.

the mature Smetana's style; but it is far more important than this. The steady rise from the gloomy minor beginning to the hopeful close, a seventh above, epitomizes Dalibor's struggle, the hero of resistance and the fighter for freedom. The motive is associated not so much with the man as with his fate, and for this reason it is never sung but heard only in the orchestra. Similarly the mutations stemming from it are associated with the destiny of the leading character and describe his changing actions and moods. Everything seems to grow from the 'fate' motive and must be measured in relation to it. Thus Dalibor, the heroic knight, before he has been committed to prison is represented by F sharp major and a bright, triumphant transformation of the initial motive:

Example 49

Smetana was certainly aware of the inexhaustible variety of melodic material that could be achieved by this organic relationship and the motives of the other characters, including that of Milada, stem from it:

Example 50

Smetana does not allow himself to be limited by this theme and subjects the basic idea to further development, using the variants for psychological suggestion or references to the hero. For example, he abbreviates the motive using only the first three degrees of the scale which, when harmonized (a), becomes a 'horn passage' lending itself to enormous possibilities not least by inversion (b) or extension (c):

Example 51 (*a*)

(*b*)

(*c*)

For the heroine Smetana reserves some of his finest metamorphoses. In Act I the motive is reworked three times and on each occasion the result is more subtle, the dramatic intention more contrasted. In example (a) we sense Milada's agitation, her anger and hate as she sweeps before the judges to testify; the second example (b) underlines her determination to revenge her brother's murderer; the third derivation[7] (c), from the final scene of Act I, expresses Milada's *volte-face* following Dalibor's intrepid confession and describes the palpitating emotion she feels for the prisoner. (See Example 52 (a), (b), (c), pp. 199, 200.)

The growing strength of Smetana's musical characterization is clear from these examples; and his ability to invest an initial germ cell with deep implications of wrath, vengeance and deliverance shows a marked advance on his earlier operatic technique and a fuller understanding of dramatic suggestion. Remarkably, the figure of Milada seemed to draw the real stuff of composition from him in a way that Dalibor did not. Though Dalibor is the hero he never dominates the

[7] This particular transformation of the theme was anticipated in the Ballade in E minor for solo piano some six years before.

Example 52 (*a*)

(*b*)

action. He is a passive, almost Italian hero,[8] and it is significant that like Leonore in *Fidelio*, and with the same undying love and devotion, Milada takes possession of the opera and the composer too. From the end of Act I she commands the stage, gaining entrance to the prison, leading the attack for Dalibor's escape and sustaining fatal wounds on his behalf. In marked contrast, Dalibor meekly offers no defence to the judges' accusations, simply accepts their verdict and makes no attempt to resist capture or avoid death.

[8] The 'Italian' influence shows itself most noticeably in the long Bellini-like melodies, harmonized in thirds, which Smetana gives his hero. Verdi's *Otello* provides a similar instance where the hero is a passive figure; but there it is Iago not Desdemona who is the active force in the tragedy.

Example 52 (c)

Two other modifications of the 'fate' motive must be mentioned: both appear in Act I and thereafter are frequently heard in the orchestra. The first, an inversion of the original motive associated with King Vladislav, is resolute and determined, full of dignity and regal brilliance and ideally suited to the image of a fifteenth-century Bohemian monarch; the second, a more lyrical transformation in the major also has a chivalrous character and represents the spirit of Dalibor's murdered companion, Zdeněk. Subsequently he is evoked by a solo violin, appropriately enough for a person who symbolizes the nation's musicality. (See Example 53 on next page.)

The remaining characters are sketched in rather less detail. Jitka, for all her faithful qualities (to some extent anticipating Liu in Puccini's *Turandot*) remains a secondary figure. But she is more than a foil to Milada's fighting heroine: her basic theme (drawn from the 'fate' motive) represents freedom and her sole aim is to liberate

Example 53 (*a*)

(*b*)

Dalibor. Like Jitka herself, her theme comes and goes but never dominates the score:

Example 54

Beneš, the gaoler, despite his stirring tribute to music and the Czech people, 'Který pak Čech by hudbu neměl rád!' ('I know no Czech who would not like music': Act II, Scene 3), does not achieve the musical stature or dignity of Beethoven's Rocco. Budivoj never emerges as a credible commander and is little more than a prop in the gloomy garrison where Dalibor is captive. Vítek also remains undistinguished. The chorus, on the other hand, plays more than a perfunctory role. It is used to represent the townsfolk, who assume the function of protagonist in the drama and only become the bearers of a mood in the tavern scene in Act II. Significantly, this is the only moment in the score which is not tragic[9] and which does not depend substantially on the 'fate' motive for its musical impetus. Elsewhere the chorus suggests the anxiety of people awaiting the result of Dalibor's trial and adds to the sad atmosphere in the castle yard in hushed whispers that anticipate the impending fate of the hero. But where Beethoven in *Fidelio* makes the chorus contemplative, bringing the prisoners from darkness into light to sing of the glories of their Creator and to comment on the redemption of man from the misery of life's unhappiness, Smetana is more literal, allowing the people to express the misery of the prisoner's life in deep dungeons and nothing more.

There is one matter, however, in which Smetana does score over Beethoven—that of musical continuity. As has been suggested, *Dalibor* is to some extent monothematic; it is also a through-composed work, resembling Weber's *Euryanthe*, and herein lies its strength. Where *Fidelio* is a numerical opera with spoken dialogue, *Dalibor* is a piece of sustained dramatic and musical action. Certainly there is more than a suggestion of this towards the end of Act I of *The Brandenburgers in Bohemia*, but Smetana had never before adopted the method so consistently or so elaborately as he does in *Dalibor*. Though there are clearly defined marches, interludes (for scene changes), recitatives, arias and ensembles,[1] each is skilfully integrated and moulded so as to lead to the next in a logical sequence and with a swiftness of intention quite absent in his earlier operas, where effect depended on the variety of musical invention and the wide range of differing thematic ideas. It is particularly in the handling of recitatives as declamation or ensemble and the treating of ensemble as large-scale scena or extended finales that Smetana lays the foundation of continuous Czech opera, making *Dalibor* the first real music drama[2] to come out of Prague.

One cannot but admire the swiftness with which the action unfolds:

[9] This is certainly the most cheerful part of the score and the only place where Smetana adopts a popular idiom. The vigorous drinking chorus looks back to a similar one in *The Bartered Bride* incorporating a number of folk-like three-bar phrase lengths, common to both.

[1] Among the ensembles there is no quartet: in *Dalibor* Smetana's favourite form is the duet and this score includes a greater number than any other he was to compose.

[2] To Smetana's critics, the fact that the score was no longer divisible into independent numbers but resembled *Tannhäuser* and *Lohengrin* only gave them more cause to dishonour him and cast him 'Wagnerian'.

it spans little more than a long day and Smetana pens detail after detail underlining the drama with unerring confidence. Several instances will make this clear. Towards the end of Act II, Dalibor and Milada confess their feelings for each other in an impassioned duet and look forward to the time when they can be united in freedom. At this point Smetana feels some extra comment is necessary, and in the last bars points the dramatic change that has occurred in their lives by a startling and unprepared modulation which jolts us into accepting their new state. The clarinets intone Dalibor's 'fate' motive; we expect a full close in the key of A flat but are thrust into A major before being knocked abruptly back into A flat. Earlier in the same duet (bars 1002–1007) Smetana uses a change of harmony to reflect the change of mood and situation. As Milada speaks to Dalibor of the liberation her plans will bring, oboes and trumpets brilliantly sing the 'fate' motive (now varied to Jitka's freedom theme) optimistically in the major; two bars later, clarinets sound the same fragment in the minor, with a degree of sad resignation, followed by a third statement on the horn—but augmented and again in the major. By a psychological use of the motive and without a word from the singers Smetana has subtly told us Dalibor's fate: he will know neither freedom nor Milada's love:

Example 55

This method of musical commentary is something Smetana almost certainly inherited from Wagner's *Lohengrin*; but *Dalibor* also shows other Wagnerian traces, especially in the way the opera begins. There is no formal overture as there is in *The Bartered Bride*, only a sixteen-bar introduction which sets the mood and leads directly to the gloomy surroundings of the courtyard where Dalibor is to be tried—a scene dimly lit by Smetana's subdued orchestral colouring. Throughout he displays great assurance of instrumentation, being more painstaking in dynamic marking and more imaginative in effect than ever before. For the first time in his scores he makes the trumpets play 'con sordino' to suggest distant fanfares (bar 1), and only before the arrival of King Vladislav, musically the brightest moment since the rise of the curtain, does he ask the players to remove their mutes. In the dungeon scene of Act II he captures the shadowy atmosphere of the damp cell and as we cross the threshold of this den of misery he evokes the prisoner's ebbing life by pitching the groping lines especially low on double basses and bassoons. As Milada awaits Dalibor's signal in Act III solo timpani, with marked quaver rhythm, suggest tension and portray her beating heart. The second act scene change from tavern to prison suggests a descent similar to that from Valhalla to Nibelheim, and though Smetana's transformation is less spectacular than Wagner's the string writing plunging into the dark labyrinth is particularly telling; as it is in Dalibor's soliloquy in Act II where a series of gently shimmering semiquaver figures evoke the vision of Zdeněk. The introduction of solo instruments associated with specific characters is another innovation (the harp for Milada, the solo violin for Zdeněk, the clarinet and horn for Dalibor); and so is the way the orchestra weaves its own lines, often independently against the voice, yet always expressing the essence of the dramatic situation even when the singer is not. Smetana's use of terse trumpet flourishes to capture the atmosphere of chivalry and provide the fundamental colour of old Czech knighthood, and his skill in grading the full orchestra to match the climax of his acts, show his growing skill as an orchestrator. Thus the Dalibor-Milada love duet[3] in Act II is built up like a number of monolithic columns of sound that seem to tower, phrase by phrase, higher and higher, like the great Gothic façade of St. Vitus's Cathedral which forms the backcloth of the drama itself.

It is ironic that a score so steeped in legend and so deeply marked with Czech imagery could have failed to attract those who attended the early performances in 1868. That Dalibor is the personification of his nation, the fighting model of what the Czechs should be, and that Zdeněk is the spirit of hope, speaking through the medium of music a message of faith and optimism seems to have eluded the first audiences completely. One can forgive them for having failed to appreciate the superbly shaped acts, the impassioned melody, or Smetana's innate sense of theatre and dramatic intensity; but it is strange his critics never perceived the inherent weaknesses of the opera—Wenzig's uneven libretto, the effeminate, passive qualities of the hero, the thinly sketched minor characters and Smetana's failure in bringing to the spirit of Zdeněk music of only an earthly nature instead of celestial harmonies. A hundred years after the event it is possible to see clearly that *Dalibor* was the object of a malicious slander campaign. His enemies condemned the work and the Wag-

[3] This duet is not only the highest peak in the whole opera but supreme among Smetana's operatic duets. It is a hymn of dramatic lyricism and seems to be modelled on Beethoven's 'O namenlose Freude' in *Fidelio*.

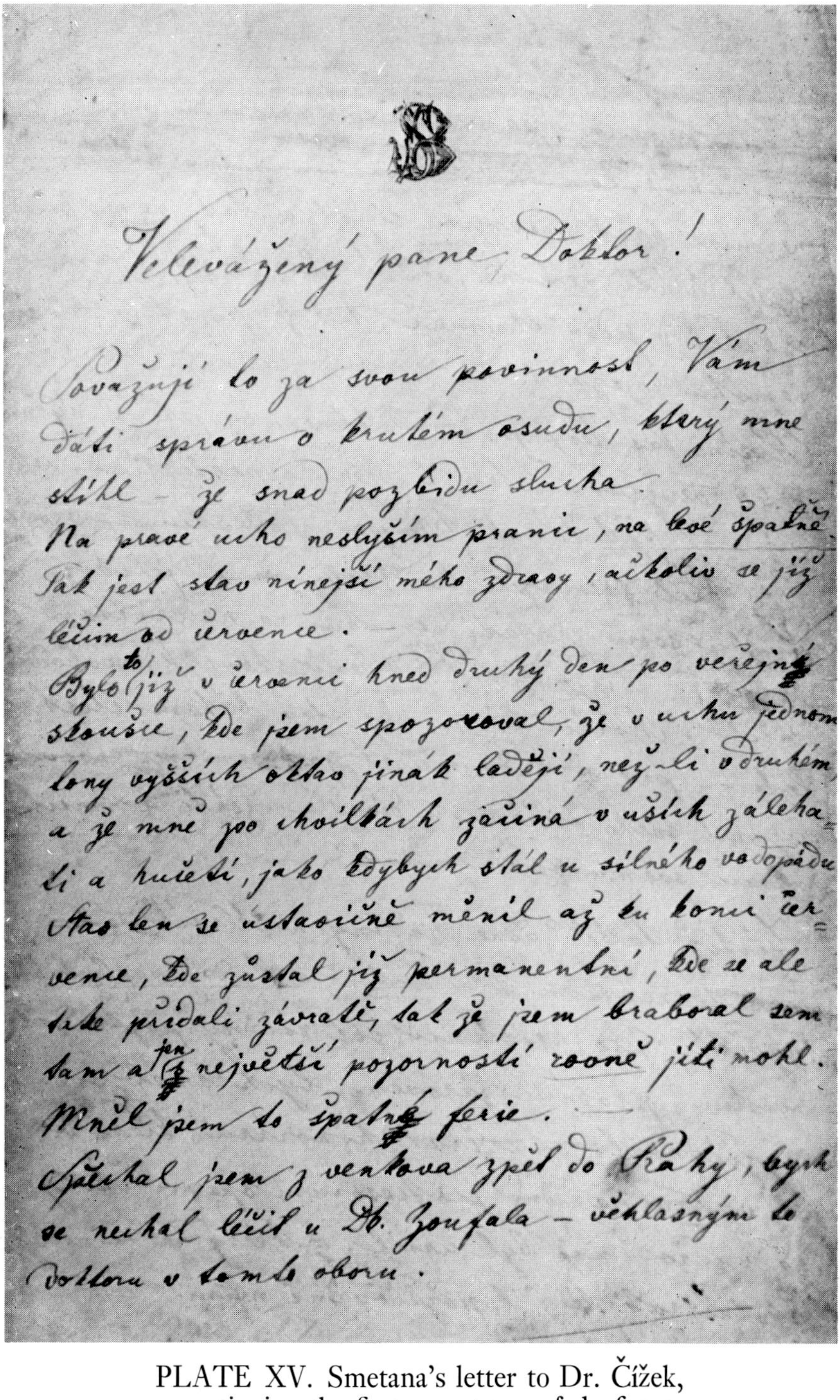

Velevážený pane Doktor!

Považuji to za svou povinnost, Vám dáti správu o krutém osudu, který mne stihl – že snad pozbydu slucha.
Na pravé ucho neslyším pranic, na levé špatně.
Tak jest stav nynější mého zdraví, ačkoliv se již léčím od července.
Bylo to již v červenci hned druhý den po veřejné zkoušce, kde jsem spozoroval, že v uchu jednom tony vyšších oktáv jinak ladějí, než-li v druhém, a že mně po chvílkách začíná v uších zaléhati a hučeti, jako kdybych stál u silného vodopádu. Stav ten se ustavičně měnil až ku konci července, kde zůstal již permanentní, kde se ale k tomu přidaly závratě, tak že jsem vrávoral sem tam a jen s největší pozorností rovně jíti mohl.
Měl jsem to špatné ferie.
Spěchal jsem z venkova zpět do Prahy, bych se nechal léčit u Dr. Zoufala – vyhlášeným to doktoru v tomto oboru.

PLATE XV. Smetana's letter to Dr. Čížek, mentioning the first symptoms of deafness (October 7th, 1874)

PLATE XVI

Smetana's pencil

nerian excuse was as good a peg as any upon which to hang their accusation. Unfortunately the score was allowed to drop from the repertoire after only a handful of performances, and even then it remained a target for hostile attacks. These almost broke the composer's spirit. Of all his progeny *Dalibor* was nearest to his heart. He became exasperated with those who launched offensive after offensive against him; but the result was not what his detractors had hoped for. Instead of intimidating him and forcing his return to the style of *The Bartered Bride* he responded in a typical manner. Impatient of public opinion as always, he flung himself with enormous energy into the sketches for a new opera, *Libuše*, built not on the lines of *The Bartered Bride* as everyone hoped, but on epic proportions which come closer to the Wagnerian concept of music drama and festival opera than anything in *Dalibor*.

NINE

'LIBUŠE'

1869–1872

SMETANA COMPLETED *Dalibor* on December 29, 1867, thirteen months after his appointment as Conductor at the Provisional Theatre. Though he had worked on this score more or less concurrently with his administrative work, he had never allowed his function as Director to assume secondary importance; and from the beginning sought to fulfil his duties as conscientiously as possible, his aim being to raise the mediocre standard inherited from Maýr to a level that would bring Prague into line with other European houses. Within days of taking up his post he transformed the theatre into a forum for new ideas. Suggestions, schedules, amendments, propositions all poured from his office in an endless stream. His most formidable task was to improve the level of soloists; for Prague, unlike the bigger German houses, could offer only small fees and Smetana realized that without substantial financial incentive good singers would look elsewhere for engagements. Early on, he suggested that funds be made available to supplement existing salaries and so attract to Prague artists of reasonable standard; but the scheme foundered and Smetana could do little to prevent frequent changes among the principals and ensemble (later he managed to build a team of directors, producers and designers who remained loyally with him until 1874). In his initial season he encountered much resistance, especially to his proposal to establish an independent school attached to the theatre where promising talents could be fostered in the correct musical climate. Enlightened as this proposal was, it failed to find favour, and was only allowed to materialize in the year before his retirement.[1]

[1] Permission was given for the school to be established on January 12, 1873, when a committee appointed Smetana Director and Professor of Theory. The teaching staff included Jan Lukes (tenor), Professor of Vocal Training;

Crushed by lack of interest in these projects, Smetana turned to more immediate matters, working hard to discipline the chorus, increasing rehearsal time, improving conditions of work. When recruiting singers and players he looked for those who were talented rather than merely able, and consequently the standard of audition was raised. Though he demanded much of his performers, they respected his musical judgement and responded to him, not least of all for abolishing Maýr's system of imposed fines:

> After the stern and domineering Maýr, who was feared by all and never overlooked even the slightest slip on anyone's part—delighting in this as he did, since he could hardly have impressed anybody by his musical qualities—the conductor's place was filled by a great creative artist who was sensitive and thoughtful towards everyone. . . . Smetana treated the musicians in the orchestra as equals and was considerate towards them all . . . he never prolonged rehearsals unreasonably, not wishing to tire the performers unnecessarily, and made everything come to life. . . . Not a single mistake or false note escaped his notice. Ragged entries immediately called forth a rap of the baton and the repetition of the passage accompanied by a reproachful glance. That was far more effective than sharp words . . . and thus he always achieved what he wanted. . .[2]

The task, however, which Smetana regarded as of prime importance and to which he devoted enormous hours of study was the creation of a representative repertoire. Under Maýr the Provisional Theatre had developed a distinct Italian bias; enterprisingly, Smetana now attempted to establish a well balanced repertoire of Italian, German and French works while ensuring Czech and other Slavonic scores (such as existed) were not neglected. How catholic was his taste can be judged by examining the theatre records between 1866 and 1872. Over six seasons, eighty-two different operas were played, all of which Smetana studied for rehearsal or performance. Of these he prepared and conducted thirty-three new productions, including the first and subsequent presentations himself.

Otilie Sklenářová-Malá (actress), mime and declamation; M. Hertzová, dance and ballet; and František Kolár, mime and movement. The first performance at the Opera School took place in July, 1874, but thereafter it failed when Smetana became deaf. Maýr had no interest in it and Pivoda tried to sabotage it as it rivalled his own institution. Many of the pupils, however, continued privately with Lukes, who set up his own school in the following year.

[2] Jiránek: *Reflections of Smetana's Pupil* (1941).

Der Freischütz	(Weber)	September 28, 186
Die Zauberflöte	(Mozart)	October 3, 1866
La Juive	(Halévy)	October 10, 1866
Lucrezia Borgia	(Bellini)	October 14, 1866
Nachtlager von Granada	(Kreutzer)	October 21, 1866
The Bartered Bride	(Smetana)	October 27, 1866
Il Trovatore	(Verdi)	October 31, 1866
La Muette de Portici	(Auber)	November 7, 1866
The Brandenburgers in Bohemia	(Smetana)	November 28, 186
Guillaume Tell	(Rossini)	December 14, 1866
A Life for the Tsar	(Glinka)	January 4, 1867
Don Giovanni	(Mozart)	March 8, 1867
Rigoletto	(Verdi)	April 13, 1867
Il Barbiere di Siviglia	(Rossini)	April 28, 1867
Lucia di Lammermoor	(Donizetti)	May 22, 1867
Les Huguenots	(Meyerbeer)	June 14, 1867
Faust	(Gounod)	July 6, 1867
Lejla	(Bendl)	January 4, 1868
Halka	(Moniusko)	February 28, 1868
Robert le Diable	(Meyerbeer)	March 20, 1868
Dalibor	(Smetana)	May 14, 1868
Le Premier Jour de Bonheur	(Auber)	September 11, 186
Le Nozze di Figaro	(Mozart)	November 6, 1868
Orfeo ed Euridice	(Gluck)	January 12, 1869
Jessonda	(Spohr)	February 26, 1869
Il Seraglio	(Mozart)	April 6, 1869
Crispino e la Comare	(L. & F. Ricci)	June 20, 1869
Roméo et Juliette	(Berlioz)	August 29, 1869
The Brandenburgers in Bohemia	(Smetana)	November 26, 186
Fidelio	(Beethoven)	January 21, 1870
Marie Potoká	(Lepold Eugen Měchura)[3]	January 13, 1871
St. John's Rapids	(Rozkošný)	October 3, 1871
Iphigénie en Aulide	(Gluck)	April 9, 1872

This substantial catalogue far outnumbers that of Maýr, in whos term of office (1862–1866) fifty-seven operas were staged (he con ducted no more than twenty productions himself). Though Smetana' list includes a generous number of French, Italian and German works

[3] Leopold Eugen Měchura (1804–1870), a lawyer as well as a composer and th first to produce a Czech opera on a theme from Pushkin.

Wagner's name is absent. Smetana never conducted any of his music dramas and Emanuel Chvála, the composer and critic, recalls that on one occasion he declared himself to be against the performance of Wagner's operas at the Provisional Theatre since they were 'foreign in their downright Germanism', and therefore 'completely unacceptable to a singing nation like the Czechs'.[4] In the light of the accusation of Wagnerism which had been launched against *Dalibor*, Smetana's reasoning seems to be too well-considered to be entirely credible, especially for one who was widely known to be an admirer of Wagner's scores. Possibly he had never seen his way clear to casting a Wagner opera from within the company as it then stood, though it is more likely he found it easier to deny charges of Wagnerism with greater confidence by restraining his taste and leaving the Prague German Theatre to mount their mediocre *Tannhäusers* and *Lohengrins*.

Today it is difficult to estimate the standard of production which Smetana achieved during his years at the Provisional Theatre. Contemporary accounts vary considerably depending on whether the writer was for or against him. We know, however, that the orchestra was not large[5] (no more than twenty-four players) and that the chorus, depending on the score to be performed, could muster sixteen singers, though they were often reinforced by members of the Hlahol. The stage was small, and stock scenery served widely differing productions, returning nightly, like the singers, with alarming regularity and increasingly worn appearance. In such impoverished conditions it is only surprising that operas were ever staged at all. Indeed, many of them were barely thrown together and one production which seems particularly to have suffered was Glinka's *A Life for the Tsar*. After attending the première in January, 1867, Balakirev exclaimed:

> What a horror it was! I have not quite come to my senses yet. The overture was so-so, but when the curtain went up—oh, horror! What costumes!! The peasants were wearing some kind of peaked caps and overcoats with white buttons, and they had beards, but not Russian ones—Jewish ones!!![6]

Balakirev was in Prague to conduct Glinka's *Ruslan and Ludmila* and became so enraged with the performance of *A Life for the Tsar* that he

[4] Bartoš: *Letters and Reminiscences* (1955).

[5] By comparison with other pit orchestras the Prague Provisional Theatre was well served. Smetana's Diary records that *The Bartered Bride* was given in February, 1878, in Mladá Boleslav with an instrumental force comprising five strings, one flute, one clarinet and harmonium.

[6] Edward Garden: *Balakirev* (1968).

insisted on Smetana being replaced by Tausig for the forthcoming *Ruslan* rehearsals. Though the management reluctantly agreed, the incident inevitably caused a deal of ill feeling between the two composers; and later Balakirev accused Smetana of sabotaging the performances with a hissing party, led by a group of Poles well-known for their anti-Russian sympathies.[7] Certainly Smetana and Balakirev remained estranged, and when *The Bartered Bride* received a rough passage at its first performance in St. Petersburg in 1871 Smetana was convinced that Balakirev was responsible for whipping up hostility.[8]

In Russia, in Prague, everywhere, it seemed Smetana was the object of scorn, complaint and criticism. He was like a whale in a fishpond. On the one hand Maýr and his followers attacked his standard of performance at the Provisional Theatre, on the other, Pivoda and Rieger condemned him for subscribing to Wagnerism. Yet despite intrigue and acrimony, malice and untruth, he continued his work at the Theatre, at the Hlahol and at the Umělecká Beseda, under whose auspices he arranged and conducted three subscription concerts in the Žofín Hall with programmes including Bruch's G minor Violin Concerto, Beethoven's Third and Sixth Symphonies, Liszt's *Tasso*, Schubert's C major Symphony and overtures by Berlioz, Schubert, Wagner and Glinka (December 5 and 12, 1869, and January 24, 1870). He still continued to teach at his Institute and with Heller set up the first free school for instructing Prague music teachers (a nineteenth-century teachers' training scheme).[9] In between he played the piano, though not in public, took great interest in political matters, read widely and devoted considerable time to composition.

After *Dalibor* he had turned his hand to a number of occasional pieces by way of relaxation, the first being a short but impressive series of *Fanfares* for a festive performance of Shakespeare's *Richard III* at the Novoměstské Theatre on April 23, 1867. (The evening began with Smetana's tone poem *Richard III*; the *Fanfares* were heard as incidental music during Act II, while between the third and fourth acts he conducted his *Shakespearean March* of 1864.) The *Fanfares*, which run to twenty-seven bars, are scored for four horns, two trumpets, three trombones and timpani; they are slight in musical value and have no thematic connexion with his earlier composition on the

[7] Garden: *op. cit.*

[8] See Chapter 7, page 171.

[9] One of Smetana's pupils at this time was Zdeněk Fibich whose leaving certificate, awarded for teaching and conducting on September 14, 1873, describes his talent as 'outstanding'.

same subject. The next work to appear was a *Divertimento on Slavonic Songs* arranged for solo křidlovka (flugel horn) and military band. The score is unfortunately lost, but from Smetana's Diary we know that it was written for the Hlahol, at one of whose garden fêtes it was performed for the first time on May 15, 1869.

Two other works occupied him during the spring of 1869: *Rybář* (*The Fisherman*) and *Libušin soud* (*Libuše's Judgement*), both designed for amateurs and given at a concert organized to raise funds for the completion of St. Vitus's Cathedral. Though the foundations had been laid in the reign of Charles IV by Matthias of Arras and building had continued under the eminent Gothic artist Peter Parler of Gmund, more than four hundred years were to pass before the Cathedral was complete.[1] On April 12, an audience, drawn mostly from the nobility, filled the Žofín Hall to hear a recital of poetry and music devised by the Prague Cathedral Association. Even before the venture, its success was assured: every seat was sold and an extra performance had to be arranged for April 13. In all ten thousand gulden were raised, and for his participation Smetana received twenty gold coins from Count Thun and a canteen of silver cutlery from the Countess Kounic.

On both occasions he conducted the orchestra of the Provisional Theatre in the accompaniments to three *tableaux vivants*, the first an arrangement of music from *The Bartered Bride* including the opening chorus, the second based on Goethe's *The Fisherman*, and the third *Libuše's Judgement*, which looked to early Bohemian history for its inspiration. Of these the first is an insignificant piece of hack-work, while the second suffers from weaknesses of thematic material and working out. Long-held pedals are firmly anchored on E flat over which a limpid figuration floats upwards from double basses to violins, with horn and harmonium filling in arpeggios, immediately suggesting the opening of *Das Rheingold*. Unfortunately, the piece never establishes itself as anything more than an accompaniment. Smetana's inspiration (or Wagner's magnetism) was soon damped, and the result is a pleasant but undistinguished piece of jobbery. The score is remarkable only inasmuch as it anticipates a watery atmosphere returning five years later in the tone poem *Vltava*.

Libuše's Judgement, the third *tableau*, is on a much higher plane. From the opening it is obvious Smetana was fired by the patriotic theme, the imperious nature of the legendary and sibylline Princess of Bohemia and though the music furnished an excellent background for the charitable entertainment of Prague's nobility, it provided far

[1] The Cathedral was finished in 1929, and consequently every architectural style is represented, from Romanesque to the modern.

more for the composer. The *tableau* was a deliberate musical study for his fourth and loftiest operatic utterance *Libuše*, and he even incorporated into the score a figure of some majesty on the trumpets which was later reworked in the opening fanfares.

For some time Smetana had considered *Libuše* as possible operatic material, and he even had in his possession a roughly shaped libretto on the theme. Indeed, something of Smetana's plans had been announced in the Press:

> Mr. Smetana, the composer, will write a solemn opera called *Libuše*, for which Wenzig will provide the text. The opera will be performed at the Coronation of the Emperor Franz Josef.

Although this statement appeared at a time when Smetana had barely mounted the first performances of *The Bartered Bride* and was still at work on *Dalibor*, he clearly had a very definite conception of the purpose to which his next opera should be put. Like all true Czechs, he fervently believed the time would come when political and social bickering between Vienna and Prague would be at an end, when the Emperor of Austria would unite the two empires by accepting Bohemia's Crown. With this in mind, *Libuše* was planned not as a repertoire opera, but as a work for special celebrations:

> I desire it to be used only for festivals which affect the whole Czech nation. *Libuše* is not an opera of the old type, but a festive *tableau*—a form of musical and dramatic sustenance.[2]

Clearly, *Libuše* had assumed a deep ceremonial significance for Smetana, and from the beginning it was his intention to endow it with a solemn ritualistic character.

Smetana was by no means the first artist to be drawn to the subject. The painter Mánes and the sculptor Ales had both celebrated the legend in their art, and the spirit of the subject had long found favour with other Bohemians following the unearthing, at Králové Dvůr and at Zelená Hora in 1817 and 1818, of fragments of ancient Bohemian literature dealing with *The Judgement of Libuše*. But the origins of the Libuše theme go far back into Czech history. One of the earliest references is to be found in the eleventh-century Latin *Chronicon Bohemorum* written by the Canon of Prague, Cosmas (1045–1125), whose three-volume work dealing with the legends of Bohemia is the most important source concerning the origin and development of the Bohemian State, and traces its history from the deluge to 1038 (Volume I), from 1038 to 1092 (Volume II) and from 1092

[2] Letter to Čech: August 17, 1883.

to 1125 (Volume III). Cosmas's writings are tales rather than history, but they undoubtedly formed a tradition, the earliest and most popular of which describes Krok, the pagan Bohemian prince who, in default of male descendants, ruled over the country with his three daughters, Kázi, Teta (or Lethka) and Libuše:

> Smaller in years but greater in wisdom . . . she was wonderful among women, chaste in body, righteous in her morals, second to none as judge over the people, affable to all and even amiable, the pride and glory of the female sex, doing wise and manly deeds; but as nobody is perfect, this so praiseworthy woman was, alas, a soothsayer. . . .

Cosmas describes Libuše's reign, her dispute with two nobles, her choice of Přemysl as consort and her founding of the City of Prague:

> Standing on a rock on Vyšehrad in the presence of her husband and the elders of the people, and incited by the spirit of prophecy, Libuše uttered this prediction: 'I see a town, the glory of which will reach the stars. There is a spot in the forest, thirty strides from this village, which the River Vltava encircles and which to the north the stream Brusnice secures by its deep valley; and to the south a rocky hill, which from its rocks takes the name of Petrin, towers above it . . . when you have reached the spot you will find a man in the midst of the forest who is working at a door-step[3] for a house. And as even mighty lords bend before a low door, so from this event you shall call the town which you shall build—Praha.' Thus they proceeded immediately to the ancient forest, and having found the sign which had been given them they built on this site Praha, the mistress of all Bohemia.

The date of the founding of Prague is uncertain, as is most information concerning this semi-mythical Princess. However, the legend in this form is the most ancient account that has come down to us and is the one upon which all subsequent ones are based over the next four hundred years, including that recorded by the sixteenth-century chronicler Hajek of Libocan (1520–1620), who, together with *Libuše* documented the sagas of *Šárka*, *Vlasta* and *Ctirad*.[4] Sometime between 1589 and 1596, Hajek's version was translated into German, in which language it became widely known outside Bohemia notably

[3] 'Prah' means 'door-step' or 'threshold'.

[4] Both *Vlasta* and *Ctirad* were considered by Smetana as possible operatic material but nothing came of the ideas. *Šárka* was, of course, to be the subject of the third tone poem in the cycle *Má Vlast*.

in a dramatized adaptation given by Veltn's group of wandering players in the region around Dresden up to 1665. Under the title *The Comedy of Libussa* [*sic*], it won enormous popularity and was considered suitable for an opera by the Italian composer Albinoni. Nothing materialized. The legend developed more as parody than history and of several comic versions that appeared the most celebrated was *The Iron Table*. Here Libuše, re-christened Orismannia, was transformed into a Sweeney Todd-like character who enticed her lover, Sigislav (a variant of Přemysl), to a cellar where, after making love to him, she murdered him.

In Bohemia, however, the subject was treated with more respect, and during the seventeenth century a number of details were added to make the plot more suitable for serious musical treatment. *La Libusa*, [*sic*] *una dramma per musica* with music by Bartolemeo Bernardi, was played throughout Bohemia by a company led by Jan Bedřich Sartorico during 1703–1704. In this version the plot was distorted to make it more attractive, and Přemsyl emerged as Libuše's secret lover instead of her husband. A more substantial setting, which also added lustre to the theme, appeared in 1723 when Fux produced his *La constanza e fortezza* based firmly on the Libuše legend. Written especially for the Coronation of the Emperor Charles VI and performed for the first time in Prague on August 28, 1723, the work is remarkable for a dramatic climax corresponding to Libuše's oracular revelations. Here Fux created a precedent which was emulated, eleven years later, by Antonio Danzi (1763–1826). Despite its title, *Praga—Nascente da Libusa e Primislao*, Danzi's opera closely adheres to Cosmas's original and was presented at the Spork Theatre, Prague, in three *tableaux*. (a) 'Libusa's choice of husband'; (b) 'The founding of Prague'; (c) 'Libusa's prophecy'. But it was not only in the field of music and opera that the legend flourished: during the reign of Maria Theresa the subject was reworked in several dramatizations, notably by Brentano (*Die Gründung Prags*), and Grillparzer (*Libussa*). Both brought to their work a high degree of dramatic concentration and to his monologues Grillparzer introduced a remarkable intensity which has led them to be favourably compared with those in Goethe's *Faust*. With Grillparzer, however, Libuše emerges rather like Carlo Gozzi's Turandot, posing riddles to the nobles of her tribe. The reverse is true of Herder, whose *Die Fürstentafel* (in his famous collection of *Volkslieder*) is more faithful to Cosmas's legend and does not attempt to hide the original inspiration of the saga.

The unearthing at Králové Dvůr and Zelená Hora of Bohemian manuscripts led to an enormous revival of interest in early literature, and though at the beginning of the nineteenth century the authenticity of the find was not in question (subsequent research has proved the fragments to be the work of forgers), these ancient relics stimulated at least four other composers to set *Libuše* to music.

The first to respond was the little-known Moravian composer Baron Eduard von Lannoy, whose two act *Libuše*, performed in Brno in 1818, treats the subject so sketchily and in such an undistinguished fashion that it failed to travel outside the Moravian capital. The next to take up the torch was Tomášek, who, for all his allegiance to the music of Mozart and Haydn turned to the Kralové Dvůr manuscript for the texts of a series of songs (1820) extolling Libuše's qualities and celebrating the glorious city she founded. In 1822 Konradin Kreutzer produced a three-act fairy-tale setting of the legend which was so successful that it quickly travelled from Vienna to Budapest, Leipzig, Frankfurt, Berlin, Amsterdam and Copenhagen. Another version which was also warmly received was by František Škroup. *Libuše's Wedding* (1832) is a free adaptation of the original, in which the heroine emerges more as a wild Amazon than a goddess. Musically, however, Škroup's setting disappoints, for instead of matching the epic nature of the subject he introduces folk melodies which stand unnaturally alongside conventional Italian tunes of the day and fail to make an integrated whole. The first complete performance was given in 1850.

The challenge facing Smetana, therefore, was enormous and that he was aware of the scale and value of his work we know from his correspondence. For this opera he believed it to be his sole responsibility to produce 'the most perfect work on the highest dramatic plane', so he wrote to Procházka on September 36, 1877; and when planning it as a series of festive *tableaux*—a number of musical and dramatic pageants depicting Bohemian life—he saw himself as the 'creator of a new kind of Czech music' and *Libuše* as a work of 'unique importance in our history and literature'.[5] Following one of the initial performances at the National Theatre, Smetana had declared his sentiments in a letter (May 26, 1882) to the Director of the Theatre Committee:

> They [the critics] consider *Libuše* to be ordinary, commonplace, even tedious; but I believe it to be the highest peak in the expression of Czech music.

That Smetana was, generally speaking, modest allows us to appreciate the force of these remarks and to understand with what seriousness he

[5] Letter to Srb-Debrnov: December 20, 1880.

approached his task. Unlike his earlier operas, which had followed hot on the heels of each other within a surprisingly short space of time, *Libuše* occupied him for more than four years, during which time he lavished the utmost care and affection on the score, shaping it with the highest intention, endeavouring to present to the nation a tribute and monument of his art.

The idea originated from Josef Wenzig who, after completing *Dalibor*, presented an outline of the text as early as April 24, 1866:

> Full of joy he came with the *Libuše* poem and read it to me saying 'If you like it take it, here it is!' I did like it, but I did not buy it, for Wenzig gave it to me and I have no claim to it financially.[6]

At this period Smetana was still drafting the music of *Dalibor* and was able to do little more than put Wenzig's treatment on one side. But it did not remain there long. So enthusiastic did he become about the subject that by the end of May he had resolved to accept the libretto and was reported in the Prague newspapers to be at work on the score.[7] In fact, three years were to pass before he actually began; for during this time he was engaged in the preparation and staging of his earlier operas as well as the revision of *The Bartered Bride*. In any case, Wenzig's German text needed to be translated into Czech and for this Ervín Špindler, who had previously collaborated on *Dalibor*, was again invited to provide the domestic version.[8] Wenzig's libretto corresponds closely to the saga recorded by Cosmas, dealing with the dispute between the brothers Šťáhlav and Chrudoš, arguing over their father's inheritance. Libuše, according to custom, orders them to divide the legacy equally, but Chrudoš, impulsive and hot tempered, is outraged by her judgement and abuses the Princess demanding that no man be ruled by a woman. Shocked, Libuše sends for Přemysl, a peasant leader working the fields in Stadice, summoning him to Vyšehrad as consort and husband. With him she founds the princely Přemyslide dynasty and thus restores order to the land.

In adapting the legend for operatic use, Wenzig incorporated two further themes which add both dramatic emotion and a thrilling

[6] Letter to Čech: August 17, 1883.

[7] *Národní Listy*: June 7, 1866.

[8] Špindler's name is missing from the score, playbills and programmes. He may in all modesty have requested that his name be omitted since Smetana had reworked part of the text himself (Act II, Scene 1); but it is more likely neither Wenzig nor the composer were anxious to publicize the fact that *Libuše*, a national epic, had begun life in a German form.

climax to the original. By introducing Krasava, one of the women in Libuše's court, and contriving for her to fall in love first with Chrudoš, who does not immediately return her feelings, and then with Šťáhlav, Wenzig develops the conflict between the two brothers by adding a romantic motivation founded on jealousy. Later, Krasava is instrumental in reconciling Chrudoš and Libuše, thus becoming one of the chief characters in the plot. For Wenzig, however, the most testing section was the culmination of the opera itself, and he devised a scene depicting Libuše's divine prophecy in which the most significant events of Czech history pass before her eyes in a number of *tableaux vivants*. In the 1860's the device of musical accompaniment to a series of posed pictures was especially popular and though Smetana had previously gained experience with *The Fisherman* and *Libuše's Judgement*, the idea of building an operatic finale on the same device was both daring and strikingly new. Wenzig selected events from Czech history which both celebrated the nation's past and prophesied its future, and deliberately chose a number of images representing the greatest champions for national freedom: Prince Břetislav, who united Bohemia and Moravia and secured his countries' borders against the two-fold Brandenburg invasion of Henry III; Jaroslav of Šternbeck, the knight who defended his country against Tartar attack; Přemysl Ottokar II, the monarch who increased the Slavonic Empire from north to south; Elizabeth of the Přemyslides, mother of Charles IV, who made Bohemia the centre of Europe and founded in 1348 the first European university; Žižka, Prokop the Great and the warriors of Hus, followed by the culminating vision of the Hussite King, George of Poděbrady (reigned 1458–1471), whom the people elevated to the throne in order to put down the revolution and bring peace to their homes. At the point where the Hapsburgs invaded the Bohemian lands, Wenzig deliberately reserved no place for a representative of the Austrian Crown; instead he proposed a portentous finale in which the Czech National Anthem, 'Kde domov můj?' ('Where is my home?'), was to be sung by the entire cast. Smetana, though captivated by the great vision of the final prophecy and warmly appreciative of the scheme, could not envisage the climax of his opera founded on a melody by another composer. To a man who from the beginning had wished to endow *Libuše* with a special character of solemnity, nobility and majesty, Škroup's anthem was unacceptable. And so was the idea of a finale based on a number of musical accompaniments to a series of *tableaux vivants*. As an alternative, Smetana proposed a dramatic monologue for *Libuše*, incorporating the images suggested by Wenzig which, after the fifth picture, would point to the Hapsburg domination in a meaningful phrase 'that the coming future conceals from my dull sight the secret of dreadful damnation'. Only at this moment did Smetana intend the prophetess to declaim the basic motive of the work—the immortality of her nation which would withstand and overcome all 'horrors of Hell'. To voice such a theme when freedom of expression was not permitted, and in a work that was planned to celebrate the Coronation of the Hapsburg, Franz Josef, was indeed brave. So also was Smetana's scheme to build the later part of the monologue on the fifteenth-century Hussite chorale, *Kdož jste Boží bojovníci!* (*Ye who are God's warriors!*).

It is likely he was attracted to the chorale more for the associations it had gained over the past centuries, when it had become the watchword in inciting people to revolt against religious and social tyrannies of church and feudal administrations, than for its musical values, considerable though these are. Smetana, who was opposed to the petty bureaucracy which prevailed in the politics of his day, was thus voicing his own discontent with existing conditions and especially with the Austro-Hungarian government which, in 1868, was attempting to limit the home-rule of non-German citizens. The Diary for August records his continued sympathies towards the radical Young Czech movement which was attacking, as best it could, the Cabinet of Friedrich von Beust. Such onslaughts resulted in persecutions. Not only were journalists arrested but those found guilty of maligning the Old Czech Party, more tolerant of the Austro-Hungarian Government, were similarly suppressed or punished. Clearly the passionate and irreconcilable opposition of the two political parties had in no way lessened over the years and again the Diary details Smetana's reaction:

> . . . the feudal and clerical Old Czech Party . . . is stronger as far as wealth and property are concerned, while the liberal Young Czech Party—although it contains a few rich people—consists of men of letters, artists and journalists. Naturally, I belong to the Young Czechs. The struggle between the two groups becomes more bitter from month to month . . . the Old Czechs, wherever they go in politics, in social life, or in the arts, endeavour to suppress everything that is carried out in the name of the Young Czech Party and to throw them out.[9]

Is it impossible that Smetana interpreted the home-rule disputes in Prague as the nineteenth-century analogy to the strife that existed between the two brothers in *Libuše*: Chrudoš, on the one hand, bringing disunion to the nation as he becomes estranged from the customs

[9] Diary: January, 1869.

and ways of his people; Šťáhlav, on the other, representing the guardian of tradition and faithful to his tribe? What is certain, however, is that *Libuše* was lit from a spark fanned by winds of topical political tension, and it remains a vision of future reconciliation, a supposition of harmony through which it is possible to appraise the greatness of the nation's future.

Precisely when Smetana began his sketches is unknown, but it is improbable that he started much before June, 1869, the date jotted in his motive book above Libuše's theme. He seems to have made rapid progress, and on September 7, 1870, *Hudební Listy* reported him to be at work on the third act. This almost certainly refers not to the definitive score but to the draft; for a careful examination of the manuscript reveals that besides making the customary through-composed pencil sketch, in some scenes he outlined an alternative version which varies considerably. For example, the thirty-two pages of rough notes end halfway through Act III (full score: page 496) and show that Přemysl's aria in the Stadice scene was initially accompanied by a solo harp in the key of D minor; now it is in C and scored for full orchestra. Originally Lutobor was to have been a baritone, but as Smetana experienced difficulty in writing for the male voice in this range he changed the part to a bass; elsewhere motives differ radically, and for his sketch Smetana drew up a working list of themes, many of which were found to be dispensable. Throughout, the pages are well studied: there are many crossings out, and alterations suggest that second thoughts were best. Unfortunately these give no indication when draft was transferred to score. All that is known is that after many interruptions and three years later, he was able to write:

> I have at last finished the opera *Libuše*: it was indeed strenuous and hard work.[1]

Early in November *Hudební Listy* announced the completion of the opera, but in fact the instrumentation of the third act was not completed until the 12th,[2] and even the fair copy of the conductor's score bears witness of further revisions (mostly in dynamic and tempo markings). The full score also shows another alteration—the dedication being simply: 'For Country and Nation'. Franz Josef's refusal to accept the Bohemian Crown caused disappointment among the Czechs, whose faith in Vienna was irrevocably shaken to the roots.

[1] Letter to Leopold Hruš: October 20, 1872.

[2] The instrumentation of Act I is dated September 2, 1871; Act II is marked February 18, 1872.

With no coronation to celebrate, Smetana was without an occasion for mounting *Libuše*, and though there was no foreseeable event for which the opera could be festively presented he refused to allow it to enter the ordinary repertoire of the Provisional Theatre. He believed it to be destined for something far greater, possibly the opening of the National Theatre, the foundations of which had recently been laid. The more he considered it, the more convinced was he that only on a spacious new stage, with modern technical facilities could his opera achieve the grandeur of presentation it deserved. Despite petitions from friends calling on him to mount *Libuše* at one of Prague's other houses, Smetana adamantly refused, regarding his work as a christening gift for the new Theatre and arguing that nothing existed which could do justice to its epic nature:

> For the sake of a few miserable gulden I will not allow a work of such importance to be swept into the company of ditties that are whistled everywhere.[3]

Commendable though this attitude may have been, it was also nothing short of obstinacy. Both the New Czech and Novoměstské Theatres accommodated a much larger audience than did the National Theatre when it was eventually opened; and it was in the New Czech Theatre that the six performances of *Libuše* were staged when the National Theatre was partly destroyed by fire on August 12, 1881. Smetana so much wanted *Libuše* to be associated with a national celebration that he withheld the score for nine years, even though there was no guarantee of performance. One cannot but admire the strength of mind behind this action, and it is hard to blame him for authorizing the overture to be performed when opportunity arose (it was heard in Prague on three occasions before the première: April 14, 1872; May 25, 1874; October 28, 1881; and twice in Nice[4] in 1875 and in 1877). The overture became more widely known after 1875 when the publisher Starý brought out the full score and parts. For Smetana this was an important event (the Prelude to *Libuše* was the first orchestral score to be published during his lifetime), but though it boosted his morale, it did little to speed the building of the National Theatre.

In 1874 Smetana became deaf.[5] Thereafter he was mentally ailing,

[3] Letter to Čech: August 17, 1883.

[4] At this time Bendl lived in Nice and occupied the post of Conductor in the residence of Baron Dervies—a wealthy Russian patron of the Arts. It was at Bendl's concerts that Smetana's overture was performed.

[5] See p. 244.

desperately poor and found work next to impossible. Though he no longer had any hope of actually hearing *Libuše*, he never gave up the desire to see it mounted and on September 14, 1879, submitted the score under a *nom de plume* in a competition organized to find the most suitable serious work for the opening of the National Theatre. Three months later *Libuše* was awarded the prize of a thousand gulden[6] with the assurance that it would be performed at the inaugural celebrations promised for the following spring.

Early in 1881 instructions were given for the constructional work to be speeded up so that the opening festivities could be made to coincide with the recently announced wedding of the Archduke Rudolf to Princess Stephanie of Belgium. It was hoped that the Royal couple would be present at the première, but the decision caused misgivings among the Young Czechs, and general alarm with the public who resented that a theatre designed for the nation should be transformed into a setting for Royal patronage. Amidst apprehension plans went ahead for the official opening, and Smetana dispatched implicit instructions to Adolf Čech, who was to conduct the first performance. Though delays caused the inaugural celebrations to be postponed three times, June 11 was finally selected for the festive opening—a date which was to coincide precisely with the wedding ceremonies of the Archduke. All augured well, but an unexpected change of heart on the part of Princess Stephanie brought chaos and confusion to the carefully organized plans. Both Royal wedding and state visit to Prague were cancelled, and as the auditorium was far from complete, the Committee contemplated postponing the opening yet again. In the event it was decided to proceed with the inauguration and so the National Theatre opened its doors on June 11 only to close them two weeks later in order to complete the decoration. While these messy arrangements cast something of a shadow across the première, the opera was a success, and the Archduke Rudolf himself made a surprise visit to Prague to be present at the first performance in the National Theatre.

For the occasion no expense had been spared. New décor constructed in Vienna at a cost of five thousand gulden, a chorus enlarged by members of the Hlahol and lesser known soloists, an orchestra augmented to a total of fifty-two, with twenty students drawn from the Conservatoire, gave the first performance added grandeur. But for Smetana it was a sad event. Though present for the first night, it is generally acknowledged that the Theatre administration omitted

[6] In the same competition Bendl received five hundred gulden for his opera *The Montenegrins* and Fibich was awarded a similar prize for the score of *Blaník*.

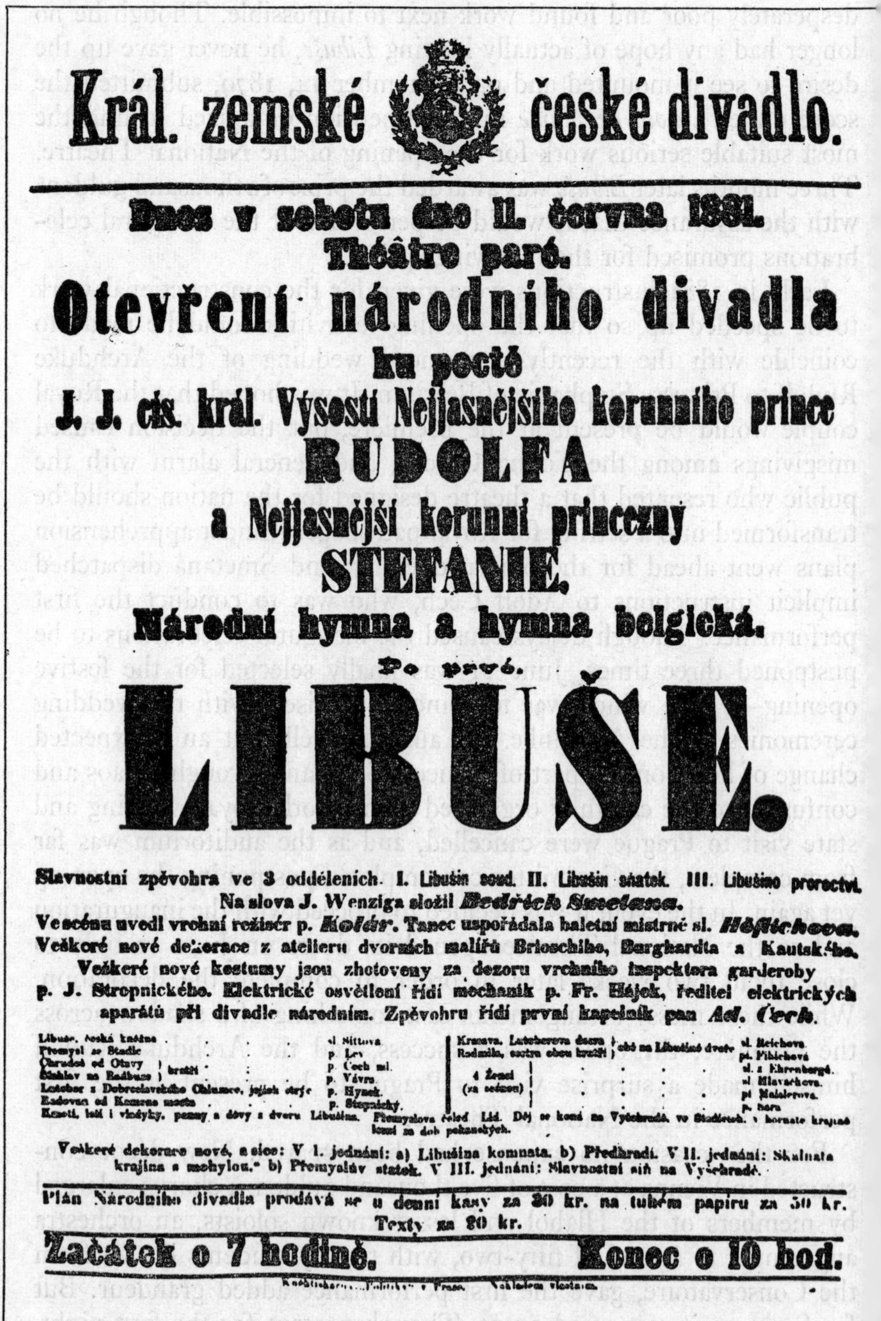

Král. zemské české divadlo.

Dnes v sobotu dne 11. června 1881.

Théâtre paré.

Otevření národního divadla

ku poctě

J. J. cís. král. Výsosti Nejjasnějšího korunního prince

RUDOLFA

a Nejjasnější korunní princezny

STEFANIE.

Národní hymna a hymna belgická.

Po prvé.

LIBUŠE.

Slavnostní zpěvohra ve 3 odděleních. I. Libušin soud. II. Libušin sňatek. III. Libušino proroctví.
Na slova J. Wenziga složil Bedřich Smetana.
Ve scénu uvodí vrchní režisér p. Kolár. Tanec uspořádala baletní mistrně sl. Hőflichova.
Veškeré nové dekerace z atelieru dvorních malířů Brioschiho, Burghardta a Kautského.
Veškeré nové kostumy jsou zhotoveny za dozoru vrchního inspektora garderoby p. J. Stropnického. Elektrické osvětlení řídí mechanik p. Fr. Hájek, ředitel elektrických aparátů při divadle národním. Zpěvohru řídí první kapelník pan Ad. Čech.

Libuše, česká kněžna	sl. Sittova	Krasava, Lutoborova dcera } obě na Libušině dvoře		sl. Reichova
Přemysl ze Stadic	p. Lev	Radmila, sestra obou bratří }		pí. Fibichová
Chrudoš od Otavy } bratří	p. Čech ml.	4 Ženci (za sedmou)		sl. z Ehrenbergů
Šťáhlav na Radbuze }	p. Vávra			sl. Hlaváčkova
Lutobor z Dobroslavského Chlumce, jejich strýc	p. Hynek			pí Maislerova
Radovan od Kamena mostu	p. Šťepanský			p. Sora

Kmeti, leši i vladyky, pánny a dívy z dvoru Libušina. Přemyslova čeleď. Lid. Děj se koná na Vyšehradě, ve Stadicích, v hornaté krajině české za dob pohanských.

Veškeré dekorace nové, a sice: V I. jednání: a) Libušina komnata. b) Předhradí. V II. jednání: Skalnatá krajina s mohylou." b) Přemyslův statek. V III. jednání: Slavnostní síň na Vyšehradě.

Plán Národního divadla prodává se u denní kasy za 20 kr. na tuhém papiru za 30 kr.
Texty za 20 kr.

Začátek o 7 hodině. Konec o 10 hod.

Poster announcing the Opening of the National Theatre, Prague with a festive performance of *Libuše* (June 11, 1881)

to send him any tickets, and since the price of admission was a hundred gulden and well outside his pocket, he was forced to gain admittance as best he could. According to an article signed with the initials 'K.C.M.' in *Dalibor* (June, 1881) 'Smetana walked along the gangway, up the stairs and into the Theatre where he wandered in front of the stage until someone in the Directors' box asked him to sit down as though they were doing him a favour'. Neither Betty Smetana nor his daughter were able to attend the gala. Moreover, nothing could now restore his hearing, and in the entire audience he was the only one not to hear a single note. He attended *Libuše* with eye and brain, following it in the dungeons of his mind, and though he sat with an 'exalted expression'[7] he was completely calm and resigned. During the first interval he was presented, with Josef Zítek,[8] to the Crown Prince,[9] but as a result of the latter's presence there was no demonstration on the part of the audience. Only after the third act, when it became known that Archduke Rudolf had left, did the applause, which had been stifled during the early part of the evening, thunder out for Smetana, who was called onto the stage for the first time in the National Theatre.[1]

Whereas *The Brandenburgers in Bohemia* unfolds like a historical novel, *The Bartered Bride* reads like an idyll, and *Dalibor* develops

[7] Zelený: *On Bedřich Smetana* (1894).

[8] Josef Zítek (1832–1909) was an outstanding Czech architect. Apart from the National Theatre he also designed the Rudolfinum in Prague, the Mill Colonnades in Karlovy Vary, and the Museum in Weimar.

[9] According to Zelený:

> 'The summons to the Royal Box came quite unexpectedly for Smetana. He was not prepared for anything of this kind. In particular he was without his hat, which had been mislaid backstage. As there was no time to fetch it, there was a moment of awkwardness which was ended by someone in the neighbouring box offering Smetana his top hat. . . . But the hat was superfluous, for it was left in the anteroom and the gentlemen were conducted into the Royal Box by the Master of Ceremonies. . . . The Crown Prince conversed with the architect Zítek, but while speaking with him looked at Smetana several times, probably enquiring about the nature of his illness, failing to understand the stage it had reached. He walked up to Smetana and standing quite close to him addressed him, after which he waited with an expectant look on his face for an answer. Smetana said: "Your Imperial Highness, I am unhappy that I cannot hear you." The Crown Prince was evidently most surprised by these words and, in the belief that he had not spoken sufficiently loudly, repeated his question. Smetana then explained that he had been completely deaf for six years. After that the Prince spoke to the Chairman of the Theatre Association about Smetana with obvious compassion.' (Zelený: *op. cit.*)

[1] Zelený: *op. cit.*

with epic pathos, it is *Libuše* alone which has the grandeur of an ode. It is not opera in the traditional sense but a magnificent pageant, a hymn to the nation, cast in six *tableaux*. If one attempts to place it in the stream of nineteenth-century opera, there are two works which appear to have fruitfully influenced it and with which it has certain affinities: Wagner's *Die Meistersinger* and Berlioz's *Les Troyens*. Though these scores are widely dissimilar, there is a common link—the epic scale on which each was conceived. Further, Smetana's dramatic idiom, looking to Wagner's on the one hand, and recalling Berlioz' prophetic princess, Cassandra, and tragic queen, Dido, on the other, makes comparison profitable, quite apart from the fact that all three operas were composed within a span of twenty years. Next to Liszt, Berlioz and Wagner were the composers whose music Smetana most admired and it is not surprising that *Libuše* bears traces of their influence.

Like Wagner, Smetana prefaces his score with a long orchestral introduction which, though it serves the function of overture, comes closer to a symphonic poem, in presenting the three motives that are to dominate the festive drama. Impressive fanfares built on a triadic figure previously used in the *tableau*, *Libuše's Judgement* (could this have been the model for the first section of Janáček's *Sinfonietta*?), establish the key of C major and Vyšehrad, Libuše's stately home high above the Vltava (see Example 56 on next page).

In the opera Smetana uses this majestic figure to symbolize the Princess's authority and several years later turned it to good use in *Vyšehrad*, the initial tone poem of the cycle *Má Vlast*. Fanfares give way to (a) Libuše's theme on the oboe, dignified and full of power, followed by (b) Přemysl's motive—a proud heroic melody on the horns that immediately establishes his manly character (see Example 57 on next page).

From these three ideas Smetana forges his musical argument, and throughout the overture his speech has a marked rhetoric; the lines are broadly sketched, the pace remains noble and unhurried. By comparison with his earlier scores, the musical textures are here noticeably more polyphonic, the interweaving of the characteristic motives being light and natural; and possibly Wagner's Prelude to *Die Meistersinger* inspired this passage where the themes of *Libuše* and Přemysl are effortlessly combined (see Example 58 on next page). The strength of *Libuše* lies not so much in the libretto but in the composer's art of depicting characters as individuals and not as dead illustrative symbols. Consequently he places enormous faith in the use of the motives announced in the Prelude, and the orchestra

Example 56

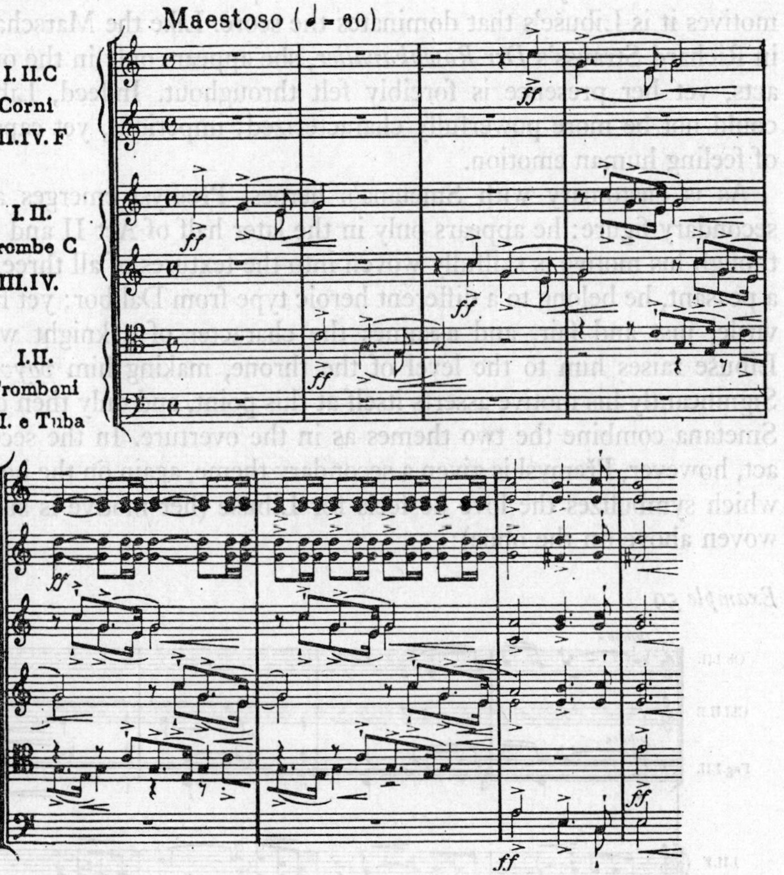

Example 57 (*a*)

(*b*)

Example 58

introduction really becomes a condensed epic in itself. Of the three motives it is Libuše's that dominates the score. Like the Marschallin in Richard Strauss's *Der Rosenkavalier*, she appears only in the outer acts, yet her presence is forcibly felt throughout. Indeed, Libuše could not be more powerfully characterized: imperious, yet capable of feeling human emotion.

As is customary with Smetana's heroes, Přemysl emerges as a secondary figure: he appears only in the later half of Act II and III, though his motive is skilfully woven into the textures of all three. As a peasant, he belong to a different heroic type from Dalibor; yet he is virile, just and fair, and assumes the character of a knight when Libuše raises him to the level of the throne, making him *voyvode*. Significantly his motive asserts itself at this point, and only then does Smetana combine the two themes as in the overture. In the second act, however, Přemysl is given a secondary theme, again on the horns, which symbolizes the love he feels for Libuše (her motive is subtly woven above on the oboe):

Example 59

The basic material for this theme was not new. Smetana had previously put it to good use in the *Album Leaf*, 'To Robert Schumann', in 1849; another *Leaf* (the one in G major) also furnished him with ideas for the dance of Přemysl's harvesters in Act II.

The other figures are less significantly characterized. Neither Krasava, Radmila, Radovan nor Lutobor have distinctive motives but the brothers Chrudoš and Šťáhlav do, and are musically well contrasted. Chrudoš, the rough warrior who has broken from his people's customs, is associated with a powerful trumpet fragment which is as abrupt and as strident as his manner:

Example 60

Šťáhlav, his rival, is less aggressive and emerges as the guardian of tradition. There is nothing defiant in his motive invariably sung by the cellos:

Example 61

In Act II, where the brothers are reunited by Krasava's confession, Smetana not only changes the instrumentation of the themes to suggest their harmonious association (cellos are replaced by clarinets, trumpets by trombones and tuba) but also combines their motives with consummate skill to show that the family rift has been healed:

Example 62

(He later repeats the device in Act III when Libuše welcomes the reunited brothers to Vyšehrad, though on this occasion Šťáhlav's motive is given to the cello.)

Like Přemysl, Chrudoš has a secondary theme but this is associated as much with his followers as it is with him. The motive denotes strife and after its first appearance in the form of a square, march-like phrase (a) is later transformed to a chromatic four-note pattern (b):

Example 63 (*a*)

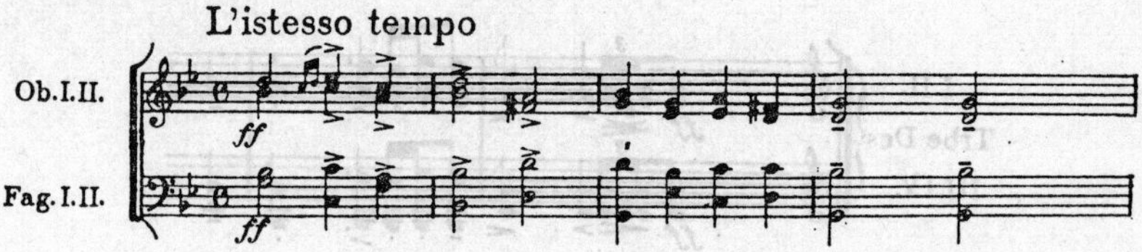

(*b*)

Similarly Šťáhlav's supporters are given a motive reflecting their disunion; and in contrast to their preceding themes, it is extended and characterized by foreboding:

Example 64

This motive is invariably sung by the chorus. It is noticeably in the dramatic choral writing that *Libuše* shows Smetana's development since his earlier scores. Here the supporters of Chrudoš and Šťáhlav become active participants in the drama, their music being full-blooded and marked to be sung with full throated vigour. The part-writing is appreciably more contrapuntal than hitherto; antiphonal effects are juxtaposed with columns of sound, and fugal episodes are alternated with homophonic phrases. The rhythms are vital, the overall effect dynamic, even explosive. Indeed, Wagner may well have been the force behind these choruses; for the brawl scene in *Die Meistersinger* showed new ways of handling great masses on stage and in score, and almost certainly Smetana had this work in mind when he composed the outburst in Act I and the homage scene in Act III. As the united tribes greet Libuše, one cannot but think by comparison of the corresponding passage in Wagner's score where the people of Nuremberg salute Hans Sachs. Yet where Wagner's idea culminates in a powerful exclamation of praise, Smetana's conception is more extended: the preparation is a gradual crescendo, the climax a lengthy peroration ending with the words 'Bud'zdráv, ó choti Libušin! Měj stále v mysli slávy čin!' (Long live Libuše's husband! May your reign always be glorious!'). This is not the only instance where *Die Meistersinger* seems to have influenced Smetana. In the climax Libuše foretells the glories of the future Czech nation and touches on the devastation that wars will bring. The final sentiment, that the Czech people shall survive all the hardships of war, seems to be modelled on Hans Sachs's address, even though he is concerned with issuing a warning about disaster threatening the German nation. But here Smetana may also have had another score in mind: Berlioz's *Les Troyens* where the glory of the future Roman capital is revealed to Dido. Certainly his long and impassioned monologues recall those written by Berlioz, and Libuše's declamations matched by a noble expression and occasional static poses, even suggest a great costumed oratorio.

Undoubtedly the most impressive of Libuše's utterances is the final one where each of her visions is evoked by a different instrumentation: Břetislav and Jitka are described with horns (later supported by trombones), and clarinets (doubled by bassoons) singing a lilting $^6_4$ phrase, made to sound archaic by the introduction of the harp; for Jaroslav of Šternbeck, strings bear the weight of the expression; Ottokar II, Elizabeth and Charles IV are introduced by the full orchestra; Žižka and the Hussites are invoked with the chorale *Ye who are God's warriors* on trombones, and later by the entire brass section; while for George of Poděbrady[2] the chorale is thundered out by full orchestra in a broad March that fulminates across the score anticipating the close of the tone poems *Tábor* and *Blaník* (so powerfully is the chorale stated at this point that three other composers were moved to incorporate it into their music: it is to be found in Dvořák's *Hussite Overture*, Suk's tone poem *Praga*, and Vítěslav Novák's *South Bohemian Suite*).

Smetana's feeling for subtle orchestral colouring is also to be found in Libuše's earlier monologues, notably that in Act I, where she sits in judgement. As she describes the rite she must perform as arbiter in the dispute the symbolic implements of justice are solemnly evoked, one by one, in the orchestra like the semi-tones of nature.

[2] Although Mussorgsky, in a burst of Pan-Slav enthusiasm, had attempted to sketch a symphonic poem on the feats of George of Poděbrady in 1867, it is unlikely this coloured Smetana's penultimate *tableau*, even though some of Mussorgsky's themes are Czech in character and may well be actual folk songs collected by Balakirev during his visits to Prague.

The lime tree is depicted by the oboe; the tablets by staccato strings; flute scales represent the rushing fire, and widely spaced arpeggios on violins and violas suggest the undefiled water. Elsewhere Smetana's gift for orchestral colouring is no less striking. For the arrival of the deputation in Act II he creates a magical effect with muted strings playing pizzicato as the procession of horses draws nearer. But the most imaginative stroke of all occurs in the Stadice scene (Act II, Scene 3) where two clarinets accompany the tracery of four solo voices (two sopranos, alto and high tenor—all behind the stage) in a delicate filigree of shifting thirds and sixths that is the real precursor of the rustic mood pictures of *Má Vlast* and the musical essence of the Bohemian countryside as interpreted by Smetana. This and Přemysl's meditation under the lime tree are among the most delicate pastoral interludes in all his music.

But the mood does not hide the diffidence Smetana felt when writing for his hero. That he was troubled creating this role and others we know from the sketches where Přemysl's part is pitched surprisingly high for a baritone. While Smetana was able to suggest alternatives for the solo lines, the duet with Libuše in Act III caused particular embarrassment, the tessitura being demanding and made more exposed by the low range of the soprano's part. Unfortunately this disturbed the composer, who had always experienced difficulties in writing love duets, be it in *The Brandenburgers in Bohemia* (where also the scene for Liduše and Tausendmark is a weak spot) or in *The Devil's Wall* where Vok emerges more as Hedvika's father than her lover. In *Libuše* the difficulty was aggravated by Smetana's inability to know how two supreme national leaders should express their intimate feelings for each other. His solution is contrived. Certainly Libuše and Přemysl declare their love, but not to each other: instead they address gods, a cumbersome and time-worn device which results in a curiously impersonal effect.

This duet apart, there is much to admire in *Libuše* and much that is new. Smetana's adventurous harmonic vocabulary has been mentioned in previous chapters, but here he seems to accept dissonance completely, using triads and combinations of notes without either preparation or resolution. Naturally, the chord structure is chromatic, and where there is no recognizable progression Smetana's system of pedals, sometimes simultaneously sounded, binds the texture. His modulations never seem planned over a long period of bars: they simply happen and are effected by a characteristic technique of sliding semitonal movement into another key, regardless of false relations or aggressive clashes that may result:

Example 65

tak sva-zek svor-no-sti ob-jí-mej
tak sva-zek svor-no-sti ob-jí-mej, ob-
tak sva-zek svorno-sti ob-jí-mej nás,
tak sva-zek svorno-sti ob-jí-mej
sf
nás, ob-jí-mej nás ob-ji-mej nás,
ji-mej nás, ob-ji-mej nás, ob-ji-mej
ob-jí-mej nás, ob-jí-mej ob-jí-mej
nás ob-jí-mej nás, ob-jí-mej nás.
sf
tak svazek svor-no-sti ob-jí-mej nás, at
nás, tak svazek svor-no-sti ob-jí-mej nás,
nás, tak sva-zek svorno-sti ob-jí-mej
tak sva-zek svorno-sti ob-jí-mej nás,
sf
cresc.
p

Example 65 (*b*)

Throughout, augmented and diminished triads are combined with so much chromatic and enharmonic alterations that Smetana is hard put to prevent his score from assuming a distinctly Wagnerian sound. Indeed, he must have found it hard to avoid the influence of the great Brünnhilde-Wotan duet in *Die Walküre* when he came to write the impassioned burial mound scene, where Krasava pleads for her father's forgiveness (Act II, Scene 1). Similarly, the bridal chamber scene in *Lohengrin* may well have furnished ideas for Libuše's maidens as they prepare the Princess for her nuptial ceremony (Act III, Scene 2).

That Smetana did not always resist external influences is not to his discredit. Possibly his admiration for the music of Liszt was as constructive as was that for Wagner, and it is not surprising that the mythological nature of the plot drew from him a powerful symphonic expression which leans more heavily on Wagner's music dramas than it does on any other composer. But where Wagner interpreted the myth as a vehicle for expressing his own symbolism and philosophy, Smetana transformed it into a peak of patriotic solemnity and festive pageantry. Unlike *Má Vlast*, *Libuše* is little known outside Czechoslavakia, yet it remains one of its composer's most significant scores, and the one he most highly esteemed. Today it holds a special place in the repertoire of the National Theatre in Prague, and though the performances there may be more numerous than the 'memorial days that touch the Czech people as a nation',[3] the enthusiasm which it rouses remains an affirmation of Bohemia's ancient glory and its future triumph.

[3] Letter to Čech: August 17, 1883.

TEN

'THE TWO WIDOWS'
1872–1874

IN THE MONTHS immediately following the première of *Dalibor* few people were aware that Smetana was working on *Libuše*. To a public who had witnessed the appearance of his first three operas within the space of what seemed little more than a few months, a new score was long overdue. It seemed strange that nothing had been announced—strange, too, that the man who had done more than any other to create National Opera in Prague should be the centre of controversy and the subject of heated polemics. Attacks which at first were directed at Smetana on a personal level grew against a background of artistic disputes and political friction between the Young Czech and Old Czech Parties, and for the root cause we need look no further than Smetana's appointment as Conductor at the Provisional Theatre. At that time his friends had included František Pivoda (1824–1898), a Moravian who, after studying composition in Vienna, had set up a second-rate singing school in Prague. He seems to have been a narrow-minded, mean and selfish man, whose enemies had nicknamed him 'Orpheus' because he was always singing his own praises to further his own ambition. Smetana had known him first at the Umělecká Beseda and later on a Committee to establish a School of Dramatic Art. Their friendship flourished, and within months Pivoda had recommended Smetana for the post of Director at the Prague Conservatoire. Though he failed to be elected, his subsequent appointment to the Provisional Theatre encouraged Pivoda to believe he could better his own position and he proposed that his own pupils be engaged at the Opera. He offered to provide an entirely new cast of principals each year, and came to regard the Provisional Theatre as the senior class of his school. Enterprising as the scheme was, Smetana refused to be associated with any form of nepotism, least of all that which flouted musical continuity or went against the idea of a permanent company. Embittered, Pivoda sought to oppose the new conductor and began to scheme, first with the displaced Maýr, then with Rieger, Intendant and leader of the Old Czechs.

The first attack came after the première of *Dalibor*, a score which split the musical world into two camps. On the one hand there were some who appreciated the real value of the work and saw it as a significant link in the chain of operas Smetana was writing; for this minority he was the light of the future, a reformer to be supported not suppressed. On the other, there were many who regarded him with suspicion, who believed him to be a disciple of Wagner, and therefore the Judas of Czech Art. Much of the discontent had emanated from *The Bartered Bride* which, after *Dalibor*, had been seized as the symbol of Czech national music. Its popular melodies, gay dances and colourful plot had created a musical cult to which everyone quickly subscribed. *The Bartered Bride* had so charmed its audiences that everything thereafter was measured by it. The people had come to regard Smetana as the creator of a true national opera: that he did not continue in the same style could only be interpreted as a betrayal and a sin against the nation.

Pivoda spitefully used this situation to start a campaign against Smetana, using *Dalibor* as a stick with which to castigate the composer. The first attack appeared in the paper *Pokrok* (*Progress*) where he detected an 'indigestible foreign influence' in *Dalibor*. Later he condemned Smetana's revisions of *The Bartered Bride* as a deliberate attempt to spoil a national work:

> *The Bartered Bride* is no longer a beautiful country girl but a painted hussy returning from the city where she has been in order to become educated and refined.

Today Pivoda's reasoning seems so childish that it is hard to believe he commanded any following at all. He seems to have possessed little more than a mediocre musical talent and disliked rich orchestral polyphony which obscured words or vocal lines. He reproached Wagner for failing to express himself in simple triads and saw in Italian opera the acme of all vocal writing: he lived for the singer, not the song, and regarded folk music as the criterion of true national art.

Despite this bigotry he was not unsuccessful in recruiting supporters to his cause and within weeks Rozkošný, Böhm, Hřímalý, Knittl, Konopašek and Jirášek, the barley dealer, were entrenched in his ranks. Smetana's followers, Fibich, Kliebert, Pech, Novotný and Pippich, retaliated, and the opposing groups mobilized their forces around two newspapers: *Dalibor*, aptly named for Smetana, and *Hudební Listy* for Pivoda. Thus, the columns of two rival journals became the soil upon which the battle for the recognition of Smetana's music was fought. This was no friendly combat but a vicious onslaught in which weapons were words, scandal and lies. There was no question of compromise. People were either for Smetana or against him. Tactfully, he seldom engaged in the polemic himself (for that matter, neither did Maýr); but when in 1869–1870 the reproaches became more infamous and spread to other journals, he felt moved to voice some defence. While Neruda and Hálek supported him in *Lumír*, the vitriolic Vlček attempted to discredit him in *Osvěta*. Cartoonists caricatured him in *Paleček*: satirists lampooned him in *Humoristicke Listy*. More serious was the introduction of political backing. During 1870 Pivoda, now joined by Durdík, renewed his attacks in *Pokrok* and *Politik*, both papers being supported by the Old Czech Party: in retaliation the Young Czechs turned to *Národní Listy*. Edited by Gustav Eim, the language became fiery, the epithets blunt. Within a short time the issue had grown to inflated proportions and clearly Smetana had now to be reckoned with. His supporters tried to prove that in establishing a true and artistic level of Czech music he was the man of the future: his enemies saw it as their duty to protect art from all foreign and progressive influences and reinstate Maýr, the man of the past. Thus the slogan 'to be for or not to be for Modern Czech Music' had particular significance at this time; and neither the maligning of Smetana's operas, nor the combined tactics of printing articles attacking him and suppressing testimony in his favour could avail long.

Smetana had always regarded composition from a nationalistic and realistic point of view, disliking abstract music and leaning towards programmatic subjects. He believed that absolute music stifled national expression and led to repetition of form and content. He approached each work with the intention that it should be unique, and reproached those who saw the future of Czech music in the creation of traditional cantatas and concertos. Not unnaturally he had turned to the tone poems of Liszt and looked to the music dramas of Wagner to broaden his musical horizon, and in so doing had provided ammunition for his adversaries. Pivoda, who had set himself up as Grand Inquisitor, attempted in a series of national trials to prove Smetana's guilt and have him excommunicated from the musical faith. He argued that nationalism in music could only be established by incorporating folk song into opera and since Smetana had spurned this in *Dalibor*, attempting to out-Wagner Wagner, he could only be proclaimed 'un-Czech'. To Pivoda, everything Germanic in life and art, thought and feeling was rotten to the core and fit only for destruction.

Consequently, Smetana's interpretation of *Fidelio* at the Provisional Theatre was dismissed as the action of a German traitor, and his reading of Beethoven's Ninth Symphony as one 'spitting abuse on religion and almighty God'. Pivoda even brought out a pamphlet based on Hanslick's criticisms of Wagner, in which he argued that Smetana's Germanization of Czech music made further development impossible. With Max Konopašek, he urged that Czech music be regarded not as an independent unit, but as part of a larger Slavonic art. Konopašek argued that the Germanism of Bohemian and Moravian folk songs made them beyond salvation and proposed a return to the basic elements of Slavonic music, namely a rusin dance from the Galizien region, called kolomejka[1] which he had recently rediscovered. Konopašek firmly believed he was striking a blow for progress and this became the centre of his thesis. In *Hudební Listy* he advocated that artists should work together to create an art-form based on the kolemejka, which would unite all Slav peoples.

Meanwhile, Rieger determined to spearhead a drive against Smetana (who had been co-opted as champion of the Young Czechs) by adopting a composer for the Old Czech Party whom he hoped could be made to overshadow his rival. In Rieger's hands, Vilém Blodek, whose opera *In the Well* had won certain critical acclaim, was a puppet to be manipulated this way or that, and through the columns of *Pokrok* and *Hudební Listy* he began to emerge as a force to be reckoned with. At the Měšťanská Beseda (the Prague Citizens' Club and meeting place of the Old Czechs) he was regarded with high hopes, but for all the publicity he received Blodek was little more than a second-rate composer, let alone a second Smetana. He was never able to approach the originality of his opponent and his tragic death[2] in 1874 forced Rieger to cultivate a replacement in Antonín Dvořák.

Over the months Pivoda had in no way mellowed, and to ensure his own position, testimonials of his abilities appeared in the Press:

> He is an artist whose pedagogic renown and experience place him in the front row of all domestic musical legions.[3]

The Old Czechs lauded him as the authority *par excellence* on Prague's musical and theatrical activities and encouraged him to intensify his

[1] Kolemejka—a quick dance in a two-in-a-measure time popular among the mountain peasants, especially in the Carpathians, Tatras and in Poland.

[2] Blodek's death in a lunatic asylum at the age of forty prevented him from completing his second comic opera *Zitek* to a libretto of Sabina. Six years later Blodek's widow invited Smetana to complete her husband's work but at the time he was engaged on *The Devil's Wall* and unable to accept.

[3] *Hudební Listy*: September, 1868.

PLATE XVII. Jabkenice: grounds and summer-house

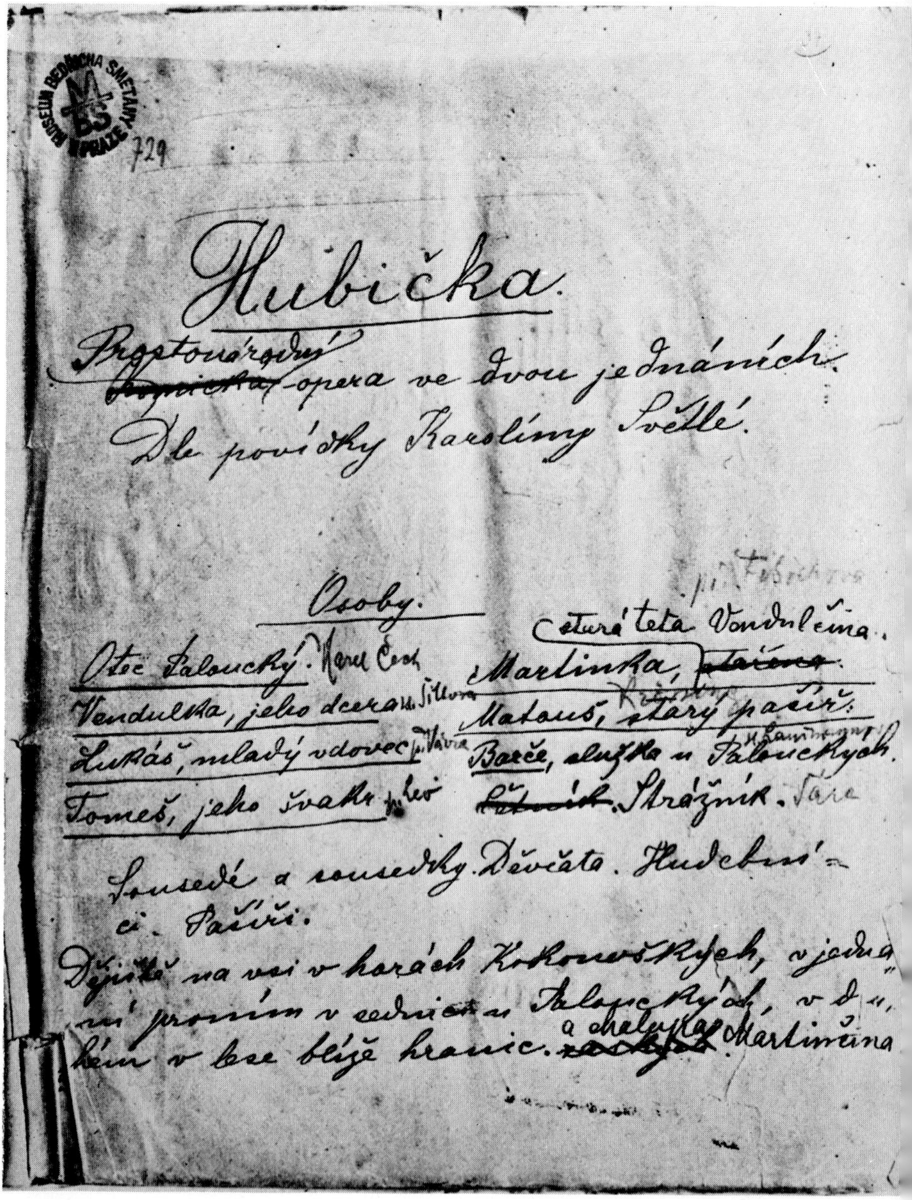

Hubička.
Prostonárodní opera ve dvou jednáních.
Dle povídky Karoliny Světlé.
Osoby.
Otec Paloucký. Karel Čech
Martinka, stará teta Vendulčina.
Vendulka, jeho dcera.
Matouš, starý pašíř.
Lukáš, mladý vdovec.
Barče, služka u Palouckých.
Tomeš, jeho švagr.
Strážník.
Sousedé a sousedky. Děvčata. Hudebníci. Pašíři.
Dějiště na vsi v horách Krkonošských, v jednání prvním v sednici u Palouckých, v druhém v lese blíže hranic a chalupa Martinčina.

PLATE XVIII. *The Kiss:* Title page of Libretto

Showing Smetana's list of characters with suggested casting

thrusts on a more personal level. Openly, he now confessed a repugnance and disgust for Smetana, envying only his beautiful wife. At forty-eight, he described him as an 'elderly composer ten years past his prime' and 'a German iconoclast revolting against feudalism and clericalism'. Next followed an offensive against his work at the Theatre. He criticized his reforms, deplored his programmes, deprecated his standard of performance. He reproached Smetana for the time spent away from the Theatre composing, and castigated his neglect of operas by native composers. But it was an accusation of indifference which most provoked Smetana, who had done more than anyone to introduce works by Rozkošný, Bendl, Blodek, Hřímalý and Šebor into the repertoire, quite apart from his own.[4] Though Pivoda was aware of these facts, his persecutions continued at such an intense pitch that Smetana considered resigning his post and contemplated a return to Sweden. Otakar Hostinský records that he was prepared for the time when he would have to leave the Provisional Theatre, and that he was ready to take up his career as a concert pianist. Josef Paleček, who was often a guest in the Smetana household, even promised to secure work for him at the Imperial Opera in St. Petersburg, where he was principal bass. Smetana's eldest daughter Žofie confirms Hostinský's account and remembers that at this time her father began to practice up to four hours each morning to regain his technique. Josef Jiránek, his friend and pupil, describes that in preparation for his Russian tour he did not spare himself five-finger exercises in double thirds, as well as restudying the concertos of Liszt, Schumann and Chopin. And all this was in order to escape allegations that he was an obstacle to the further development of musical talents and had monopolized the musical scene for too long.

In December the situation became grave:

> My enemies (headed by Rieger) have done their best with the Theatre Association to bring about my dismissal and re-establish Mayr in my place. Half Prague is talking about it and singers, orchestras, journalists, critics and subscribers are doing their best to see that this happens. Articles are being written everywhere.[5]

[4] In the period 1866–1874, over two hundred performances were given of works by Czech composers:

> Four operas by Šebor were performed a total of forty-five times. Two operas by Bendl received nineteen performances, of which fifteen were of *Lejla*. Two operas by Rozkošný received twenty-eight hearings. Blodek's *In the Well* was heard thirty times and Hřímalý's *Enchanted Prince* fifteen. *The Bartered Bride* was given forty-nine times, *The Brandenburgers in Bohemia* eight, *Dalibor* eleven, and *The Two Widows* six times.

[5] Diary: December 6, 1872.

Indeed they were, and a letter signed by nearly seventy season-ticket holders demanded his resignation; the Press urged Maýr's return 'to allow Mr. Smetana more time for composition'; Pivoda, descending to gutter level, cunningly stressed the composer's advancing years and cast doubts as to his sanity; Rieger announced that Maýr was ready to take over from Smetana should his health deteriorate. On the surface Rieger seemed certain of success. But neither he, Maýr nor Pivoda had allowed for public opinion. Hastily, Smetana's friends came to his defence. A number of handbills were printed and prominently displayed in the windows of Grégr and Dattel's publishing house; friends campaigned on his behalf, some of them picketing passers-by to rally to his side. At the end of the first day two hundred signatures had been collected, and by the beginning of the second week over two thousand had registered their support. The petition was delivered in person to Rieger, but the bitter campaign was only interrupted, not halted.

Depressed, dispirited, apparently dishonoured, Smetana arrived at the Provisional Theatre on December 12 to conduct a routine performance of Auber's *La Muette de Portici*. The occasion proved to be quite different from what he was expecting. On walking into the pit he was greeted with a tumultuous ovation from artists, orchestra and audience:

> There were three wreaths on my desk, each with the inscription 'Remain with us in the Theatre and give yourself to the Nation'. As I stepped onto the rostrum they sounded a fanfare and everyone rose to their feet. The public also rose and there were shouts of 'Bravo' and 'We won't let you go!' This continued for some ten minutes during which I had to keep bowing and acknowledging them.[6]

Earlier, a manifesto signed by thirty-five musicians, including Fibich, Dvořák, Heller, Foerster and Hřímalý, all supporting his policy and demanding greater powers for his position, was delivered to the Intendant and the Directors:

> What Smetana is to our music in general he is doubly to our dramatic art. It is therefore vital that our Operatic Institute keeps the services of a composer who has done the most to ensure the gratifying development of our operatic literature in these difficult times. Mr. Smetana left his position abroad and hastened here to Prague to lay the foundation of our future

[6] Diary: December 12, 1872.

> dramatic national music . . . with *The Bartered Bride* he blazed a trail for Czech light opera, indeed we may say he is the creator of that genre. In *The Brandenburgers in Bohemia* and *Dalibor* he has given no less splendid proof of his conscious and determined striving towards a goal. . . . We declare that should the time come when someone who does not (if we do not wish to say 'cannot') compare with him, either from the point of view of artistic training or as regards his activities as composer, we shall be forced to the depressing conclusion that real art finds no honour or recognition at home and that, therefore, our own honourable strivings have an uncertain future. And just as we have full confidence in Mr. Smetana, we would, on the other hand, have to be very mistrustful of anyone who was put in his place against unanimous convictions and despite the protests of the circle of musicians whose word will not be regarded as lacking in weight in this matter. . . . In short the opera composers among us would hesitate to entrust their works to the hands of a conductor whom they might have to pronounce as unfit for the job.

These campaigns were widely reported in the Press, and on December 14 Jan Neruda made an impressive appraisal of Smetana's work and achievement in *Národní Listy* in which he argued that the people had done harm to themselves and to the nation by recognizing neither Smetana nor his art. On the same day the orchestra presented a declaration to the Theatre Committee pledging support for their Musical Director:

> We ask the Committee to accept our grateful thanks for the present situation which is crowned by wonderful achievements. From the moment when the Committee engaged Mr. Smetana, our excellent and irreplaceable leader, our art was elevated by his clear efforts to a level from which only genuine artistic results can flow. We are enthusiastic about his conducting and all our leanings are towards him. We want only to fulfil his slightest wish with our fullest abilities. In Mr. Smetana we see ourselves united in one person, and in friendship. In him we see a reflection of all our spiritual efforts; for he is the guiding star to all enterprise. He should stay with us from year to year for the glory of the Czech nation. Glory to Smetana!

For all its exaggerated tone, this tribute of loyalty did much to restore Smetana's confidence. But his decision to stay as conductor was greeted by new charges of incompetence from Pivoda and his claque. National trials continued. Demonstrations followed. Close friends urged Smetana to assert his position by producing the recently-completed *Libuše*; but at a time when he was being made the martyr for Czech art he realized that the appearance of this particular score could do nothing but increase hostilities.

For some time, however, Hostinský and Neruda had pressed him to write an opera in a new vein which would silence his critics, reaffirm his image in the public eye, and stabilize his position at the theatre. Adolf Čech, had offered to take the administrative burden from his shoulders. The idea of composing another opera was certainly not new, and for several months Smetana had been searching for a suitable plot. He had even invited the young poet Eliška Krásnohorská, a member of his choir, to provide a libretto similar to *Lejla*, with which Bendl had recently won enormous success. She duly complied and suggested a plot based on the life of Lumír, the Slavonic bard; but this suggestion failed to attract the composer, who was much more interested in *Vlasta*, a mythological subject close in spirit and time to *Libuše*. Unfortunately this was promised to Hynek Palla, and as Krásnohorská had nothing ready, she could only offer to alter *Lumír* until it pleased Smetana. Though he re-read the text he failed to respond to its austere nature, and six months were to pass until April 21, 1871, when he received a new libretto based on Shakespeare's *Twelfth Night*, entitled *Sebastian and Viola*. About this he was more enthusiastic, and by May 11 the outline had been transformed to rough draft. On June 29 Smetana wrote to Krásnohorská accepting the poem but asking for cuts to be made. As these were substantial and would involve a certain delay she attempted to persuade Palla to relinquish *Vlasta*, upon which Smetana had so set his heart. In exchange she offered her fifth libretto, *Cassandra*, but Palla refused to co-operate. Disappointed, Smetana resolved to wait until *Sebastian and Viola* was in a more advanced state.

Being the centre of a ruthless altercation in which his own position was becoming less certain under the pressure of Pivoda's pejorative attacks, Smetana naturally preferred to push Krásnohorská's librettos to one side; in any case he had long set his heart on writing something more sophisticated than *The Bartered Bride*, which he had lately come to despise. Possibly Hřímalý's *Enchanted Prince*, Auber's *Le Domino Noir* or Halévy's *L'Éclair* had aroused in him a desire to try his hand at a lighter type of drawing-room opera; but with so much scandal in the air the time hardly seemed right. Yet the more he considered it the more convinced was he that a new opera would silence his enemies, providing it could be in a different style. By chance, he hit on a frivolous one-act comedy by the French playwright

Jean Pierre Félicien Mallefille (1813–1868). Written in 1859 and presented at the Théâtre Français in the following year, *Les deux Veuves* became one of the brightest successes in Paris. In June 1862, it reached the German stage and a few months later arrived in Prague in a German translation. After a space of six years it was revived in Czech at the Provisional Theatre and during the summer months played to full houses in a triple bill with Herion's *Who's Going to Die?* and Suppé's operetta *Zehn Mädchen und kein Mann*. Smetana may well have seen it at this time or read about it in *Národní Listy*. Certainly he had access to the scripts at the Theatre and may even have kept the play in mind for future operatic use. At precisely what stage he decided to set it to music is uncertain: all we know is that Mallefille's comedy became the instrument of his defiance sometime during the spring of 1873.

The Diary, which reveals as much information about the composition of *Dvě vdovy* (*The Two Widows*) as any of his operas, is curiously vague as to the origins of the text. We do not know if Smetana invited his librettist Emanuel Züngl to co-operate with him or if Züngl offered him a fully-drafted scheme before composition, though the former is more likely. Züngl (1840–1894), like Smetana's previous collaborators, was not a professional poet, but a linguist who earned his living as a freelance writer, and approached his work with the speed of a journalist. He enlarged the action from one act to two, added an opening and closing chorus, and gave the whole a local flavour with Czech names and a Bohemian setting. Only minor details in the French text were omitted, and while some extra verses were added for arias and ensembles, the essential conversational dialogue of Mallefille's original remains. Though Züngl's copy of the libretto shows traces of his having worked at a considerable pace, he succeeded in preserving wit and removed many of the vulgarities present in the French text.

Smetana began work on July 16, 1873, and composed at a rate quite unprecedented in his career. By September 5 the newspaper *Dalibor* announced he was engaged on a new opera (erroneously, to a libretto by Krásnohorská) and that he had proceeded as far as Act II. The manuscript vocal score bears witness of his rapid progress, the final page of the first act being inscribed:

> Begun July 16 and finished August 30 after fourteen days' holiday in Vienna where I attended the World Exhibition.

This refers only to the completion of the vocal draft, for another inscription records that the orchestration of Act I was completed on

November 13, 1873. So confident was he that he seems, more or less, to have dispensed with sketches altogether. Unless others have been lost, only four page of rough notes, and those appertaining to a later revision, have come down to us. As was his usual practice, he took themes previously noted in his motive book for the substance of his creative thought, selecting those he considered most appropriate to the style of his plot: the Act I, Scene 5, quartet theme, 'Ó Jakou tíseň' ('Oh, what anxiety') dates from June, 1863; the principal melody of the Act II, Scene 2, duet, 'Ruzhodnuto uzavřeno' ('It's decided, it's completed') from September, 1864; and the polka tune, for Ladislav and Anežka, from August, 1866.

While these provided Smetana with some of his basic material, this does not account for the remarkable speed at which *The Two Widows* was composed. By January 15, 1874, the instrumentation of Act II was complete and the opera announced for performance in the spring. At the end of February the score[7] was in rehearsal and on March 27 the curtain rose at the Provisional Theatre for the première, which was also Smetana's Benefit:

> *The Two Widows* filled the house and received a most excellent performance. After each item there was warm applause and at the end of both acts the composer had to appear on the stage. He was given a silver laurel wreath and a silver baton. Smetana was so long on the platform that it made a fitting reward to the ridiculous and outrageous attacks he has received elsewhere.[8]

The success of the new opera was immediate. In his Diary Smetana called it 'perfect'. Hans von Bülow exclaimed that the nineteenth century had not seen an opera with which it could be compared; and Jan Neruda described it as 'springing from the soul of the nation . . . the work of a genius who has shown the direction Czech opera must follow'.[9] Though these comments did much to boost Smetana's morale they did little to silence his enemies: on the contrary, his name became the subject of renewed bitterness. *The Two Widows* was seen as the work of a Wagner disciple; its idiom was considered too progressive, its style incomprehensible. Pivoda again accused him of teutonic influences and Rieger continued to canvas for Maýr's return as Chief Conductor:

[7] The manuscript score is written in violet ink. This may well have been a stroke of affectation on Smetana's part, but since the staves are printed in brown rather than black it is possible that violet ink showed up better to a man whose sight was failing fast.

[8] *Dalibor*: March 28, 1874. [9] *Národní Listy*: March 28, 1874.

I am again persecuted in the Press by Pivoda, Rieger and Maýr. They claim that Maýr was more active and diligent than I. In a reply to *Hudenbí Listy* and *Politik* I have corrected the slanders printed by Pivoda and Lindhart, but they have published my letter with comments more insulting and mendacious than before.[1]

The cause of these attacks was rooted not only in the success of *The Two Widows*, which received five performances between March and May, but also in Smetana's salary, which was increased to two thousand gulden a year. Annoyed, Pivoda produced a ruthless attack in *Politik* which appeared anonymously:

At the Opera whom have we gained since 1866? The Conductor Mr. Smetana who has an enormous salary as composer, Conductor, Artistic Director and Director of the Opera School. As a composer his activities are negligible. In 1866, *The Brandenburgers in Bohemia* and *The Bartered Bride* were already finished. Since then only *Dalibor* and *The Two Widows* have appeared. In eight years he has written two operas! And of all his works only *The Bartered Bride* has held the stage. As Conductor he is known by name only in the theatre handbook. The public see him more frequently in the Café Bendl reading the papers, or at home resting his jangled nerves. The Theatre is in a desolate state and his constitution is so frail that he does not want to see a baton, let alone hold a rehearsal. Everything is left to the deputy conductor, Adolf Čech. As Artistic Director Smetana is even more inactive—and for the same reasons. But as Director of the Opera School he has an immense timetable: two lectures since the School began. And for these he receives six hundred gulden—that is three hundred gulden for each. Indeed, more than a princely reward! How this Opera School is progressing under his direction was demonstrated at their fiasco in the Provisional Theatre recently. In short, the Principal Conductor must be considered a nothing—a zero—a blank! From time to time he asks the Committee for a prolongation of his contract, and the raising of his salary which Dr. Čížek, the Chairman, agrees to make. Mr. Smetana is the first person to regard the Theatre as his home and an institute for pathological idiots.[2]

The stab was exquisite in its calculated cruelty and perfect in timing; but ironically it was not attacks such as these which forced Smetana to relinquish his post. The tragedy that had overtaken Beethoven was now repeated in Smetana:

[1] Diary: April, 1874.

[2] *Politik*: September 12, 1874.

. . . It is my cruel destiny that I may lose my hearing. In my right ear I hear nothing, and in the left very little. So I am going deaf. This is the state of my health, of which since July I have tried to cure myself. It was in July,[3] the second day, that I noted the higher octaves in my ear were tuned at a different pitch. From time to time I had a rushing noise in my ears as if I was standing near a forceful waterfall. The condition was continuously changing until the end of the month when it became permanent, being accompanied by spells of giddiness. I began to reel and only by concentrating all my strength could I manage to walk straight.[4] I had a bad holiday and rushed from the country to Prague to see Dr. Zoufal,[5] the well known specialist. Now I am his patient. He allows me to make no effort[6] and no music. I can neither play nor listen to playing. A fair-sized choir becomes a hotchpotch of sound and I'm unable to distinguish one voice from another. For this reason I ask you to inform the Committee of my sad state and unhappiness. For me this is a tragedy. Since I cannot continue in my present position I beg the Committee to release me for a certain time from conducting all rehearsals. If my condition deteriorates within three months then I must resign my office and accept my sad fate. As I cannot give lessons and have no means of supporting my family I ask you to send part of last year's fee from the Opera School, which is still outstanding. Dr. Zoufal is willing to provide any certificate you may require as to my distressing condition.[7]

Over the next few weeks Smetana's condition remained unchanged, but on October 8 his hearing in the left ear improved slightly:

For the first time for ages I can hear all the octaves, in their

[3] The Diary for July includes the following entry for the 28th:

My hearing is failing and at the same time my head seems to be spinning. I feel giddy. It started during a short duck-shooting expedition when the weather had suddenly changed.

[4] According to the Diary for August 1, the rushing in his head was so great that he could hardly work. In the same entry he wrote 'I must see a doctor!'

[5] On August 5 he consulted Dr. Emanuel Zoufal (1837–1910) the eminent German ear, nose and throat specialist. His Diary records that 'Dr. Zoufal ordered me to stay in Prague so that he can keep me under observation for a few days'. On August 8 he visited the specialist again and noted that 'the ear trouble is caused by catarrh: for the time being I am trying inhalations'.

[6] Because of his persistent ear trouble Smetana's Diary entry for August 2[illegible] notes that he was unable to take part in the hare hunting as was his usual practice.

[7] Letter to Dr. Čížek: September 5, 1874.

> proper balance. Previously they were completely jumbled up, but I still cannot hear anything in my right ear.[8]

During the next fourteen days there was sufficient amelioration to allow him to attend, and hear, a performance of Delibes's opera *Le Roi l'a dit* at the Provisional Theatre:

> The opera had pleased me so much that after the fifth act I returned home and extemporized fantasies at the keyboard for over an hour. On the morning of October 20, 1874, I awoke stone deaf, unable to hear anything in either left or right ears.[9]

While its continuous flow and tender lyricism suggest that *The Two Widows* was written in one stretch of time, and at one of the happiest periods of the composer's life, nothing could be further from the truth. Indeed, *The Two Widows* underwent considerable revision before it emerged in its third form, in 1882 and the version which Smetana heard for the last time on May 11, 1874, differed considerably from the definitive score of 1877. Though it was the basis for all later versions, it was shorter and more chamber-like than the one we know today. Originally there were four principals and a chorus, and the action proceeded with spoken prose between the musical items. With two overtures, one prefacing each act, there were only thirteen musical numbers, but one of them, the quartet which concludes Act I, ran to a hundred and twenty-seven bars.

With Smetana's enforced retirement in 1874, the problem of survival became increasingly difficult. To deafness was added financial hardship and when, in 1877, the Committee of the Provisional Theatre ceased all payments to him he was forced to negotiate a new agreement. In return for a miserable pittance he ceded the performing rights in all his operas, and agreed to revise *The Two Widows* which had lain unperformed for three years.

> To show my goodwill to the Theatre, I have consented to rework the score of *The Two Widows*. I hope it will be finished soon because I have signed away the rights of performance without royalty.[1]

In this new version Smetana wanted to rectify flaws and weaknesses that had been noted in the early performances. He was anxious to bring the score into line with his previous operas by substituting

[8] Diary: October, 1874.
[9] Letter to J. Finch Thorne: December 11, 1881.
[1] Letter to Krásnohorská: July 10, 1877.

sung recitative for spoken prose. Moreover, he hoped to stress its national elements and as this entailed two scenes being enlarged, he invited Züngl to work with him again, even though he had been able to offer only sixty gulden for his contribution in 1874. In the second version Züngl was no longer translator but collaborator, condensing dialogue into verse ready for recitative. He created an extra song for Ladislav; a new finale for Act I (it became the most extended ensemble in the opera); two new characters, Lidunka and Toník, and a trio for them and Mumlal. It is difficult to know how much Züngl worked on his own initiative, but it is likely many suggestions emanated from Smetana himself. In all, the changes add up to twenty-eight pages of new text which the composer 'worked on with enthusiasm'.[2] Again there are no sketches and few dates with which to trace his progress. We know, however, that Act I was finished on June 28, 1877, and that Act II followed a fortnight later on July 13. The material seems to have been newly composed except for a waltz-like motive (jotted in the motive book in February, 1876) which Smetana put to good use in Ladislav's song in the second act:

> I hope it will be successful. I believe this scene with Ladislav behind the stage to be similar to the lullaby in *The Kiss*. The piece is in a national idiom and, though I say it myself, this is a new Czech song. The recitatives are not as easy to compose as one might have hoped. Some are *secco* but in others, where there are references to former songs and motivs and a greater characterization, the work has been difficult, becoming more important in value than in normal opera. The Act I finale and Act II trio are now in a national idiom.[3]

In spite of difficulties and the fact that Smetana could no longer work with his previous facility, he was able to deliver the new version to the Provisional Theatre on August 15. Secretly, he hoped he would now be in a stronger position to demand payment of his salary, which had been withheld for several months. But with Mayŕ returned as Conductor,[4] Smetana received little sympathy and his score was left to collect dust until March 15, 1878, when Čech re-introduced it to the repertoire. By this time public opinion had improved for Smetana

[2] Letter to Züngl: July 16, 1877. [3] Letter to Züngl: July 16, 1877.

[4] Mayŕ returned to the Provisional Theatre in October, 1874, but left in the summer of 1875 to work at the Prague Turc Arena Theatre. His place was taken by Adolf Čech, who chose Fibich as his deputy. When the Turc Arena was closed in 1877, Mayŕ was reappointed to the Provisional Theatre, Fibich resigned, and Čech was obliged to become Mayŕ's assistant.

and *The Two Widows* emerged as something of a triumph; but even so, it survived only six hearings and the score again failed to make any lasting impression on the public. During 1879 it was dropped altogether and in 1880 was heard only twice (up to the time of Smetana's death it had been given no more than fifteen times). Despite his work on the second version, *The Two Widows* remained a disappointment; but its fate was not yet sealed. Through the recommendation of Ludevít Procházka (Smetana's former pupil then living in Hamburg), Benhard Pollini,[5] Director of the Town Theatre, took an interest in Smetana's score and began to negotiate for the rights of performance in Hamburg. Procházka, acting on Smetana's behalf, opened discussions in May, 1880, but since both composer and Pollini wanted the best of the bargain, matters dragged on until July 26, 1881, when a one-sided settlement was concluded. Finally, Smetana conceded all performing rights for six per cent of the gross takings and an advance of one thousand gulden, providing the opera was mounted before the end of the year.

Apart from the thousand gulden, Smetana originally demanded a ten per cent royalty for each performance of *The Two Widows*, but Pollini argued that since he paid Wagner only eight per cent for *Der Ring des Nibelungen* Smetana's request was unreasonable. The usual Hamburg royalty was five per cent (Nessler received this for his *Pied Piper of Hamelin*) but through Procházka's bargaining Smetana was eventually offered an extra one per cent. In the event, however, Pollini, a shrewd Jew, wrote into the contract a covering clause whereby the percentage was to be divided between composer and Director; and so poor Smetana was cheated of half his royalty. After three performances in Hamburg and one in Altona this brought him the meagre sum of seventy-eight marks. Smetana despaired:

> This is really not worth all the trouble taken to ensure my opera the honour of being performed a few times in Hamburg. Our travelling theatre companies run by Pištěk[6] and Švanda[7]

[5] Pollini—his real name was Baruch Pohl—started his career as a singer, but later turned to managing an Italian opera company in Lvová. He moved to Hamburg in 1874.

[6] Pištěk was co-director ofŠvanda's touring company; later he became manager of an opera company in Brno.

[7] Pavel Švanda (1825–1891) was a writer, producer and Dramaturg of the New Czech Theatre under Thomé. In 1868 he became director of an independent touring company. In 1871 he was active in erecting Prague's Turc Arena Theatre; a year later he opened the Winter Theatre in the Smíchov district of Prague. He still maintained his interest in the touring group mounting *The*

pay better royalties than this![8]

Various setbacks hindered production, but eventually, on Decembe 28, 1881, *The Two Widows* made its début on the Hamburg stag conducted by Josef Sucher and produced by Hock, with choreo graphy by Merjacková. Smetana did not attend the first night but h quickly learnt that it had made some impact on the public and in th Press:

> Smetana's light opera *The Two Widows*, a superb musical pla in the style of Auber, is original because of its Slav melodi inventiveness and its masterly craftsmanship. It has made th most delightful impression. Humour, wit and liveliness wi ensure its success everywhere.[9]

Though *The Two Widows* was given four times, Pollini made n effort to revive the production (had he done so he would have bee obliged to pay Smetana an additional thousand gulden for anythin after the sixth performance). Annoyed by Pollini's cunning, Smetan became enraged on learning that his opera had been staged in a three act form, and in an unauthorized translation by Roderick Fels. German version made by Josef Srb-Debrnov had been found totall unworkable, and Fels (his real name was Rosenfeld), a self-style expert on theatrical matters, had been invited to rewrite the tex In his enthusiasm he had not only stressed the comic rather than th drawing-room element, but turned Smetana's operatta into music comedy. Moreover, he had changed the period from the 1860's to th Rococo, and the setting from Bohemia to France. But it was not th France of Mallefille's original: instead, the action was played out i the Provençal Castle of Alvadois, the characters being elevated to noble milieu, with names more appropriate to their station. Karolin became Charlotte d'Alvardois, and Anežka, the other widow, Blank de Chateaubleu; Ladislav, the amorous suitor, became the brother in-law of Blanka and was called Alfredo de Chateaubleu. Mumla the gamekeeper, emerged as Grognard; Lidunka as Mignette, an Toník as François. Furthermore, Fels proceeded to shorten the firs

Bartered Bride and *The Kiss* in Plzeň in June, 1880. His last project was th planning of Prague's Summer Theatre but he died before the scheme could b completed.

[8] Letter to Procházka: February 21, 1882.

[9] Ludwig Hartman: *Dresden Nachrichten* (December, 1881). Hartman (183 1919) had been a pupil of Liszt and Moschles and was a writer and critic Dresden. He became a convinced supporter of Smetana's music, translatin *The Kiss* and *Libuše* into German and making an analysis of *The Kiss* and *T Bartered Bride*.

.ct, pausing after the quartet (Smetana's first version had also ended ıere); he repositioned the first-act finale so that it followed Mumlal's .ria and made a fitting conclusion to his second act; the third act ›egan with the trio and continued to the end of the opera. This was nutilation indeed, and deeply offended, Smetana objected:

> . . . those gentlemen in Hamburg wish to degrade my opera and turn it into a farce with music *à la* Lecocq, Delibes or Offenbach! . . . In *The Two Widows* I purposely gave the music a certain style so that the elegance of the drawing-room should be joined with tenderness and nobility.[1]

This was not his sole complaint. It seems that Pollini had secretly ıegotiated with Bote and Bock for the publication of the opera in Fels's 'ersion. Unfortunately for Pollini, Bote and Bock felt unable to bring he score out until certain weaknesses had been removed, and they now tipulated the inclusion of several new numbers. For this, Smetana ıad to be involved. Not surprisingly, he rounded on Procházka:

> My music is Czech and I emphatically demand that it remain as I wrote it. Nothing can be changed or added. I am willing to allow scenes to be shortened . . . but I protest against additions . . . I shall not add a single note, for the opera was not composed for such a vulgar end! I protest against changes. In this way my music is degraded to the level of street-songs. . . . In Prague the original will always be kept and Mr. Bock is mistaken if he thinks I am ready to change even a single quaver, let alone add one! His knowledge of dramatic expression in music is limited to pause signs for cadenzas at the end of arias, where the singers yell for applause; and if the success of my opera depends on pauses and applause, then I am sorry for it![2]

'eeling that Smetana had completely misunderstood the situation 'rocházka hastily invited him to confer with Bote and Bock, Fels and Iartman:

> . . . In your interest and those of your heirs Mr. Bock urges you to allow certain changes to be made so that the opera as a whole may be improved. Fels' reworking urgently demands the return of the main characters at the end of Act I. The piece has certainly gained a great deal but still needs a few details to be altered. I propose you come to Dresden at the expense of Mr. Bock so that we may examine this matter together.[3]

[1] Letter to Procházka: February 21, 1882.
[2] Letter to Procházka: February 21, 1882
[3] Letter from Procházka: March, 1882.

Owing to a certain stubbornness which he found hard to overcome Smetana refused to entertain the matter further, but in August, 1882, he was prevailed upon to change his mind:

> My health is such that I can now visit Dresden and I am willing to accept reasonable alterations. But it is impossible to compose new items for it as it stands. Since 1874, when I first prepared *The Two Widows*, I did not see it until last year [August 18, 1881] when it was presented on the Emperor's birthday. The style of the opera is now strange to me and I fear if additional pieces are to be added that it would generally be felt that they belong neither musically nor dramatically to the original. Anyway I cannot bother myself until I learn the conditions that await me in Dresden!

He journeyed to Dresden on August 26, and following vigorous discussions agreed, with considerable reluctance, to write a new trio for the first act (it was finally placed at the end of Scene 3), and a more brilliant ending to Anežka's aria in Act II (he erased the original A minor close, added a twelve-bar transition and a 'piu animato' in C major running to some thirty-eight bars with an *ad libitum* cadenza and an optional C in alt.). To the suggestion that he should compose an aria for Toník, newly-named Jean, and authorize the change of Ladislav's name to Heinrich von Budona he flatly refused; and not even the receipt of four verses of a couplet intended for Jean made him deviate:

> For the sake of its greater success I have submitted to changes and am employed on this work. I hope to be able to send you the new number next week. I have had everything translated into Czech since I cannot allow myself to compose to a German text. Now I must point out that since I was under no obligation to add numbers, I wish to be paid for this. . . . The trio and end of Anežka's aria (in Czech!) you shall have soon—but the couplet for Jean I cannot and will not compose! I cannot work on such a frivolous and coarse text which is written in the style of a Viennese ballad singer. Such music disgusts me and I should thereby only prove to the whole world that for money I am willing to write anything they want of me! I am therefore returning to you the text of this couplet.[4]

Smetana fulfilled his side of the agreement but composed the two items with little enthusiasm, adding over the score of the trio 'written

[4] Letter to Procházka: August 31, 1882.

at the request of the Germans'. He could muster little interest in these additions, and even failed to have them copied. He valued the opera only in its second version (1877), and neither accepted Fels's Hamburg performing edition, nor his tasteless text, which he called 'impious and irreverent'. But for all his efforts Smetana never saw *The Two Widows* in print (only the Overture and Polka were published in 1882), the vocal score appeared in 1893, and then in a revision by Josef Zubattý. For this the action was again restored to Bohemia (Rožmberk) but the period remained Rococo; and the names of the characters were also changed along with Ladislav's relationship to the widows. Ironically, the name Roderick Fels (he committed suicide in 1883) appears nowhere on the title page. But Bote and Bock's publication of the score did not settle the form of *The Two Widows*. In 1892 another version was staged, this time in Prague, with radical cuts and additions which transformed the piece entirely. An extra ball-room scene with music culled from various sources was thought to add lustre to Smetana's score. The Waltz was used as an independent overture and new recitatives and modernized dialogue were interpolated by Novotný. Sadly, this travesty remained in the repertoire of the National Theatre until 1902, when the piece was dropped for a number of years; only in 1923 was the version of 1877 restored.[5]

For Smetana the composition of *The Two Widows* was a light-hearted relaxation between two epics, *Libuše* and *Má Vlast*. By comparison we cannot but think of Mozart who, after the demands of *Don Giovanni* suddenly dismissed all problems to work in a less serious vein on *Così fan tutte*. Surprisingly, *The Two Widows* has much in common with Mozart's *Così*, not least of all the society in which both pieces are enacted. Here Smetana entered the fashionable world of the aristocracy; however, it is not the sundrenched Neapolitan atmosphere of Mozart, but rather the lush bourgeoisie of Bohemian forest estates which finds its parallel in the works of the Czech playwright Alois Šmilovský. Smetana more than surpasses his contemporary in both elegance and style and fashions a richly-coloured milieu which fits Mallefille's drawing-room elegance as well as Mozart's prettily painted backcloth of the Bay of Naples suits Da Ponte's masquerade. Similarly the two operas are close in time: both plots are revealed and resolved in the space of one long day and are set in the period in which they were written. Da Ponte's references in *Così* (through the voice of Despina) to the presence of Balkan

[5] A table tracing the chequered growth of Smetana's fifth opera will be found in Appendix E.

magnates in Naples is as topical, or as realistic, as Mumlal's allusions to the emancipation of women, and Karoline's indirect hint of self-government in *The Two Widows*. Such textual niceties can only have been made anachronisms when the period was changed to the Rococo or the Empire; and it was for this reason, as well as the fact that he wanted to write a 'present day' opera, that Smetana objected to alterations in the Hamburg production. From the start he had set out to create a sophisticated drawing-room entertainment in which the predominating elements were dignity and elegance. Into this frame he worked figures typical of the day—two rich widows, Podhajský, a landowner connected with society, and Mumlal, a civilized but slow-witted gamekeeper in the employ of nobility. These are sketched, not on a huge canvas, but intimately and with the refinement of a miniature. There is nothing frivolous or farcical about the situations in *The Two Widows*. Possibly Smetana intended his audiences to smile rather than laugh; for he evolved a specially piquant conversation-piece with delicate, almost fragile, musical invention married to a light form of characterization which makes for the most charming kind of humoresque.

With the exception of Karoline Záleská, the characters are unreal. She manipulates the actions of the others like a puppeteer, and though her colleagues express a wide range of emotions they never reveal any great depth. Karoline has a parallel in Don Alfonso in *Così*, who similarly dictates the actions of two pairs of lovers, and Fiordiligi and Dorabella might well have been the models for Smetana's own two widows. Significantly, he selects the same type of voice for his leading ladies, soprano for Karoline (Fiordiligi) and mezzo-soprano for Anežka (Dorabella), and develops the two characters, making each a foil to the other. On the one hand Karoline is witty, charming, something of a coquette, every inch a merry widow and very much in control of all situations. She is resourceful and spontaneous, and her lines contain the most charming touches of delicate *coloratura* which ideally point her carefree, vivacious disposition. It is Karoline who dominates the action and it is her theme which is strongly felt in much of the music, including the Act II overture. There, the short staccato motive mirrors the agile steps with which she moves:

Example 66

Anežka, on the other hand, is more serious-minded, a reticent, almost morose cousin, inconsolable, dolefully faithful to her widowhood and mourning her late husband's memory with a sense of devotion that rarely allows her to give vent to her emotions. Podhajský has a certain blandness, but he never emerges as anything but a cardboard lover, only too willing to play 'prisoner' to Karoline's 'judge' so as to further his plea for Anežka. Mumlal (his name means 'mumbler') is little more than a prop; but despite the comic relief his part inevitably brings, he is not the descendant of Kecal in *The Bartered Bride*. Dullard he may be, yet he has nothing of the marriage-broker's bluff, ill-mannered tomfoolery. Mumlal knows how to adapt himself to society, neither playing the clown nor descending to the level of a country bumpkin. Toník, the junior hand, and Lidunka, the innkeeper's daughter, are not soloists in the real sense of the word; but they emerge as leaders of the chorus and embellish the ensembles (their kissing scene with Mumlal in Act II is best seen as an ornament to the main action). Similarly, the chorus, though it reflects an initial atmosphere—the gaiety of a beautiful morning, and later transports everyone in a spirited zákolanskou (a polka-like dance) in the brilliant Act II finale—never participates in the action as it does in *The Bartered Bride*. Possibly, following Mozart's example in *Così*, Smetana decided to regard the chorus in a passive, almost functional fashion, allowing it to suggest the mood and nothing more. In this way it becomes part of a *tableau*—an appendage to the setting, preparing each act for the course of the action and concluding it in an appropriate fashion.

With little to commend it dramatically and an apparently huge debt to *Così fan tutte*, we may well ask what it is that makes this essay in drawing-room style one of Smetana's most endearing works. When, however, one examines the wealth of invention and the polished technique with which the score has been put together, one realizes that here Smetana was working in a style which he found hard to equal again. Though he succeeds in portraying the psychological states of mind of his leading characters, often (as in the case of Anežka) with considerable emotional depth, it is his skill in moulding musical textures into integrated paraphrases which makes the opera so remarkable. After the restraint imposed by *Dalibor* and *Libuše*, where he expressed himself on a heroic, lofty plane, this score shows a complete renaissance of the composer's basic feeling for life. By returning to everyday situations he rediscovered an elegant world of brightness, peace and gaiety which allowed him to imbue his music with an abundance of sensitive and profoundly lyrical perceptions that echo the charming poetic Polkas called *Memories of Bohemia*, written in 1863.

Unlike either *Dalibor* or *Libuše*, *The Two Widows* is a number opera, with set pieces which eschew any attempt at a continuous flow of ideas. Certainly the recitatives introduce significant musical strands heard in earlier or later parts, and make for some unity, but each section is marked off from the next by a double bar and a full close. Throughout these sections Smetana evokes a range of musical experience, the tender and intimate, the rich and noble, all of which mirror the dignity of his drawing-room setting. In *The Two Widows* he depends on a scheme of working motives representing his principal characters, but these are fewer than before and more economically used. In the first act it is the theme associated with Podhajský that commands the musical argument since initially he is established as a potential conqueror. In Act II, however, where he becomes the object of Karoline's ploy, his motive loses its importance and as the widow supervises the action it is her theme that assumes significance until it dominates the entire score. Another characteristic theme which emerges with distinction and grows from the exuberant overture is the motive of arrest which reappears at the moment of Podhajský's capture:

Example 67

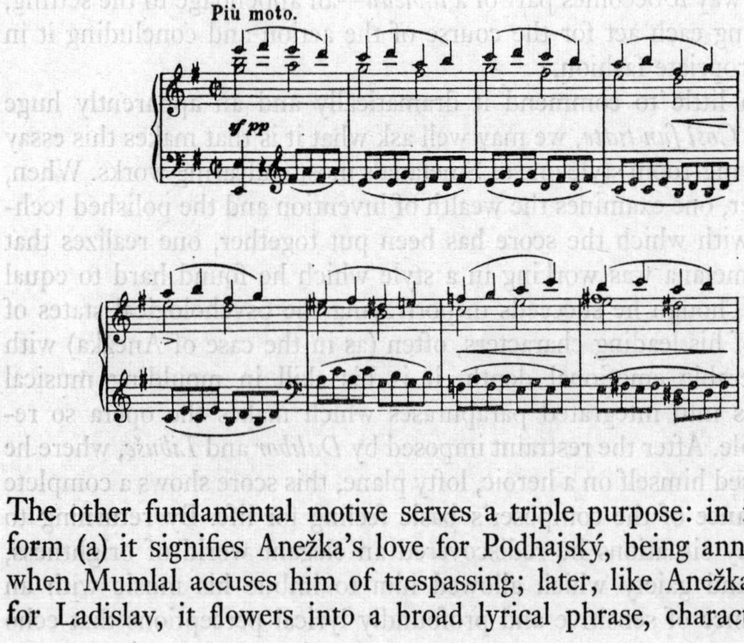

The other fundamental motive serves a triple purpose: in its first form (a) it signifies Anežka's love for Podhajský, being announced when Mumlal accuses him of trespassing; later, like Anežka's love for Ladislav, it flowers into a broad lyrical phrase, characterizing the doleful widow herself (b); and finally it is parodied and transformed to denote Podhajský's mock trial (c):

Example 68

(*a*)

(*b*)

(*c*)

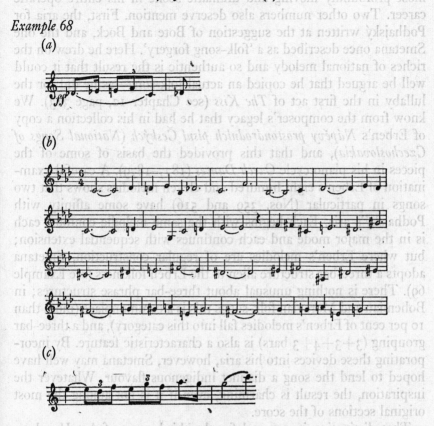

This is not an isolated case of Smetana's use of parody. In the second act duet for Karoline and Anežka (Scene 2) he skilfully reintroduces a playful scherzo, previously given to Karoline in Act I, to point her independent attitude of mind. As Anežka in a show of pique loses control of her emotions, she hurls the same idea at her cousin with as much abuse as she can muster. The resulting show of temperament is brilliantly calculated and particularly amusing as the two widows become rival prima donnas, seemingly irreconcilable. Their duet is one of the highlights in the score: another occurs in the same act following Anežka's rejection of Podhajský. In a long recitative and aria (Scene 5) she laments her plight in what becomes the equivalent of a classical monologue, moving through a range of human emotions from self-pity and desolation to resentment, jealousy and rage. Here, in an otherwise light-hearted plot, is a musical description of a woman deprived of love, and without hope. Seemingly the situation touched in Smetana a nerve that led him to produce the most profoundly moving and dramatic scene in his entire operatic career. Two other numbers also deserve mention. First, the aria for Podhajský written at the suggestion of Bote and Bock, and the one Smetana once described as a 'folk-song forgery'. Here he drew on the riches of national melody and so authentic is the result that it could well be argued that he copied an actual folk-song—as he did for the lullaby in the first act of *The Kiss* (see Chapter 12, page 313). We know from the composer's legacy that he had in his collection a copy of Erben's *Nápěvy prostonárodních písní Českých* (*National Songs of Czechoslovakia*), and that this provided the basis of some of the pieces in his piano cycle *Czech Dances* (1877–1879). A careful examination of Erben's eight hundred and eleven melodies shows that two songs in particular (Nos. 359 and 516) have some affinity with Podhajský's aria. Each begins with the same melodic contour, each is in the major mode and each continues with sequential extension; but where Erben's melodies are of regular construction, Smetana adopts a three-bar structure alien to the Erben folkiness (see Example 69). There is nothing unusual about three-bar phrase structures; in Bohemian and Moravian folk-songs this is a commonplace (more than 10 per cent of Erben's melodies fall into this category), and a three-bar grouping (3+3+4+3 bars) is also a characteristic feature. By incorporating these devices into his aria, however, Smetana may well have hoped to lend the song a distinct indigenous flavour. Whatever the inspiration, the result is charming, even if it is not among the most original sections of the score.

That distinction is reserved for the third scene of Act II, where Podhajský declares his love for Anežka. Risking ridicule and rejection he begs to know what hope remains for his heart. Other composers faced with this situation might well have launched into Italian operatic convention with full-throated fervour; but Smetana, possibly realizing that this scene was the most crucial in the opera and therefore the most difficult to handle, responded in an untypical fashion by turning it into a 'melodrama'. Instead of allowing Podhajský to bemoan his miserable state he instructs him to speak over a delicate accompaniment on the strings and woodwind. This was no innovation. The modern melodrama is thought to have been the creation of Jiří Benda (1722–1795), who, in calling his works 'duodramas', evolved a genre far removed from a play linked by songs and musical interludes. His *Ariadne* (1774), *Medea* (1775), *Pygmalion* (1779) and *Almansor and Nadire* (1779), which were much admired by Mozart, develop a technique of accompanied recitation, in which the orchestra

Example 69

(*a*)

(*b*)

(*c*)

is used as the medium of emotional expression instead of the voice. It is precisely this scheme which Smetana introduces in *The Two Widows*, and at a time when Benda's work was all but forgotten. Though Benda's music is more likely to be the dominant influence behind this scene, Smetana may well have had in mind other recent usages, such as the grave-digging scene in *Fidelio*, the incantation scene in *Der Freischütz*, some passages of *Egmont*, or even the third act of *La Traviata* where the dying Violetta, presumably too weak to sing her farewells, speaks them above a suitably pathetic accompaniment. Benda, a Slav by birth and servant of a German princeling, was the pioneer and motive force behind the eighteenth-century melodrama. Smetana, however, was the first important Bohemian composer to extend the technique to opera. Although his use of the melodrama is slight (it returns in none of the later scores), it is tellingly worked and subtly points Podhajský's case. Probably, its appearance in *The Two Widows* stimulated the younger generation of composers. Fibich, Smetana's pupil, was quick to seize the opportunity to revitalize the form in his *Christmas Eve*, *Eternity*, *Water-sprite*, *Hakon* and the epic trilogy *Hippodamia* (1890–1892), and later Kovařovic and Foerster popularized the form, making it into something of Czech tradition in *The Three Riders* (1887), *The Legend of St. Julia* (1891), and *Princess Dandelion* (1897). Outside Bohemia, Richard Strauss, a great admirer of Smetana's music (he was the first to conduct the complete *Má Vlast* cycle in Germany and invariably informed the Director of the National Theatre of his intention to visit Prague with the request that *The Two Widows* be played during his stay), may well have drawn on the basic idea for his own melodrama *Enoch Arden*; as may Humperdinck for his *Königskinder* of 1897, though there is no evidence that he ever attended a performance of Smetana's opera in Prague.

In *The Two Widows* Smetana reached a peak which he found hard to achieve again. Despite a certain artificiality of the comedy and its small-scale plot, or possibly because of it, he was able to provide a sparkling gem of intimate humour which not only equals the inventiveness of *The Bartered Bride* but in some respects surpasses it. *The Two Widows* has none of the ethnographical colouring of the earlier score and similarly the characters never become curiosities of folklore: they remain puppets who charm us not through their manipulated actions but because of the purity of their musical expression. Though Smetana was to learn, in *The Kiss*, *The Secret* and *The Devil's Wall*, how to handle recitatives with greater skill, he found it difficult to supersede the fluency of thought and piquancy of scoring which makes the arias and ensembles in *The Two Widows* so memorable. One could hardly expect otherwise when deafness robbed him of his hearing shattered his world and broke his spirit. *The Two Widows* was not immediately followed by another opera but by a period of desolation, medical treatment and rehabilitation, during which something of his faith in human nature was restored. Gradually, he regained his ability to compose; but he was a changed man, shy, withdrawn, suffering from mental depression, and afraid to write choral works or pieces of a subjective nature. Slowly he learnt to accept that he could follow his works only in his eye and brain. He persevered and produced, not because of human suffering but through it, one of the most significant works in his entire catalogue: the symphonic cycle *Má Vlast*. Here he not only extols his country but penetrates the very roots of Czech national feeling by celebrating everything that is dear to the people, their legends, landscapes, history and the prophetic vision of their future.

ELEVEN

DEAFNESS AND RETIREMENT

1874–1875

'MÁ VLAST'

ON OCTOBER 20, 1874, a veil fell abruptly over Smetana's activities—activities which had completely revitalized Prague's artistic life and laid the foundations of modern Czech music. Now fifty, he was quite deaf. He suffered continual pain, with the same rushing in the ears which had tormented him in the preceding weeks. An ether dressing applied through tubes failed to ease his state:

> I am to stay at home for almost a week. I cannot go out and have my ears wrapped in cotton wool since I must have complete quiet. I fear the worst—that I will become permanently deaf. I can hear nothing at all. How long will this last? If only I could be healed! And what if I do not get better?[1]

He could distinguish neither word nor note, even with an ear trumpet, and his family and close friends could communicate only in writing. His doctor experimented with a number of treatments, including the insertion of small tubes into the nostrils, which permitted air to be inhaled more directly. But this therapy was ineffectual:

> My ear infection is now as it was at the beginning of the month. I hear nothing in either right or left sides. Dr. Zoufal still has hope but I despair! If only the rushing would stop![2]

The rushing never did stop. According to a letter written on December 11, 1881, to J. Finch Thorne in Tasmania,

> . . . it remains until now and continues day and night without ceasing. It is even stronger when my head is active and less noticeable when I am quiet. When I compose it is always in evidence.

[1] Diary: October 30, 1874. [2] Diary: November 30, 1874.

Despite these pitiful entries he was able to work, and on November 18 recorded the completion of his symphonic poem *Vyšehrad* 'begun at the end of September'. Two days later he took up his pen again, this time on a second tone poem, *Vltava*. At one of the saddest periods of his life he managed to overcome adversity and misfortune, concentrating his creative powers to celebrate, in *Má Vlast*, the glories of Bohemia. In this cycle he transforms shadows of personal darkness and misery to a paean of praise.

The genesis of the six symphonic poems is confused, but certainly the period of gestation is close to *Libuše*, in which Smetana moulded his personal form of expression into a manifestation of heroism and faith in the future of the Czech nation. It was directly from this ideology that the basic scheme of *Má Vlast* was born: both opera and symphonic cycle are a glorification of the country and its people, and significantly they are bound by the same period of time. After many wearisome interruptions Smetana put the finishing touches to *Libuše* on November 12, 1872; but five days before, on November 7, a review had appeared in *Hudební Listy* announcing him to be at work on the symphonic poems *Vyšehrad* and *Vltava*. It is obvious that even with the pressure of his latest opera he had been looking to the future and had a very clear idea of the programme content these tone poems should have. Almost certainly their growth springs from deeper roots than any of his previous mood pictures.

Possibly one movement of the cycle was motivated by an excursion made in the company of his friends, Ludevít Procházka and Mořic Anger,[3] to the Šumava Valley in 1867. Between August 26 and 31 Smetana was the guest of Anger's parents in Sušice, and it was from here he made an outing to Černěk's sawmill at Hirschenstein on the 28th. This picturesque countryside, laced with numerous brooks like the Křemelná, is divided by two fast-flowing streams—one cold, and other warm—and, according to Anger, it was at the confluence of the Vydra with the Otava, that the first ideas for his tone poem sprang to life:

> Here he heard the gentle poetic song of the two rippling streams. He stood there deep in thought. He sat down, stayed motionless as though in a trance. Looking around the enchantingly lovely countryside he followed the Otava, accompanying it in spirit to the spot where it joins the Vltava, and within him sounded the

[3] Anger (1844–1905) was a violinist in the pit orchestra of the Provisional Theatre from 1862 to 1868. He later took up conducting and joined the staff of the National Theatre in 1881.

first chords of the two motifs which intertwine, and increase, and later grow and swell into a mighty melodic stream.[4]

In the years between this excursion and the newspaper report, Smetana had produced several scores including the *tableau vivant* based on Goethe's *The Fisherman* where the watery figuration distinctly anticipates the description of the river in the tone poem. Though this may well have been important in preparing him for work on *Vltava*, another outing, this time to the St. John Rapids (a fast-flowing section of the river before it reaches Prague), made the inspiration indelible:

> Today I took an excursion to the St. John Rapids where I sailed in a boat through the huge waves at high water: the view of the landscape on either side was both beautiful and grand.[5]

While these natural stimuli stirred him in *Vltava*, *Vyšehrad* sprang from another source, namely *Libuše*. Not only is the action of the opera set on Vyšehrad, the high rock overlooking Prague, but Act II introduces the Vyšehrad theme itself. As Radovan addresses Přemysl, the future husband of Princess Libuše, his words 'Máš zasednouti na bělouše, až ranní zoře bude kvést ve slávě branou Vyšehradskou' ('You shall ride triumphantly through the arch of Vyšehrad on a white horse') are accompanied by this theme:

Example 70

[4] R. G. Kronbauer: *What Mořic Anger Told me*.
[5] Diary: August 14, 1870.

For Smetana this phrase became the musical symbol of Vyšehrad's past glories, reappearing in the tone poem thus:

Example 71

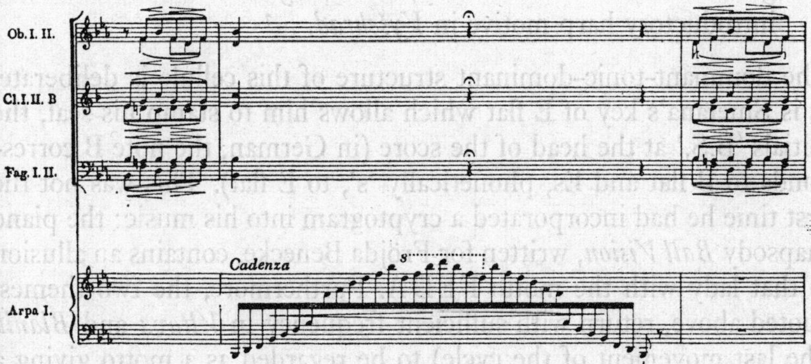

Curiously, this theme assumes secondary importance in the symphonic poem, being invariably preceded by a series of four chords on the second harp (a) which is derived from the 'glory theme' (b) in *Libuše* (Act III: bars 128–30) where the Princess refers to Krok and his reign in Vyšehrad:

Example 72

(*a*)

(*b*)

But that the origin of this theme emanates from *Libuše* is contradicted by Smetana's friend Zelený:

> On October 20, 1874,[6] Smetana was irritated by a persistent four-note germ cell which recurred in his head until it engraved itself in his memory, becoming the foundation of the introductory harp motive in *Vyšehrad*. . .[7]

The dominant-tonic-dominant structure of this cellule is deliberate, as is Smetana's key of E flat which allows him to stamp his seal, the initials 'B.S.' at the head of the score (in German, the note B corresponds to B flat and Es, phonetically 's', to E flat). This was not the first time he had incorporated a cryptogram into his music: the piano rhapsody *Ball Vision*, written for Fröjda Benecke, contains an allusion to that lady with the motto FEDA. Furthermore, the two themes, quoted above, return with sufficient frequency in *Vltava* and *Blaník* (the last movement of the cycle) to be regarded as a motto giving a ritualistic and formal unity. But these are not the only links which exist between the opera and the tone poems: the idyllic idea of nature and the symbolic lime tree in *Libuše* (Act II) are paralleled in the peaceful evocation of nature in *Vltava*; Krasava's love for Chrudoš at the burial mound (Act II, Scene 1) is mirrored in Šárka's wild Amazonian passion for Ctirad in the tone poem; the sunny atmosphere and dance of the reapers in the Stadice scene (Act III) is reflected in the sun-drenched folk elements of *Z Českých luhů a hájů* (*From Bohemia's Woods and Fields*); and the reappearance in *Tábor* and *Blaník* of the Hussite chorale with which Smetana epitomizes the Czech nation in *Libuše* all mark the connexion and pose the question: at what stage did work really begin on the cycle?

The 1874 Diary establishes that *Vyšehrad* was started 'at the end of September'; but the autograph manuscript (preserved in the Smetana Museum in Prague) reveals that the opening bars are not only inconsistently written by comparison with the remainder of the score, but are noted in a different coloured ink (the opening cadenza for harp is considerably shorter than the version we know today). Could this be accounted for if the score had been started some time before November, 1872? Most of the pages are worked in violet ink, a working habit in which Smetana indulged from December,

[6] It is almost certain that when Smetana revealed this information he mistook the date. October 20 was, in fact, the day on which he became deaf. The late Vladimír Helfert believed this incident, if it happened at all, to have occurred some time well before the first signs of deafness.

[7] Zelený: *On Bedřich Smetana* (1894).

1872, until May, 1878 (*Tábor*, the final movement of the cycle is finished in black ink), but since the opening sheets are clearly set out it could well be that the composition was begun some time before the Diary entry of 1874. If this were the case, it makes the musical connexions between *Libuše* and *Vyšehrad* more logical; it explains how the composer, smitten by deafness, was able to produce a large orchestral score in an otherwise astonishingly short period; it corresponds in time to the *Hudební Listy* announcement of November, 1872; and accounts for the opening cadenza (originally for one harp and written in black) being extended by cadenzas for a second harp and in violet ink. In 1872, the orchestra at the Provisional Theatre included only one harp; but by 1873, when the Philharmonic Society was founded, Smetana had at his disposal a total of fifty musicians including those drawn from the German Opera House and two harps;[8] and the first 'combined' concert in which two harps were utilized was given on March 16, 1873, a date that lends force to Smetana's alterations in violet ink.

If, as it now seems, *Vyšehrad* was begun in 1872, we might well ask why he put the work on one side for two years. Possibly the anti-Smetana campaigns, and the desire to write a lighter opera (*The Two Widows*), distracted him; but could the appearance of an austere symphonic poem, based on a mythological subject have silenced his enemies; or would they have interpreted his use of another legend as Wagnerian and therefore un-Czech? All that is certain is that during these two years the initial idea grew in scale; and from an article written by V. J. Novotný and published in the periodical *Dalibor* (June 27, 1873), we know that a whole cycle had not only been envisaged but was actually in the process of 'being composed'. Smetana was reported to be at work on a series of musical pictures of 'Czech glories and defeats'. The cycle was to take as its subjects Říp, the mountain near Rodniče where, in the year 860 A.D., the first Czech settlers made their home by founding a village on its slopes (Říp is also believed to have been the burial ground of the first Czech Father and the legendary home of Přemysl who is said to have been ploughing two kilometres below the summit when he received the summons from Libuše); Vyšehrad, the rock; Vltava, the river; and Lipany, the field where Czechs slaughtered Czechs in civil war during the battle of Bílá Hora (1620).

[8] In Smetana's lifetime his enemies attempted to prove that the harp cadenza in *Vyšehrad* had been copied from Dvořák's *Slavonic Rhapsody* in A flat, Opus 45, No. 3. Such critics failed to notice that Dvořák's piece was not composed until the autumn of 1878, four years after Smetana's tone poem.

Of these subjects, only two materialized, but Novotný's statement is also important in giving the cycle's title for the first time: it was to be called simply *Vlast* (*Country*), not *Má Vlast*. This apart, the announcement supports the belief that *Vyšehrad* was begun in the autumn of 1872 and thus exonerates Smetana from any suggestions of plagiarism; for by an unfortunate coincidence Fibich's tone poem *Záboj, Slavoj and Luděk* (1873) includes a note-for-note echo of the *Vyšehrad* theme.

Smetana completed *Vyšehrad* on November 18, 1874, and two days later began *Vltava*. Within three weeks this too was finished and in the New Year, he began *Šárka*, the third part of his cycle, completing the scoring on February 25. When drafting *Vlast*, Smetana had had a four-movement scheme in mind and in the fourth poem he hoped to 'depict Czech life in song and dance'.[9] This materialized in *From Bohemia's Woods and Fields*, begun on June 3, 1875, and finished in score on October 18, 1875.

With this fourth poem Smetana closed the cycle. Newspapers referred to it as a tetralogy. The composer turned to a set of piano pieces called *Dreams* and a new opera entitled *The Kiss*. But at the back of his mind lurked the idea of extending the existing cycle of tone poems. Details were announced in Procházka's review following the first performance of *Šárka*, published in *Národní Listy* on March 23, 1877, when he alluded to a sequel to *Vlast* directly asking: 'What would Smetana be able to make of the heroic personalities of the famous Hussite period?' It is almost certain this was neither impulse nor challenge on Procházka's part but a well-timed reflection of the composer's own remarks. Smetana's correspondence confirms as much:

> I have completed in these three years of deafness more than I had otherwise done in ten; besides many piano pieces, I have written the tetralogy for large orchestra with the title *Vlast* (*Vaterland*) . . . these pieces have been performed in Prague with unexpected success, and the great climax in the coda of *From Bohemia's Woods and Fields* is persuading me not to finish here, but to enlarge the cycle with other movements. . .[1]

It was only in the summer of 1878, however, that Smetana was able to concentrate his efforts on these extra sections and not until December 13 that he could put the finishing touches to the fifth part *Tábor*. With failing health he began to prepare *Blaník*, and on

[9] Letter to Procházka: December 9, 1874.

[1] Letter to C. Maria Savenau: November 19, 1877.

January 1, 1879, the magazine *Dalibor* published a progress report:

> Smetana is composing a new trilogy of symphonic poems, *Tábor*, *Blaník* and others in which he will glorify the fundamental ideas of the Hussite movement: freedom and liberty as signs of victory.

Eight days later, the composer was moved to correct the reporter:

> It is not meant to be a new trilogy as erroneously stated in *Dalibor*, but an extension and sequel to the old tetralogy *Vlast*: Numbers Five and Six, *Tábor* and *Blaník*. I have finished *Tábor* and work now on *Blaník*. In both poems I am using the Hussite chorale '*Ye who are God's warriors*'. In *Tábor* the hymn dominates the entire composition, while in *Blaník* the theme appears only in part, the last verse . . . becoming the motif of a triumphal finale.[2]

Smetana finished the instrumentation of *Blaník* on March 9, 1879, and above the title wrote the inscription *Vlast*. The other parts of the cycle bear the words 'Na vlast' tvoří celek' ('Following Parts of Country'); but the pronoun 'Má' appears nowhere in the title. It seems to have been added only as an afterthought. At the age of ninety, Heinrich Damisch, writing a commemorative article on Prince Alexander Thun-Taxis[3] suggests that it was Smetana's patron himself who prompted the composer to enlarge the title with the world 'Má', and though this is not impossible, it is curious that none of Smetana's correspondence contains a reference to the cycle in this form before May 8, 1883, when an isolated letter, addressed to Anna Trnobranská, includes the pronoun for the first time. It is more likely, however, that the stimulus came not from the composer but from his enterprising publisher Urbánek, who, six weeks before bringing out *Vyšehrad* arranged in a four-handed piano duet, had an announcement inserted in the Press:

> Mr. Smetana has decided to dedicate his cycle of symphonic poems *Má Vlast* to the city of Prague.[4]

But Smetana had actually decided to dedicate his cycle 'To the city of Prague' twelve months before this announcement appeared:

> I wish to give this work to Prague since it was the city in which I

[2] Letter to Hostinský: January 9, 1879.
[3] *Österreichische Musikzeitschrift* (1960: page 340).
[4] *Dalibor*: December 13, 1879.

> received my musical education, where for many years I performed officially and where I was smitten with deafness. I ask you to accept this offering and to place my scores in the city archive.[5]

The warm response which had greeted the first four poems[6] was renewed for the première of *Tábor* and *Blaník*, given on January 4, 1880, at a festive concert organized to commemorate the fiftieth year of Smetana's artistic activity, but the pieces were not heard again until Adolf Čech conducted the first complete performance of the cycle on November 5, 1882. The occasion was a triumph and one of the most stirring successes of Smetana's career:

> Since the opening of the National Theatre there has never been such an exalted mood among any Czech assembly. The solemn chords of *Vyšehrad* . . . raised us to such a degree of enthusiasm that immediately after its moving conclusion the cry 'Smetana' rang from the hundreds who were there. After *Vltava* a hurricane of applause broke loose and his name resounded on every side amidst cheers. . . . Everyone rose to his feet and the same unending storm of applause was repeated after each of the six parts. . . . At the end of *Blaník* the audience was beside itself and the people could not bring themselves to take leave of the composer.[7]

The Press were equally enthusiastic and friends urged him to write a new series of poems associated with Vlasta (the Amazonian sister of Šárka and the subject of an operatic text by Krásnohorská, previously rejected by Smetana). Again this failed to appeal, and the composer was even unmoved by a letter from Srb-Debrnov (November 15, 1882) in which he outlined Záboj, Svatopluk, Čestmír and Říp as suitable material for a second tetralogy.

Possibly Smetana felt the subjects too close in ethos to *Vyšehrad*, and perhaps he considered a setting of *Záboj* unwise in view of Fibich's own treatment of it. Whatever the reason, he abandoned the project, contenting himself with the preparation of *Má Vlast* for publication. He had recently negotiated with Urbánek to bring out the orchestral material as well as a four-handed piano version; but it

[5] Letter from Smetana: October 14, 1878

[6] *Vyšehrad* was performed in Prague on March 14, 1875; *Vltava* on April 4, 1875; *From Bohemia's Woods and Fields* on December 10, 1876; and *Šárka* on March 17, 1877.

[7] Zelený: *On Bedřich Smetana* (1894).

Smetana laying the foundation stone, May 1868

Destruction by fire, 1881

PLATE XIX. The National Theatre in Prague

Emmy Destinn as Mařenka

Karel Čech as Kecal

Marie Sittová as Mařenka

Jindřich Mošna as Circus Chief

PLATE XX. Opera stars, *The Bartered Bride*

was not until 1880–1881 that full scores of *Vyšehrad*, *Vltava* and *From Bohemia's Woods and Fields* appeared (*Šárka* was not issued until 1890, and *Tábor* and *Blaník* followed only in 1892 and 1894 respectively). Though the appearance in score of the first parts did much to popularize Smetana's name, it did little to ease his impoverished financial state: for the piano arrangement of each movement he received a mere thirty gulden, while for the full scores he accepted forty, bringing him a total of four hundred and twenty gulden, without the possibility of royalties. So keen had he been to see his works receive the distinction of print, and so unrealistic was his business sense, that he had offered Bote and Bock in Hamburg the exclusive right of publication 'in return for a few free copies'.[8] It was only towards the end of his life, when he discovered the fee Dvořák was receiving from Simrock in Berlin, that he realized how unwise he had been. Ironically, at a time when he needed every kreutzer to live, he threw away his finest achievement, not for the price of a symphony but barely that of a song.

Má Vlast is far from being a song, and though Smetana in the course of the poems sings of the monumentality of his homeland, the nation, the country and its people, the work is really a six-movement symphony, bound by a cyclic device and a sequence of pictures. Broadly, he paints three basic scenes: two rich frescoes prompted by legend, which like *Libuše* owe their inspiration to an interest in ancient literary manuscripts, namely *Vyšehrad* and *Šárka*; two portraits in oils founded on old masters, and drawn from Palacký's *History of the Czech Nation* (this accounts for *Tábor* and *Blaník*); and two delicate watercolours inspired by the Czech countryside, its rivers, valleys, and above all by its people. It was precisely such scenes which Smetana had known in his childhood and memories of them that he reproduced in *Vltava* and *From Bohemia's Woods and Fields*.

Though *Má Vlast* covers an extraordinarily diverse number of ideas and moods stemming from the very roots of the Czech myth, its heroic past, the beauty of its nature, the life of the country folk and finally the prophetic vision of the nation, it stands as a unique musical conception. Each part is integrated into the general structure of the cycle so as to grow organically from the mysterious, austere tones of *Vyšehrad*, through the passionate *Šárka*, to the epic and gloriously triumphant finale of *Blaník*. Yet *Má Vlast* remains unashamed programme music written under the influence of the neo-Romantic school. Admittedly the Swedish tone poems had also

[8] Letter to Srb-Debrnov: October 16, 1878.

been written under the same banner, but *Má Vlast* penetrates far deeper than anything there. Undeniably *Wallenstein's Camp* shows the composer scratching the surface of a literary theme directly associated with Bohemia's past, but it was essentially a passing phase which helped him to come to grips with the problems of creating the symphonic poem, and little more. After returning from Sweden, Smetana wrote operas manifesting the dramatic and patriotic character of his country; but he soon found that these were not ideal vehicles for displaying his patriotism. Much remained unsaid; and what could not be conveyed in an opera libretto could be more adequately expressed in the free forms of the symphonic poem. But where Liszt and the neo-Romantics selected subjects ideally suited to literal musical description, Smetana penetrated far deeper by choosing programmes that did not obviously lend themselves to musical treatment—the glorification of Bohemia, its natural beauties, the perpetuation of its individuality. In *Má Vlast* Smetana emerges as a national artist, but he was not content merely to describe his homeland: like Beethoven in the Pastoral Symphony his aim was *mehr Empfindung als Malerei* ('more an expression of feeling than a representation'); and various letters preserved in the Smetana Museum show his willingness to do just this. Possibly the narrowness of Prague's musical life, the unlikelihood of repeat performances and the desire not to be misunderstood led him to write for each poem a commentary which he sent to Urbánek with an undated letter, sometime towards the end of May, 1879. In spite, or perhaps because, of their terse simplicity, these explanatory notes remain one of the most characteristic and authoritative statements from the composer's pen.

Vyšehrad

> The harps of the bards begin; a bard sings of the events that have taken place on Vyšehrad, of the glory, splendour, tournaments and battles, and finally of its downfall and ruin. The composition ends on an elegiac note.

Vyšehrad is the name given to the high rock on the outskirts of Prague, which falls steeply to the Vltava and guards its entry into the capital. According to legend it was the seat of Bohemian princes, and the court of Libuše, even before the descendents of the Přemyslides built Prague Castle, and the legendary symbol of Czech history. In Smetana's day Vyšehrad did not create an imposing picture of past glories. It was surrounded by fortifications erected in the reign of

Maria Theresa and used in the nineteenth century as a fort and arsenal. Anxious to avoid 'present-day' appearances he strikingly begins his poem with a salutation to the past: the ancient world of Lumír, the Slavonic bard, is evoked by harps (a mark of style previously used in the tone poem *Hakon Jarl*) which intone the motives of 'Vyšehrad' and 'glory'. Thus Smetana begins to describe not only the ancient castle, but what for him was a symbol of the Czech state.

Vyšehrad is cast in sonata form with a number of images corresponding to the basic A-B-A scheme. The exposition seems to suggest an atmosphere of pagan and mythological times; the development describes something of the combats and chivalrous deeds that passed within its castle's walls; the recapitulation reconsiders the memories of bygone glories.

As was the case in *Richard III*, Smetana here adopts a monothematic working method, endowing the motives from *Libuše* ('Vyšehrad' and 'glory') with the function of first and second subjects, and he even observes the tonic-dominant key relationship (E flat and B flat). In the first eighty bars these ideas are simply presented in an instrumentation that is austere, yet noble. For his central episode the basic germ cells are subjected to a number of characteristic transformations: (a) rhythmic alteration (diminution and augmentation); (b) phrase extension; (c) melodic alteration by inversion; and (d) a combination of these devices (see Example 73 overleaf).

In marked contrast, the second section depends on counterpoint for its impetus. The music is busier, the rhythms more sharply pointed, the textures more fragmentary. Here also the orchestration is more highly charged, and where before the harps bound the various strands, it is the strings which bear the weight of the argument, with trumpets invoking pageantry, and triangle and cymbal adding the clash of arms to knightly tournaments and deeds of valour. Seemingly all this belongs to the reign of George of Poděbrady and it is an echo of his music from Libuše's visionary apotheosis that returns at the climax reflecting Vyšehrad's glory. But the most dramatic moment of the score is yet to come. At the point depicting Vyšehrad's downfall, Smetana writes a ten-bar transition built on a series of descending chromatic sequences which are onomatopoeic in function. The device is simple, the image of catastrophe. Like Valhalla, Vyšehrad crumbles irrevocably to dust, to emerge in the final pages as a ruined monument of Bohemia's past, a relic of former triumphs and defeats.

Example 73

(a)

(b)

(c)

Più allegro (a 2 battute) e poco agitato

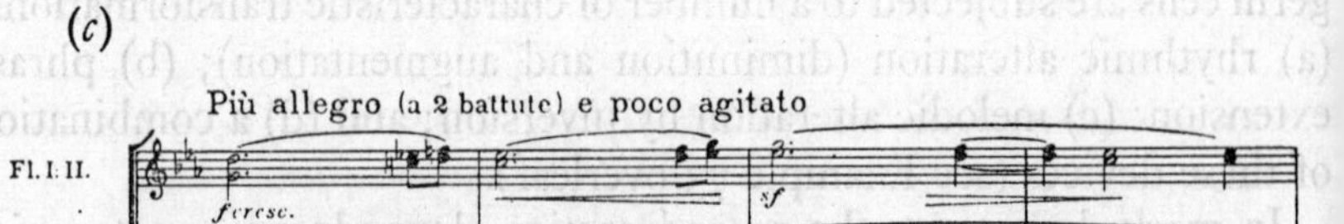

(d)

Più allegro (a 2 battute) e poco agitato

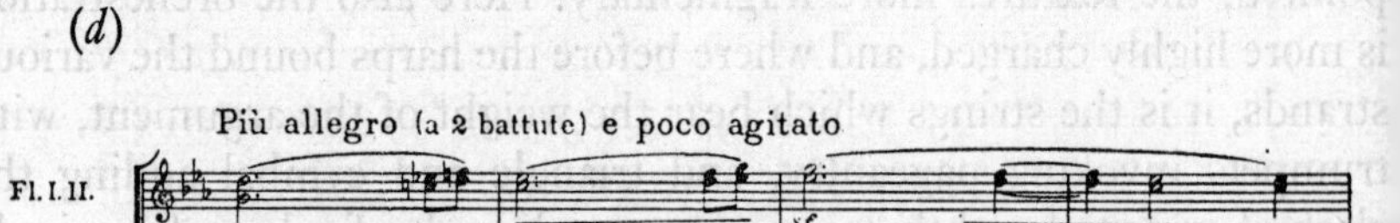

Più allegro (a 2 battute) e poco agitato

Vltava

> The composition depicts the course of the river, from its beginning where two brooks, one cold, the other warm, join a stream, running through forests and meadows and a lovely countryside where merry feasts are celebrated; water-sprites dance in the moonlight; on nearby rocks can be seen the outline of ruined castles, proudly soaring into the sky. Vltava swirls through the St. John Rapids and flows in a broad stream towards Prague. It passes Vyšehrad and disappears majestically into the distance, where it joins the Elbe.

Possibly anticipating the change progress would bring to the Vltava and the original character of the region, Smetana adds to his score notes indicating the course of the river, winding southwards from the Šumava Mountains, through central Bohemia and Prague to form a confluence with the Elbe at Mělník. *Vltava* is programme music of the first order, falling into eight clearly-defined episodes:

(a) First and second sources flowing into the Vltava itself.	Bars 1–79	E minor
(b) Forest and hunting.	Bars 80–117	C major
(c) Rustic village wedding.	Bars 118–180	G major
(d) Moonlight and dance of water sprites.	Bars 181–238	A flat major
(e) Vltava returns.	Bars 239–270	E minor
(f) St. John Rapids.	Bars 271–332	E major
(g) Vltava in broad stream.	Bars 333–358	E major
(h) Vltava salutes Vyšehrad and flows by.	Bars 359–427	E major

Despite these divisions, he gives his poem a certain thematic unity and though the return of the 'Vltava' theme suggests rondo form it is more subtly conceived. Apart from section 'c' the music is bound by a constant musical figuration, a characteristic semiquaver motive, which may have been coloured by the second theme in Mendelssohn's overture *Fingal's Cave*, representing the river, that is omnipresent and from which other material can be traced. Heard on flutes in the opening bars (a) and then inverted on clarinets (b), it suggests the cold and warm springs. From these fragments Smetana develops a wealth of ideas including one on cellos and basses (c) which forms the basis of the section 'f' (St. John Rapids), and another that flows into the 'Vltava' theme itself (d) (see Example 74 overleaf).

Example 74

(*a*)

(*b*)

(*c*)

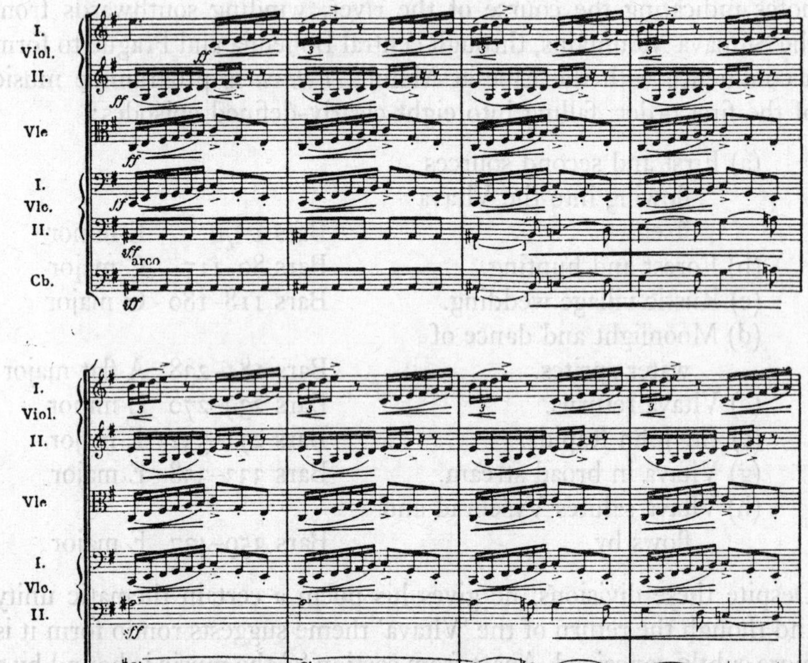

(*d*)

It is generally thought that the theme Smetana chose to represent the great Bohemian river is a Bohemian folk song, and indeed it is sung today throughout Czechoslovakia to the rhyme 'Kočka leze dírou, pes oknem' ('The cat crawls through the hole, and the dog through the window'); but in Smetana's copy of Erben's collection of national folk songs, the melody accompanying 'Kočka leze dírou' appears to have no connexion with the Vltava tune whatsoever:

Example 75

Possibly the folk poem was added to Smetana's melody some time after it had become popular, just as lyrics have been fitted to certain orchestral works of Tchaikovsky in our own day; but there is no disputing an indigenous folkiness of the 'Vltava' theme. Of Erben's eight hundred and eleven melodies, not one can be said to be the model of Smetana's and this suggests that the theme is either original or a 'folk song forgery'; yet it appears in neither Smetana's motive book nor his sketches. In fact, the 'Vltava' theme is a folk song but it comes not from a collection of Bohemian melodies, but a group of Swedish songs made by Geijer and Afzelius in 1814–1816. It was from this source that the playwright Dahlgren and the composer Randel had taken material for the folk play *Värmlänningarna* (*The Vermland People*), of 1846. Now there would seem to be nothing singularly remarkable about this, except that during his stay in Sweden, Smetana had become acquainted with Dahlgren, who also resided in Göteborg, and particularly with his sister-in-law, Bina, a pupil at his Institute, who had occasionally recited 'local' poems to him to stimulate an interest in Swedish literature. Smetana may not have known the Geijer-Afzelius collection but almost certainly he knew Dahlgren's play and the most popular song in it: 'Ack Varmeland du sköna' (see Example 76 overleaf).

Though twelve years or more had elapsed since his Swedish days, he had not forgotten this melody and may well have drawn on his memory of it when writing the 'Vltava' theme, just as Sibelius was to do with the Bohemian folk song which forms the basis of the oboe melody in the trio of his Second Symphony:

Example 76

Rosa Newmarch has described *Vltava* as 'topographical music',[9] but it is far more than this. Indeed, it may be less realistic than the tone poems of Liszt, but it possesses an atmosphere far richer and more deeply felt than anything in those works. Here there is a noticeable sense of development as the stream rushes through dense forests and peaceful countryside towards the city; we sense the hunt, delightfully evoked by horn fanfares; join the rustic wedding ceremony with its typical Polka rhythm and melody moving in parallel thirds and sixths over a drone bass; we observe Vltava's moonlit banks where the veiled quality of the string writing looks forward to the nocturnal mood picture of Dvořák's water sprites in the opera *Rusalka*; we experience the excitement of the St. John Rapids, forceably suggested by trombones, and are swept with the torrents towards Vyšehrad, powerfully evoked by a majestic restatement of the 'glory' theme from the preceding movement.

In *Vltava*, Smetana discovered for the first time how to marry his intimate knowledge of the Bohemian countryside with a rich musical imagery, describing nature. In the succeding tone poem he turned from pastoral subjects to legendary personalities.

Šárka

This poem depicts not the landscape but the story of *Šárka*. It begins with a portrayal of the enraged girl swearing vengeance

[9] Newmarch: *The Music of Czechoslovakia* (1942).

> on the whole male race for the infidelity of her lover. From afar is heard the arrival of armed men led by Ctirad who has come to punish Šárka and her rebel maidens. In the distance Ctirad hears the feigned cries of a girl [Šárka] bound to a tree. On seeing her he is overcome by her beauty and so inflamed with love that he is moved to free her. By means of a previously prepared philtre, she intoxicates Ctirad and his men who finally fall asleep. As she blows her horn (a pre-arranged signal) the rebel maidens, hidden in nearby rocks, rush to the spot and commit the bloody deed. The horror of general slaughter and passion and fury of Šárka's fulfilled revenge form the end of the composition.

On the outskirts of Prague (not far from its airport) is the wild, rocky valley known as Šárka, originally associated with the legend of the Bohemian Amazon. Following the death of Princess Libuše, Sárka led the women from the court of the Přemyslides in rebellion against the absolute rule of men, fighting for the supremacy of the female race. It is her fighting spirit and passionate beauty that Smetana describes in his composition.

Like its predecessor, *Šárka* is also episodic; but where *Vltava* depended on a florid semiquaver figure for its unity, here the various sections are divided from each other so that the piece emerges as a short five-movement symphony in which material from the first part is repeated in the last. The stormy introduction, portraying the enraged manhater, is followed by a march representing Ctirad and his men; an episode marked 'moderato ma con calore' forms the slow movement, describing Ctirad's love for Šárka; a scherzo evokes the drunken warriors; the finale deals with the Amazon's insatiable fury, the frenzy of the massacre and Šárka's bloody revenge. Though each part is independent of every other, the sections are linked by a number of recitative-like transitions. A solo clarinet represents Šárka herself and joins march to love scene; Ctirad, first depicted by the solo cello then by solo violin, binds love scene to scherzo; a final clarinet flourish connects scherzo to finale, and by quoting a phrase previously associated with the hero he suggests Šárka's fleeting womanly weakness, perhaps a passionate regret, before she gives the fateful signal. Thus, Smetana not only lends his music continuity but adds a psychological significance to the drama, expressing the inner voices of his two principal characters and contrasting each with thematic material which reflects his or her different personalities. Šárka's music is characterized by craggy intervals, syncopated rhythms and a full-blooded, almost wild instrumental sound (a);

Ctirad and his love for the Amazon by a warm lyricism generally associated with the strings and marked 'amoroso' (b):

Example 77

(*a*)

(*b*)

The score abounds in the most felicitous pictorial detail, notably in the scherzo where Smetana depicts the drunken stupor of the warriors leaping to an irregular polka (curiously the theme used here returns, slightly modified, in *The Kiss* to depict Lukáš's drunkenness):

Example 78

(*a*)

(*b*)

Later he captures the sense of evil preceding Šárka's treacherous onslaught, and by skilfully employing the dark colours of the woodwind in their lowest register with ominous string tremolandos he evokes the foreboding of destruction. Earlier he stresses three exposed C naturals, on bassoons, to depict the snoring of Ctirad's men, and in the final section suggests the panic of battle in a multi-rhythmic coda with abrupt alterations from A major to A minor in the final bars which look forward to the violent tonal changes at the end of Richard Strauss's *Elektra*.

From Bohemia's Woods and Fields

> This is a painting of the feelings that fill one when gazing at the Bohemian landscape. On all sides singing, both gay and melancholic, resounds from fields and woods: the forest regions, depicted on the solo horn; the gay, fertile lowlands of the Elbe valley are the subject of rejoicing. Everyone may draw his own

picture according to his own imagination; for the poet has an open path before him, even though he must follow the individual parts of the work.

Where *Vltava* was a musical reflection of the great Bohemian river, *From Bohemia's Woods and Fields* is a symphonic picture of Smetana's experiences of the Czech countryside. It is not intended to be an impression of general pastoral views, but a personification of rustic surroundings in which the composer had once lived, and where he had observed country folk, their customs and lore. In *Vltava* Smetana followed, as realistically as he could, the course of a river; here he wanders down hills, through wooded valleys into charming villages, but all in the recesses of his memory.

Although he invites 'everyone to draw his own picture' he did in fact provide his friend Zelený with a more specific programme:

> The beginning is powerful and intended to convey the impression as one steps into the country for the first time. . . . The music moves from G minor to G major as a naïve country girl is pictured walking through the fields. In the $\frac{3}{4}$ section we sense the beauty of nature at noon on a summer's day when the sun is directly overhead. In the forest it is as shadowy as twilight and only a shaft of light can penetrate the trees. The continuous phrase

Example 79

> suggests the twittering of birds and over this emerges the F major motive, a big contrapuntal task, but one which I easily made. The G minor motive represents harvest time and a rustic feast or any kind of peasant merrymaking.[1]

Clearly Smetana regards the symphonic poem as a vehicle for expressing his philosophy of life, and like Beethoven in the Pastoral Symphony he is both pantheist and optimist, worshipping on the one hand, the universe and nature, and on the other confessing his joy in living. In effect, *From Bohemia's Woods and Fields* is a symbolic hymn to nature, an apotheosis of life's gaiety, expressed in song and dance. It falls into three sections, the first of which presents motives

[1] Zelený: *On Bedřich Smetana* (1894).

of the countryside (a), the country girl and her song (b), the sounds of nature (c) and nature itself (d):

Example 80

(*a*)

(*b*)

(*c*)

(*d*)

For the central episode (it serves the function of a trio), motives (a) and (b) are transformed into a polka which is extended with motive (d) to make the finale. Formally, the piece is awkward, but in technique and imagery it is outstanding. The music seems to grow organically from example (a) and exploits processes of imitation, augmentation, diminution and fugal activity. Where the previous movements of the cycle were conceived in broad homophonic sentences, *From Bohemia's Woods and Fields* is worked out in polyphonic phrases; and as a result of this linear thinking the harmonic logic tends to be more adventurous and less well tempered than hitherto. The clash of semitones and simultaneously sounded pedals lend the music a dissonance which in places anticipates the wild evocations of nature in Sibelius's tone poem *Tapiola*. But where Sibelius paints a picture of dark, brooding, Scandinavian forests, Smetana uses his orchestra no less imaginatively and no less successfully to create bright, optimistic recollections of his native Bohemia.

Tábor

(*Kdož jste Boží bojovníci*)
(*Ye who are God's warriors*)

> The whole composition is based on this majestic chorale. It was undoubtedly in the town of Tábor, the seat of the Hussites, that this stirring hymn resounded most powerfully and most frequently. The piece depicts the strong will to win battles, and the dogged perseverance of the Táborites, and it is on this level that the poem ends. It cannot be analysed in detail, because it expresses the glory and renown of the Hussite struggle and the indestructible character of the Hussite warriors.

The poem takes its name from the medieval town in southern Bohemia which, for the Hussites whose home it became, was a fortress of freedom and religion. In Czech tradition Tábor became the symbol of supreme revolutionary opposition, and the chorale *Ye who are God's warriors* the anthem of the movement and seal of its cause. Here, then, Smetana is describing neither landscape nor town, neither nature nor legend: instead he paints a picture of the faith of men, and significantly prefaces the manuscript with these words:

> Their character cannot be broken: firm, constant,
> determined, persevering, unyielding and stubborn.

It was precisely these characteristics which Smetana tried to reflect in his music and he deliberately built his musical conception on the chorale which to him expressed the unbroken loyalty of the followers of Jan Hus.

The symphonic poem is derived from the various stanzas of the hymn and is to some extent monothematic, treating the chorale as an ostinato and theme for variation. The piece falls into two sections, one static, the other dynamic. Programmatically it is possible to see the first as a picture of faithful 'warriors' and the principle for which they fought, the second as an analogue of their battles. But Smetana, a non-practising Christian, was not concerned with the religious implications of the Hussite movement, only their ethic ideals; and consequently he uses the chorale to express both creed and combat. The text of the hymn falls into three stanzas, each of which corresponds to an essential motive in the words, namely command, prayer and fulfilment:

Command: Ye who are God's warriors and of his law,
Prayer: pray to God for help and have faith in him;
Fulfilment: that finally with him you will be victorious.

For Smetana the outer lines were the most fruitful. In the first he saw constancy, determination and perseverence—qualities which he stresses in the initial bars with the fourfold insistence of the opening notes, firmly anchored in the Dorian mode. The second line was possibly too passive in quality to offer much substance to his granite-like development, but from the last with its augmented fourth (F B♮) he quarried material well suited to the idea of battle and military movement:

Example 81

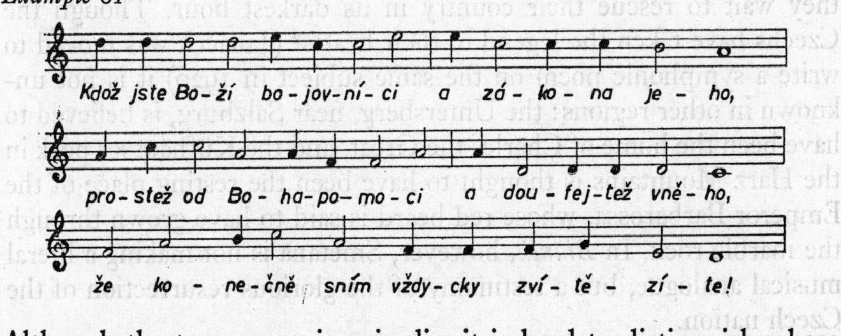

Although the tone poem is episodic, it is hard to distinguish where one section ends and the other begins because it is designed as a type of palindrome:

1st line: 2nd line: Chorale complete: 3rd line //
3rd line: 2nd line: Chorale complete: 1st line

The scheme is completely different from anything Smetana had worked before, and while the final bars reflect something of the Hussites' pugnacious character, they are strangely inconclusive. The weakness is only corrected in *Blaník*, which is really the continuation of *Tábor*.

Blaník

> *Blaník* begins where the preceding composition ends. Following their eventual defeat, the Hussite heroes took refuge in Blaník Mountain where, in heavy slumber, they wait for the moment when they will be called to the aid of their country. Hence the chorale, which was used as the basic motive in *Tábor*, is used as the foundation of this piece, namely, *Ye who are God's warriors*. It is on the basis of this melody, the Hussite chorale, that the resurrection of the Czech nation, its future happiness and glory, will develop. With this victorious hymn, written in the form of a march, the composition ends, and with it the whole cycle of *Vlast*. As a brief intermezzo we hear a short idyll, a description of the Blaník region where a little shepherd boy plays a pipe while the echo gently floats back to him.

Smetana's symphonic poem suggests first the geography then the legend with which it is associated, and almost certainly he was inspired by his childhood recollections of Růžková Lhotice, where he had lived close to Blaník Mountain for several years. In this area he had come to know at first hand the fifteenth-century legend concerning the band of knights who marched into the Mountain where they wait to rescue their country in its darkest hour. Though the Czechs have taken the legend to their hearts[2] (Janáček was moved to write a symphonic poem on the same subject in 1920) it is not unknown in other regions: the Üntersberg, near Salzburg, is believed to have been the home of Charles the Great, and the Küfhäusser peak in the Harz Mountains is thought to have been the resting place of the Emperor Barbarossa, whose red beard is said to have grown through the marble rock. In *Blaník*, however, Smetana is not making a literal musical analogue, but a testimony of the glorious resurrection of the Czech nation.

From the beginning we are made aware that *Blaník* is the continuation of *Tábor*: the Dorian mode persists, and the opening stanza of

[2] During the 1914–1918 World War, when the First Czech Republic was about to be established, the legions which formed in Russia, France and Italy to fight against Austria called themselves the 'Knights of Blaník'.

the chorale returns with a fourfold repetition of the initial notes, hammered out on horns and trumpets. Thereafter the music develops through a series of March-like episodes and interludes. In all, there are five Marches, and the three intermezzos occur between the first and second, the third and fourth, and the fifth and sixth Marches. The bulk of the musical material for these is drawn from the chorale itself.

From the opening of the chorale, Smetana fashions a striking theme which depicts the Hussites in the bowels of Blaník. The way the theme hovers between D and F looks back to the music of George of Poděbrady in the final apotheosis of *Libuše*:

Example 82

March No. 2, an extension of the first, elaborates the same material with a triplet figuration. For the third episode, however, a new element appears, derived from the final line of the chorale and extended by several bars:

Example 83

[*cont. overleaf*

The outer stanzas of the chorale are again suited to Smetana's conception of Hussite warriors and their quest for ultimate freedom, while the second assumes the nature of a 'peace' motive forming the basis of a more reflective episode:

Example 84

In the second half, Smetana abandons the chorale in favour of pastoral melody, treated canonically to suggest the shepherd piping on the mountain slopes and listening to the echo of his own music

Example 85

Here the composer may well have had earlier pastoral movements in mind; but though he writes in the same manner as Berlioz in the *Symphonie Fantastique*, his outlook is different. Where Berlioz depicts two shepherds responding to each other antiphonally, Smetana suggests a solitary figure listening to the sounds of nature. For his final interlude he returns to the type of contrapuntal expertise which marked the Prelude to *Libuše*, and in order to stress the musical importance which the chorale and 'Vyšehrad' theme play in the entire cycle, he combines the two simultaneously. While woodwinds and strings sing the 'Vyšehrad' theme, horns, trumpets and trombones solemnly intone the chorale (three bars later the two motives are driven home again, but with the instrumentation reversed). So, with the reintroduction of the 'Vyšehrad' theme in Blaník, Smetana gives his symphonic poem a definite cyclic purpose.

But *Má Vlast* is important for a number of reasons other than this. Though each part has its own character, it is the overall feeling which makes the cycle tower above the rest of Smetana's compositions. Each poem is programmatic, yet each deals with a different programme, be it history, descriptions of past glories, the prophecy of a better future, or evocations of scenery, landscapes or the people who dwell there. While this invests the subject matter with contrast, Smetana emphasizes it by varying the instrumentation in each movement. The most colourful is *Vltava*, where harp and woodwind combine in a surging mood picture of the great river. In *Šárka* (perhaps the most highly-charged of all the movements) it is the violins which predominate. In *Tábor* and *Blaník*, the brass lend weight to the musical argument, while in *Vyšehrad* it is the harp that evokes the mythological past and adds a fullness to the otherwise classical clarity of the scoring.

Má Vlast is the first important work belonging to Smetana's maturity which is not shackled by words. Here he is able to speak for himself without the aid of a librettist, and significantly he develops a form of polyphony curiously absent from his operatic music. In these symphonic poems his essentially direct harmonic and melodic thought is made more intricate as a result of his linear approach. That he had always previously thought in terms of the simplest means of expression we know from his correspondence:

> . . . the style of my music in this opera [*The Devil's Wall*] is Smetanesque: that is the drawing together of simple melodies and straightforward harmonies, formed into a considered plan of construction . . . the style has been proved in my comic and serious operas. . . .[3]

But in *Má Vlast* polyphonic ideas are infinitely more adventurous than hitherto: double and triple counterpoint are commonplaces in *Vyšehrad* (central episode), in *Vltava* (St. John Rapids), in *Šárka* (the slaughter scene); in *Tábor* and *Blaník* there are numerous canons; the drinking section in *Šárka* is worked out fugally and the description of nature's sounds in *From Bohemia's Woods and Fields* develops an eight-bar fugue subject through a five-part exposition. Similarly, the rhythms are more irregular than in the earlier works. The march and polka continue to figure largely in his scheme, but here he seems to enjoy the sheer exuberance of cross-rhythms, couplets against triplets, endless syncopation, more than previously. The symphonic poems abound in multi-rhythmic patterns. *Vltava*'s water-sprites present no less than four different rhythmic units simultaneously and other examples are to be found in *Šárka* and *Blaník* where the rhythmic invention for the triangle alone is quite remarkable.

With *Má Vlast* Smetana emerged as a mature and original composer of orchestral music, much nearer to the Berlioz of the *Symphonie Fantastique* than to the tone poems of Liszt. In these six pieces he not only shows his developing style, which looks forward to the works of the last years, but proves his ability to endow music with a sense of its having been drawn from Czech life. It is this which gives the cycle its individuality and its permanent place in the repertoire of symphonic music.

[3] Letter to Čech: July 4, 1882.

TWELVE

A RETURN TO THE STAGE 1876

'THE KISS'

WITH THE COMPLETION of *Vltava* it seemed that Smetana had risen above the terrible blow fate had dealt him. Though he appeared cheerful in company, with his family he was deeply depressed. He shouted without realizing it, became irritable with friends, and was short with his children. The reinstatement of Maýr at the Provisional Theatre angered him, as did the wholesale dismissal of artists who had shown especial sympathy towards him during his term of office. The news, in late December, that one singer had hanged himself following the abrupt termination of his contract shocked Smetana deeply:

> Now the Christmas season will be a sad one for me. I can attend neither concert nor opera since my deafness is as before.[1]

While his ear complaint caused continual pain, his own personal situation brought new anxieties: to deafness was added the further anxiety of financial insecurity. Smetana had never been rich, and though he had held the leading musical post in Prague he had saved little, depending on royalties[2] and receipts for the luxuries of life. From the monthly accounts, noted in his Diaries, we can see that even at the height of his career his income had barely covered expenses.

[1] Diary: December 14, 1874.

[2] Between 1866 and 1875 Smetana had received the following sums in royalties from the Provisional Theatre:

Brandenburgers in Bohemia	758.38
The Bartered Bride	2,131.51
Dalibor	498.66
The Two Widows	615.66
	4,004.21 gulden

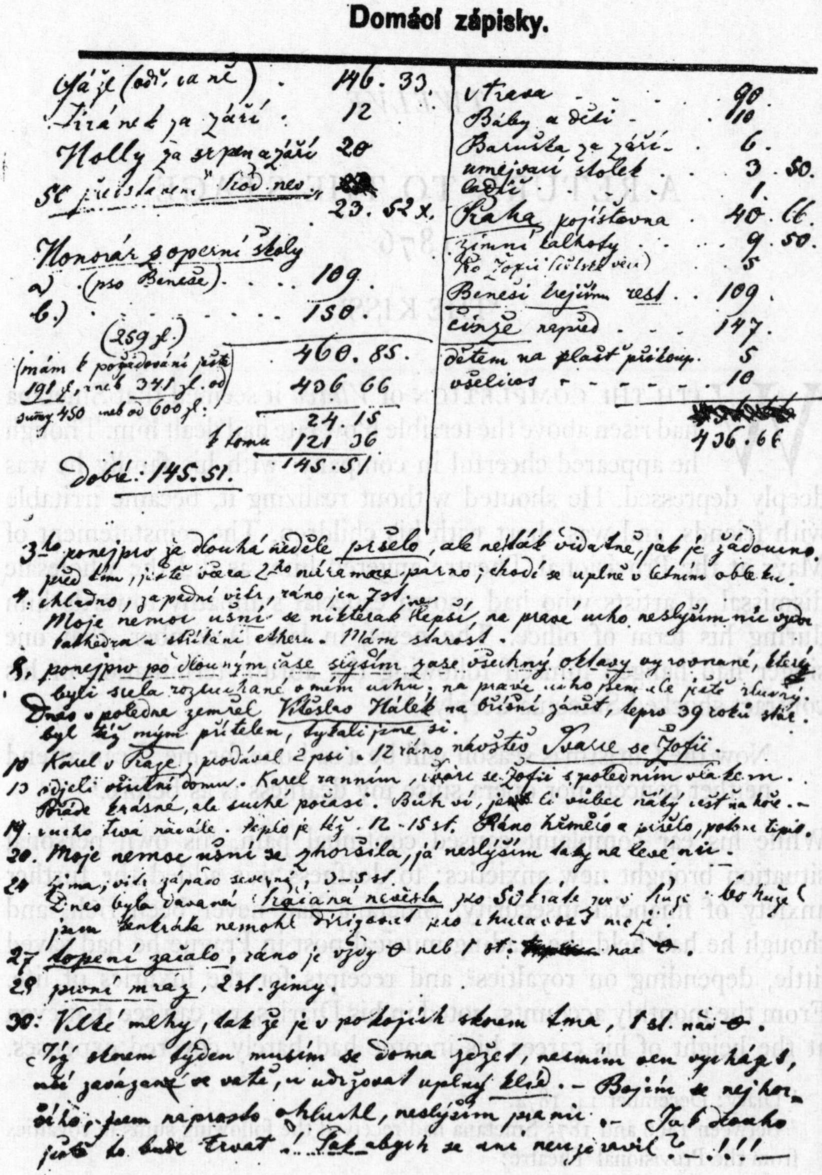

A page from Smetana's Diary in which his monthly accounts and daily activities are noted.

In March, 1874, after an expenditure of four hundred and thirty-one gulden, fifty-one kreutzer, the amount remaining from his salary, lessons and performing rights from *The Two Widows* was five gulden, eighteen kreutzer:

Receipts	*Gulden*	*Expenses*	*Gulden*
Salary	158.83	Food	95.00
Jiránek	22.00	Jiránek	6.00
From Count Nostitz	58.00	Baruška [cook]	6.00
Private lesson	12.00	Babi and the children	10.00
Third performance of *The Two Widows*	100.00	Dattel [publisher]	40.00
		Insurance Company 'Praha'	40.66
From Thun [pupil]	36.00	Wine	6.50
From Lobkovic [pupil]	36.00	Shoes	2.00
Fourth Performance of *The Two Widows*	13.86	Trip to Ovčarý and back	6.00
		To Žofie	10.00
		Trip to see Rudolf	8.00
		To Matice Hudební [Society]	3.00
		Trousers and vests	12.00
		Hat and scarf	10.00
		For Tomášek's party	5.00
		Rent in advance [for 3 months]	147.00
		Score of Tausig's *Studies*	4.35
		Medicine	20.00
	436.69		431.51

In February, his daughter Žofie married the forester Josef Schwarz, and the reception had cost Smetana two thousand, two hundred and fifteen gulden, of which six hundred and thirty-eight were drawn from his savings. Over the next months he barely kept his head above water: there were few performances of his operas and by the autumn he was heavily in debt. In November his expenses totalled three hundred and twenty-nine gulden, forty-two kreutzer, against which his receipts were only one hundred and sixty-eight gulden, thirty-three kreutzer (see next page).

With a deficit of one hundred and sixty-one gulden, nine kreutzer, and few savings, his concern for the future grew acute, and in December he wrote to Čeněk Bubeníček (Chairman of the Provisional Theatre from 1873 to 1876), asking for his position to be clarified and a salary fitting his post to be fixed. With the return of Maýr, however, the members of the Theatre Association were drawn from the Old Czech Party and their reaction to Smetana was naturally unsympathetic, even hostile. Their recommendation that he should

Receipts	*Gulden*	*Expenses*	*Gulden*
Salary without deductions	146.33	Food	90.00
From Jiránek [for October]	12.00	Betty and children	10.00
		Baruška [cook]	6.00
From Holý	10.00	Wreath for grave	1.00
		Games for children	4.00
		Insurance company 'Kotva'	16.58
		Piano tuner and grave digger	4.00
		Záložna [savings bank]	136.84
		To Baruška—six per cent interest for loan	18.00
		For Betty's birthday	10.00
		Teacher for children: October	6.00
		Medicine [2 bottles per week]	8.00
		Shoes for Zdenka	4.00
		Loan to Florian	15.00
	168.33		329.42

serve the Theatre through his compositions in return for a yearly salary of twelve hundred gulden naturally provoked him:

> ... Twelve hundred gulden! If I am to be condemned to a slow death by starvation then this is enough, but whether this is an incentive to compose is another matter. I think that poverty, misery and continuous worry for daily bread will hardly inspire me to work. I have no wish to become bitter and because of my great respect for you. . . . I shall say no more about my painful feelings on the subject. In order that the Association may know how little is needed to put everything right I herewith submit my requests:
>
> (a) That my former salary be paid for December of last year.
>
> (b) That a salary of fifteen hundred gulden be fixed for the duration of the Association and that my pension contributions be maintained.
>
> (c) That I be paid compensation for the Benefit still outstanding to me for 1874, which is mine according to contract up to a guaranteed sum of one hundred and fifty gulden.
>
> In exchange, I am willing to allow my existing operas to be performed without royalty, and future works according to special agreement. I shall place my manuscript scores at your disposal

for this purpose until the Association has had them copied as their property. Only on the above conditions can I conform to the wishes of the Association and serve the Theatre.[3]

The Theatre Association was not, however, disposed to grant this request and, within weeks, Bubeníček urged him to reconsider the previous terms:

> . . . As the deficit at the Theatre is great, the possibility exists that the Association might be less generous and readily accept your refusal whereby you would get into fresh difficulties since there is no hope you could achieve better results by taking the matter to a court of law. . . . The Theatre is bringing in less during the present crisis and you must realize that twelve hundred gulden for the mere right to perform your works, of which only one or two are box office successes, is no small amount. In the eyes of impartial observers I am sure the Association is behaving quite reasonably towards you and I ask you to let me have your decision without delay.[4]

Faced with a clear ultimatum, Smetana had little option but to accept and on February 3, 1875, he signed away the performing rights on his five operas, for the sum of one hundred gulden a month—a paltry figure far below that paid even to second-rate singers at the Provisional Theatre. Not knowing how he would keep house and home together he became despondent, suffering attacks of vertigo which sometimes prevented him from leaving his bed. He was cheered only by the visits of friends and former pupils, but such occasions tended to become ordeals, both emotional and physical. Communication was difficult and tiring:

> . . . I had visits from nobility, the Thun and Lobkovic families were here to express their sympathy for my illness, but we could say nothing and only exchanged written words. My ears are always the same. I hear nothing.[5]

From a letter written to his daughters we know something of how he passed his time:

> My former pupils came to see me—all the countesses tried to make me happy, but it's a pity they can't save me from misery. I write sheets of questions when they are here since without writing we cannot communicate. In the morning I compose or

[3] Letter to Čeněk Bubeníček: January 6, 1875.
[4] Letter to Smetana: January, 1875. [5] Diary: February, 1875.

> read and then I exercise my fingers to keep up my technique. . . . In the afternoon I stroll through Prague or read in the Café. At home I feel bored. When it is dark I go to bed and dream, for only then do I forget my sickness and life of pain.[6]

From the recollections of the poet Ladislav Quis (1846–1913) we know that Smetana was a sorry sight at this time. His ears were plugged with cotton wool and firmly bandaged, and though he was only fifty he appeared twenty years older. His figure had shrunk, his face was worn by pain, his eyes tired from worry, his hair now streaked with grey. It was little wonder people sympathized with him and wanted to help him. The first to do so was his former pupil, Countess Elizabeth Kounic (*née* Thun) who organized at her home a concert performed by members of the aristocracy and pupils of the deaf composer:

> Today a recital was arranged by the Countess Kounic for my benefit. When she handed me eighteen hundred gulden she wept. Afterwards she spent over an hour with me writing more than a sheet of questions. She promises to come again.[7]

She did, and though her generosity eased Smetana's peace of mind, the event did not go unnoticed in the Press. In *Politik* and *Hudební Listy* Pivoda spat further abuse and rekindled the furnace of hatred:

> The papers are furious that a concert was given at Kounic's place to aid me. They argue that the Association has behaved in so noble a fashion towards me as has never been equalled in the Theatre, and that with my twelve hundred gulden I am more than well off, and so on. . .[8]

Pivoda's callous attacks were swiftly silenced by Jan Neruda on February 28, when *Národní Listy* published a lengthy defence of the composer in which he observed that it was not the Czech people themselves who had supported Smetana at his worst moment, but representatives of Bohemian society. Neruda's article hit hard at Pivoda's partisans and the sting may even have prompted Fröjda Benecke to make a positive effort to help the ailing musician. Despite the passage of time she still felt an immense affection for him—her letters reveal as much—and she quickly organized a fund among Smetana's Swedish pupils and friends, raising the sum of thirteen hundred gulden which was sent to him at the end of March, with

[6] Letter to Smetana's daughters: February 1, 1875.
[7] Diary: February 23, 1875. [8] Diary: February 27, 1875.

the express purpose of being used for medical attention. He willingly accepted and on April 18 travelled overnight to Würzburg where he submitted himself to the ear specialist Dr. Tröltsch. For five anxious days he underwent a series of tests, but Tröltsch was able neither to diagnose cause nor recommend cure. He confirmed that there was an infection, that the 'ear drums should be left open',[9] and dispatched the patient to consult the eminent aural specialist Dr. Politzer, in Vienna. Here Smetana fared little better. Politzer was as baffled as Tröltsch, but on May 5 he diagnosed paralysis of the inner auditory nerve and, after further examination, prescribed a form of 'electric treatment and exercises'.[1] He also recommended the use of an ear trumpet but Smetana, knowing this contraption to be futile, returned to Prague on the 9th, where, two weeks later, he entered Dr. Zoufal's clinic.

On the night of May 23 a fierce storm raged over Prague, but though he could see the lightning and rain, he was unable to hear the thunder or the howling wind which swept the city for hours. Afterwards, he walked through the deserted streets 'for the last time before treatment'.[2] Dr. Zoufal's therapy began on May 24, and for the next four weeks he was confined to a room where neither noise nor light could penetrate the solid walls. He was attended by Baruška Pospíšlová, who applied paste and ointment to his neck and body, and returned only to serve his meals; but nervous tension and mental anxiety prevented him from eating regularly and he soon grew emaciated:

> They have begun the treatment—rubbing ointment behind the ears and smearing it all over my body. I am isolated here and must remain so for a month or more. To play the piano is forbidden and I am not even allowed to speak. May the good Lord help me![3]

During the next four weeks he was a prisoner in Dr. Zoufal's clinic, where not even his family could visit him. On May 31, the paste dressing was washed from his body, but later a new lotion was applied. Unfortunately, his Diary for this period is uninformative as to how he spent his time, and though he recorded details of the warm weather, there is nothing of a personal nature apart from the remark noted on the 31st: 'my ears seem more peaceful'. That he did not expect this solitary ordeal we know from an undated letter

[9] Diary: April 25, 1875.
[1] Diary: May 6, 1875.
[2] Diary: May 23, 1875.
[3] Diary: May 30, 1875.

written by his wife, who was staying with her children outside Prague:

> I never imagined you would have to endure such treatment. It is cruel and I cannot see how it can possibly be good for you to be so entirely without fresh air in such beautiful spring weather. But the doctor must know what he is about, and if he did not believe that it would help you he would not impose such merciless treatments on you. You have borne a great deal already with your illness and, God willing, it will be the last trial you will have to bear before recovering.

Though Smetana was not in great physical pain, he suffered from his confined surroundings. For nearly thirty days he existed in one small room, able to move only when the rushing in his head abated. On June 4, he was washed and re-examined only to be freshly smeared with the thick ointment. There was no improvement. On June 15 he noted in the Diary that Dr. Zoufal had ordered the treatment to continue for a further five or six weeks. 'May the good Lord give me strength!' is his pathetic exclamation. To his wife he turned rarely for sympathy or comfort, but to his children he poured out the wretchedness of his miserable world:

> . . . I am condemned to interminable loneliness. Since I am neither allowed to move from the room nor talk to anyone, and no-one is permitted to see me, I begin to wonder if I will ever speak again, indeed, if I will ever move, let alone hear again. I sit for hours staring into space and it seems as if I have been alone for nearly six months. You can hardly imagine how I long to have news from you, how I long to see you, how I long to forget my misery. Oh, God, if only I could hear again! . . .[4]

After further examinations on June 21, Dr. Zoufal order the smearing treatment to stop and, perhaps realizing that little could be done to improve his patient's condition, which seemed to be more deeply rooted than the ear trouble at first appeared, he allowed him to leave the clinic. On June 24, Smetana took the air for the first time for over a month:

> I have been out for a walk for the first time after four and a half weeks of being shut up in my room, but the weather was too hot for me and I was forced to return home because it was so stormy.[5]

[4] Letter to Božena and Zdenka Smetana: June 20, 1875.

[5] Diary: June 29, 1875.

Four days later he ventured out again, this time to see horse-racing; but the strain was considerable. He was overcome by the oppressive weather and so soaked in perspiration that he had to abandon his outing. At home he seemed morose. His family was at a loss to know how to relieve his depression, but a change of position for his son-in-law, Josef Schwarz, offered a solution. Early in June he had been appointed forester on the country estate of Count Thun-Taxis in Jabkenice, a small village twenty-five miles north of Prague, and it was here that he and his wife now lived in the spacious keeper's lodge, surrounded by large, rich game reserves. On July 1 they invited Smetana to be their guest; and hoping that a change of environment would help him become his former self, the composer and his family moved to Jabkenice, where a large first-floor room with windows overlooking the garden had been prepared. In this peaceful, rustic setting he began to feel more at ease. He played skittles with Božena and Zdenka; planted two trees named after them; rambled through the lovely countryside; explored the deep forests laced with streams, and fished in the many small lakes where on warm days he liked to swim. Sometimes he would accompany his son-in-law on partridge shoots or deer hunts, though he always remained an observer and never took an active part. Despite the stimulations of country life, he was unable to accept the quiet, leisurely surroundings for long periods and began to thirst for city life. Early in August he spent several days in Prague, and in September paid a second visit. He generally returned to the country in the highest spirits and following one such expedition began work on a cycle of piano pieces, the first to be written since the *Memories of Bohemia* of 1863. Although he had produced a *Concert Fantasy on Bohemian Folk Songs*, and a *Fantasia* on themes from *Dalibor* (it had appeared in the magazine *Dalibor* in February, 1873, with the intention of popularizing the opera), this new cycle, entitled *Sny* (*Dreams*), was his most important contribution to piano literature for thirteen years.

Though Smetana no longer played the piano in public, he had never lost his technique. Even when deaf he was able to perform, and eye-witnesses confirm that only his touch was heavier than before. From his Diary we know he began work on *Dreams* around August 5, and composed with speed (the first four movements were completed by August 19, the remaining pieces being finished on September 14, after another visit to Prague). The *Dreams* are dedicated to his former pupils who had done so much to ease his financial situation. Numbers 1, 2 and 3 are inscribed to the Thuns; Numbers 4 and 5 to the Nostitz family, and Number 6 to the House of Lobkowitz. Here, Smetana was acknowledging his appreciation, but the cycle is more than just a thanksgiving offering. The very titles suggest a deeper significance and seem to reflect the composer's unhappy state. These are not light-hearted pieces, but serious-minded, deeply searching utterances lasting nearly thirty minutes in performance. In time and spirit, they come close to *Má Vlast* and are best seen as a reflective cycle of tone poems for the piano. 'Faded Happiness', the first, could well be a portrait of the composer's former triumphs. Like *Vyšehrad*, it is an evocation of past glories, beginning with a slow cadenza that recalls distant memories. A Chopin-like andante, sighing wistfully, leads to a bravura passage suggesting Smetana the virtuoso; but like his own pianistic career this section is short-lived, making way for a return of the andante, now abbreviated. The *Dream* ends with a fortissimo crash which salutes the past without contemplating the future. 'Consolation', the Second *Dream*, owes nothing to Liszt's pieces of the same name but looks to Chopin's Nocturnes for its inspiration. It is subjective, withdrawn in expression, and with a central episode that is more rhapsodic than chimerical. 'In the Drawing-Room' is a picture of sadness. Throughout, the mood is one of loneliness and dejection, with an elegiac, introvert melody that suggests Smetana communing with himself and painting a picture of his own drawing-room, which for him had become a silent cell. The next piece, 'In Bohemia' (subtitled 'In the country') brings relief to the preceding gloom and looks forward to the tone poem *From Bohemia's Woods and Fields*. The *Dream* is warm and sunny. Muted unisons at the beginning suggest shepherds piping: a polka movement in the middle section fleetingly gives way to pastoral figuration. 'By the castle' might well be a dream-like remembrance of Wallenstein's castle in Litomyšl, where Smetana spent his childhood, or of Prague castle which provided the backcloth for *Dalibor*. Whatever the inspiration it is a highly charged rhapsody, full of march-like rhythms and dissonant harmonies. After completing the cycle the composer sent the score to his pupil, Josef Jiránek, with the request that he play through the pieces before submitting them to the publisher, E. M. Starý.[6] On a cursory examination, however, Jiránek failed to appreciate many of the harmonic niceties and wrote to Smetana drawing his attention to numerous 'illogical' points. This action not only enraged the composer but provoked him to reprove Jiránek:

[6] Though Starý agreed to publish the pieces, four years were to pass before they appeared in print, and before Smetana received his fee: twenty gulden for each *Dream*.

> . . . I do not ask you to correct anything in these pieces and I do not send them to you for your comments. I never even considered whether they would please you or not. If . . . you have not arrived at the stage where you understand all the possibilities of harmony or its combinations, then I am sorry for you, and more so since you are my pupil! . . . I cannot understand how you could want to correct me. Should I perhaps have the pieces published with the note 'Composed by B. Smetana and corrected by J. Jiránek'? You will allow me to explain these 'terrible dissonances' to you when next I come to Prague. For the moment kindly leave them as they are and give the manuscript to Mr. Starý.[7]

Dissonances apart, the *Dream* is heroic and massive. The final piece, 'Harvest', marks a return to optimism, being a polka in the form of a lively scherzo. Its wild, Dionysiac vigour soon shakes off the initial dream-like qualities, becoming a fantastic vision of dizzy energy, anticipating (by three years) the Skočná and Dupák in the *Czech Dances* and (by fourteen years) the finale of Dvořák's Eighth Symphony. For Smetana 'Harvest' was a triumph of composition. Despite his infirmity, he was able to command a keyboard style which was a development of the dazzling display pieces of the 1850's. The cycle will always hold an important place in his output, for in the course of its six movements he rediscovered his former confidence and forecast his future strength.

Smetana stayed in Jabkenice until mid-October. After completing *From Bohemia's Woods and Fields* on the 18th, he returned to Prague where, on the 22nd, he again became a patient in Dr. Zoufal's clinic. On this occasion he was not submitted to the isolation of a darkened room, nor did he have to endure the evil-smelling dressing which had previously been smeared over his body; instead, he underwent electric shock treatment[8] which it was hoped would stimulate the paralysed acoustic nerves. But Smetana failed to respond and at the beginning of November he returned to his flat, as deaf and as helpless as before. Racked by doubts, nervous and depressed, he found it hard to attune himself to city life. Gradually he found relief and solace in Prague itself—the streets, the banks of the Vltava and the Bendl

[7] Letter to Jiránek: October 7, 1875.

[8] On September 1, he noted in his Diary that Dr. Zoufal was proposing to bring some new electric apparatus from Leipzig, which he hoped to be able to operate himself, and thus spare Smetana the trouble and expense of journeying to Germany.

Café where reading his newspaper. he was a familiar, if pathetic figure, Though he could not easily communicate with people, he enjoyed company and would often take it into his head to call unexpectedly on former friends and pupils.

One person with whom he now renewed his acquaintance was Eliška Krásnohorská,[9] the poetess, whose libretto *Sebastian and Viola* had so interested him in 1871. At that time she had lived in Plzeň, but from 1874 had made her home in Prague where she was Editor of the women's newspaper, *Ženský Listy*. In the intervening years she had devised a text on the Blaník theme for Fibich, and had reworked her original draft of Shakespeare's *Twelfth Night*, which she sent to Smetana early in 1874. His illness and subsequent retirement from the Provisional Theatre had prevented his working on it, but on August 21, 1875, the newspaper *Dalibor* reported him to be sketching a new opera called *Sebastian and Viola*. It is impossible to know how reliable this information was; certainly he was in touch with Krásnohorská at this time and it was she who suggested he should read the folk novel by Karolina Světlá called *Hubička* (*The Kiss*) in order to assess its potential for operatic treatment. Smetana had asked for something 'of a national character that comes from the people'. He did not know of Světla's work. Eliška Krásnohorská tells us more:

> I lent him a copy of Světlá's book straightaway so that he could read it. This the Master did, returning it quickly saying he could find no trace of the essence of music or song in *The Kiss*. . . . I knew at once the way the wind was blowing [Smetana had discussed *The Kiss* with the journalist Eim] and it was useless to fight against the influence of a friend by reason or argument, so I did all that could be done with pencil and paper to bring Smetana to realize that *The Kiss* was indeed rich in subjects for songs. I even drew up a draft of the first act in order to induce him to form a musical idea of it. But all was in vain. The Master would not retreat an inch. Determined Smetana should not become a prey to those who fight only with pens, I adopted a drastic measure. Then and there I put the courting scene into verse, including the duet 'We belong to each other', and the very next time he came to see me I handed him this sample. The effect was immediate and tremendous. 'But that already plays

[9] Eliška Krásnohorská, *née* Pech (1847–1925), was a Czech writer, poetess and author of the librettos of Smetana's last three operas as well as the incomplete *Viola*.

Emmy Destinn as Milada
in *Dalibor*

Vilemina Hájková and Vilém Žitek
as the Hostess and the Builder in
The Secret

Emmy Destinn as Libuše

Marie Sittová as Vendulka
in *The Kiss*

PLATE XXI. Opera stars, *Dalibor*, *The Secret*, *Libuše*, *The Kiss*

Polka

Skipping dance

PLATE XXII. Old Czech dances

and sings', he shouted delightedly. 'All we need now is music paper and it is ready. How did you manage to put music into it? It is as though it was already composed!' It is indeed true that when I wrote *The Kiss* certain tunes were running through my head of which, of course, I did not boast to the Master. To me they were proof that the theme of *The Kiss* might well have been created to be set to music.[1]

Somehow Krásnohorská's simple but effecting verses touched a vein in Smetana, who grasped the essence and scope of the plot and excitedly began to write the new opera:

I have begun to sketch *The Kiss* by Miss Krásnohorská, but at the same time I continue work on *Viola*.[2]

That he was enthusiastic about this new project we know again from Krásnohorská:

He did not realize how loudly he shouted, and to my embarrassment he would stop me in the street and declare how happy he was that I had given him *The Kiss*—something many a passer-by interpreted quite differently and therefore turned to look at me quite curiously. I pointed this out to him, but in vain. . . . During the time he was writing this enchanting work the Master seemed rejuvenated. He would often stand in my room in front of the mirror, laughing and threatening his reflection with his finger, saying: 'That's supposed to be me, that grey headed old badger who's looking at me from the mirror. Don't you believe it, that mirror's no good! I feel like a youth of seventeen, not like that bespectacled old grandfather with whiskers!'[3]

But not everything in the libretto was to his liking and towards the middle of December, 1875, he returned the text to Krásnohorská, asking for new ensembles and other revisions to be made:

I have tried very hard to alter the text as you asked. I wanted to give it an independent ensemble, but this would have marred the comic element in Act II. Instead I have added a duet for the women, another for the men, and a trio for Vendulka, Martinka and Matouš. . . . Indeed, you were right when you said that *The Kiss* is very different from *Viola*, the verses of which are perhaps too lyrical. *Viola* demands a more romantic idealization, *The Kiss* a more realistic one. Perhaps I have been more successful in

[1] Bartoš: *Letters and Reminiscences* (1955). [2] Diary: November 20, 1875.
[3] Bartoš: *op. cit.*

writing *The Kiss* than *Viola* because the scenes alternate more smoothly.[4]

In spite of her additions, Smetana was not entirely satisfied with the scenario and began to revise it himself in the New Year:

I work on the libretto of *The Kiss*. . . . Please God let me succeed with it.[5]

Meanwhile Krásnohorská, who in response to his earlier demands was working on *Viola*, had developed misgivings as to what he might be doing to her text and pleaded with the composer to exercise care:

In Act II, when Vendulka comes out of the woods, I beg you not to let Lukáš approach her asking forgiveness. Had she granted this, he could not logically reject her kiss. He does this out of remorse because he has no right to the kiss. . . . Please leave this scene as I wrote it, otherwise the critics will say it is too contrived and they will tear my eyes out. As for *Viola*, I beg you to give me more time. I have made some changes but before I can continue I must re-read the original Shakespeare.[6]

Though certain sections of the poem still remained incomplete, Smetana began to draft the music towards the end of 1875. The pencil sketches are contained on thirteen pages in very small writing but, unfortunately, four sheets are missing. Musically, they are the most fully worked of any for his operas, proceeding very nearly to the end of the text. According to Adolf Čech, he began with the scene which most interested him—the smugglers' chorus in Act II—and set out with the intention of making *The Kiss* the sister of *The Bartered Bride*. He composed with speed and enthusiasm, and by February 29 was able to note:

Miss Krásnohorská, with her brother Jindřich Pech and Mr. Novotný, were here to listen to the draft of *The Kiss* which is almost complete.[7]

On the following day Krásnohorská was moved to write a lengthy appraisal in which she expressed her thanks and added:

You told us it was nothing but an outline—yes, but what a masterly outline! We were able to see what an original, refreshing spirit, what natural and irresistible humour, what a splendid kind of lovely, natural, true Czech melodiousness will

[4] Letter to Smetana: December 17, 1875.
[5] Diary: January 11, 1876.
[6] Letter to Smetana: February 27, 1876.
[7] Diary: February 29, 1876.

> permeate the entire opera. I expected much, but what I heard surpassed my expectations. You were indeed right in proposing that we should call *The Kiss* a simple national opera. I believe that in a very short while it will truly take root in the nation, and that we shall soon hear it sung among the people.[8]

Though Smetana recorded at the end of February that the opera was almost complete, nearly five more months were to elapse before he was able to finish the scoring:

> It is done and in the evening I played the first act to Betty who liked it.[9]

Although *The Kiss* sounds as if it was composed at one of the most peaceful periods of Smetana's life, nothing could be further from the truth. At the time he was putting the finishing touches to the instrumentation of Act I (March 27, 1876), he was ailing badly and a patient at Dr. Zoufal's clinic where he received regular electric-shock treatment. There could be no improvement in his health, and possibly he began to realize that the nature of his infection was more serious than he had been told:

> If my disease is incurable then I would prefer to be liberated from this painful life as soon as possible.[1]

To his worries were added new financial problems: for in spite of the agreement which Smetana had signed with the Committee of the Provisional Theatre, his salary for March was withheld. His protests brought no satisfaction:

> The way Maýr treats me is really abominable! I still have no salary. He puts me off daily. Today is the last on which all members of the Theatre receive their pay for the final week in March and now he sends me a message telling me he has nothing to do with it, that I should see Dr. Dašek, and that they have no money at present.[2]

Nothing came at all, and his financial position became so critically strained that on April 11 he was obliged to give notice to the landlord of his Prague flat and make arrangements to live permanently at his daughter's home in Jabkenice. Secretly he hoped this could be avoided, but he was unable to impose his will, and by the end of May he was still without money. The situation was grave. Though he hung

[8] Letter from Krásnohorská: March 1, 1876.
[9] Diary: July 29, 1876.
[1] Diary: March 2, 1876.
[2] Diary: April 10, 1876.

on, the Theatre Association ignored him completely. He despaired of making any headway by appeal or argument against the chicaneries of Rieger. Finally, on June 3, unable to maintain his position any longer, he swallowed his pride and humbly moved to the country, which now became his home.

In Jabkenice Smetana occupied the same sunny, upstairs room he had used before. It was narrow and long and served the dual purpose of bedroom and study. The adjoining room, which housed a grand piano, was light and spacious and became a drawing-cum-music room. Though the family ate together, Smetana seems to have been cut off from his wife and children, who occupied a different part of the house. He lived in a silent world of his own and, though some of the financial strain was eased by his leaving Prague, he was still at a loss to know if and when the Provisional Theatre would honour his contract. He clung on desperately, and seven more weeks were to pass before, on July 26, he received a back payment of one hundred gulden—his salary for March. For a hundred and fifty days he had existed without funds and it is not surprising this tension took its toll of his weak frame. He was nervous and ill, and only gradually was able to regain his spirits. To financial worries were now added personal problems with Betty.

At this time he badly needed the warm security of a home and the cosseting and comforts of a devoted wife, but in Jabkenice he rarely found either. For several years his relationship with Betty had been deteriorating. In the past she had always shown him more respect than love, and now, as he dwindled to a shadow of his former self, all sense of loyalty slipped away. They lived apart. Contact with his wife riled him. There were daily differences, misunderstandings, constant rows. Often Schwarz and Žofie were the sadly perturbed witnesses of scenes of horrible recrimination, and only from Smetana's Diary can we catch a glimpse of his unhappiness:

> A fateful day. Betty has rotted and destroyed in me all future hope.[3]

> It was cold and raining outside and, like the clouds above, everything in my heart was grey and desolate. She again pointed out to me how little she loves me. . . . All hopes of improving my cruel state have vanished for ever.[4]

> Betty walked with me to Národice . . . it was a fateful day and full of unhappiness.[5]

[3] Diary: July 7, 1876. [4] Diary: July 19, 1876. [5] Diary: August 10, 1876.

> Today I had a great row with Betty, who now refuses to visit me in my room.[6]
>
> Yet another row with Betty—this time in a furious rage![7]

It is impossible to know which of the two was to blame, for they were like instruments out of tune with each other. There were faults on both sides, and it can only have been humiliating for Betty, who had known society and wealth, to be reduced to accept charity—and the charity of a step-daughter. Neither can it have been easy for her to live with a man who was suffering from a serious infection, the first outward sign of which had been the loss of his hearing. Possibly she had realized that his complaint might be more serious than mere deafness. Perhaps her bitterness was rooted here, and this could well have been the spark before the final bursting into flame of a long smouldering resentment. But to regard him with disgust and repulsion was unforgivable. Certainly, Smetana cannot have been an easy companion: short-tempered, erratic, airing his peculiarities, shouting without knowing it and demanding constant attention, he made her life unbearable. Little wonder their early days in Jabkenice were difficult. However, the delightful country surroundings afforded him the chance of getting away from Betty, and on occasions he travelled in his son-in-law's cart to Jičín, to Kutná Hora and to Čáslav. In summer he bathed in the small pools, went for walks to the beautiful Dobrovice Valley where he enjoyed the sight of wandering game, and sometimes attended a circus or play at the local theatre 'where the amateurs made me laugh a lot and helped me to forget'.[8]

In the autumn his spirits were raised by the news that *The Kiss* was to receive its first performance under Adolf Čech on November 7. Following considerable publicity the Provisional Theatre was packed to capacity with an enthusiastic audience. As Josef Foerster was later to recall:

> The overture was enough to rouse the liveliest response—yes, the audience tried to insist on it being repeated. Čech, the conductor, thanked them several times, but the applause did not cease. The overture was not repeated but the duet for Tomeš and Lukáš had to be sung twice, and there were not a few who listened with tears in their eyes. The splendid figure of the stubborn peasant, Paloucký, aroused enthusiasm immediately and was compared with the figure of Kecal. The betrothal scene unfolded in all its poetic beauty . . . words fail me when I attempt to describe the

[6] Diary: September 18, 1876. [7] Diary: September 19, 1876.
[8] Diary: September 8, 1876.

> picture by the side of the cradle. Here composer and poet vied with one another and revelled in creating scenes of lofty and consecrated poetry. . . . The conclusion was in sharp contrast; the theatre stormed and cheered; the artists acknowledged their thanks, accepting flowers and homage. Finally Smetana himself appeared, small, pale, diffident, his mouth set in bitter lines. . . . Laurel wreaths flew from the boxes over the heads of those in the stalls to his feet, bouquets were thrown from all sides. The shouts and applause were unending. But the Master, who had created and caught with untiring hand this unearthly beauty of heavenly sound, the Master, who had poured into every bar such a wealth of feeling, heard nothing. Then scarves began to wave, the audience rose to its feet, and Smetana waved gently to the audience. . . . Unforgettable moments.

Indeed, Smetana was deeply touched by the reception of *The Kiss*, though less so by some aspects of the production:

> The décor was poor, the first act being badly designed. Over two shoemakers' stools someone had draped a cardboard box to suggest a farmer's painted chest, with a saint and soldier stuck on it for decoration. But worse was to come. Act II filled the stage with unreal mountains and false mounds, and the smugglers scene took on a very comic effect. Since the stage was so shallow all the action took place at the footlights. As for the costumes, there was only one new creation in the whole wardrobe. Most of the cast wore velvet jackets in colours and cuts more suited to German farmers than Bohemian country folk.[9]

The second performance, however, confirmed the excellent musical impressions, the quality of singing making up for any shortcomings in scenic presentation. To Smetana's surprise *The Kiss* was a triumph:

> A huge celebration in the theatre for my benefit. I was called time and again onto the stage. Many deputations and countless laurel wreaths were presented to me on the platform, greetings recited in verse by the tragedian Mrs. Malá, and so on. Truly a great reward for my efforts.[1]

And from an official report made by the Board of Management to the Governor of Bohemia we can gauge the enthusiasm of the audience on this occasion:

> The performance concluded with a festive ovation for Smetana and the sold-out and overcrowded house was in a holiday mood.

[9] *Lumír*, No. 587: 1876. [1] Diary: November 14, 1876.

The opera was received with stormy enthusiasm, both the Drinking Chorus and Act II duet being encored. The soloists were called back many times. After Act I Smetana, led by the producer, appeared on stage to the roll of a drum. Deputations presented him with wreaths and flowers: from the National Theatre Committee a wreath of laurel; from the National Club, a silver wreath; from the region of Říp another laurel wreath presented by Karel Sladkovský, and from *Národní Listy*, Litomyšl, the Citizens of Louny, the Umělecká Beseda and the Academic Readers' Club and other unnamed admirers more laurel wreaths including some from the orchestra decorated with national colours. Following the ovation Smetana was called on stage five times and again at the end. Backstage he was presented with gifts of honour including forty gulden, two hundred gold coins which lay in a gilded silver box. Later the patriots of Rodnice sent him ten gulden and the Umělecká Beseda honoured him with a considerable sum.

On the following day he returned to Jabkenice to find numerous telegrams awaiting him from every town. At last he was victorious. During November and December *The Kiss* was given eleven times, always to capacity houses, with the result that his strained financial straits were eased (for the first three performances he received a total of ninety-five gulden; for the fourth, thirty-eight gulden, eighty-nine kreutzer; for the fifth, sixty-one gulden; for the sixth, thirty-four gulden, forty-one kreutzer; for the seventh, sixty-one gulden, twenty kreutzer; for the eighth, fifty-eight gulden, eighty-seven kreutzer; for the ninth, fifty-eight gulden, forty-nine kreutzer; and from his Benefit, one hundred and forty-seven gulden, thirty-six kreutzer). For the first time since his deafness the tide of his fortune seemed to have turned. Smetana could at last enjoy the fruits of his hard work. The Diary records that 'Christmas was a rich feast'[2] and the success of

[2] From Jiránek's *Memoirs and Correspondence* (Prague, 1957) it is possible to learn how Smetana spent this Christmas:

> The Master himself took a hand in dressing the Christmas tree; he fixed the small wax candles and lit them and it was he who rang the bell for the Christchild after the evening meal. On this evening the Master was happier than he had been for a long time. The momentary disappointment of the children when they had not seen the golden piglet run past the wall, a thing promised to them if they were good and if they refrained from eating before supper, . . . was quickly forgotten the moment they saw the tree, hung with many coloured home-made paper chains and laden down with gold and silver nuts, apples and sweets, resplendent in the flickering lights of the candles. And as for the presents, mostly toys, what joy they gave! . . . After the gifts

The Kiss spilled over into the New Year. There were fresh telegrams, 'new wreaths, including a silver one, and certain boroughs and committees have accorded me honorary citizenship. I have even been called the founder of National Music'.[3] Yet although theatre trains brought hundreds of country folk to Prague especially to see *The Kiss*, Smetana doubted its lasting success:

> If a work of art wins public favour at one go, this is not the best sign for the lasting recognition of the piece; for the taste of the audience is not the real criterion of the merit of the work.[4]

Possibly he had misgivings about the slight, almost naïve, action of the plot. Lukáš, a widower, wants to kiss Vendulka at their betrothal but she insists on waiting until after the wedding: they quarrel, only to make it up at the final curtain. Further episodes are provided by Lukáš's baby (by his first wife) over whose cradle Vendulka sings a lullaby, and by Martinka, Vendulka's aunt, who engages in part-time smuggling. Certainly the framework is slender, but as a musical experience it is a very different matter. That Smetana has produced a score so warm, genial, felicitous and enchanting is one of the miracles of music when one remembers that because of his total deafness he was 'unable to hear even one of the thousands of notes I have written down in *The Kiss*'.[5]

Krásnohorská's rustic plot may be simple and parochial, but her characters belong to a different world from those in *The Bartered Bride*. Where, for instance, Jeník and Mařenka come from the Bohemian countryside, Lukáš and Vendulka inhabit a mountain region near the Saxon border (the region in which *Der Freischütz* is also set): where, for example, Kecal and Vašek play out a broad comedy in *The Bartered Bride*, Paloucký and Tomeš emerge in *The Kiss* as endearing figures in a charming *tableau* of Bohemian morals.

had been handed out, we returned to the dining-room where we joined in the customary Christmas Eve card-game 'Black Peter'. Whoever was the loser had to have his forehead blackened with a cork held over the flame of a candle and this caused tremendous merriment on the part of the others. Smetana laughed most heartily and Madame Smetana, herself, did the 'branding'. Amongst his children Smetana became a carefree, happy child. When later the Christchild brought a little theatre, with paper figures which had been cut out, stuck on to cardboard and fixed up with wire, the Master himself gave performances from memory of plays by Klicpera and Kopecký.

[3] Letter to Charlotte Valentin: January 29, 1877.

[4] Undated letter to Krásnohorská.

[5] Letter to Charlotte Valentin: January 29, 1877.

From the beginning the overture (which was written last and finished on August 31, 1876) supplies the key to the mood of the work: it is genial, yet expressive. Generally Smetana was not in favour of orchestral preludes (he felt they belonged more to the concert hall than the opera house) and though he tried to avoid them in his serious dramatic works he admitted they served a function in the lighter ones by introducing the principal thematic material related to the body of the music. The overture to *The Kiss* is no exception, being built on four motives which play an important part in the opera itself:

Example 86

(*a*)

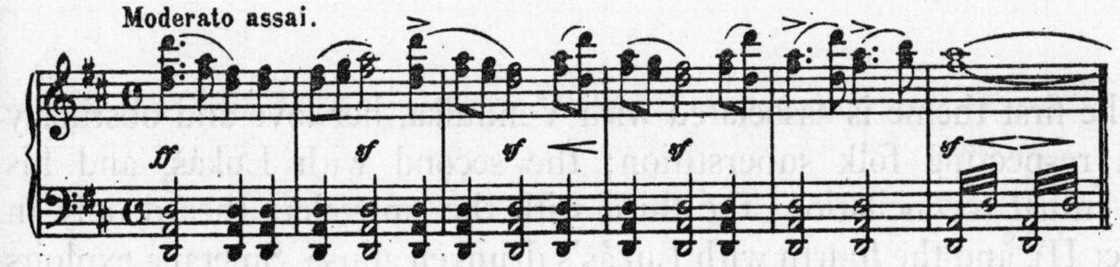

(*b*)

(*c*)

cont. overleaf

(*d*)

The first theme is associated with Vendulka, her love and obstinacy in respecting folk superstition; the second with Lukáš, and his eventual reconcilation; the third with the smugglers (heard only in Act II), and the fourth with Lukáš's drunken abuse. Smetana exploits these motives neither symbolically nor as a means of identification, as he had in *The Brandenburgers in Bohemia*, and he makes no attempt to transform them or build whole symphonic structures from them, as he did in *Dalibor* or *Libuše*. Instead he is concerned with the portrayal of character and in *The Kiss* the leading figures emerge more realistically than ever before. There is no sense of Smetana exaggerating his characters; on the contrary, they are developed according to their lights and with a sense of spontaneity which makes them entirely credible even in the subsidiary roles. Martinka, the ageing aunt who enjoys her smuggling on the quiet, is depicted by a continuous quaver movement which illustrates her breathlessness and her small rapid footsteps: and Paloucký—afraid of the noise of the outside world, serious and slightly ponderous, the guardian of commonsense and a prototype of the Czech chronicler—is made endearing by the repeated appearance of the interval of a seventh which distinguishes much of his music (see Example 87).

Tomeš, the bridegroom's friend, for all his matchmaking schemes, is one of the most successful baritone roles Smetana ever wrote, and even Barče has some charming moments in her Act III *coloratura* aria; but in an opera which revolves around the lovers all other figures merge into the background. Lukáš and Vendulka are the central figures, but they are no village Romeo and Juliet. When Lukáš rushes off to the nearby inn before insulting Vendulka, he acts according to his kind; and when Vendulka shows her maternal instincts by adopting Lukáš's baby she too is equally true to her type.

Example 87

(*a*)

(*b*)

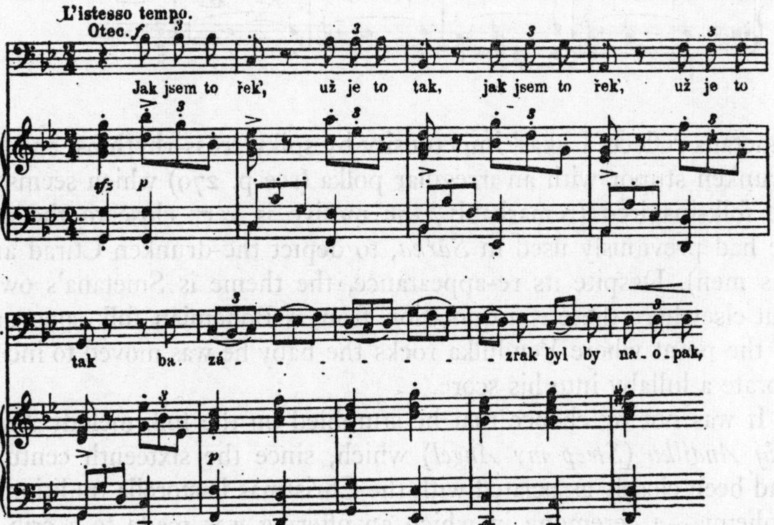

Here the feeling emanates from the folk, and above all *The Kiss* is about elemental joys and quarrels, its leading figures being the musical counterpart of the chief characters in Němcová's folk-play, *Babička* (*The Grandmother*). For his hero and heroine Smetana produced some of his most enchanting and tender melodies. There is a southern warmth about their music, with impassioned outbursts for Lukáš and an almost Schubertian freshness in Vendulka's soaring arias. Yet despite this, the music remains essentially Czech and nothing could be more so than the lovely first act duet where lilting parallel thirds and sixths point the lovers' initial harmony:

Example 88

Smetana reflects Lukáš' impetuosity by spiky cross-rhythms, and his drunken stupor with an irregular polka (see p. 279) which seems to be folk-inspired (remarkably, the motive is very close to the one he had previously used in *Šárka*, to depict the drunken Ctirad and his men). Despite its re-appearance, the theme is Smetana's own; but elsewhere there is a quotation from a Bohemian folk song and at the point where Vendulka rocks the baby he was moved to incorporate a lullaby into his score.

It was not by chance that he stumbled on the folk melody *Hajej můj Andílku* (*Sleep my Angel*) which, since the sixteenth century, had been closely associated with the Christmas Pastorella tradition in Bohemia—a ceremony in which an offering was made to a crib in adoration of the Infant King. Sixteenth-century accounts record that the singing of *Hajej můj Andílku* was an integral part of the proceedings and later, in the seventeenth and eighteenth centuries, women are reported to have brought dolls to church, rocking them in their arms during devotions, to the accompaniment of this lullaby. While the crib became the focal point of the action, the essential feature of the custom was the addressing of a lullaby to the Infant, and throughout Bohemia *Hajej můj Andílku* was the traditional melody employed. Thus it had become an accepted lullaby long before the time of Smetana, who was by no means the first to incorporate it into secular music. In fact, the seventeenth-century Bohemian composer Pavel

Vejvanovský had introduced it in his *Sonata a 7* (1666), his *Sonata a 10* (1666), his *Serenada* for four violas, two trumpets and cembalo (1670) and the *Sonata Natalis* (1674); and it can also be found in the last movement of Bach's *Pastorale* for organ (BWV. 590); the third movement of Mozart's *Galimathias Musicum* (K. 32); Michael Haydn's *Pastorella* and *Motetta Germanica*: *Lauft Ihr hirten all zugleich* and in the Intermezzo *Trinkgern* by J. E. Eberlin. Following Smetana, Brahms incorporated it into his *Geistliches Wiegenlied* (Opus 91, No. 2); Hugo Wolf utilized it in his *Christlied* for soloist, chorus and orchestra, and Max Reger in his *Mariä Wiegenlied* (Opus 76).

In *The Kiss*, Smetana makes no attempt to disguise the folk origins of the lullaby, copying it note-for-note and word-for-word from Žižka and Schottky's collection of national songs. And it is at this point in the score that his skill as a craftsman is best seen; for he follows *Hajej můj Andílku* with another lullaby, this time of his own composition, which seems to grow imperceptibly from the indigenous idiom of the first:

Example 89

(*a*)

(b)

Though *The Kiss* is notable for the way the central figures emerge with a sense of reality, it is remarkable in being the first Smetana opera to treat large scenes as entities and not, as in the case of *The Bartered Bride* and *The Two Widows*, as mere songs and choruses. Indeed, so continuous is the musical flow that it would have been possible to play *The Kiss* without intervals had the Provisional Theatre been equipped with facilities for rapid scene changes (Smetana may well have had this idea in mind, as Wagner had in *Der fliegende Holländer*, for he deliberately begins his second act with precisely the same music which closes the first.)

In *The Kiss* human relations are clearly of a profounder nature and consequently Smetana allows them to develop not in formal set pieces, but with a continuity and integration that he had rarely achieved before. A patch of recitative is a rarity: invariably arioso leads imperceptibly to aria, or ensemble, and thence to an orchestral meditation in which the composer voices moments of passion and tenderness. Here we realize Smetana is a master of the art of dramatic transition, and his gift for creating an atmosphere by using the most subtle instrumental colours to depict nature, scenery and man's relationship to both. Perhaps the rustic setting of Jabkenice, where the music was written, impregnated itself on his mind, and this may well have contributed to the feeling of natural Romanticism in Act II—the wood by night, Vendulka's fear as she wanders through the deep forest and the dawn breaking in Act II, where the secrecy of night disappears with the first glow of morning light. Again, one has only to examine the opening of the second act to appreciate how skilfully Smetana has evoked a nocturnal forest atmosphere, with the smugglers stealthily moving in the shadows. In choosing a four-bar ostinato-cum-passacaglia (it is maintained for nearly seventy bars) he establishes a mood which reminds us of another smugglers scene—that in *Carmen* where Bizet also uses a four-bar ostinato to create a similar sense of suspense. Though *Carmen* had been written a year before *The Kiss*, it is unlikely that Smetana would have known Bizet's work. Even if he heard about it, he can have had little opportunity of seeing the score, and it is all the more singular that the two composers should have shed similar tears when creating similar scenes.

Throughout *The Kiss* Smetana had been so successful in marrying words with harmony, melody with instrumentation, that one feels the composer had rarely before used his art to conceal art. Possibly he realized this too; for when pressed to select the most beautiful moment in all his works, he chose Vendulka's lovely meditation in Act I (Scene 4). Today it might seem curious that he chose nothing from *The Bartered Bride*, the work which had done more than any other to establish his name as a leading composer in Bohemia. But for Smetana *The Kiss* was a work apart. Its humour is totally different, it is less naïve and its characters are not portrayed as clowns. The sufferings of Vendulka and Lukáš are almost real, and from the beginning we sense the opera is not a comedy, but a humorous play shot with pathos in which the situations, rather than characters, provide the humour. Rosa Newmarch aptly summed it up when she said, 'Tears and smiles alternate throughout the score'.[6] Indeed, they

[6] Newmarch: *The Music of Czechoslovakia* (1942).

do, and light-hearted gaiety mingles with a touch of poignant, but tender, melancholy—a melancholy which almost, but not quite, breaks the balance of radiance and shadow which permeates the score.

Tragically, increasing deafness and cerebral complications were to rob Smetana's later works of the very qualities which make *The Kiss* so endearing, and because some commentators see it as the last work to be written before his mental collapse, the opera has assumed a special place in his output. But to appraise it so is to underrate his last two operas and the works of the final years.

THIRTEEN

'THE SECRET'
1876–1878

SMETANA'S first major triumph over adversity was *The Kiss* and within weeks of completing the overture he flung himself into another composition, turning for the first time since 1855 to the field of chamber music. Then the tragic death of his five-year-old daughter had torn from him the turbulent Piano Trio in G minor, a landmark in his career; now, twenty-one years later, the cruel blows of fate led him to produce one of his most heartfelt works, the Quartet in E minor, his first real string quartet, significantly entitled *Z mého života* (*From My Life*). Begun in October, 1876, the first two movements were ready in score by the 30th and the last two by December 29. Where in *Má Vlast* Smetana had spoken with the force of an orator, a singer and prophet, in the Quartet he began to sink into himself, seeking in his inner nature calm for his wounded spirit. He began to think in a subjective, intimate way, communing with himself and speaking of himself as much as he had hitherto refrained from doing. Now he liked to recall his past, his childhood, the joys of his youth, the happiness of his loves, his triumphs and successes. In this way he was able to stifle the depression which threatened the clarity of his reason, and it is not surprising that the E minor Quartet reflects the loneliness and desolation he was experiencing in Jabkenice. But the work reveals more than this. From the outset of his career Smetana had always been attracted to compositions with specific, descriptive aims; and he brought to his chamber music a profound autobiographical and distinctly programmatic background. Because of its personal, almost visionary form of expression, the Quartet is a 'remembrance of my life and the catastrophe of complete deafness'.[1] In 1878 he described it as 'more or less a private composition, and therefore deliberately written for four instruments conversing among themselves about the things

[1] Letter to Srb-Debrnov: February 10, 1879.

that torture me, and no more'. Indeed, the Quartet may be 'private', but Smetana was nevertheless moved to divulge its programme to Srb-Debrnov:

> As regards my Quartet I gladly leave others to judge its style, and I shall not be in the least angry if this style does not find favour or is considered contrary to what was hitherto regarded as 'quartet style'. I did not set out to write a quartet according to recipe or custom in the usual forms. . . . With me the form of every composition is dictated by the subject itself and thus the Quartet, too, shaped its own form. My intention was to paint a tone picture of my life. The first movement depicts my youthful leanings towards art, the Romantic atmosphere, the inexpressible yearning for something I could neither express nor define, and also a kind of warning of my future misfortune:

Example 90

> The long insistent note in the finale owes its origin to this. It is the fateful ringing in my ears of the high-pitched tones which, in 1874, announced the beginning of my deafness. I permitted myself this little joke because it was so disastrous to me. The second movement, a quasi-polka, brings to my mind the joyful days of youth when I composed dance tunes and was known everywhere as a passionate lover of dancing. The third movement (the one which, in the opinion of the gentlemen who play this Quartet, is unperformable) reminds me of the happiness of my first love, the girl who later became my first wife. The fourth movement describes the discovery that I could treat national elements in music, and my joy in following this path until it was checked by the catastrophe of the onset of my deafness, the outlook into the sad future, the tiny rays of hope of recovery; but remembering all the promise of my early career, a feeling of painful regret.[2]

It was only to be expected that Smetana's Quartet should assume a

[2] Letter to Srb-Debrnov: April 12, 1878.

highly personal form; his creative thought, whether in opera or symphonic poem, was inevitably concerned with the expression of extra-musical ideas. Once this is accepted the E minor Quartet can be seen as a 'classical' piece of chamber music. The first movement is in modified sonata form, with a principal theme representing 'fate' and a second subject suggesting the composer's romantic yearning; a stormy development leads directly to the recapitulation of the second subject, not the first. The second movement is a scherzo-polka with fugal imitations that recall the opening of *The Bartered Bride* overture, and a subsidiary idea suggesting a post-horn fanfare, the part being marked 'solo quasi Tromba':

Example 91

The third movement is a combination of song-like episodes and variations, while the finale (again in sonata form) evokes memories of Kecal from *The Bartered Bride*:

Example 92

(*a*)

(*b*)

and later introduces the tragedy of Smetana's life. The use of bowed tremolos, striking enharmonic changes, and a plaintive recitative utterance below the high, piercing E announces that fate has overtaken him, and the quiet ending possibly reflects his acceptance of his cruel destiny:

Example 93

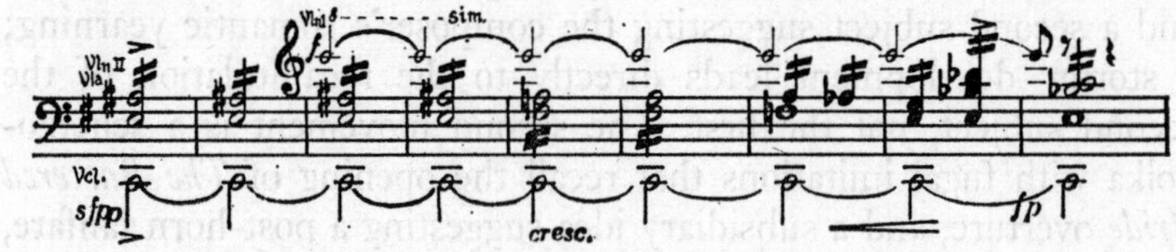

The Quartet in E minor is a remarkable score, which initiated a whole series of Czech chamber works in which composers were moved to record their private feelings in music: Fibich's *Moods, Impressions and Memories* (for piano) is a musical diary of his affair with Anežka Schulzová, as is his Piano Quintet in D (1894); Janáček's Quartet, *Intimate Letters*, a record of his love for Kamila Stoesslová; and Martinů's Fifth Quartet of his love for his pupil, Víetězslava Kaprálová. But this is only incidental. Smetana's work is more important for the style of quartet writings which it established for Dvořák (the opening of the so-called American Quartet, op. 97, seems to be modelled on Smetana's work), Suk and the second generation of Czech composers. Indeed, so advanced was the idiom considered to be that the Prague Chamber Music Association, to whom the score had been submitted, rejected it on grounds of doubtful 'orchestral' style and insuperable technical difficulties. Deeply wounded, the composer sought the advice of Ferdinand Heller, and even contemplated revising the score. Happily, however, he left it in its original form and two years later it was presented for the first time in the Konvikt Hall as part of a concert sponsored by the Umělecká Beseda.[3] Though its individuality was acknowledged from the start, it met with little understanding and only slowly became recognized as one of the most valuable works of nineteenth-century chamber music.[4]

[3] Although the Quartet had been given privately in Srb-Debrnov's flat in 1878 by V. Novotný, Vašá Laub, Tomaš Kovařovic, with the young Dvořák playing the viola, it was not performed publicly until March 29, 1879, when the players were Ferdinand Lachner, Jan Pelikán, Josef Krehan and Alois Neruda.

[4] It was not until May 17, 1880, when he received a letter from August Kömpel in Weimar, that Smetana realized how successful his Quartet was in performance. Kömpel writes:

> We, the Weimar Quartet, cannot resist the urge to tell you what rare enjoyment the performance of this original and vigorous work gave us. We played

Despite the initial rejection of his Quartet, Smetana continued to work quietly and in isolation, making a piano reduction of *The Kiss* and sketching a new four-part male chorus, for the Hlahol, called *Píseň na moři* (*Song of the Sea*). The impulse had come from Srb-Debrnov,[5] who, in December, 1876, had suggested a setting of Víetězslav Hálek's[6] *Black Flag* (the title was later changed to *Song of the Sea*). At first Smetana hesitated, feeling that Bendl, Dvořák or Fibich would be better suited to the task, but Srb-Debrnov persisted, and on January 26, 1877, the composer responded with a colourful tone poem for male voices. Hálek was a lover of nature, and in nature found his finest expression. In this particular poem he epitomizes the sea, the rich images and metaphors being ideally suited to reviving Smetana's vivid memories of his journeys between Göteborg and Prague. Hálek's poem released in him his most idyllic form of expression and prompted him to write programme music, conveying all the bustle of port life as a ship sets sail, the emotions of parting, the pangs of loneliness, the gay atmosphere on board, man's impressions of vastness as he gazes at the limitless horizon and, finally, his disembarking to a cheerful welcome. Though Smetana sings of foreign seas and distant lands, the music is unmistakably Czech, and includes folk dances like the skočná, the sousedská and polka; and there is even an echo of the halekačky—a cross between a yodel and an exultant exclamation normally to the word 'Halo'. This was used as much by farmhands on mountain slopes as it was by boatmen on Bohemian

> it before Liszt . . . who was most warmly appreciative of your work. Though your beautiful String Quartet is quite difficult, it captivates and holds the imagination from beginning to end, and it is indeed impossible to decide which of the movements is to be preferred. Our sincere thanks for this most welcome enrichment of chamber music literature.

[5] Smetana feared he would be unable to complete the piece since he had not worked on

> . . . anything of the kind for so long and because my illness does not permit me to compose uninterruptedly for more than an hour. I always have to stop when the buzzing starts in my ears. I therefore can only work for short intervals and have to avoid great exertion.
>
> (Letter to Srb-Debrnov: December 20, 1876)

[6] Hálek (1835–1874) studied philosophy at the Charles University before turning to journalism and becoming Editor of the magazine *Máj*. Later he produced a collection of poems, of which his most important cycles are *Evening Songs* and *In Nature*. Following these, there was a group of epic ballades and plays which emphasize his growing interest in social and political matters. He opposed the lofty style of Czech Romanticism, favouring instead a more realistic, colloquial, even racy form of expression.

rivers and served a functional purpose, whether in locating herds of cattle in foggy valleys or giving orders to deckhands on board ship.

The music, much of which is essentially chordal in style, falls into a number of clearly defined episodes, each corresponding to a descriptive scene. Technically the chorus is demanding, with a tessitura for the tenors that ranges up to top C sharp—a feature which, at its first performance on March 4, 1877, led to its being considered too virtuosic and outside the scope of Prague's amateur choirs.

Moved by the quality of Hálek's verse, Smetana was impelled to set his *Večerní písně* (*Evening Songs*), not for choir but for solo voice with piano accompaniment. When recalling how prolifically the Romantic composers expressed themselves in song, it seems curious how very much smaller is Smetana's body of music for the human voice than that for the piano. It is as if he was able to sing of human joys or sorrows without needing a poet's verse to clarify his meaning; for, apart from the early songs, written during his apprenticeship with Proksch, and an isolated ballad (based on a Swedish folk song) for the historical drama *Baron Goertz* by Emmanuel Bozděch, nothing came from his pen until this masterly collection. Here Smetana succeeds in matching the sweetness, simplicity and tenderness of Hálek's verse, producing five pieces which possess an almost classic beauty. This short cycle belongs to the autumn of the composer's life, and is tinged with sadness and shadow (significantly, each song is marked to be performed at a slow or moderate tempo, the fastest indication being Allegretto). In the opening songs 'Kdo v zlaté struny zahrátzná' ('Who Can Play the Golden Harp') and 'Nekamenujte proroky!' ('Stone not the Prophet!'), there is a simple hymn-like quality which gives way to more muted tones in 'Mmě zdálose' ('I Dreamt'). Beneath the soaring melody of 'Hej, jaká' ('Oh, What Joy!') there is a suggestion of a polka, and in the final song, 'Z svých písní trůn Tiudělám' ('I Will Make You a Throne'), a sense of optimism which permeates the veiled nature of the poem. In these fine pieces, Smetana sings the praises of all that was close to him in life—music, song, dance, a beloved wife, and his loyalty to the native land, elements which led him to produce a finely-wrought collection where words and harmony are ideally matched.

Yet, regrettably, Smetana's relationship with his second wife was less well matched. The Diaries for 1876–1878 shows a continuing estrangement from Betty, and differences of opinion were a daily occurrence. Though he was learning to lip-read, he was still dependent on writing-pads for communication and was despairingly conscious of being caught in a net of misunderstanding and misrepresentation from which there was no escape:

> Today I wrote an important letter to Betty concerning our future—but for that I hold no hope![7]

During the summer matters became more serious. On July 18 he noted that he had been shown proof of her hatred and on August 4, after a family outing to the Cirque Carré, Betty refused to allow him to sleep in the same hotel room as herself and the children, forcing him to share accommodation with Baruška the cook. A violent outburst followed on the 5th, this time because his wife refused to let him 'waste' money on visits to Prague, and again on the 9th because she would not permit him to travel there alone; nor would she agree to accompany him. On September 1, there were further scenes:

> Betty, Lizi, Schwarz and myself were all involved in a violent row. I wanted to leave here for ever but Betty saw how serious were my intentions and became cooler. May God prevent it from happening again![8]

Their quarrels became more frequent, being aggravated by renewed financial strain. Four months before, a new nine-member Committee at the Provisional Theatre had returned Dašek as Chairman and Maýr as conductor. At one meeting Wirsing had proposed that Smetana's salary should be reduced by four hundred gulden, since only *The Bartered Bride* was a box-office success. 'They play my operas but they don't pay me, neither do they honour my contract', is the sad entry in his Diary.[9] Weeks went by and despite urgent petitions on Smetana's part, the Theatre continued to deny him, refusing to pay his salary on the grounds that his agreement would first have to be revised:

> This is the second month I have had nothing from the Theatre and clearly my reward is to grow hungry and miserable.[1]

The Committee remained insensitive to his pleas and in a state of concern he turned to Procházka:

> I am still a miserable invalid, an unhappy creature full of fears for my own, and my family's future. . . . Not only do I suffer from my illness, but I also have to contend with the worries of living. Since May I have had no salary. Dr. Dašek has stopped all

[7] Diary: April 29, 1877.
[8] Diary: September, 1877.
[9] Diary: June 15, 1877.
[1] Diary: July 28, 1877.

means of existence until such a time as a new agreement shall be approved by a new Committee. I waited vainly until today for this approval, and am thereby plunged into the deepest anxiety. . . . I swallowed my pride and humbled myself, begging the management to leave matters as they stood—that is to say for a salary of twelve hundred gulden. . . . In addition, I paid personal visits to Dašek and Ignác Schick [Editor of the newspaper *Politik*], where I was most affably received and put off by fine words. . . . Beethoven received a pension, the only condition being that he should remain in Austria. For less I have conceded the rights on four major operas. . . . I am bitter about this and do not know what to do. If they leave me without money for another month I shall have to move. I can't possibly stay with my son-in-law since he depends only on his wages. But now I have nothing, I can contribute nothing. Where can I go? I know not—unless it be to beg![2]

Procházka was able to offer little assistance and, though he petitioned Dašek and Schick on Smetana's behalf, there was no improvement. Full of fear for his future, the composer wrote again:

I shall be most grateful if you can help me bring matters speedily to a head. The whole business is most distasteful to those gentlemen. I am a great burden to them. They would gladly be rid of me, and I, believe me, would be delighted not to have to ask anything from those who so clearly give me to understand that it is only alms that they offer me. What a sad fate and in my old age! Of what have I been guilty that I am now little better than a beggar?—perhaps of devoting all my energies to my homeland rather than to foreign countries? The Association has put on my operas during the entire period that my salary was stopped, and not a kreutzer have they sent me. Now I am without a single heller![3]

Smetana remained in this difficult state until November when he finally received a hundred gulden and a new contract:

I had to agree to give them all my operas except *Libuše* for an annual salary of twelve hundred gulden. From May until today they have ignored me, refusing to pay me even though my operas have been performed. What misery have I suffered![4]

[2] Letter to Procházka: September 26, 1877.
[3] Letter to Procházka: October 10, 1877.
[4] Diary: November 5, 1877.

But this was not the only misery that he was compelled to endure. Though he had now been deaf for three years, time had neither healed his ears nor made his lot more bearable. He continued to have medical treatment and on November 7 travelled to Lamberk to consult Klima, a quack doctor on leave from the Ruskych Hulano (a regiment of Russian Hussars) who was confident he could cure the composer's deafness:

> I came to Lamberk for the operation. First Klima pierced me behind the ears with an instrument called a bunky [a long, sharp needle], and then in the neck. He oiled my ears and neck, and promised that within three days I would be able to hear again. Now I wait patiently in my room.[5]

For the next two days there is no entry in the Diary, but on the 10th Smetana recorded:

> The result of my operation is *nulla*. Instead of being able to hear again I have only a swollen neck. I am as deaf as before and Klima cannot understand why I do not hear. For my part, I cannot understand how he could have cured me.

To a swollen neck were added attacks of vertigo and fainting. There was neither improvement nor remedy, yet seven months later he returned to Lamberk for further butchery:

> The piercing treatment behind the neck has begun again and there is a sharp buzzing sensation in my ears. I am unable to sleep at night.[6]

For the next five days he submitted himself to Klima's crudities and on June 12 had to be put to bed in a state of nervous exhaustion. He was confined to the house with swollen legs for three weeks and acute attacks of giddiness prevented his returning to Jabkenice until July 3.

Back in the forester's lodge little had changed. Bitter family differences remained. The Provisional Theatre continued to dishonour their agreement and though he had relinquished the rights of performance on *The Kiss* in addition to his earlier operas he was still without regular salary. It was even proposed that his Benefit should be cancelled. In an attempt to set his affairs in order once and for all, Smetana addressed himself to the lawyer Dr. Robert Nittinger (1838–1906), Secretary of the Theatre Association:

> I do not wish to become bitter, but I would merely point out

[5] Diary: November 7, 1877. [6] Diary: June 7, 1878.

> that I value my works more highly than does the Directorate of the Theatre. . . . The Committee gives me a pension of twelve hundred gulden a year of which, after tax, and other deductions, only eleven hundred gulden remain. But unhappily I also have a family; there are five of us and I have to feed us all. I can do this only because my son-in-law is able to take us in and I contribute half my salary towards our board. The possibility of being able to improve my position, add to my income and thus be able to buy a book or two for the children, was a great incentive to tireless work. The anticipation of Benefit royalties drove me to work diligently in spite of my disability, which allows me to write only in snatches. If you rob me of this incentive to increase my income then you rob me of all desire to compose anything further. I believe my compositions would bring in ten times as much each year if only the Director would perform them; but though they are played occasionally, they lie for the most part collecting dust in the Theatre archives. . . . Let old Smetana be content with the crumbs that are left over, they say. No, gentlemen, no! I am grateful for the salary which I regard as a national reward. But in exchange I allow you to perform my five operas for nothing. Gentlemen, we are quits! . . . I give you five operas and in return I insist you pay me eleven hundred gulden a year. This is final![7]

In such circumstances, it is surprising he was able to summon any powers of concentration at all, let alone put his mind to music. His nervous system had deteriorated so much that intensive work caused giddiness and a strong buzzing in the head. Though he could sit at his desk for no more than one hour each day, he clung to composition, and against doctor's orders gave himself to the score of his seventh opera *Tajemství* (*The Secret*).

Following the success of *The Kiss*, it was only natural that Smetana would want to work with Eliška Krásnohorská again. He had learnt to rely on her instinct, judgement and dramatic imagination. But the faith which he placed in her was the cause of friction and recrimination. She was reproached for not having provided in *The Kiss* a large-scale text worthy of Smetana's art; and while Betty saw Krásnohorská as a rival, journalists resented her success particularly because she was a women. But she continued working for the composer, more out of devotion than ambition, refusing payment for her librettos. When Smetana invited her to choose a new operatic

[7] Letter to Robert Nittinger: July 16, 1878.

subject she quickly suggested a folk tale called *Šotek*[8] (literally *The Dwarf* or *The Gnome*), a plot steeped in witchcraft and wizardry; but this was abandoned for another legend—*The Cantor and the Fairy*. This, too, was short-lived and on November 22, 1876, she outlined her latest idea:

> I have put *The Cantor and the Fairy* on one side and am full of enthusiasm for a new play, about spells and fairies, but based on country life, with comic and romantic situations. How do you like *The Secret* for the title? I propose to place the action in the region you know and like: the famous Bezděz,[9] the ruins of which you can see from a hill in Jabkenice. For the rest, even for you this will be a secret! The plot will be newly invented and fully worked out by myself. I hope it will have a certain effect and I will try hard to achieve this. For me, it will be difficult to equal *The Kiss*, but for you, however, with your ceaseless fantasy, it will be easy.[1]

The Diary and letters for 1876 reveal nothing further about *The Secret*, and it was not until July 18, 1877, that Smetana acknowledged receipt of part of the text:

> I am speaking your verses to Act I aloud and am persuaded that in this work I shall forget my deplorably sad state.[2]

Five days later he began the pencil sketches,[3] but work was difficult and his rate of progress slow; by September 30, he was barely halfway through the first act. Having no more verses to hand he began the scoring, and completed the first eight pages on October 2:

> I work when and as I can at our latest opera, but dizziness and vertigo trouble me greatly. I have got as far as Skřivánek's song of the lark, but there is much more to compose than in *The Kiss*, and many more ensembles. I should like to get to the solo passages, but I fear the music is too serious. How could it be

[8] For further details see Appendix F.

[9] Bezděz (Boesig) was once a Royal Castle in northern Bohemia, not far from Doksy. *The Secret* is set in the town of Bělá at the foot of the Bezděz itself.

[1] Letter from Krásnohorská: November 22, 1876.

[2] Letter to Krásnohorská: July 18, 1877.

[3] The opera and overture are contained on eleven sheets of manuscript paper and, as had become customary with Smetana's jottings, the draft registers little more than the vocal outlines and the essential chord structure. The instrumentation was left until last and more independent parts were either cursorily indicated or referred to as 'etc'. But Smetana remained flexible; the text is frequently worded in a different way from that which he had originally set down.

> otherwise when inside I know only suffering. I don't want to bore you with my troubles, I only wish to work without pain or sorrow. But fate and those men at the Theatre prevent it. I am without salary and when I see what the future offers me—nothing but poverty and misery—I lose all joy in writing. My former happiness is drowned by despair. But despite this, please send me Act II of *The Secret*. When I create a musical fantasy I forget everything that persecutes me in my old age.[4]

Krásnohorská duly complied. On October 19 Acts II and III arrived, and a day later Smetana expressed his pleasure with the new text:

> I have quickly finished Act I and omitted only a few lines [four in all] so that your entire libretto is in score, including the Rose-Boniface duet which you indicated as a possible cut. As you know, my financial position is poor, but nevertheless I would like to reward you and pay you something for this libretto. I shall be grateful to know what figure you ask. I shall also tell the Theatre to allow you the rights of publication, otherwise I cannot permit *The Secret* to be performed. Act I is now being copied for you by Zdenka. . . . To me, Act II seems more noble and tender than comic; but in Act III comedy returns. What I fear most, however, are the ensembles. Is it laziness or old age that makes me uneasy when working on these parts? I can't tell you how I feel when I finish such a scene where everyone has been running about. Afterwards I breathe more freely, and each aria seems to come more easily.[5]

On October 23, 1877, Krásnohorská sent details of the period she thought most suitable for *The Secret*, bringing her original idea forward to the 1800's, sympathizing with the composer's difficulties, and promising to make fewer ensembles in their next collaboration, *Viola*.

For the next three months Smetana worked on the opera as often as his health would permit, and by January 31, 1878, had Act I in score, and the sketch of Act II in pencil:

> The duets for Blaženka and Vítek are now properly written, but I fear my style is insufficiently comic. Perhaps I'm wrong? I no longer possess a sense of humour and something Kalina sings has set me thinking that the opera could well be called *Poklad* (*The Treasure*) instead. Don't you think this more effective? I would not dare change your title, but is mine not perhaps more

[4] Letter to Krásnohorská: October 2, 1877.
[5] Letter to Krásnohorská October: 20, 1877.

attractive? I read with joy that you have something new for me; I only returned *Viola* because I had hoped to cross the Czech frontier of music. Now I no longer have that wish. I am old with no certainty of ever being able to hear again. I must be content with what I have in my homeland. Please do not bother with *Viola* but choose, instead, whatever pleases you. Do remember: fewer ensembles and much less chorus than in *The Secret*. I can only write such sections in a polyphonic style and that is long and tiring, especially with so many people on stage. I would also like to work on a comic character like Dr. Bartolo or the Mayor in *Czaar und Zimmerman*: these stand by themselves and therefore can be made the most of. . . . I would so much like to try this; for up to now I have never composed in this genre. I don't want a mere copy—you must create something quite original for me.[6]

The feeling which composer and librettist seemed to share was quite exceptional, and throughout their correspondence one is conscious of a unity of thought, and a harmony of intention. Krásnohorská's understanding of the sick composer was indeed penetrating; her tact and skill in handling him, sometimes against his will, was remarkable and often charming:

The title *The Treasure* is splendid; but would not the public expect to see a real treasure? I always believed *Old Love* would be suitable, but perhaps *The Secret* is best after all, because we have already let this enter the minds of the people. One asks the name of Smetana's next opera and the other replies: 'It is a secret!' So at first they wonder, then they ponder, then finally they laugh. It is as much a joke as was *The Kiss*. For the new opera I promise to create fewer characters. The main figure will be an old bachelor, called Viloušek, who has never married because he is too fussy, and too prim and proper. When he finally decides to take a wife his choice is made difficult since he has fallen in love with two pretty girls, neither of whom is attracted to him. . . . This does not seem to be a very new subject, but as I envisage it, with comic incidents and different humorous characters, it could have a considerable effect. And I will find an arch-comic type for you . . . from the Czech countryside. Would you be against a country parson—not a parody—but a kind-hearted, serious man who advises everyone?[7]

[6] Letter to Krásnohorská: January 31, 1878.
[7] Letter from Krásnohorská: February 1, 1878.

The day before receiving this Smetana had finished the pencil sketch of Act II of *The Secret* and noted in his Diary that the first fifty-six pages were ready in score. The remainder of the instrumentation for the second act was completed on April 4, that of Act III on May 31. There only remained to be written the overture (finished on July 15, 1878) before the new opera could be delivered to Adolf Čech on August 4. The première was announced for September 18 in the New Czech Theatre, and at the beginning of the month Smetana had set out his requirements:

> I am glad everyone seems to like the latest opera and the two motives on which the piece is built. . . . For the scene in Act II where Kalina falls asleep I have spoken already to the producer and have asked for children to represent the gnomes with faces like little old men. The chorus of basses are to sing behind the stage, and when Kalina wakes up the ghosts must disappear, but not before. . . . Let it be clearly understood that I need a full orchestra with the largest string section, namely 6/6/4/3/3 players, and Skřivánek must be accompanied by a guitar. Also, the ballet should be classic in style and not merely a series of jumps for comic phantoms.[8]

Accordingly, the string section was enlarged by members of the Prague Salon Octet and the permanent chorus, which at this time numbered only sixteen, was also increased by members of the Hlahol; but despite this and a thoroughly rehearsed production by Edmund Chvalovský (1843–1934), the success of the first night was marred by poor attendance. The second performance on September 20 fared little better, and it was only at the third, Smetana's Benefit, that the public began to respond:

> The house was full and I had to go onto the stage and bow and receive presentations of wreaths and flowers.[9]

Unfortunately this show of enthusiasm did not last long. *The Secret* failed to become the box office success for which Smetana had hoped, and it was dropped from the repertoire after twelve hearings (during the last six years of the composer's life it was given no more than a dozen times). Possibly the audience, which had warmed to the spontaneous gaiety of *The Bartered Bride*, failed to understand the serious-minded *Secret*, which is touched more than ever by melancholy and a pessimistic view of life. Where, for instance, *The Bartered Bride* was written as a comedy in the full flowering of Smetana's

[8] Letter to Čech: September 4, 1878. [9] Diary: September 23, 1878.

creative powers, *The Secret* is less immediate in its appeal, being a deeper, more consciously mature, almost elegiac offering which penetrates a romantic sphere and turns from reality to the supernatural. Neither critics nor public were enthusiastic about the new opera, and though the composer added an extra aria for Kalina in Act II, the general reaction was indifference. While recognizing that Smetana had maintained a place in Czech music, Pivoda believed *The Secret* to be 'well below the level of *The Bartered Bride*'.[1] Others found Krásnohorská's libretto uneven, and several of Smetana's closest friends urged him to look elsewhere for a collaborator:

> I wish only one thing, that you could find a text on the same level as your music, namely a good libretto for a serious opera. Certainly Eliška Krásnohorská writes fine Czech texts, but has she sufficient dramatic power to follow you further? I doubt it! I hope I'm wrong. If you would like an introduction to another writer I will willingly arrange this with pleasure, and I will look for a new text myself. The slightest service I can do for you will be an honour.[2]

Despite this Smetana felt a degree of loyalty to his librettist, and after presenting her with a silver coffee service engraved with her name together with those of the two operas on which she had worked, he sent the following undated letter from which it can be seen that he had come to regard her as an essential part of their collaboration:

> What shall I do with these critics? Is it easy to have a coat made by somebody else? People do not realize what it means to create a huge opera, and especially for one who is worn out by deafness and sorrow. They all want me to break away from something which has grown between us. I have become attached to your verses and to the music I feel instinctively to be in them. I can find this nowhere else.

The Secret is another story of Bohemian life, but its subject matter is less touching and far more serious than Smetana's previous operas. Unlike *The Kiss*, it depends hardly at all on the irony of temperament. The plot, which owes a debt to La Fontaine's fable *Les Femmes et le Secret*, comprises a number of thumbnail sketches of Bohemian village life, revolving round the trivial conflicts of two Aldermen and a Romeo and Juliet-like motive, based on the secret love of Vítek for Blaženka. These two elements form the shell of the drama;

[1] *Věstník Divadelni a Hudební*—No. 15/16: 1878.
[2] Undated letter from Hostinský.

but Smetana preferred to concentrate on its serious core, treating Kalina's desire for wealth and his wounded pride as the principal theme. Yet, with the exception of the young lovers, the remaining figures belong to comic country types—a boasting veteran soldier, a drink-loving ballad-singer, a hopelessly amorous spinster, a gossiping builder. The comedy springs not from these characters, but from their situations and though it is often a trifle heavy handed, it is never unkind. Here Smetana seems to delve more deeply below the surface of his characters, discovering in them traits and conflicts of which the librettist had probably been unaware, emphasizing certain supernatural forces to a greater degree than ever before. There is also a marked insistence on folk lore and idiom, and Krásnohorská's text offered various opportunities for exploring these riches. The names Kalina and Malina literally mean 'snowdrop' and 'raspberry', their bickering lines sometimes suggest a Cox-and-Box-like play on words (a), while Skřivánek, the wandering folk singer and the symbol of freedom, is the Czech for 'lark' (b) (his first-act ballad sarcastically mocks first the flower, then the fruit) and has a popular folk-song flavour that may well have been inspired by the Bohemian melody, *Včera neděle byla* (*Yesterday was Sunday*):

Example 94

(*a*)

(*b*)

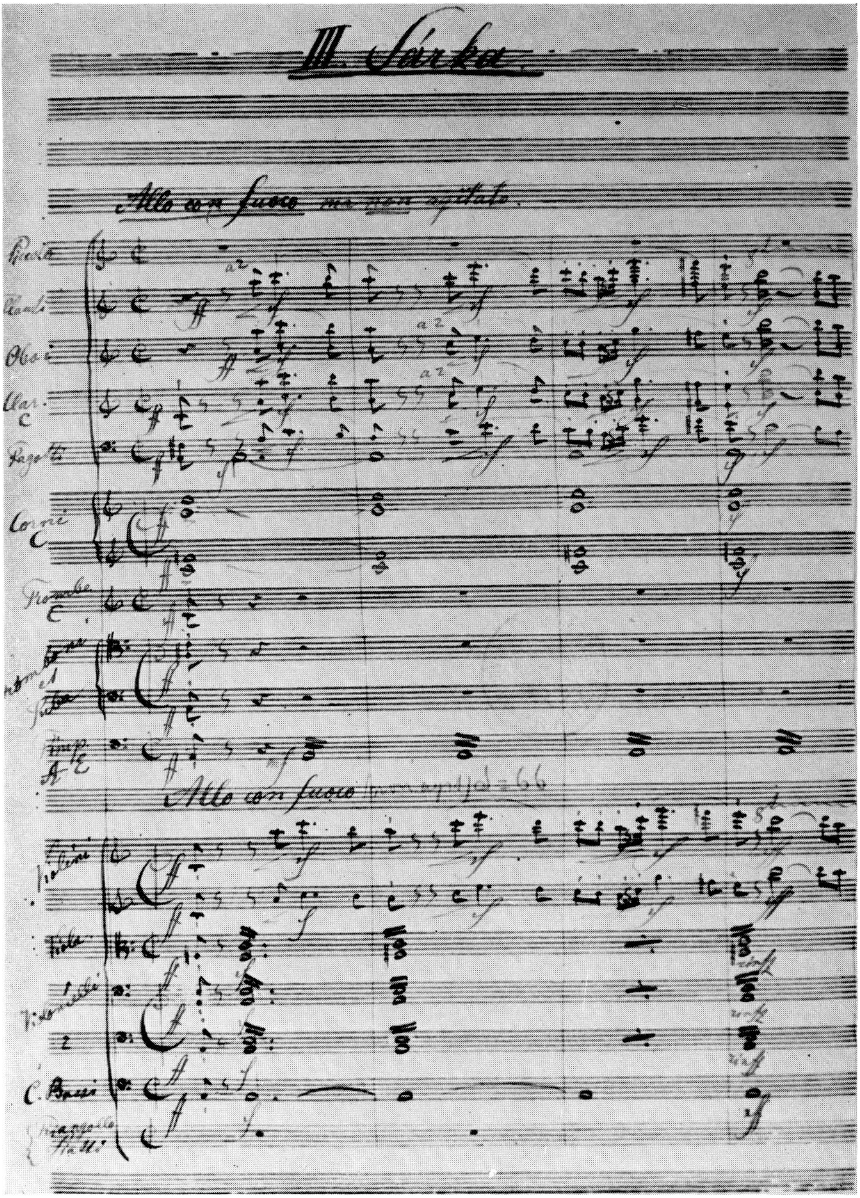

PLATE XXIII. Manuscript score of Má Vlast

PLATE XXIV. Pages from the unfinished opera, *Viola*
with inscriptions 'Glory to Viola' written in a time of mental confusion

In Act I (Scene 4), the introduction of the *dudy* leads to a boisterous folk-dance over a pedal drone which lasts for a hundred bars; and earlier, in Scene 1, the picture of threshers at work on the corn is a direct invitation to depict their busy flails by wooden blocks in the orchestra (they are maintained for a ninety-bar period). The procession of pilgrims in Act II is another invitation to incorporate a rustic feeling into the music; and though Smetana does not actually use a traditional hymn at this point, his chorale-like melody, to the words 'Matičko Boží, obětuj milosti své mně zář!' ('Mother of God, graciously show us your face!'), could well be a paraphrase or remembrance of a tune that local carillon ringers used to play at the church in Loreta, near Vlašim, where Smetana spent part of his childhood.

Apart from these charming details, *The Secret* is essentially a serious work which does not reveal its beauties as readily as *The Kiss*; neither does it have quite the same unity or spontaneous flow of ideas that distinguishes the earlier work, even though it is bound by two significant motives. Smetana develops much of his music organically from two themes,[3] the one representing the ideas of secret and treasure, the other Kalina himself:

Example 95

(*a*)

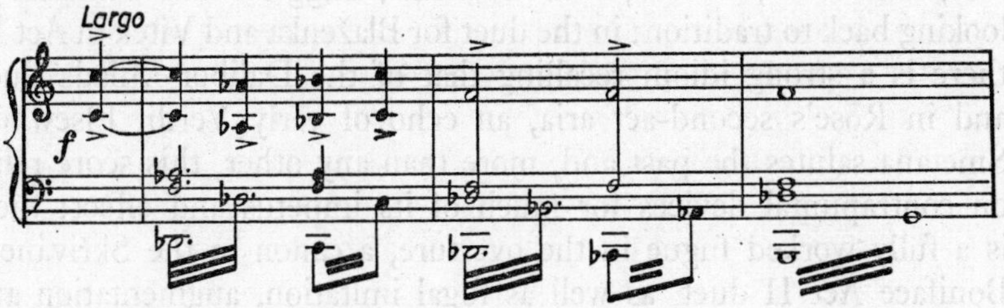

(*b*)

[3] Significantly the contour of these motives had been anticipated in the tone poem *From Bohemia's Woods and Fields* several years before, when Smetana had written this phrase:

Remarkably, the 'secret' motive, when transformed, also typifies Rose, the ghost of Friar Barnabáš, the band of gnomes and dwarfs (a) and the idea of the 'joke' (b) which the Friar is playing on Kalina:

Example 96

(*a*)

(*b*)

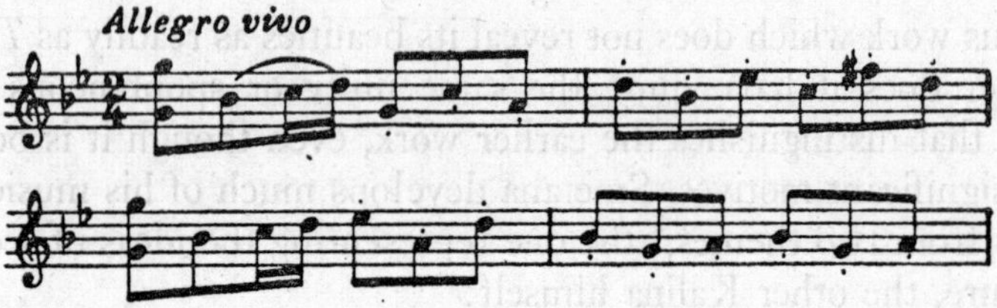

Though these transformations tend to give the score a symphonic semblance, the introduction of set pieces and formal arias for Boniface, Skřivánek, Kalina, and Blaženka, suggest that Smetana is looking back to tradition: in the duet for Blaženka and Vítek in Act II, there is a strong idiom recalling that of the Dalibor-Milada duet, and in Rose's second-act aria, an echo of early Verdi. Elsewhere Smetana salutes the past and, more than any other, this score relies on contrapuntal devices for much of its impetus and effect: there is a fully-worked fugue in the overture, a canon in the Skřivánek–Boniface Act II duet, as well as fugal imitation, augmentation and diminution (notably for the apparition of the gnomes in Act II). Possibly Smetana's desire to convince himself that he was capable of writing complicated music, and weaving a tissue from an intricate network of motives, led him to exercise his craft in this way; but it could be argued that in counterpoint he found a safe, almost mechanical form of composition, and was relying on academic principles more than his ear. But where *The Secret* does show an advance on the previous operas is in the handling of the chorus and ensembles.

We know from Smetana's correspondence with Krásnohorská that it was precisely these sections of the score which he found difficult; yet, ironically, these are the places which stand out as the most memorable. One might have predicted that for the rival groups centred around Kalina and Malina, Smetana would adopt antiphonal exchanges (he had resorted to this device with considerable success in *Libuše*) but one would not have expected the effect to be so overwhelming, so immediate or so full of impact as it is. These ensembles erupt without preparation, and though the writing is complex (often in twelve or more parts), there is a rhythmic urgency which propels the music and makes them brilliant gems in a somewhat dull setting. If there is a reservation it is that such passages are all too short-lived, and that they reflect none of the malicious or hostile tones suggested in the text. Neither, for that matter, is there anything sinister in the gnomes' scene in Act II; on the contrary, their music is charming rather than frightening and, though it seems to look back to the will-o'-the-wisps' music in the last act of Nicolai's *Die Lustigen Weiber von Windsor*, it possesses no inherent element of terror. Perhaps this was deliberate on Smetana's part; for had he not specifically requested children wearing masks to portray this vision? Certainly his music has a childlike playfulness which is wholly endearing.

Delightful though this is, one of the most original sections is to be found at the end of Act I, where the composer engages in the most subtle forms of sound perspective and looks back to the tone poem *From Bohemia's Woods and Fields*.[4] While Blaženka and Vítek steal a kiss in the moonlight, Skřivánek and the night-watchman announce Kalina's secret through a megaphone, from various levels of the tower. Though there are clearly two divergent elements here, the quartet of voices is skilfully bound by the motive of the 'secret', with neither party disturbing or paying attention to the other.

Despite some trivialities in the libretto and the variable style of much of the music, Smetana spent an extraordinary amount of care and time on the score. Working with painful slowness, he took nearly a year to complete the first act—the shortest of the three, moreover. Regrettably, much of the music is uneven and occasionally a sense of fatigue or nervous tension hangs over the score, like a thin veil which never quite shuts out the composer's former brilliance, but just dims it.

[4] At the point where the night-watchman announces Kalina's secret from the tower, Smetana writes an augmented version of the theme he had several years before, put to good use in the tone poem *From Bohemia's Woods and Fields* and later in *Blaník*.

FOURTEEN

'THE DEVIL'S WALL'
1879–1882

A SMALL SHRIVELLED figure of a man, huddled in a lon heavy coat trimmed with fur, walked falteringly through th streets of Prague. The coat had seen better days, and so had th wearer. Submerged in his own silent world of illusions and frenzie imaginings the man, looking seventy, possibly more, with a bowl hat pulled well down over his lined face, wandered aimlessly, ack nowledging neither friends nor passersby who pointed with alarm t his dishevelled appearance. It was a sorrowful sight for those wh recognized Smetana's genius. His face was an album in which enemie had written their signatures with slanderous attacks. Emaciate burdened with worry as he was, and with the chill hands of exhaustio and depression upon him, few would have believed that this was th man who had laid the foundations of modern Czech music, the ma who had raised critics against him in every quarter of the cit Smetana was fifty-five. He walked slowly, placing one foot uncer tainly in front of the other; with an extravagant sweep of his hat or flamboyant gesture of his cane he would greet strangers, starin through them; he seemed dead to reality, oblivious of weathe crowds or circumstances. He wandered dangerously in the stree and over railway lines,[1] yet he could not tear himself away from th city that had witnessed his triumphs and defeats and was now th only place in which he could fructify during his fallow seasons. F Smetana Prague was a paradise, a cloud cuckoo land, a place escape from the boredom and bedlam of Jabkenice. Along thorough fares and in cafés he became a familiar but sad figure, making use his stay to refresh his tired and burdened mind with the most varie forms of amusement. In the morning he would read newspapers i

[1] On August 20, 1881, he narrowly escaped death at Neratovice Station whe he failed to see several railway carriages hurtling towards him. Despite attempted warning having failed, he managed to reach safety in the nick of tim

the coffee houses and spend the best part of the afternoon in the same way. Later in the day he liked to stroll, mingling with the people or staring at the Vltava from its tree-lined banks. In the evening he would go unannounced and unnoticed to the theatre, watching the audience as much as the stage, though he seldom stayed beyond the first act unless there was promise of sumptuous scenery, parades, battles or ballets. He even developed a special taste for children's plays and fairy tales:

> Just imagine a deaf all but dead brain to which neither the scraping of instruments, the hum of voices, nor any living sound can penetrate! At least I must see something, to feast my eyes on something childlike. I only have to look, and the more colourful it is the less I miss my hearing.[2]

When in Prague he would often visit the music section of the Umělecká Beseda of which he was honorary chairman; but when he was in attendance there was only one item on the agenda—to listen to Smetana. He enjoyed speaking and though we know from Ladislav Dolanský (1857–1910)[3] that his voice now fluctuated peculiarly to unnatural heights and depths, he would recall his life and compositions, and was moved to play the piano, demonstrating the history of the sonata or the development of the symphony. Zelený testifies that he still possessed a phenomenal memory, being able to perform without preparation compositions he had not heard for years, and undoubtedly had not seen either; and from Josef Foerster we learn that:

> . . . his supple hands touched the keys so lightly, and his perfect rhythmic playing, his stirring delivery quick with feeling, held everyone spellbound.[4]

But neither Foerster nor Zelený realized that in his country retreat Smetana had begun work on a collection of dances for piano which had helped him to maintain his technique and keep his hands in trim. Smetana started to sketch a set of four *České Tance* (*Czech Dances*) at the beginning of April, 1877, and completed them within the month:

> Each is a polka and a continuation of the style of my earlier polkas written years ago. Those who know my previous pieces will recognize my progress in this genre.[5]

[2] Undated letter to Krásnohorská.
[3] Dolanský: *Hudební Pameti* (*Musical Memories*) (1949).
[4] Bartoš: *Letters and Reminiscences* (1955).
[5] Letter to Urbánek: March 2, 1879.

Indeed, the pieces are similar, but those who noted a new vitality in the Polkas of the 1850's could hardly have foreseen what the fully developed genre would become. Certainly the Polka in F looks back to the melody of the *Album Leaf* in D, and the *Poetic Polka* in A flat, and the appearance of two trio sections in the new B flat Polka is a reprise of the structural scheme employed in the second movement of the early G minor Piano Trio. Of the four pieces only the third is fast, the others being muted and reflective. The set, however, is typically Czech and demonstrates that despite his handicap the composer was still able to write delightful miniatures:

Example 97

Apart from this F major Polka (sometimes known as *Caprice Bohemien*) the cycle failed to catch the public's attention and like *Dreams*, the *Four Czech Dances* remained unperformed and unpublished for some time. Smetana began to resent the neglect into which his pieces had fallen and possibly felt affronted by the popularity that Dvořák was winning with his *Moravian Duets* and *Slavonic Dances*. Though he had recently been spared the calumny of Pivoda and Maýr, Smetana was still the victim of attacks by Rieger, who having set up a scarecrow of his own which he took to be the image of Smetana, now proceeded to demolish it in the belief that he was disposing of Smetana himself. Next, Rieger adopted Dvořák as musical champion of the Old Czech Party, and in order to foster his new protegé, he contrived for his own daughter, the poetess Marie Červinková-Riegrová, to collaborate with Dvořák on a new opera. Once accepted in German musical circles it was only to be expected that Dvořák's compositions should be revalued in Bohemia where he was beginning to be regarded as the leading force of Czech music. To his cause Rieger now enlisted the aid of the young Leoš Janáček who, as Editor of the Brno *Hudební Listy*, denounced Smetana by the misrepresentation of fact and the sophistry of dialectic. It is regrettable that a man of Janácek's undoubted talent should have allowed himself to lapse into promoting Dvořák's compositions at Smetana's expense; but this was only to be expected in view of Janáček's[6] unconditional allegiance to Dvorák (the two musicians maintained a lively personal relationship, stayed in each other's apartments and spent holidays together). What is more Janáček had made Brno the centre of a Dvořák cult.[7] That Smetana was passionately interested in Dvořák, whose star was beginning to eclipse his own, we know from the zoologist and palaeontologist František Bayer (1854–1936), who brought Smetana a copy of the *Slavonic Dances* (Opus 46) as soon as they were published by Simrock in August, 1878. Though he affirms[8] that the composer praised Dvořák's spate of melodies and the Beethovian development of his themes, it is almost certain he regarded him with rivalry and suspicion.[9]

[6] The influence of Dvořák on Janáček's youthful works was quite overwhelming. The *Four Male Choruses* (1885), the opera *Šárka* and the oratorio *Amarus* (1898) are all dedicated to Dvořák. Moreover, he considered Dvořák, not Smetana, to be the sole representative of Czech music and said as much at a lecture in Brno in March, 1882. When Janáček was invited to commemorate the hundredth performance of *The Bartered Bride* in Brno, he declined the proposal, and only two years after Smetana's death did Brno honour his memory with a performance of the E minor Quartet, poorly rehearsed and given in the absence of Janáček. Unfortunately Janáček cannot be entirely exonerated from the reproach of obstinacy; for however cogently he tried to rationalize his critical objections to Smetana, the fact remains that he could not, or would not, understand Smetana's style, which was founded on the neo-Romantic school.

[7] In April, 1877, Janáček performed Dvořák's *Serenade for Strings*; in 1878 Brno heard the *Moravian Duets*, and *Four Slavonic Dances*, and later on the *Slavonic Rhapsodies*, the *Czech Suite*, the Symphonies in F, D and A minor, *The Spectre's Bride* and *Stabat Mater*. A rich selection by comparison with Smetana's works of which, between 1880 and 1886, *Vltava* was heard twice, *Vyšehrad* once.

[8] Bartoš: *Letters and Reminiscences* (1955).

[9] Smetana had observed Dvořák's progress with interest, watching him graduate from the orchestra of the Provisional Theatre, where, as a violist he had played under Smetana's baton, to a composer of the first rank. In a letter written to

Smetana now planned to make a 'comeback', so he told Urbánek, by composing a set of Czech Dances 'with their original names' which could be published singly or collectively, for one or two pianos or for orchestra. Smetana continues:

> I think this would be a good idea, for every Czech should know these dances. When Dvořák calls his pieces by the general title *Slavonic Dances*, no-one knows which particular dance forms they are, or if they really exist. Instead, I shall show the special names we Czechs give our national dances, so please tell me if you like this idea so that I can begin work.[1]

Urbánek did like Smetana's scheme, and in the summer he started work on a suite of pieces which incorporates Bohemia's most celebrated dance forms. He outlined six types, intending to write two of each:

(a) Individual dances for a man or woman.
(b) Dances for pairs of men renouncing love.
(c) Dances for pairs of men declaring love.
(d) Dances for pairs of women renouncing love.
(e) Dances for pairs of women declaring love.
(f) Collective dances for men and women.

Some of the pieces were to be based on folk melodies drawn from Erben's collection and others from an eighty-year-old teacher called Suchý, who had retired to a small cottage opposite the Forester's Lodge at Jabkenice. Suchý, a self-taught violinist, provided Smetana with a wealth of information relating to traditional Bohemian-Moravian dances; and according to Josef Schwarz he even demonstrated the steps himself, scribbling down various rhythms and folk tunes which may have provided the inspiration for the later pieces.[2] After a deal of research, however, Smetana was still short of material for categories (d) and (e) and resolved to rearrange the cycle, reducing the movements to ten, and omitting the rejdovák and chimney-sweep's dance which he had previously earmarked for inclusion.

Procházka on December 23, 1879, he refers to Dvořák as 'this jester' and implies that he has copied certain effects from him: 'He has introduced various instrumental devices in his third *Rhapsody* as novelties—I mean the place where the harp alone begins the movement and is later joined by the orchestra; and in other similar things which Smetana, that's me, has already created! But as his works have appeared in print before mine, I shall be the one to be called plagiarist.' Smetana was convinced that Dvořák had the opening of *Vyšehrad* in mind when he composed his third *Rhapsody*, which also begins with a harp cadenza.

[1] Letter to Urbánek: April 22, 1879. [2] Bartoš: *op. cit.*

The cycle opens with a furiant, a fiery, impulsive peasant dance in fast triple-measure such as Smetana had already used in *The Bartered Bride*. It dates from the time of the French occupation of Bohemia, when it was spelt Fouriant, but has no etymological connexion with 'fury'. Originally it was performed exclusively by men as an expression of indignation for Bohemia's invasion, its syncopated rhythms reflecting the stubborn character of the oppressed. By choosing it as his first movement Smetana was ensured that the cycle had a vital beginning; while the sudden major-minor flashes lend the music a resolute defiance. Though he jotted down Erben's folk melody at the top of his page, he chose not to copy it note for note, but used it as a theme for variation:

Example 98

(*a*)

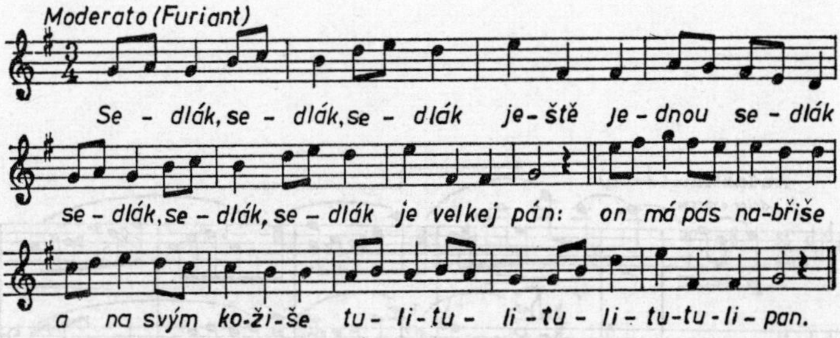

(*b*)

'Slepička' ('Little Hen'), the second movement, is a girl's dance in the style of a polka in which the trio is transformed into a dazzling showpiece recalling the bravura compositions of Liszt; but despite its appealing folk idiom it does not draw on any specific national melody. By contrast 'Oves' ('Oats') incorporates a folk song of renounced love and Smetana records his debt to Erben by indicating the title and opening lines of the text on his score:

> I was sowing yesterday and today,
> but I won't love you any more, my sweetheart.
> No, I won't love you ever again!

Example 99

(*a*)

(*b*)

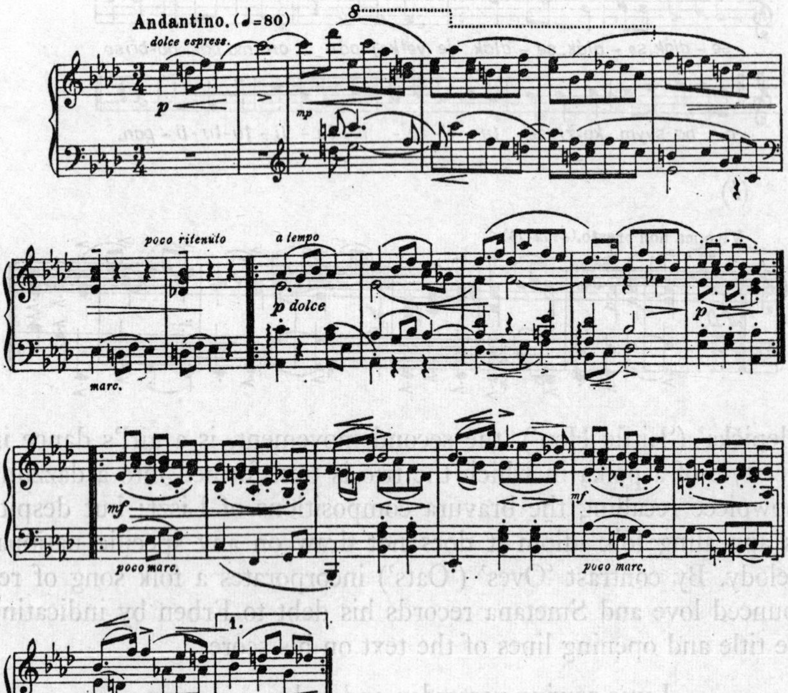

'Medvěd' ('The Bear') draws on a traditional folk dance called bavorák, a robust piece in alternating triple/duple time. Here Smetana deliberately attempts to capture the sense of irony which mirrors the folk text and paints the bear-like steps of the young girl's boyfriend:

> I won't marry you my dear,
> because you look just like a bear.
> A bear has hairy legs but you have also a cursed heart!

Example 100

In the middle section he abandons Erben's melody and over a sixty-bar *dudy* drone writes a bucolic trio that is one of his most delightful creations. 'Cibulička' ('Little Onion') is the most widely known of Bohemian folk songs, and in choosing it for his fifth dance Smetana was certain of lending his cycle popular appeal. Wisely, he treats it in a series of simple guises in which the embellishment never conceals the original. 'Dupák', the next piece, is a stamping dance for men in fast duple time that closely resembles a scherzo-polka. It is an exciting, though demanding, display piece in double octaves, nicely combining the brilliance of a Liszt étude with the acid humour of the folk text:

> Wait until you are a hundred before you marry.
> When you have lost all your teeth—
> they won't hurt you any more!

Musically, Smetana seems to have been impressed only by the rhythm of the last bar of Erben's folk tune which he transforms thus:

Example 101

(*a*)

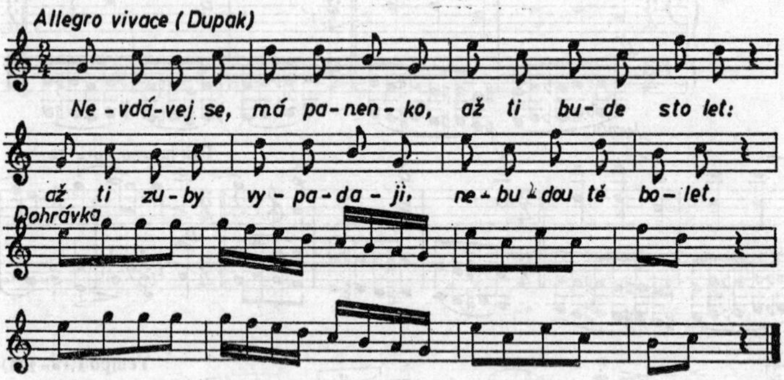

(*b*)

'Hulán' ('The Lancer'), a female dance both sad and reflective, provides a welcome foil to the preceding boisterousness and aptly mirrors the reflective nature of the folk poetry:

I had a sweetheart—a Lancer was he.
I liked him dearly and gave him my silver ring.
Now Lancer and ring are no more!

Inspired by Erben's folk song No. 379, and treated as a theme for variation, Smetana produces a delicate tracery of virtuoso filigree, demonstrating that he was still the possessor of a formidable technique. 'Obročák', the eighth piece, is a turning dance for women in fast duple time, and though it closely resembles the style of a polka Smetana uses it to depict two girls: the first is rich and orders her boy-friend 'Not to go there, better come here' (Erben No. 541); the second is poor, but her beauty and natural charm (Erben No. 114, *Haj jusy ze pšenice*: *Hey, geese, come out of the corn*), win the composer's heart and dominate the score. The penultimate movement, 'Sousedská', is a slow waltz, such as Smetana had used in the third part of *Wedding Scenes* (1849). Here he writes a free fantasia which owes no debt to Erben; and neither does the final piece, 'Skočná', a wild, dynamic stamping dance in duple time with a three-bar phrase structure, that has all the breathless energy of the most brilliant polkas:

Example 102

The skočná was traditionally a peasant dance and Smetana had incorporated it into his work twice before—in Act I of *The Brandenburgers in Bohemia* and for the 'Dance of the Comedians' in

The Bartered Bride. In both cases it was used as an invitation to dance, but here, full of leaps and swirling, insatiable rhythms, it is the epitome of rejoicing. Direct in folk idiom, and rich in invention, the suite represents the highest form of dance music to come from Smetana's pen; but the pieces are not imitations, nor are they merely coloured by folk characteristics as are some of Dvořák, Brahms or Grieg. These are glittering paraphrases of a virtuoso order, conceived in the most masterly fashion and founded on genuine folk forms which interpret the national spirit. Sadly, the *Czech Dances* are little known in the West. They would make a welcome addition to the concert pianist's repertoire, being challenging and rewarding for the artist and a source of endless delight for the listener.

While he was completing his *Czech Dances* Smetana was invited to compose another dance, this time for orchestra, to celebrate the thirtieth anniversary of the founding of the Národní Beseda. At the inaugural meeting in 1849 his Polka in D, later named *Našim děvám* (*To Our Girls*), had been performed; but now he felt too old, too much out of sorts to write cheerful ballroom music. For Smetana this appeared to be nothing more than a thankless chore, but on realizing that the event was being organized to raise funds for the building of the National Theatre, he agreed to write a 'ballroom polka' which he called *Venkovanka* (*The Country Woman*), taking as his theme part of an unfinished piano work of the 1850's. He revised it, composed a new trio, and gave it an orchestral dressing; but that he approached this task with a certain lack of enthusiasm he confessed to Srb:

> Please give my Polka (*Venkovanka*) to the Národní Beseda. What a composition it is—the damned thing! Indeed, it's a weight off my mind.[3]

In the event, Smetana's Polka opened the Jubilee Ball on December 28, 1879. It was followed by a Waltz by Fibich, a Mazurka by Novotný, a Quadrille by Kovařovice, a Polka by Laube, a Quadrille by Hauser, a Polka by Jiránek, a Mazurka by Knittl, a Sousedská by Chvala, two Waltzes by Dvořák and Šebor, a Galop by Rozkošný and a final Mazurka by Kovařovice.

Another score to which Smetana returned, after a gulf of ten or more years, was the Cantata *Česká píseň* (*Song of the Czechs*), which he revised for a performance also arranged to raise money for the National Theatre fund. His catalogue contains only one work for chorus and orchestra, but this, like *The Bartered Bride*, suffered a chequered history, proceeding through various stages before emerging

[3] Letter to Srb-Debrnov: November 13, 1879.

in its final form. The text had been written by the patriotic priest and revivalist Jan Jindřich Marek, whose verses Smetana had put to good use in 1860 when Ludevít Procházka had invited him to produce an unaccompanied chorus for men's voices. Though he had set the text to music as Opus 17, it was neither published nor performed. Eight years were to pass before he rearranged the original for mixed choir with piano accompaniment, and yet another two before *Song of the Czechs* was performed for the first time on May 16, 1870. On this occasion three hundred men and a hundred women joined to sing it; but realizing that on this scale, even with a harmonium, the accompaniment was ineffective, Smetana resolved to score it for full orchestra. Another eight years were to elapse before he fulfilled his task. Though the Cantata did not appear in its definitive form until 1878, the use of this title should not lead us to expect a liturgical work. Smetana, for whom Christianity in particular or religion in general had little appeal, never produced a sacred work, and *Song of the Czechs* is a very positive, secular offering. An orchestral introduction leads to four separate 'songs': the first serious, extolling the Czech landscape; the second, a lyrical love song for female voices; the third a dramatic song for men only; and the finale, a national patriotic song for full chorus which ends with a full-blooded coda recalling the introduction. Work on the Cantata was followed by a cycle of part-songs commissioned by Heller with performance by school children in mind. While Smetana would have preferred to write for women's voices, and in four parts rather than three, he found himself stirred by Sládek's *Přiletěly vlaštovičky* (*The Swallows have Come*) and *Za hory slunce zapadá* (*Sunset*), and Peček's *Má hvězda* (*My Star*), and responded with three charming miniatures. Although the songs are slight in length and musical value, *The Swallows have come* is interesting for the way a Polka theme, previously exploited in the *Song of the Czechs*, is reworked; and *Sunset* for its sad turn of melody which proclaims the composer of the String Quartet in D minor of 1883.

Another poem which drew from him a simple, yet strong, setting was Srb-Debrnov's *Věno* (*Dedication* or *Dowry*), written in 1880. Here Smetana writes not a personal inscription but a musical dedication to his native land, and celebrates Czech song in a fashion quite different from the earlier Cantata, announcing his principal theme in the old Czech motto: 'Through song to the heart, through the heart to the country'. Technically the piece is less demanding than his previous choral works, being designed in ternary form for mass singing with broad homophonic passages that come close to the style of an anthem. Possibly, because of its directness and telling simplicity, the work has come to be regarded as a national hymn and is one of the most popular items in the Czech repertoire.

Less fortunate was Smetana's next chorus, *Modlitba* (*Prayer*), also written to a poem by Srb-Debrnov. Despite its title, the piece was created neither for church nor cathedral, but for a choral festival in 1880. This short, expressive utterance is built on two entreaties: the first for peace, the other for the well-being of the homeland. Into this Smetana incorporated stanzas of the eleventh-century chorale, *Hospodine Pomiluj Ny*!, the Slav equivalent of *Kyrie Eleison*, treating each directly so as to express the basic idea of Srb's poem: the salvation of mankind.

The end of the Seventies saw a decline in the disputes over Smetana's music. He was awarded the presidency of numerous choral unions, and the honorary citizenships of a number of Bohemian towns. In September, 1880, his birthplace, Litomyšl, fêted him with celebrations, a banquet and the unveiling of a plaque[4] in his honour; and eight months before, Prague had marked the occasion of his fiftieth anniversary as a performer with a midday jubilee concert in the Žofín Hall at which Čech conducted *Vyšehrad*, the first performances of *Tábor* and *Blaník*, as well as *Song of the Czechs*. In the same programme the *Evening Songs* were presented for the first time by Lev and Sitt, and to conclude Smetana returned to the keyboard for Chopin's Nocturne in B, and his own Polka in A minor:

> Even though deaf, he played with such originality, feeling and expression that he clearly towered above all other pianists. Considering his state, he produced a rich range of dynamic nuances which were as astonishing as was his technical perfection. It was touching to see an artist whose performances so excited the public, especially when they realized that not one of the sounds which he charmed from the instrument could ever penetrate his soul. Many wept for Smetana's tragic fate.[5]

In the evening *The Kiss* was revived at the Provisional Theatre for his Benefit, and though he was able to note that the events had been exceptionally successful and that his efforts did not warrant so much praise,[6] he was unable to rid his mind of gloom and trepidation. While

[4] At the Smetana celebrations, the castle authorities refused to allow a plaque to be put on the brewery in which the composer had been born. Instead it was unveiled on a house in the square where Smetana's parents had previously lived. Later the plaque was affixed to the wall of the castle brewery, and the room in which he was born was opened to the public.

[5] *Česky Noviny*: January 6, 1180. [6] Diary: February 18, 1880.

the tributes showered on him cheered him, they were unable to relieve his pessimism or the depressing rut of daily routine. On the surface, his lot was a pleasant one. He rose at eight-thirty, walked after breakfast, worked up to lunch-time, dozed in the afternoon, took tea at four, played with the children until dinner, and indulged in a game of cards or chess before retiring to bed (at nine o'clock in winter, and ten in summer). He enjoyed a glass of wine, liked beer, smoked a cigar every day and relished his favourite dish škubánky (potato dumplings). Yet in this relaxed, almost dignified, atmosphere he never found real contentment. On the contrary, he was often irritable, nervous, depressed. While the 1880's marked the beginnings of relative peace between the Old and Young Czech Parties, for Smetana there was no reconciliation either with his wife or his own painful condition. He began to slow down; composition became something of an ordeal; he noticed that his musical memory was getting weaker, that the periods in which he was able to work continuously were becoming shorter. He suffered further attacks of vertigo, hallucinations, even premonitions of death. The omens of fate were against him. His doctors recommended rest and quiet, ordering him to work for no more than an hour each day. But he defied the limitations imposed on him and, at the cost of exacting even greater strain, began two new compositions—a chamber work and an opera.

Z domoviny (*From my Home*), two duets for violin and piano, is not on the same level as the rest of Smetana's chamber music. Dedicated to Alexander Thun-Taxis (who, in acknowledgement, sent the composer an ivory snuff box embellished with Czech garnets), these simple, genial confessions are an intimate pendant to the tone poem *From Bohemia's Woods and Fields*, and sing of the same lyrical yearning for the homeland. The first duo, in three sections, vacillates between major and minor tonalities (a characteristic feature of Moravian folk song), while the second piece, more complex in form, contains several marks of Smetana's musical maturity—a canonic pastorella, looking back to the one in *Blaník*, a wild skočná reminiscent of that in *The Brandenburgers in Bohemia*, and a melodic echo of the song *Sadness of a Deserted One*.

While these duets are to some extent backward looking, the reverse is true of his last complete opera *Čertova stěna* (*The Devil's Wall*). Following his work on *The Secret*, he had invited Eliška Krásnohorská to provide the text of another opera, which he hoped to dedicate to her in admiration and gratitude:

> I was touched by your kind thought to honour me publicly and I

> thank you for your intention, but please do not bother. I am not eager to see myself distinguished in this way, neither am I ambitious, except for those whom I like and who are my betters. For your next opera . . . I have an idea (perhaps exploited elsewhere, I don't know?) about a father's love for his priceless daughter. I would give the daughter not only the tenor whom she loves, but also two other rival admirers who would both be in each other's way. The piece, which could be called *The Rivals*, would be comic and chivalrous.[7]

Though Smetana would willingly have taken up the text of *Viola* at this time, Krásnohorská sent him instead *The Dancing Master*; but feeling this to be too close to Jonas's operetta, *Gavotte* (1873), and Delibes's *Le Roi l'a dit*, she again offered him *The Rivals*.

Set in the Middle Ages, it deals with two suitors, Achille, a young army officer, and Burian, a rich elderly burger. First they attempt to bribe a dressmaker, then a shoemaker to press their cause with Milinka, the beautiful heroine. Bored, as one attempts to outwit the other, she resolves to end the affair by eloping with her own secret lover. Whether it was on account of its similarities to Shakespeare's *The Taming of the Shrew*, or for some other reason, Smetana failed to respond to the plot. Much more to his liking was a new sketch called *Vok of Rožmberk* which Krásnohorská fashioned from factual material gleaned in 1879, from František Dvorský, historian and librarian at the Prague City Archives. Previously Dvorský had occupied similar offices in Třeboň and Jindřichův Hradec, and from him she had learnt of the founding of the Abbey at Vyše Brod, which forms the historical backcloth to her drama, later re-named *The Devil's Wall*, after the great barrier of rocks that stretches across the Vltava at Vyše Brod like the piers of a ruined bridge, which tradition says was thrown across the river in prehistoric times by the Devil himself.

Krásnohorská took as her theme the conflict between the Church and Hell, and attempted to make the founding of the Abbey and the destruction of the bridge by the Devil the dénouement. Not unnaturally the plot, which was the most fantastic Smetana had ever received, fascinated him as much for its dark, evil mood as for its diabolistic suggestiveness. It was inevitable that he should respond in this way, for the nocturnal scenes in *The Kiss* and the shadowy forest atmosphere inspired by smugglers and superstition had created a precedent as well as a train of thought which had developed in *The Secret*, with its

[7] Letter from Krásnohorská: November 15, 1878.

mysterious gnome-like phantoms and the ghost of Friar Barnabáš, Furthermore, *Tábor* and *Blaník* had dealt with the ghostly knights. doomed to suffer for their former deeds until the time should come for them to save their country from destruction. And it was not for nothing that the leader of the Knights of Blaník was Oldřich of Rožmberk, the ancestor of Krásnohorská's hero, Vok.

From his first reading of the draft, Smetana had a clear notion of the form the libretto should take. Early in 1879 he had asked the poet to provide him not with a serious interpretation but with a light, comic treatment of the plot. Astonished that he should have come to see what was essentially a stern, almost solemn, drama with romantic relief as a light parody, she attempted to emphasize the implication of her play:

> I can't bring myself to do what you ask. For me to write something that is full of humour and wit and without any serious situation is impossible and out of the question. I cannot do again what I did in *The Kiss* and *The Secret*, even though they were more serious-minded than the work you now want to compose. . . . I realize that I don't have the slightest drop of French comic spirit in me, and I know that my humour is always heavy, almost sad . . . but if only you knew how hard I had to work to create something in that vein!! Meanwhile, could you not compose some more of your wonderful tone poems while I try to rethink the text? If you ask me for a style of wit and gaiety, you ask a great deal—almost as if you wanted a bear to sing the role of the Queen of the Night in *Die Zauberflöte*. So 'bear-like' will my libretto be![8]

With a mentality like Smetana's no amount of letters or assurances would have carried conviction on a matter seen by her from a completely different angle from his own. He was adamant. He renewed his request for a humorous libretto and in the meantime began to sketch a number of themes for the new opera. Though, much against her will, Krásnohorská spent the next eight months refashioning the text so as to include the various elements Smetana had demanded, it was not until September 9 that she was able to return it to him:

> I expect the text will cause you less trouble than it has me, and I trust this devilish piece will spoil your life less than it has mine! I hope you are happier with the musical ideas that have emerged from your fantasy. Sometimes an artist feels that to create a work is like swallowing poison, but when another examines

[8] Letter from Krásnohorská: January 29, 1879.

it he is enthusiastic about it. And so it will be with your ideas. . . . Please will you make the following alteration. Helena's name should read Hedvika. For the vision in Act II, I had *Faust* or *Egmont* in mind; for like Egmont, Jarek is asleep and sees his love in a dream. I have stolen this fully consciously and for the following reason: I have a certain confidence in the theatrical directors who know how to produce *Faust* and *Egmont* by heart. If I made this scene otherwise then it would be a mess, as it was with the painted chest in *The Kiss*. . . . The vision or dream should fade and change, but on our small stage and with other classical productions how can this work? I saw something similar and quite tasteless in Dvořák's *Armide*, and Wagner's *Tannhäuser* at the German Theatre. I wondered why it could not have been staged more tastefully for the same cost. Shall I provide the vision or can you illustrate this in purely musical terms? You must decide. . . . I also wanted the Devil to play dice in Act III, but people will say this is copied from *Robert le Diable* so, instead, I have made him play draughts! Apart from other faults, the libretto is too long, but you can always shorten it as you wish.[9]

Though Krásnohorská tactfully allowed Smetana to alter the text as he desired, she had no idea how radically his original conception of the plot was changing. He now seemed to be probing beneath the surface, and was penetrating the souls of the characters, approaching them with a seriousness quite different from his earlier ideas. By some curious mental quirk he had come to regard the text as containing a personal, almost autobiographical, significance, and he may well have seen in the ageing Vok and the young woman whom he had previously loved, a picture of himself enveloped by memories of his past happiness. Certainly the subject contains a deal of Smetana's own world—a world in which he longed not only for the understanding of society, but especially for that of his first wife whom he had dearly loved. That he pined for her in this opera we know; for he gave one of the soprano roles the name Katuška (the Czech diminutive of Kateřina), and endowed her music with tones of innermost lyrical beauty, looking back to his youth and the happy years he had spent with his own Kateřina.

He began composition slowly and with difficulty; and it was not until the following February that he could report the completion of the Act I pencil sketch:

I have finished the first act, but not in score. . . . What I'm

[9] Letter from Krásnohorská: September 9, 1879.

pleased about is that I'm enjoying my work which goes well. I think Vok's aria is beautiful and when I sing it to myself I am transported by it. I hope you will like it too. This is not a formal aria, but adheres closely to the text and brings me to tears since it comes from the heart, and reflects my unhappy state. I hope the rest will be equally successful and I'm more than content with your verses which, in themselves, are so musical. I think the opera could be very original, but many critics will find it a puzzle; for they will look for a Czech style only in the songs and not in the declamation of words. I have previously introduced so much Czech song into my dramatic works that I feel I can now finally allow myself to create melody on the basis of the written words. Today I have finished the first scene of Act II and, without modesty, I am overjoyed with it. I would so much like to complete the entire work. I am taking from your draft only the essential words and fear that Act II will cause a deal of trouble.[1]

Smetana's failing health made progress arduous, and we can only admire the continuing tenacity with which he struggled on. Over the next seven months he corresponded hardly at all with his librettist, and it was not until October that he invited her to hear the piano draft of the new opera. Although she had provided him with a witty comedy in which the Devil disguised as a hermit gives saintly advice and lures people to sin and ruin, Smetana had substantially transformed the character of her play, so that instead of a humorous pastiche it emerged as a serious drama, the reflective and solemn tones of which went completely against the text. Possibly the changes were to be found in Smetana's innermost being; for not only deafness and encroaching old age with its attendant troubles but the whole outside world made his life almost unbearable.

In his early years he had known both hardship and cruel want, and though he was by no means destitute, his tired mind, tormented by financial disputes with the Provisional Theatre Association, led him to live in constant fear of starvation. Coupled with his own personal unhappiness, this made the composition of a light comedy impossible. Unfortunately Krásnohorská failed to appreciate his situation. Shocked to see how her work had been transformed she expressed her discontent in no uncertain terms:

Honoured Sir,

From the literary point of view, *The Devil's Wall* is quite

[1] Letter to Krásnohorská: February 16, 1880.

> dreadful and I must bear the entire responsibility for it. . . . The whole text was written at great length so you could choose to omit what you wished. You are indeed free to take everything from me—every thing, that is, except one! Though I know that the opera will be charming from your point of view, from the point of view of the poet, and as a serious historical document, it will be ghastly! Please allow me to explain in the Preface that my text began life as a comedy—I cannot agree to less, because a serious subject of this kind, I will not and cannot have on my conscience. Mr. Smetana has every right to rework a libretto as he wishes, but no one will forgive me if I seriously describe Vok in this way, and if I seriously provide a combat between Hell and the Church, as in a religious play! No!! It would provoke so much laughter that not even you could allow it. I will not force you into comedy or humour just for me when you are possessed by romantic ideas. I leave the outcome to you and your music. Do with the text what you will![2]

It seems unlikely that Smetana was able to defend his changes since he may well have been unaware of them himself. Certainly his relationship with Krásnohorská broke down at this time, and for the next eighteen months both parties maintained a stubborn silence, refusing to correspond and avoiding each other in Prague. Krásnohorská's pride was deeply wounded. Smetana's friends urged him to break from her for all time. The Press widely publicized the fact that he was considering two new librettos, Julius Zeyer's *Šárka* (later set by Janáček), and *The End of Vlasta* by Karl Pippich (later accepted by Ostrčil); but neither attracted him. His course was firmly set on *The Devil's Wall*. Quietly, and with increasing slowness, he assumed the task of librettist as well as composer, making drastic cuts in the original sketch[3] and omitting seventy-eight verses from Act I, two hundred and three from Act II, and two hundred and eleven from Act III. That he experienced setbacks through illness we know from his letters to Srb-Debrnov, upon whom he began to depend more and more not only for artistic advice but for the supervision of his business affairs:

> I work on *The Devil's Wall* with difficulty. I would like so much to earn more money for a smaller composition. But with what and

[2] Letter from Krásnohorská: October 29, 1880.

[3] Despite wholesale cuts, Smetana's pencil sketches run to three thousand, three hundred and thirteen bars, to which he added a further twenty-five in the final score.

> where? I can't produce music out of my sleeve as Dvořák does, because I want my scores to have a certain artistic value. I'm hindered by deafness, but I have so great an esteem for art that I can only write when the ideas are worthwhile, interesting and outstanding. This does not happen every day and that's a pity, for there is always debt.[4]

To Adolf Čech he admitted that the score was very complicated and to Srb he confessed the need of making even more cuts so that the public would not find 'this enormous work too long'.[5] During the summer he continued to battle with Krásnohorská's verses, but his growing confusion led him to shift the dramatic emphasis still further, so that the music began to emerge not as a reflection of the poetry, but as its antithesis:

> I am lacking both quietness and time, and only after long intervals can I work. I have a great and complex task on hand. Truly I regard with horror the ordeals that await me. How I wish my friends would not force me to compose in times of sickness and distress, and in my disagreeable and depressed state. What I need is a permanent rest from all this, in the literal sense.[6]

Smetana's spirits seem to have been at their lowest ebb at this time, and he may well have been looking to death as a happy release from his morose and dejected condition. He complained that deafness was no joke for a musician,[7] and though he had lived in a world of silence for more than seven years, he still hoped to regain his hearing. Early in December, experiments at Dr. Zoufal's clinic in Prague with a 'dentiphone'—a sophisticated ear-trumpet—failed to bring any relief, and he returned to Jabkenice where he was confined to bed for several weeks with bouts of giddiness and spots before the eyes. The doctor was his most frequent visitor. From Zelený we know Smetana suffered from bronchial catarrh with the result that he was frequently unable to communicate with those who tended him. When he spoke loudly, which he did unconsciously, he experienced pains in the throat[8] which lasted many hours. Strain and discomfort

[4] Letter to Srb-Debrnov: November 28, 1880.
[5] Letter to Srb-Debrnov: March 16, 1881.
[6] Letter to Špindler: November 9, 1881.
[7] Letter to F. Bayer: December 20, 1881.
[8] On August 23, 1882, he complained in a letter to Procházka that:

> . . . my health is worse, I feel prickly all over my body and most of all in the windpipe. Sometimes I gasp for air as my windpipe becomes blocked and I suffocate for a moment or so. I have become nervous and there is little chance of working!

made work next to impossible. When composing, he would often sing, without realizing it, until exhaustion of the vocal chords brought him to a sudden halt. Though his doctors prescribed 'Hungarian water' to purify his system and ease his condition, there was little improvement. To general internal disorders were added lapses of memory. He found it difficult to recall the music he had already committed to paper and was obliged to re-read his previous notes. With this extra strain he sometimes wrote no more than four new bars a day. Clearly, *The Devil's Wall* was becoming a heroic struggle:

> I lost a fortnight's work because of illness and have not been able to continue as quickly as I would have liked. I still have the last scenes to compose which are very difficult. No previous opera ever cost me so much time or energy![9]

In the New Year Smetana summoned all his concentration to complete the opera, and after four months put the finishing touches to the full score on April 17, 1882 (Act I had been completed in score in March, 1881, and Act II on September 15 of the same year). Though exhausted by his efforts, he was not dissatisfied with the results, and confessed as much to Adolf Čech:

> The music is difficult, particularly in regard to intonation and harmony, though it teems with delightful melodies. The parts can all be said to be worthwhile. Naturally I am only speaking about the music. Since it gives me considerable pleasure, I take the liberty of writing this as a recommendation to the singers.[1]

Four days earlier he had expressed similar sentiments to Srb-Debrnov:

> Though the finale gave me the most trouble, I do not doubt the musical effect. . . . The style of my opera is really quite extraordinary, . . . the more I examine it the more convinced I am that the music is good, and that it could have been composed in no other way. The songs are eminently singable and will delight you. The orchestration, too, is colourful and so varied that I marvel how I had the patience to work it out. Now, you see, I praise my opera, but only to you, dear friend, who really understand and admire my music.[2]

Several weeks after completing his eighth opera, Smetana was honoured at a celebration to mark the hundredth performance of

[9] Letter to Srb-Debrnov: December 23, 1881.
[1] Letter to Čech: April 24, 1882. [2] Letter to Srb-Debrnov: April 20, 1882.

The Bartered Bride (the first Czech opera to receive the distinction of so many performances), and on May 7, the New Czech Theatre was crowded as never before. 'Anyone who could remain unmoved during the final loud rejoicing', wrote Ludwig Hartmann in the *Dresdener Nachrichten*, 'would have to be without a heart and without any artistic perception or understanding'. The ovations following the performance seemed to convey the enthusiasm of the entire nation and, touched by the warmth of the occasion, the ageing composer looked forward to the première of *The Devil's Wall*, for which he hoped there would be a similar demonstration.

Secretly he had always wanted to present to his country a work of great proportions and lasting significance, and in the new opera he believed he had achieved this goal. The first night was announced for October 29, but instead of a triumph, the opera was an undistinguished failure. For Smetana's Benefit (November 3) the house was barely a third full. From the very beginning it appears the opera was under-rehearsed, misunderstood and shabbily serviced. Stock scenery and old costumes made *The Devil's Wall* a sad addition to a repertoire that included Dvořák's brilliant *Dimitri*, upon which Rieger and Maýr had lavished the utmost care and expense only a few months before. For Smetana, the failure of *The Devil's Wall* was the most crushing blow in his artistic career. Zelený believed that the faults which quite wrecked the music came from the Theatre, whose careless and slovenly stage presentation left an ineradicable mark on the Prague public and even provoked laughter at the most serious moments of the drama. An examination of the first night reviews reveal the neglect and clumsy treatment surrounding the production:

> It has been many years since we saw such a hotchpotch as we did in *The Devil's Wall* last evening. Not only were the costumes well-worn and threadbare, but the scenery depicted the Vltava, by some unhappy perspective, flowing upside down! To this were added antique statues from the garden of some knight or other, and a procession composed of thirteenth-century Jews with whom the Director makes the same endless procession in all countries, nations and times. From rocks appeared sheep, but sheep with the heads of poodles and bodies of lions! Now when all these 'visions' appeared in a supposedly serious scene [the Devil's song in Act III] it is not surprising they caused so much hectic laughter that the music was completely drowned. And this was the setting for Smetana's new opera![3]

[3] *Národní Listy*: October 30, 1882.

Nové české divadlo.

Dnes v neděli 29. října 1882. – Mimo předplacení.

Po prvé:

Čertova stěna

Komicko-romantická opera ve 3 dějstvích. Text od **Elišky Krásnohorské.**
Hudbu složil **Bedřich Smetana.**
Ve scénu uvedl regisseur pan **Fr. Hynek.** *Nové dekorace* maloval malíř král. českého divadla zemského pan **J. F. Haiss.** *Elektrické osvětlení* řídí mechanik pan **Hájek.** Zpěvohru řídí první kapelník pan **Adolf Čech.**

OSOBY:

Vok Vítkovic, pán z Růže, nejvyšší maršálek království českého	p. Lev.	Michálek, hradní na Rožmberce	p. Krössing.
Záviš, jeho strýc	pí. Fibichova.	Katuška, jeho dcera	sl. Sittova.
Jarek, rytíř ve službě Vokově	p. Vávra.	Beneš, poustevník	p. Hynek.
Hedvika, hraběnka ze Šauenburka	sl. Reichova.	Rarach	p. Chlumecký.

Poslové krále Přemysla Otakara II. Rytíři a ženská družina hraběnčina. Lid hradní a selský. Pekelné příšery
Dějiště: V 1. a 2. jednání Rožmberk, v 3. jednání: Čertova stěna. Čas děje: polovice 13. století.

„Pekelný tanec", uspořádaný baletním mistrem panem **V. Reisingerem**, tančí: slečny **Keplerova, ze Schöpfů, Zieglerova a sbor baletní.**

Pan K. Čech jest churav.

Vstupenky prodávají se od 9 do 1 hodiny spolední v král. zem. českém divadle a od 6 hod. v Novém českém divadle.

Začátek v 7 hodin. Konec před 10. hod.

Zítra v pondělí dne 30. října 1882 35. hra v předplacení.

Po druhé.

PODSKALÁK.

Poster announcing the première of Smetana's last complete opera—*The Devil's Wall* at the New Czech Theatre, Prague (October 29, 1882)

Ironically, this was just the sort of review Smetana might well have written himself some seventeen years earlier, when he was striving for recognition as a columnist. Now history seemed to be repeating itself; but the boot was on the other foot, and it hurt. According to Josef Foerster, however, it was not only the décor which incited derision but the singers themselves:

> There was Beneš (played by Hynek), and the Devil (sung by Chlumský), and according to the text the two were identical in appearance and voice. Even the singers, so they assured us, could not distinguish one from the other—but somehow the entire scene assumed an unbelievably farcical effect for Mr. Hynek was small and fat and Mr. Chlumský was tall and thin, and neither resembled the other, not even in the smallest detail.

The opera was condemned. The libretto[4] was considered uneven, illogical and without development. How right Krásnohorská had been when she complained that people would ridicule her and that *The Devil's Wall* would spoil part of Smetana's life! It had. What he did not anticipate, however, was the indifference with which the public received him and his new music. When he was called on stage at the end of the first act on November 3, his Benefit, the applause was barely polite. He was presented with neither bouquet nor wreath. As the curtain fell he was heard to mutter to himself: 'Now I am so very old I will never write again—they want nothing more from me'.[5] Afterwards he laconically recorded in his Diary: 'My Benefit was miserable'. This was the last bitter drop in a cup already full. To an artist who for years had known theatre practice on both sides of the curtain, this apathetic attitude could only be interpreted as deliberate humiliation, the more hurtful following the recent *Bartered Bride* celebrations. Indignant that he should have been ostracized by friends and followers alike, he bitterly castigated all those who had valued him only as long as his national works had benefited them:

> If I had never been recognized then I should go to the grave with the knowledge that I had worked as best I knew how. But first of all they raised me up to giddy heights, then they dropped me. . . . People are cross with me that it was quickly rehearsed

[4] Hartmann, writing in the *Dresdener Nachrichten*, described his impression: . . . the verses are so bound to a national legend, and by a lady whose treatment is so clumsy, that it becomes incredible and incomprehensible. One can speak only of a local success for the composer, which is to be regretted. There can be no hope of bringing this opera to Germany. . .

[5] Zelený: *On Bedřich Smetana* (1894).

> and that I tolerated the décor. Procházka[6] has written to me from Dresden with much offence and rudeness, reproaching me that Devils no longer exist, not even on the stage. . . . Indeed, I should have withdrawn the score after the first performance because it was so badly given.[7]

Reproaches and recriminations from close friends, in addition to a total lack of understanding on the part of the public, failed to shake Smetana's conviction that *The Devil's Wall* was a valuable work; but it was long before it was recognized, and for many years it suffered a fate similar to that of *Dalibor*, except that its rejection came when Smetana was handicapped by tragic infirmity. Ironically, the only person who seemed to stand by him at this time was Krásnohorská. Dishonoured and scorned, she sacrificed her reputation for that of the composer. While she could easily have published her original version of the text with Smetana's letters and thus cleared her name, she preferred to remain silent, often burning valuable documents lest they should incriminate Smetana. Though she was unfairly attacked by Prague literary circles for her work on *The Devil's Wall*, she was nevertheless imaginative and skilled in her craft; indeed, two of her works[8] were awarded prizes when submitted to a competition under a *nom de plume*.

The Devil's Wall is the most complex of Smetana's operas, the plot being deliberately involved since the interest of the work is to keep the spectator from immediately guessing which of the two doubles, the Devil or the Hermit, is the cause of all evil. Thus there is confusion as to whether the Devil is masquerading as the Hermit or vice versa, and the hidden enigma is the key to solving the inherent riddle of the plot. Despite its complexity, Smetana's treatment is not at all confused, and the music never emerges as the work of a crazed mind; on the contrary, the most striking quality of the score is its nobility and dignity. The short, powerful overture, written as

[6] On November 7, 1882, Procházka complained:

> . . . the libretto of *The Devil's Wall* is so naïve that it can only be laughed at. To allow the Devil to appear on the stage in the nineteenth century is both daring and adventurous especially when presented in such a crude fashion! It would have been sufficient had he appeared only in the finale. How stupid it would seem to a foreign audience that the powerful Vok has to discuss his plans for marriage with his followers. It is a pity you have given so much to this feeble text!

[7] Letter to Srb-Debrnov: November 11, 1882.

[8] *The Child of Tábor*, previously offered to Smetana, and *Karel Škretá*, which was later set by Bendl.

an afterthought, shows with what exalted tones Smetana approached this score, and it is only in the scenes with Míchálek that he relaxes his intensely serious grip. Unfortunately he was not able to sustain his musical invention on a consistently high level, and though opera was the sphere in which he was most completely at home, *The Devil's Wall* shows him to be occasionally ill at ease. Where, for instance, his earlier stage works can be seen as broad, flowing rivers, this one emerges as a stream whose beauty is sometimes obscured as it is forced underground, or deflected. But at intervals, where Smetana's inspiration takes possession of him, it broadens into a beautiful lake.

The Devil's Wall is an uneven work which shows him first breaking new ground and, possibly because his infirmity made him uncertain of himself, falling back on conventional characters drawn from his gallery of operatic types. Consequently, we find ourselves in a world of operatic oaths and their evasions, trick parodies and villainous intrigues. In Míchálek we discover a comic strain developed from Kecal, through Paloucký and Boniface, who appears here as a parody of a thirteenth-century knight; in Katuška we find a lively figure who dominates the opera and is the courtly cousin of Mařenka or Vendulka; Jarek is a lyrical lover who, having recently won his spurs, is both spirited and dashing, and clearly related to Vítek in *The Secret*; Hedvika, for all her Senta-like qualities in redeeming Vok at the eleventh hour, and the motive of child-like charm she brings to the score, is the offspring of Liduše, or a more naïve Milada. For his other characters, however, Smetana was unable to draw on the catalogue of wares used in previous operas, and in creating Vok (was perhaps Olbram in *The Brandenburgers in Bohemia* his ancestor?), the Hermit and the Devil, he broke new ground.

As mentioned above, the figure of Vok was one with which Smetana became personally identified, and the role is particularly rich in the lyricism of an ageing man, and his dream of the young woman whom he had loved in his youth. Despite these autobiographical elements, Vok is really a pendant of *Der fliegende Holländer*; like the Dutchman he looks for a bride but is rejected by all until Hedvika risks her life to save him. Smetana, however, brings to the part more of himself than Wagner did in *Holländer*, and in none of the previous operas is so much care bestowed on a single role. Here Smetana seems unable to content himself with the usual marks or comments. Instead he is moved to supplement the score with unusually detailed instructions, pointing the need for keeping to the exact notation in the more passionate passages, and even thinking out new indications so as to express with greater precision the emotional colouring of his thoughts.

Throughout, Vok's music is marked by profound seriousness and a sad yearning as if, in the autumn of his life, Smetana was harking back to his former happiness, and the memories of his faded youth. The music is distinguished by subdued warmth and tenderness and, following Jarek's confession and oath in Act I (Scene 5), Vok is so touched by this sacrifice that only the orchestra can voice his sentiments:

Example 103

It is notably in his aria, 'Jen jediná mě ženy krásná tvář tak dojala' ('Only one lovely woman's beauty touched me so'), that Smetana really opens his heart and pours out a passionate flow of melody which is the high-water mark of the opera. Vok's part is rich in melody, but so, also, is Jarek's and that of Katuška, whose soaring phrases allow light to shine through the score. But it is particularly in his portrayal of the Devil and the Hermit that Smetana achieved his most daring and perhaps most penetrating creations. While he was experienced in painting the world of knights and nobility (*The Brandenburgers* and *Dalibor* both have chivalry as a backdrop to their respective dramas) apart from *Macbeth* he had never before attempted to represent evil in music, even though the phantoms in *The Secret* show his leaning towards the supernatural. Of operatic Devils that existed at this time, Smetana certainly knew Meyerbeer's, Gounod's, and Weber's (though, of course, Samiel only speaks), and perhaps wisely avoided these types, preferring to look elsewhere. Instead of turning to the well-meaning and stupid Devil of Czech fairy tales and treating him as an object of ridicule and comic relief, as Dvořák was to do in *The Devil and Kate*, he created a half-crazed demon, possibly descended from Berlioz's Mephistopheles, intent on possessing all human souls, and whose greatest pleasure is to provoke chaos. Smetana's Devil is a scheming ghoul who preys on the weak Hermit, Beneš, by impersonating him. Musically he is represented by three motives: the first two, suggesting demonic laughter, flash across the score like forked lightning; the third, by subtle harmonization and enharmonic and chromatic alteration symbolizes the Devil in all his cunning:

Example 104

(*a*)

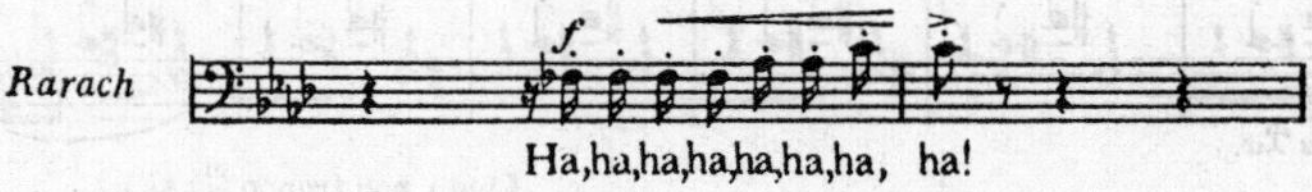

(*b*)

(*c*)

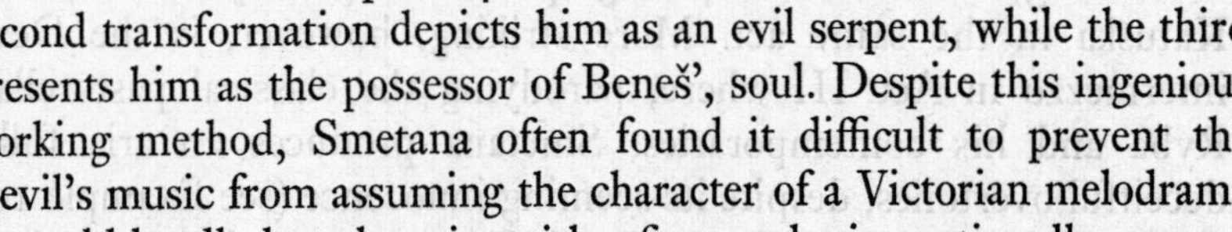

In its first form Example 104c shows the Devil as a weak schemer; the second transformation depicts him as an evil serpent, while the third presents him as the possessor of Beneš', soul. Despite this ingenious working method, Smetana often found it difficult to prevent the Devil's music from assuming the character of a Victorian melodrama (it could hardly be otherwise with a figure who is continually appearing and disappearing through trap doors to the accompaniment of loud peals of laughter). However, he is most successful in suggesting the powers of evil by advanced harmonic thought. Earlier in his career he had used dissonance to depict Macbeth's confrontation with the Witches: now he resorted to it again, but on a larger canvas. By employing augmented and diminished triads as a harmonic commonplace and suspensions, appoggiaturas, accented passing notes (often sounded simultaneously), he gives this music a distinct feeling of atonality. Little wonder Smetana's first critics found the opening of Act II, built predominantly on augmented chords, difficult to understand:

Example 105

Almost certainly, Smetana conceived the Devil's music around the tritone (the augmented fourth) in a deliberate use of the interval once known as the *diabolus in musica*; and, significantly, when Beneš is possessed of the Devil, his music is marked by similar characteristics. But in the moments when one would expect Smetana's imagination to have been fired by the situation, the challenge of depicting Hellish ferment and cataclysmic explosion, he is oddly disappointing. The second act transformation from the shepherd's hovel to Rožmberk castle has nothing of the dramatic genius with which Wagner dissolved Brünnhilde's rock to the Hall of the Gibichungs in *Götterdämmerung*, nor is there anything spell-binding for Jarek's vision of Katuška in the same act. More striking, however, is the Devil's intermezzo in Act III where, parodying the classical pastorella of Ryba and his contemporaries, Smetana produces an aria full of deceitful overtones, despite its seeming innocence (see Example 106).

At a time when the Young Czech Party was gaining ground, not least of all for its liberal attitude to religious matters, Smetana gives his score a certain topicality by mocking religious institutions and poking fun at the Church (in Act III he allows the Hermit to confess not to a priest but to a burgrave). All this was certainly appreciated by the younger element in Prague, but less immediate in its appeal was

PLATE XXV. Smetana in 1880, aged 56

PLATE XXVI. Jabkenice, Smetana's last home

Example 106

Smetana's masterstroke—the music which accompanies the building of the Devil's Wall across the Vltava and the rise of the waters. At the point where the Devil's followers pile boulder on boulder to hold back the course of the river, Smetana creates a nightmare of dissonance and savage disorder in the orchestra. His melodic lines become craggy and include leaps of ninths and false relations, his rhythms are distorted with cross-patterns and syncopations, but despite his forceful imagination he cannot prevent this Vltava music from assuming a diabolistic waltz-like quality that may well have been coloured by Liszt's *Mephisto* pieces and seems to echo the principal theme from Smetana's own tone poem *Vltava* (see Example 107, pp. 366–7).

In this scene Smetana's instrumentation is at its most vivid, and though the forces are no larger than normal, he tends to extend the perspective outwards (as Janáček was to do) so that the piccolo playing in its highest register and the double basses in their lowest range make for a richer palette. Possibly the triangle and cymbal could have been handled more sparingly, but overall the scoring is eminently

Example 107

(*a*)

(b)

Più vivo.
sf
(♩= 116.)
poco a poco dim. e languentando
espress.
poco rallent.
dim
p
rall
Vivo. (♩= 69.)
Cor.
f
ff Tr.
Sm. D.
sf tr
Sm.
D.
ff
sf
p
cresc.
Tutti.
ff
sff
dim.
p rit.
sffz

clear, bright and economic, many arias and duets being accompanied only by strings with woodwind interjections. There are fewer recitatives in *The Devil's Wall* than in previous operas and those that exist are skilfully integrated into the fabric so that arioso leads imperceptibly to ensemble. Smetana emerges once again as a master of dramatic transition. Fewer, too, are the choruses and ensembles. Since these sections had caused him considerable embarrassment in *The Secret*, it was only to be expected that here they should be minimized, and for the first time in his operatic career he omits to set the mood and atmosphere of each act with a characteristic chorus. Only at the close of Act III does he revert to a conventional celebratory stanza to establish an air of general rejoicing before the curtain falls. Elsewhere, the music for the knights is less exuberant than it was in *Dalibor*, assuming an almost perfunctory nature; but for the chorus of peasants Smetana is more at home creating echo devices and charming melodies in parallel thirds and sixths which give this music its typically Czech hallmark:

Example 108

The Devil's Wall is one of the most individual operas Smetana wrote but it is a flawed and uneven work, lacking the spontaneity and ease of his earlier scores. Despite the conflict of music and verse, the opera contains much that is striking and many things which are puzzling, especially on first acquaintance. Though Smetana's swan-song, it is far from being the work of a confused mind. The fact remains that as a result of its advanced harmonic thought *The Devil's Wall* is an enigma—an enigma which cannot be solved on one hearing and a cursory glance at the score. It is a work requiring deep concentration and renewed probing, and only then will it reveal its secrets.

FIFTEEN

MADNESS AND DEATH
1883–1884

FOR SMETANA THE reception of *The Devil's Wall* was like the sudden harsh awakening from a dream. It shattered his life. His whole world collapsed, leaving him an outcast, deserted and unwanted. In the peaceful countryside of Jabkenice he existed in an atmosphere which afforded little peace. Dishonoured and dispirited, he sank a deeper shaft into himself and, where before he had found consolation in reading and composing, he now sat staring aimlessly before him, an ageing figure whom fate had treated more than harshly. To bitterness were added resentment, indignation, even apathy; but worst of all boredom. Contact with people caused a protective withdrawal of himself to the inner recesses of his being, gazing out from which upon the ordinary world of man everything seemed curiously unreal. While the rustic surroundings had previously helped him to relax, he now began to distrust them, seeing in the shadows evil spirits tormenting his walks. Invariably they drove him back to his room where, in a fit of trembling, he shut himself up for hours. The illusions soon passed. At first he told no-one of these strange visions, merely noting their occurrence in his Diary; but as they became increasingly frequent his solitude was invaded by formless voices or veiled processions of beautiful women to whom he bowed affably before sending them on their way to Prague to seek better company. He began to confide in Srb-Debrnov who became his most trusted friend and the strongest prop on which he could lean. To Srb he disclosed his personal affairs, and to him he confessed his most dreaded fear—madness. As early as 1879 he had had a premonition that deafness would lead to insanity and he intimated as much to Jan Neruda:

> I am downhearted and fear the worst. I'm terrified I shall go mad and have become so downcast that I sit for hours doing nothing, unable to think about anything except my unhappiness.[1]

[1] Letter to Neruda: February 25, 1879.

Since that time his apprehension had in no way been allayed. On the contrary, the hallucinations occurred more frequently as his physical condition deteriorated. He was erratic, depressed and obstinate. He longed to return to Prague and his letters to Srb, with whom he corresponded once, sometimes twice, a week repeatedly urged him to find a small flat with simple furniture (a bed and desk), where he could be at his ease 'away from home'.[2] He pleaded to be allowed to stay in Srb's rooms for three or four weeks[3] but nothing materialized and new complications prevented him from travelling. To the rushing in his head and the giddiness before the eyes were added a hoarseness in the voice, pains in the throat, and chronic bronchial catarrh. He complained of insomnia, a heavy cough, of breathing like a consumptive, and worst of all, acute stiffness and cramp which seemed to be sapping all the strength from his frail body. There followed financial worries created by his brother Karel, who in order to educate his son in Tábor, had mortgaged his property and accumulated considerable debts. To avert disaster, Smetana secretly begged Srb's help:

> I have sent my savings book to Prague for the four per cent interest to be made up under the name of Oskar Dagmar. Please withdraw three hundred gulden from my account and send it, recorded delivery, to my brother Karel who has bad debts. From one loan he apparently paid another, and out of his pension money the interest of yet another. Now he fears his debtors will make him surrender his pension rights. He needs three hundred gulden desperately by December 1. No one else can help. . . . He has explained everything and hopes to repay me in instalments of twenty-five gulden.[4]

Certainly his brother's financial affairs concerned him deeply and he now feared for his own future. The royalties from *The Devil's Wall* were non-existent. He lived in dread of starvation, of want and poverty, and these apprehensions may well have accelerated the first of a series of fits which he now suffered:

> I am gravely ill with cramp in the brain. No, don't be afraid, it has come only once, and at midday. I was bringing a libretto to my wife when suddenly, and without pain, I began to stammer

[2] Letter to Srb-Debrnov: July 2, 1882.
[3] Letter to Srb-Debrnov: July 14, 1882.
[4] Letter to Srb-Debrnov: November 27, 1882.

incomprehensible syllables: *a-a-tě-tě-tě* and could say nothing else. They saw my efforts to speak. My tongue was pressed down on one side and I could not say what I wanted nor what I was bringing to her. At first they thought I was joking, but when my eyes and face were contorted on one side they recognized that something serious had happened. After an hour and a half I could speak again, and only then did they tell me how I had looked. So far there has been no repetition, but the children firmly believe me to be mad![5]

This was not to be the only attack; within days he was stricken again, this time more seriously:

After the last episode my condition has deteriorated and now a great change has come over me. Recently, one evening, I lost my voice and all power and possibility of expressing my thoughts. I was not even able to speak what came into my head. I forgot the names of the contemporary and historic personalities and nothing but *tjě*, *tjě*, *njě*, could I utter, with long pauses in between and my mouth wide open. No-one knew what to do. They were just going to send for the doctor (it was quite late in the evening) when, suddenly, all the sickness disappeared and I was able to read and remember everyone's names. About a week later, this repeated itself, but to a much worse degree. I could not speak a single word. They put me to bed where I began, slowly, to recover. The doctor has forbidden me to drink wine, beer or spirits, and he explains that I have blood pressure on the brain, that I might easily lose my memory and even go mad! The work done by the brain, the incessant deafness with no assistance from the aural nerves, drove a strong stream of blood to the brain which became rigid and refused to understand anything at that moment. The doctor forbids me to read for more than a quarter of an hour and has completely forbidden me to do anything with music unless I wish to deprive myself of my entire musical talent. I must think of nothing. I may not even read or imagine, in my own mind, compositions or works of others. This state must last a year. . . . Clearly, moments of happiness are becoming more and more rare. . . . Please do not tell my family that I'm writing to you in this way, and not a word to my brother Karel. Excuse me, I can say no more since my head not only buzzes, but speaks with many voices, and whistles, and all the time they mock and laugh at me and call me a blockhead. Goodbye! I

[5] Letter to Srb-Debrnov: November 30, 1882.

> write no more for I feel in my inner self a great and grave struggle taking place. Don't pity me! I am prepared, for it is my fate.[6]

Although doctors ordered 'Hungarian water' to cleanse his body, nothing was prescribed for what seems to have been a stroke. One half of his face remained contorted and his speech was more pronouncedly slurred than before. He was subjected to attacks of trembling and seems to have been seized by an abnormal terror of hunger. Gradually he was beginning to lose his sense of judgement and often, in the company of friends, his mind would wander. Zelený testifies that he was perscuted by 'bad dreams' during the day, and haunted by cruel visions at night. Clearly his sickness was more deep-rooted and he intimated as much to Srb:

> Spiritually I'm depressed and if I stay here much longer I will be convinced that I have an infection. My appetite is good, but my body and brain are sick.[7]

His family were at a loss to know how to tend him as he began to crack under mental pressures. Contrary to his previous nature, he developed a ruthless mania for self-exaltation; he demanded to manage his own affairs; insisted on having more money; pestered to be allowed to return to Prague. Yet he was incapable of looking after himself, and his wife and son-in-law were obliged to take a firm control of family affairs. Unfortunately, Betty was so repelled by his infected frame that it was as much as she could do to bring herself to be in the same room with him, let alone nurse him. For years their relationship had hovered on the brink of disaster: now, in a crescendo of discontent it foundered completely. His reason became clouded, and he regarded her only as an obstacle to future progress, intent on ruining him and all he had worked for:

> Now I have distressing domestic troubles with my wife! After the hundredth performance of *The Bartered Bride* I was given a national gift, a savings book containing two thousand, five hundred gulden, three credit bonds, each for a hundred gulden, and some other money; but as my room in Jabkenice can easily be visited by thieves or robbers, I entrusted this gift to the care of my wife. Recently I wanted to have the book taken to Prague so that interest could be calculated, but my plans were opposed by my hard-headed partner who refused to show it to me. As a result of my excited nerves I was enraged. Eventually she gave me

[6] Letter to Srb-Debrnov: December 9, 1882.
[7] Letter to Srb-Debrnov: December 30, 1882.

an account of goods bought with her money which she considered to be a loan and not a gift. . . . Now she wants to hold this book permanently. I must go to a lawyer for advice. She had no dowry when she married me, and in linen or furniture she had nothing either. I have sustained the entire family with my money and, even in my dreams, I could not imagine that a wife would act so wickedly and unlovingly towards me! Following this theft I am in tears, and am torn to pieces. I am so distracted that I cannot work.[8]

The same events looked at through different eyes can often bear a very different interpretation. To Smetana, irreparable mischief had been done, but it seems unlikely that Betty would actually have taken money from her husband. A letter from Schwarz to Smetana attempts to clarify the rift, reminding him that he himself gave the savings book to her keeping. Smetana refused to accept the facts. Certainly money was hard to come by and possibly following an incident when he had been found distributing coins to children in the streets of Jabkenice, Betty had resolved to take a stronger hand. It may well have been for this reason that his resentment had grown. Forces irreconcilable by nature once unleashed and coming to a clash can result in nothing but catastrophe. The incident was the last drop that made a cup already full at last overflow. The two were estranged for six weeks. Smetana travelled to Prague to discuss with Srb the possibilities of divorce:

> I can't tell you I am fit again, but I can tell you I am able to look after myself, and that there will be no more scenes. I must live quietly. Srb has asked me to do everything to make a peaceful settlement between you and me, otherwise it would be known all over Bohemia that my wife would not return the reward which was given to me for my work. There would be a scandal if it were not returned. . . . I leave you my savings book, but look after it and don't spend the money recklessly. What you need you will always have from me, provided you behave as my wife and keep the peace. I cannot live under the same roof as a person who hates and persecutes me. . . . I look for some lines from you, but I don't force you to write to me.
>
> Yours, from the first moment of our meeting until today faithfully,
>
> Bedřich Smetana.[9]

[8] Letter to Srb-Debrnov: January 24, 1883.
[9] Undated letter to Betty Smetana.

Away from Betty, Smetana was able to shake off the boredom he had known in the country and recharge his life's batteries with new surroundings and the company of trusted friends:

> I have come to Prague to convalesce in the colourful city which is so different from our exceedingly dull summer existence. I'm as ill as before, but this change of location, away from tedium, will help me to find a new purpose in life. My family resent me coming to you because they fear I will waste everything on nothing. If my wife could shut me up in the smallest closet she would do just that, so I shall not squander what little I earn.[1]

As always, the shops, the people, the general hubbub stimulated him, and proved as beneficial as any tonic. With Srb he went to plays, to the opera, to various clubs of which he was still a member; but, though he was recognized and welcomed, he was a sad sight. At a gathering called in honour of Saint-Saëns's visit to Prague, Smetana obstinately refused to meet the guest until he finally grasped that his continued absence would cause great offence. On another occasion his friend Adolf Heyduk[2] was greeted as a complete stranger. Clearly such lapses of memory were embarrassing for all concerned. Contemporary accounts confirm that Smetana's appearance had changed radically by this time. Zelený testifies that he walked through crowded streets on the hottest of days in a fur-trimmed coat, and that he acknowledged passers-by with a low bow of the head and an inane expression. Nevertheless, Prague revitalized him and on returning to the solitude of Jabkenice he was able to turn once again to music, but not immediately to composition.

First he took up his motive book, given to him in 1858 and in which he had jotted down a hundred and fifty-six themes over a period of twenty-two years. This important document reveals a varied series of musical impressions and impulses which often served to create his most significant works. The last motive to be entered is dated November 15, 1880; but not everything before this was clearly catalogued or documented, and he now found time to go diligently through the book indicating, in blue crayon, those ideas which had been used and the works in which they appear. He also incorporated certain personal remarks over appropriate themes, such as 'Deafness came here', and 'In all these pieces I was said to have been ingenious'; elsewhere we

[1] Undated letter to Srb-Debrnov.

[2] Heyduk (1835–1923), the idealist poet and author of the libretto *The Will of the Ancestors*, later set to music by Ostrčil.

learn that a motive, originally set down in 1856, had been intended for a violin concerto which never materialized:

Example 109

Occasionally a title is marked over a phrase incorrectly, but the rest is mostly accurate. Apart from documenting his themes, the real purpose seems to have been to gather material that could be put to good use in the compositions he was now hoping to write.

The first piece, for which he summoned all his courage, was the String Quartet in D minor, written in secret and against his doctors' orders. It was begun at a time when work was limited to a few minutes each day, and that he composed with painful slowness and great difficulty we know from his letters where he acknowledged his inability to jot down more than one line of manuscript at a session:

> I can't write quickly without moving my head or disturbing my nerves. The Quartet is finished except for the finale, but to find a real conclusion with chords and cadences is difficult. At times I get confused, but I no longer have spots before my eyes and the rushing in my ears is less forceful. Alas, I tend to lose my memory when composing so that if a movement is too long I cannot remember the principal melody. If the working out takes some time I forget the qualities of the melody and look on it as if it were the work of a stranger. How weak my memory is!

> I tend to lose track of ideas, but in spite of this I want to work and perhaps will be victorious in my struggle.[3]

The D minor Quartet, completed on March 12, is an intensely emotional and soulful work, beginning where the first left off. Clearly, Smetana takes up his pen after the catastrophe of his deafness:

> Imagine a whirlwind of music in a person who hears nothing, no-one has the slightest notion how musical ideas run away from a person who is deaf, and if I don't commit them to paper immediately, I can't remember how they were even half a day later. And to think that once my memory was called phenomenal!![4]

Despite its confessional nature, the Quartet is less obviously autobiographical than *From my Life*. It contains flashes of charming inchoate melody, swift changes of mood and rhythmic impulses which come and go with no ordered design. Yet though Smetana's brain was too weary to face the problems of co-ordinating the complex development, the thematic material is far from obscure or morbid. The first movement has the same tragic quality as the earlier Quartet, but is built on a germ-cell (a), transformed into two other ideas, (b) and (c). A central episode replaces the conventional development and leads to a return of the three ideas, but in the reverse order:

Example 110

That Smetana was concerned about the first movement we know from his correspondence:

> . . . as regards the style of this movement I am in a quandary; it is quite extraordinary and difficult to understand. A kind of conflict dominates which, it seems to me, will present great problems, especially for the players. All this is the result of my unhappy life. I now feel tired and sleepy and I fear that I'm slowly losing the vividness of musical thought. It seems that

[3] Letter to Srb-Debrnov: February 27, 1883.
[4] Zelený: *On Bedřich Smetana* (1894).

> everything I work out in my mind's eye is covered with a hazy mist of depression and pain. I think I am at the end of all original creation and soon my talent will be silenced for ever.[5]

Despite this foreboding, his tormented brain refused to rest. In the second movement, the most immediately appealing of the four, he wrote a miniature polka, the melodic idea of which dates from thirty years before, with a graceful lullaby as its central trio. The third movement is more complex, being sunless and bearing traces of the nervous fatigue that beset him at this time. It comprises a number of fugal and march-like episodes and leads, without break, to a turbulent finale which develops the harmonic idiom of the last act of *The Devil's Wall* and is almost perfunctory in its terseness. The Quartet in D minor is a brief, but characteristic work; and though Smetana later found it 'good and full of melodious moments, emotions and novelty', it is clearly the testimony of his triumph over adversity. It has achieved less popularity than its sister-work and, possibly because its technical difficulties and occasional dissonances anticipate the twentieth century and the chamber works of Novák and Suk, it was misunderstood at its first performance (at an Umělecká Beseda concert on January 3, 1884, when the executants were F. Lachner, J. Raušer, J. Krehan and A. Neruda). One composer who quickly recognized its inherent musicality, however, was Arnold Schoenberg, who considered it to have been written years ahead of its time.

After the D minor Quartet Smetana turned to the field of choral music, producing a four-part setting for male chorus of Srb-Debrnov's poem *Naše píseň* (*Our Song*). This is the last of Smetana's works for choir and though it was composed during his illness, it is neither halting in character, nor tragic in nature. On the contrary, it is a celebratory work extolling the joys of Czech song and dance, significantly written in a light polka style which incorporates a certain amount of polyphonic weaving. Smetana later believed the part-writing to be 'entangled', and hoped to simplify the piece by re-arranging it for full chorus; but Srb, convinced that it was satisfactory as it was, proposed that it should be performed at the re-opening of the National Theatre. Unfortunately the work was thought unsuitable, and its subsequent disappearance and rediscovery delayed the première until 1924.

Following his work on the D minor Quartet and *Our Song* which was, for the most part done in secret, Smetana was again the victim of severe bouts of depression:

[5] Letter to Srb-Debrnov: July 14, 1883.

> My disease is drawing a host of others in its wake, troublesome auxiliary complaints, which are all due to nervous irritation. For this reason I have been unable to read anything which might activate the fantastic side of my brain. This would cause other morbid conditions and the doctors have forbidden me to write or even think. They have not, however, forbidden me to listen . . . for one mightier than they has done so already . . . I, a musician, have had my hearing destroyed. Why, I have never even heard the little voices of my own grandchildren! This is spiritual mourning . . . if martyrs are still born, then I am the unhappiest of them all, for fate has sentenced me to a silent tomb where voices are unknown.[1]

Despite his morbid spirits he began to compose again and the work which occupied much of his time was the symphonic poem *Pražsky karneval* (*Prague Carnival*), the genesis of which can be traced to 1878 when, on February 25, he wrote to Ludevít Procházka:

> I would like to write an orchestral tone poem called *Bohemian Carnival* or *Prague Carnival*, in which not only Czech dances, but also small themes and certain characters from my operas will appear in the guise of masks. I don't think the idea is bad. The type and form are quite new. I'm sure it could arouse interest and might even bring me in some money!

When recalling that it had been his intention to orchestrate the cycle of *Czech Dances*, it may not be unfair to see *Prague Carnival* as a continuation of the same idea, but on a sophisticated, more extended level; for it was not only to be a collection of orchestral dances, but also a set of symphonic poems and the counterpart of *Má Vlast*. In *Prague Carnival* the basic element was to have been the dance (almost certainly Smetana hoped to equal the popularity of Dvořák's *Slavonic Dances*) and each section was intended to exploit a different form. Thus, the dances provide the basis upon which a precise programme of events would be developed, and contain all the bustle and excitement that a carnival brings. He planned to precede the dances with an Introduction to open the festivity and describe the masked crowd, jostling excitedly before the entry of the dancers who begin a dignified polonaise. In June 1883, he was able to write to Adolf Čech that the various scenes of *Carnival* would be performable separately or as a whole, like the movements of *Má Vlast*, and that the dances could be played in any order. Five weeks later, Smetana informed Srb that he had completed the 'complicated Introduction'

[1] Letter to Anna Trnobranska: May 8, 1883.

and worked 'three-quarters of the Polonaise in score'. But at this point he laid it to one side since he found it 'tiring to write in too many voices', and because he suffered from the strain of 'unifying so many thoughts for the different characters'.[6] For the Polonaise he took a forty-eight-bar section entered in his motive book on March 14, 1858—the first musical idea to be written there—and from the same source selected a number of short themes, mostly of a waltz-like character, which he proposed working into the subsequent dances. The plan of writing further sections of the cycle remained unfulfilled as a deterioration in his health made composition arduous. And it was not until September 1, 1883, that he was able to inform Srb that 'the last note in the score of *Prague Carnival*—No. 1: Polonaise—has been written today'. In fact, parts of the instrumentation had still to be filled in and another fortnight was to pass before the score was really complete.

It is to be regretted that the promise of Smetana's plan did not materialize; for the intention of linking the cycle with characteristic and recognizable motives drawn from the operas, and possibly *Má Vlast*, was unique and would have stamped the 'symphonic fantasy' with an indelible hallmark of Smetana's style. As it stands, the Introduction and Polonaise are striking both in orchestral presentation and harmonic thought, but at the première, on March 2, 1884, they were coolly received and greeted with suspicion. Srb found the piece 'a little strange' with 'some suprising dissonances' which resulted, in fact, from copying errors in the parts. Others were less charitable, and Dr. Josef Theurer later recalled it as the most painful moment of his life:

> After attending the première of *Prague Carnival* we went away dejected and depressed. We had heard cacophony and dissonance. It was incomprehensible. Only the effect of his mental disease could have made him use the drums and battery of percussion in such an unaccustomed fashion.[7]

Another eye-witness, Hynek Palla (Krásnohorská's brother-in-law), also found the work beyond comprehension:

> Sounds seemed to be flying through the air in a surprising fashion. The whole was disjointed in spite of the polonaise form, and it was considered to be the work of a madman and therefore an embarrassment.[8]

[6] Letter to Srb-Debrnov: July 23, 1883.
[7] Dolanský: *Hudební Pameti* (*Musical Memories*) (1944).
[8] M. Očalik: *Krásnohorská and Smetana* (1940).

It is hard to conceive how this score could have been so misunderstood; for *Prague Carnival* is really the work of a highly imaginative and skilled craftsman. That the music contained a wealth of innaccuracies contributed to a false impression, and Smetana even confessed certain difficulties in transferring key and time signatures from score to parts, where he had to 'guess many accidentals'.[9] Errors apart, the most serious cause of failure was in the choice of conductor. A disagreement with Adolf Čech had led to Mořic Anger being entrusted with the first performance. Unfortunately he was, at this time, inexperienced and at a loss to know how to tackle a new and complex score like *Prague Carnival*.

Indeed, the score is complex and needs virtuoso performers to ensure its brilliant effect; for it is noticeably more fragmentary than anything in *Má Vlast*, with tricky ensembles and intricate cross-rhythms of irregular length which look back to the piano fantasy, *Macbeth and the Witches*. However, the variety of this music is enormous, and in the numerous episodes gaiety alternates with pensiveness, lyricism with reckless abandon. Although there is a feeling of mass movement, in which various musical strands emerge and disappear like fleeting figures on a dance floor, there are no broad melodies in the conventional sense and even the Polonaise, which is the antithesis of those of Chopin, or Tchaikovsky in *Eugene Onegin*, is fashioned in a highly personal way from a number of terse cellules which are often more rhythmic than melodic. Clearly this is only a remembrance of a ball, a feverish, subjective vision drawn from the depths of Smetana's imagination. The textures are noticeably more polyphonic than those in *Má Vlast*, and the harmony, depending a great deal on the augmented triad for its intensity, is a continuation of the idiom established in *The Devil's Wall*. There is nothing outrageous in *Prague Carnival* and the score, which is striking in its orchestral presentation and use of the solo violin, is important for linking neo-Romantic music with the second generation of Czech composers.

Smetana never completed the cycle, and the main reason for his waning interest seems to have been *Viola*, which he began to hear in his head:

> I can't tell you how I am carried away by the beauty of the scenes I have sketched and already finished. Now I work every day on the opera and just scribbling on the paper makes me confused or dizzy.[1]

[9] Letter to Srb-Debrnov: September 1, 1883.
[1] Letter to Srb-Debrnov: July 23, 1883.

The idea of composing an opera on a Shakespearean theme had haunted him for twelve years or more, and judging from the fragments of Smetana's version of *Twelfth Night*, we are certainly the poorer for not having the entire opera. He first became interested in Krásnohorská's text, *Sebastian and Viola*, in April, 1871, when working on *Libuše*. By June he had accepted it in principle, though he stipulated certain cuts and asked for the general outline to be reworked.[2] Possibly he had intended to begin the score after *The Kiss*, but revision of the libretto (now called simply *Viola*) and Krásnohorská's enthusiasm for *The Secret* caused further delays. Somehow she had never warmed to the nature of the plot and her letters clearly reveal a preference for a 'national play touched with lyricism or comedy':

> I have an attractive libretto quite different from the others and I would like to prepare this instead of *Viola*. *Viola* does not really excite me, perhaps because it deals with a lovesick girl dressed in man's apparel—and I don't like this either on the stage or in reality. As you asked, I have begun *Viola*, and will finish it after *The Secret*. But since *Viola* does not really come from the heart people will surely condemn me, even hang and ridicule me for it! Shall I prepare something new or must I really stay with *Viola*, with whom you seem to be infatuated? I don't reproach you since I know men have different tastes from women, whether on Parnassus or beneath it! But for this 'masculine taste' I cannot make an exception, not even for Mr. Smetana![3]

Krásnohorská's subsequent eagerness for *Vok of Rožmberk* and her estrangement from the composer caused the postponement of their collaboration on the new opera. It was not until February, 1882, at a time when Smetana was engaged on the third act of *The Devil's Wall*, that he began to reconsider *Viola* as a suitable subject for a competition organized to select the best opera for the re-opening of the burnt-out National Theatre. In reply to a courteous letter seeking advice, Krásnohorská still showed little enthusiasm for the venture:

> . . . You know I don't like *Viola* and I even suspect my libretto. I am convinced that nothing good can result from this old-fashioned text, should it come before the public's eye. It would cost me considerable personal effort and I would have to suppress

[2] See Appendix F for details of the Krásnohorská-Smetana correspondence.
[3] Letter from Krásnohorská: January 25, 1878.

a great deal to give you permission to use it for a competition. Were it not for the fact that you have already composed certain parts, I would never accept the responsibility against my own taste or judgement. I don't wish to offend you or stand in your way . . . so please continue composing and competing, as you wish. I will not be the cause of your loss. Fortunately, the competition is devised so that music can be awarded the prize even if the text is bad—so even a text less good than *Viola* would not be a deterrent to the jury because the librettos will be considered separately. . . . If you have made up your mind to compete, then I can only congratulate your certain victory in advance. However, I would have preferred you to have had a better text, and not one which is merely a sad accessory to your music. I would not have advised you to take *Viola* and I wish you had chosen another scenario. I know full well you have other plots in mind [*Šárka* and *The End of Vlasta*] through which you could easily fulfil your ideas. You are eager to find pagan Czech subjects and I can't understand why you do not select one of those. . . . Perhaps they have faults, but possibly both would be better than Wenzig's *Libuše*, or at least as good! You know how people treat librettists nowadays—it is a nonsense and I have decided to write no more texts. It is unnecessary when philosophers begin to write poetry, and now I hear Mr. Hostinský has produced a text which is said to be a model libretto, so painfully absent before! He has given Fibich his *Bride of Messina*. Now there's a good address for you, honourable sir! For our unhappy *Viola* I have made further alterations, and from the many ensembles you can strike out the ones you do not like and turn the verses into arias or dialogue. If you have five people on stage they need not sing the whole text as written. . . . I don't impose any conditions on you and I don't ask for anything in return; but what I would have liked is for my goodwill to be recognized and an acknowledgement that I contributed something to you. If I were to write another libretto then I should ask payment from the Theatre—but as I have said, I will not write any more texts. I have little time and my literary duties cause me considerable troubles. . . . For *Viola*, it would be best if you could send me a copy of the text as it now stands. This I must have if I am to be of service to you and make alterations. But major changes are impossible, otherwise the entire verse must be reworked. The changes should be limited to details![4]

[4] Letter from Krásnohorská: February 23, 1882.

Clearly Krásnohorská was deeply offended, and on reading that she was willing to fulfil only the minimum obligation, Smetana himself must have been saddened. He resolved not to enter the competition. Instead he returned to *The Devil's Wall*, but like Verdi after the initial failure of *Falstaff*, he composed only as a pastime. Smetana did not take up *Viola* again until April, 1883. Then it was not a question of starting from scratch, for the sketches show he had begun the draft as early as 1875–1876, when he was working on *Má Vlast* and *The Kiss*. It is impossible to date them precisely, but that they cover several periods is certain since the writing is in various coloured inks, and on different types of manuscript paper. A letter to Srb, dated April 3, 1883, mentions the beginning of *Viola*, 'marked with a noisy tremolando', the sketch of which he had mislaid. Four days later he wrote again to Srb:

> I forgot to ask if you have any sketches for *Viola*: they contain my first ideas and impressions, and I need the musical scene of the first act and the motive of the storm and sea. If you can't find them I must begin again or invent other themes, and this would be a burden I would much dislike.[5]

Happily, Smetana found the sketches himself and during May began work in earnest. Progress was slow. He met with constant setbacks especially as his memory was beginning to fail him:

> My whole family fears that I could possibly lose my ability to read and write, and that I could become an idiot. I work secretly in short periods, and not as before. I will have to struggle with this large score for at least a year, but in between I shall come to Prague to give my art a fresh impulse and get a new momentum for my life![6]

Despite his condition, he remained cheerful and worked at *Viola* with real enthusiasm:

> You will soon know the charming richness of the ideas and the many motives which will transport the hearer. How I would like to see the score come to life, not with sad scenes but happy ones.[7]

Clearly, *Viola* had taken possession of him and he laboured on it every day, spending the evenings analysing the motives 'to see if I

[5] Letter to Srb-Debrnov: April 7, 1883.
[6] Letter to Srb-Debrnov: July 24, 1883.
[7] Letter to Srb-Debrnov: September, 1883.

like them'![8] Not even the retirement of Maýr[9] from the National Theatre, and the appointment of a new Director, František Šubert (1849–1915), who increased Smetana's pension to fifteen hundred gulden a year, could entice him from the new opera for anything but a few moments. Only the reopening of the National Theatre itself, with a revival of *Libuše* (for which he had had to fight[1]), seduced him away from *Viola*. He attended the *Libuše* rehearsals, staying on to see the first performance on November 18, and later the one hundred and seventeenth presentation of *The Bartered Bride* (the first to be given in the reconstructed National Theatre). But despite the benevolent attitude which Šubert showed him (he had also raised the royalties for *Libuše* from sixty to one hundred gulden), he was overlooked at the official opening ceremony, and was forced to beg for admittance: 'Maybe some corner can be found where I should not be in anybody's way, possibly behind a pillar, because the tickets, which cost forty or fifty gulden each, are otherwise beyond my means.'[2] While in Prague he used his time to enjoy the entertainment, and good food and wine:

> . . . the very things my wife is against because they cost money which she says we do not have and which she will not allow me to spend. She does not understand that I must have variety, even if it is only three weeks in the Prague streets, in order to stimulate my interest in my work.[3]

[8] Letter to Srb-Debrnov: December, 1883.

[9] Maýr was finally replaced by Adolf Čech in May, 1883.

[1] During the months before the second opening of the National Theatre, Smetana's enemies had urged that the inaugural performance be devoted not to *Libuše*, but to Dvořák's *Dmitri*. On July 10, 1881, Smetana had made his feelings known to Srb-Debrnov when he wrote:

> It cannot be a matter of indifference to me that the second, and as the whole world is being told, the real and only valid inauguration of the Czech Theatre to be celebrated by the Nation, is not to be opened by the work which was saved for the purpose for whole decades, destined and written for it—namely *Libuše*. Is it my fault that the first inauguration was not the real, but only the official one? Is *Libuše* now to be pushed aside after it was so successful, being fitted for a solemn occasion both as regards its content and its style? Is, I repeat, this opera to serve simply as a stop-gap for other solemn events? . . . I want *Libuše* to be given again and in the same way as on the first inaugural day, and later according to the whims of the gentlemen who rule the Theatre. I do not mind if the very next opera performed is one by my rivals!

[2] Letter to Šubert: November 11, 1883.

[3] Letter to Srb-Debrnov: September, 1883.

Back in Jabkenice in the solitude of his soul he could indulge himself to the full in his self-absorption for *Viola*. He attempted to integrate the first four scenes, but as illness forced him to leave greater intervals between composition, he jumped haphazardly from one section to another, working erratically in piano and orchestral score as his fancy took him. The extant material comprises sixty-seven pages of fragments, in which the same verses are often set to music in two, sometimes three, different versions. In all they total three hundred and sixty-three bars, of which two hundred and seventy-six are scored:

Bars 1–256	Scenes 1 and 2 are complete in full score, in addition to part of Scene 3.
Bars 257–264	Three sheets of piano score.
Bars 265–267	A section in which the voice and string parts are indicated, but the remainder of the instrumentation is only suggested.
Bars 268–363	Exist only as an outline for voice and piano.

The score is a remarkable document which, in its many errors in notation, text and stage instruction, reveals how Smetana's mind was deteriorating at this time. In Scene 2, he mistakes Sebastian for Viola and confuses Antonio with Mark. In the piano draft he writes the word 'šlechetnik' for 'nobleman', while in the orchestral setting it appears as 'schlakenstrik'. Often he indicates the continuation of a part by drawing a wavy line and, elsewhere, adds a number of remarks in either Czech, German, French or Italian, or a mixture of each. Yet the fragments contain sections which are clearly conceived and sometimes both beautiful and daring. Clearly, *Viola* cannot be dismissed merely as a record of a diseased mind just because it is only a fragment. His contemporaries were mistaken in regarding the rich and dramatic strokes in the opening pages as a continuation of *The Devil's Wall*. It is not. The first scene dates from the Seventies. There is no overture. The beginning is immediate and stark. The curtain rises on a highly-charged storm in which the chorus—divided into six parts—observes the tempest and shipwreck, against a wild orchestral accompaniment (see Example 111).

In Scene 2, the rescued Sebastian enters with Antonio, and Scene 3 introduces Viola and Mark. Scene 4 stops short after Orsino's thirty-second bar and, tantalizing though this is, sufficient is recorded to reveal that for his principal theme Smetana had once more dipped into his notebook, where the Orsino motive was jotted down in 1871. For Viola and Sebastian, however, he selected not two themes but

Example 111

one, fashioning the music from a phrase which fuses their fate both musically and dramatically. Possibly he intended to build the bulk of his ideas monothematically from this, as he had with Milada and Dalibor; for in the second and third scenes, the theme is transformed as shown in Example 112 overleaf.

Though it is impossible to assess the work critically on the basis of the three hundred and sixty-three bars which exist, at least one can point to the many lyrical passages and striking harmonic combinations and marvel at the courageous concentration of a man whose mind and body were close to the point of disintegration. Though he began to

Example 112

(*a*)

(*b*)

grow feeble and was confined to the house, he still felt an intense warmth for *Viola*, revealing his passion for the score to Srb in letters which show his difficulty in committing logical ideas to paper:

> *Viola*—up to now—is from no composer in my style, be it Czech, Yugoslav, or Illyrian, neither forged nor understood. I'm looking forward to playing you the first act with its melodic motive and varied scenery [*sic*!].[4]

A few days later and against doctor's orders, he managed to find notepaper and envelopes (it seems they had been locked away by his family so that he should not strain his mind with the effort of writing) and scribbled again to Srb. This time the content is more confused:

> My breast overflows with pride that this distinguished art was bestowed on me. Oh, Viola, tell the gentlemen in Prague how my soul is moved to tears—tears—tears. From Act I I send you

[4] Letter to Srb-Debrnov: 'After Christmas', 1883.

divine melodies so you can enjoy these parts in full delight. . . Some transform me into an angel—nothing else from the beginning—the numbers do not exist. It will not set the world on fire, but it will awaken admiration. Glory to *Viola*![5]

Clearly his mind was not merely confined by its limitations but poisoned by disease. He was unstable, but in his moments of reason, which were becoming increasingly few, he turned again and again to *Viola*. It is difficult to know when he last worked on it, but a significant valedictory remark, scrawled in Czech across the final page in a wild hand, mentions 'January, 1884':

Glory—Viloa [*sic*!] eternally sh[ould?]
glorious glory bare! Glory to her.
Today in January, 1884, public performance
for merited musicians through me all concerts,
theatres and operas—Glory.

Prophetically, the final words are: 'Poslední Arch'—'The final sheet'. This was Smetana's last gallows' grin at life.

But the score of *Viola* was not the only document on which he scribbled. A programme book, brought to him on the eve of his sixtieth birthday concert,[6] which he was too sick to attend, was drawn over with meaningless crayon when shown to him; and so was the draft of a Symphony on which he had also been working simultaneously with *Viola*. The earliest reference to this is in a letter to Srb written on July 24, 1883; but over the next six months he managed to proceed no further than the first four pages of pencil notes. Curiously, at this time he returned to a form which he had avoided since the ill-fated *Triumphal Symphony* of 1846. This new work was to have been a *Grosse Sinfonie* for piccolo, flutes, oboes, clarinets, bassoons, two horns, two trumpets, three trombones and tuba. The percussion was to comprise timpani and tenor, bass and side drums, while the violins were to be divided into four parts and the violas and cellos into two. Where the score of *Viola* predominantly favours the strings, the *Sinfonie* sketch contains more woodwind writing, but there is not enough for any critical appraisal. What is remarkable, however, is the inscription scribbled on the first page: 'Viola als muster'—'Viola as the example'. Whether this applies to the opera or the instrument it is impossible to tell. Apart from a few bars of notes on

[5] Letter to Srb-Debrnov: January 8, 1884.

[6] The concert, arranged by Srb at the Žofín Hall on March 2, 1884, included the *Festive Overture* (1849), *Wallenstein's Camp*, a group of piano pieces, two songs, *Vyšehrad* and the première of *Prague Carnival*.

the second and third pages, there are two tempo indications, but on the fourth page this instruction is to be found:

> 'Mit leichtem graziösem Strich, voll Bewunderung und Ehrfurcht.'
> ('With light, gracious bowing, full of admiration and humility.')

Three Italian terms suggest Smetana may have had a premonition that this was to be his last score: he was getting slower, quieter and would soon be dried up: Ritenuto, Diminuendo e Secco.

The sketch of the Symphony was probably the last music he saw, but there are in existence a number of undated letters which, from their confused content, can only have been written in late January or early February, 1884. From these it can be seen that his relationship with Betty had collapsed completely: 'All gaiety has gone from our lives . . . we live amidst domestic crises. . . . I am on the edge of despair.' That he still feared starvation, not knowing from where the next coin would come, can be seen in other letters:

> I dare not think how I will live. The salary gave me money, these joys, so it is until today, so it is, only exception is one hundred and fourteen zlati a month—did not do my wish. Divided into thirty days, no-one gets anything from it for the month. Could go begging as before, they hope for this. They will get, or from another, so they laugh. I wait and wait, if I will receive something? Need is destroyed in everyone. It will last a year like this, but with us it is not otherwise. The theatre calls it salary, but I don't thank you for such a life. . . What will be when February will always be February? I ask for a quick answer to this because, for the next months, March, April, May and St John's Day—and what comes after that? January, January, January. I think that January. . . . Everywhere and as long as someone wants, but no money can be found anywhere. . .[7]

An undated note to Čech shows his obsession with money and a higher pension; another letter to his son-in-law accuses his wife of stealing a purse of gold coins; another to Srb pleads for help. He insists on re-installing his 'reign' in the household; he longs to oust Betty, who has 'ruined' him; he sees *The Kiss*, *The Secret* and *The Devil's Wall* as the greatest masterpieces of all time; and of Viola: 'You don't know it yet, but everything is bewitched, beautiful, enchanted'.

In the middle of February a radical change came over him. He

[7] Undated letter to Srb-Debrnov.

lost the power of thinking rationally, of expressing himself logically, or articulating clearly. His voice was hoarse. His doctors diagnosed paralysis of the larynx. He became stiff. He could no longer write. He grew violent. The gun which had been kept by his bedside, to protect him from the visions that plagued him, was removed lest he should attack his wife, the sight of whom made him vicious. He trembled. He babbled senselessly. He destroyed everything that came within his reach.

During the daytime he was tended not by his wife but by a servant in Schwarz's employ, František Moucha, and at night Anna Čapek guarded him in case he should fall from the window as he waved to the countless processions of unknown admirers who, in his diseased mind, entered his room through closed doors. When he could no longer walk he suffered the most painful bouts of indigestion, hysterically refusing to eat, to be fed, to be washed or cleaned. He vomited. He grew weaker. Only in delirium was he spared the vile nightmares that tortured him daily. Clearly he could no longer be nursed in this dreadful condition, and for the safety of his family, he was removed to the Prague Lunatic Asylum in Kateřinsky:

> On a rainy day, April 23 it was, Mr. Schwarz helped Smetana into his long, warm coat. In front of the wooden steps leading to the house stood the carriage, and on the box sat Josef Bíma, holding the reins. Slowly the forester carried Smetana to the carriage and I stood by, holding two rugs. Smetana sat in the carriage, insensible to all around him. His daughter, Mrs. Schwarz, stood a little way off, crying as though her heart would break. . . . As Mr. Schwarz climbed into the carriage on Mr. Smetana's left, Mr. Srb-Debrnov got in opposite. We all began to weep as they pulled away and the Master left Jabkenice for ever.[8]

It was only Smetana's wrecked body which arrived in Prague on April 23, for his mind had already departed by the fourth page of the *Grosse Sinfonie*.

In the Kateřinsky Asylum he was placed in Room 172, where Dr. Václav Walter tended him:

> He was muddled and confused, and sat nervously on the couch tossing this way, turning that. He was a babbling old man whose mind was completely demented. He was restless, yet he could not stand or keep quiet. He persisted in giving no-one a moment's

[8] Bartoš: *Letters and Reminiscences* (1955).

rest. To pacify him was impossible since he was stone deaf. Fortunately he was feeble and could easily be overcome. He refused to take food, or be fed. From the beginning his speech was paralytically slurred and, day by day, it became more difficult to understand what he was trying to say. He recognized no-one and there were no bright intervals, only fainting fits and hallucinations. There could be no hope for, physically, he was only skin and bone and a picture of sad decay. Slowly he was fading away, yet with his right hand he continued to conduct and beat time, and by growling he tried to imitate musical instruments. And in the middle of it all he suddenly shouted out with unusual force 'Bamm!', like the bang of a drum, but more often he just shrieked with an uneven panting as only paralytics laugh.[9]

Following an examination on April 23, his condition was recorded in the Hospital Register:

> The patient is undernourished. His body shakes. He is so weak he cannot stand. He lies on his bed, huddled up, and stays awake at night jabbering and shouting nonsense. He swallows with difficulty and articulates only with the greatest effort. His bladder is paralysed and he refuses to have his urine removed. . . . The right corner of his mouth is sunken. When he tries to speak, the left side is paralysed. As he gets out of bed he falls on the floor. He seems to be persecuted by hostile phantoms.

Further reports on April 25, 28 and May 2, show little change; but on May 7 he was found to be unclean, with a deteriorating pulse. Over the next few days Drs. Čumpelík and Füstl scrutinized his condition closely and found him to be weakening crucially:

> His complexion is pale and he sleeps hardly at all. He often shouts for several hours and in his delirium cries out the names of Liszt, Wagner, the Emperor and Crown Prince. He is dirty. He refuses to look at water. When he attempts to clean himself he calls out for help, yet runs away when it comes. He fails to recognize either his children or his neighbours, and makes disorder by breaking everything within reach, and smashing windows.[1]

In this prison-like cell Smetana still clung to life. For five days he battled with crazed apparitions like the ones that had plagued Kalina

[9] V. Balthasar: *Bedřich Smetana* (1924). [1] Balthasar: *op. cit.*

in *The Secret* or were conjured up in *The Devil's Wall*; but these were different. No matter how often Smetana rung down the curtain in his diseased mind, he could never dispel the hideous visions that now possessed him.

On the evening of May 10 the news went around Prague that Smetana was nearing the end. His friends knew no peace.

On May 12, 1884, Smetana's death was expected in the morning. The light had gone from his eyes; the nervous tension had changed to apathy; his hands trembled gently. His head, with its sharp lines and seared complexion, lay on a cushion like an old wood-carving of the head of a martyr. His chin sagged; his mouth half opened; his breath slowly faded. It was five-thirty on a Monday afternoon.

The hospital certificate records the cause of death as *Dementia Senilis*, but among his family he was known to have been the victim of a more cruel disease which had not only caused his deafness, but sapped his blood and finally penetrated his brain. He died of syphilis.

Neither friend nor relative was with him in the last moments, and when Zelený arrived later the same afternoon, he found Smetana at peace:

> His head rested heavily on a pillow, and the silver of his long beard could hardly be distinguished from the white of the bed clothes. Over his forehead fell wisps of hair and strands of longer grey hair. Only the fists clenched on his chest proved that his tortured body had not given up without resistance. Alone, separated from his family, far from friends, isolated from all who loved him, our Master left the fame of this life. But his wonder-working hand was not yet cold and already the quiet tears of the most peaceful of farewells were trickling over it.[2]

Three days later a solemn funeral procession, accompanied by a cloud of smoking torches carried by members of the Hlahol, left the Church of the Mother of God in the Old Town Square. The occasion was one of national mourning. A catafalque laden with hundreds of wreaths moved to the muffled tones of Horák's *Miserere* and the March from *Dalibor*. At the National Theatre fanfares saluted the cortège as it passed on its way to the cemetery at Vyšehrad, the final resting place. By an ironic quirk of fate the National Theatre had arranged a performance of *The Bartered Bride* on the very evening of the funeral. It was not cancelled. And though it seemed as if a

[2] Zelený: *On Bedřich Smetana* (1894).

black veil had been draped before the stage, and tears darkened the eyes of the hundreds who were present, this joyful score was the most fitting memorial to the man who had dedicated his life to the Theatre and the foundations of modern Czech music.

GENEALOGICAL TREE

FRANTIŠEK SMETANA
26:10:1777–12:6:1857

I ANNA BARTONIČKOVÁ
?

II LUDMILA EXNEROVÁ
1779–13:9:1820

III BARBORA LYNKOVÁ
1792–20:11:1864

II	JOSEFA b. 1810 d. 1811	ANNA b. 1813 d. 1858	FRANTIŠEK b. 1813 d. 1813	KLÁRA b. 1815 d. 1888	ŽOFIE b. 1816 d. 1895	MARIE b. 1817 d. ?	LUDMILA b. 1819 d. ?	FRANTIŠKA b. 1810 d. 1820

III	ALBERTÍNA b. 1821 d. 1875?	FRANTIŠKA b. 1823 d. 1823	BEDŘICH b. 1824 d. 1884	ANTONÍN b. 1825 d. 1881	FRANTIŠEK b. 1826 d. 1827	BARBORA b. 1827 d. 1899	JINDRIŠKA (Jetty) b. 1828 d. 1828	KAREL b. 1830 d. 1907	ANTONIE b. 1831 d. 1831	FRANTIŠKA b. 1833 d. 1901

BEDŘICH SMETANA
2:3:1824–12:5:1884

I KATEŘINA KOLÁŘOVÁ
5:3:1827–19:7:1859

II BARBORA FERDINANDIOVÁ
10:11:1840–14:12:1908

I	BEDŘIŠKA b. 1851 d. 1855	GABRIELA b. 1852 d. 1854	ŽOFIE b. 1853 d. 1902 (Married JOSEF SCHWARZ 3:2:1874)	KATEŘINA b. 1855 d. 1856

II	ZDENKA b. 1861 (Married ADOLF HEJDUŠEK 1:7:1889)	BOŽENA b. 1863 (Married KAREL GRAF)

APPENDIX B

CATALOGUE OF ALBUM LEAVES

Key Scheme	*Sequence*	*Number of parts*	*Smetana's numbering*	*Smetana's arrangement*	*Leaves omitted in final edition*	*Leaves published in Smetana's lifetime*	*Posthumous publications*
1 C major	1	I/1	1	Op. 2, No. 1		Kistner, 1851	
2 A minor	2	I/2	2	Op. 2, No. 2		Kistner, 1851	
3 G major	3	I/3	3	Op. 2, No. 3		Kistner, 1851	
4			9		Album Leaf in G major		U.B., 1903 (Umelěcká Beseda)
5 E minor	4	I/4	4	Op. 2, No. 4		Kistner, 1851	
6 D major	5	I/5	5	Op. 2, No. 5		Kistner, 1851	
7 B minor	6	I/6	6	Op. 2, No. 6		Kistner, 1851	
8			11		Album Leaf in B minor		U.B., 1903
9 A major	7	II/1	—	Op. 3, No. 2		Hallberger, 1857	
10			7		Album Leaf in A major		Curwen, 1958
11 F sharp minor	8	II/2	2	Op. 4, No. 1		Veit, 1858	
12			8		Album Leaf in F sharp minor		Unpublished

13	E major	9	II/3	3	Op. 3, No. 1		Hallberger, 1857	
14				3		Album Leaf in E major		Unpublished
15	C sharp minor	10	II/4	4	Op, 3, No. 3			U.B., 1903
16	B major	11	II/5	5	Op. 4, No. 2		Veit, 1858	
17	G sharp minor	12	II/6	6	Op. 4, No. 4		Veit, 1858	
18				6		Album Leaf in G sharp minor		Unpublished
19				12	Op. 5, No. 2		Veit, 1858	
20	F sharp major	13	III/1	13	Op. 5, No. 1		Veit, 1858	
21	E flat minor	14	III/2	14		Album Leaf in E flat minor		U.B., 1903
22	D flat major	15	III/3	15	Op. 5, No. 3		Veit, 1858	
23	B flat minor	16	III/4	16		Album Leaf in B flat minor		U.B., 1903
24	A flat major	17	III/5	17	Op. 4, No. 3		Veit, 1858	
25	F minor	18	III/6	18	Op. 5, No. 4		Veit, 1858	
26	E flat major	19	IV/1	13		Andante in E flat major	Christoph-Kuhe, 1856	
27	C minor	20	IV/2					Unpublished

APPENDIX B (*cont.*)

Key Scheme	*Sequence*	*Number of parts*	*Smetana's numbering*	*Smetana's arrangement*	*Leaves omitted in final edition*	*Leaves published in Smetana's lifetime*	*Posthumous publications*
28 B flat major	21	IV/3	22		Album Leaf in B flat major		Curwen, 1958
29			21		Toccatina in B flat major		U.B., 1903
30 G minor	22	IV/4	10		Album Leaf in G minor		U.B., 1903
31 F major	23						Unpublished
32 D minor	24						Unpublished

APPENDIX C

THE GENESIS OF *THE BARTERED BRIDE*

VERSION I *in 2 Acts*	*VERSION II* *in 2 Acts*	*VERSION III* *in 2 Acts*	*VERSION IV* *in 3 acts*	*VERSION V* *in 3 Acts*
1st Performance: May 30, 1866 Provisional Theatre— Number of performances: 2	1st Performance: October, 27 1866 Provisional Theatre— Number of performances: 13	1st Performance: January 29, 1869 Provisional Theatre— Number of performances: 4	1st Performance: June 1, 1869 Provisional Theatre— Number of performances: 9	1st Performance: September 25, 1870 Provisional Theatre.
OVERTURE ACT I A Village Green	OVERTURE ACT I A Village Green	OVERTURE ACT I A Village Green	OVERTURE ACT I A Village Green	OVERTURE ACT I A Village Green
SCENE 1 Mařenka, Jeník, Villagers and Farmers	SCENE 1 Mařenka, Jeník, Villagers and Farmers	SCENE 1 Mařenka, Jeník, Villagers and Farmers	SCENE 1 Mařenka, Jeník, Villagers and Farmers	SCENE 1 Mařenka, Jeník, Villagers and Farmers
CHORUS: 'Let's rejoice and be merry' *Proč bychom se netěšili*	CHORUS: 'Let's rejoice and be merry' *Proč bychom se netěšili*	CHORUS: 'Let's rejoice and be merry' *Proč bychom se netěšili*	CHORUS: 'Let's rejoice and be merry' *Proč bychom se netěšili*	CHORUS: 'Let's rejoice and be merry *Proč bychom se netěšili*
SCENE 2 Mařenka and Jeník	SCENE 2 Mařenka and Jeník	SCENE 2 Mařenka and Jeník	SCENE 2 Mařenka and Jeník	SCENE 2 Mařenka and Jeník
DIALOGUE:	DIALOGUE:	DIALOGUE:	DIALOGUE:	RECITATIVE: 'It will happen as I have been told' *Tak tedy přece*

APPENDIX C (cont.)

VERSION I *in 2 Acts*	*VERSION II* *in 2 Acts*	*VERSION III* *in 2 Acts*	*VERSION IV* *in 3 Acts*	*VERSION V* *in 3 Acts*
1st Performance: May 30, 1866 Provisional Theatre— Number of performances: 2	1st Performance: October 27, 1866 Provisional Theatre— Number of performances: 13	1st Performance: January 29, 1869 Provisional Theatre— Number of performances: 4	1st Performance: June 1, 1869 Provisional Theatre— Number of performances: 9	1st Performance: September 25, 1870 Provisional Theatre.
ARIA: 'If I should ever learn anything like that about you' *Kdybych se co takového*	ARIA: 'If I should ever learn anything like that about you' *Kdybych se co takového*	ARIA: 'If I should ever learn anything like that about you' *Kdybych se co takového*	ARIA: 'If I should ever learn anything like that about you' *Kdybych se co takového*	ARIA: 'If I should ever learn anything like that about you' *Kdybych se co takového*
DIALOGUE:	DIALOGUE:	DIALOGUE:	DIALOGUE:	RECITATIVE: 'At last it is true. Your past life seems veiled in a sort of mystery' *Konečně je celá minulost tvá*
DUET: 'While a mother's love means blessing' *Jako matka požehnáním*	DUET: 'While a mother's love means blessing' *Jako matka požehnáním*	DUET: 'While a mother's love means blessing' *Jako matka požehnáním*	DUET: 'While a mother's love means blessing' *Jako matka požehnáním*	DUET: 'While a mother's love means blessing' *Jako matka požehnáním*
LEADING TO: 'Faithful love can't be marred' *Věrné milování*	LEADING TO: 'Faithful love can't be marred' *Věrné milování*	LEADING TO: 'Faithful love can't be marred' *Věrné milování*	LEADING TO: 'Faithful love can't be marred' *Věrné milování*	LEADING TO: 'Faithful love can't be marred' *Věrné milování*
SCENE 3 Ludmila, Krušina, Kecal	SCENE 3 Ludmila, Krušina, Kecal	SCENE 3 Ludmila, Krušina, Kecal	SCENE 3 Ludmila, Krušina, Kecal	SCENE 3 Ludmila, Krušina, Kecal

TRIO: 'As I was saying my good fellow, you have pledged your word' *Jak vám pravím, pane kmotře*	TRIO: 'As I was saying my good fellow, you have pledged your word' *Jak vám pravím, pane kmotře*	TRIO: 'As I was saying my good fellow, you have pledged your word' *Jak vám pravím, pane kmotře*	TRIO: 'As I was saying my good fellow, you have pledged your word' *Jak vám pravím, pane kmotře*	TRIO: 'As I was saying my good fellow, you have pledged your word' *Jak vám pravím, pane kmotře*
DIALOGUE:	DIALOGUE:	DIALOGUE:	DIALOGUE:	RECITATIVE: 'Of course I know Tobiáš Mícha' *Ovšem Tobiáše Míchu znám*
TRIO: 'He's a nice boy, well brought up and decent' *Mladík slušný*	TRIO: 'He's a nice boy, well brought up and decent' *Mladík slušný*	TRIO: 'He's a nice boy, well brought up and decent' *Mladík slušný*	TRIO: 'He's a nice boy, well brought up and decent' *Mladík slušný*	TRIO: 'He's a nice boy, well brought up and decent' *Mladík slušný*
SCENE 4 Mařenka, plus the foregoing	SCENE 4 Mařenka, plus the foregoing	SCENE 4 Mařenka, plus the foregoing	SCENE 4 Mařenka, plus the foregoing	SCENE 4 Mařenka, plus the foregoing
QUARTET: 'Here she is now, let's talk to her' *Tu ji máme*	QUARTET: 'Here she is now, let's talk to her' *Tu ji máme*	QUARTET: 'Here she is now, let's talk to her' *Tu ji máme*	QUARTET: 'Here she is now, let's talk to her' *Tu ji máme*	QUARTET: 'Here she is now, let's talk to her' *Tu ji máme*
DIALOGUE:	DIALOGUE:	DIALOGUE:	DIALOGUE:	RECITATIVE: 'Jeník won't give in, I know' *Jeník neupustí to vím*
			SCENE 5 POLKA FURIANT	SCENE 5 POLKA
			ACT II An Inn SCENE I Chorus of villagers, Jeník and Kecal	ACT II An Inn SCENE I Chorus of villagers, Jeník and Kecal
			CHORUS: 'To beer' *To pivečko*	CHORUS: 'To beer' *To pivečko*

APPENDIX C (*cont.*)

VERSION I *in 2 Acts*	*VERSION II* *in 2 Acts*	*VERSION III* *in 2 Acts*	*VERSION IV* *in 3 Acts*	*VERSION V* *in 3 Acts*
1st Performance: May 30, 1866 Provisional Theatre— Number of performances: 2	1st Performance: October 27, 1866 Provisional Theatre— Number of performances: 13	1st Performance: January 29, 1869 Provisional Theatre— Number of performances: 4	1st Performance: June 1, 1869 Provisional Theatre— Number of performances: 9	1st Performance: September 25, 1870 Provisional Theatre.
				FURIANT
SCENE 5 Vašek	SCENE 5 Vašek	SCENE 5 Vašek	SCENE 2 Vašek	SCENE 2 Vašek
ARIA: 'My mother said to me' *Ma-Ma-Ma-Matička*	ARIA: 'My mother said to me' *Ma-Ma-Ma-Matička*	ARIA: 'My mother said to me' *Ma-Ma-Ma-Matička*	ARIA: 'My mother said to me' *Ma-Ma-Ma-Matička*	ARIA: 'My mother said to me' *Ma-Ma-Ma-Matička*
SCENE 6 Mařenka and Vašek	SCENE 6 Mařenka and Vašek	SCENE 6 Mařenka and Vašek	SCENE 3 Mařenka and Vašek	SCENE 3 Mařenka and Vašek
DIALOGUE:	DIALOGUE:	DIALOGUE:	DIALOGUE:	RECITATIVE: 'Surely you are Mařenka's bridegroom' *Vy jste zajisté ženich*
DUET: 'I know of a maiden fair' *Známt' já jednu dívčinu*	DUET: 'I know of a maiden fair' *Známt' já jednu dívčinu*	DUET: 'I know of a maiden fair' *Známt' já jednu dívčinu*	DUET: 'I know of a maiden fair' *Známt' já jednu dívčinu*	DUET: 'I know of a maiden fair' *Známt' já jednu dívčinu*
		CHANGE OF SCENE At the inn		
		SCENE 7 Chorus of villagers, Jeník and Kecal		
		CHORUS: 'To beer' *To pivečko*		

Scene 7 Jeník and Kecal	Scene 7 Jeník and Kecal	Scene 8 Jeník and Kecal	Scene 4 Jeník and Kecal	Scene 4 Jeník and Kecal
				Recitative: 'As I was saying, she's lovely, sweet and rich' *Jak pravím, hezká je hadná, bohátá*
Duet: 'Now sir, listen to a word or two. I know a maiden' *Nuže, milý chasníku, Znám jednu dívku*	Duet: 'Now sir, listen to a word or two. I know a maiden' *Nuže, milý chasníku, Znám jednu dívku*	Duet: 'Now sir, listen to a word or two. I know a maiden' *Nuže, milý chasníku, Znám jednu dívku*	Duet: 'Now, sir, listen to a word or two. I know a maiden' *Nuže, milý chasníku, Znám jednu dívku*	Duet: 'Now sir, listen to a word or two. I know a maiden' *Nuže, milý chasníku, Znám jednu dívku*
Dialogue: 'As I was saying, she's lovely, sweet and rich' *Jak pramím, nezka, je hodna bohátá*	Dialogue: 'As I was saying, she's lovely, sweet and rich' *Jak pramím, nezka, je hodna bohátá*	Dialogue: 'As I was saying, she's lovely, sweet and rich' *Jak pramím, nezka, je hodna bohátá*	Dialogue: 'As I was saying, she's lovely, sweet and rich' *Jak pramím, nezka, je hodna bohátá*	
Dialogue: 'If you renounce Mařenka I shall pay you' *Odřekneš—il se Mařenky*	Dialogue: 'If you renounce Mařenka I shall pay you' *Odřekneš—il se Mařenky*	Dialogue: 'If you renounce Mařenka I shall pay you' *Odřekneš—il se Mařenky*	Dialogue: 'If you renounce Mařenka I shall pay you' *Odřekneš—il se Mařenky*	Recitative: 'If you renounce Mařenka I shall pay you *Odřekneš—il se Mařenky*
Scene 8 Jeník Aria: 'When you discover whom you've bought' *Až uzříš—Jak možná věřit*	Scene 8 Jeník Aria: 'When you discover whom you've bought' *Až uzříš—Jak možná věřit*	Scene 9 Jeník Aria: 'When you discover whom you've bought' *Až uzříš—Jak možná věřit*	Scene 5 Jeník Aria: 'When you discover whom you've bought' *Až uzříš—Jak možná věřit*	Scene 5 Jeník Aria: 'When you discover whom you've bought' *Až uzříš—Jak možná věřit*
Scene 9: Finale Jeník, Krušina, Kecal	Scene 9: Finale Jeník, Krušina, Kecal	Scene 9: Finale Jeník, Krušina, Kecal	Scene 9: Finale Jeník, Krušina, Kecal	Scene 9: Finale Jeník, Krušina, Kecal

APPENDIX C (*cont.*)

VERSION I *in 2 Acts*	*VERSION II* *in 2 Acts*	*VERSION III* *in 2 Acts*	*VERSION IV* *in 3 Acts*	*VERSION V* *in 3 Acts*
1st Performance: May 30, 1866 Provisional Theatre— Number of performances: 2	1st Performance: October 27, 1866 Provisional Theatre— Number of performances: 13	1st Performance: January 29, 1869 Provisional Theatre— Number of performances: 4	1st Performance: June 1, 1869 Provisional Theatre— Number of performances: 9	1st Performance: September 25, 1870 Provisional Theatre.
ENSEMBLE: 'Come inside and listen to me' *Pojd'te, lidičky*	ENSEMBLE: 'Come inside and listen to me' *Pojd'te, lidičky*	ENSEMBLE: 'Come inside and listen to me' *Pojd'te, lidičky*	ENSEMBLE: 'Come inside and listen to me' *Pojd'te, lidičky*	ENSEMBLE: 'Come inside and listen to me' *Pojd'te lidičky*
ACT II A Village Green	ACT II A Village Green	ACT II A Village Green	ACT III A Village Green	ACT III A Village Green
		SCENE 1 CHORUS: POLKA		
SCENE 1 Vašek ARIA: 'I can't get it out of my head' *To-to mi v hlavě le-leží*	SCENE 1 Vašek ARIA: 'I can't get it out of my head' *To-to mi v hlavě le-leží*	SCENE 2 Vašek ARIA: 'I can't get it out of my head' *To-to mi v hlave le-leží*	SCENE 1 Vašek ARIA: 'I can't get it out of my head' *To-to mi v hlavě le-leží*	SCENE 1 Vašek ARIA: 'I can't get it out of my head' *To-to mi v hlavě le-leží*
SCENE 2 Principal, Comedians, Esmeralda, Indian, Vašek	SCENE 2 Principal, Comedians, Esmeralda, Indian, Vašek	SCENE 2 Principal, Comedians, Esmeralda, Indian, Vašek	SCENE 2 Principal, Comedians, Esmeralda, Indian, Vašek	SCENE 2 Principal, Comedians, Esmeralda, Indian, Vašek
			MARCH OF THE COMEDIANS	MARCH OF THE COMEDIANS
DIALOGUE:	DIALOGUE:	DIALOGUE:	DIALOGUE:	RECITATIVE: 'We publically announce' *Ohlašvjeme slavnému publikum*

	Gipsy Dance (from ballet music of *The Brandenburgers in Bohemia*, Act I).		Skočná (Ballet: Dance of the Comedians)	Skočná (Ballet: Dance of the Comedians)
Principal and Esmeralda	Principal and Esmeralda	Principal and Esmeralda		
Couplet: 'He pretends he's a good boy' *Ten staví se svatouškem*	Couplet: 'He pretends he's a good boy' *Ten staví se svatouškem*	Couplet: 'He pretends he's a good boy' *Ten staví se svatouškem* (Dropped after 7:2:1869)	———	———
Dialogue:	dialogue:	Dialogue:	Dialogue:	Recitative: 'Oh, oh, that will be nice, and the Indian girl too' *Je-je-je-je-je, to bude hezké*
Principal and Esmeralda	Principal and Esmeralda	Principal and Exmeralda	Principal and Esmeralda	Principal and Esmeralda
Duet: 'We'll make a pretty little thing out of you' *Milostné zviřátko*	Duet: 'We'll make a pretty little thing out of you' *Milostné zviřátko*	Duet: 'We'll make a pretty little thing out of you' *Milostné zviřátko*	Duet: 'We'll make a pretty little thing out of you' *Milostné zviřátko*	Duet: 'We'll make a pretty little thing out of you' *Milostné zviřátko*
Scene 3 Háta, Vašek, Mícha, Kecal	Scene 3 Háta, Vašek, Mícha, Kecal	Scene 4 Háta, Vašek, Mícha, Kecal	Scene 3 Háta, Vašek, Mícha, Kecal	Scene 3 Háta, Vašek, Mícha, Kecal
Dialogue:	Dialogue:	Dialogue:	Dialogue:	Recitative: 'Oh dear, all of them want to love me!' *Oh, já ne-ne-nešťastný*
QUARTET: 'He does not want her. What has happened?' *Aj! Jakže? jakže?*	QUARTET: 'He does not want her. What has happened?' *Aj! Jakže? jakže?*	QUARTET: 'He does not want her. What has happened?' *Aj! Jakže? jakže?*	QUARTET: 'He does not want her. What has happened?' *Aj! Jakže? jakže?*	QUARTET: 'He does not want her. What has happened?' *Aj! Jakže? jakže?*
Scene 4 Mařenka, Ludmila, Krušina, Háta, Mícha, Kecal	Scene 4 Mařenka, Ludmila, Krušina, Háta, Mícha, Kecal	Scene 5 Mařenka, Ludmila, Krušina, Háta, Mícha, Kecal	Scene 4 Mařenka, Ludmila, Krušina, Háta, Mícha, Kecal	Scene 4 Mařenka, Ludmila, Krušina Háta, Mícha, Kecal

APPENDIX C (*cont.*)

VERSION I *in 2 Acts*	*VERSION II* *in 2 Acts*	*VERSION III* *in 2 Acts*	*VERSION IV* *in 3 Acts*	*VERSION V* *in 3 Acts*
1st Performance: May 30, 1866 Provisional Theatre— Number of performances: 2	1st Performance: October 27, 1866 Provisional Theatre— Number of performances: 13	1st Performance: January 29, 1869 Provisional Theatre— Number of performances: 4	1st Performance: June 1, 1869 Provisional Theatre— Number of performances: 9	1st Performance: September 25, 1870 Provisional Theatre.
ENSEMBLE: 'No, no, I don't believe it. It's just an ugly dream' *Ne, ne, tomu nevěřím*	ENSEMBLE: 'No, no, I don't believe it. It's just an ugly dream' *Ne, ne, tomu nevěřím*	ENSEMBLE: 'No, no, I don't believe it. It's just an ugly dream' *Ne, ne, tomu nevěřím*	ENSEMBLE: 'No, no, I don't believe it. It's just an ugly dream' *Ne, ne, tomu nevěřím*	ENSEMBLE: 'No, no, I don't believe it. It's just an ugly dream' *Ne, ne, tomu nevěřím*
SCENE 5 Vašek, with the foregoing 'Tell me what you want' *Co . . . co pořáde chcete?*	SCENE 5 Vašek, with the foregoing 'Tell me what you want' *Co . . . co pořáde chcete?*	SCENE 6 Vašek, with the foregoing 'Tell me what you want' *Co . . . co pořáde chcete?*	SCENE 5 Vašek, with the foregoing 'Tell me what you want' *Co . . . co pořáde chcete?*	SCENE 5 Vašek, with the foregoing 'Tell me what you want' *Co . . . co pořáde chcete?*
SEXTET: 'Make your mind up, Mařenka' *Rozmysli si, Mařenko*	SEXTET: 'Make your mind up, Mařenka' *Rozmysli si, Mařenko*	SEXTET: 'Make your mind up, Mařenka' *Rozmysli si, Mařenko*	SEXTET: 'Make your mind up, Mařenka' *Rozmysli si, Mařenko*	SEXTET: 'Make your mind up, Mařenka' *Rozmysli si, Mařenko*
SCENE 6 Mařenka alone	SCENE 6 Mařenka alone	SCENE 7 Mařenka alone	SCENE 6 Mařenka alone	SCENE 6 Mařenka alone
ARIA: 'Oh, what grief!' *Ó, jaký žal!* ONLY TO THE WORDS: 'How I long to know the truth at this moment' *O kyz se mi v nesnází té skutečná pravda zjeví*	ARIA: 'Oh, what grief!' *Ó, jaký žal!*	ARIA: 'Oh, what grief!' *Ó, jaký žal!*	ARIA: 'Oh, what grief' *Ó, jaký žal!*	ARIA: 'Oh, what grief!' *Ó, jaký žal!*

		ARIA EXTENDED: 'That dream of love!' *Ten lásky sen*	ARIA EXTENDED: 'That dream of love!' *Ten lásky sen*	ARIA EXTENDED: 'That dream of love!' *Ten lásky sen*
SCENE 7 Mařenka and Jeník	SCENE 7 Mařenka and Jeník	SCENE 8 Mařenka and Jeník	SCENE 7 Mařenka and Jeník	SCENE 7 Mařenka and Jeník
DUET: 'Mařenka mine!' *Mařenko má!* 'Are you such a stubborn lass?' *Tak, tvrdošíjná, dívko, jsi?*	DUET: Mařenka mine!' *Mařenko má!* 'Are you such a stubborn lass?' *Tak, tvrdošíjná, dívko, jsi?*	DUET: 'Mařenka mine!' *Mařenko má!* 'Are you such a stubborn lass' *Tak, tvrdošíjná, dívko, jsi?*	DUET: 'Mařenka mine!' *Mařenkao má!* 'Are you such a stubborn lass?' *Tak, tvrdošíjná, dívko, jsi?*	DUET: 'Mařenka mine!' *Mařenko má!* 'Are you such a stubborn lass?' *Tak, tvrdošíjná, dívko, jsi?*
SCENE 8 Mařenka, Jeník, Kecal	SCENE 8 Mařenka, Jeník, Kecal	SCENE 9 Mařenka, Jeník, Kecal	SCENE 8 Mařenka, Jeník, Kecal	SCENE 8 Mařenka, Jeník, Kecal
DIALOGUE:	DIALOGUE:	DIALOGUE:	DIALOGUE:	RECITATIVE: 'Well, you are still here' *Hle, hle, chas íku*
TRIO: 'Calm down and trust me' *Utiš se, dívko*	TRIO: 'Calm down and trust me' *Utiš se, dívko*	TRIO: 'Calm down and trust me' *Utiš se, dívko*	TRIO: 'Calm down and trust me' *Utiš se, dívko*	TRIO: 'Calm down and trust me' *Utiš se, dívko*
SCENE 9 FINALE: Mařenka, Ludmila, Háta, Jeník, Krušina, Mícha, Kecal and Choir	SCENE 9 FINALE: Mařenka, Ludmila, Háta Jeník, Krušina, Mícha, Kecal and Choir	SCENE 10 FINALE: Mařenka, Ludmila, Háta Jeník, Krušina, Mícha, Kecal and Choir	SCENE 9 FINALE: Mařenka, Ludmila, Háta, Jeník, Krušina, Mícha Kecal and Choir	SCENE 9 FINALE: Mařenka, Ludmila, Háta Jeník, Krušina, Mícha, Kecal and Choir
ENSEMBLE: 'What have you decided Mařenka?' *Jak jsi se, Mařenko rozmyslila?*	ENSEMBLE: 'What have you decided Mařenka?' *Jak jsi se, Mařenko rozmyslila?*	ENSEMBLE: 'What have you decided Mařenka?' *Jak jsi, se Mařenko rozmyslila?*	ENSEMBLE: 'What have you decided Mařenka?' *Jak jsi se, Mařenko rozmyslila?*	ENSEBMLE: 'What have you decided Mařenka?' *Jak jsi se, Mařenko rozmyslila?*
SCENE 10 The foregoing with Vašek and the children	SCENE 10 The foregoing with Vašek and the children	SCENE 11 The foregoing with Vašek and the children	SCENE 10 The foregoing with Vašek and the children	SCENE 10 The foregoing with Vašek and the children

APPENDIX C (*cont.*)

VERSION I *in 2 Acts*	*VERSION II* *in 2 Acts*	*VERSION III* *in 2 Acts*	*VERSION IV* *in 3 Acts*	*VERSION V* *in 3 Acts*
1st Performance: May 30, 1866 Provisional Theatre— Number of performances: 2	1st Performance: October 27, 1866 Provisional Theatre— Number of performances: 13	1st Performance: January 29, 1869 Provisional Theatre— Number of performances: 4	1st Performance: June 1, 1869 Provisional Theatre— Number of performances: 9	1st Performance: September 25, 1870 Provisional Theatre.
DIALOGUE:	DIALOGUE:	DIALOGUE:	DIALOGUE:	RECITATIVE: 'Don't be afraid. I'm not a bear!' *Ne–nebojte se!*
CONCLUSION: ENSEMBLE: 'He's not grown up yet!' *Pomněte, kmotře* CHORUS: 'A good cause has won and faithful love has triumphed' *Dobrá věc se podařila*	CONCLUSION: ENSEMBLE: 'He's not grown up yet!' *Pomněte, kmotře* CHORUS: 'A good cause has won and faithful love has triumphed' *Dobrá věc se podařila*	CONCLUSION: ENSEMBLE: 'He's not grown up yet!' *Pomněte, kmotře* CHORUS: 'A good cause has won and faithful love has triumphed' *Dobrá věc se podařila*	CONCLUSION: ENSEMBLE: 'He's not grown up yet!' *Pomněte, kmotře* CHORUS: 'A good cause has won and faithful love has triumphed' *Dobrá věc se podařila*	CONCLUSION: ENSEMBLE: 'He's not grown up yet!' *Pomněte, kmotře* CHORUS: 'A good cause has won and faithful love has triumphed' *Dobrá věc se podařila*

THE BARTERED BRIDE COUPLET

PRINCIPÁL, ESMERALDA
KUPLET
Moderato
Flauti I.II.
Oboi I.II.
Clarinetti I.II. C
Fagotti I.II.
Corni I.II. C
Timpani C, G
ESMERALDA
PRINCIPÁL
Violini I. II.
Viole
Violoncelli
Contrabassi
poco rall.
Cl.I.II.C
Cor.I.II.C
Principál
1. Ten sta - ví se sva - tou - škem, se sva - tou - škem, o - či - ma krou - tí,
2. Mno - hý, jenž se do - ma, jenž se do - ma jen mazlí s svou že - nou, svou že - nou,
Viol. I. II.
Vle
Vlc.
Cb.
[a tempo]
1. však hle - dí, kde ko - ho by, kde ko - ho by mo - hl o - hnou - til
2. na u - li - ci, na u - li - ci pá - lí za každou fi - fle - nou,

APPENDIX D (cont.)

80
Fl.I.II.
Ob.I.II.
Cl.I.II.C
Fag.I.II.
Cor.I.II.C
Timp.C,G
Esmeralda
vša-dy za larvou tvář ji-ná se kry-je a, a, a před svě-tem,
Principál
vša-dy, vša-dy, vša-dy a před světem hra-je se jen ko-me-di-e,
I.
Viol.
II.
Vle
Vlc.
Cb.
Fl.I.II.
Ob.I.II.
Cl.I.II.C
Fag.I.II.
Cor.I.II.C
Timp.C,G
Esmeralda
před svě-tem hra-je se jen ko-me-di-e, ko-me-di-e, ko-me-di-e,
Principál
ko-me-di-e, ko-me-di-e, ko-me-di-
I.
Viol.
II.
Vle
Vlc.
Cb.

APPENDIX D (*cont.*)

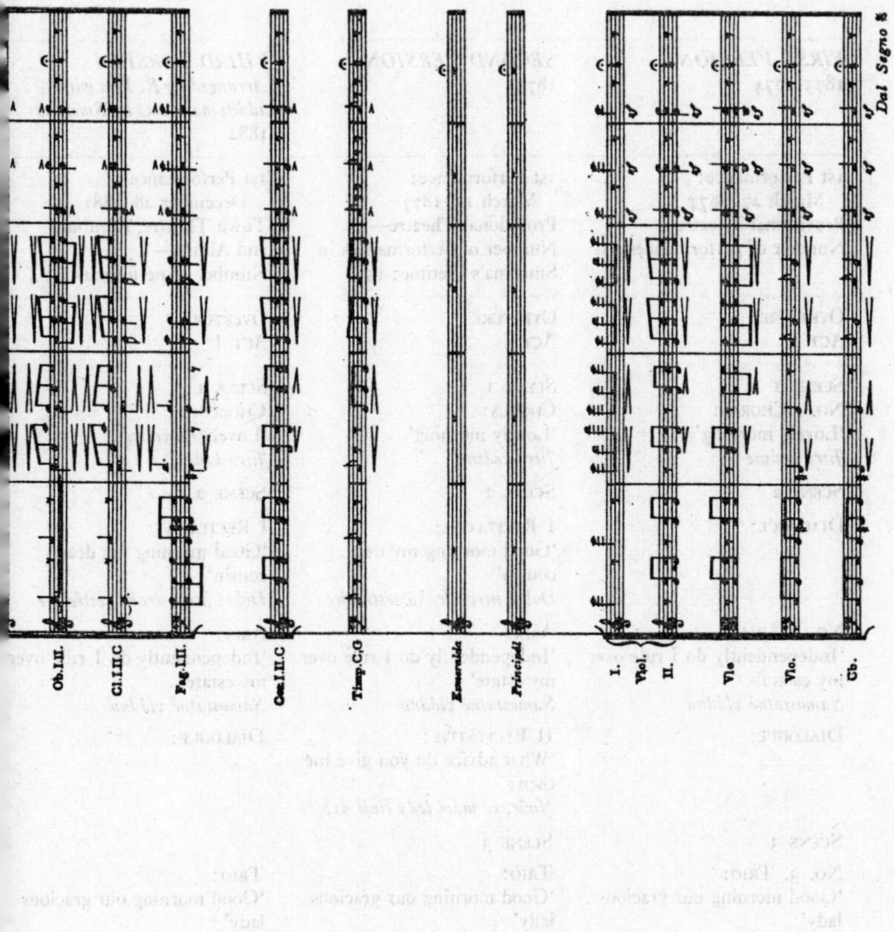
Ob.I.II.
Cl.I.II.C
Fag.I.II.
Cor.I.II.C
Timp.C.G
I.
Viol.
II.
Vla
Vlc.
Cb.
Dal Segno

APPENDIX E

GENESIS OF *THE TWO WIDOWS*

FIRST VERSION 1873–1874	*SECOND VERSION* 1877	*THIRD VERSION* *Arranged by R. Fels with additional items by Smetana* 1882
1st Performance: March 27, 1874 Provisional Theatre— Number of performances: 6	1st Performance: March 15, 1877 Provisional Theatre— Number of performances in Smetana's lifetime: 15	1st Performance: December 28, 1881 Town Theatre, Hamburg and Altona— Number of performances: 4
OVERTURE ACT I	OVERTURE ACT I	OVERTURE ACT I
SCENE 1	SCENE 1	SCENE 1
NO. 1 CHORUS: 'Lovely morning' *Jitro krásné*	CHORUS: 'Lovely morning' *Jitro krásné*	CHORUS: 'Lovely morning' *Jitro krásné*
SCENE 2	SCENE 2	SCENE 2
DIALOGUE:	I RECITATIVE: 'Good morning my dear cousin' *Dobré jitro, drahá sestřenice*	I RECITATIVE: 'Good morning my dear cousin' *Dobré jitro, drahá sestřenice*
NO. 2 ARIA: 'Independently do I rule over my estate' *Samostatně vládnu*	ARIA: 'Independently do I rule over my estate' *Samostatně vládnu*	ARIA: 'Independently do I rule over my estate' *Samostatně vládnu*
DIALOGUE:	II RECITATIVE: 'What advice do you give me then?' *Nuže, co mám ledy činit as?*	DIALOGUE:
SCENE 3	SCENE 3	
NO. 3. TRIO: 'Good morning our gracious lady' *Dobré jitro milostiva pani!*	TRIO: 'Good morning our gracious lady' *Dobré jitro milostiva pani!*	TRIO: 'Good morning our gracious lady' *Dobré jitro milostiva pani!*
DIALOGUE:	III RECITATIVE: 'His only virtue is that he never hits anything' *Jedinou to jeho ctností*	III RECITATIVE: 'His only virtue is that he never hits anything' *Jedinou to jeho ctností*

FIRST VERSION 1873–1874	*SECOND VERSION* 1877	*THIRD VERSION* *Arranged by R. Fels with additional items by Smetana* 1882
		TRIO: *Vždyt' pytlák, neumí-li střílet*
SCENE 4	SCENE 4	SCENE 3
DIALOGUE:		
No. 4. DUET: 'How much longer must I wait before meeting someone?' *Dlouho-li zde budu bloudit?*	DUET: 'How much longer must I wait before meeting someone?' *Dlouho-li zde buhu bloudit?*	DUET: 'How much longer must I wait before meeting someone?' *Dlouho-li-zde budu bloudit?*
SCENE 5	SCENE 5	SCENE 4
DIALOGUE:		DIALOGUE:
		SCENE 5
	IV RECITATIVE: 'All's well, good lady!' *V pořádku vše, milospaní!*	IV RECITATIVE: 'All's well, good lady!' *V pořádku vše, milospaní!*
SCENE 6	SCENE 6	SCENE 6
No. 5. QUARTET: 'He's waiting at the door!' *Vězeň přede dveřmi tam!*	QUARTET: 'He's waiting at the door!' *Vězeň přede dveřmi tam!*	QUARTET: 'He's waiting at the door!' *Vězeň přede dveřmi tam!*
END OF ACT I		END OF ACT I
	SCENE 7 FINALE: 'Here you are Mumlal, we want to ask you something.' *Mumlal, tu vás máme něco se vás pozeptáme'*	
	END OF ACT I	
ACT II	ACT II	ACT II
PRELUDE	PRELUDE	PRELUDE
SCENE 1	SCENE 1	SCENE 1
	ARIA: 'When May comes' *Když zavítá máj*	ARIA: 'When May comes' *Když zavítá máj*
		SCENE 2
DIALOGUE:	I RECITATIVE: 'Fancy keeping that man here!' *Nechati zde muže toho!*	DIALOGUE:
		SCENE 3 DIALOGUE:
SCENE 2	SCENE 2	SCENE 4
DUET: 'There's no longer any doubt' *Není pochybností více*	DUET: 'There's no longer any doubt' *Není pochybností více*	DUET: 'There's no longer any doubt' *Není pochybností více*

FIRST VERSION 1873–1874	*SECOND VERSION* 1877	*THIRD VERSION* *Arranged by R. Fels with additional items by Smetana* 1882
SCENE 3 NO. 6. MELODRAMA/DUET: 'Poem!' *Báseň!*	SCENE 3 MELODRAMA/DUET: 'Poem!' *Báseň!*	SCENE 5 MELODRAMA/DUET: 'Poem!' *Báseň!*
SCENE 4 DIALOGUE:	SCENE 4 II RECITATIVE: 'Halt my dear! What do I see?' *Stůjte, pane! Jakže? Muzno-li?*	SCENE 6 II RECITATIVE: 'Halt my dear! What do I see?' *Stůjte, pane! Jakže? Muzno-li?*
SCENE 5 NO. 7. RECITATIVE AND ARIA: 'There they depart together' *Odcházejí spolu*	SCENE 5 RECITATIVE AND ARIA: 'There they depart together' *Odcházejí spolu*	RECITATIVE AND ARIA: 'There they depart together' *Odcházejí spolu* WITH NEW ENDING
SCENE 6 DIALOGUE:	SCENE 6 III RECITATIVE: 'Well here you are!' *Dobře, výborně!*	SCENE 7 DIALOGUE:
NO. 8. ARIA: 'No matter what rouses my anger' *Necht' cokoliv mne zlobí* DIALOGUE:	ARIA: 'No matter what rouses my anger' *Necht' cokoliv mne zlobí* IV RECITATIVE: 'You dear old man' *Milování hodný příteli*	ARIA: 'No matter what rouses my anger' *Necht' cokoliv mne zlobí*
		SCENE 8 FINALE FROM ACT I: 'Here you are Mumlal, we want to ask you something' *Mumlal, tu vás máme* END OF ACT II
		ACT III
	SCENE 7 TRIO: 'What's the matter?' *Co to, holka, co to?*	SCENE 1 TRIO: 'What's the matter?' *Co to, holka, co to?*
SCENE 7 DIALOGUE:	SCENE 8 V RECITATIVE: 'Go into the kitchen, and make them hurry the dinner, Mumlal' *Zabruč, Mumlale, jim medvědem*	SCENE 2 V RECITATIVE: 'Go into the kitchen, and make them hurry the dinner, Mumlal' *Zabruč, Mumlale, jim medvědem*

FIRST VERSION 1873–1874	*SECOND VERSION* 1877	*THIRD VERSION* *Arranged by R. Fels with additional items by Smetana* 1882
SCENE 8	SCENE 9	SCENE 3
No. 9. QUARTET: 'Ah, what a painful surprise.' *Jaké to, ach, překvapení*	QUARTET: 'Ah, what a painful surprise.' *Jaké to, ach, překvapení*	QUARTET: 'Ah, what a painful surprise.' *Jaké to, ach, překvapení*
		DIALOGUE:
		SCENE 4
DIALOGUE:	VI RECITATIVE: 'My gracious lady' *Milostivá, Milostivá* (98 bars)	VI RECITATIVE: 'My gracious lady' *Milostivá, Milostivá* (78 bars)
SCENE 9		SCENE 5
DIALOGUE:		VI RECITATIVE CONTINUED: (20 BARS)
SCENE 10	SCENE 10	SCENE 6
FINALE: CHORUS AND ENSEMBLE 'Our Lord must surely love us' *Musí nás mít Pán Bůh rád*	FINALE: CHORUS AND ENSEMBLE 'Our Lord must surely love us' *Musí nás mít Pán Bůh rád*	FINALE: CHORUS AND ENSEMBLE 'Our Lord must surely love us' *Musí nás mít Pán Bůh rád*
END OF ACT II	END OF ACT II	END OF ACT III

APPENDIX F

EXTRACTS FROM THE CORRESPONDENCE BETWEEN ELIŠKÁ KRÁSNOHORSKÁ AND BEDŘICH SMETANA

THE Smetana Museum in Prague contains twenty-eight letters in Krásnohorská's hand. Though these cover a period of nearly twenty years, only eight of Smetana's replies have been preserved—the rest having been destroyed in 1910 by Krásnohorská herself. The first letter to deal in any detail with their collaboration is dated April 26, 1871, and refers to the sketch of Shakespeare's *Twelfth Night*, later renamed *Viola*:

> Esteemed and Honourable Sir,
> I promise to be witty, gay and full of fun. I'll try not to offend Shakespeare, but I cannot do justice to the text with all its detail as it stands. I must be free to omit and add that which is suitable for a comedy and an opera. I have jotted down the voices I have in mind for the characters and I'm wondering if you would like to choose any other. . . . Please tell me if you want me to squeeze in more arias or songs, or anything similar. Shall we include dialogue or not? It is important to know this now. Not everyone should speak, but the comic figures—Tobias, Andrew and Mary—are half actors, half singers, and for these we could well use dialogue. Please tell me what changes you want before I start the libretto. There is nothing more annoying than having to change something once it has been settled!

Smetana's reply is missing, but Krásnohorská's letter of May 11 is intact.

> Esteemed and Honourable Sir,
> If all composers answered as you do then I would be happy and it would be a delight to write librettos. . . . I'm glad you like the first act [of *Sebastian and Viola*]. I had to consider it very carefully. Your reaction to the second and third acts fills me with joy. That you wish to suppress the chorus for the sake of dramatic vividness makes you a paragon among operatic composers! Most people cannot imagine a finale without a rousing chorus, and the

poet, whether he wants it or not, even though it spoils the scene, is obliged to drag the singers onto the stage by their hair! It is said that a finale without chorus has no effect, but let's not speak about such an old-fashioned idea. . . . I cannot prescribe the musical form. You must do that. As for the canon, I only indicated this because in Shakespeare's work they sing it as such, and it really has a comic effect in the play. All that is necessary is that they sing and make a noise to infuriate Malvolio. Canon or no—it matters little! But may I make another suggestion? Could not a ballet be incorporated here with success? Tobias could possibly call through the window to passersby in Italian peasant costume and ask them to perform a humourous dance. This could be very picturesque and provide Andrew Aguecheek with an opportunity to be light-hearted and Malvolio to be furious. Malvolio could then send the people away with Jupiter's thundering! A ballet in Act II (in front of Orsino's Palace) would weaken the dramatic structure; but I must confess that a formal, almost solemn dance does not appeal to me, especially in the poor way it would be danced on our stage. . . . The title should include both names because the similarity of Sebastian and Viola is the root of all conflict; but the fact remains that Sebastian is the ugliest of names. We cannot re-baptize him, so Sebastian he must remain!

On June 29, 1871, Krásnohorská sent Smetana a draft text with this letter:

As you asked, I have incorporated the ballet into Act III. Since the first and second acts are already long, this now makes the last more balanced. If you would prefer it to be placed in Act II, at the point where the people greet the Duke, then it could go immediately after the quintet in Scene 5. Could not the people return from the Palace and, after taking refreshment, begin to dance? I assure you the ballet is quite tolerable either at the beginning or the end of the act, but in the middle of the scene it will disrupt the action. For the plot itself, Shakespeare did not bother to explain why Viola acts so adventurously. I have no intention of going against Shakespeare, but I have given as the main motive her love for her brother. . . . I beg you sustain the same character in the music and keep my ideas in mind. . . . I have tried to give Viola a simple character since I wanted to make her situation touching rather than comic. Her only humourous moments are in Act II, Scene 5, where she has to fight a duel, and in the last scene when Mark is unable to distinguish Viola from Sebastian. This comedy cannot be avoided. Surely there can be no objection to this. I have done everything to make this delicate situation as tasteful as possible and I have dressed it in the purest robe of innocence I can find. I could help Olivia only by making the hot-blooded Sebastian fall in love with her immediately. Now what do you say to Malvolio singing a serenade? I was puzzled how to portray his decisive action and show that he is suspected of madness. This charming figure would be bizarre enough in a romantic costume, with flowers on his chest, a ribbon around his neck and a guitar under his pelerine. To treat this scene as Shakespeare does is impossible because even the sharpest wit loses its effect when sung. The situation itself must be comic and the player must be seen rather than heard. . . . Perhaps the text is too long. I have indicated in pencil the places where cuts can be made, or the text changed. I think it is better for the musician to have more text in hand so that the hero is not obliged to repeat the verse fourteen times as Adolar does in Weber's *Euryanthe*. His phrase 'I trust in God and my Euryanthe' even surpasses your famous Kecal! Having written *Viola* (she has become very dear to me) I want only to hear her brought to life by your genius. I hope you will ask Paleček to sing the role of Malvolio and for Viola will find an actress who not only looks like, but sings like, an angel.

Smetana's work on *Libuše* and *The Two Widows* made him put *Sebastian and Viola* aside, and his deafness in 1874 brought his activities to a standstill. It was only in November, 1875, that he began to correspond with Krásnohorská again. The subject of their letters, however, was not *Šebastian and Viola* but a new opera—*The Kiss*:

I have tried very carefully to rework the text as you asked. I wanted to give it unity, but I felt this would mar the comic element, and so in Act II I have added one duet for the women, another for the men, and a trio for Vendulka, Martinka and Matouš. You have judged correctly that *The Kiss* is very different from *Sebastian and Viola*, where the text is perhaps too lyrical. There, if you permit, I would make several changes in the parts you have not yet composed and which I hope will give the principal scenes greater dramatic strength. I realize now how little I knew when I wrote *Viola*! Or am I mistaken? Is not *The Kiss* written in a more gratifying way than *Viola*? Viola demands a romantic idealization while *The Kiss* a realistic one. I don't know in which I have been most successful. You ask me why *The Kiss* is less formal than *Viola*, and perhaps it's because the scenes alternate more smoothly.

Though Krásnohorská asked for more time to make the changes in *Viola* effective (letter: February 27, 1876), she was able to offer

Smetana a new subject; and in a letter dated May 26, 1876, she outlined details of a new libretto entitled *Šotek* (*The Dwarf*).

> The main characters are Kazisvetka—a witch, a ghost, a rich farmer who later becomes a judge, his wife, a young servant called Franče who falls in love with Emanek, Emanek's father, a nightwatchman, and a thrifty bachelor. . . . The plot concerns the witch who has a scheme to spoil the happiness of Franče and Emanek; in a dream the farmer learns that Franče possesses a little Šotek [a lucky omen], and consequently he resolves to bind her to his service, refusing to allow her to marry. Overnight the farmer is appointed Judge and, attributing his turn of fortune to the presence of the Šotek, he decides to regard Franče as a daughter. His wife interprets his affection for Franče as a sign of her husband's faithlessness. Meanwhile the farmer tries to prevent anybody from seeing Franče, especially Emanek. Secretly, however, he manages to meet his sweetheart every evening by the well and is encouraged to do so by the farmer's wife, who knows nothing of the Šotek and tries to hasten Franče's wedding in order to save her own marriage. She even offers Emanek a dowry to take Franče off her hands. The farmer, suspecting foul play, engages a nightwatchman to spy on the lovers, but he falls asleep after climbing into a lilac tree and consuming a bottle of wine. The witch visits the thrifty bachelor in a dream informing him that Franče has a Šotek and that if he marries her he will become the richest man in the land. The bachelor immediately resolves to court Franče. In the bachelor, the farmer has a more persistent rival than Emanek, and when Franče goes to the well she is not only fondled by Emanek on one side, but caressed by the bachelor on the other. The farmer, believing that the Šotek has left, sees the well as the source of all evil and orders it to be filled in. The bachelor maintains that the well is his property. Emanek's father claims it belongs to him and a trial follows in which the farmer has to decide the verdict. There is no evidence to prove who the rightful owner is, and the farmer orders the well to be blocked up. The villagers rebel and form a barricade. At midnight on May 1 the witches hold their Sabbath and cast a spell which dries up all the water. The nightwatchman returns but, being drunk, falls into the well again. Franče arrives and, by making a sign of the Cross, traps the witch in the well. Emanek joins Franče and together they try to resolve the situation. Emanek frees the nightwatchman, captures the witch and forces her to remove the spell from the well. The witch advises the farmer not to interfere in the affairs of Franče and Emanek and places the lucky Šotek in the possession of the farmer's wife. The opera ends happily with the marriage

> of the young couple. . . . This is only a rough sketch but I could alter it if you wished or offer you another text entitled *The Cantor and the Fairy*. As for *Viola*, it still needs many alterations. Please never speak again of offering me payment for my texts. For me it is a joy to work with you!

After completing *The Kiss* (to a libretto by Eliška Krásnohorská) Smetana turned his attention to *The Secret*. Before committing himself fully to this new score he was obliged to rework sections of *The Two Widows*. This letter to Krásnohorská (dated July 18, 1877) tells us more:

> Dear Friend!
>
> One thing I ask of you is to omit your flowery form of address: 'Esteemed and Honourable Sir!'! This frightens me! Should I not, therefore, call you the same: 'Esteemed and Honourable Miss!'? Call me: 'Dear friend!'. Thank you for the tale which you sent my daughter. Everyone likes your story about the wind. I shall read it later when I am more rested. . . . At present I am depressed and worn by the question of existence. Since May I have had no salary. Dr. Dašek has stopped it until my contract with the Theatre can be rearranged. I am unable to ask for money from my son-in-law for, with his modest income, he can barely support his own family let alone me. In spite of my humiliating prayers the Theatre Committee treat me unfairly. All the glory I had with *The Kiss* last November goes for nothing. They sentence me to starve! To show my kindness I have agreed to rework *The Two Widows* and let them have it without payment. Züngl has addd twenty-eight more pages of text, which equals more than one-and-a-half acts of the opera! Apart from recitatives, there are two new characters, and a new Act I Finale, new arias, a trio and more ensembles. I began to work immediately, but without enthusiasm. I could not write to you before since my mind was torn to shreds. I was overworked, depressed almost to the point of desperation. Not content with my fate, I wait to become a human being again—but I wait in vain. Since yesterday I have been reciting *The Secret* aloud and I am convinced that in this work I shall forget my unhappy circumstances.

Despite failing health and financial hardship Smetana struggled with *The Secret*; but he was also disturbed by the attention which the young Antonín Dvořák was winning with his latest compositions. On February 27, 1828, Krásnohorská wrote to Smetana:

> . . . You told me after the première of *The Kiss* that Dvořák showed you a certain animosity and a lack of understanding.

The irony of fate is that he must hear from all sides that he has taken your *Kiss* as his model. Despite his gifts, he never met with as much success as when he followed in Smetana's footsteps—Smetana, who seemed to him too simple-minded and too original! Dvořák's operas are beautiful mosaics, but not paintings as are yours. Despite an obvious talent he is neither poet, dramatist nor musical architect. These qualities are not lacking in some part, but totally. I see the difference between *The Kiss* and *The Peasant a Rogue* as between a masterpiece and an improvisation. He has borrowed from your Act I duet in *The Bartered Bride*. Other parts are almost copies! I don't wonder he was seduced; for his libretto is very similar to your Act I of *The Bride*. First a gay chorus, then a lament by the girl, then a duet for the girl with her lover, then an intervention by the father and the suggestion of a rich bridegroom, and so on! But happily there are also exceptions. The melodies are truly Dvořák's and have their own character—wild, exuberantly gay, with marked rhythms and stormy tempi which give the opera a certain monotony, for really soft, tender moments are missing. The most firmly-drawn character is the Duke. He has a noble, almost Chopin-like character which does not change so kaleidoscopically as those of the other persons. Your poetic and profoundly dramatic qualities are the crown of your art, which so far has not been reflected, even minutely, in the work of Dvořák. He is, nevertheless, very interesting musically. Perhaps he lacks a general literary education, and it is to be regretted that his gifts are modelled on your works! . . . Though I liked the music of his choruses in *The Peasant a Rogue*, I learnt to value your merits all the more and quoted to myself Wagner's words: 'Ehrt mir die Meister' [a misquotation from *Die Meistersinger*].

On March 1, 1878, Smetana replied:

. . . Your remarks about Dvořák show your good sense and just criticism! You so correctly assessed what is missing—general education! He's a gifted musician, but with little else, and so, alas, are the rest of the younger composers! Apart from music they have had no other education, and even then it is one-sided. Harmony, counterpoint and instrumentation are the sum total! They lack knowledge of form, working out of motives, how to create melodies from themes which grow phrase by phrase into transitions or periods, not to mention the aesthetic side of the art! They only study this superficially when they have to write songs or choruses for an opera. But this does not apply to Dvořák. Judging from his work he seems to have studied musical

> form, but what he lacks is what you so cogently expressed. The declamation of Dvořák's texts is really ordinary, almost banal. Something like this should not be allowed!

Although Smetana and Krásnohorská continued to correspond about their final collaboration, *The Devil's Wall* (see Chapter 14), few of their letters have been preserved. In a note written to Smetana on October 17, 1878, Krásnohorská gives a possible explanation:

> . . . Please destroy all my letters wherein people's names are mentioned or personalities involved. Our correspondence should be like a dialogue: it should be whispered and never written. But I am forced to put pen to paper and, if the letters remain, this can only mean the beginning of gossip!

The following is a list of Eliška Krásnohorská's literary works with the names of the composers who set them to music:

Břetislav	(Bendl)
Blaník	(Fibich)
The Devil's Wall	(Smetana)
The Child of Tábor	(Bendl)
The Kiss	(Smetana)
Cassandra	(Hynek Palla)
Karel Škretá	(Bendl)
Lejla	(Bendl)
Sebastian and Viola (later *Viola*)	(Smetana)
The Secret	(Smetana)

Suggested plots by Eliška Krásnohorská:

Lumír
The Cantor and the Fairy
The Rivals
Šotek
The Dancing Master
Vilousek
Vok of Rožmberk
(later *The Devil's Wall*)
Harant's Wife

APPENDIX G

WORKS IN ORDER OF COMPOSITION

Since most of Smetana's manuscripts are clearly dated, it is possible to arrange his works chronologically with considerable certainty. The following table places each piece within the year or years in which it was composed and brings up to date the catalogue of one hundred and thirty-five compositions listed by Karel Teige in his *Contributions to the Artistic work of B. Smetana* (1896).

1832
Little Galop for Piano

1839
Polka for Quartet
Osmanen Polka for Quartet
String Quartet in D♭ minor

1839–1840
Waltz for Quartet
Overture for Quartet
Fantasia on motives from Bellini's *Il Pirata* for Quartet
Variations on motives from Bellini's *I Montecchi ed i Capuletti* for Piano
Variations on a theme from Bellini's *I Montecchi ed i Capuletti* for Piano

1840
Introduction and Adagio for Piano
Memories of Nové Město for Piano four hands (lost)
Galop di Bravoura for Piano
Louisa's Polka for Piano
Dahlia Polka for Piano
The Wanderer—song to words of Schiller's *Der Pilgrim*

1841
Marina Polka for Piano
Polčinka (*Grand Polka*) in B minor for Piano (fragment)
Waltz in A♭ major for Piano
Galop in B major for Piano
Waltz in A♭ major for Piano
Nocturne in F♯ major for Piano
Song in Memory of St. John of Nepomuk (lost)
Kateřina Polka for Piano
Elizabeth Polka for Piano
Impromptu in E♭ minor for Piano
Impromptu in B minor for Piano

1842
Impromptu in A♭ major for Piano
Bravoura Waltz in C♯ minor for Piano
Klara Quadrille for Piano
From a Student's Life—Polka for Piano
Galop Bajadérek for Orchestra
Minuet in B♭ major for Orchestra

1842–1843
Fantasia on *Sil jsem proso* (*I was sowing millet*) for Violin and Piano

1842?
Overture in C minor for Piano (four hands)

1842–1843
Overture in A major for Piano (four hands)

1843
Quadrille in F major for Piano
Quadrille in B♭ major for Piano
Song without Words for Piano
Étude for Piano (left hand)
Rhapsody for Piano
Memories of Plzeň—Polka for Piano

1844
Tragic March in F Minor for Piano
Album Leaf in B♭ major (fragment)
Album Leaf in C major (fragment)
Five Waltzes for Piano
Album Leaf for Kateřina Kolářová for Piano
Bagatelles and Impromptus—eight pieces for Piano

1845
Composition in C in 'Song Form' for Piano
Tragic March in F minor for Piano
Album Leaf for Elizabeth Thun for Piano
Lesson in E♭ major for Piano (fragment
Nocturne in E♭ major for Piano
Composition in C major for Piano
Composition in C minor for Piano
Album Leaf for Josefina Finkeová for Piano
Album Leaf for Jean Kunz for Piano
Figurations on the Chorale *Bože milostivy bud a vlidny* for Piano
Exercises on the building of musical periods for Piano
Nine fugal expositions for Piano (fragments)
Vivace in F major for Piano
Andante in F major for Piano
March in F major for Piano
March in C minor for Piano
Album Leaves in F major, F minor, D major, D minor, G minor, G♭ major, F♯ major, D major (all fragments)
March of the Warriors for Piano
Country March in B♭ major for Piano
Four-voiced Fugue in C major for Piano
Four-voiced Fugue in A minor for Piano
Pensée Fugitive-Album Leaf for Piano
Four-voiced Fugue in G major for Piano
Three-voiced Fugue in E minor for Piano
Four-voiced Fugue in D major for Piano
Double Fugue in B major for Piano
Four-voiced Fugue in D major for Piano
Four-voiced Fugue in A major for Piano
Eighteen Canons for Piano
Double Fugue in F♯ minor for Piano
Four-voiced Fugue in E major for Piano
Double Fugue in C♯ minor
Triumphal March in E major

1846
Four Canons for Piano
Étude in C in the form of a Prelude for Piano
Étude in A minor in Song form for Piano
Forty-eight Variations on a theme in F major for Piano
Characteristic Variations on the Czech National Song *Sil jsem proso* (*I was sowing millet*) for Piano
Rondo in C major for Piano
Rondo in A minor for Piano
Rondo in F major for Piano
Rondo in D minor for Piano
Composition in Sonata Form in C major for Piano
Composition in Sonata Form in B♭ major for Piano
Composition in Sonata Form in A major for Piano
Composition in Sonata Form in D major for Piano (unfinished)
Composition in Sonata Form in B♭ major for Piano (fragment)

Three Songs with Piano Accompaniment:
Liebchen's Blick (B. Breiger)
Lebewohl (W. Melhop)
Schmerz der Trennung (C. M. Wieland)
Four-part Chorale: *Jesu meine Freude* (SATB)
Four-voiced Fugue: *Ich hoffe auf den Herrn* (SATB)
Introduction and Fugue: *Lobet den Herrn* (SATB)
Double Chorus: *Heilig, Heilig ist der Herr Zabaoth* (SATB)
Polka in E♭ major for Piano.
Fantasia on Four Bohemian Folk Songs for Piano (lost)
Sonata in G minor for Piano
Scapulis Suis: Offertory for SATB, Organ and Chamber Orchestra
Meditabitur in mandatis tuis: Offertory for SATB, Organ and Chamber Orchestra
Einladung: Song with Piano Accompaniment (J. G. Jacobi)
Six Preludes for Organ

1848
Six Characteristic Pieces for Piano, Op. 1.
March for the Prague Students' Legion for Military Band
March for the National Guard for Military Band
Hymn in Honour of the Bohemian King (lost)
The Death of Jan of Husinec for Chorus (lost)
Patriotic Chorus (lost)
Song of Freedom for Voice and Piano

1849
Wedding Scenes—three pieces for Piano
No. 1 Wedding Procession
No. 2 Bride and Groom
No. 3 Wedding Merriment
Overture in D major for Orchestra
Album Leaf in B♭ major for Piano
Album Leaf in C (Prelude for Piano), Op. No. 1
Album Leaf in A minor (Chanson for Piano), Op. 2, No. 2
Album Leaf in G major (Vivace for Piano), Op. 2, No. 3
Album Leaf in E minor (Allegro for Piano), Op. 2, No. 4
Album Leaf in D major (Moderato for Piano), Op. 2, No. 5
Album Leaf in B minor (Andante for Piano), Op. 2, No. 6
Album Leaf 'To Robert Schumann' for Piano, Op. 3, No. 1
Album Leaf 'Song of the Traveller' for Piano, Op. 3, No. 2
Album Leaf 'A roaring, whirling hissing can be heard' for Piano, Op. 3, No. 3
Sketches, Op. 4
Album Leaf in F♯ minor (Prelude for Piano) Op. 4, No. 1
Album Leaf in B major (Idyll for Piano), Op. 4, No. 2
Album Leaf in A♭ major (Remembrance for Piano), Op. 4, No. 3
Album Leaf in G♯ minor for Piano (Persevering Effort). Op. 4, No. 4
Sketches, Op. 5
Album Leaf in F♯ major (Scherzo-Polka for Piano), Op. 5, No. 1
Album Leaf in G♯ minor (Melancholy for Piano), Op. 5, No. 2
Album Leaf in D♭ major (Landscape for Piano), Op. 5, No. 3
Album Leaf in F minor (Rhapsody for Piano), Op. 5, No. 4
Album Leaf in B minor for Piano
Toccatina in B♭ major for Piano
Album Leaf in G major for Piano
Album Leaf in G minor for Piano
Album Leaf in E♭ minor for Piano
Album Leaf in B minor for Piano
Polka in D for Orchestra (later entitled *To our Girls*
Allegro Capriccioso in B♭ minor for Piano

1849–1850
Mladí (*Youth*)*:* Rondo for Two Pianos (eight hands)
Sonata in E minor for Two Pianos (eight hands)
A Well of Melody Rondo for Two Pianos (eight hands) (Prelude, Capriccio, Finale)
Beethoven: *Fidelio* and *Coriolan* overtures (arranged for Two Pianos) (eight hands)

1850
Sonata for Two Pianos (incomplete sketch)
Weber: *Jubel-Overtüre* arranged for Two Pianos (eight hands)

1851–1852
Prelude (?) in D minor for large Orchestra (three unconnected fragments)

1852
Polka in E major for Piano
Polka in G minor for Piano
Polka in A major for Piano (completed in 1883)
Polka in F minor for Piano

1853
Song with Piano Accompaniment: *Liebesfrühling* (F. Rückert)

1853–1854
Festive or *Triumphal Symphony* for large Orchestra, Op. 6

1854
Three Salon Polkas, Op. 7
(1) F♯ major; (2) F minor
(3) E major
Three Poetic Polkas, Op. 8
(1) E♭ major; (2) G minor;
(3) A♭ major

1855
Schumann: Canonic Studies—arranged for Two Pianos (four hands)
Wagner: *Tannhäuser* Prelude—arranged for Four Pianos (sixteen hands)
Beethoven: March from *The Ruins of Athens*—arranged for Four Pianos (sixteen hands)

1855–1856
Trio in G minor for Piano, Violin and Cello

1856
Cadenzas to Mozart's Piano Concerto in D minor (K. 466); C minor (K491); B♭ major (K595)
Andante in E♭ major for Piano

1857
Frithjof: incomplete fragment for Orchestra
The Viking's Voyage: incomplete fragment for Orchestra
Richard III: Symphonic Poem for Orchestra

1857–1858
Cid Campeador e Zimene: incomplete Fantasia for Piano
Transcription of Schubert's 'Der Neugierige' for Piano
Transcription of Schubert's 'Thränenregen' for Piano (lost)

1858
Ball-Vision: Polka—Rhapsody in C for Piano
Capriccio in A minor for Piano
Étude in C major for Piano

1858–1859?
Beethoven: *Egmont* Overture arranged for Two Pianos (eight hands)

1858
Ballade in E minor for Piano (incomplete sketch)
Mendelssohn: *Fingal's Cave* Overture—arranged for Four Pianos (sixteen hands)
Spontini: *Ferdinand Cortez* Overture—arranged for Four Pianos (sixteen hands)

1859–1860
Wallenstein's Camp: Symphonic Poem for Orchestra

1859
Macbeth and the Witches: Piano Fantasia
Bettina Polka for Piano
Étude in G♯: (*On the Sea Shore*) for Piano, Op. 17

1860
Memories of Bohemia: Two Polkas for Piano, Op. 12 No 1 A minor; No. 2 E minor.
Memories of Bohemia: Two Polkas for Piano Op. 13 No. 1 E minor; No. 2 E♭ major
Song of the Czechs: Cantata for TTBB (Version I)

1860–1861
Cadenza for Beethoven's Piano Concerto in C minor (Op. 37)

1861–1862
Hakon Jarl: Symphonic Poem for Orchestra

1862
Fantasia on Czech National Songs for Piano
Album Leaf in C major (for Marie Proksch) for Piano
Doktor Faust: Overture to a Puppet Play by M. Kopecký for small Orchestra
The Three Riders: Ballade for TTBB to words by J. V. Jahn

1863
Oldřich and Božena: Overture to a Puppet Play by M. Kopecký for small Orchestra

1863–1864
The Brandenburgers in Bohemia: Opera in Three Acts to a libretto by K. Sabina
The Bartered Bride: Overture arranged for piano (four hands)

1864
Shakespearean March for large Orchestra
The Renegade: Double Chorus for TTTT BBBB to words by A. L. Metlinský (later rearranged for TTBB)

1864–1870
The Bartered Bride: Opera in Three Acts to a libretto by K. Sabina

1866–1867
Dalibor: Opera in Three Acts to a libretto by J. Wenzig

1867
Fanfares for Shakespeare's *Richard III*
Incidental Song for the tragedy *Baron Goertz* to words E. Bozděch

1867–1868
Song of the Czechs: Cantata for SATB with Piano (Version II)

1868
Fantasia on themes from the Opera *Dalibor* for Piano
Festive Overture in C for large Orchestra
The Peasant: Chorus for TTBB to words by V. Trnobranský

1869
The Bartered Bride: Tableau Vivant for Chamber Orchester arranged from music to the opera.
The Fisherman: Tableau Vivant for Chamber Orchestra
Libuše's Judgement: Tableau Vivant for Chamber Orchestra
Divertimento on Slavonic Songs for solo Flugel Horn and Brass Accompaniment (lost)

1869–1872
Libuše: Opera in Three Acts to a libretto by J. Wenzig

1870
Festive Chorus for TTBB to words by E. Züngl

1874–1878
The Two Widows: Opera in Two Acts to a libretto by E. Züngl

1873
Fantasia on themes from the Opera *Libuše* for Piano

1874–1879
Má Vlast: Six Symphonic Poems for Orchestra

Vyšehrad
Vltava
Šárka
From Bohemia's Wood and Fields
Tábor
Blaník

1875
Dreams: Six Pieces for Piano

1875–1876
The Kiss: Opera in Two Acts to a libretto by E. Krásnohorská

1876
String Quartet in E minor: *From my Life*

1877
Song of the Sea: Chorus for TTBB to words by V. Hálek

1877–1878
The Secret: Opera in Three Acts to a libretto by E. Krásnohorská
Czech Dances: Four Polkas for Piano
(1) F♯ minor; (2) A minor; (3) F major; (4) B♭ major

1878
Three Choruses for Female Voices: *My Star* (SSA) to words by B. Peska
The Swallows have come (SSA) to words by J. V. Sládek
Sunset (SSA) to words by J. V. Sládek
Song of the Czechs: Cantata for SATB and Orchestra (Version III)

1878–1879
Czech Dances: Ten Pieces for Piano
Furiant
Slepička
Oves
Medvěd
Cibulička
Dupák
Hulán
Obkročák
Sousedská
Skočná

1879
Evening Songs: Five Songs for Voice and Piano to words by V. Hálek
Venkovanka: Polka for Orchestra

1879–1882
The Devil's Wall: Opera in Three Acts to a libretto by E. Krásnohorská
Andante in F minor for Piano

1880
From my Homeland: Two Duos for Violin and Piano
Dedication: Chorus for TTBB to words by J. Srb-Debrnov
Prayer: Chorus for TTBB to words by J. Srb-Debrnov

1881
Romance in G minor for Piano

1883
String Quartet in D minor
Two Slogans for Chorus (TTBB) to words by J. Srb-Debrnov
Our Song: Chorus (TTBB) to words by J. Srb-Debrnov
Prague Karneval: Introduction and Polonaise for large Orchestra

1871–1884
Viola: projected Opera in Three Acts to a libretto by E. Krásnohorská

1883–1884
Symphony—incomplete fragment for Orchestra

APPENDIX H

LIST OF WORKS

OPERAS

Braniboři v Čechách (*The Brandenburgers in Bohemia*)

Opera in Three Acts. Text by K. Sabina. Composed 1863. Produced Prague January 5, 1866. Provisional Theatre.

Volfram	(bass)	František Hynek
Oldřich	(baritone)	Petr Doubravský
Junoš	(tenor)	Jindřich Polák
Tausendmark	(baritone)	Josef Lev
Varneman	(tenor)	Josef Lukes
Jíra	(tenor)	Arnošt Grund
Liduše	(soprano)	Isabella Ferenczyová
Vlčenka	(soprano)	Josefina Procházková
Děčana	(contralto)	Marie Pisařovicová
Old Man	(bass)	Josef Paleček
Biřic	(bass)	Josef Čapek

Chorus

Orchestra: Piccolo, Two Flutes, Two Oboes, Two Clarinets, Two Bassoons, Four Horns, Two Trumpets, Three Trombones, Tuba, Timpani, Triangle, Cymbal, Bass Drum, Strings.
Stage Band: Trumpet, Side Drum.

Prodaná nevěsta (*The Bartered Bride*)

Opera in Three Acts. Text by K. Sabina. Composed 1864–1870. Produced Prague May 30, 1866. Provisional Theatre.

Krušina	(baritone)	Josef Paleček
Ludmila	(soprano)	Marie Procházková
Mařenka	(soprano)	Eleonora von Ehrenberg
Mícha	(bass)	Vojtěch Šebesta
Háta	(mezzo-soprano)	Marie Pisařovicová
Vašek	(tenor)	Josef Kysela
Jeník	(tenor)	Jindřich Polák
Kecal	(bass)	František Hynek
Comedian	(tenor)	Jindřich Mošna

Esmeralda	(soprano)	Terezie Ledererová
Indian	(bass)	Josef Křtín

Chorus

Orchestra: Piccolo, Two Flutes, Two Oboes, Two Clarinets, Two Bassoons, Four Horns, Two Trumpets, Three Trombones, Timpani, Cymbal, Bass Drums, Tambourine, Strings.
Stage Band: Piccolo, Trumpet, Tambourine, Cymbal, Bass Drum.

Dalibor

Opera in Three Acts. Text by J. Wenzig. Composed 1867. Produced Prague June 6, 1868. Novoměstské Theatre.

Vladislav	(baritone)	Josef Lev
Dalibor	(tenor)	Josef Lukes
Budivoj	(baritone)	Vojtěch Šebesta
Beneš	(bass)	Josef Palěcek
Vítek	(tenor)	Vitka Antonín Barcal
Milada	(soprano)	Emilie Benevicová-Mikova
Jitka	(soprano)	Eleonora von Ehrenberg

Chorus

Orchestra: Piccolo, Two Flutes, Two Oboes, Two Clarinets, Two Bassoons, Four Horns, Two Trumpets, Three Trombones, Tuba, Timpani Triangle, Cymbal, Bass Drum, Tambourine, Harp, Strings.
Stage Band: Eight Trumpets, Three Trombones, Tuba, Bells.

Libuše

Opera in Three Acts. Text by J. Wenzig. Composed 1868–1872. Produced Prague June 11, 1881. National Theatre.

Libuše	(soprano)	Marie Sittová
Přemysl	(baritone)	Josef Lev
Chrudoš	(bass)	Karel Čech
Šťáhlav	(tenor)	Antonín Vávra
Lutobor	(bass)	František Hynek
Radovan	(baritone)	Leopold Stropnický
Krasava	(soprano)	Irma Reichová
Radmila	(contralto)	Betty Fibichová
Reapers	(soprano)	Eleonora von Ehrenberg
	(soprano)	Ema Meislerová
	(contralto)	Anna Hlaváčková
	(tenor)	Jan Šára

Chorus

Orchestra: Piccolo, Two Flutes, Two Oboes, Two Clarinets, Two Bassoons, Four Horns, Four Trumpets, Three Trombones, Tuba, Timpani, Triangle, Cymbal, Bass Drum, Harp, Strings.
Stage Band: Four Trumpets, Two Trombones.

Dvě vdovy (*The Two Widows*)

Opera in Two Acts. Text by E. Züngl after Mallefille. Composed 1873–1874. Produced Prague March 27, 1874. Provisional Theatre.

Karoline Záleská	(soprano)	Tereza Boschetiová
Anežka Miletinská	(mezzo-soprano)	Marie Sittová
Ladislav Podhajský	(tenor)	Antonín Vávra
Mumlal	(bass)	Karel Čech
Lidunka	(soprano)	Marie Laušmannová
Toník	(tenor)	Jan Šára

Chorus

Orchestra: Two Flutes, Two Oboes, Two Clarinets, Two Bassoons, Four Horns, Two Trumpets, Three Trombones, Timpani, Triangle, Strings.

Hubička (*The Kiss*)

Opera in Two Acts, Text by E. Krásnohorská after K. Světlá. Composed 1875–1876. Produced Prague November 7, 1876. Provisional Theatre.

Paloucký	(bass)	Karel Čech
Vendulka	(soprano)	Marie Sittová
Lukáš	(tenor)	Antonín Vávra
Tomeš	(baritone)	Josef Lev
Martinka	(contralto)	Marie Cach
Matouš	(bass)	František Mares
Barče	(soprano)	Marie Laušmannova
Guard	(tenor)	Jan Šára

Chorus

Orchestra: Piccolo, Two Flutes, Two Oboes, Two Clarinets, Two Bassoons, Four Horns, Two Trumpets, Three Trombones, Timpani, Triangle, Strings.

Tajemství (*The Secret*)

Opera in Three Acts. Text by E. Krásnohorská. Composed 1877–1878. Produced Prague August 18, 1878. Nové České Theatre.

Malina	(bass)	František Mareš
Kalina	(baritone)	Josef Lev
Rose	(contralto)	Betty Fibichová
Blaženka	(soprano)	Marie Sittová
Vítek	(tenor)	Antonín Vávra
Boniface	(bass)	Karel Čech
Skřivánek	(tenor)	Adolf Krössing
The Builder	(baritone)	Leopold Stropnický
The Hostess	(soprano)	A. Märzová
Jirka (The Night-watchman)	(tenor)	Jan Šára
Friar Barnabáš	(bass)	Ferdinand Koubek

Chorus

Orchestra: Two Flutes, Two Oboes, Two Clarinets, Two Bassoons, Four Horns, Two Trumpets, Three Trombones, Timpani, Bells, Guitar, Wooden Blocks, Strings.

Čertova stěna (*The Devil's Wall*)

Opera in Three Acts. Text by E. Krásnohorská. Composed 1879–1882. Produced Prague October 29, 1882. Nové České Theatre.

Vok Vítkovic	(baritone)	Josef Lev
Záviš Vítkovic	(contralto)	Betty Fibichová
Jarek	(tenor)	Antonín Vávra
Hedvika	(soprano)	Irma Reichová
Míchálek	(tenor)	Adolf Krössing
Katuška	(soprano)	Marie Sittová
Beneš	(bass)	František Hynek
The Devil	(bass)	Josef Chlumský
Chorus		

Orchestra: Piccolo, Two Flutes, Two Oboes, Two Clarinets, Two Bassoons, Four Horns, Two Trumpets, Three Trombones, Timpani, Triangle, Cymbal, Harp, Strings.
Stage Band: Two Trombones.

Viola

Projected Opera in Three Acts. Text by E. Krásnohorská after Shakespeare. Sketched 1871–1884. Incomplete fragment.

Orsino	(tenor)
Viola	(mezzo-soprano)
Sebastian	(mezzo-soprano)
Olivia	(mezzo-soprano)
Tobias	(baritone)
Andrew	(tenor)
Malvolio	(baritone)
Marie	(soprano)
Sasek	(baritone)
Antonio	(bass)
Mark	(bass)
Chorus	

CHORAL WORKS

Chorale: *Jesu meine Freude* (SATB)	1846
Choral Fugue: *Ich hoffe auf den Herrn* (SATB)	
Introduction and Fugue: *Lobet den Herrn* (SATB)	
Double Chorus: *Heilig, Heilig, ist der Herr Zabaoth* (SATB)	
Offertory: *Scapulis Suis* (SATB, Organ and Chamber Orchestra)	
Offertory: *Meditabitur in Mandatis Tuis* (SATB, Organ and Chamber Orchestra)	
Song in Honour of the Bohemian King	1848 (lost)
Patriotic Chorus	(lost)
The Death of Jan of Husinec for Chorus	(lost)
Píseň svobody (*Song of Freedom*) for Massed Voices	
Česká píseň (*Song of the Czechs*): Chorus for TTBB	1860

Tři jezdci (*The Three Riders*): Chorus for TTBB 1862
Odrolilec (*The Renegade*): Double Chorus for TTTTBBBB (later rearranged for TTBB) 1864
Česká píseň (*Song of the Czechs*): rearranged for SATB with Piano 1867
Rolnická (*The Peasant*): Chorus for TTBB 1868
Slavonostní sbor (*Festive Chorus*) for TTBB 1870
Piseň na moři (*Song of the Sea*): Chorus for TTBB 1877
Má hvězda (*My Star*): Chorus for SSA 1878
Přiletěly vlaštovičky (*The Swallows Have Come*): Chorus for SSA
Za hory slunce zapadá (*Sunset*): Chorus for SSA
Česká píseň (*Song of the Czechs*): Cantata for SATB with Orchestra 1878–1879
Věno (*Dedication* or *Dowry*): Chorus for TTBB 1880
Modlitba (*The Prayer*): Chorus for TTBB
Dvě hesla (*Two Slogans*): Choruses for TTBB 1883
Naše píseň (*Our Song*): Chorus for TTBB

SONGS

Poutník (*The Wanderer*) Schiller's *Der Pilgrim* for Voice and Piano 1846
Liebchen's Blick (Breiger) for Voice and Piano
Lebewohl! (Melhop) for Voice and Piano
Schmerz der Trennung (Wieland) for Voice and Piano
Einladung (Jacobi) for Voice and Piano)
Liebesfrühling (Rückert) for Voice and Piano 1853
Incidental Song to the tragedy *Baron Goertz* 1867
Večerní písně (*Evening Songs*) (Hálek): Five Songs for Voice and Piano 1879

(1) Kdo v zlaté struny zahrátzná? (Who can play the golden harp?)
(2) Nekamenutje proroky! (Stone not the Prophet!)
(3) Mmě zdálose (I dreamt)
(4) Hej, jaká radost v kole! (Oh, What joy!)
(5) Z svých písní trůn Tiuděiám (I will make you a Home)

CHAMBER MUSIC

Polka for String Quartet 1839
Osmanen Polka for String Quartet
String Quartet in D♭ minor
Waltz for String Quartet 1839–1840
Overture for String Quartet
Fantasia on motives from Bellini's *Il Pirata* for String Quartet 1840
Fantasia on *Sil jsem proso* (*I was sowing millett*) for Violin and Piano 1842–1843
Trio in G minor for Piano, Violin and Cello 1865–1866
String Quartet No. 1 in E minor: *Z mého života* (*From my Life*) 1876

Z domoviny (*From my Home*): Two Duets for Violin and Piano 1880
String Quartet No. 2 in D minor 1883

SYMPHONIES

Slavnostní Symfonie (*Festive* or *Triumphal Symphony*) for large Orchestra 1853–1854
Grosse Sinfonie (*Grand Symphony*)—sketch of part of the first movement 1883–1884

ORCHESTRAL WORKS

Galop bajadérek (*Bajader's Galop*) 1842
Minuet in B♭ major
Pochod Pražské studentské legie (*March for the Prague Students' Legion*) arranged for Military Band by Jan Pavlis 1848
Pochod Národní gardy (*March for the National Guard*) arranged for Military Band by Jan Pavlis
Polka in D major—later entitled *Našim děvám* (*To Our Girls*) 1849
Overture in D major for large Orchestra
Prelude in D minor—Three unconnected fragments for Orchestra
Frithjof—incomplete fragment for Orchestra 1857
Plavba vikingů (*The Viking's Voyage*)—incomplete fragment for Orchestra
Richard III—Symphonic Poem after Shakespeare
Valdštýnův tabor (*Wallenstein's Camp*)—Symphonic Poem after Schiller 1859–1860
Hakon Jarl—Symphonic Poem after Oehlenschläger 1861–1862
Doktor Faust—Overture to a Puppet Play by M. Kopecký for Chamber Orchestra 1862
Oldřich and Božena—Overture to a Puppet Play by M. Kopecký for Chamber Orchestra 1863
Pochod k slavností Shakespearove (*Shakespearean March*) for large Orchestra
Fanfares for Shakespeare's *Richard III* 1867
Slavnosti předehra (*Festive Overture*) in C major 1868
Prodaná nevěsta (*The Bartered Bride*)—Tableau Vivant for Chamber Orchestra 1869
Rybář (*The Fisherman*)—Tableau Vivant for Chamber Orchestra
Libušin soud (*Libuše's Judgement*)—Tableau Vivant for Orchestra
Divertimento on Slavonic Songs for solo Flugel Horn with Brass Accompaniment (lost)
Má Vlast (*My Country*)—A Cycle of Six Symphonic Poems 1874–1879

(1) Vyšehrad
(2) Vltava
(3) Šárka
(4) Z Českých luhů a hájů (From Bohemia's Woods and Fields)

(5) Tábor
(6) Blaník

Venkovanka (*The Country Woman*)—Polka for Orchestra 1879
Pražský karneval (*Prague Carnival*)—Introduction and Polonaise for Orchestra 1883

PIANO WORKS

Kvapiček (*Little Galop*) 1832
Variations on motives from Bellini's *I Montecchi ed i Capuletti* 1839–1840
Variations on a theme from Bellini's *I Montecchi ed i Capuletti*
Vzpomínka na Nové Město (*Memories of Nové Město*) four hands (lost)
Introduction and Adagio
Louisa's Polka in E♭ major
Jiřinková Polka (*Dahlia Polka*) in D major 1840
Galop di Bravoura
Marina Polka
Polčinka (*Grand Polka*) in B minor 1841
Waltz in A♭ major
Galop in B major
Waltz in A♭ major
Nocturne in F♯ major
Kateřina Polka
Elizabeth Polka
Impromptu in E♭ minor
Impromptu in B minor
Impromptu in A♭ major
Bravoura Waltz in C♯ minor 1842
Klara Quadrille
Ze studentského života (*From a Student's Life*)—Polka in C major
Overture in C minor (four hands)
Overture in A major (four hands) 1843
Quadrille in F major
Quadrille in B♭ major
Duo beze slov (Song without Words)
Étude for the left hand
Rhapsody
Vzpomínka na Plzeň (*Memories of Plzeň*)—Polka in E♭
Tragic March in F minor 1844
Album Leaf in B♭ major (fragment)
Album Leaf in C major (fragment)
Five Waltzes
Album Leaf for Kateřina Kolářová
Eight Bagatelles and Impromptus:

(1) Novinnost (Innocence)
(2) Sklíčenost (Dejection)
(3) Idyla (Idyll)
(4) Touha (Desire)

(5) Radose (Joy)
(6) Pohadka (Fairy Tale)
(7) Laska (Love)
(8) Nesvár (Discord)

Composition in C in 'Song Form' 1845
Tragic March in F minor
Album Leaf for Elizabeth Thun
Lesson in E♭ major (fragment)
Nocturne in E♭ major
Composition in C major
Composition in C minor
Album Leaf for Josefina Finkeová
Album Leaf for Jean Kunz
Figuration on the Chorale *Bože milostivy bud a vlidny*
Exercises on the building of musical periods
Nine fugal expositions
Vivace in F major
Andante in F major
March in F major
March in C minor
Eight Album Leaves (all fragments)
(1) F major; (2) F minor; (3) D major; (4) D minor;
(5) G minor; (6) G♭ minor; (7) F♯ major; (8) D major
March of the Warriors
Country March in B♭ major
Four-Voiced Fugue in C major
Four-Voiced Fugue in A minor
Pensée Fugitive (Album Leaf)
Four-voiced Fugue in G major
Three-voiced Fugue in E minor
Four-voiced Fugue in D major
Double Fugue in B major
Four-voiced Fugue in D major
Four-voiced Fugue in A major
Eighteen Canons
Double Fugue in F♯ minor
Four-voiced Fugue in E major
Double Fugue in C♯ minor
Triumphal March in E major
Four Canons 1846
Étude in C in the form of a Prelude
Étude in A minor in Song form
Forty-eight Variations on a theme in F major
Characteristic Variations on the Czech National Song: *Sil jsem proso* (*I was sowing millet*)
Rondo in C major
Rondo in A minor
Rondo in F major
Rondo in D minor

Composition in Sonata Form in C major
Composition in Sonata Form in B♭
Composition in Sonata Form in A major
Composition in Sonata Form in D major (unfinished)
Composition in Sonata Form in B♭ major (fragment)
Polka in E♭ major
Fantasia on Four Bohemian Folk Songs (lost)
Sonata in G minor
Six Characteristic Pieces, Op. 1 1848

(1) V lese (In the Wood)
(2) Vznikajicivašeň (Rising Passion)
(3) Pastýřka (Shepherdess)
(4) Touha (Desire)
(5) Valečník (Soldier)
(6) Zoufalstvi (Despair)

Svatební scény (*Wedding Scenes*) 1849

(1) Svatební průvod (Wedding Procession)
(2) Zenich a nevěsta (Bride and Groom)
(3) Svatební veseli (Wedding Merriment)

Album Leaf in B♭ major
Album Leaf in C major (Prelude), Op. 2, No. 1
Album Leaf in A minor (Chanson), Op. 2, No. 2
Album Leaf in G major (Vivace), Op. 2, No. 3
Album Leaf in E minor (Allegro), Op. 2, No. 4
Album Leaf in D major (Moderato), Op. No. 5
Album Leaf in B minor (Andante), Op. 2, No. 6
Album Leaf 'To Robert Schumann', Op. 3, No. 1
Album Leaf 'Song of the Traveller', Op. 3, No. 2
Album Leaf 'A roaring, whirling hissing can be heard', Op. 3, No. 3

Črty (*Sketches*), Op. 4
Album Leaf in F♯ minor (Prelude), Op. 4, No. 1
Album Leaf in B major (Idyll), Op. 4, No. 2
Album Leaf in A♭ major (Remembrance), Op. 4 No. 3
Album Leaf in G♯ minor (Persevering effort), Op. 4, No. 4

Črty (*Sketches*), Op. 5
Album Lead in F♯ major (Scherzo-Polka), Op. 5, No. 1
Album Leaf in G♯ minor (Melancholy), Op. 5, No. 2
Album Leaf in D♭ major (Landscape), Op. 5, No. 3
Album Leaf in F minor (Rhapsody), Op. 5, No. 4

Album Leaf in B minor
Toccatina in B♭ major
Album Leaf in G major
Album Leaf in G minor
Album Leaf in E♭ minor
Album Leaf in B♭ minor
Allegro Capriccioso in B♭ minor
Polka in E major 1852–1853
Polka in G minor

Polka in A major (completed in 1883)
Polka in F minor
Three Salon Polkas, Op. 7 — 1854
(1) F♯ major; (2) F minor; (3) E major
Three Poetic Polkas, Op. 8
(1) E♭ major; (2) G major; (3) A♭ minor
Andante in E♭ major — 1856
Cid Campeador e Zimene (incomplete Fantasia) — 1857–1858
Vidění na plese (*Ball-Vision*)—Polka-Rhapsody in C major — 1858
Capriccio in A minor
Étude in C major
Ballade in E minor (incomplete sketch) — 1859
Macbeth a čarodějnice (*Macbeth and the Witches*)
Bettina Polka in C major — 1858–1859
Na břehu mořském (*On the Sea Shore*)—Etude in G♯ major, Op. 17 — 1859
Vzpomínky na Čechy (*Memories of Bohemia*), Op. 12
(1) Polka in A minor
(2) Polka in E minor

Vzpomínky na Čechy (*Memories of Bohemia*), Op. 13
(1) Polka in E minor
(2) Polka in E♭ major

Album Leaf in C major (for Marie Proksch) for Piano — 1862
Fantasia on Themes from the Opera *Dalibor* — 1868
Fantasia on Themes from the Opera *Libuše* — 1873
Sny (*Dreams*)—Six Characteristic Pieces — 1875
(1) Zaniklé štěstí (Faded Happiness)
(2) Ütěcha (Consolation)
(3) V Čechách (In Bohemia)
(4) V salóně (In the Drawing-Room)
(5) Před hradem (Near the Castle)
(6) Slavnost Ceskych (Bohemian Festival)

Czech Dances—Four Polkas — 1878
(1) F♯ minor
(2) A minor
(3) F major
(4) B♭ major

Czech Dances—Ten Characteristic Pieces — 1878–1879
(1) Furiant
(2) Slepička (Little Hen)
(3) Oves (Oats)
(4) Medvěd (The Bear)
(5) Cibulička (Little Onion)
(6) Dupák
(7) Hulán (The Lancer)
(8) Obkročák
(9) Sousedská
(10) Skočná

Andante in F minor	1880
Romance in G minor	1880

WORKS FOR TWO PIANOS

Mladí (*Youth*)—Rondo for eight hands	1849–50
Sonata in E minor for eight hands	
A Well of Melody for eight hands	
Sonata for eight hands (incomplete fragment)	

ARRANGEMENTS AND TRANSCRIPTIONS

Weber: *Jubel-Overtüre* arranged for Two Pianos (eight hands)	1850
Schumann: Canonic Studies arranged for Two Pianos (eight hands)	1855
Wagner: *Tannhäuser* Prelude for arranged Four Pianos (sixteen hands)	1855
Beethoven: March from *The Ruins of Athens* for Four Pianos (sixteen hands)	
Transcription of Schubert's 'Der Neugierige' for Piano (two hands)	1857
Transcription of Schubert's 'Thränenragen' for Piano (two hands)	1857 (lost)
Mendelssohn- *Fingal's Cave* Overture arranged for Four Pianos (sixteen hands)	1858?
Spontini: *Ferdinand Cortez* Overture arranged for Four Pianos (sixteen hands)	1858?
Beethoven: *Fidelio*, *Coriolan* and *Egmont* Overtures arranged for Four Pianos (sixteen hands)	1850–1858?
Smetana: *The Bartered Bride* Overture arranged for Piano (four hands)	1863

CADENZAS FOR PIANO

Cadenzas for Mozart's Piano Concerto in D minor (K. 466); C minor (K491); B♭ major (K595)	1856
Cadenza for Beethoven's Piano Concerto in C minor (op. 37)	1860–1861

WORKS FOR ORGAN

Six Preludes	1846

APPENDIX I

OPERA SYNOPSES

The Brandenburgers in Bohemia

Act I. Scene 1. Volfram Olbramavič (bass), Mayor of Prague, is in heated discussion with a group of Bohemian Knights, led by Oldřich Rokycanský (baritone). They are debating the state of the country recently overrun by Brandenburger hordes. Oldřich describes the atrocities—murders, abductions, looting of monasteries—which have become daily occurrences. He favours combat and urges Volfram to drive the invaders out. The Knights support him, but the peace-loving Volfram advises reconciliation and a bloodless settlement. All is not lost, he argues: the infant heir to the throne lives in a castle near Prague protected by loyal Czechs; he begs the Knights be patient. In Scene 2 Junoš (tenor), a young citizen, brings news of fresh attacks: there is pillaging and killing in the streets, he reports, with many of Prague's German burghers playing a prominent part in the fighting. Worse, the infant heir and his mother have been kidnapped. Enraged, Volfram orders the Knights to act immediately and quell the uprising. Scene 3. As they leave the garden, Liduše (soprano), the eldest of Volfram's three daughters, enters. Concerned that Junoš should have left without seeing her, and unaware of the latest disturbance, she reproaches his apparent neglect. She expresses the love she feels for him and concludes with a prayer for peace in the troubled land. In Scene 4 she is interrupted by Tausendmark (baritone), a Prague citizen in league with the invaders who cares nothing for the Bohemian-Brandenburg quarrels. While Liduše taunts him for not supporting the Bohemians in Prague, Tausendmark describes his affections for the girl who has captured his heart. Liduše resolutely declares that the Vltava shall change its colour before she consents to marry Tausendmark, whom she orders to return to his Brandenburg friends. Scene 5 introduces Liduše's two sisters, Vlčenka (soprano) and Děčana (contralto). Accompanied by a group of peasants, they warn their sister that soldiers are plundering the estate. In Scene 6, Tausend-mark, anxious to revenge Liduše's rebuff, bargains with the Brandenburgers agreeing they shall take as loot everything in Volfram's home except th three daughters whom he reserves for himself. Liduše and her sisters ar held captive as the alarm is raised in the village. Scene 7—a crowded square in Prague. It is night and the people angrily express their discontent with the Brandenburgers and their supporters, the treacherous Prague burghers. Jíra (tenor) a runaway serf, is elected leader of the Bohemians and his first action is to incite the townsfolk to raid the cellars of the rich. Having satisfied their empty stomachs, the mob dance exultantly and (Scene 8) seeing themselves the equal of lords they elevate Jíra as King of the Beggars. Liduše, having escaped from Tausendmark (Scene 9), appeals to the crowd to save her sisters. Jíra agrees to help and in Scene 10 captures Tausendmark's sword by trickery. Disorder breaks out, and only ceases when Volfram, Oldřich and Junoš arrive with their followers. As the Brandenburgers scatter, taking as hostages the three girls, Tausendmark seizes the opportunity to accuse Jíra and the rabble of abducting the Mayor's daughters. The crowd protests; but Volfram, anxious for the safety of his children, believes Tausendmark's story and orders Jíra's arrest.

Act II. Scene 1. In a village on the outskirts of Prague the peasants, hungry and desperate, are forced to leave their homes. Led by an old man (bass), the people chant a chorale and beg God's mercy. Their prayers for peace are interrupted by a new Brandenburger raid. Scene 2. Having dispersed the crowd, Captain Varneman (tenor) brings the three abducted girls to the village where he orders the old man to prepare a place in which they can be safely guarded. In Scene 3 a Herald (bass) proclaims that mandatory rule is at an end and foreigners and armed forces are compelled to evacuate the Bohemian lands within three days. The villagers are delighted at the prospect of freedom, but Varneman asserts his authority and insists that everyone obey his orders for the next seventy-two hours. The old man is despatched to Prague to inform the Mayor that his daughters are in the custody of the Brandenburg Captain and that they will remain so until his demands for ransom are met. Scene 4. In a court-room in Prague Town Hall, Jíra is tried by Volfram and sentenced to death; later Tausendmark is entrusted with the task of freeing Liduše and her sisters. In Scene 5, Junoš forces his way into the Hall and attempts to convince the Court of Jíra's innocence; he announces the arrival of the old man bearing a message from Varneman, who demands from Volfram a ransom for the freedom of his daughters. When Tausendmark is delegated to receive the message on Volfram's behalf, Junoš begs the court dismiss the foreign traitor. His warning is ignored, and Jíra is flung into prison. Scene 6 is set in the Brandenburg camp where Děčana and her sisters lament their fate. Anxiously they await news of their father. All seems lost. Only Liduše remains hopeful. Meanwhile Junoš, by picking up the Brandenburger's tracks, has found his way to the village where, in Scene 7, he reveals himself to Liduše. He confirms his love and promises to free her. Junoš hides. In Scene 8, Varneman threatens to keep the daughters for himself unless Volfram sends the ransom money. Liduše protests, preferring death to dishonour; and convinced that her father will save them, she succeeds in allaying the fears of her sisters.

Act III. Scene 1. It is evening and Tausendmark comes to the village to remind Varneman that his detachment must leave at once. He describes how the old man has spread news that the Captain has abducted the Mayor's daughters and that the people now seek vengeance. Tausendmark bargains with Varneman, offering him three hundred gold pieces for the hostages. Varneman accepts but on learning that Tausendmark also seeks safety outside Bohemia he refuses to keep his word. The Captain is adamant: he takes both the money and the girls, explaining that thousands of foreign murders could harm Bohemia no more than one villain like Tausendmark. Scene 2. Left to lament his fate, Tausendmark resolves to steal the girls; he enlists the help of the old man, who has returned from Prague. In Scene 3 Liduše and her sisters are startled by the old man, whose real intention is to foil Tausendmark and set them free. Accompanied by his son, he helps Děčana and Vlčenka to escape (Scene 4) but before Liduše can follow them Tausendmark forces her into the bushes. On hearing screams Varneman rushes to the spot (Scene 5) but is puzzled to find the place deserted. In Scene 6, Junoš and a band of people arrive, and after questioning Varneman they join forces to find Tausendmark. Scene 7 describes their search for Liduše, Scene 8 Jíra's capture of Tausendmark, and Scene 9 the reunion of the three sisters. Volfram orders the Brandenburgers to leave for good and exonerates Jíra of guilt, offering him a home on his estate. The opera ends with an exultant chorus celebrating the protectors of the glorious Bohemian Lands.

The Bartered Bride

The central characters in this episode from peasant life are Jeník, son of the farmer Tobiaš Mícha (by his first wife) and Mařenka, daughter of the farmer Krušina. Before the rise of the curtain Jeník, driven away by his step-mother Háta, has taken work in the neighbouring village where he has found and fallen in love with Mařenka; and Kecal, the local marriage broker, who has earmarked Vašek, Mícha's second son by his marriage to Háta, as a suitable partner for Mařenka.

Act I. Scene 1. A group of villagers are celebrating a parish fair and urge everyone to be merry and enjoy himself. Mařenka (soprano) is melancholy, for her parents have told her that she is to meet her future husband. Jeník (tenor) tries to console her and the chorus press her to join the dance and abandon cares. She remains sad. In Scene 2 she ponders how to tell her father that the love she feels is only for Jeník and she pleads for an assurance that he will be true to her. The couple declare their feeling for each other. Scene 3. Ludmila (soprano), Krušina (baritone) and Kecal (bass) discuss Mařenka's marriage and question the broker who it is that has been chosen for their future son-in-law. Kecal proposes Vašek and sings the virtues of Tobiaš Mícha's second son. When Mařenka enters (Scene 4) and the marriage proposition is put before her she makes it clear that she has no intention of accepting Vašek, whom she has never met. Though her heart is already promised, Kecal insists she renounces Jeník and produces a contract, drawn up with

Mícha (bass) many years before. The more Kecal claims it to be binding, the less notice Mařenka takes of it. As the villagers return (Scene 5) the broker suggests the respective parents retire to discuss the matter further, while he himself offers to come to some agreement with Jeník at the Inn. The act closes with a lively Polka.

Act II is set in the Inn where village locals extol the delights of drinking. Jeník tells Kecal that love tastes better than any wine but the chorus exclaim that beer, being a heaven-sent gift, supersedes all. Someone strikes up a furiant and the people dance onto the green. Scene 2. Vašek enters. He is shy and slow, and stutters that his mother wants him to marry Mařenka, a girl he has never seen. His stammerings are interrupted by Mařenka herself (Scene 3) who, pretending to be someone else, mischievously misleads her simple listener into believing that Mařenka is an evil girl who would stop at nothing. As she advances towards him Vašek declares his feelings for his newly found friend and willingly promises to renounce Mařenka for ever. Thanking fate for the good fortune that has brought him such a beauty he rushes from the Inn as Kecal and Jeník enter. Scene 4. The cunning broker schemes to make Jeník relinquish Mařenka, but not even the description of a wealthy and delightful maiden whom he knows nor the offer of a bribe can shake Jeník's irrefutable faith in the girl he really loves. Only when he learns that Mařenka must marry the son of Tobiaš Mícha by settlement (Scene 5) does he accept Kecal's three hundred gulden and agree to sign a contract ceding Mařenka to no-one but Mícha's son. Kecal calls the villagers to witness the contract being signed (Scene 6) and, horrified, they reproach Jeník for his rascally actions, driving him out with the chorus: 'Prodal svou milou za tři sta, nenít' věru drahá. Hanba hanba!' ('He has sold his sweetheart for three hundred gulden. Shame on him!')

Act III. Vašek, alone on the village green, contemplates what fate will befall him if he marries the evil Mařenka. His musings are interrupted by the arrival of a troupe of travelling players who give the farm-hands a preview of their act (Skočná—'Dance of the Comedians'). As the troupe prepares for the evening performance (Scene 2) Vašek is attracted to the lovely Esmeralda, a tightrope walker, but is prevented from pursuing her by an Indian who discloses that one of their company has become so drunk that he is unable to perform (Scene 3). The principal comedian and Esmeralda hatch a plot in which Vašek is persuaded to dress up as a bear and deputize for the drunken man. His reward is to be Esmeralda herself and he willingly agrees to dance a Can-Can in public. Vašek is joined by his parents and Kecal (Scene 4) who insist he signs the contract binding himself to Mařenka. This he refuses to do arguing that Mařenka would only poison him if he married her. The astonished parents suspect madness, the wily Kecal trickery. Mařenka wanders onto the green, dazed that Jeník should have deceived and deserted her. (Scene 5). Only when she sees the contract with his signature can she accept what has happened. Kecal urges her to sign the agreement and marry Vašek but she protests. With Vašek's arrival the scheme by which Mařenka has tricked him becomes known, and on learning who Mařenka really is he eagerly changes his opinion of her. Dispirited and crestfallen (Scene 6), Mařenka begs time to consider the situation while Kecal and the parents press her to make up her mind. She gives way to sorrow and reflects how blissful life would have been had her dream of love come true. Jeník enters (Scene 7) but is repulsed by Mařenka who denounces him. He attempts to explain what has happened but is thwarted by Kecal (Scene 8) who renews his scheme to win Mařenka for Vašek. Tension heaves below the surface. Jeník tries to clarify the misunderstanding but Mařenka in a show of temper refuses to listen and angrily fetches her parents. Scene 9. The disturbance grows and as the villagers gather they learn that Mařenka is consenting to a union with Vašek to spite Jeník. The timely arrival of Tobiaš Mícha and Háta reveals Jeník's true identity and confusion is unconfounded. Kecal, realizing he has been tricked, rushes away and Jeník explains his ruse was devised only to save Mařenka from Vašek. Deeply offended, Háta insists that Vašek marries Mařenka after all, but the proceedings are interrupted by a bear running wild across the green (Scene 10). Alarm turns to merriment when the bear is discovered to be the disguised Vašek who has brought shame on his family and ridicule on himself. Krušina argues that Vašek is clearly much too young to settle down and asks Micha to bestow his blessing on Mařenka and Jeník. The parents agree and the villagers celebrate the triumph of faithful love with a rousing chorus.

Dalibor

Act I. Scene 1. People gather in the courtyard of Prague Castle to witness Dalibor's trial. Jitka (soprano), an orphan who has been protected by Dalibor and has lived on his estate, urges the townsfolk to rebel and rescue the brave knight. Trumpet fanfares announce the solemn procession of judges (Scene 2) who take their places on either side of the throne as King Vladislav (baritone) arrives in state. He accuses Dalibor of disturbing the peace, attacking Ploškovice Castle and murdering the Burgrave. Milada (soprano), the Burgrave's sister, testifies to Dalibor's guilt (Scene 3) and after describing the bloody fight in Ploškovice and the killing of her brother she demands that the prisoner be punished for his crime. Vladislav promises that justice shall be done and Jitka expresses fear for the condemned man's life. In Scene 4 Dalibor (tenor) is led in and after confessing, he explains that plunder and murder were committed in revenge for injustice (the killing of his friend Zdeněk). There can be no mercy for Dalibor and the judges pronounce sentence: he is to be imprisoned until death claims him by starvation. For Dalibor, however, death is not something to be feared: he welcomes the release from life that will bring him to Zdeněk and defiantly asks that he be taken quickly. Milada, hearing his fearless reply, feels her hatred change to pity and senses a new emotion whose nature she dare not admit even to herself. In Scene 5 she implores the King's mercy begging for Dalibor's life, but the judges reject her plea. The Court is dismissed. Milada can do no more. She laments the fate of the heroic knight (Scene 6) who through her actions is condemned to death. Jitka, however, remaining after the crowd has dispersed, refuses to believe that all is lost and outlines a plan to liberate Dalibor. She explains how he might be rescued with the aid of loyal supporters and the act ends with Milada's promise to help.

Act II. Scene 1 is set in a tavern on the outskirts of the city where Dalibor's followers and armed retainers are drinking. The beer has gone to their heads and they sing a lively chorus. They are interrupted by the arrival of Jitka who has come to discuss with her lover, Vítek (tenor), a plan for Dalibor's release. She describes how Milada's hate has turned to love, her anger to sorrow and how, disguised as a wandering boy musician, she has won the confidence of Dalibor's gaoler and thus entered the prison. In Scene 2 Jitka persuades Vítek to assist and he immediately enlists the help of Dalibor's followers. They toast Jitka (Scene 3) and pledge their support to the cause of liberty. Scene 4. In the gaoler's quarters, Budivoj (bass), the Captain of the Guard, urges the gaoler Beneš (bass) to take extra precautions in securing the prisoner as Dalibor's supporters are at large in the town and could well storm the castle. Beneš guarantees Dalibor's safe custody and explains that he has taken on an orphan boy to help keep guard. Satisfied, the Captain leaves. In Scene 5 the gaoler laments his sad lot. The 'boy' enters (Scene 6) and professing to be the dutiful assistant offers to complete the old man's routine by securing Dalibor's dungeon for the night. Beneš gratefully accepts and asks for a violin to be taken to the prisoner to help him pass away the time. As he goes to find the instrument Milada expresses her passionate feelings for Dalibor and prays she may yet be able to save him (Scene 7). Beneš returns with the violin (Scene 8) and directs her to the dungeon steps. The scene changes to Dalibor's cell where the sleeping knight is awakened by a sudden shaft of light in which the ghost of Zdeněk is seen playing his violin (Scene 9). Startled by the apparition, Dalibor meditates on the fate which has brought him to the prison and is so overcome by the vision that he is hardly aware that Milada has entered the cell (Scene 10). She offers him the violin and in a long confession discloses her identity and declares her love. Attributing her change of feeling to the supernatural intervention of Zdeněk, Dalibor regards her as his salvation and looks forward to freedom and happiness.

Act III. Scene 1 is set in the Royal Hall. Budivoj warns the King that Dalibor's followers are preparing to release their master by force. He summons Beneš who describes how the disguised Milada has duped him to gain entry to the prisoner's cell and that a plan has been hatched for Dalibor's escape. As the King weighs the duties of a just sovereign (Scene 2) the judges urge execution. Vladislav hesitates. He is loth to see the brave knight slain. The judges predict treason and bloodshed in the city and the King is prevailed upon to sign the death sentence. Scene 3 is again set in Dalibor's dungeon. He sings of the freedom which awaits him outside where Milada, Jitka and her faithful followers have gathered. He is on the point of playing a prepared signal on his violin (previously arranged with Milada) when a string breaks. Dalibor interprets this as a bad omen and as he contemplates what action he shall take Budivoj rushes into the cell, seizes the prisoner and announces his execution. On hearing this sentence Dalibor finds comfort in the fact that he will soon be reunited with the spirit of Zdeněk. Outside the castle (Scene 4) Milada, no longer disguised, waits for Dalibor's signal; but instead of the strains of a violin she hears only the tolling of the death knell which accompanies the chanting of monks as Dalibor is led to the place of execution. With sword in hand, Vítek at her side, she orders an advance. Dalibor's supporters rush the castle guard but they cannot break the lines. Milada is wounded and Dalibor, no longer wishing to live, allows himself to be stabbed. As Milada dies in his arms he valiantly waits for the time when he can join her and Zdeněk in death.

Libuše

Act I. Libuše's Hall at Vyšehrad overlooking the Vltava Valley. Scene 1 Libuše (soprano), attended by a group of maidens and priestesses, is listening patiently as Radmila (contralto) complains that her brothers Chrudoš (bass) and Šťáhlav (tenor) are disputing their father's heritage. She begs for help. Tolerantly, Libuše promises to bring the brothers and their quarrel before her court, and in an impassioned prayer invokes the god's protection:

> May the Lord's powers bring about good
> and produce plenty for all men.
> May concern and love lead the people forward
> and proclaim the glory of its future days.
> Oh, ye Gods, hear my prayer and protect our land.

A horn fanfare summons Libuše and her maidens to the court but as they proceed from the Hall, Krasava (soprano), daughter of the sage Lutobor (uncle of the brothers Chrudoš and Šťáhlav), remains to lament her state (Scene 2). She confesses her love for Chrudoš, and discloses that in order to provoke a declaration from him she has falsely favoured his brother. Her monologue of guilt is interrupted by the return of Radmila who is alarmed to see Krasava, whom she regards as a sister, so distressed. Promising to reveal her secret at some later time, Krasava drags Radmila from the Hall. Scene 3 is set in an open space on the Vyšehrad. The court is dominated by a sacred lime tree (a symbol of the Czech nation as the oak is an emblem of the English). Within its shadow stands Libuše's throne, and on either side two groups of opposing elders, the supporters of Chrudoš and Šťáhlav. While the chorus describe how conflict has split their tribe, the elders assert that a male ruler would govern with a firmer hand than the peace-loving Princess. As the two brothers adamantly refuse to be reconciled, Lutobor (bass) tells Radovan (baritone), an adviser, how Libuše frequently rides to Stadice on a white horse to seek advice on matters of government from Přemysl. Fanfares announce the Princess's arrival (Scene 4) and ascending the throne she outlines the litigation, summoning the brothers to submit their arguments. Chrudoš, a rough and imperious warrior, claims the entire heritage, quoting in his defence a similar law prevalent among German clans. Šťáhlav, less violent, recognizes only native custom and promises to respect Libuše's judgement. After consideration she proclaims that the brothers shall inherit equal shares of the legacy and orders them to live in peace. As the judges endorse this ruling the enraged Chrudoš violently abuses Libuše:

> Man can only man obey
> for his fist is strong.
> I despise your ruling since
> it comes from a woman.

He insolently refuses to obey her verdict and storms from the court. Indignantly the chorus voices its horror and Lutobor swears revenge. Libuše, deeply wounded, but with great dignity, abdicates:

> Let henceforth with an iron hand my husband rule!
> You yourselves shall elect him, and he shall
> rule over you and avenge me.
> Indeed, I shall marry him.

Quietly the people urge her to choose a consort and promise to accept whomsoever she shall elect as Prince. After pondering her choice, she announces that Přemysl, a virtuous peasant, shall become her partner and the act ends with a chorus of exultation.

Act II is set in a gloomy mountain forest close to the burial ground of the ancestors of Chrudoš and Šťáhlav. Lutobor enters with Krasava, who has confessed to the offence which has brought jealousy and dispute between the brothers and the people. Angrily, Lutobor reproaches her for her duplicity: she is ordered to conciliate her lover and heal the quarrel on pain of banishment. Krasava explains she really loves Chrudoš and that her thoughtless actions were dictated only by the selfish desire to make him disclose his feelings for her. She admits her blame and implores forgiveness. Šťáhlav enters with Radmila and together they beg Lutobor to exercise compassion. He promises to pardon Krasava providing she can make Chrudoš

> . . . forego defiance, renounce all violent deeds,
> submit to our Princess and beg her grace.

Lutobor storms into the forest, and Chrudoš, deep in thought, approaches the burial mound (Scene 2). Sorrowfully, he recalls Krasava's betrayal and obdurately curses Libuše and the entire female race, swearing neither to make peace nor do homage. Krasava emerges from the shadows, begging forgiveness and imploring love. Angrily, he rebukes her falsehood and faithlessness.

She pleads for Chrudoš's heart or that a sword be thrust through her own. Overcome by emotion he absolves her, promising to be reconciled with his brother. Radmila, Lutobor and Šťáhlav return and embrace. Scene 3 is located in the peaceful countryside at Stadice where, among lime trees, Přemysl has made his home. It is noon. In the distance four farmhands sing whilst they gather the harvest. Přemysl, lost in meditation, contemplates Libuše's beauty and expresses his hope of gaining her love, but his thoughts are broken by the harvesters who come to celebrate both their labour and their lord. Their festivity is halted as Přemysl bids them listen to the murmuring of the lime trees, which he declares to be the sacred symbol of his people. His ruminations are interrupted by the hum of voices and ringing fanfares which announce the arrival of a deputation from Vyšehrad. Ceremoniously, Radovan invites Přemysl to mount the white horse Libuše has sent him and ride with them through the city gate where he is to become her consort. In Scene 5, Přemysl prepares to leave Stadice. The crowd acclaim him as Libuše's husband and protector and ruler of them all. Deeply moved, he bids farewell, ready to defend the peace of the land which he feels to be threatened by Chrudoš's revolt.

Act III opens in Libuše's chamber in Vyšehrad where she welcomes the reconciled brothers:

> Peace is made between the two.
> Peace is made between the maiden and her lover.
> Resolved is the strife that parted them and
> again we are united in concord.

As she gives Krasava to Chrudoš, trumpets announce Přemysl's arrival, and all but the Princess leave to greet him. Alone (Scene 2), she prays for happiness, invoking the memory of her father, Krok, that he may intercede for the future peace of her country. The soliloquy is broken by twelve maidens (Scene 3) who prepare Libuše for her wedding. Fanfares herald the coming of Přemysl. Scene 4. People assemble in the great court to welcome the new Prince. Přemysl enters and Chrudoš's pride rises, threatening to make him break his oath of allegiance. Libuše joins her consort on the throne and listens while Přemysl swears to rule with wisdom and justice (Scene 5). When he summons Chrudoš, Přemysl's act is one of clemency; he stops him from humbling himself at Libuše's feet and elevates him as his equal. The crowd burst into a chorus of acclamation during which the prophetic spirit takes possession of the Princess. In her vision, the great line of destiny is revealed and gazing into the future, one by one six glorious pictures come before her eyes: Břetislav and Jitka, Jaroslav of Šternbeck, Otakar II, Charles IV, Žižka the Hussite and George of Poděbrady. To the strains of the Hussite chorale *Kdož jste Boží bojovníci* (*Ye who are God's warriors*), Libuše proclaims that the Czech people shall never perish and that they shall resist all the horrors of Hell. A powerful chorus reiterates this phrase and the opera ends with a triumphant paean of thanksgiving.

The Two Widows

Act I. The action takes place on the spacious country estate of Karoline Záleská (soprano), a beautiful young widow and rich landowner. It is midsummer. Scene 1. A group of villagers make their way onto the veranda of the garden pavilion, inviting Karoline to a ball arranged to celebrate harvest festival. She promises to attend and bring her widowed cousin, Anežka Miletinská (mezzo-soprano). Following the death of her husband, Karoline has administered the estate and borne herself with carefree dignity: Anežka, on the other hand, regards mourning as an obligation, performing the rite dutifully, avoiding society and attiring herself in black. Scene 2. Karoline endeavours to hearten her by extolling the advantages of freedom and independence which widowhood can bring. She describes her energy in managing the estate and urges her melancholy cousin to join the gaiety of the Harvest Ball. Scene 3. Mumlal (bass), a morose, grumbling gamekeeper who disapproves of amorous affairs because his wife beats him continuously, condemns those who flirt and praises Anežka as the exemplar of all widows. To him, her resigned bearing, vigorous self-discipline and unshakeable devotion to the memory of her late husband seem beyond reproach. Mumlal has actually come not to praise Anežka, but to report the presence of a suspicious poacher, recklessly exploiting the preserves. Mumlal's description of the trespasser—handsome, thirty and a very bad shot—arouses Anežka's curiosity. Could it, she wonders, be Ladislav Podhajský (tenor), whom she has secretly admired for years? Karoline, perceiving her agitation, orders the intruder be brought before her, and Mumlal, boasting of his courage, leaves to accomplish the task. In Scene 4 Karoline discloses her scheme:

> If he greets us we shall answer.
> If he's a bore we shall send him home.
> If he's a learned man he'll amuse us.
> If he's gallant you shall fall in love with him!

Astounded at her cousin's immodest suggestion Anežka retires, while Karoline gleefully withdraws to the pavilion. Scene 5 deals with the arrest. Mumlal is terrified Podhajský may do him harm, while he in turn is anxious that he may not gain admittance to the house. He attempts to provoke Mumlal into action by bribery. On receipt of a coin, the gamekeeper promises to lead the relieved and eager prisoner to the ladies' presence. While Mumlal describes his own 'tiger-like bravery' (Scene 6) the two widows turn the veranda into a court room where they propose to try the interloper. Karoline is to be the judge and Anežka the jury; Ladislav willingly submits to all the business of a mock trial, introducing himself as a rich landowner, and a huntsman vainly pursuing a shy doe. Scene 7. Karoline enters into the spirit of the charade, mischievously cross-examining Podhajský, while Anežka, realizing she is the victim of this amorous poacher, grows uneasy. Ladislav admits both his guilt and his love, and Karoline sentences him to pay a fine in favour of the poor.

She orders him to be detained in the adjoining blue room. Mystified at the proceedings, Mumlal escorts the prisoner out. Finale: on returning to the veranda he is confronted by a group of villagers led by Toník (tenor) and his young bride Lidunka (soprano) who demand to know the prisoner's identity. Lidunka, recognizing Ladislav's actions to be 'those of a man in love', strikes up a lively chorus in praise of this heaven-sent gift.

Act II is set in the large hall of Karoline's house. While Ladislav sings a romance on the terrace, Anežka listens inside with rapt attention. Karoline, observing her, inadvertently touches Anežka and notes her ardent expression change to one of feigned indifference. Anežka accuses her cousin of irresponsible behaviour. She argues that a young man confined in the house of two widows can only encourage gossip. Anežka fears for their safety and Karoline is moved to call Mumlal's protection. The gamekeeper joins them explaining how the prisoner, on being shown to his room, called his liveried manservant waiting in the garden. Karoline, assuming Ladislav's visit to have a specific purpose, declares that he must be in love with one of them (Scene 2). Does Anežka want him or shall Karoline take him? Anežka denies any interest in the man, but in order to provoke a declaration of her true feelings, Karoline pretends to be infatuated by Ladislav herself. Is he not handsome, young and rich, and is she not a widow? The two quarrel. Karoline praises his manly appearance and Anežka mocks her cousin's change of heart. Ladislav discovers Anežka alone (Scene 3). He explains that he has come only on her account, and that her cold indifference pains him. He declares his love and begs for some recognition; but Anežka offers only friendship. Unable to bear this cruel decision, he makes as if to leave (Scene 4), but is stopped by Karoline, who invites him to escort her to the Ball. In Scene 5, Anežka rebukes her frivolous cousin and laments her own loneliness and self-imposed punishment. Her grief is interrupted by Mumlal (Scene 6) who relates that Karoline's flirting with Ladislav can only signify a wedding within the month. Anežka is scandalized and the gamekeeper, denouncing women like Karoline as godless, describes how he would deal with such creatures if only he had the chance. His bluff good humour cheers Anežka who retires to her room. Meanwhile, Toník pursues Lidunka from the ball-room in an attempt to snatch a kiss from her (Scene 7); but Mumlal, deciding to stop any licentious behaviour, comes between them as they are about to embrace. The couple round on him and drive him away. Karoline returns from the ball-room with Ladislav (Scene 8) who acknowledges it is love that has brought him to the house. The widow, interpreting his confession as a personal declaration of his feelings for her, is touched, but Ladislav realizes his tactless mistake and attempts to clarify the misunderstanding. On bended knee he begs Karoline's forgiveness, but is interrupted by Anežka (Scene 9), robed in a magnificent gown adorned with gardenias. On seeing Ladislav in a position which she interprets as a proposal of marriage she screams, bringing Mumlal to the hall. The two widows reproach each other for duplicity. Ladislav bemoans his misfortune and Mumlal decries Anežka's conduct as an offence against morality. Anežka, unaware that Ladislav overhears her, now admits the love she has felt for Podhajský but has denied in respect for the memory of her late husband. Karoline discloses that her ploy was designed only to force a confession from her cousin, and instantly Ladislav offers himself and his possessions in exchange for Anežka's heart. Her consent is Mumlal's cue to announce the banquet, and (Finale) the chorus celebrate not only the harvest but the engagement of the young couple.

The Kiss

Act I. The curtain rises on Paloucký's living-room where Martinka (contralto) excitedly announces that Tomeš (baritone) is bringing his brother-in-law, the widower Lukáš (tenor), to ask for Vendulka's hand in marriage. Vendulka (soprano), cannot believe that the rich young farmer, who married another girl in order to obey his parents, has come to court her so soon after laying his first wife to rest. Paloucký (bass) urges Vendulka to accept Lukáš if she will have him and his baby. Barče (soprano), the maid, shows the two visitors into the room (Scene 2) and a group of curious villagers crowd in behind. Tomeš explains that his brother-in-law wishes to take Vendulka, the girl he has always loved, for wife (Scene 3). Paloucký consents somewhat grudgingly, and Lukáš, a hothead, questions his attitude. Paloucký has to admit that neither party is ideally suited to the other, since both are stubborn, pigheaded and impatient. Should not this alone unite them? pleads Lukáš. The fathers nods disapprovingly and insists that they would never be free from quarrels. Lukáš sneers and boasts that mountains must crumble to dust before their first misunderstanding. Vendulka enters (Scene 4) blissfully content that at last she will be united with the man she loves; but as he attempts to seal their betrothal with a kiss, she resists and a quarrel flares up. At first Lukáš assumes she is only teasing, but Paloucký repeats his warning and Tomeš and the chorus, after drinking a toast to the engaged couple, leave them to unravel their differences. Though Vendulka willingly offers to mother Lukáš's child (Scene 5), she refuses to accept his kiss explaining that before the wedding it would be a mark of disrespect to the memory of his first wife, and an ill omen to spurn folk superstition. Vendulka is adamant. The misunderstanding grows into a heated argument and finally she drives Lukáš from the house. Paloucký, with some satisfaction, declares he was right after all (Scene 6), and Vendulka, wondering if Lukáš has behaved out of stubbornness or from outraged vanity, questions the wisdom of her actions (Scene 7). She ponders whether to call him back, but on learning from Martinka that he is drinking in a local tavern, she prepares to rock Lukáš's child to sleep. After singing a lullaby she herself becomes drowsy. The sound of music outside her window (Scene 8) rouses her and she is shocked to see a drunken Lukáš flirting with the village girls. Shamed by his conduct (Scene 9) she hurriedly packs a bundle of clothes and rushes from the house to join the band of smugglers, of which her aunt is a member.

Act II is set in a dense forest. It is night and Matouš (bass) leads the smugglers, with their contraband, to hiding. As Lukáš comes into the clearing, the smugglers dive for cover. Full of remorse, Lukáš expresses his sorrow for abusing Vendulka (Scene 2) but his lament is interrupted by the arrival of Tomeš, who has been searching for his brother-in-law. Scene 3. Lukáš explains the cause of his grief and threatens to kill himself. Tomeš reasons with him and suggests he asks Vendulka's forgiveness instead; but for Lukáš the shame and disgrace are too much. Tomeš, however, has the upper hand and persuades him to visit Vendulka and to have faith in true love. The band of smugglers creep from their hiding in time to rendezvous with Martinka. At first Matouš is suspicious of Martinka's trembling accomplice (Scene 5), but on learning who Vendulka is he announces that this will be her first and last adventure, and hints that a reconciliation with Lukáš is in the offing (for he has overheard the previous conversation between Tomeš and Lukáš). Matouš and Martinka exchange parcels and go their way, but the women are stopped by a frontier guard who interrogates them. The ever resourceful Martinka succeeds in duping him by a ruse with a basket of apples and admonishes her niece to torment Lukáš no longer. Scene 7. A clearing outside Paloucký's house. Barče salutes the lark and greets the morning. Scene 8. Matouš, Tomeš and the villagers gather to witness Lukáš's confession of guilt and Vendulka's act of forgiveness, and on seeing him (Scene 9) she rushes into his arms and attempts to embrace him. Lukáš quickly frees himself, refusing to be kissed. Neither Martinka, Matouš, Tomeš nor Paloucký can understand this form of reconciliation. With the neighbours, they accuse Lukáš of provoking new strife. He confesses his guilt, makes an apology and is reunited with Vendulka. The couple seal their love with a kiss and the onlookers sing a chorus wishing them good health and happiness.

The Secret

The Secret is another story of Bohemian life but its subject matter is less simple or touching than that of *The Kiss*, and far more serious. Twenty years before the action begins, Kalina (baritone), the son of a poor peasant, had fallen in love with Rose Malina (mezzo-soprano), the daughter of a rich farmer, and ventured to ask for her hand in marriage. Having been rejected by Rose's parents on account of his low station he married the humblest girl he could find purely out of spite. Rose, however, who loved Kalina, has remained faithful to him. Secretly, she suspects him; for before his death, Friar Barnabáš (baritone) divulged that Kalina had failed to act on secret advice which, if followed, would have led to reconciliation with Malina's family and marriage with Rose. Time has not healed her heart and she lives unhappily with her brother who, like Kalina, has recently been elected an Alderman of the town. Enmity prevails between the two. They oppose each other in public and thus divide the community. Kalina is now a widower and his son, Vítek (tenor), a forester, is deeply in love with Blaženka (soprano), Malina's only daughter. Despite position and rank, Kalina is still poor, but in an effort to create the impression of wealth he has ordered a new house to be built in the square, where the action of Act I is located.

It is harvest time and villagers praise God for the crop which is both plentiful and rich (Scene 1). Boniface (baritone), a bachelor and old soldier who secretly hopes to win Rose for himself, teases her about her former love for Kalina; but with Rose, only hatred remains. As Malina and Kalina leave the Town Hall (Scene 2) a Builder (baritone) and some bricklayers come from Kalina's new house telling him their work is complete. Malina and his followers mock their rival for attempting to show off. Kalina pretentiously rewards the Builder with a purse, bragging loudly that his wealth is greater than anybody else's. Not to be thwarted, Malina produces riches which he distributes to a group of threshers who run from the barn. Kalina calls the Hostess (soprano) to bring drinks for his friends, and Malina orders beer for his supporters. Rushed off her feet, she does not know which group to serve first and as Kalina and Malina grow impatient they hurl abuse at each other. Scene 3. Respite occurs with the arrival of the folk-singer, Skřivánek (tenor). First Kalina, then Malina, press money into his hand, bribing him to sing a song in their favour; but having taken something from both parties Skřivánek is obliged to extemporize a ballad in which he honours the two, but not before mocking them for their feudal squabbles. Hoping to bring them to their senses, he points out the futility of their quarrel; but Rose chides the singer for impertinence, Boniface defends her, Kalina refuses to marry her and Malina despairs of any solution. Chaos develops. Only the arrival of a bagpiper and a group of dancers restores peace to the community. Malina and the threshers join in the dance but, when Kalina and the Builder attempt to stop the merriment (Scene 4), a brawl begins. Blaženka and Vítek succeed in quelling the rioters and send them to their homes (Scene 5). Left alone, the young couple declare their love for each other and lament that family differences prevent their union. Scene 6. Boniface, who has tried to carry off a broken plank from Kalina's old house, returns with a piece of paper which he has found thrust in a crack. It contains a message apparently intended for Kalina, and written in the hand of the late Friar Barnabáš. Kalina discloses to Vítek, the manner of acquiring a great treasure, but stipulates that the details must remain a secret. Boniface, overhearing the word 'secret' (Scene 7), spreads the rumour that Kalina is to inherit secret treasure. He first tells the Builder, who tells the Hostess (Scene 8), who tells a woman drawing water from the well, who tells Jirka (tenor), the Nightwatchman and Bell Ringer, who announces to the whole town, through his megaphone, that Kalina has a secret. And thus are secrets kept in all villages.

Act II is set on the slopes of the Bezděz Mountain, near the ruined castle. It is evening. Kalina, acting on the instructions in the message, has come to find the promised treasure. After contemplating the power of gold, he falls asleep but is tormented by gnomes and dwarfs who whirl around the ghost of Friar Barnabáš (baritone), seen emerging from a crevice in the rock (Scene

2). This fantastic vision is exorcized only by a procession of pilgrims (Scene 3) making their way to a chapel in the ruins. Their hymn wakes the startled Kalina who, fearing for his safety, follows the procession. Blaženka has seized the opportunity of joining the pilgrims in order to meet Vítek at a discreet place near the mountain top. Scene 4. The two passionately declare their feelings for each other. Scene 5. They are not only discovered by Boniface, who betrays them to Rose, Kalina, and Malina, but succeeds in making a public scandal of their innocent flirtation, thus strengthening the enmity between the two families. Skřivánek, the Builder, and the chorus lend their support, but when Blaženka begs for the family rift to be forgotten, Rose denounces Vítek as the faithless son of a faithless father. Vítek, abused by both sets of parents, decides to break from his family and urges Blaženka to join him. Secretly, Rose admires Vítek's daring action and laments that her own love for Kalina had not proceeded in the same direction. She is joined by Boniface (Scene 6), who offers himself in return for her love. Scene 7. They are interrupted by Kalina who, with lantern and spade, has come to dig for treasure. He reads the instructions aloud: 'Your road to happiness leads you underground through the secret passage—where to enter is clearly marked, and there you can find your treasure.' As he descends, the gnomes and dwarfs return to torment him. Terrified for Kalina's safety, Rose rushes to prevent him, but unable to stand before her as a beggar, he disappears into the rocks.

Act III is located in a room in Malina's house where the family, farmhands and neighbours are helping to sort hops. The Builder urges Blaženka to entertain them and, fighting her emotion, she sings about unrequited love. Her song ends in a flood of tears. Vítek comes to say farewell, before leaving to make his fortune (Scene 2). He promises to marry Blaženka within the year if he succeeds and Rose, touched by his stand, pleads with Malina not to allow narrowmindedness to ruin the happiness of the young couple. He agrees to their wedding, provided that Kalina comes in person to arrange the ceremony. But this can never happen, exclaims Boniface, 'for the devil must have swallowed him on his treasure-hunting expedition'. He divulges Kalina's 'secret' to the remaining few who do not already know it, and the mysterious details of Barnabáš's message sends a chill through the superstitious peasants. It is midnight. Sounds of banging behind the stove seize the room with fear and everyone believes the house to be haunted. The hop sorters invite Skřivánek to ward off evil spirits with a song; but the banging persists and when the room is plunged into darkness all except Rose run into the square for safety. Scene 3. Suddenly, the door behind the stove splits open and with lantern and spade in hand, Kalina emerges to claim the treasure that awaits him. Clearly Friar Barnabáš's secret passage led only to Malina's house where Rose, the greatest treasure and better than any gold, stands before her blundering lover. In Scene 4 the 'secret' and family feuds are resolved to the satisfaction of everyone except Boniface. Vítek takes Blaženka, Kalina promises to marry Rose, and the villagers look forward to a more harmonious life and sing a chorus of reconcilation which acknowledges that true love can never be forgotten.

The Devil's Wall

Act I. Scene 1 is set on the banks of the Vltava in front of the castle of Rožmberk in southern Bohemia. Míchálek (tenor), and Jarek (tenor), lament their failure to find a suitable partner for Vok Vítkovic (baritone), Lord of Růže. The two knights have been unsuccessful in presenting Vok's suit to the widow, Madalena. Pitying Vok, Jarek swears to forego marriage to Katuška (soprano) until his master finds a partner. This oath has been overheard by the Devil (bass), who inhabits the area in the disguise of the Hermit Beneš (bass) so as to lead people astray. The Devil is the double of the Hermit and when Beneš enters it is impossible to distinguish one from the other. The two begin to dispute which of them is the Saint, and which the Devil; but it appears neither is saintly for the Devil is interested only in leading people into sin and Beneš in furthering his own selfish ends. Scene 2. Katuška, Míchálek's daughter, has had a premonition that Jarek will forsake her and fights back tears as a chorus of maidens greet the morning. Katuška enquires as to Jarek's whereabouts and is reunited with him in Scene 3. The details of his oath fall heavily on her. She fears they can never be wed, but Jarek comforts her, and declares his intention to marry when he can. The Devil, disguised as the Hermit, reappears to bless the couple. Trumpets blaze the arrival of Vok. Decorated boats appear on the river, girls strew flowers on its banks and a magnificent procession halts in front of the castle. Scene 4. While Záviš (contralto), Vok's nephew, proclaims the place to be a paradise, Vok hopefully enquires about the widow Madalena. On learning that he has been rejected, he swears to remain celibate. Míchálek admonishes him to marry as soon as possible and the Devil, again in the guise of the Hermit, maliciously urges him to ask for Katuška's hand. Dragged before him, she refuses to disclose the name of her lover. Later, when Katuška rushes to Jarek, Vok realizes where her heart is pledged and orders the wedding to be celebrated the same day. The Devil, still masquerading as Beneš, promises to unite the couple but Katuška, conscious of Jarek's oath, refuses to proceed with the ceremony. Míchálek describes how Jarek has sworn to abstain from matrimony, and deeply touched, Vok dismisses the gathering. Scene 5. The Devil (alias Beneš) promises to release Jarek from his oath on condition that Vok appoints him Abbot of the recently completed Abbey. Scene 6. A messenger delivers the will of the late Countess Sauenberg, whom Vok had loved in former years and who, when dying entrusted Hedvika, an orphan to his protection. The Devil urges him to bring this charge to Rožmberk and Vok explains how he himself felt like an orphan when rejected by the Countess. As a memorial to her love he has built the Abbey above the castle. He orders Záviš to escort the girl to his court. Scene 7. The Devil enters with Beneš, who is powerless to exorcise evil because he is guilty of egoism himself: he confesses that he [Beneš] deliberately ruined the prospects of Vok's marriage with the Lady Madelina in order to secure Vok's wealth to endow the Abbey and have himself appointed Abbot. He tries to drive his opponent from the castle with the sign of the Cross, but the Devil calls down the powers of darkness and brews a storm which terrifies the Hermit, and drives him from the scene instead.

Act II is set in a shepherd's hut to which Jarek has come for shelter. He is now a pilgrim, fighting to keep his oath. Tormented by thoughts of Katuška, he turns to the moon, begging for peace of mind. As he falls asleep the Devil appears disguised as a shepherd. Anticipating the time when Jarek's soul will be his property, he conjures a vision of the Rožmberk landscape where, on a boulder overlooking the Vltava, Katuška is seen surrounded by peasants who attempt to console her. Suddenly, the Devil transforms the hut into a magnificent hall in Rožmberk where Jarek is discovered dozing against a pillar. Scene 2. Míchálek falls prey to a sudden desire for wealth and laments not having forced Katuška to marry Vok; in this way he would have raised himself to the station of Chief Marshall. Scene 3. Katuška enters accompanied by the Devil (in the form of the Hermit). She implores him to exert his powers so that Vok shall marry soon, for only in this way can she be reunited with Jarek. Míchálek enquires of Beneš (alias the Devil) if Katuška's betrothal to Vok is really impossible, and seeing the sleeping Jarek attempts to use the situation to make his daughter renounce him in favour of Vok. Jarek's awakening forestalls him. Scene 4. Záviš, who has brought Hedvika to the castle, enters with Vok. Finding in her face an irresistible charm reminiscent of that he had known in the Countess Sauenberg years before, Vok falls helplessly in love with Hedvika who, accompanied by her retinue, comes into the hall (Scene 5). Though Vok tries to receive her like a daughter, he cannot prevent himself from looking on her as his future wife. Scene 6. The Devil and Beneš attempt to persuade him to create one of them Abbot and though Vok sees only one figure at a time (believing it to be the same person) when the Devil speaks, Beneš recedes into the background and vice versa. While the Hermit advises Vok to renounce the world so as to release Jarek from his oath, the Devil urges him to take the cloth so as to give his soul to the Church in whom he will find the most "faithful bride". Vok, believing Hedvika could never love him, declares his intention to enter the Church. Scene 7. His followers entreat him to reconsider the situation and he makes his decision conditional: should any woman who loves him dare come to him in the Abbey before he takes his vows he promises to marry her. In this way he gives Hedvika the opportunity of deciding his fate.

Act III is set beside the Vltava where a footbridge leads to the Abbey, high above the rocks. Along the river bank are boulders and one resembling an anvil denotes the so-called Devil's Chancel, near Vyše Brod. As Vok and Záviš take leave of each other, Záviš admits that Hedvika loves his master. Unconvinced, Vok climbs to the Abbey. Scene 2. Jarek, Katuška and Hedvika appear and on seeing Vok in the distance, Hedvika openly declares her love for him. Záviš attempts to take the news to Vok, but is prevented from crossing the river by Míchálek (Scene 3). Instead, Záviš runs after Hedvika so that she may bring Vok back from the Abbey herself. Beneš enters. Acknowledging his guilt he begs Míchálek to hear his confession and absolve him from sin. Míchálek agrees to act as confessor, and listens to the Hermit's plan to retrieve Hedvika so that all may be saved. As Beneš guards the bridge to prevent the Devil from entering the Abbey, Míchálek schemes to bring Katuška to Vok, so that she may become mistress of Rožmberk. In Scene 4, Beneš is confronted by the Devil disguised as a shepherd and accompanied by a herd of sheep. As he tries to clamber over the bridge, Beneš forces him back. Scene 5. A chorus of girls from the village arrive anxious to obtain Vok's hand in marriage but they, too, are chased back by their boy-friends who tease them for having fickle intentions. Amid thunder and lightning (Scene 6), the Devil appears on the Chancel Seat and in an interlude, the sheep are transformed into Hellish monsters, dancing over the rocks. The Devil orders them to lift the boulders and build a dam across the river. The waters rise and both Vok and the Abbey are imperilled. Steadily, the number of monsters grows and with them the waves. Hedvika, sensing Vok's danger, climbs over the rocks while the storm thickens and the waves surge above. Followed by Jarek and strengthened by her love, she eludes the Devil's snares and reaches the Abbey as Beneš causes the dam to tumble with a sign of the Cross (Scene 8). The Devil is swept into the vortex and as the storm abates, bells are heard chiming from the Abbey. Scene 9. Hedvika is reunited with Vok, and Katuška with Jarek. A deputation of envoys from the King of Bohemia deliver a mission appointing Vok Viceroy of Austria and Carinthia. The opera ends with a powerful chorus praising true love and honesty.

APPENDIX J

SELECT BIBLIOGRAPHY

The principal source material for the life of Smetana consists of his Diaries, letters and critical writings, most of which are preserved in the Smetana Museum, Prague. The Diaries have never been published. Apart from a selection of letters edited by F. Bartoš and Z. Němec, *Z dopisů B. Smetany* (*From Smetana's Letters*) (Prague, 1947), available only in Czech, and *Smetana ve vzpomínkách a dopisech* (*Smetana in Reminiscences and Letters*) (Prague, 1955), edited by F. Bartoš and available in English, no other general collection of the correspondence has been made. The following volumes, however, have appeared in Czech and include some of Smetana's letters:

M. Očadlík: *Soupis dopisů B. Smetany* (*A List of Smetana's Letters*) (Prague, 1960)

V. Balthasar: *Bedřich Smetana* (*On Bedřich Smetana*) (Prague, 1924) containing Smetana's correspondence with Srb-Debrnov

A. Kraus: *Smetana v Göteborgu—Smetanova švédská korespondence* (*Smetana in Göteborg—Smetana's Swedish Correspondence*) (Prague, 1925)

J. Jiránek: *Vzpomínky a korespondence s B. Smetanou* (*Memories of and Correspondence with B. Smetana*) (Prague, 1957)

J. Löwenbach: *B. Smetana a Dr. L. Procházka* (*Correspondence of B. Smetana and Dr. L. Procházka*) (Prague, 1914)

M. Očadlík: *E. Krásnohorská a B. Smetana* (*Correspondence of E. Krásnohorská and B. Smetana*) (Prague, 1940)

K. Teige: *Příspěvky k životopisu a umělecké činnosti B. Smetany* (*Contributions to the Biography and Artistic Work of B. Smetana*) Volume II (Prague, 1896)

Zelenka-L. Lerando: *B. Smetana a E. Züngl* (*Correspondence of B. Smetana and E. Züngl*) (Prague, 1903)

Smetana's reviews and critiques for *Národní Listy* and other newspapers have been comprehensively collected by V. H. Jarka: *Kritické dílo B. Smetany* (1858–1865) (*Critical Works of B. Smetana*) (1858–1865) (Prague, 1948).

The standard Czech biography, prepared by Z. Nejedlý, *Bedřich Smetana* Volumes I–VII (Prague, 1950–1954), deals only with the years 1824–1843, and Nejedlý's *Smetana—Doba zrání* (*Smetana—The Period of Maturity*) (Prague, 1962) continues the life story up to 1862. These works are available only in Czech, but an abridged biography by Nejedlý was printed in English in 1924, and Rosa Newmarch's *The Music of Czechoslovakia* contains an interesting, if brief, account of the composer's career. In Czechoslovakia no complete full-length study exists, but the following Czech editions deal with certain aspects of the composer's work:

L. Dolanský: *Hudební paměti* (*Musical Memories*) (Prague, 1949)

O. Hostinský: *B. Smetana a jeho boj o českou moderní hudbu* (*Smetana and His Fight for Modern Czech Music*) (Prague, 1901)

M. Očadlík: *Smetana—tvůrce české národní hudby* (*Smetana, the Creator of Czech National Music*) (Prague, 1949)

K. Teige: *Příspěvky k životopisu a umělecké činnosti B. Smetany* (*Contributions to the Biography and Artistic Work of B. Smetana*) Volume I (Prague, 1893)

M. Malý: *Nástin života a díla B. Smetany* (*An Outline of the Life and Work of B. Smetana*) (Prague, 1954–1956)

M. Očadlík: *Klavírní dílo B. Smetany* (*Smetana's Piano Works*) (Prague, 1961)

M. Očadlík: *Svět Orchestru—Česká hudba* (*The World of the Orchestra—Czech Music*) (Prague, 1961)

M. Očadlík: *Smetanova Má Vlast* (*On Smetana's Má Vlast*) (Prague, 1953)

O. Zich: *Symfonické básně Smetanovy* (*Smetana's Symphonic Poems*) (Prague, 1949)

O. Kredba: *Klavírní trio B. Smetany* (*Smetana's Piano Trio*) (Prague, 1944)

O. Šourek: *Komorní skladby B. Smetany* (*Smetana's Chamber Compositions*) (Prague, 1945)

J. Plavec: *Smetanova tvorba sborová* (*Smetana's Choral Works*) (Prague, 1954)

P. Pražák: *Zpěvohry Smetanovy* (*Smetana's Operas*) Volumes I–IV (Prague, 1948)

V. Helfert: *Tvůrčí rozvoj B. Smetany* (*The Creative Development of B. Smetana*) (Prague, 1924)

J. Racek: *Idea vlasti, národa a slávy v díle B. Smetany* (*The Idea of Country, Nation and Glory in Smetana's Work*) (Prague, 1947)

A. Sychra: *O hudbu zítřka* (*The Music of Tomorrow*) (Prague, 1952)

A collection of articles on Smetana's music by Vladimír Helfert will be found in the appendix of Helfert's *Friedrich Smetana* (Leipzig, 1956), available in a German translation.

INDEX

All works are listed under their composers